MW01556571

Executive Compensation Answer Book

Fourth Edition

Executive Compensation Answer Book

Fourth Edition

Bruce Overton
Susan E. Stoffer

A PANEL PUBLICATION
ASPEN PUBLISHERS, INC.

Copyright © 2000 by PANEL PUBLISHERS
A Division of Aspen Publishers, Inc.
A Wolters Kluwer Company
www.panelpublishers.com

ISBN 0-7355-0494-6

Printed in the United States of America

About Panel Publishers

Panel Publishers—comprising the former Prentice Hall Law & Business, Little, Brown and Company's Professional Division, and Wiley Law Publications—is a leading publisher of authoritative and timely treatises, practice manuals, information services, and journals written by specialists to assist attorneys, financial and tax advisors, and other business professionals. Our mission is to provide practical, solution-based how-to information keyed to the latest legislative, judicial, and regulatory developments.

We offer publications in the areas of compensation and benefits, pensions, payroll, employment, civil rights, taxation, estate planning, and elder law. Other Panel products on related topics include:

Books and Manuals

> Officer Compensation Report
> The Pension Answer Book*
> Pension Distribution Answer Book
> Pension Investment Handbook
> 401(k) Answer Book*
> Estate and Retirement Planning Answer Book
> Nonqualified Deferred Compensation Answer Book

Periodicals and Electronic Titles

> Journal of Deferred Compensation
> Journal of Pension Benefits
> Compensation & Benefits Management
> Pension Plan Administrator
> Panel Pension Library on CD-ROM

Companion volume of Forms & Worksheets available.

PANEL PUBLISHERS
A Division of Aspen Publishers, Inc.
Practical Solutions for Legal and Business Professionals
www.panelpublishers.com

v

SUBSCRIPTION NOTICE

This Panel product is updated periodically with supplements to reflect important changes in the subject matter. If you purchased this product directly from Panel Publishers, we have already recorded your subscription for this update service.

If, however, you purchased this product from a bookstore and wish to receive future updates and revised or related volumes billed separately with a 30-day examination review, please contact our Customer Service Department at 1-800-234-1660, or send your name, company name (if applicable), address, and the title of the product to:

PANEL PUBLISHERS
A Division of Aspen Publishers, Inc.
7201 McKinney Circle
Frederick, MD 21704

Introduction

The *Executive Compensation Answer Book, Fourth Edition* has been revised and updated to reflect the changing world of executive compensation. Subscribers now have current information and resource material on all of the broad areas that affect executive pay. This includes the range of direct compensation—from base salary to long-term incentives; the range of indirect compensation—from perquisites to supplemental benefits; the range of executive pay practices in small and large companies; and executive pay as well as outside director pay. The addition of an experienced legal professional as co-author has significantly expanded the book's use as an authoritative resource on executive compensation.

The new and critical issues that are now part of this *Fourth Edition* are:

- A discussion of total compensation strategies for executives in small and large companies, company divisions, and the executive compensation strategy issues during a restructuring, merger, or acquisition.

- Company responses to executive compensation regulations from the Financial Accounting Standards Board (FAS Ruling #123); from the Securities Exchange Commission (Rule 16b-3); and from the Internal Revenue Service (Code Section 162(m)).

- A detailed discussion of the new FICA withholding rules for nonqualified deferred compensation plans.

- Current trends in executive compensation to include performance-based stock awards, economic profit plans, higher levels and the different mix of executive compensation, the transferability of stock options, and the use of reload stock options.

- Expanded coverage of deferred compensation and supplemental retirement plans for executives in chapter 9, which includes descriptions of insurance-based and non–insurance-based funding alternatives.

- An expanded discussion of special early retirement programs, including the requirements for valid waivers of claims under the Older Workers Benefit Protection Act.

- An updated discussion of deferred compensation techniques for non-profit organizations, including an example of a Code Section 457(f) deferred compensation plan.

- A thorough explanation of "golden parachute" regulations and examples of recent court cases and IRS rulings on Code Section 280G.

- Complete description of ERISA reporting and disclosure requirements for all top hat plans and a discussion of 401(k) wrap plans, including summaries of IRS private letter rulings on the subject.

- Numerous examples of executive compensation plans and sample disclosure statements in company proxies to include annual incentives, stock award plans, outside director plans, economic profit plans, etc.

The *Executive Compensation Answer Book* offers authoritative guidance on how to establish structured executive compensation programs that will help companies attract and retain executives, to motivate them to achieve key company objectives, and to insure that companies will receive the best possible return on compensation and benefit dollars. The *Fourth Edition* also has straightforward answers to questions in these areas of executive compensation:

- Base salary, annual incentives, long-term incentives including stock award plans, and perquisites.

- The accounting and tax treatment of these executive compensation programs.

- Alternative types of incentive and stock award plans and their advantages and disadvantages.

- Specific descriptions of stock options, restricted stock, premium options, discounted stock options, stock purchase plans, phantom and shadow stock plans, performance share plans, stock appreciation rights, and book value plans.
- Executive compensation for international executives.
- How executive compensation is different in not-for-profit organizations, private versus public companies, and large versus small companies.

The questions and answers on these and many other executive compensation issues are intended to provide the reader with the information necessary to design, implement, and administer plans. The authors hope that the *Fourth Edition* will be a significant reference tool and practical guide for all those involved in executive pay.

Bruce Overton
Susan E. Stoffer
October 1999

Acknowledgments

The authors would like to acknowledge the contributions of Mr. Ryan Coker to the *Executive Compensation Book*. Mr. Coker is a Partner with The Benefit Company and has received CLU, ChFC, and EAP designations. His knowledge of executive benefits was a valuable asset in the revisions to chapter 9 of this book. Mr. Coker has over 25 years experience in executive compensation, strategic benefit planning, business insurance, and retirement and estate planning.

The authors also wish to express gratitude to Ellen Ros and Dancy Burns of Aspen Publishers for their guidance, assistance, and patience as we prepared this *Fourth Edition.*

About the Authors

BRUCE OVERTON is the President of Overton Consulting, Inc. an executive compensation consulting firm located in Atlanta, Georgia. Mr. Overton is also on the staff of The Benefit Company, a human resource consulting firm, in Atlanta, Georgia, where he heads their Executive Compensation Division. He was formerly an elected Vice President of Human Resources with RJR Nabisco and he served as their top compensation executive for over 10 years. In that capacity he oversaw worldwide compensation policy and advised the Compensation Committee of the Board Directors. He has also served in various human resource positions with Xerox Corporation and he practiced as an executive compensation consultant with Sibson & Company where he was a Partner for six years. Mr. Overton is a former President and Board Chairman of the American Compensation Association where he was also awarded a life membership. He has published numerous articles on personnel and compensation issues and currently writes the monthly *Executive Compensation Update* for Aspen Law & Business. He is a graduate of Widener University in Pennsylvania.

Mr. Overton previously authored the *Executive Compensation Answer Book, Second Edition* and the *Executive Compensation Answer Book, Third Edition.*

SUSAN E. STOFFER is a member of the Compensation, Benefits and ERISA Litigation practice group in the Atlanta, Georgia office of the law firm of Kilpatrick Stockton LLP. Ms. Stoffer concentrates her practice on ERISA and employee compensation and benefits, with an emphasis on qualified and nonqualified retirement plans, executive compensation, health and welfare plans and benefits aspects of mergers and acquisitions. She is an alumna of the University of Illinois and received her J.D. from Fordham University School of Law. Prior to her move to Atlanta, Ms. Stoffer practiced for several years with a large international law firm based in New York and served Time Warner Inc. as employee benefits counsel during its merger/transition period. She is a frequent speaker at seminars covering a variety of compensation and benefits topics and has authored numerous articles on employee benefits topics.

How to Use This Book

The *Executive Compensation Answer Book, Fourth Edition* uses clear, precise language and avoids technical jargon wherever possible. The question-and-answer format, with its breadth of coverage and plain-language explanations, effectively conveys the complex and essential subject matter of executive compensation and makes the material readily accessible.

To provide additional assistance in locating related topics, the *Fourth Edition* makes use of an extensive system of cross-referencing.

Question-and-Answer Format. The question-and-answer format, with its breadth of coverage and concise, plain-language explanations, effectively conveys the complex and essential subject matter of executive compensation, while providing quickly accessible, straightforward answers to common concerns.

Detailed Listing of Questions. The detailed listing of questions that follows the table of contents at the front of the book is designed to help the reader locate specific areas of immediate interest. This listing functions as a detailed table of contents and provides the specific question that you are researching as well as the page number on which the answer appears.

Appendices. For the reader's convenience, valuable resource material and sample documents have been provided in the appendices that precede the Index.

Index. At the back of the book is a detailed key-word index that is provided as a further aid to locating specific topical information. All references in the Index are to question number rather than to page number.

The *Executive Compensation Answer Book, Fourth Edition* is intended to provide you with a comprehensive set of answers to the issues you face when designing or evaluating your company's executive compensation philosophy.

Contents

List of Questions xxix

CHAPTER 1

Fundamental Concepts of Executive Compensation . 1-1

    Total Compensation Issues 1-2

    Base Salary 1-12

    Incentive Plans 1-14

    Tax Considerations 1-21

    Accounting Considerations 1-29

CHAPTER 2

Private Versus Public Companies 2-1

    General Considerations 2-2

Stock-Based Plans 2-4

S Corporations 2-6

SEC Regulations 2-11

Proxy Rules 2-18

CHAPTER 3

Base Salary 3-1

Establishing Base Salary 3-2

Job Evaluation 3-3

Salary Increases 3-9

Salary Banding; Other Increases 3-10

CHAPTER 4

Annual Incentives 4-1

General Considerations 4-2

Plan Design 4-10

Performance Measures 4-23

Performance Standards 4-29

Funding Incentive Plans 4-33

Contents

CHAPTER **5**

Long-Term Incentive Plans 5-1

General Considerations 5-2

Plan Comparisons 5-12

Compensation Philosophy 5-21

Plan Design 5-23

Stock Options 5-26

Omnibus Plan 5-29

Tax Considerations 5-30

Stock Option Exercise 5-35

Plan Administration 5-40

CHAPTER **6**

Purchase Plans 6-1

General Considerations 6-2

Incentive Stock Options 6-3

Nonstatutory Stock Options 6-10

Discounted Stock Options 6-16

Premium Stock Options 6-19

Option Reloads 6-22

Book Value Purchase Plans 6-24

Convertible Debentures 6-27

Junior Stock Plans 6-30

Performance-Based Stock Options 6-32

CHAPTER 7

Appreciation and Full-Value Plans 7-1

Appreciation Plans 7-2

Stock Appreciation Rights 7-2

Book Value Appreciation Rights 7-10

Full-Value Plans 7-12

Phantom Stock Plans 7-13

Restricted Stock Grants 7-18

Performance Unit Plans 7-21

Performance Share Plans 7-23

CHAPTER 8

Combination Long-Term Plans 8-1

General Considerations 8-1

Performance Share/Stock Option Plans . . .   8-3

Restricted Stock/Stock Option Plans   8-7

SAR/Stock Option Plans   8-11

CHAPTER **9**

Executive Benefit Plans   9-1

General Considerations   9-2

Qualified Retirement Plans   9-3

Nonqualified Retirement Plans   9-5

Tax Considerations   9-13

Funding Arrangements   9-21

Insurance-related Nonqualified Deferred
Compensation Plans   9-24

Split-Dollar Life Insurance   9-27

Executive Disability Income Insurance . . .   9-30

ERISA Considerations   9-32

Other Considerations   9-38

CHAPTER **10**

Perquisites and Other Benefits   10-1

General Considerations 10-1

Tax and Accounting Impact 10-11

Contracts 10-16

CHAPTER 11

Building a Total Compensation Strategy 11-1

General Considerations 11-2

Compensation Factors 11-3

Benefit Factors 11-6

Other Factors 11-9

Determining the Mix 11-10

Developing a Total Strategy 11-14

Approval and Implementation 11-15

Examples of Strategy Statements 11-17

CHAPTER 12

Small Company Considerations 12-1

General Considerations 12-1

New Venture Businesses 12-9

Contents

CHAPTER **13**

Board of Directors' Compensation 13-1

General Considerations 13-2

Outside vs. Inside Directors 13-3

Compensation Methods 13-6

Other Benefits 13-8

CHAPTER **14**

Executive Compensation in the Not-For-Profit
Organization 14-1

General Considerations 14-1

Base Salary 14-5

Annual Incentives 14-6

Long-Term Incentives 14-10

Perquisites 14-11

CHAPTER **15**

Special Early Retirement Programs 15-1

Overview 15-2

Severance Programs 15-3

Planning Early Retirement Programs 15-4

CHAPTER 16

U. S. Executives Working Overseas 16-1

General Considerations 16-2

Tax Considerations 16-9

Special Compensation 16-16

CHAPTER 17

Executive Compensation in the Public Sector 17-1

CHAPTER 18

Compensation for Temporary Executives 18-1

General Considerations 18-2

Incentives and Benefits 18-7

Federal Protection 18-9

Conversion to Full-Time Status 18-9

Current Litigation 18-10

CHAPTER 19

Economic Profit-Based Incentive Plans 19-1

Overview 19-2

Implementation 19-8

Case Studies 19-16

CHAPTER **20**

Trends in Executive Compensation   20-1

Total Cash Compensation   20-1

Long-Term Compensation   20-10

Regulatory Issues   20-18

Outside Directors   20-25

CHAPTER **21**

Compensation for Division Executives   21-1

Base Salary   21-1

Annual Incentives   21-3

Long-Term Incentives   21-6

Benefits and Perquisites   21-15

CHAPTER **22**

Small-Company Versus Large-Company Practices . .   22-1

Total Cash Compensation   22-1

Long-Term Plans   22-8

Benefits and Perquisites   22-13

CHAPTER **23**

Executive Compensation Practices During a Restructuring 23-1

Overview 23-1

Base Salary 23-12

Short-term Incentives 23-15

Long-term Incentives 23-20

Benefits and Perquisites 23-25

APPENDIX **A**

IRS Model Rabbi Trust Arrangement A-1

APPENDIX **B**

Sample Compensation Agreements B-1

Attachment 1

Sample Proxy Disclosure B-77

APPENDIX **C**

Sample Severance and Noncompetition Agreement . . C-1

APPENDIX **D**

Sample Employment Agreements D-1

Contents

APPENDIX **E**

Sample Shareholder-Approved Annual Incentive
Compensation Plan E-1

    Fortune Brands, Inc. Annual Executive
    Incentive Compensation Plan E-2

APPENDIX **F**

Sample Compensation Plan for Outside Directors . . .   F-1

    Dupont Stock Accumulation and Deferred
    Compensation Plan for Directors F-1

APPENDIX **G**

Sample Proposal to Increase the Number of Shares
Used in an Executive Compensation Plan G-1

    Proposal to Amend the 1992 Executive
    Long-Term Incentive Plan by Increasing the
    Number of Shares Available for Issuance . .   G-1

APPENDIX **H**

Sample Proposal of Shareholder-Approved
Performance-Based Compensation Plan as Defined
under Code Section 162(m) H-1

    Amendment to the Incentive Compensation
    Plan for Officers of The Boeing Company . . .   H-2

    Attachment 1

    Incentive Compensation Plan for Officers
    and Employees of The Boeing Company
    and Subsidiaries (As Amended and
    Restated) H-5

APPENDIX I

Economic Value-Added Bonus Plan I-1

APPENDIX J

W. R. Grace Stock Incentive Plan J-1

APPENDIX K

Apple Computer, Inc. Senior Officers Restricted Performance Share Plan K-1

APPENDIX L

Code Section 162(m): Recent IRS Rulings L-1

Letter Ruling 9924007 . . . .   L-1

Letter Ruling 9921032 . . . .   L-2

Letter Ruling 9910011 . . . .   L-2

Letter Ruling 9811029 . . . .   L-2

Letter Ruling 9801043 . . . .   L-3

APPENDIX M

Code Section 280G: Cases and IRS Rulings M-1

Letter Rulings 9920009, 9915021 . . . .   M-1

Letter Ruling 9905012 . . . .   M-1

Letter Ruling 9822029 . . . .   M-1

Contents

Letter Ruling 9610022 . . . . M-2

Sullivan v. Easco Corporation (662 F Supp 1396 (D Md 1987)) M-2

Worth v. Huntington Bancshares, Incorporated (43 Ohio St 3d 192, 540 NE2d 249 (1989)) M-2

Cline v. Commissioner (34 F3d 480 (7th Cir 1994)) M-2

APPENDIX **N**

Sample Deferred Compensation Plan for Non-Profit Organization N-1

INDEX IN-1

List of Questions

Chapter 1 Fundamental Concepts of Executive Compensation

Total Compensation Issues

Q 1:1   What is total remuneration? **1-2**

Q 1:2   How does base salary meet the needs of executives as
    well as the company? **1-2**

Q 1:3   How do annual and long-term incentives meet the needs
    of executives and the company? **1-2**

Q 1:4   How do benefits and perquisites satisfy executive needs?   **1-3**

Q 1:5   How do companies express the value of all elements of
    executive compensation? **1-3**

Q 1:6   What is total cash compensation? **1-5**

Q 1:7   What is total compensation? **1-5**

Q 1:8   What are some of the factors that affect total
    compensation? **1-5**

Q 1:9   How does the type of executive responsibility affect total
    compensation? **1-5**

Q 1:10   How does level within the organization affect an
    executive's total compensation? **1-6**

Q 1:11   How does the type of industry affect an executive's total
    compensation? **1-8**

Q 1:12   How do supply and demand factors influence total
    compensation? **1-8**

Q 1:13   How does company size influence total compensation? .   **1-9**

Q 1:14   How does company performance affect total
compensation? **1-10**

Q 1:15   Does executive performance affect total compensation? .   **1-11**

Base Salary

Q 1:16   Does geographic location affect an executive's base
salary? **1-12**

Q 1:17   How is base salary related to the other components of
total compensation for executives? **1-12**

Q 1:18   How can base salary be used to determine the mix of total
compensation? **1-13**

Incentive Plans

Q 1:19   What is the rationale for having an incentive plan? **1-14**

Q 1:20   Are annual incentive plans appropriate for all types of
organizations? **1-14**

Q 1:21   What characteristics identify organizations for which
annual incentive plans are feasible? **1-14**

Q 1:22   How can companies deal with executives' focusing on the
short run at the expense of long-term performance in
their efforts to receive high annual payout? **1-15**

Q 1:23   What is the typical relationship between annual and
long-term incentives? **1-16**

Q 1:24   What are some basic guidelines for incentive plan design?   **1-16**

Q 1:25   Typically, who is eligible for incentive plan participation? .   **1-17**

Q 1:26   How do executive compensation programs differ in
emerging or start-up companies? **1-18**

Q 1:27   How does corporate philosophy affect the method of
compensation chosen? **1-19**

Q 1:28   What are the objectives of long-term incentive plans? . . .   **1-19**

Q 1:29   What is the difference between annual incentive plans and
long-term incentive plans? **1-20**

Q 1:30   Are stock plans considered incentive plans? **1-21**

Tax Considerations

Q 1:31   What are the general tax implications of different forms of
compensation? **1-21**

Q 1:32   What is unreasonable compensation? **1-22**

Q 1:33   What happens if an executive's compensation is deemed
unreasonable? **1-22**

Q 1:34   What are the limitations on compensation deductions under Code Section 162(m)? **1-23**

Q 1:35   Should executive compensation plans be changed in response to the Code Section 162(m) "caps" on executive pay? **1-26**

Q 1:36   What is ordinary income? **1-26**

Q 1:37   What are capital gains? **1-26**

Q 1:38   What was the rationale for favorable capital gains treatment? **1-27**

Q 1:39   How do tax rates affect executive compensation planning?   **1-27**

Q 1:40   What is the effective tax rate? **1-28**

Q 1:41   What is the marginal tax rate? **1-28**

Q 1:42   What is the alternative minimum tax? **1-29**

Accounting Considerations

Q 1:43   What are the general accounting implications of the different forms of compensation? **1-29**

Q 1:44   What accounting statements contain compensation expenses? **1-30**

Q 1:45   What is the accounting for stock awards? **1-30**

Q 1:46   How does APB 25 compare to FAS 123? **1-32**

Q 1:47   What changes in APB 25 were implemented by the FASB under FAS 123? **1-32**

Q 1:48   What stock plans are included in FAS 123? **1-33**

Q 1:49   How is the fair value calculated under FAS 123? **1-34**

Q 1:50   How do some of these fair value determination models work? **1-35**

Q 1:51   What are the disclosure requirements of FAS 123? **1-37**

Q 1:52   What are the FASB guidelines on EPS calculations that are to be used in company financial statements? **1-37**

Chapter 2 Private Versus Public Companies

General Considerations

Q 2:1   What is a public or publicly traded company? **2-2**

Q 2:2   What is a private or privately held company? **2-2**

Q 2:3   What is a closely held company? **2-2**

Q 2:4   Is a privately held company always a closely held company? **2-2**

Q 2:5   Do executive compensation programs in privately held companies differ from those in publicly traded companies? **2-3**

Stock-Based Plans

Q 2:6   Do privately held companies use stock-based capital accumulation programs to structure their executive compensation arrangements? **2-4**

Q 2:7   What are the most common forms of long-term incentives in private companies? **2-4**

Q 2:8   Are there problems with using stock plans in private companies? **2-4**

Q 2:9   What conditions are typically included in a buy-back agreement? **2-5**

Q 2:10   Is there a negative effect if a privately held company does not provide long-term incentive plans? **2-6**

S Corporations

Q 2:11   What is a Subchapter S corporation? **2-6**

Q 2:12   How does a company elect to become a Subchapter S corporation? **2-7**

Q 2:13   Does electing S corporation status have an impact on executive compensation? **2-7**

Q 2:14   Does the issue of unreasonable compensation affect publicly traded companies differently from privately held and S corporations? **2-9**

SEC Regulations

Q 2:15   What is the Securities Act of 1933, and how does it affect executive compensation? **2-11**

Q 2:16   What is the Securities Exchange Act of 1934, and how does it affect executive compensation? **2-12**

Q 2:17   How can a company avoid application of the 1933 Act? . . **2-12**

Q 2:18   What are the basic rules under Section 16 of the 1934 Act? **2-13**

Q 2:19   Who is subject to the Section 16 reporting rules? **2-13**

Q 2:20   What are the most significant effects of the Section 16 rules from a compensation perspective? **2-15**

Q 2:21 What actions are needed in order to give certain transactions the benefits of Rule 16b-3? **2-17**

Q 2:22 Can the Board of Directors or Shareholders ratify a stock option grant after the fact? **2-18**

Proxy Rules

Q 2:23 What are the shareholder proxy and the proxy statement? **2-18**

Q 2:24 How do the SEC proxy reporting requirements affect executive compensation? **2-19**

Q 2:25 What is the compensation committee of the board and what role does it play in executive compensation? **2-20**

Q 2:26 What rules govern the SEC proxy reporting requirements? **2-22**

Q 2:27 What disclosure information charts must be included with proxy statements? **2-22**

Q 2:28 What other executive compensation information must be disclosed in the proxy statement? **2-23**

Q 2:29 How should public companies determine the future value of stock options and its effect on executive compensation? **2-25**

Q 2:30 How can companies reduce negative media and shareholder reaction to major stock option exercises by executives in years when company earnings are flat or down from previous years? **2-25**

Q 2:31 How does the disclosure requirement for a company performance comparison graph affect the amount of executive compensation awarded? **2-26**

Q 2:32 How do the SEC proxy reporting rules generally affect the design of executive compensation programs? **2-27**

Chapter 3   Base Salary

Establishing Base Salary

Q 3:1 How is an executive's base salary set? **3-2**

Q 3:2 How do companies decide on salaries or salary ranges for executives? **3-2**

Job Evaluation

Q 3:3 What is job evaluation? **3-3**

Q 3:4 How does the ranking system work? **3-3**

Q 3:5	How does a classification system work?	3-5
Q 3:6	How does the point factor approach work?	3-5
Q 3:7	How does factor comparison work?	3-6
Q 3:8	How do companies establish labor market values for executive positions?	3-7
Q 3:9	How do most companies position their executive base salary and annual incentive against labor market competitors?	3-8
Q 3:10	Are there reasons for paying base salaries above or below a competitive average?	3-9

Salary Increases
| Q 3:11 | Do merit increases motivate executives? . . . . | 3-9 |
| Q 3:12 | How can companies reduce the inflationary impact of annual base salary increases? . . . . | 3-10 |

Salary Banding; Other Increases
Q 3:13	Are there alternatives to base salary ranges and merit pay for executives?	3-10
Q 3:14	What are some positive company experiences with salary banding?	3-12
Q 3:15	What are some negative company experiences with salary banding?	3-13
Q 3:16	What have been company experiences with economic pay increases?	3-13

Chapter 4 Annual Incentives

General Considerations

Q 4:1	How is short-term or annual incentive defined?	4-2
Q 4:2	How prevalent are annual incentive plans?	4-3
Q 4:3	What is the rationale for having an annual incentive plan? .	4-3
Q 4:4	How is eligibility in annual incentive plans typically determined?	4-4
Q 4:5	Which forms of payment are typically used in an annual incentive plan?	4-5
Q 4:6	Are annual incentive plan payments pensionable compensation?	4-7

Q 4:7   What is the tax impact of annual incentive plans on the
          executive? **4-7**

Q 4:8   What is the accounting treatment for annual incentive
          plans? **4-8**

Q 4:9   Is shareholder approval required for annual incentive
          plans? **4-9**

Plan Design

Q 4:10   What are the key issues in the design of an annual
          incentive program? **4-10**

Q 4:11   What are the basic plan designs for annual incentive
          plans? **4-11**

Q 4:12   How does a profit sharing plan operate? **4-11**

Q 4:13   What are the advantages of a profit sharing plan? **4-12**

Q 4:14   What are the disadvantages of a profit sharing plan? . . .   **4-12**

Q 4:15   How does a growth or improvement plan operate? **4-13**

Q 4:16   What are the advantages of a growth or improvement plan?   **4-14**

Q 4:17   What are the disadvantages of a growth or improvement
          plan? **4-14**

Q 4:18   How does the target performance plan work? **4-14**

Q 4:19   What are the advantages of a target performance plan? .   **4-16**

Q 4:20   What are the disadvantages of a target performance plan?   **4-16**

Q 4:21   How does a peer company performance plan operate? . .   **4-16**

Q 4:22   What are the advantages of a peer company performance
          plan? **4-17**

Q 4:23   What are the disadvantages of a peer comparison plan? .   **4-17**

Q 4:24   What are the key features of a matrix plan? **4-18**

Q 4:25   What are the advantages of a matrix plan? **4-19**

Q 4:26   What are the disadvantages of a matrix plan? **4-19**

Q 4:27   What is a discretionary plan? **4-19**

Q 4:28   What are the advantages of a discretionary plan? **4-19**

Q 4:29   What are the disadvantages of a discretionary plan? . . .   **4-20**

Q 4:30   Are executives categorized as U.S. expatriates included in
          annual incentive compensation programs? **4-20**

Q 4:31   Do companies with international operations include local
          national executives in incentive compensation plans? . .   **4-21**

Q 4:32   Can incentive compensation plans be utilized in new
          ventures/start-up businesses? **4-21**

Q 4:33   How can annual incentives for executives be distinguished from those for mid-level managers? **4-21**

Q 4:34   How can short-term incentive plans be integrated with executive compensation plans during a merger of two companies? **4-22**

Performance Measures

Q 4:35   What types of performance measures are commonly used in annual incentive plans? **4-23**

Q 4:36   What are some examples of quantitative performance measures? **4-23**

Q 4:37   What financial performance measures are commonly used in annual incentive plans? **4-23**

Q 4:38   What is earnings per share and how is it calculated? . . .   **4-24**

Q 4:39   What is return on assets and how is it calculated? **4-25**

Q 4:40   How is return on equity calculated? **4-25**

Q 4:41   How is return on capital calculated? **4-25**

Q 4:42   What nonfinancial performance measures are commonly used in annual incentive plans? **4-26**

Q 4:43   What is the difficulty of using performance measures in annual incentive plans? **4-27**

Q 4:44   How does a company decide whether the incentive programs should be based on group or individual performance? **4-27**

Q 4:45   How do performance measures vary by group or organizational level? **4-28**

Q 4:46   What performance measures work best for a manufacturing organization? **4-28**

Q 4:47   What performance measures work best in financial institutions? **4-29**

Q 4:48   Which performance measures are best for a service company? **4-29**

Performance Standards

Q 4:49   What are the basic methods of comparing performance in annual incentive plans? **4-29**

Q 4:50   How does the look forward approach to performance comparison work? **4-30**

Q 4:51   How does the peer group approach to performance comparison work? **4-30**

Q 4:52   How does the look back approach to performance comparison work? **4-30**

Q 4:53   How does the percentage of profits approach to performance comparison work? **4-31**

Q 4:54   May performance maximums be set for annual incentive plans? **4-31**

Q 4:55   Do companies typically establish a threshold performance level in annual incentive award plans? **4-31**

Q 4:56   How can appropriate performance standards be determined? **4-32**

Funding Incentive Plans

Q 4:57   How do companies determine the size of award appropriate in annual incentive compensation plans? . . **4-33**

Q 4:58   What factors drive the amount of annual incentive amounts paid to executives? **4-33**

Q 4:59   How does the pool method operate when used in determining incentive funds? **4-34**

Q 4:60   Are there advantages to the pool method? **4-35**

Q 4:61   Are there disadvantages to the pool method? **4-35**

Q 4:62   How is the participant method used in determining incentive pools? **4-35**

Q 4:63   Are there advantages to the participant method? **4-36**

Q 4:64   Are there disadvantages to the participant method? **4-36**

Q 4:65   Do incentive plans have maximum or caps on incentive payments? **4-36**

Chapter 5 Long-Term Incentive Plans

General Considerations

Q 5:1   What are long-term incentive plans? **5-2**

Q 5:2   What are the characteristics of long-term incentive plans? **5-2**

Q 5:3   How is eligibility for participation in long-term plans determined? **5-2**

Q 5:4   How prevalent are long-term incentive plans? **5-3**

Q 5:5   What is the rationale for having a long-term incentive plan? **5-3**

Q 5:6   What should be considered in selecting a long-term incentive plan? **5-5**

Q 5:7   What are the principal types of long-term incentive plans?   **5-7**

Q 5:8   What new forms of long-term incentive are currently
         emerging? **5-8**

Q 5:9   What is economic value-added? **5-9**

Q 5:10   How do EVA plans work? **5-10**

Q 5:11   What is shareholder value? **5-11**

Q 5:12   How do shareholder value plans work? **5-11**

Q 5:13   What is a long-term performance plan? **5-12**

Q 5:14   What is a stock option plan? **5-12**

Plan Comparisons

Q 5:15   What is the advantage of a stock option plan over a
         long-term performance plan? **5-12**

Q 5:16   What are the advantages of a stock option plan over a
         restricted share plan? **5-13**

Q 5:17   What is the disadvantage of stock options compared to
         long-term performance plans? **5-13**

Q 5:18   Are there disadvantages to using stock options as
         compared to restricted stock? **5-14**

Q 5:19   Under what circumstances is a performance plan the best
         type of long-term incentive for a company to select? . .   **5-14**

Q 5:20   Under what circumstances are stock-based plans the best
         form of long-term incentive for a company to select? . .   **5-15**

Q 5:21   How can companies get executives to own stock? **5-15**

Q 5:22   What are the advantages of shareholder value/EVA plans
         over stock plans? **5-16**

Q 5:23   What are the advantages of shareholder value/EVA plans
         over performance plans? **5-17**

Q 5:24   What are the general rules regarding taxation of long-term
         incentive plans? **5-17**

Q 5:25   What are the basic accounting issues for a long-term
         incentive plan? **5-18**

Q 5:26   How does the Black-Scholes option pricing model work? .   **5-20**

Compensation Philosophy

Q 5:27   How should a corporate compensation philosophy be
         utilized in plan design? **5-21**

Q 5:28   What is the primary disadvantage of long-term
         performance plans? **5-22**

Plan Design

Q 5:29   How do companies typically determine the amount of the long-term incentive payout or grant? **5-23**

Q 5:30   How does the salary multiple approach work in determining the size of long-term incentive awards? . . . **5-24**

Q 5:31   How does the targeted income approach work in determining the size of a long-term incentive award? . . **5-25**

Stock Options

Q 5:32   What are the different types of stock options? **5-26**

Q 5:33   What is the typical exercise period for a stock option? . . **5-26**

Q 5:34   What is the rationale behind using stock-based plans? . . **5-27**

Q 5:35   Under what conditions are stock options effective? **5-28**

Q 5:36   In what cases are stock options ineffective? **5-28**

Q 5:37   How do companies determine the number of shares to reserve for stock option plans? **5-28**

Omnibus Plan

Q 5:38   What is an omnibus plan? **5-29**

Tax Considerations

Q 5:39   How does the tax doctrine of constructive receipt affect a long-term incentive plan? **5-30**

Q 5:40   What are some of the conditions that create a substantial risk of forfeiture in a long-term incentive plan? **5-31**

Q 5:41   What are some of the conditions that do not create a substantial risk of forfeiture in a long-term incentive plan? **5-31**

Q 5:42   What is the general tax effect of a stock option? **5-32**

Q 5:43   What is the general tax effect of a stock appreciation right? **5-33**

Q 5:44   What is the general tax effect of a restricted stock grant? . **5-33**

Q 5:45   What is the general tax effect of a performance plan award? **5-33**

Q 5:46   How does the constructive receipt doctrine affect deferred compensation? **5-34**

Q 5:47   What is the economic benefit theory? **5-34**

Q 5:48   What is a Code Section 83(b) election? **5-35**

Stock Option Exercise

Q 5:49   What are the different ways an employee can pay the exercise price of a stock option? **5-35**

Q 5:50   How do the Section 16 rules of the SEC affect stock plans and the way employees can pay for stock? **5-36**

Q 5:51   What is a cashless option exercise? **5-36**

Q 5:52   What is Regulation T, and what is its effect on executive compensation? **5-37**

Q 5:53   What is a stock swap? **5-37**

Q 5:54   What is a pyramiding stock swap exercise? **5-38**

Q 5:55   What is the tax treatment of a stock swap or pyramiding exercise? **5-38**

Q 5:56   Are there drawbacks to a pyramiding exercise or stock swap? **5-39**

Plan Administration

Q 5:57   What is needed to institute a long-term incentive plan? . .   **5-40**

Q 5:58   What is needed to amend a long-term incentive plan? . .   **5-41**

Q 5:59   What information about a long-term incentive must be disclosed in a company's proxy statement? **5-41**

Q 5:60   How should long-term incentive compensation plans be handled during a merger of two companies? **5-42**

Q 5:61   How should deferred compensation be integrated during a merger of two companies? **5-43**

Q 5:62   What is an example of integration of deferred accounts? .   **5-44**

Chapter 6   Purchase Plans

General Considerations

Q 6:1   What is a purchase plan? **6-2**

Q 6:2   What are the different types of purchase plans? **6-2**

Q 6:3   What are the fundamental differences between different types of purchase plans? **6-2**

Q 6:4   How are stock option exercise prices set? **6-2**

Q 6:5   How long is the typical option exercise period? **6-3**

Incentive Stock Options

Q 6:6	What is an incentive stock option?	6-3
Q 6:7	What is the tax treatment of an ISO?	6-5
Q 6:8	What is the effect of the alternative minimum tax on the tax treatment of an ISO?	6-6
Q 6:9	What is the accounting impact of an ISO?	6-8
Q 6:10	What approach is used in calculating the fully diluted earnings per share for an ISO?	6-8
Q 6:11	How prevalent are ISOs?	6-9
Q 6:12	What are the advantages of an ISO?	6-9
Q 6:13	What are the primary disadvantages of an ISO?	6-10

Nonstatutory Stock Options

Q 6:14	What is a nonstatutory stock option?	6-10
Q 6:15	How prevalent are nonstatutory stock options?	6-11
Q 6:16	What is the accounting treatment of a nonstatutory stock option?	6-11
Q 6:17	How does a company calculate dilution with a nonqualified stock option?	6-12
Q 6:18	What is the tax treatment of a nonstatutory stock option? .	6-12
Q 6:19	What are the advantages of nonqualified stock options? .	6-13
Q 6:20	What are the disadvantages of the nonqualified stock option?	6-14
Q 6:21	Can features be added to nonstatutory stock options to offset the withholding burden?	6-14
Q 6:22	How do ISOs compare with nonstatutory stock options? .	6-15

Discounted Stock Options

Q 6:23	What is a discounted stock option?	6-16
Q 6:24	How prevalent are DSO plans?	6-17
Q 6:25	What is the tax treatment for a DSO?	6-17
Q 6:26	What is the accounting impact of a DSO?	6-17
Q 6:27	What are the advantages of a DSO plan?	6-18
Q 6:28	What are the disadvantages of a DSO plan?	6-18
Q 6:29	How deeply can DSOs be discounted?	6-19

Premium Stock Options

Q 6:30	What is a premium stock option?	6-19

Q 6:31 How is the premium established on a premium stock option? **6-20**

Q 6:32 How prevalent are premium stock options? **6-21**

Q 6:33 What is the accounting impact of a premium stock option? **6-21**

Q 6:34 What is the tax treatment of a premium stock option? . . . **6-21**

Q 6:35 What is the advantage of a premium stock option? **6-21**

Q 6:36 What is the disadvantage of a premium stock option? . . . **6-22**

Option Reloads

Q 6:37 What is an option reload plan? **6-22**

Q 6:38 What is the accounting impact of a reload option? **6-23**

Q 6:39 What is the tax treatment of a reload option? **6-23**

Q 6:40 What are the advantages of an option reload provision? . **6-23**

Q 6:41 What are the disadvantages of an option reload plan? . . **6-24**

Book Value Purchase Plans

Q 6:42 What is a book value purchase plan? **6-24**

Q 6:43 What is the accounting impact of a book value purchase plan? **6-25**

Q 6:44 What is the tax treatment of a book value purchase plan? . **6-25**

Q 6:45 What are the advantages of a book value plan? **6-26**

Q 6:46 What are the disadvantages of a book value plan? **6-26**

Q 6:47 For what type of companies does a book value plan make sense? **6-26**

Convertible Debentures

Q 6:48 What is a convertible debenture? **6-27**

Q 6:49 Is shareholder approval required to issue convertible debentures? **6-28**

Q 6:50 What is the accounting impact of a convertible debenture? **6-28**

Q 6:51 What is the tax treatment of a convertible debenture? . . . **6-29**

Q 6:52 What is the EPS impact of a convertible debenture? . . . **6-29**

Q 6:53 What are the advantages of a convertible debenture program? **6-29**

Q 6:54 What are the disadvantages of a convertible debenture program? **6-30**

Q 6:55 For what type of company does a convertible debenture plan make sense? **6-30**

Junior Stock Plans

Q 6:56	What is a junior stock plan?	6-30
Q 6:57	What are the advantages of a junior stock plan?	6-31
Q 6:58	What are the disadvantages of a junior stock plan?	6-31
Q 6:59	How prevalent are junior common stock plans?	6-32

Performance-Based Stock Options

Q 6:60	What are performance-based stock options?	6-32
Q 6:61	What are the advantages of performance-based stock options?	6-32
Q 6:62	What are the disadvantages of performance-based stock options?	6-33
Q 6:63	What are the tax consequences of performance-based stock options?	6-34
Q 6:64	What is the accounting treatment of a performance-based stock option?	6-34
Q 6:65	What is an indexed stock option?	6-35

Chapter 7   Appreciation and Full-Value Plans

Appreciation Plans

Q 7:1	What are appreciation plans?	7-2
Q 7:2	What are examples of appreciation plans?	7-2

Stock Appreciation Rights

Q 7:3	What is a stock appreciation right?	7-2
Q 7:4	How do the SEC Section 16 rules affect SARs?	7-4
Q 7:5	How prevalent are SARs?	7-5
Q 7:6	Should the SAR be eliminated now that the cashless exercise is possible?	7-5
Q 7:7	What is the accounting impact of an SAR plan?	7-5
Q 7:8	What is the tax treatment of an SAR plan?	7-7
Q 7:9	When do SARs typically vest?	7-8
Q 7:10	What are the advantages of an SAR plan?	7-8
Q 7:11	Are there disadvantages to using SARs?	7-9
Q 7:12	For what type of company does an SAR make sense? . .	7-10

Book Value Appreciation Rights

Q 7:13   What is a book value appreciation right? **7-10**

Q 7:14   What is the accounting impact of a book value
appreciation right? **7-11**

Q 7:15   What is the tax treatment of a book value appreciation
right? **7-11**

Q 7:16   What are the advantages of book value appreciation
rights? **7-11**

Q 7:17   Are there disadvantages to book value appreciation rights?   **7-12**

Full-Value Plans

Q 7:18   What are full-value plans? **7-12**

Q 7:19   Why would a company choose to implement a full-value
plan rather than a purchase plan? **7-12**

Phantom Stock Plans

Q 7:20   What is a phantom stock plan? **7-13**

Q 7:21   Are dividends paid on phantom stock? **7-15**

Q 7:22   How prevalent are phantom stock plans? **7-15**

Q 7:23   What is the accounting impact of a phantom stock plan? .   **7-16**

Q 7:24   What is the tax treatment of a phantom stock plan? **7-16**

Q 7:25   What are the advantages of a phantom stock plan? **7-16**

Q 7:26   Are there disadvantages to a phantom stock plan? **7-17**

Q 7:27   When do phantom stock units typically vest? **7-17**

Q 7:28   For what type of company does a phantom stock plan
make sense? **7-17**

Q 7:29   What is a shadow stock plan? **7-18**

Restricted Stock Grants

Q 7:30   What is a restricted stock grant? **7-18**

Q 7:31   How prevalent are restricted stock grants? **7-18**

Q 7:32   What is the accounting impact of a restricted stock grant?   **7-19**

Q 7:33   What is the tax treatment of a restricted stock grant? . . .   **7-19**

Q 7:34   How does a Code Section 83(b) election affect a restricted
stock grant? **7-20**

Q 7:35   What is the typical vesting period for a restricted stock
grant? **7-20**

Q 7:36   What are the advantages of a restricted stock grant? . . .   **7-20**

Q 7:37   Are there disadvantages to a restricted stock grant?   . . .   **7-21**
Q 7:38   For what types of companies do restricted stock grants
              make sense? **7-21**

Performance Unit Plans

Q 7:39   What is a performance unit plan? **7-21**
Q 7:40   How are performance measures established for a
              performance unit plan? **7-22**
Q 7:41   What is the accounting impact of a performance unit plan?   **7-22**
Q 7:42   What is the tax treatment of a performance unit plan? . . .   **7-22**
Q 7:43   What is the typical award period for a performance unit
              plan? **7-23**
Q 7:44   What are the advantages of a performance unit plan? . . .   **7-23**
Q 7:45   Are there disadvantages to instituting a performance unit
              plan? **7-23**

Performance Share Plans

Q 7:46   What is a performance share plan? **7-23**
Q 7:47   What is the tax treatment of a performance share grant?   .   **7-24**
Q 7:48   What is the accounting treatment of a performance share?   **7-24**

Chapter 8   Combination Long-Term Plans

General Considerations

Q 8:1   What is a tandem plan? **8-1**
Q 8.2   What is a parallel plan? **8-2**
Q 8:3   Are there advantages to creating tandem or parallel
              combination plans? **8-2**
Q 8:4   Are there disadvantages to tandem and parallel
              combination plans? **8-2**
Q 8:5   What compensation combinations are the most common
              in combination long-term plans? **8-3**

Performance Share/Stock Option Plans

Q 8:6   What are combination stock option and performance
              plans? **8-3**

Q 8:7 What is the accounting impact of combination performance share and stock option plans? **8-4**

Q 8:8 What is the tax treatment of combination performance share and stock option plans? **8-6**

Q 8:9 Are there advantages to a combination plan of performance shares and stock options? **8-6**

Q 8:10 Are there disadvantages to the combination performance share and stock option plan? **8-7**

Q 8:11 For what type of company does a combination performance share and stock option plan make sense? .   **8-7**

Restricted Stock/Stock Option Plans

Q 8:12 What is a tandem restricted stock/stock option plan? . . .   **8-7**

Q 8:13 Can a parallel grant be made of restricted shares and stock option shares? **8-8**

Q 8:14 What is the accounting impact of a combination restricted stock/stock option plan? **8-9**

Q 8:15 What is the tax treatment of a combination restricted stock/stock option plan? **8-9**

Q 8:16 What are the advantages of a combination restricted stock/stock option plan? **8-10**

Q 8:17 What are the disadvantages of the combination restricted stock/stock option plan? **8-10**

Q 8:18 For what type of company does a restricted stock/stock option plan make sense? **8-11**

SAR/Stock Option Plans

Q 8:19 What is a tandem SAR/stock option plan? **8-11**

Q 8:20 What is a parallel SAR/stock option plan? **8-12**

Q 8:21 How prevalent are SAR/stock option plans? **8-12**

Q 8:22 What is the accounting impact of combination SAR/stock option plans? **8-13**

Q 8:23 What is the tax treatment of combination SAR/stock option plans? **8-13**

Chapter 9 Executive Benefit Plans

General Considerations

Q 9:1 Why are executive benefit plans so important? **9-2**

Q 9:2 How do traditional benefit programs fail executives? . . . **9-2**

Q 9:3 How do these executive benefit programs fit into overall compensation? **9-3**

Qualified Retirement Plans

Q 9:4 What makes a retirement plan *qualified*? **9-3**

Q 9:5 Why is *qualification* of a retirement plan desirable? **9-3**

Q 9:6 Are there limits on contributions and benefits under a qualified retirement plan? **9-4**

Nonqualified Retirement Plans

Q 9:7 Can compensation and benefits be deferred outside of a qualified retirement plan? **9-5**

Q 9:8 What are the primary approaches for deferring compensation? **9-6**

Q 9:9 What is a nonqualified deferred compensation plan? . . . **9-6**

Q 9:10 How does a nonqualified deferred compensation plan differ from a qualified plan? **9-7**

Q 9:11 What do nonqualified deferred compensation plans typically provide? **9-7**

Q 9:12 What is the rationale for creating nonqualified deferred compensation plans for executives? **9-7**

Q 9:13 What are the typical objectives of the executive in deferring income under a nonqualified deferred compensation plan? **9-8**

Q 9:14 What are the typical objectives of the company in providing a deferral program? **9-8**

Q 9:15 Who can generally benefit under a nonqualified deferred compensation plan? **9-8**

Q 9:16 Are there different types of nonqualified deferred compensation plans? **9-9**

Q 9:17 What factors must be considered by a company in determining the appropriateness of a deferred compensation plan? **9-12**

Tax Considerations

Q 9:18 How are nonqualified plans treated for tax purposes? . . . **9-13**

Q 9:19 What is an example of the tax treatment on company contributions to a nonqualified plan? **9-13**

Q 9:20 Are contributions to a funded plan treated differently than contributions to an unfunded plan? **9-15**

Q 9:21 How are employers who establish funded excess benefit plans treated for tax purposes? **9-15**

Q 9:22 How are employees who benefit from excess benefit plans treated for tax purposes? **9-16**

Q 9:23 Are contributions made pursuant to a nonqualified deferred compensation plan includible in an employee's income under the constructive receipt doctrine? **9-16**

Q 9:24 Are contributions made pursuant to a nonqualified deferred compensation plan includible in the employee's income under the economic benefit doctrine? **9-16**

Q 9:25 How does Code Section 83 apply to property transfers to an employee in exchange for the performance of services? **9-17**

Q 9:26 What are the tax consequences under a Code Section 457 plan? **9-18**

Q 9:27 When are deferred compensation arrangements subject to FICA and FUTA taxes? **9-18**

Funding Arrangements

Q 9:28 What is a rabbi escrow agreement? **9-21**

Q 9:29 What is a rabbi trust? **9-21**

Q 9:30 What is a secular trust? **9-23**

Q 9:31 What are the major distinctions between a secular trust and a rabbi trust? **9-23**

Q 9:32 Can life insurance also be used by an employer to fulfill its promise to an employee? **9-24**

Insurance-related Nonqualified Deferred Compensation Plans

Q 9:33 How is life insurance used by an employer to fulfill its promise to an employee? **9-24**

Q 9:34 Can life insurance other than COLI be utilized to fund nonqualified deferred compensation programs? **9-25**

Q 9:35 What is the difference between COLI and *retail* life insurance contracts? 9-26

Q 9:36 What are the advantages of using employee-owned life insurance to fund nonqualified deferred compensation benefits? 9-26

Split-Dollar Life Insurance

Q 9:37 What is split-dollar life insurance? 9-27

Q 9:38 How is split-dollar treated under ERISA? 9-27

Q 9:39 How does the policy splitting occur? 9-27

Q 9:40 Must the executive pay his part of the premium? 9-28

Q 9:41 How is the policy split accomplished? 9-28

Q 9:42 What happens when the executive retires? 9-28

Q 9:43 What are common split-dollar applications? 9-28

Q 9:44 What problems do executives experience in group term life insurance plans? 9-29

Q 9:45 Why is split-dollar effective in replacing group term coverage? 9-29

Q 9:46 Why is split-dollar useful in estate planning? 9-29

Q 9:47 How can split-dollar enhance a nonqualified retirement plan? 9-30

Executive Disability Income Insurance

Q 9:48 How does an executive disability income insurance plan work? 9-30

Q 9:49 What legal framework should exist to minimize taxation of executive disability plans? 9-31

Q 9:50 How are benefits taxed to the executive? 9-31

Q 9:51 How are premiums taxed to the executive and the employer? 9-31

Q 9:52 Are executive disability premiums more expensive than LTD? 9-31

Q 9:53 Do executive disability income plan have to be funded by the employer? 9-32

ERISA Considerations

Q 9:54 What are the general ERISA requirements for a nonqualified deferred compensation plan? 9-32

Q 9:55 What are the general participation, vesting, and funding requirements for a nonqualified deferred compensation plan? **9-34**

Q 9:56 What are the general fiduciary issues for a nonqualified deferred compensation plan? **9-34**

Q 9:57 Is plan termination insurance needed for a nonqualified plan? **9-34**

Q 9:58 For purposes of ERISA Title I, is a nonqualified deferred compensation plan generally considered funded or unfunded? **9-35**

Q 9:59 What is the difference between a funded and an unfunded plan? **9-35**

Q 9:60 For purposes of ERISA Title I, are plans affected by whether or not they are considered funded or unfunded? **9-35**

Q 9:61 Does an employer inadvertently create a top hat plan that is subject to ERISA requirements when it provides benefits to one executive under an employment contract? **9-36**

Q 9:62 How does the employer pay the benefits provided by a top hat plan? **9-36**

Q 9:63 Can employer assurances be made that future benefits will be paid without subjecting employees to current taxation? **9-36**

Q 9:64 Is a top hat plan a funded or unfunded plan for purposes of Title I of ERISA? **9-37**

Q 9:65 Are contributions to an unfunded top hat plan treated differently than contributions to a funded top hat plan? . **9-37**

Q 9:66 Is an excess benefit plan subject to the ERISA Title I requirements? **9-37**

Q 9:67 Is an excess benefit plan subject to the participation, vesting, and funding requirements imposed by Title I of ERISA? **9-38**

Q 9:68 Is an excess benefit plan subject to the reporting and disclosure requirements imposed by Title I of ERISA? . . **9-38**

Other Considerations

Q 9:69 Is a nonqualified deferred compensation plan a security subject to SEC registration? **9-38**

l

Chapter 10 Perquisites and Other Benefits

General Considerations

Q 10:1   What is an executive perquisite? **10-1**

Q 10:2   What are examples of executive perquisites? **10-2**

Q 10:3   How are cellular phone perquisites typically provided? . . **10-3**

Q 10:4   How do companies structure company car programs for executives? **10-3**

Q 10:5   How do companies provide country club/luncheon club perquisites? **10-4**

Q 10:6   How are financial planning programs provided to executives? **10-4**

Q 10:7   Do expense accounts for entertainment purposes have maximums? **10-6**

Q 10:8   What is the typical amount of severance in a severance contract for an executive? **10-6**

Q 10:9   What are typical amounts of supplemental life insurance for executives? **10-7**

Q 10:10   What are typical supplemental executive retirement plan benefit amounts? **10-7**

Q 10:11   How do companies conduct an analysis of executive perquisites provided in competitive companies? **10-8**

Q 10:12   How are executive perquisites valued? **10-8**

Q 10:13   How do companies select executive perquisites? **10-10**

Tax and Accounting Impact

Q 10:14   What are the tax regulations on the reimbursement of travel expenses? **10-11**

Q 10:15   What are the tax regulations on the reimbursement of entertainment expenses? **10-12**

Q 10:16   What are the tax regulations on the reimbursement of club memberships? **10-12**

Q 10:17   What are the tax regulations on company cars? **10-13**

Q 10:18   What are the tax regulations on company payments of car/cellular phones and laptop computers? **10-14**

Q 10:19   What are the tax regulations on company payments of supplemental life insurance for executives? **10-14**

Q 10:20   What are the tax regulations on the executive perquisites of company planes and first-class travel? **10-15**

Q 10:21   What are the tax regulations on the executive financial planning perquisite? **10-15**

Q 10:22   What is the accounting treatment of executive perquisites? **10-16**

Contracts

Q 10:23   What are the types of executive contracts? **10-16**

Q 10:24   How does a company select the type of executive contract? **10-17**

Q 10:25   What are the advantages of an employment agreement? . **10-17**

Q 10:26   What are the disadvantages of an employment agreement? **10-17**

Q 10:27   Are noncompete clauses enforceable? **10-18**

Q 10:28   Are employment agreements enforceable? **10-18**

Q 10:29   What is a golden parachute? **10-19**

Q 10:30   What is a silver parachute? **10-20**

Q 10:31   What is a tin parachute? **10-20**

Q 10:32   How is a change of control defined? **10-20**

Q 10:33   What are the advantages and disadvantages of golden parachutes? **10-20**

Q 10:34   What government regulations impact golden parachute payments? **10-21**

Q 10:35   What are payments "in the nature of compensation"? . . . **10-21**

Q 10:36   Who is a "disqualified individual"? **10-22**

Q 10:37   When do the golden parachute tax rules apply? **10-22**

Q 10:38   What is an "excess parachute payment"? **10-23**

Q 10:39   Are there certain types of payments not considered to be parachute payments? **10-23**

Q 10:40   What are payments "contingent" on a change of control? . **10-23**

Q 10:41   How is the "excess parachute payment" calculated? . . . **10-24**

Q 10:42   Are certain types of payments not subject to a change of control but still considered as parachute payments? . . **10-25**

Q 10:43   How are stock options treated for parachute purposes? . **10-25**

Q 10:44   Are parachute payments subject to tax withholding rules? **10-25**

Q 10:45   Is there a way to avoid the 20 percent excise tax on excess parachute payments? **10-26**

Q 10:46   What is an example of a golden parachute payment? . . . **10-26**

Q 10:47   What are typical provisions in a retirement contract? . . . **10-27**

Q 10:48   Why do companies use retirement contracts for executives? **10-28**

Q 10:49   What are the advantages and disadvantages of retirement
           contracts? **10-28**

Q 10:50   What is an example of an executive retirement contract? .   **10-29**

Chapter 11 Building a Total Compensation Strategy

General Considerations

Q 11:1   What is a total compensation strategy? **11-2**

Q 11:2   What elements of executive compensation are included in
           a total compensation strategy statement? **11-2**

Q 11:3   What are the business purposes of a total compensation
           strategy? **11-2**

Compensation Factors

Q 11:4   What factors determine a total compensation strategy? . .   **11-3**

Q 11:5   How does a company's philosophy affect its total
           compensation strategy? **11-3**

Q 11:6   How can a company's mission or vision statement affect
           its total compensation strategy? **11-4**

Q 11:7   How can a company's business plan affect a total
           compensation strategy? **11-4**

Q 11:8   How can a company's life cycle affect its total
           compensation strategy? **11-5**

Q 11:9   How do internal factors affect a company's total
           compensation strategy? **11-5**

Q 11:10   How do external factors affect a company's total
           compensation strategy? **11-6**

Benefit Factors

Q 11:11   What benefit programs should be included in a total
           compensation strategy statement? **11-6**

Q 11:12   How can health care plan benefits and costs affect a total
           compensation strategy statement? **11-7**

Q 11:13   How can retirement benefits affect a company's total
           compensation strategy statement? **11-7**

Q 11:14   How can life insurance and disability insurance affect a
           company's total compensation strategy statement? **11-8**

Q 11:15   How can capital accumulation plans affect a company's
total compensation strategy statement? **11-8**

Other Factors
Q 11:16   Can total compensation strategies vary by company
business unit? **11-9**
Q 11:17   Can total compensation strategies be developed for
international businesses? **11-10**

Determining the Mix
Q 11:18   How can a company determine the proper mix of
executive compensation elements in a total
compensation strategy statement? **11-10**
Q 11:19   How should companies define competitive labor markets?   **11-11**
Q 11:20   Should all companies establish a total compensation
strategy to pay at the 50th percentile of labor market
competitors? **11-12**
Q 11:21   How can a company decide on the type of short-term
incentive? **11-12**
Q 11:22   How can companies decide on the best type of long-term
incentive? **11-13**

Developing a Total Strategy
Q 11:23   What should be included in a total compensation strategy
statement? **11-14**

Approval and Implementation
Q 11:24   Who should approve a total compensation strategy? . . .   **11-15**
Q 11:25   How should a total compensation strategy be
communicated to executives? **11-15**

Examples of Strategy Statements
Q 11:26   What is an example of a total compensation strategy
statement for a small company? **11-17**
Q 11:27   What is an example of a total compensation strategy
statement for a large company? **11-18**
Q 11:28   What is an example of a total compensation strategy
statement in an entrepreneurial, high-growth company? .   **11-19**

Chapter 12 Small Company Considerations

General Considerations

Q 12:1   How does the mix of executive compensation elements
           differ in small companies? **12-1**

Q 12:2   How do small companies with less sophisticated business
           performance measures establish annual incentives?   . .   **12-2**

Q 12:3   How can small companies with a small human resources
           staff determine appropriate compensation levels? **12-3**

Q 12:4   What form of long-term incentive is most appropriate for
           small companies? **12-3**

Q 12:5   How can small companies attract high-quality people
           without offering competitive base salary and bonus
           amounts? **12-4**

Q 12:6   How can small companies offer competitive executive
           retirement plans without incurring significant costs? . . .   **12-5**

Q 12:7   When and how do family-owned companies provide stock
           to non-family members? **12-6**

Q 12:8   What total compensation strategies are used in small
           companies? **12-6**

Q 12:9   How do small, high-growth companies establish
           competitive values on executives when their companies
           are doubling in size every one or two years? **12-7**

Q 12:10   Are design issues for annual incentive compensation plans
           different in the small company? **12-8**

Q 12:11   How are executive benefits and perquisites different in the
           small company? **12-9**

New Venture Businesses

Q 12:12   How Is incentive compensation structured in new venture
           businesses? **12-9**

Q 12:13   How are base salary and benefits structured in new
           venture businesses? **12-10**

Chapter 13 Board of Directors' Compensation

General Considerations

Q 13:1   How does a company choose the members of its board of
           directors? **13-2**

Q 13:2   What is the role of a company board of directors?   13-2

Outside vs. Inside Directors
Q 13:3   Why would a company choose to have outside directors?   13-3
Q 13:4   What are the typical compensation elements for directors?   13-4
Q 13:5   Are inside directors compensated specifically for their
            activities as directors?   13-5
Q 13:6   How much do outside directors receive for their services?   13-5

Compensation Methods
Q 13:7   How is director income taxed?   13-6
Q 13:8   What methods are used in deferring compensation for
            directors?   13-6
Q 13:9   In what types of performance-based plans do directors
            participate?   13-6
Q 13:10   How are stock options used in compensating directors? .   13-7
Q 13:11   How do the Section 16 rules apply to directors' options? .   13-8
Q 13:12   Do companies provide "regular" stock plans for directors?   13-8
Q 13:13   Can tandem SARs/stock options be granted to directors?   13-8

Other Benefits
Q 13:14   What other benefits are typically provided to directors? . .   13-8
Q 13:15   Do companies provide retirement benefits for their
            directors?   13-9
Q 13:16   Can Keogh plans be utilized by outside board members? .   13-9
Q 13:17   Can Keogh plans be utilized by insider board members? .   13-9
Q 13:18   What are some new trends in board of director
            compensation?   13-10
Q 13:19   Do outside directors get perquisites?   13-10

Chapter 14 Executive Compensation in the Not-For-Profit Organization

General Considerations
Q 14:1   What is a not-for-profit company?   14-1
Q 14:2   How does the mix of executive compensation elements
            differ in a not-for-profit company?   14-2

Q 14:3 How do the business objectives of executive compensation plans differ in a not-for-profit company? . **14-2**

Q 14:4 Does the size of the organization affect executive compensation in a not-for-profit organization? **14-4**

Q 14:5 Does the type of not-for-profit organization affect the level of executive compensation? **14-4**

Q 14:6 Does geographical location affect executive compensation in the not-for-profit company? **14-5**

Base Salary

Q 14:7 How are base salary ranges established in not-for-profit companies? **14-5**

Q 14:8 Are merit increases to base salary used in not-for-profit companies? **14-6**

Annual Incentives

Q 14:9 What is the prevalence of annual incentive plans in not-for-profit companies? **14-6**

Q 14:10 Does the size of the annual incentive award in the not-for-profit company differ from that in the for-profit company? **14-7**

Q 14:11 What performance measures are typically used in the annual incentive plans of not-for-profit companies? . . . **14-7**

Q 14:12 How is eligibility determined for annual incentive plans in not-for-profit companies? **14-7**

Q 14:13 What regulations guide incentive compensation plans for tho not-for-profit company? **14-8**

Long-Term Incentives

Q 14:14 What types of long-term incentive plans are prevalent in not-for-profit companies? **14-10**

Perquisites

Q 14:15 What types of perquisites are prevalent in not-for-profit companies? **14-11**

Q 14:16 What are the requirements for establishing a "bona fide severance plan" in a not-for-profit organization? **14-11**

Chapter 15 Special Early Retirement Programs

Overview

Q 15:1   How does a special early retirement window program work
under an existing retirement plan? **15-2**

Q 15:2   Why do companies offer special early retirement window
programs? **15-2**

Severance Programs

Q 15:3   Do companies offer special severance programs along
with special early retirement programs? **15-3**

Q 15:4   What are the typical severance benefits used along with a
special early retirement program? **15-3**

Planning Early Retirement Programs

Q 15:5   How do companies fund special early retirement
programs? **15-4**

Q 15:6   What, if any, are the negative consequences to companies
that implement special early retirement programs, and
how can these consequences be handled? **15-4**

Q 15:7   Are there any negative consequences to employees who
accept a special early retirement program? **15-5**

Q 15:8   What are the ERISA and Internal Revenue Code
implications of a special early retirement program under
a qualified pension plan? **15-6**

Q 15:9   Do companies require employees who elect a special
early retirement benefit to sign noncompete and/or
nonlitigation agreements? **15-8**

Q 15:10   Do companies provide medical benefits along with a
special early retirement program? **15-9**

Q 15:11   Are there special ERISA rules to consider if the company
wishes to provide an early retirement incentive program
outside of a qualified retirement plan? **15-10**

Chapter 16 U. S. Executives Working Overseas

General Considerations

Q 16:1   What is an executive expatriate? **16-2**

Q 16:2   What are the typical elements of an executive expatriate compensation package?   16-2

Q 16:3   What is a foreign service premium?   16-3

Q 16:4   What is a hardship allowance?   16-3

Q 16:5   What is a cost of living allowance?   16-3

Q 16:6   What is a housing allowance?   16-5

Q 16:7   Do executive expatriates receive reimbursement of any home sale or other relocation costs when they take an overseas assignment?   16-6

Q 16:8   What is a home rental program?   16-8

Q 16:9   What is an education allowance?   16-8

Q 16:10   What is language training?   16-8

Q 16:11   What is home leave?   16-9

Tax Considerations

Q 16:12   What is tax equalization?   16-9

Q 16:13   What is tax-free income?   16-11

Q 16:14   What is spendable income?   16-12

Q 16:15   What are foreign earned income exclusions?   16-13

Q 16:16   How can executive expatriates avoid taxes when on overseas assignment?   16-14

Q 16:17   Can an executive expatriate avoid capital gains tax on the sale of a home while on overseas assignment?   16-16

Special Compensation

Q 16:18   Are executive expatriates protected against currency fluctuations?   16-16

Q 16:19   What is a completion bonus?   16-17

Q 16:20   Can stock options be granted to executive expatriate? . .   16-17

Q 16:21   What are free-standing stock appreciation rights?   16-18

Q 16:22   Can long-term bonus plans be used for executive expatriates?   16-18

Q 16:23   Can annual incentive plans be used for executive expatriates?   16-19

Q 16:24   What kind of medical benefits are provided to executive expatriates?   16-19

Q 16:25   What happens to an executive expatriate's pension plan while on overseas assignment?   16-20

Q 16:26 How are life insurance and disability established for
executive expatriates? **16-20**

Q 16:27 What perquisites are provided to executive expatriates? . **16-20**

Q 16:28 What is done for executive expatriates upon repatriation? . **16-21**

Q 16:29 What special compensation is provided to an executive
expatriate who takes a second overseas assignment? . . **16-22**

Q 16:30 What are the elements of a net to net compensation
program? **16-22**

Q 16:31 What are the typical elements of a modified home country
balance sheet compensation program? **16-24**

Q 16:32 Is there a checklist of issues that should be considered by
a company and/or executive in developing an executive
expatriate compensation program? **16-24**

Chapter 17 Executive Compensation in the Public Sector

Q 17:1 What is the driving philosophy behind executive
compensation in the public sector versus that in the
private sector? **17-1**

Q 17:2 How is base salary different in the public sector
organization than in the private sector organization? . . **17-2**

Q 17:3 Are job evaluation systems used for executive positions in
public sector organizations? **17-3**

Q 17:4 Can merit increases to base salary work for executive
positions in public sector organizations? **17-3**

Q 17:5 What are the advantages and disadvantages of
tenure-based pay increase systems? **17-4**

Q 17:6 Why do public sector organizations prefer a tenure-based
pay increase system? **17-5**

Q 17:7 Are salary ranges used in the public sector? **17-6**

Q 17:8 Are annual incentives used in public sector organizations? **17-7**

Q 17:9 Are long-term performance plans or stock award plans
used in public organizations? **17-7**

Q 17:10 Are insured benefits in the public sector better than those
in private companies? **17-8**

Q 17:11 Are retirement plans in the public sector better than those
in private companies? **17-8**

Q 17:12 Can supplemental retirement plans be used in public
sector organizations? **17-9**

Q 17:13   Are public sector organizations subject to Title VII of the Civil Rights Act of 1964, the Fair Labor Standards Act, Americans with Disabilities Act, Age Discrimination in Employment Act, or other such regulations? **17-9**

Q 17:14   Do public sector executives have perquisites? **17-10**

Q 17:15   How can compensation plans be used to attract high-quality executives into the public sector? **17-10**

Chapter 18 Compensation for Temporary Executives

General Considerations

Q 18:1   What is a temporary executive? **18-2**

Q 18:2   Are temporary executives independent contractors? . . . **18-2**

Q 18:3   What are the advantages and disadvantages of being an independent contractor to the executive? **18-3**

Q 18:4   What are the advantages and disadvantages of independent contractors to a company? **18-3**

Q 18:5   What is the difference between a short-term and long-term temporary assignment? **18-4**

Q 18:6   What is outsourcing? **18-4**

Q 18:7   What are other alternatives to outsourcing? **18-5**

Q 18:8   How do temporary executives obtain an assignment? . . . **18-5**

Q 18:9   Can temporary executives be placed on an overseas assignment? **18-6**

Q 18:10   How is base salary determined for temporary executives? **18-6**

Incentives and Benefits

Q 18:11   Are temporary executives provided with incentive compensation? **18-7**

Q 18:12   Are temporary executives provided with stock awards? . . **18-8**

Q 18:13   Are temporary executives provided with perquisites? . . . **18-8**

Q 18:14   What insured benefits are provided to temporary executives? **18-8**

Q 18:15   Are temporary executives provided with retirement benefits? **18-9**

Federal Protection

Q 18:16   Are temporary executives subject to federal regulations on
          equal pay, age, etc.?   18-9

Conversion to Full-Time Status

Q 18:17   Can temporary executives be converted to full-time status?   18-9
Q 18:18   If a temporary executive converts to a full-time employee,
          are there benefit issues that arise?   18-10

Current Litigation

Q 18:19   How does the *Microsoft* case affect the temporary
          employee arena?   18-10

Chapter 19 Economic Profit-Based Incentive Plans

Overview

Q 19:1   What is economic profit?   19-2
Q 19:2   What is economic value-added?   19-3
Q 19:3   How is economic profit used in executive compensation
          plans?   19-3
Q 19:4   What are the advantages of economic profit plans?   19-5
Q 19:5   What are the disadvantages of economic profit plans? . .   19-5
Q 19:6   What impact do executives have on economic profit? . . .   19-6
Q 19:7   Can executives affect the cost of capital?   19-7
Q 19:8   Can economic profit be used in divisions or strategic
          business units?   19-7
Q 19:9   Can economic profit plans be used with other annual or
          long-term incentive plans?   19-8

Implementation

Q 19:10   What steps are necessary to implement an economic profit
          plan?   19-8
Q 19:11   How is economic profit performance correlated to
          compensation?   19-10
Q 19:12   How are payments made for economic profit awards that
          are earned as part of a long-term incentive plan?   19-11

Q 19:13   How are economic profit plans communicated to
           executives?   19-14
Q 19:14   May nonexecutives participate in economic profit plans? .   19-15
Q 19:15   Should economic profit plans have a fixed term?   19-15

Case Studies

Q 19:16   What are some examples of companies that have used
           economic profit or EVA plans?   19-16
Q 19:17   How can economic profit plans be used to help a
           company accomplish a business turnaround?   19-17
Q 19:18   How can economic profit plans be used to help a
           company overcome significant competitive pressure? . .   19-20
Q 19:19   What is an example of an economic profit plan that was
           unsuccessful?   19-22

Chapter 20   Trends in Executive Compensation

Total Cash Compensation

Q 20:1   How are base salary levels changing for executive
           positions in large companies?   20-1
Q 20:2   How are base salary levels changing for executive
           positions in small companies?   20-3
Q 20:3   Is the $1 million cap on the deductibility of executive pay in
           public companies having any influence on executive
           base salary levels?   20-5
Q 20:4   How are annual bonus levels changing in large
           companies?   20-6
Q 20:5   How are annual bonus levels changing in small
           companies?   20-7
Q 20:6   How are annual incentive practices changing?   20-7
Q 20:7   What changes are occurring in the mix of base salary and
           annual incentive for executive positions?   20-9

Long-Term Compensation

Q 20:8   How are stock award levels changing for executive
           positions?   20-10
Q 20:9   Does the use of performance-based stock options
           continue as a trend?   20-13

Q 20:10   Have noncompete clauses been used in stock award plans? **20-14**

Q 20:11   Are economic value-added (EVA) plans continuing as a trend? **20-14**

Q 20:12   Are reload stock features continuing as a trend? **20-15**

Q 20:13   Do many companies use stock ownership guidelines for executives? **20-15**

Q 20:14   Are any executive loans still used in long-term plans? . . . **20-16**

Q 20:15   Are stock cancel and reissue plans still used? **20-17**

Q 20:16   What are other trends in long-term incentives? **20-18**

Regulatory Issues

Q 20:17   What has been the reaction to FAS 123 on the accounting for stock options? **20-18**

Q 20:18   Have the SEC regulations on the reporting of public company performance comparisons in annual proxies had an impact on executive compensation? **20-19**

Q 20:19   Has the capital gains tax rate decrease to 20 percent had any effect on executive pay? **20-21**

Q 20:20   Will more executives be subject to the alternative minimum tax (AMT) if the use of ISOs increases in response to a lower capital gains tax? **20-22**

Q 20:21   What new regulations are pending? **20-23**

Q 20:22   Do current regulations allow stock options to be transferred? **20-23**

Q 20:23   With greater use of stock plans, is dilution a new issue in executive compensation that needs to be regulated? . . **20-24**

Outside Directors

Q 20:24   How are remuneration levels changing for outside directors? **20-25**

Q 20:25   Are retirement plans still commonly established for outside directors? **20-26**

Q 20:26   Are stock awards common for outside directors? **20-27**

Q 20:27   Are outside directors typically provided with benefits? . . **20-28**

Q 20:28   Do outside directors receive change-of-control benefits? . **20-28**

Chapter 21 Compensation for Division Executives

Base Salary

Q 21:1   What is a division executive? **21-1**

Q 21:2   How is base salary different for division executives? . . . **21-2**

Annual Incentives

Q 21:3   How are annual incentive amounts different for division
executives? **21-3**

Q 21:4   Is the mix of total cash compensation changing for division
executives? **21-4**

Q 21:5   Should division executives have their annual incentive
determined from division or corporate results? **21-5**

Long-Term Incentives

Q 21:6   How are levels of long-term incentives different for division
executives? **21-6**

Q 21:7   Should division executives have their long-term incentive
determined from division or corporate results? **21-6**

Q 21:8   How can long-term incentives be changed from stock
options to incentives based on division results? **21-8**

Q 21:9   What is the best way to design a payout schedule for a
long-term incentive plan that is based on division results? **21-8**

Q 21:10   Can value-added performance measures be used in
long-term incentives? **21-10**

Q 21:11   What is an example of a value-added performance
measure in a division? **21-10**

Q 21:12   How do companies determine the cost of capital? **21-12**

Q 21:13   Can division-based incentive plans be the same for an
executive's annual incentive and long-term incentive? . . **21-13**

Q 21:14   Can division-based incentive plans be used in not-for-profit
organizations? **21-14**

Q 21:15   Can division-based incentive plans be used in international
organizations? **21-14**

Q 21:16   What are the disadvantages of division-based incentive
compensation plans? **21-14**

Benefits and Perquisites

Q 21:17   What perquisites are typically provided to division executives? **21-15**

Q 21:18   Are division executives subject to the same regulatory constraints as corporate executives? **21-15**

Q 21:19   Is the compensation of division executives included in public company proxies if they are one of the five highest paid employees? **21-16**

Q 21:20   Are there differences in the total compensation of division executives based on degree of autonomy? **21-16**

Chapter 22   Small-Company Versus Large-Company Practices

Total Cash Compensation

Q 22:1   How do small and large companies define executives? . .   **22-1**

Q 22:2   How do base salary levels in a small company compare to those in a large company? **22-2**

Q 22:3   How do annual incentive amounts in a small company compare to those in a large company? **22-3**

Q 22:4   What are typical amounts of total cash compensation in small and large companies? **22-5**

Q 22:5   What are typical annual incentive amounts as a percentage of base salary for both small and large companies? **22-6**

Q 22:6   How are annual incentive plans structured in small and large companies? **22-7**

Long-Term Plans

Q 22:7   How many shares as a percentage of the total shares outstanding are reserved for executive compensation plans? **22-8**

Q 22:8   What are the typical targeted amounts of incentive used in long-term incentive plans for small and large companies?   **22-9**

Q 22:9   What is the typical mix of executive compensation elements in small and large companies? **22-10**

Q 22:10   How do small and large companies calculate the value of stock options? **22-11**

Q 22:11   How are long-term performance plans structured in small
           and large companies? **22-12**

Benefits and Perquisites

Q 22:12   How do executive perquisites differ between small and
           large companies? **22-13**
Q 22:13   How are supplemental retirement plans typically
           structured in small and large companies? **22-14**
Q 22:14   How are benefits different in small versus large
           companies? **22-15**

Chapter 23   Executive Compensation Practices During a Restructuring

Overview

Q 23:1   What is a restructuring? **23-1**
Q 23:2   What are some examples of companies that have
           undergone restructurings? **23-2**
Q 23:3   What issues must be considered when reviewing executive
           pay strategy during a restructuring? **23-3**
Q 23:4   What issues are unique to a restructuring involving an
           acquisition? **23-6**
Q 23:5   What issues are unique to a restructuring involving a
           merger? **23-7**
Q 23:6   How are levels of compensation established for executives
           in separate business units or departments within a
           restructured company? **23-10**
Q 23:7   If the company requires executives to be transferable
           between business units or departments, how is the
           executive compensation strategy affected? **23-11**
Q 23:8   How should supplemental benefits and perquisites be
           handled in a restructuring? **23-11**

Base Salary

Q 23:9   How should executive positions be classified for base
           salary purposes following a restructuring? **23-12**
Q 23:10   Should salary ranges be dictated by industry practices,
           location, or job responsibilities? **23-14**

Q 23:11   Should salary administration practices be the same or
           different after a corporate restructuring? **23-14**

Short-term Incentives

Q 23:12   Should eligibility for annual incentives be affected by a
           restructuring? **23-15**

Q 23:13   Should short-term incentive plans be the same between
           company businesses or should they be designed to
           support different business unit objectives? **23-16**

Q 23:14   After a restructuring, how are potential award levels
           determined for annual incentives? **23-16**

Q 23:15   What performance measures are used by restructured
           companies? **23-17**

Q 23:16   If different goals are used among business units after a
           restructuring, how can a company achieve equity in the
           annual incentive program? **23-18**

Q 23:17   Is it possible for one business unit to have a performance
           target plan and another business unit to have a
           discretionary plan? **23-19**

Q 23:18   Who should approve annual incentive payments in a
           restructured company? **23-19**

Long-term Incentives

Q 23:19   How are long-term incentive plans affected by a
           restructuring? **23-20**

Q 23:20   Should long-term incentive plans be the same between
           business units or departments? **23-21**

Q 23:21   How do restructured companies determine the size of
           long-term incentive awards? **23-22**

Q 23:22   Is the number of shares used in executive long-term plans,
           as a percentage of the total shares outstanding, greater
           in a restructured company? **23-24**

Q 23:23   Does a restructuring prompt changes in award frequency
           and terms in long-term incentive plans? **23-24**

Benefits and Perquisites

Q 23:24   How do executive benefits and perquisites change during
           a restructuring? **23-25**

Q 23:25   Does eligibility for executive benefits and/or perquisites
change during a restructuring? **23-26**

Q 23:26   What perquisites are most commonly added or improved
during a restructuring? **23-27**

Chapter 1

Fundamental Concepts of Executive Compensation

The growth and development of a company can be greatly assisted if quality executives can be secured and retained. Efficiently designed executive compensation programs are an important factor in a company's ability to recruit and retain an executive team. A typical executive compensation package consists of a base salary, annual incentives, long-term incentives, benefits, and perquisites. The cost to the company and the value to the executives of long-term incentives and executive benefits continue to grow. The design of executive compensation packages is driven by competitive practices, tax and accounting rules and regulations, and company values and strategies. This chapter addresses the fundamental concepts in executive compensation.

Total Compensation Issues 1-2
Base Salary 1-12
Incentive Plans 1-14
Tax Considerations 1-21
Accounting Considerations 1-29

Total Compensation Issues

Q 1:1   What is total remuneration?

Total remuneration is generally defined as a combination of five factors:

- Base salary
- Annual incentives
- Long-term incentives
- Benefits
- Perquisites

Each of the elements of the total remuneration package meets a different executive need as well as a company need.

Q 1:2   How does base salary meet the needs of executives as well as the company?

Base salary supports the executive's lifestyle, providing the cash to meet day-to-day expenses. From the company's point of view it is a fixed cost for services rendered. It also can represent the minimum rate that the company is willing to pay for a given job.

Q 1:3   How do annual and long-term incentives meet the needs of executives and the company?

Annual incentives supplement base salary and provide lump-sum payments to executives based on their achievement of annual goals (which are generally stated in the company's annual business plan). These incentive payments can also be provided on a monthly or quarterly basis. Annual, quarterly, or monthly incentives provide the company with an excellent means of motivating executives to achieve specific and critical company goals. The term "annual incentive" has the same meaning as the term "annual bonus."

Long-term incentive programs (i.e., plans that have an award period of two years or more) provide executives with the wherewithal to accumulate capital and build an estate. They can serve as a significant means of retaining key executive talent. Long-term incentives are provided in the form of cash payments or stock payments; therefore, significant rises in stock prices can result in quite significant amounts of compensation. The term "long-term incentive" has the same meaning as the term "long-term income."

Q 1:4   How do benefits and perquisites satisfy executive needs?

Benefit programs provide financial security in the case of death, disability, sickness, or retirement, while perquisites, such as club memberships, first-class air travel, company cars, financial planning, supplemental retirement, and supplemental insurance, are special entitlement programs made available to a select group of executives.

Q 1:5   How do companies express the value of all elements of executive compensation?

Elements of the total compensation package can be expressed as a percentage of base salary. This analysis can be represented by the following:

Total Compensation as a Percentage of Base Salary	$100,000 Base Salary	$250,000 Base Salary
Base Salary	100%	100%
Annual Incentives	30%	40%
Annual Value of Long-Term Incentives	35%	50%
Benefits	30%	30%
Perquisites	10%	15%
Total Compensation	205%	235%

Companies also express the mix of executive compensation elements as a percentage of total compensation. This is shown in Chart 1-1.

1-3

Chart 1-1. Total Mix of Executive Compensation for CEO Position

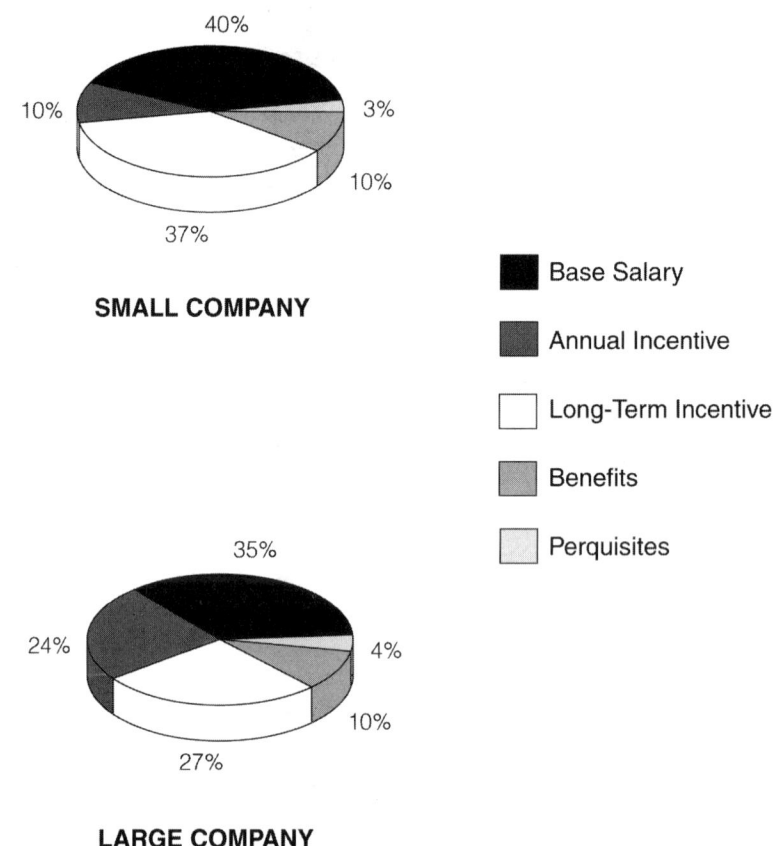

40%

10%   3%

                       10%

37%

SMALL COMPANY

■ Base Salary

■ Annual Incentive

□ Long-Term Incentive

▨ Benefits

□ Perquisites

35%

24%   4%

                       10%

27%

LARGE COMPANY

Source: Management Performance International, Inc.

Q 1:6 What is total cash compensation?

Total cash compensation (also known as total direct compensation) is the sum of annual base salary plus annual payments from any short-term incentive compensation plan. This can be measured by using targeted or actual annual short-term incentives plus base salary. Most companies establish executive compensation levels by reviewing their own business needs and by reviewing competitive total cash compensation practices using *actual* short-term incentive amounts paid, not *targeted* amounts.

Q 1:7 What is total compensation?

Total compensation is the sum of annual base salary plus annual payments from any short-term incentive compensation plan plus annual payments (or the annualized value of potential payments) from any long-term incentive or stock award plan.

Q 1:8 What are some of the factors that affect total compensation?

The following six factors have some impact on executive compensation:

- Job responsibility
- Level of job within the organization
- Type of industry
- Supply and demand factors in the labor market
- Size of organization
- Company and executive performance

All other factors being constant, job responsibility and organizational size have the most significant impact on the total compensation for any executive.

Q 1:9 How does the type of executive responsibility affect total compensation?

The executive's necessary skills and responsibilities and expected achievements have a significant effect on total compensation. For example, a vice president of finance typically receives a higher total compensation package than a vice president of human resources because most companies consider the human resources position less complex and easier to learn and the finance position more critical to the success of the business operation. Functional responsibilities in a job therefore have a direct impact on an executive's total compensation.

In most companies the chief executive officer's (CEO's) compensation is the foundation upon which the balance of a company's compensation practices and pay levels are based. The compensation for executives who report to the CEO will show a constant pattern; their compensation is expressed as a percentage of the CEO's. It is thus extremely important to establish a proper value for the CEO and to consider the relationship between the compensation of this CEO and that of other executives in the organization. Chart 1-2 presents average compensation of executive positions as a percentage of average CEO base salary and total compensation, as reported in *2000 Officer Compensation Report*. (*The Officer Compensation Report* offers comprehensive annual labor market data on top executive positions in small and medium-sized companies.) [M. Meltzer, H. Goldsmith, and M. Meller, *2000 Officer Compensation Report* (New York: Panel Publishers 2000) EXEC-29]

Q 1:10   How does level within the organization affect an executive's total compensation?

The closer an executive's position is to the top position in the organization (usually the CEO), the more likely that the total compensation will be higher.

Example. The Vice President of Engineering in Company A reports to the Chief Operating Officer, who in turn reports to the Chief Executive Officer. The Vice President of Engineering in Company B reports directly to the Chief Executive Officer. Assume that both companies have the same sales volume and the same number of employees. The Vice President of Engineering for Company B (who is closer in reporting structure to the CEO) will receive a higher base salary, a greater bonus eligibility, a more lucrative capital accumulation plan, and probably have access to more perquisites. Part of this is caused by the organizational-level salary differentials

Chart 1-2. Median Officer Compensation as a Percentage of Average CEO Compensation

	Percent of Median Base Salary 1999 (Bonus Ineligible)	Percent of Median Base Salary 1999 (Bonus Eligible)	Percent of Median Bonus 1999 (Bonus Eligible)	Percent of Median Total Direct Comp 1999 (For Bonus Eligible Execs who received bonuses)
CEO/Pres	100.00	100.00	100.00	100.00
COO	74.07	73.68	73.33	71.89
Fin/Acctg Exec	70.37	59.47	36.00	51.60
Sales/Mktg Exec	69.14	54.21	34.67	49.82
Mfg/Prod Exec	58.02	46.32	24.00	41.64

that most companies attempt to maintain. Part of it is also caused by the organizational perspective that the closer an executive is to the CEO in reporting relationship, the more impact that executive has on the company's performance and, therefore, the greater his or her compensation should be.

Q 1:11   How does the type of industry affect an executive's total compensation?

The industry in which an executive is employed has an impact on the total compensation of the executive for two main reasons. First, executives generally are compensated more highly in industries where companies tend to have larger sales volume or assets (see Q 1:13). Industries with larger companies, such as petroleum manufacturing and energy, will therefore generally provide higher compensation packages than industries like health care and banking, which traditionally compensate executives at a lower rate.

Second, companies with higher profit margins tend to have higher total executive compensation packages. For example, an executive in the pharmaceutical industry would tend to be paid at a higher rate than an executive in another consumer product company because the higher profit margins in this industry drive higher amounts of total compensation.

Planning Tip. One way to determine the industry for comparison is to find out which companies your current executives were hired from, and which companies hire your former executives.

Q 1:12   How do supply and demand factors influence total compensation?

Because executive talent is a free market commodity, its price varies according to the classic laws of supply and demand. At various times during the past 30 years financial executives have been more in demand than marketing executives, while at other times during that same period, the reverse has been true. This demand occurs not only in the general economy and specific industries, but also in the life cycle of a given company. For example, companies in a growth cycle tend to recruit executives heavily, while companies in a mature or declining cycle do not recruit as heavily.

When executives are in high demand, total compensation increases in order to attract them. This can have a compounding effect on the compensation levels of long-time company executives, whose compensation should stay equitable with that of newly hired executives. Companies in a recruiting mode need to project these associated costs so that this can be budgeted and planned in advance.

Q 1:13   How does company size influence total compensation?

Two CEOs with similar responsibilities can have two totally different total compensation packages based entirely on the size of their organizations. The executive in a company that has greater sales volume typically receives higher total cash compensation than the executive in a smaller company. Companies believe that because such executives have a greater magnitude of accountability, they should be more highly paid. This reality is reflected in the labor market and in all surveys of executive compensation.

Example. Consider the case of a CEO in a $10 billion company versus that of a CEO of a $1 billion company. The CEO in the company with the significantly higher sales volume, the $10 billion company, will be more highly paid. Taking this point further, assume that the CEO in the $10 billion company has a division president who manages a $1 billion business. Compare the compensation of such a division president with that of a chief executive officer of a $1 billion company. The CEO will be more highly paid than the division president because this individual reports directly to the board of directors, not to a corporate CEO. The issue of accountability, the fact that there is one less reporting level, has a direct impact on total compensation (see Q 1:10).

Company growth, acquisition, or divestiture can compound the difficulty of determining executive compensation. For example, whenever a corporation decides to divest itself of poorly performing companies, should it reduce CEO salary because company size has decreased? Or, if the CEO acquires a new subsidiary company with a large revenue (but perhaps no profits), does the company automatically increase CEO salary?

The answer to both of these questions is no, not at the time. If acquisitions and divestitures continue, over time this will affect the level of total compensation, because company size is a major influence on executive pay.

Numerous charts in *The Officer Compensation Report* show how CEO compensation varies by company size (i.e., the larger the company, the higher the total compensation).

Q 1:14   How does company performance affect total compensation?

Corporations, consulting firms, academic institutions, and the media have actively tried for years to correlate executive pay with company performance. Every spring, the media publishes executive compensation data on public companies to support this correlation.

Annual incentive plans, if properly designed, call for incentives to rise and fall with company performance. Clearly this is the intent of any executive compensation program. Most studies relating total cash compensation to performance will show that annual incentives are usually slightly higher in successful firms than in unsuccessful firms (of course, surveys vary in their definitions of successful and unsuccessful firms). Performance can, however, be difficult to evaluate. Consider the case where a company with a 2 percent profit margin increases that profit margin to 3 percent. Contrast this with a similar company in a similar business that increases its profit margin from 10 percent to 15 percent. Both companies have achieved increases of 50 percent in their profit margins. Some would argue that executive compensation increases in each company should be the same, because performance was the same. Others would argue, however, that executive compensation increases in the company that increases its profit margin from 10 percent to 15 percent should be significantly higher because profit percentages are higher.

Most companies resolve this difficulty by using two main criteria to set performance goals with their boards of directors: (1) improvement over the prior year and (2) positive comparison to similar companies. These two dimensions of performance can be useful criteria to support increases in an executive's total compensation.

Moreover, they provide a solid link between executive and company performance and executive total compensation.

Long-term income programs also correlate positively with company performance because they are based on the appreciation of a company's stock value; therefore, payments to executives from a long-term stock award program will increase, as will the appreciation in company stock held by shareholders. Because executive performance can affect stock price, there can be a correlation between executive pay and company performance as measured in stock price.

Not all components of executive compensation are tied to performance. Base salary, benefits, and perquisites serve other purposes such as financial security and supporting a day-to-day standard of living.

Q 1:15   Does executive performance affect total compensation?

As is the case with company performance (see Q 1:14), executive performance, as measured in short- and long-term incentive plans, can also affect total compensation.

Example. Executive A in Company A receives a stock option to purchase 1,000 shares at $5 per share. Executive B in Company B also receives a stock option to purchase 1,000 shares of stock at the same price. The stock in Company A increases to $10 per share, while the stock in Company B increases to $15 per share. If both executives exercise their rights to purchase these shares, Executive A has received a value of $5,000 ($5 per share × 1,000 shares), while Executive B has a value of $10,000 ($10 per share × 1,000 shares).

The effect of executive performance on total compensation can also be illustrated by the huge stock grants that have been made to some CEOs in the past few years. One example is the CEO of Coca-Cola, Roberto Goizueta, who received an outright grant of 1.2 million shares of Coca-Cola stock worth, at the time, $80 million. At a shareholders meeting, Mr. Goizueta pointed out to great acclaim that during his term as CEO the total value of the company stock had risen $500 million. Jumbo stock grants have also been made to Michael Eisner of Disney and Lee Iacocca of Chrysler, to name a few.

Base Salary

Q 1:16   Does geographic location affect an executive's base salary?

Surprisingly, no. For example, it is generally argued that it costs more to live in New York City than in Atlanta, Georgia. A comparison of compensation levels for comparable positions in comparably sized organizations shows, however, that New York City pay premiums are less than 10 percent higher than compensation in Atlanta, substantially less than the approximately 30 to 40 percent cost-of-living differential that exists between the two cities. (Although surveys show little noticeable geographic difference in total compensation for executives, this is not the case for lower-level management positions and nonexempt or hourly positions.)

It should be noted, however, that executives do receive substantial relocation benefits whenever they are asked to move from a low cost-of-living area to a high cost-of-living area. As mentioned in Q 1:12, executives in high demand will often be provided with large base salary increases as well as front-end hiring bonuses, and special benefits and perquisites, to attract them to a company. This is another reason that geographic pay differentials are not a major factor in executive base salary.

Q 1:17   How is base salary related to the other components of total compensation for executives?

Because annual incentives and in some cases long-term incentives can be targeted as a percentage of base salary, total cash compensation as well as total compensation can vary significantly between executive jobs with significant differences in base salary.

Example. An executive with a base salary of $100,000 might typically have a targeted annual bonus award of 25 percent of base, or $25,000, and a targeted annual long-term incentive award of 30 percent, or $30,000. Thus the level of base salary in most companies is used to drive the amount of total compensation.

For this reason, most companies will provide executive base salary amounts that are close to targeted competitive levels.

Q 1:18   How can base salary be used to determine the mix of total compensation?

Because base salary is used as the foundation for the annual and long-term incentive portions of total compensation, it will have a direct effect on the mix of total compensation (i.e., annual bonus and long-term incentive).

Example. A company desires a total compensation strategy that will provide an executive with amounts of annual bonus and long-term incentive that will equal annual base salary. If this executive has a base salary of $200,000, then the targeted annual bonus could be 50 percent ($100,000), and the targeted annual award from the long-term incentive could also be 50 percent ($100,000), for a total of $200,000. The mix of total compensation meets company objectives.

In establishing the mix of total compensation, companies will typically deviate from average competitive total compensation by 10 percent. Assume a typical annual incentive for a CEO of 40 percent of base salary when the annual base salary is $200,000 (Company C). Further, assume that the annualized long-term incentive plan has a goal of providing 50 percent of base salary. The executive in Company A who is paid a lower base salary of $180,000 (10 percent below the competitive labor market) has a significantly lower total compensation than the executive in Company B who is paid a base salary of $220,000, or 10 percent above the competitive labor market.

Total Compensation Element	Company A	Company B	Company C
Base Salary	$180,000	$220,000	$200,000
40% Annual Incentive	72,000	88,000	80,000
50% Long-Term Incentive	90,000	110,000	100,000
Total Compensation	$342,000	$418,000	$380,000

Planning Tip. When establishing base salary, companies should consider the desired level and mix of total compensation. The mix of base salary, annual incentive, and long-term incentive can vary provided the total compensation remains competitive.

Incentive Plans

Q 1:19 What is the rationale for having an incentive plan?

There are several reasons why companies have incentive plans. Incentive payments have proven to be one of the most effective ways to motivate executives to focus on specific corporate performance objectives. These plans also help companies gain a competitive advantage or avoid a competitive disadvantage in terms of recruiting and retaining employees; many companies today offer some sort of incentive plan to their executives, especially in cases where base salary levels are perceived as below the market rate. As a variable form of compensation, incentive payments are reduced or eliminated as corporate performance declines; this affords a measure of safety to the company. Also, the use of incentive payments may benefit the company's cash flow either because payments are deferred until the end of a year or because they are made in company stock.

Another rationale for having incentive plans is that if executives can make decisions and judgments that affect year-to-year company results, it makes sense for these executives to have a significant part of their current earnings dependent upon the achievement of these results.

Q 1:20 Are annual incentive plans appropriate for all types of organizations?

No. In small organizations where results are not always measurable, annual incentive plans are difficult to implement and manage. They are usually not appropriate for rapidly growing companies either, because it is difficult for these companies to set realistic goals on a year-to-year basis. The lack of an annual incentive plan in fast-growth companies can typically be offset, however, by lucrative long-term plans.

Q 1:21 What characteristics identify organizations for which annual incentive plans are feasible?

Several characteristics identify those companies and/or industries for which incentive plans are more feasible:

1. Numerous short-term decisions affect company profits. In this case, executives tend to be motivated to achieve short-term profits, and their success can be judged in a relatively short time (i.e., one year or less). This is important because profit is a common performance measure in short-term incentive plans. Executives want to earn money from short-term incentive plans, so they tend to go for short-term profit.

2. The organization is decentralized. Executives have clearly defined areas of profit and loss responsibility and individuals, not committees, have the authority to make decisions and implement them.

3. The accounting and economic data used to evaluate performance are available and accessible. Too often, this characteristic is overlooked.

4. The management team is goal-oriented. This management attitude emphasizes executive focus on specific business activities that will produce overall success for the company.

5. Base salary is set below market level, but annual incentives are used to compensate for the variance.

Q 1:22 How can companies deal with executives' focusing on the short run at the expense of long-term performance in their efforts to receive high annual payout?

Annual incentives can create an overemphasis on short-term performance. For example, if the executive has no long-term objectives, or if current long-term objectives give executives the opportunity to achieve short-term results at the expense of, or in lieu of, long-term results, then these objectives should be changed. Companies should provide short-term incentive plan objectives that are integrated with long-term incentive plan objectives.

Planning Tip. One plan design method of ensuring that executives do not overemphasize annual performance is to make sure that the sum of the annual rewards over a period of time is less than the probable long-term plan payout. Consider a CEO who is currently earning a base salary of $200,000 and is eligible for an annual incentive plan payment of 50 percent of that base and is also eligible for a long-term plan that will pay out in five years.

Annual Year	Base*	Incentive
1999	$200,000	$100,000
2001	214,000	107,000
2002	228,980	114,490
2003	245,008	122,504
2004	262,158	131,079

*Assume 7% annual salary adjustment.

The long-term plan should be designed so that if performance expectations are met both on an annual and long-term basis, the long-term plan should pay out at least $575,073 (sum of annual incentive payouts) and probably 150 percent of that amount, or $862,609. With such a large long-term payout, the financial incentive will weigh toward the long term.

Q 1:23 What is the typical relationship between annual and long-term incentives?

Most companies both small and large will focus on the long-term performance of their executives. Therefore, most executives receive compensation from long-term incentive plans that is equal to or greater (on an annualized basis) than that received from the annual incentive compensation plan.

For example:

	Base Salary	Bonus %	Long-Term %
Executive A	$100,000	25%	25%
Executive B	$200,000	30%	35%
Executive C	$300,000	40%	50%

Q 1:24 What are some basic guidelines for incentive plan design?

Obviously, all incentive plans must be tailored to the company's policies and to its financial and operating circumstances. To help focus on these issues, many companies develop a written compensation philosophy statement (see Chapter 11, "Building a Total Compensation Strategy Statement," and Q 1:27). This statement, which documents the values and the unique operating circumstances of the company as they relate to the compensation of executives, can be used as a guide in the development of incentive programs. For example, if a company's compensation philosophy states that the organization values teamwork and group performance, it clearly would be inappropriate to develop an incentive program emphasizing individual performance.

Q 1:25   Typically, who is eligible for incentive plan participation?

The percentage of executives participating in annual incentive plans varies greatly between companies and within industries. As a rough rule of thumb, 1 percent of employees in an organization are eligible to participate. Two principal factors affecting the extent of eligibility in incentive plans are whether the company is capital-intensive or people-intensive, and whether the company is centralized or decentralized. Highly capital-intensive industries have proportionately fewer individuals eligible for incentive plans than do people-intensive industries. Centralized companies also have fewer individuals eligible for incentive plans than do decentralized companies.

Companies should consider two primary criteria when determining eligibility for incentive plans. First, they should include those executives who can make decisions that affect the results of the company overall or its business units in a significant way. Second, companies should also consider competitive practices. If certain executive positions normally participate in incentive plans in other organizations, then these positions must be closely scrutinized to determine whether such individuals should participate in company incentive plans.

While eligibility may be somewhat arbitrary, it is typically based on one or more of the following criteria:

- Salary level, for example, "all employees who earn $60,000 or more per year"

- Salary grade, for example, "all employees who are in compensation grade 20 or higher"
- Organizational level, for example, "all executives who report directly to the chief executive or chief operating officer"
- Combination approaches, for example, "all executives who are in grade 20 or higher and report directly to the chief executive or chief operating officer"

Each of these approaches has distinct disadvantages. Salary level favors those disciplines with high market worth and may not reflect potential impact on company performance. Salary grade cutoff favors the market value considerations that went into designing the salary structure, and puts pressure on the job evaluation program to evaluate many jobs at the minimum grade level required for eligibility in the annual incentive plan. Finally, the organizational level approach can result in the inclusion of executives with relatively minor responsibilities and the exclusion of those executives who have substantial organizational impact.

Planning Tip. Most companies are now using a combination of two or more criteria to guide incentive plan eligibility. For example, a job must be evaluated in job level 10 and report to the president. (Q 4:51 also includes a discussion of incentive plan design issues.)

Q 1:26   How do executive compensation programs differ in emerging or start-up companies?

Stock-based plans are a common component of an executive compensation program in both young and mature companies. Stock-based plans are even more crucial to start-up and emerging companies because many start-up companies and emerging companies cannot offer competitive base salary and benefits to executives. In addition, annual incentive plans that pay out in cash can be large cash drains to a start-up company.

The start-up or emerging company can, however, offer something that the mature company may not be able to offer: a chance for the executive to build wealth through stock ownership, if and when the company succeeds. This is particularly common in the field of high technology where stock-based compensation is often a significant part of the total package. This package is regularly offered not only to executives, but to other key managers and technical staff as well.

Q 1:27   How does corporate philosophy affect the method of compensation chosen?

A company's philosophy includes a number of statements on company values, beliefs, and principles that should guide the development of executive compensation plans. For example:

- Is the organization risk-oriented or risk-averse?
- Does the organization focus on individual achievement or teamwork?
- What performance measures relate directly or indirectly to the company's values and beliefs?

These internal organizational values, expressed in a compensation philosophy statement, should be as important as competitive issues in determining the appropriate design of an executive compensation program.

Planning Tip. Distribute your company's corporate compensation philosophy annually to your top executives and members of the board of directors in order to generate a discussion of current and/or new executive compensation plans and how they can be a tool to support the company's philosophy.

Q 1:28   What are the objectives of long-term incentive plans?

Companies use long-term incentive plans for the following reasons:

1. *Encourage executives to increase shareholder value.* Some companies believe that their primary purpose is to deliver financial returns to shareholders. Long-term incentive plans are an excellent tool for getting executives to focus on this business objective, particularly if shareholder value is the performance measure used in the long-term incentive and/or if stock is the main vehicle in the long-term plan.

2. *Motivate executives to achieve the long-term goals of the company.* These goals might be increasing company net worth, or more specific business goals like the development or introduction of a new product or service, the construction of a new facility, research projects, or the acquisition or divestiture of a profit center.

3. *Retain executives.* The retention of key executives is a critical human resource issue in most companies. This retention is achieved by offering substantial opportunities for gains in personal capital and net worth to the executive. The degree of gain is typically performance-based and therefore dependent upon achieving goals or increasing stock/shareholder value.

4. *Make executives owners/entrepreneurial owners of the business.* Companies achieve this primarily with stock options and stock award plans. Companies also encourage a feeling of entrepreneurial ownership in their executives by planning and investing in long-term business strategies with executives and by sharing in the profitability of business success with executives. An example is the development and introduction of a product expansion in a consumer product company or the expansion of a menu item in a food service company. Both have been done by companies jointly with executives (and with executive investment) by making them part of the entire process.

Q 1:29 What is the difference between annual incentive plans and long-term incentive plans?

Annual or "short-term" incentive plans typically cover a company's 12-month fiscal year. Some companies use six- or 18-month periods that relate directly to their executive measurement periods. An example is a company in the fashion industry where success is measured every six months. For such a company, the annual/short-term incentive plan is broken down into two six-month periods.

Long-term incentive plans cover a two- to three-year or greater period. Stock plans typically have a ten-year award period, but vest after three to four years, while performance plans typically correspond to the company's strategic planning period, i.e., a three-to-four-year period.

Q 1:30   Are stock plans considered incentive plans?

Yes, in practice, companies consider stock plans to be incentive plans because they motivate executives to increase stock price. Also, the Internal Revenue Service (IRS) states in its clarifications of Internal Revenue Code (Code) Section 162(m) that stock plans are considered "performance-based" plans and they can be excluded from compensation amounts subject to the $1 million cap on the tax deductibility of executive compensation for a public company's top five executives (see Qs 1:34 and 1:35).

Tax Considerations

Q 1:31   What are the general tax implications of different forms of compensation?

As a general rule, amounts paid by companies to their employees as compensation are tax deductible to the companies, as long as certain requirements are met:

1. The compensation must be an ordinary and necessary business expense.
2. The compensation must be reasonable in amount.
3. The compensation must be paid in the taxable year that the company takes a tax deduction.

The timing of the compensation deduction to the company may vary from the time that the services were rendered, although in all cases it will be at the same time that an executive incurs an ordinary income tax obligation.

Example. Executive A earns compensation in 1994, and receives this compensation in 1994. The executive incurs an ordinary income tax obligation in 1994, and the company can also take a tax deduction from the revenue base on which it calculates its corporate tax in 1994.

Executive B earns compensation in 1994, but defers receipt, in accordance with tax laws, to 1996. The executive incurs an ordinary income tax obligation in 1996, and the company can also take a tax deduction in 1996.

Q 1:32   What is unreasonable compensation?

In order to be tax deductible to the company, the compensation package of key executives must be reasonable. The IRS determines reasonableness using a number of key factors, including:

- Compensation paid to executives in similar jobs in similar organizations
- Executive qualifications, such as previous experience and academic credentials
- Size and complexity of the business
- Executive duties

The IRS will also take into account the nature of the compensation in determining whether it is reasonable. Incentive compensation, which is usually compensation that is contingent on the company's future performance, can generally be given in amounts that would be considered unreasonable if paid to the executive in the form of salary. This is because the executive is risking part of his or her compensation based upon the company's performance and should be entitled to a greater reward based on that performance.

Questions regarding the reasonableness of compensation most often arise in connection with payments made to shareholder-executives of a closely held corporation (see Q 2:14), especially where those shareholder-executives own a substantial part of the stock of their employer. This is because it is unclear in this situation whether the compensation is actually a disguised distribution of profits rather than true compensation. Therefore, the IRS closely scrutinizes situations where compensation or bonuses are proportionate to the amount of stock owned and/or where the company is generating profits but paying nominal or no dividends to its shareholders.

Q 1:33   What happens if an executive's compensation is deemed unreasonable?

If the IRS determines that the compensation paid to an executive, including deferred and incentive compensation, is unreasonable, the alleged excess will not be deductible to the company unless the company is able to prove that the compensation is in fact reasonable.

The executive would, of course, be taxed on the amounts received, whether or not deductible by the company.

Where the IRS disallows a compensation deduction, the company will typically have to pay back taxes and, in some cases, a penalty. In small, private companies, this can become a major financial hardship.

Q 1:34   What are the limitations on compensation deductions under Code Section 162(m)?

Effective for tax years beginning on or after January 1, 1994, a publicly held corporation will be denied a deduction for any compensation over $1 million paid to a CEO or any other individual whose compensation is required to be reported to shareholders in the corporation's proxy statement under the Securities Exchange Act of 1934 (i.e., the four highest compensated officers other than the CEO). This legal limitation was added by the Omnibus Budget Reconciliation Act of 1993 in the form of Code Section 162(m).

1. Code Section 162(m) applies to all publicly held corporations. The definition of public company includes affiliate or subsidiary companies unless these companies are publicly owned and report as a separate corporation. The determination as to whether a corporation is publicly held is made on the basis of the facts on the last day of the corporation's taxable year. Private companies that become public during a fiscal year have relief in that the $1 million limit does not apply to the compensation plans for the top five executives that were in effect prior to the initial public offering (IPO), provided that these compensation plans were described in the IPO prospectus. Similarly, a corporation that goes private during a taxable year will not be subject to Code Section 162(m) for that year.

2. A covered employee for purposes of Code Section 162(m) for any given year must be employed as a "covered employee" (i.e., the CEO and the four highest compensated officers other than the CEO) on the last day of the taxable year. For example, an officer who retires during the fiscal year is not included as a covered employee for purposes of applying the $1 million limit for the taxable year; therefore, if a retiring CEO received a

nonperformance-based retirement payment from a supplemental retirement plan in the fiscal year, the company would not be subject to the deduction limit on these payments because the retiring CEO is not a "covered employee" that year. A recent IRS letter ruling (Ltr Rul 199910011) states the IRS position that corporate officers who resign before the last day of the taxable year with no intent to resume their duties as officers will not be "covered employees" for that year. (See Appendix L for other recent rulings with respect to Code Section 162(m).)

3. All "applicable compensation" is included in the company's calculation for the top five executives. Exceptions to applicable compensation are as follows:

   a. Compensation payable under a written binding contract in effect on February 17, 1993, provided that contract was not modified thereafter in any material respect before compensation was paid.

   b. Contributions to or distributions from a tax-qualified plan (e.g., retirement, 401(k) deferrals, company match)

   c. Excludable fringe benefits

   d. Commission-based compensation (limited to compensation directly related to income generated by the individual, i.e., without broad-based performance standards such as performance of a business unit or division)

   e. Performance-based compensation

To qualify for performance-based compensation, companies must observe the following criteria:

1. Compensation plans must be written, approved by shareholders, and administered by two or more nonemployee directors.

2. Performance goals under compensation plans must be established in writing by a nonemployee compensation committee of the board of directors prior to the rendering of services to which the performance goal relates, and must use objective measurement criteria.

3. The achievement of goals must be certified, in writing, by the outside directors who administer the plan before such compensation can be paid.

Performance-based compensation does not generally include base salary, but can be in the form of an annual incentive. The regulations under Code Section 162(m) contain an unusual provision on annual incentives: Whenever an individual executive is paid a percentage of a bonus plan, then the sum of all individual executive bonus percentages cannot exceed 100 percent of the pool; if one executive's portion of the bonus pool is decreased, then another person's cannot be increased. This seems most illogical. This rule does not apply to any compensation paid prior to January 1, 2001 under a bonus pool based on pre-December 20, 1995 performance.

Stock options and other stock appreciation rights are specifically identified as being performance-based, provided that the exercise price is equal to the fair market value of the stock on the grant date and the shareholder approval and outside director requirements are met.

Compensation plans or agreements approved by shareholders prior to December 20, 1993 are exempt from the limit of $1 million on the company's tax deductibility (provided that such plans or agreements are administered by outside disinterested directors). Such plans or agreements cannot be modified materially.

Restricted stock plans are generally not treated as being performance-based compensation. In order to receive that designation, the vesting criteria must be based solely upon attainment of performance goals (i.e., not on years of service).

Code Section 162(m)(4)(F) provides for coordination of the $1 million cap on deductions with the excess parachute rules under Code Section 280G.

The Securities and Exchange Commission (SEC) also requires public companies to comment on their adherence to Code Section 162(m) during their discussion of executive compensation in each year's proxy report to shareholders; therefore, in addition to the potential loss of a tax deduction, public companies might also face negative reaction from shareholders, employees, and the media if executive compensation does not qualify for a tax deduction. The perception is that compensation is excessive. Moreover, shareholders could decide to file a lawsuit that might charge members of the board of directors with waste or mismanagement of company assets/revenue.

Q 1:35   Should executive compensation plans be changed in response to the Code Section 162(m) "caps" on executive pay?

Some company executives are concerned that the Code Section 162(m) rules will serve to limit their pay. This does not appear to be the case. A review of 200 recent company proxies shows that all companies are commenting on Code Section 162(m), and all have executive compensation plans that allow a tax deduction.

The regulations permit flexibility as to the type of compensation that is offered to executives. Specifically, the regulations exclude performance-based pay in the calculation of compensation that is subject to the $1 million cap. The IRS has stated that stock plans are performance-based. Long-term performance plans and annual bonus plans are also typically performance-based, because award levels are determined based on the achievement of predetermined goals.

Most compensation experts believe that companies will continue emphasizing stock plans and performance-based long-term and short-term incentive plans; therefore, total compensation opportunities should not decrease because of caps on the deductibility of executive compensation.

Q 1:36   What is ordinary income?

Ordinary income is earned income subject to the ordinary income tax that does not qualify as capital gains. The current ordinary income tax rates range from 15 percent to 39.6 percent, depending on taxable income and filing status (e.g., single, married).

Q 1:37   What are capital gains?

Capital gains are gains from capital assets (e.g., real estate, stock). Currently the capital gains tax of 28 percent (20 percent if asset is held for at least 18 months) is slightly lower than the ordinary income tax rate for most executives.

Q 1:38 What was the rationale for favorable capital gains treatment?

The capital gains treatment had been intended to encourage risk-taking by investors. In addition, the favorable capital gains tax rate recognized that appreciation in value over a long period should not be taxed in full in the year of the income receipt. There was a substantial reduction in tax rates provided by the Tax Reform Act of 1986 (TRA '86). At that time, Congress concluded that it was no longer necessary to provide preferential treatment for capital gains, and it established a capital gains tax rate at the same rate as that of ordinary income tax, 28 percent. Then in 1993, Congress passed the Omnibus Budget Reconciliation Act, which left the capital gains tax rate at 28 percent but raised the maximum ordinary income tax rate to 39.6 percent in 1994.

Q 1:39 How do tax rates affect executive compensation planning?

The capital gains tax is more favorable for executives, and the only form of executive compensation that offers capital gains tax on all values received is the incentive stock option (ISO) (see discussions at Qs 5:32 and 6:6). If held for one year after purchase (two years after grant), the ISO defers tax until the shares of stock are sold and offers capital gains on the entire spread (option price versus sales price). The ISO is an excellent means of providing executives with tax-effective compensation, particularly if higher tax rates prevail in future years, which most experts believe will happen.

Another way to offer tax-effective compensation opportunities for executives is to allow for income deferral, with the expectation that the executive's ordinary income tax bracket at retirement will be lower than his or her current ordinary income tax level. The primary forms of income deferral, discussed in Chapters 9 and 10, are non-qualified income deferral plans and life insurance plans.

Many executives ask for compensation programs that are tax-effective, meaning that they provide the executive with capital gains tax (at 28 percent) rather than ordinary income tax (at 39.6 percent). Cash compensation is always taxed at ordinary income tax rates; therefore, it has no tax advantage for the executive.

Stock, which is a capital asset, is subject to capital gains tax rates after being held for one year; therefore stock awards, when earned, can provide capital gains tax rates for executives.

There is one exception to this rule. ISOs, discussed in subsequent chapters of this book, can under certain circumstances provide executives with capital gains tax treatment before ownership occurs. This means that as a stock award increases in value (i.e., appreciates in price), this value, when received by the executive, is taxed at capital gains rates. (See Chapters 5 and 6.)

In concept, tax rates should not be a factor in executive compensation planning; however, it is one of many practical considerations in the selection of executive compensation plans and plan provisions.

Q 1:40   What is the effective tax rate?

The effective tax rate is the rate the executive pays on all of his or her income, typically measured as adjusted gross income. For example, if the executive's adjusted gross income was $200,000 and the amount of tax was $40,000, the effective tax rate is 20 percent ($200,000 ÷ $40,000).

Q 1:41   What is the marginal tax rate?

The marginal tax rate is the rate the executive pays on the next dollar that is earned. That rate can be used to calculate the net value of an increase in compensation. For example, if an executive with a salary of $200,000 is to receive an increase of 5 percent or $10,000, and if this executive is at a marginal tax rate of 28 percent, then the net value of the salary increase to the executive is $7,200 ($10,000 − $2,800).

The marginal tax rate is also used to determine the value of a tax deduction to the executive. For example, if an executive's marginal tax rate is 28 percent, a $1,000 deduction saves the executive 28 percent in taxes or $280 ($1,000 × 28%).

Q 1:42   What is the alternative minimum tax?

The alternative minimum tax (AMT) is a second method of calcu-lating an executive's tax liability. The AMT is sometimes called the add-back tax, because its calculation involves adding back adjust-ments and deductions that are allowed under the ordinary income tax calculation. The AMT is designed to ensure that all high-income executives bear at least a minimum level of the federal tax burden. An executive must use the AMT calculation to determine taxes due when primary sources of income are tax-sheltered or subject to favorable tax treatment. Such situations may occur when a large portion of income has been realized through stock option gains or certain tax-sheltered investments, or where a large portion of income has been protected by tax shelters.

The AMT requires that an affected executive calculate his or her tax liability under AMT rules, and then calculate tax liability under ordinary income tax rules. The executive then pays the higher of the two tax obligations.

Accounting Considerations

Q 1:43   What are the general accounting implications of the different forms of compensation?

Unlike tax laws, which establish a taxable event when compensa-tion is paid, accounting regulations, established by the Financial Accounting Standards Board (FASB), require companies to accrue compensation costs on accounting statements as they are earned; therefore, a company may not be able to take a tax deduction (from the revenue base used to calculate annual corporate taxes) for execu-tive compensation earned in a given year. The same company will be required under FASB regulations to reduce revenue reported in the same year by that same amount of executive compensation. For example: An executive earns a $30,000 bonus in 1997, but, in accord-ance with tax regulations, defers receipt of this bonus to 1999. The company must deduct $30,000 from its accounting statements for the year 1997. The company does not get to take a tax deduction for this same amount until 1999. Therefore, companies keep two sets of financial statements, one for tax purposes and one for accounting purposes.

Q 1:44   What accounting statements contain compensation expenses?

Both the income statement (profit and loss statement) and the balance sheet statement contain compensation expenses. The income statement reflects company revenues and expenses over a fixed period—a fiscal year, which is any 12-month period. The income statement documents all sources of company income, as well as all company expenses, including compensation expenses, in order to arrive at a net income or a net loss for the period. Included under operating expenses (also known as selling, general, and administrative costs) are compensation expenses and cash payments earned by an executive, as well as accruals for long-term cash payments that companies expect to pay to executives in the future (long-term incentive payments are accrued and charged to the income statement during the period in which they are earned).

At the end of the period of the income statement, any accrued compensation expenses are transferred to the balance sheet and carried as a liability. The balance sheet reflects company assets, liabilities, and equity or net worth. The sum of liabilities and equity will always equal the sum of total assets.

Q 1:45   What is the accounting for stock awards?

Companies may select one of two ways to establish the accounting treatment of stock awards (both stock option grants and full-value stock grants). The first is to follow APB 25, and the second is to follow FAS 123.

The Financial Accounting Standards Board continues to allow companies to select APB 25, created by its predecessor organization the Accounting Principles Board (APB). Under APB 25, companies must accrue compensation costs for stock awards based on the measurement principle. The measurement principle states that compensation costs will be determined on the measurement date, when two factors are known: (1) the number of shares that the executive is eligible to receive and (2) the price per share to be paid by the executive.

The compensation cost for stock awards is calculated as the difference on this date between the value of the stock award (the number of shares multiplied by their current market value) and the cost of the shares to the executive (the number of shares multiplied by the price per share to be paid by the executive).

Example: APB 25. A company grants an executive the right to purchase 1,000 stock option shares at $20 per share, which is the current market value. The accounting charge to the company's income statement is zero, calculated as follows: The value of the shares can be determined on the date of grant, and that amount is $20,000 (1,000 shares × the $20 fair market value). The cost to the executive can also be determined on this date, and is $20,000 (1,000 shares × the $20 option price to the executive). $20,000 − $20,000 = $0.

If that company granted an executive the right to purchase 1,000 stock option shares at a price of $15 per share, when the fair market value is $20 per share, the company must accrue a charge to its income statement of $5,000. The value of the shares on the date of grant is $20,000 (1,000 shares × $20). The cost to the executive on this date is $15,000 (1,000 shares × $15). $20,000 − $15,000 = $5,000.

Under the FASB ruling known as FAS 123, a company may elect to establish a "fair market value" of a stock award at the time of grant and accrue this cost on the company's income statement over the period that the stock award vests. The FASB suggests that companies use a stock pricing model to establish the "fair value." (See Q 1:49 as to the specific criteria such a stock pricing model should meet.) If a company does not select FAS 123, it must include a footnote in its financial statements that shows the earnings per share (EPS) impact that would have occurred if the stock award had been assigned a fair value that was charged to the company's earnings.

Example: FAS 123. A company grants an executive the right to purchase 1,000 stock option shares at $20 per share, which is the current market value. The accounting charge to the company's income statement is $7 per share or $7,000 (1,000 shares × $7), which must be accrued over the vesting period of the stock option.

The fair value of $7 per share was determined by reducing the executive's option price of $20 by the present value of that price, discounted back from the expected exercises/purchase date to the date of grant. This amount was further reduced by the present value of the expected stream of dividends over the expected term of the grant. (See Q 1:46.)

Many large human resource consulting firms and CPA firms offer computer discs with an option pricing model such as Black-Scholes. These are most valuable in calculating a fair value for stock awards. Every executive compensation administrator should have one.

Q 1:46   How does APB 25 compare to FAS 123?

The following chart compares key features of the two accounting regulations with an impact on stock awards.

Provision	APB 25	FAS 123
1. Date for measuring compensation cost	Date that stock price and number of shares are known	Date of grant
2. Definition of measurement	Market value minus amount to be paid by executive	Fair value as determined by an option pricing model
3. Accrual period	Vesting period	Vesting period
4. Impact on income	Footnote	Charged as statement expense

Q 1:47   What changes in APB 25 were implemented by the FASB under FAS 123?

FAS 123 significantly changed the accounting for stock plans in 1996. Under FAS 123, both private and public companies must select either APB 25 or FAS 123 as the basis for determining the charge to company earnings on any awards from a stock plan. If companies decide to use FAS 123, they must establish a "fair value" of the stock grant and charge their income statement with this fair value over the vesting period of the stock award.

Acceptable option pricing models such as Black-Scholes (see Q 5:26), the binomial option model, and the minimum value method have been identified by FASB as acceptable methods for determining fair value.

Companies that elect to continue using APB 25 are required to show the impact that a fair value measure of any stock award grant would have on its earnings per share. This impact is to be shown as a footnote to the income statement.

An important caveat to this choice is that whatever alternative a company may select for the reporting of stock options must also be used for the reporting of other forms of long-term incentive, such as performance plans, stock appreciation rights (SARs), and other variable awards.

FAS 123 also requires expanded disclosure of company practices on the accounting for stock award plans.

For companies that elect to use FAS 123, the effective date for implementation is in fiscal years beginning after December 15, 1995. For companies that elect to continue using APB 25, the effective date for implementation is in fiscal years beginning after December 15, 1994.

Q 1:48   What stock plans are included in FAS 123?

Stock plans are defined in FAS 123 as including stock options, performance-based stock options, stock appreciation rights, performance shares, restricted stock, stock purchase plans, and any other equity award to employees. Employee stock ownership plans (ESOPs) are not included in FAS 123.

Companies that use multiple forms of stock awards for executives have a challenging decision on the election of accounting methods, because a company must choose one accounting method for all stock plans. For example, if a company provides executives with both stock options and performance shares, it cannot choose APB 25 for the stock options and FAS 123 for the performance shares.

Example. A company grants an executive 1,000 stock option shares at $20/share when the current market value of the shares is also $20. The same executive is also granted 1,000 performance shares when the company's stock price is $20.

Under previous accounting regulations, the company would apply APB 25 to the stock options and have no charge to earnings because they were granted at the current fair market value. The company would then use FAS 28 and establish a charge to earnings for the actual amount earned from the performance shares, i.e., $20,000 (1,000 shares × $20) or greater if the stock price goes up during the award period.

Under current accounting regulations, the company must choose either FAS 123 or APB 25 for both grants. Clearly the company would like to use APB 25 for the stock option because it will result in no charge to earnings. The company would prefer FAS 123 for the performance shares, because the charge to earnings will be less than $20,000. Under Black-Scholes or most other option pricing models, the charge to earnings is less because in calculating the fair value the company is able to calculate a discounted present value and further discount for the value of dividends. The actual charge depends on the assumptions used. Unfortunately, the company cannot use APB 25 for the stock options and FAS 123 for the performance shares.

Companies with multiple forms of stock grant will want to do some in-depth analysis of the impact that these new accounting regulations will have on current and future year costs to the income statement.

Q 1:49   How is the fair value calculated under FAS 123?

FAS 123 requires that the following assumptions be used in determining the fair value of a stock award:

1. The expected life of the stock award;
2. The expected volatility of the company's stock price (public companies only);
3. The expected dividend yield of company stock during the expected life of the stock award;

4. The risk-free interest rate during the expected life of the stock award;

5. The current price of the stock award; and

6. The price that the executive will pay for the stock.

The FASB has stated that a company can use any stock model in establishing the fair value of a stock grant as long as it meets these criteria. One exception noted by the FASB is that private companies may use the less complicated minimum value method for establishing the fair value of a stock award. Most large companies already use the Black-Scholes option pricing method, and most small companies are using the minimum value method. Another alternative is the binomial stock price model.

Both the binomial models and Black-Scholes take into account the statistical probability of stock volatility or the extent to which a company's stock price will increase or decrease in the future. Small or private companies do not have to factor-in stock volatility; therefore, they have no need to use Black-Scholes or the binomial methods.

Q 1:50   How do some of these fair value determination models work?

The minimum value method is calculated by taking the present value of the executive's purchase price of the stock grant and adding the present value of expected dividends (if any), and then subtracting this from the current price of a company share of stock.

Example 1: Minimum Value Method.

Present value of executive's option price	$30
Present value of expected dividends	0
Current stock price	$40
Fair value per share ($40 – $30)	$10

The calculation of fair value under both Black-Scholes and the binomial models is much more complicated. Following are some examples of Black-Scholes:

Example 2: Black-Scholes.

Black-Scholes

Purchase Price	$40
Expected Life	5 Years
Volatility	1.25
Dividends	3%/Year
Risk-Free Rate of Return	7%
Fair Value	$11.50

Black-Scholes Without Volatility

Purchase Price	$40
Expected Life	5 Years
Volatility	-0-
Dividends	3%/Year
Risk-Free Rate of Return	7%
Fair Value	$7

Black-Scholes Without Dividends or Volatility

Purchase Price	$40
Expected Life	5 Years
Volatility	-0-
Dividends	-0-
Risk-Free Rate of Return	7%
Fair Value	$9

Planning Tip. The previous examples show that:

1. The higher the dividend, the lower the fair value.
2. The higher the volatility, the higher the fair value.
3. The lower the fair value, the lower the charge to the company's income statement.

These examples illustrate the type of analysis companies will need to conduct in order to make an informed decision on the accounting impact of stock award plans.

Q 1:51   What are the disclosure requirements of FAS 123?

All assumptions used in calculating fair value by a company must be disclosed in the company's financial statements. This disclosure must include:

1. A description of the accounting method chosen by the company for all stock grants.

2. A description of the assumptions used in calculating the fair value amount to be accrued on the income statement, shown as a footnote on the income statement.

3. A description of the stock plan, to include the type of award, the terms of the award, the vesting provision, and the number of shares authorized under the plan.

4. For stock options, the weighted average fair value of all stock options granted during the year. If the option exercise price is different than the current market value of the stock, then the fair value of all stock option grants must be reported separately for each grant that year.

5. For stock options, the number of shares and the weighted average option exercise price for all shares granted, forfeited or expired, and exercised.

6. For other stock grants, the weighted average fair value at the date of grant.

These disclosures are similar to those required by the Securities Exchange Commission on executive compensation.

Q 1:52   What are the FASB guidelines on EPS calculations that are to be used in company financial statements?

Such earnings per share calculation methods are "basic earnings per share" and "diluted earnings per share." Basic EPS does not include any common stock equivalents and is simply net income divided by common shares outstanding, using a weighted average common shares during the reporting period.

The fully diluted EPS calculation method is essentially the same method as that described in Q 1:49, and it therefore does include common shares equivalents using the treasury stock method.

Companies are required to report both basic and diluted earnings per share. Obviously, the FASB wants to show investors the potential dilutive impact of company stock option plans (or other share equivalents) in these calculations.

Chapter 2

Private Versus Public Companies

Privately held and closely held companies have unique organizational characteristics that typically require a significantly different approach to executive compensation. Frequently, an executive compensation plan that is effective and appropriate in publicly traded organizations will be neither effective nor appropriate in privately held companies. The use of stock-based plans, for instance, so common in publicly traded companies, is much less common in private companies. Annual incentive plans, which are common in large organizations, are difficult to make effective in small start-up companies. This chapter compares the different ways in which private and public companies approach executive compensation program design, as well as general plan design and competitive practices. It also provides information on the regulations of the Securities and Exchange Commission (SEC) that apply to public companies. The regulations under Section 16 of the Securities Exchange Act of 1934 (1934 Act) have direct impact on the design and reporting of executive compensation in public companies.

General Considerations   2-2
Stock-Based Plans   2-4
S Corporations   2-6
SEC Regulations   2-11
Proxy Rules   2-18

General Considerations

Q 2:1   What is a public or publicly traded company?

A company is publicly traded if it has a class of equity securities that is registered under the Securities Exchange Act of 1934 (the 1934 Act) and, as a result, is subject to the ongoing disclosure and reporting requirements of the 1934 Act.

Equity securities must be registered under the 1934 Act either if (1) a public offering of those securities is made under the Securities Act of 1933 (the 1933 Act) or (2) the company in question has more than $1 million in total assets *and* more than 500 shareholders of any one class of its equity securities. Rules and regulations under the 1934 Act provide that a company is exempt from the registration requirement if it has total assets of $10 million or less. In addition, the rules provide that a foreign private issuer is exempt from the registration requirement if fewer than 300 of its shareholders reside in the United States. The 1933 Act generally requires any sale of or offer to sell securities to be registered with the Securities and Exchange Commission (SEC) unless a specific exemption from registration is available.

Q 2:2   What is a private or privately held company?

A company is privately held if none of its equity securities are registered under the 1934 Act.

Q 2:3   What is a closely held company?

A closely held company is one in which management and ownership are substantially the same. The term *closely held corporation* is derived from the fact that the company's stock is held closely by a few individuals. Such companies are frequently referred to as *close corporations* or *family corporations*.

Q 2:4   Is a privately held company always a closely held company?

No, although these terms are often incorrectly used interchangeably. A closely held company will always be a privately held company, because in a private company it is possible to limit the shareholders; however, in a public company public shares cannot be held by a few close individuals. Anyone can own shares in a public company.

A privately held company will not necessarily be closely held, because some of the shareholders may be very independent.

Q 2:5 Do executive compensation programs in privately held companies differ from those in publicly traded companies?

In many cases they do, because the underlying motivations of executive compensation programs differ in public and private companies. A public company's primary motivation in instituting a compensation program is to offer executives enough compensation to retain them and motivate them to work their hardest toward achieving the company's strategic goals. This motivation exists already for owner-executives of a small private company because they already have a substantial stake in the company's stock ownership and, therefore, in ensuring that the company achieves its strategic goals. As a result, many small private companies will concentrate on rewarding their owner-executives for their efforts through perquisites. In large privately held companies, the business value and underlying motivations of executive compensation programs are similar to those in public companies, because most executives are not owners.

Another difference between private and public companies is that in privately held companies, base salaries for executives appear to be somewhat higher, but total cash compensation (salary plus bonus) is lower. This reflects the limited cash available and the career caps that exist in some private companies that are family-owned. The career caps reflect the fact that in many privately held companies the top positions are available only to family members of the primary owners.

Where annual incentive plans are used in privately held companies, they do not significantly differ in design from those used in publicly traded companies. Privately held companies, however, tend to place more emphasis on internally set performance objectives than on external performance measures such as earnings per share, peer comparisons, and cash flow. Book value growth appears frequently as a performance measure for private companies.

Stock-Based Plans

Q 2:6   Do privately held companies use stock-based capital accumulation programs to structure their executive compensation arrangements?

Yes, but not as frequently as public companies. Some owners do not wish to grant options widely to their nonowner-employees because they do not want a substantial increase in the number of owners. If a privately held company does use a stock-based capital accumulation program, it tends to distribute more shares to fewer executives than a publicly traded company would. Furthermore, the private company would certainly be well advised to keep the number of shareholders comfortably below 500 to prevent triggering reporting requirements under the 1934 Act.

Q 2:7   What are the most common forms of long-term incentives in private companies?

The most frequently used long-term incentives in closely held companies are book value plans (see Q 6:42), performance units plans (see Q 7:39), and phantom stock plans (see Q 7:20). If stock-based plans are offered, they are almost always accompanied by buy-back provisions.

Q 2:8   Are there problems with using stock plans in private companies?

There are several reasons stock option plans and stock-based plans are used less frequently in privately held companies. One reason, as stated in Q 2:6, is that an executive compensation plan that uses stock eventually results in a minority shareholder position for a number of executives, with all the rights that this position entails, including the right to vote stock, review financial records, and attend shareholder meetings. This may not be appealing to the majority owners, both because their ownership becomes diluted and they have additional people to answer to. In addition, this minority ownership can lead to an unfriendly minority shareholder if the executive is terminated or leaves the firm to join a competitor, although this problem may be avoided through the use of restrictive buy-back agreements.

Such agreements typically obligate executives to sell their stock back to the company or the majority shareholder following termination of employment, or allow currently employed executives to liquidate their investment. Restrictive buy-back agreements also typically allow the buy-back to take place over a reasonable period of time to avoid the cash burden to the company owners that could result from an obligation to purchase the stock immediately.

Privately held companies may also avoid the use of stock-based plans so they do not have to value the stock to establish the purchase price. A private company must hire an outside party to determine the value of its shares. As a result, the buy-back agreement usually stipulates a formula price or method by which the purchase price is to be determined at the time of sale, at specified intervals during the award period, and at the end of the award period.

Planning Tip. Phantom plans used by privately held companies can be exactly like those used by publicly traded companies, with an exception: Executives are able to sell their shares only to the company. The requirement is typically enforced by granting the company a right of first refusal. The company may also want to specify financing terms as part of the repurchase agreement. This permits it to settle the executive's interests over a number of years to minimize the impact of an immediate cash drain.

Q 2:9 What conditions are typically included in a buy-back agreement?

An executive may be awarded company shares with the following provisos:

1. The executive may sell the shares if one of the following events occurs:

    a. Death, disability, or early or normal retirement

    b. Voluntary termination or involuntary termination if other than for cause

    c. The completion of ten years of service after stock ownership occurs

2. If the executive then wishes to sell such shares, he or she must first offer the company the opportunity to purchase all of the shares. The purchase offer period will extend for 75 days after

one of the events occurs. If the company does not exercise its right to buy the shares by then, the executive may sell or transfer ownership at any time.

3. If the shares are sold to the company after a public offering has been completed, the price per share will be the average high and low trading price of the shares on the effective date of the sale as reported on the stock exchange. If the shares are sold to the company prior to a public offering, the price will be calculated as of the last stock valuation conducted by the company. These valuations are conducted by the company each quarter of the fiscal year. In all cases, the executive will be eligible for a payment per share equal to the price at the time of sale minus the price he or she paid at the time ownership occurred.

Q 2:10   Is there a negative effect if a privately held company does not provide long-term incentive plans?

Yes. By not providing long-term incentive programs, privately held companies are denying themselves an important tool to recruit, retain, and direct executive talent. They are also probably paying more than is necessary in fixed cash compensation and are losing the opportunity to put executives in the same boat as the owners.

Virtually all types of privately held companies can offer meaningful capital accumulation plans to key executives, the most prevalent type of which is a cash-based, long-term phantom stock plan (see Q 7:20).

S Corporations

Q 2:11   What is a Subchapter S corporation?

The Internal Revenue Code (the Code) permits shareholders of certain privately held companies to elect to be taxed as though the shareholders were carrying on their activities as partners. In such a case, the shareholders are taxed directly on the earnings of the company in proportion to their ownership of stock. As a result of this election, the shareholders avoid the double taxation of corporate earnings (first, at the corporate level on the company's earnings and, second, at the individual level when those earnings are distributed to the shareholders in the form of dividends) by passing the tax obligations through to themselves.

Q 2:12   How does a company elect to become a Subchapter S corporation?

A corporation becomes a Subchapter S corporation (S corporation) by filing an S corporation election under Code Section 1362(a). That election may be made only by a corporation that meets all of the following eligibility requirements:

1. It must be a corporation organized under the laws of the United States.
2. It cannot have more than 75 shareholders.
3. Its shareholders must be individuals, estates, or certain trusts.
4. It cannot have more than one class of stock.
5. It cannot have a nonresident as a shareholder.

Furthermore, certain types of companies are ineligible for S corporation treatment regardless of whether they meet the above criteria. Such companies include financial institutions, insurance companies, corporations under a Code Section 936 election (regarding Puerto Rico and possession tax credits), or a domestic international sales corporation (DISC) or former DISC. An S corporation may own 100 percent of the stock of a "qualified subchapter S subsidiary." In such circumstances, the subsidiary is not treated as a separate corporation, and all assets, liabilities, and items of income, deduction, and credit of the subsidiary are treated as if they were of the parent S corporation. An S corporation is also allowed to own 80 percent or more of the stock of a C corporation. The parent S corporation cannot join the C corporation in any consolidated tax returns.

Q 2:13   Does electing S corporation status have an impact on executive compensation?

Yes. An S corporation must be careful in implementing a stock-based plan because it risks losing its S corporation status if it violates one of the eligibility requirements (see Q 2:12). The number of executives entitled to participate in such a plan must be limited because the number of shareholders of an S corporation is limited. The plan must be monitored to ensure that it does not, by design or unintentionally, create a second class of stock.

The events that create a second class of stock are not always clear. The use of restricted shares may constitute a second class of stock where shares that are issued are subject to such substantial conditions or restrictions that they are deemed not to have the same rights to corporate assets as other, unrestricted company stock. Certain restrictions can, however, be imposed without creating a second class of stock. Such restrictions include:

1. Requiring the executive to obtain corporate consent before selling the shares to a third party

2. Requiring the executive to resell the shares to the company at a specified price, even if that price is less than the fair market value of the shares

3. Providing that the executive will forfeit the shares if he or she quits or is fired for good cause

Typically, an S corporation will choose to avoid the problems associated with stock-based plans by using related devices such as stock appreciation rights (SARs) and phantom stock plans (see Qs 7:3, 7:20).

The election of S corporation status also has an impact on the adoption of other nonqualified deferred compensation vehicles such as rabbi trusts or corporate-owned life insurance, although these vehicles are rarely used by S corporations because they have little value to the owner-executive of an S corporation. They are of little value because the S corporation is not a tax-shielding entity like a regular corporation. The owner-executives are currently taxed, like partners, on the income held by the company or paid in the form of insurance premiums.

An advantage of S corporation status can be the category of income received by executives. Direct compensation (salary, bonus, etc.) is of course taxable to the executive, a tax deduction to the company, and subject to FICA payment by both the executive and the company. Dividends are also taxable to the executive; however, they are not a tax deduction to the company nor subject to FICA for the executive or the company. The income category of dividends can therefore represent a substantial savings in FICA payments to the S corporation and the executive.

One caution regarding this strategy is that an S corporation cannot categorize all income as dividends just to avoid FICA tax. There must be a logical basis for the company to distinguish between direct compensation and dividends. For example, a professional services company may pay its executives a fixed salary and target bonus as direct compensation in anticipation of expected revenue and net income. An unusually profitable year might then result in a substantial dividend due to the unusual level of company success.

Q 2:14   Does the issue of unreasonable compensation affect publicly traded companies differently from privately held and S corporations?

Technically, no; in practice, yes. The requirement that compensation be reasonable applies universally to all companies. There is nothing in the Code or Treasury regulations that limits the application of unreasonable compensation issues to privately held companies. In practice, however, it is almost exclusively privately held companies that are challenged on this issue. The reason for this seemingly selective application is that there is far greater potential for and likelihood of abuse of a privately held company, where the owner-executives typically have the power to fix their own compensation and to control the company's dividend-paying policy. Furthermore, the requirement that a publicly traded corporation disclose the profit it earns each year, as well as the compensation it pays to its top executives, acts as a natural barrier against the payment of excessive salaries.

S corporations, although privately held, are generally exempt from this special scrutiny because there is no reason for the owner-executives to try to classify dividend payments as compensation unless the compensation in question is of a type (e.g., retirement plan contributions or deferred compensation) that affects the company's tax situation and the tax deductibility of compensation. The S corporation and the C corporation can easily trigger an unreasonable compensation issue: The owner-executive can classify dividends as salary in order to obtain a tax deduction for the company. If the IRS believes this to be the case, it can declare the salary unreasonable, in which case the salary becomes classified as dividends, and the company loses its tax deduction. This is very serious to a C corporation because it loses the tax deduction and pays a higher tax, and the owner-executive still pays tax on the dividend payments as he or she would if they were salary. In an S corporation, corporate income is taxed as ordinary income to the executive; therefore, no reason exists to reclassify income from dividends to salary.

This is in contrast to another strategy in which the owner-executive classifies salary as dividends to avoid (1) payment by the company and by the individual executive of FICA and FUTA (federal unemployment) taxes, and (2) federal withholding tax requirements that are applicable to compensation payments (see Q 2:13). The IRS will not raise an unreasonable compensation issue over this; however, the IRS may raise the issue that salary payments may have been misclassified to avoid taxation. Owner-executives are wise to seek advice and counsel from tax attorneys or CPAs on these complex issues.

When the IRS makes a determination of unreasonable compensation, it is presumed to be correct; therefore, the burden of proving that the payments are reasonable falls on the company and the owner-executive. In any compensation arrangement between a privately held company and its owner-executives, it is also assumed that arm's-length bargaining did not occur. This increases the likelihood that compensation will be found to be unreasonable. Each case is decided, however, on its own facts, a practice generally seen as more favorable to the executive and the company because it gives more latitude to each company. Unfortunately, as a result, there are no firm guidelines or precedents to rely on in analyzing a reasonable compensation issue, because each situation is different.

Planning Tip. An important strategy in any unreasonable compensation claim by the IRS is for the company or owner-executive to present labor market information on typical (reasonable) total compensation payments made to similar executives in similar companies over an extended period of time (e.g., five to ten years). The next step is to compare total compensation actually paid to the executive over this period to competitive total compensation that would typically have been provided over the same period of time.

SEC Regulations

Q 2:15   What is the Securities Act of 1933, and how does it affect executive compensation?

The 1933 Act sets forth the principal federal rules governing the issuance and sale of securities in the United States. The 1933 Act governs the sale, or offer to sell, by a company of shares of its stock to the public.

Under the 1933 Act, every offer and sale of a security must be registered with the SEC unless the offer and sale are exempt from registration. Exemptions are available for certain offers and sales made pursuant to tax-qualified retirement plans (provided that employee contributions are not allocated to investment in employer securities) or occurring solely within a single state. The so-called "private placement" exemption may also be available for private companies under Rule 701, permitting a certain limited amount of stock to be sold (or subject to an offer to sell, such as a stock option) in any 12-month period under a written employee benefit plan or employment contract. Nonprofit corporations may also be exempt from registration.

Rule 16a provides that certain transactions are exempt from Section 16(a) reporting requirements. The exempted transactions include, but are not limited to, stock splits and stock dividends, acquisitions of stock under a dividend reinvestment plan, and the employer's contributions under a tax-qualified employee benefit plan, which is invested in company stock (although any subsequent transfer of such contributions by the participant out of the company stock fund would be subject to Section 16(a) reporting).

Rule 144 under the 1933 Act allows the executive of a public company to hold securities that have not been registered under the 1933 Act, also known as *restricted securities*, for a minimum of two years, at which time the executive may resell the shares to the public subject to the volume limitation and other manner-of-sale requirements of Rule 144. After the securities have been held for three years, they may be transferred without regard to the volume limitations.

Q 2:16   What is the Securities Exchange Act of 1934, and how does it affect executive compensation?

The 1934 Act contains the reporting rules that must be followed by a company whose shares are held by the public. The basic principle is that everyone who buys and sells shares of the company's stock must have access to the same information concerning the company at the same time. This principle prevents certain categories of people, referred to as *insiders*, from profiting at the public's expense from any information that they have gained solely by reason of their position with the company. Therefore, a publicly traded company must file quarterly and annual statements containing audited financial statements and must notify the public of any material changes in its business or operations. Furthermore, the publicly traded company's executive officers and directors are prohibited from buying or selling shares of company stock if they have any material information that has not yet been disclosed to the public.

The 1934 Act's primary effects on executive compensation arise from the fact that the company must disclose the compensation paid each year to its most highly compensated employees and from the presumption set forth in Section 16 of the 1934 Act and the rules promulgated under that section that an insider who buys and sells stock in a six-month period is trading on inside information.

Q 2:17   How can a company avoid application of the 1933 Act?

The 1933 Act applies to the sale of, or offer to sell, stock to the public. In order to avoid the requirements of the 1933 Act a company must remain private and not offer its shares to the public. A company thereby avoids the extensive disclosure requirements outlined in Q 2:16. These include insider restrictions on the purchase and sale of stock (buy and sell transactions cannot occur within six months of each other) and the required registration with the SEC of any such stock sale or purchase. The 1933 Act also requires that executive compensation for the top five highly compensated executives be disclosed to the public. These disclosure rules are discussed in Qs 2:23 through 2:32.

As noted in Q 2:15, a company can also avoid application of the 1933 Act by utilizing its principal exemption for private offerings—that is, sales of stock that are made without an offering to the general public. This exemption is available to both publicly traded companies and privately held corporations.

Q 2:18   What are the basic rules under Section 16 of the 1934 Act?

Section 16 of the 1934 Act is designed to minimize the unfair use of inside information, which is information that is not available to the public. This is accomplished through the interaction of Section 16(a), which defines the term *insider* and states that an insider must promptly disclose all transactions in company stock, and Section 16(b), which states that any profits made by an insider from transactions involving a purchase and sale of company stock within any six-month period must be returned to the company. Any combination of purchase and sale within the six-month period will result in a violation of Section 16(b) (known as the *short-swing trading violation*), regardless of how long the shares being sold have been held or whether the executive in fact possessed material nonpublic information. The amount of profit earned will be calculated by the method producing the highest recovery for the company: The highest sale price will be matched with the lowest purchase price in the period.

Because certain stock transactions are not likely to result in abuse of insider information, Rule 16b-3 exempts these transactions from Section 16 coverage. These include stock transactions within certain employee benefit plans that allow executive participation. Rule 16b-3 also allows insiders to exercise an SAR, for cash, during a window period, which is the third through the 12th working day following the release of quarterly earnings.

Q 2:19   Who is subject to the Section 16 reporting rules?

The Section 16 rules define an insider to include directors, executive officers, and holders of 10 percent or more of the outstanding shares of a company's stock. The term *executive officers* includes "presidents or vice presidents who are in charge of a principal business unit, division, or function, and other persons who perform similar policy-making functions." [Note 33 to SEC Release No 34-28869] Specifically included in this category are the company's principal financial officer and principal accounting officer or controller. Executive officers of parent or subsidiary companies can also be considered executive officers of the company itself if they perform the described functions.

The definition of *10 percent owner* is tied directly to the definition provided in Section 13(d) of the 1933 Act. Essentially, the opportunity, directly or indirectly, to profit or share in the applicable transaction, or the right to vote or direct the voting of shares, constitutes ownership of the shares.

Under the Section 16(a) reporting requirements, an insider files SEC Form 3 at the time he or she becomes an insider, setting forth the number of shares of company stock he or she owns (including shares held by his or her spouse, children, and any other relative living in the household), as well as the number of shares he or she is then entitled to acquire on the exercise of any option or other right. Any changes are then reported on SEC Form 4 within the first ten days of the month following the month in which the transaction takes place, except for the changes that are exempt from Section 16(b) liability, which may be voluntarily reported immediately but otherwise are to be reported on the first SEC Form 4 that the insider is otherwise required to file or on SEC Form 5 filed within 45 days after the end of the company's fiscal year. An important sanction contained in Section 16(a) is the obligation of the company to report, in the annual information that it provides to its shareholders, not only any violations by any of its insiders of the short-swing profit rules of Section 16, but also any lapses or mistakes in the filing of the disclosure reports.

One of the most significant concepts under Section 16(b) involves the treatment of the acquisition and exercise of options and other derivative securities. Under the rules, generally, the granting of a stock option, warrant, or other convertible security is deemed to be a purchase event for purposes of Section 16(b). The subsequent exercise of the option, warrant, or conversion of the convertible security is not a purchase event for the purposes of Section 16(b).

Rule 16b-3 provides guidelines for certain employee benefit plans, including stock option plans, where participation is not deemed to be subject to the abuse of insider information. As long as these plans meet the guidelines of Rule 16b-3, grants of options and other securities will not be deemed to be purchases of the securities for purposes of Section 16(b), although they will be subject to Section 16(a) reporting requirements.

Rule 16b-3 exempts the following transactions in employer securities from being "matched" with non-exempt opposite-way transactions for purposes of determining Section 16(b) liability:

1. All transactions within a tax-qualified employee benefit plan, an excess benefit plan or a Code Section 423 stock purchase plan, other than "discretionary transactions" are exempt.

2. A "discretionary transaction" (intra-plan transfer in or out of a company stock fund directed by the participant or cash in-service distribution out of the company stock fund) is exempt if it occurs at least six months after any opposite-way transaction within *any* company plan (i.e., not matched with open market purchases or sales). Plan distributions on account of death, disability, retirement, or termination of employment are generally not considered to be "discretionary transactions."

3. Option grants or stock awards are exempt if the transaction is approved by a Board committee consisting of at least two outside directors, or the transaction is approved by a majority vote of shareholders, or the security is held for at least six months after acquisition (for stock options, a holding period of at least six months between option grant and the sale of the stock acquired on exercise).

4. Sales of stock to the company generally are exempt if such transactions are Board approved (can be by a committee of outside directors) or shareholder approved (by majority vote) in advance. This exemption covers transactions such as cashless exercises and tax withholding from shares.

Q 2:20   What are the most significant effects of the Section 16 rules from a compensation perspective?

The rules exempting the exercise of stock options from consideration as an insider purchase event under Section 16(b) allow an insider to exercise an option and sell shares of stock (to pay for that exercise) simultaneously. Thus, many compensation devices designed to provide the executive with cash to exercise his or her options, such as the SAR, are no longer needed.

From a corporate perspective, there are two important implications of the Section 16(b) rules for both insiders and companies:

1. If an insider exercises a stock option before six months has expired since the date of grant (the purchase event) and immediately sells the shares (a sale event), a violation of Section 16(b) has occurred.

2. If an insider sells owned shares (a sale event), is then provided with a stock option grant (a purchase event) within six months, and the option shares were not issued under an exempted 16b-3 plan, a violation of Section 16(b) may have occurred. Under an exempted 16b-3 plan, stock option shares are granted by disinterested parties (outside members of a company's board of directors who typically are members of the board compensation committee) or issued under a plan approved by shareholders.

Example 1. Executive A, an insider, receives a stock option grant of 1,000 shares at a purchase price of $15 per share on May 1, 1998. On August 1, 1998, the executive exercises the option. On September 1, 1998, the executive sells the shares at $25 per share. The executive has violated Section 16(b) because he did not hold the shares for six months from the date of grant (the purchase date of May 1, 1998) when he sold them on September 1, five months after the purchase date. As an insider, Executive A is required to hold shares for six months after a purchase event before a sale event can occur in order to avoid Section 16(b) liability.

Example 2. Executive B, an insider, sells previously owned shares (a sale event) on February 1, 1998. On May 1, 1998, Executive B is provided with a stock option grant of 1,000 shares, with an option price of $15 per share. The new stock option shares are non-16b-3 stock option grants. As a result, Executive B has violated Section 16(b) because a purchase event (the granting of the new stock option shares) has occurred within six months of a sale event (the sale of shares on February 1, 1998). If, however, those stock option shares had been 16b-3 plan shares, the executive would not have violated Section 16(b), because the stock option shares granted on May 1, 1998 (a purchase event), would not be matched against shares sold on February 1, 1998.

Example 3. Executive C, an insider, sells previously owned shares on February 1, 1998. On May 1, 1998, Executive C is provided with a stock option grant of 1,000 shares, at an option price of $15. These stock option shares are 16b-3 plan shares. On August 1, 1998, C exercises the right to purchase these shares, and then sells these shares on September 1, 1998. As a result, C has violated Section 16(b) because the sale event on September 1, 1998, occurred within six months of the purchase event (the granting of the stock option shares on May 1, 1998).

Example 4. Executive D is provided with a stock option grant of 1,000 shares on May 1, 1998, at an option price of $15 per share. These stock option shares are 16b-3 plan shares. On August 1, 1998, the executive exercises the stock option at $20 per share. On November 1, 1998, the executive sells these shares (a sale event) at $25 per share. Executive D has not violated Section 16(b) because six months have transpired between the sale date of the shares (November 1, 1998) and the purchase of these shares (the grant date of May 1, 1998).

Q 2:21 What actions are needed in order to give certain transactions the benefits of Rule 16b-3?

Under Rule 16b-3, a stock plan qualifies for an exemption to Section 16(b) if it meets the following criteria: Executives must be granted stock options by a group of nonemployee directors. The term *nonemployee director* excludes former company officers who become outside directors, consultants, lawyers, bankers, and others who earn more than $60,000 from the company, and any person employed by the company who earns more than 5 percent of the gross revenue.

Shareholder approval is not required (although it is an alternative approval process) for Section 16(b) purposes; however, shareholder approval is still required by other regulatory organizations such as the stock exchanges (if stock is part of the plan), under certain state corporate laws, and by the IRS. Code Section 422 requires companies who have incentive stock options to have shareholder approval. Code Section 423 requires shareholder approval for stock purchase plans.

Code Section 162(m) requires shareholder approval for certain exemptions from the $1 million cap on deductible compensation.

If a stock option plan meets these basic requirements, grants made under the plan to insiders as defined in Section 16(a) will be exempt transactions under Section 16(b) as long as the insider holds the stock for six months from the date of grant (the purchase event). Thus, a stock option granted to an insider is not deemed to be a purchase that will be matched to a sale (Section 16(b) provision) as long the insider does not sell the stock option shares for six months after the grant.

Q 2:22 Can the Board of Directors or Shareholders ratify a stock option grant after the fact?

Under Rule 16b-3, in order for option grants and stock awards, other than "discretionary transactions," to be considered exempt from Section 16(b) matching, approval must be given by the Board of Directors (either by the full Board or by a committee of two or more nonemployee directors) in advance. Shareholder approval is required not later than the next annual meeting of shareholders.

Proxy Rules

Q 2:23 What are the shareholder proxy and the proxy statement?

A shareholder's proxy authorizes its holder to vote on behalf of the shareholder at the annual shareholders' meeting. In voting by proxy, the shareholder instructs the company as to how his or her votes should be recorded on any business issue on the shareholders' meeting agenda, which is mailed to all shareholders in the proxy statement. This proxy method was developed because of the difficulties that would be involved if shareholders had to vote directly on all corporate matters discussed at the annual meeting of shareholders, including the annual election of directors. The 1934 Act regulates the solicitation of proxy votes by public companies by requiring that the shareholder be furnished with enough information to make an informed decision on all voting issues. Section 14 of the 1934 Act specifies that no proxy may be solicited unless it is preceded or accompanied by a proxy statement.

The contents of the proxy statement will vary each year, depending on the issues to be discussed at the meeting. If a proxy is sought for approval of the election of specified directors, the proxy statement must disclose specific information about them, including their backgrounds, company committee service, and company shares owned. When the company seeks approval for new executive compensation plans, or new or additional shares of stock to be used in executive compensation programs, the proxy statement must include information on the plans being presented for approval (e.g., copies of the plan text, or a version of the current plan with proposed amendments clearly marked). Sample compensation plans presented to shareholders for consideration at an annual meeting are provided in Appendix B.

Each national stock exchange (e.g., NYSE, NASDAQ) also requires shareholder approval of any executive compensation plan that will pay awards in stock. Public company shareholders must therefore approve the specific amounts of stock to be used in executive compensation plans. The shares are expressed as a percentage of total shares outstanding.

The annual company proxy statement is also used to disclose compensation paid to the company's most highly compensated officers, and the methods used to determine amount of pay and benefits. Proxy statements also include amounts of compensation and benefits provided to nonemployee outside directors.

Q 2:24 How do the SEC proxy reporting requirements affect executive compensation?

The SEC issues reporting rules for companies to use in summarizing executive compensation in proxy statements (see Qs 2:23–2:32). These requirements are generally believed to act as a control on the level of executive compensation. Because disclosures of executive compensation must be made clear and concise and the reasoning behind executive compensation programs must also be explained in detail, shareholders can use this information at any time to initiate a court action challenging the amounts and types of compensation provided to executives, just as the IRS can challenge compensation as being unreasonable. Such a shareholder suit could be extremely embarrassing to a corporation, especially when publicized by the media. Shareholder challenges to compensation are actually quite rare, and are almost never successful, since executive compensation levels are determined by a disinterested group of outside, nonemployee directors of the company and the primary holders of company shares of stock are typically pro-management people and/or organizations.

Challenges to executive pay can also come from the media, from a group of dissident shareholders or from hostile takeover groups. The media have, in recent years, developed numerous methods to compare executive compensation pay levels to company performance, and have been quick to point out any inconsistencies. The SEC proxy recording requirements therefore include specific comparisons of company pay to company performance so that this key relationship is visible and easy to understand.

Tables of the top five executives' pay must clearly identify current and historical levels of pay. Details of this information are discussed in Q 2:27. The media and all investors can compare this information to the company performance charts discussed in Q 2:28. High performance should correlate to increases in pay; low performance should correlate to no increases in pay. But of even greater significance is that board compensation committees must prepare a narrative explaining the basis for executive pay.

Most believe that this will have a major effect on company outside directors who determine executive compensation, typically those on the company's compensation committee of the board of directors (see Q 2:25), and that they will be much more interested and dutiful in fulfilling their responsibilities for establishing executive pay and benefit levels and programs.

Q 2:25 What is the compensation committee of the board and what role does it play in executive compensation?

The typical compensation committee is a specially designated committee of nonemployee members of the board of directors who are considered disinterested parties because they do not benefit personally from any compensation decisions by the committee.

Board compensation committees generally perform the following types of duties and responsibilities:

- Approve levels of executive compensation and benefits
- Approve executive compensation and benefit programs
- Review executive and nonexecutive compensation and benefit policy and program design strategy
- Approve individual grants of stock options, including the number of shares, the price per share, the award period, and other similar design issues relevant to stock award plans
- Approve the specific type of long-term incentive plan to be used for company executives (e.g., stock options, restricted stock, performance shares)

In fulfilling these responsibilities, members of a compensation committee represent the shareholders in assuring the appropriateness and equity of executive pay and in ensuring that executive compensation programs attract, motivate, and retain executives within the company so that company goals beneficial to shareholders are achieved. In this capacity, board compensation committees are both extremely powerful and function in a fishbowl, in that all of their decisions are subject to the evaluation, scrutiny, and audit of all shareholders, as well as the media. Moreover, during corporate restructuring, such as a merger, acquisition, or recapitalization, board compensation committees are asked to deal with many difficult compensation issues such as golden parachutes, the disposal of compensation programs that are no longer needed, and maintaining the equity of executive pay plans where only some executives receive buyouts from existing compensation programs. In some cases, they significantly influence the determination of future company owner ship via their approval of executive compensation programs that involve equity or ownership in the company. As a result, in recent years many board compensation committees have turned more extensively to survey data and outside compensation consultants in order to enhance their contribution to executive compensation decisions, as illustrated in the brief extract from an actual company proxy statement that follows:

> The compensation for the top five officers consists of base salary, annual bonus, long-term bonus, share options, and other benefits. Studies are conducted periodically by an outside con-

sulting firm of 24 companies in the electronics field, 19 of which are in the S&P Electronic Subgroup Index shown in the performance graph on the previous page. This study uses regression analysis techniques that relate our company's size and performance to those in other companies, and the compensation committee considers the results of these studies in determining appropriate compensation levels for the CEO.

Q 2:26   What rules govern the SEC proxy reporting requirements?

The SEC proxy reporting rules are contained in Item 402 of Regulation S-K of the 1934 Act. In addition, Securities Act Release No. 7497 contains the "plain English" rules for reporting purposes.

Q 2:27   What disclosure information charts must be included with proxy statements?

The SEC rules provide that several charts, in addition to the charts on the top five company executives, must be included in proxy statements. These charts are:

1. A summary chart of base salary, annual bonus, stock awards, other forms of long-term income, and other annual compensation (i.e., the cost of providing perquisites and personal benefits, tax gross-ups, discounts on purchases of company stock, and any other preferential interest or dividend payments provided to executives). This information must cover the top five executives for the past three years.

2. A table on stock option/SAR grants made during the last fiscal year. While this essentially repeats some of the information in the summary compensation table, its coverage is more extensive. Companies are required to estimate the future value of stock options either by using assumptions of company stock appreciation at both 5 and 10 percent yearly increases in value over the term of the option, or by using another recognized option evaluation technique such as the Black-Scholes method (see Q 5:26). A similar table is to be provided for long-term incentive plans (performance units/performance share plans) showing the number of shares, the performance period, and

estimated future payouts using threshold, target, and maximum payout levels.

3. A special table on the aggregated stock option/SARs exercised during the last fiscal year for each of the top five executives. This table is to include the number of shares acquired or exercised during the last fiscal year, the actual value realized by the individual executive, the number of unexercised options or SAR shares at the end of the fiscal year, and the number and value of both exercisable and nonexercisable shares at the end of the fiscal year.

4. A table of estimated retirement benefits for the executives named in the summary compensation table. This table is also to show annual retirement benefits payable to executives at various levels of credited earnings under the company's qualified pension plan, and to indicate whether supplemental retirement plans are provided to participating executives (the top five and the other levels represented). The number of years of service credited for pension plan purposes to each of the top five executives is also to be indicated.

Q 2:28   What other executive compensation information must be disclosed in the proxy statement?

Executive compensation information that must be disclosed in the proxy statement includes the following:

1. The compensation committee of the board must submit a report indicating the members of the committee and discussing the committee's strategies in determining executive compensation and benefits, including the extent to which such compensation is performance-related and the performance measures considered. Specifically, this portion of the proxy statement must include a discussion of the chief executive officer's (CEO's) compensation, and how the specific level of pay and benefits for this position was established by the committee. The specific stock or long-term incentive awards provided to the CEO and the rationale for these awards is also to be included in this report.

2. Compensation committee interlocks are also to be disclosed. Interlocks are members of the compensation committee who also serve as a partner of a major company supplier, law firm, or financial institution, or a CEO of another company for which the company CEO serves on the board compensation committee.

3. A performance graph must be prepared comparing the company's total shareholder return against a performance indicator of the overall stock market as published by the Standard & Poor's 500 Index or other similar index. A second performance graph is also to be prepared, comparing total shareholder return for that company against a selected group of peer companies, again using some form of recognized industry index or similar published index relevant to that company's industry or line of business. Total shareholder return is generally understood to mean stock price appreciation plus dividends paid during each fiscal year shown by the graph. These graphs are to reflect the five-year cumulative shareholder return.

4. Employment contracts and arrangements are to be discussed for the company CEO and other top four executives shown in the proxy statement. This includes special severance or change-of-control agreements for these executives, as well as special severance benefits to other key management employees.

5. Pay of outside directors is to be summarized in the proxy statement, although individual director amounts need not be specified. Director fees, retainers, stock awards, retirement plans, deferral arrangements, and even charitable or legacy programs are included in this section of the proxy statement.

6. An option/SAR repricing report on all executives included in the proxy statement must be provided. This describes the events triggering the option repricing, the options currently being repriced, and similar actions taken during the last 120 months, and includes a ten-year option/SAR table showing the name, date, number of option/SARs repriced, market price at the time of repricing, exercise price at the time of repricing, new exercise price, and length of the original option term remaining on the date of repricing. Obviously, the SEC is trying to discourage companies from repricing stock options and SARs, since this alternative is not available to other shareholders.

These SEC executive compensation reporting rules may serve to drive the design features in company executive compensation programs, particularly annual incentives (see Chapter 4) and long-term incentives (see Chapters 5 through 8).

Examples of selected compensation disclosure provisions contained in actual proxy statements filed with the SEC can be found in Appendix B, Attachment 1.

Q 2:29   How should public companies determine the future value of stock options and its effect on executive compensation?

Under the SEC proxy reporting rules, approximately 60 percent of all companies project stock growth at 5 to 10 percent per year during the option award period using an SEC-suggested method. The remaining 40 percent of all companies use the Black-Scholes option pricing model (see Q 5:26).

These stock growth projections serve only to predict the future compensation of the top five executives in the company. The stock appreciation actually realized by the executives when they complete a purchase and subsequent sale of the stock options can be unpredictable. Historically, some companies have had no stock growth over the entire stock award period; other companies have had 100 percent or greater growth.

Despite the difficulty of projecting stock growth, public companies should recognize that the SEC regulations give them reason to weight the top executives' total compensation package in favor of stock options or similar stock grants. If future compensation of top executives is related to stock growth (whatever that growth may be), there will be little media criticism of executive compensation because as the executive gains from stock appreciation so does the shareholder.

Q 2:30   How can companies reduce negative media and shareholder reaction to major stock option exercises by executives in years when company earnings are flat or down from previous years?

The following alternatives should be considered:

1. Communicate the importance of stock option exercise timing to the executive. Before the 1990s, the timing of stock option exercises was rarely an issue in executive compensation administration because CEO compensation was neither a major topic of media analysis, discussion, and articles nor as available for public scrutiny. Companies must sensitize executives to and train them on this issue. While this alternative places new requirements on the executive, it allows more positive acceptance and cooperation from the media and more responsiveness from executives.

2. Establish minimum exercise provisions for each stock option grant. Assume that an executive receives a 10,000-share stock option grant. The stock options vest 20 percent per year or 100 percent after five years, and the award period of the stock option is ten years. A company could require the executive to exercise a minimum of 20 percent of those stock option shares each year from year 6 through year 10.

3. Require approval by a board compensation committee (see Q 2:25) on all stock option exercises by the company's top five executives. This will obviously serve to increase executive focus on the issue of stock option timing, although it does take away flexibility.

4. Provide more flexible post-termination/retirement exercise provisions for the top five executives. A company could allow a retiring executive to exercise vested stock options for a three- to five-year period after retirement, at which point the exercise transaction would not be included in company proxies.

Q 2:31 How does the disclosure requirement for a company performance comparison graph affect the amount of executive compensation awarded?

The SEC proxy reporting rules call for the development of a performance graph that compares company stock performance to a broad index of stock growth in other companies and stock performance of a relevant peer group (see Q 2:28). Company stock performance graphs have an even greater impact than the stock growth charts. If the graphs show low company stock performance relative to the broad market or peer group index, any increases in total cash compensation (salary plus bonus) or in total compensation (total cash plus long-term incentive) could raise numerous questions from shareholders and the media. Therefore, companies must ensure that there is a correlation between the stock performance graphs and actual total cash compensation provided and reported on the top five executives in each year's annual proxy. For example, if a stock performance graph shows a 5 percent decline in the company's position, actual total cash compensation should also show some decline from the previous year, or the company's board compensation committee should provide a good reason why lower compensation should not follow lower performance. This would be the logic of the shareholders, media people, and other investors who review company stock performance graphs.

This issue is of critical importance, and many board compensation committees will want to analyze the graphs each time they are asked to make key executive compensation decisions. These regulations could also be a catalyst for improving the correlation of executive compensation and performance in public companies.

Q 2:32   How do the SEC proxy reporting rules generally affect the design of executive compensation programs?

The following results are obvious from reading and reviewing a wide variety of proxies:

1. The purpose and business value are confirmed for each element of executive compensation, and the company's total compensation strategy (see also Chapter 11) is clarified.

2. Board compensation committee members have increased their involvement in the review and approval of executive compensation and benefit programs. Communication among those who develop and administer executive compensation programs within the company, outside consultants who advise the company, and board compensation committee members has created a clear rationale for executive compensation programs.

3. Company performance measures have been evaluated and confirmed; moreover, their use in executive compensation programs is very clear, since the performance graphs required by the proxy rules put a definite focus on the comparison of

executive pay versus company performance as measured in total shareholder return.

4. More frequent monitoring of executive compensation programs by company management and board compensation committee members is expected to occur during the year to ensure that the pay for performance comparisons reported in the proxy are being followed and achieved within the company. Any increase in executive compensation when company stock price and/or performance decreases would produce a significant negative shareholder and media response.

5. The company strategies developed for the executive pay programs must have continuity and staying power; board compensation committee members will not be willing to make constant program changes each year, simply because these changes have to be explained in the proxy.

It is clear that the detailed proxy reporting rules, and related access to the details of public company executive compensation programs, are a major factor in executive compensation program design and will continue to be for many years to come.

Chapter 3

Base Salary

Base salary represents the single largest element of the total compensation package, which consists of salary, annual and long-term incentives, benefits, and perquisites. Base salary is still the principal method of compensating executives. Because annual and long-term incentives are frequently developed as a percentage of base salary, an inappropriate base salary can have a compounding effect on the total executive pay plan. From a business standpoint, the ideal base salary is the one that, at the lowest cost to the company, leaves the executive in a posture of aggressive contentment—content enough not to seek other opportunities, but aggressive in the desire to earn the incentive portions of the total compensation package. This chapter provides information on how companies establish internally equitable and externally competitive base salaries.

Establishing Base Salary   3-2
Job Evaluation   3-3
Salary Increases   3-9
Salary Banding; Other Increases   3-10

Establishing Base Salary

Q 3:1   How is an executive's base salary set?

Base salary is the amount of fixed cash compensation that is paid to an executive on a periodic basis that represents income that is not at risk. The board of directors of the company typically sets the base salary of the chief executive officer (CEO) using market data obtained by the board. There is a growing tendency, because of board liability concerns, to use outside consultants to provide competitive compensation data from several independent sources for this purpose as well. The company's compensation specialist frequently collects all such appropriate competitive practices information.

The other executive salaries are normally established by the CEO, who may or may not present this information for approval to the board of directors. The CEO receives the market data and either formally or informally reviews the executive's performance.

Q 3:2   How do companies decide on salaries or salary ranges for executives?

Two approaches are typically used to peg the value of an executive position. Internal equity is determined by some form of job evaluation process and attempts, without any external reference, to determine which executive positions have more value to the corporation. External equity is determined by some method of data collection to establish what similar companies are paying for similar positions. The process of establishing external equity is referred to as market pricing. These two approaches, which are generally used in combination, often give conflicting rankings of positions and therefore act to counterbalance each other. Using either formal statistical techniques or a more subjective management decision process, a dollar value range is then assigned to each executive position. Typically, clusters of similarly valued positions are assigned to one salary range.

It is important to note, however, that in some industries base salary may be set at significantly lower levels than indicated by either the internal or external equity approach (see Q 3:10). Where this is the case, bonuses are often used to compensate for the variance (see Chapters 4 and 5).

Job Evaluation

Q 3:3 What is job evaluation?

Job evaluation is the process that establishes a position's internal relative worth to a company by measuring a position's duties against a predetermined yardstick. Job evaluation measures job worth in an internal sense rather than in an economic or social one.

A company establishes the economic worth of a position by looking outside the organization to see what the market is paying for a position; social worth is a function of the external perception of the importance of the contributions of a specific person or occupation. The internal concept of job worth involves the scope of responsibility or difficulty of assignments. Market worth, social worth, and internal value are not identical and may not correlate.

This lack of correlation is one of the difficulties of job evaluation. As a result, there are hundreds of different methods of job evaluation, and all of them measure job responsibilities against a different pre-established yardstick. They differ in (1) whether they measure the whole job or elements of the job and (2) how they assign values to the steps on the yardstick.

The four basic approaches to job evaluation are:

- Ranking system
- Classification system
- Point evaluation
- Factor comparison system

Q 3:4 How does the ranking system work?

In this approach, the chief company executive, usually with the help of the chief human resource executive, simply ranks one executive position against another. The CEO compares the two positions

Chart 3-1. Job Evaluation Methodology for Executives

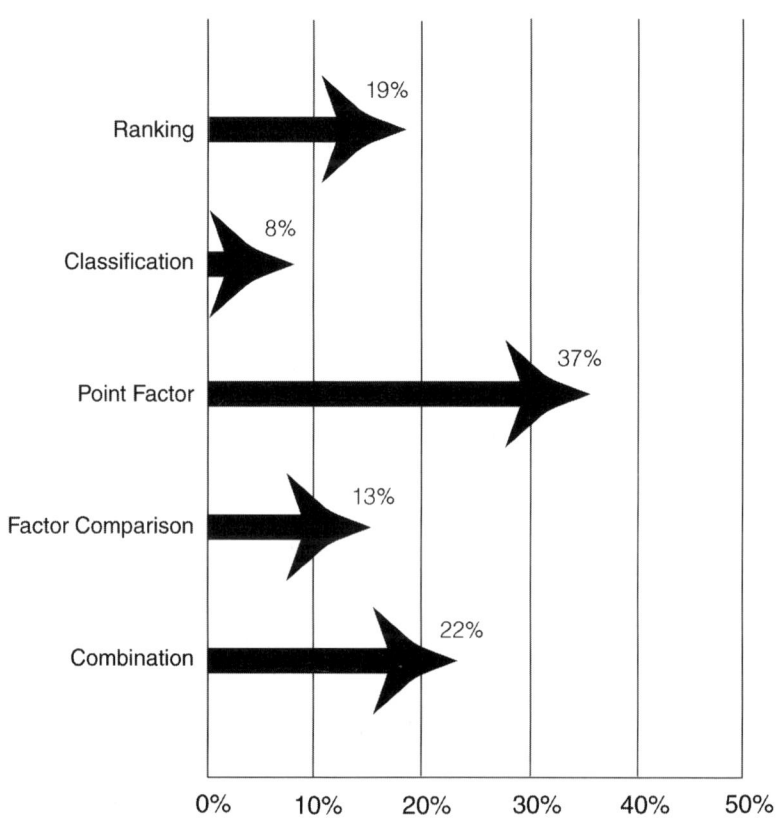

Source: Miller Mason & Dickenson, 1991.

and decides which is more difficult or important. A third position is compared to the first two and so on until all jobs have been ranked. The advantage and disadvantage of this approach is its simplicity.

Q 3:5 How does a classification system work?

In a classification system, each job is measured against a predetermined scale whose various categories define the overall value of the positions. The CEO, or a committee of company employees, typically compares each job against the scale and assigns each executive position to the grade that best describes the position.

Q 3:6 How does the point factor approach work?

The point factor system, which is the most widely used approach to job evaluation, measures a position against a series of factors (e.g., administrative responsibility, technical expertise, financial impact), with each factor having a scale of points for the degree that each applies to a specific job. A company can choose the degrees for each factor and assign points on a scale based on relative value to the company. The scale defines values and degrees of each factor. Many companies use plans developed by consulting firms that have predetermined factors and factor values for each degree.

Example. One such plan assesses the following job factors:

1. *Administrative Responsibility.* Degree of managerial responsibility over people and/or business functions, and the degree of human relations knowledge required in the job

2. *Technical Expertise.* Depth and breadth of skill and knowledge of a business function(s) required in the job

3. *Financial Impact.* Magnitude of the impact that the job has on company operations

The first factor, administrative responsibility, is assigned factor degrees as follows:

	Scope of Management				
Independence of Action	Minor Individual Contributor	Moderate Department Level	Diverse Multi-Department	Complex Multi-Function	Corporate Management
1. Follows established procedures	30	60	90	120	150
2. Wide variety of decisions	60	90	120	150	180
3. Decides from general policies	90	120	150	180	210
4. Complex problems requiring creative judgment	120	150	180	210	240

Q 3:7 How does factor comparison work?

The factor comparison job evaluation approach is similar to the point factor approach except that it ranks positions based on selected factors, without definitions or values for the various degrees. The CEO would analyze and rank all positions in terms of one factor, then all positions in terms of the second factor. Only after all positions are evaluated are the points assigned for each factor. The points are added to get the positions' overall relative value.

Example. The following chart highlights the same job factors as in Q 3:6, but rather than assigning factor degrees, the company assigns points as follows:

	Factor		
Points	Administrative Responsibilities	Technical Expert	Financial Impact
60	Research Fellow	—	—
90	—	—	Research Fellow
120	Director Finance	Director Finance	—
150	—	VP Marketing	Director Finance
180	VP Marketing	Research Fellow	VP Marketing

Q 3:8 How do companies establish labor market values for executive positions?

Market pricing is the name of the process used by companies to value the "outside" or labor market value of executives. Companies can use labor market comparisons either to establish the value of points used in a job evaluation plan or simply to value executive jobs directly from the market pricing process. Pricing executive positions is a critical activity. The first step in this process is for a company to establish a list of competitive companies by determining the previous employers of current company executives and determining the companies that provide similar products and/or services (see Q 1:11).

The next step is to establish a match between the responsibilities of the company's executive positions and the responsibilities of similar positions in competitor companies. This process will be kept manageable by using market pricing only for "benchmark jobs" (jobs that are common to most companies, easy to define, and represent various company functions and organization levels). Matches should not be based on job titles and will rarely reflect education and experience for executive jobs. (For non-executive jobs, education and experience can, however, be very relevant. For example, in major job families like engineers, research associates, or accountants, base salary surveys will frequently show a direct relationship between salary and level of education and number of years of experience. This is not used for executive jobs because the more relevant factor that drives the value of a job is the degree of responsibility.) When matching executive jobs, the key six to eight major responsibilities in each executive position should be identified, with matching positions having at least 75 percent of the same responsibilities. Data should be collected on base salary and annual incentives (i.e., total cash compensation) for each of these positions.

Many surveys are available for use in market pricing positions. A number of companies also conduct their own customized surveys throughout competitor companies to establish the labor market value of executive positions. It is important to note, as well, that a company's compensation philosophy may affect market pricing. For example, if a company has a high-growth, high-risk pay philosophy and views its labor market as "leadership" or "innovative" companies, then this could affect the selection of competitor companies.

Once labor market data is gathered, companies use it to either value job evaluation points and then convert points to a salary range or they use the data directly in establishing a salary range for each position.

Q 3:9   How do most companies position their executive base salary and annual incentive against labor market competitors?

Once a company has "market priced" total cash compensation, (see Q 3:8), it must decide on a market value from the survey. Consider a CEO salary survey of five companies:

Company	Base Salary	Annual Incentive	Total Cash Compensation
A	$180,000	45%	$261,000
B	$170,000	50%	$255,000
C	$230,000	35%	$310,500
D	$200,000	40%	$280,000
E	$220,000	40%	$308,000

The median base salary is $200,000, while the median total cash compensation is $280,000.

It is not appropriate to determine a company's base salary position without considering annual incentive because some competitors may structure their compensation packages differently; for instance, some companies pay a lower base but higher bonus than competitors, and vice versa. This can be countered by establishing the position of both pay elements at the same time; this is usually done by using the median survey base salary to establish a company's salary range midpoint and the median survey annual incentive to establish the company's target annual incentive. The company must decide how competitive its executive compensation should be with the median survey amounts. If the median (50th percentile) survey data are not consistent with the company's pay philosophy, then another market value should be utilized (see also Q 3:12).

Q 3:10   Are there reasons for paying base salaries above or below a competitive average?

Yes. If an executive's base salary is 10 percent above or below the average competitive base salary as reported in a salary survey, then that executive's base salary is competitive. The best survey data are accurate at plus or minus 10 percent, and most companies establish salary ranges for executives that are plus or minus 20 percent from competitive data to allow for performance and job tenure differences among executives.

A company may need to pay a high base salary if it has no annual incentive or long-term incentive plans. If other aspects of a company make it unattractive as an employer, it may have to pay a premium base salary. For example, if the company is experiencing financial difficulties or if it is in a geographically isolated area, it may have to pay a premium to attract executives. A company in a slow- or no-growth environment may have to pay a premium to compensate for limited career promotion opportunities.

The other extreme of high base-paying companies are high-growth companies that offer low base salaries in exchange for substantial long-term compensation and career movement opportunities. In high-growth companies, promotions and promotional salary adjustment can compensate for lower competitive salaries.

Salary Increases

Q 3:11   Do merit increases motivate executives?

Some companies have concluded that merit increases do not motivate executives. This is a recent trend. The logic behind this conclusion is that executives are motivated instead by annual and long-term incentives, which can be substantial in comparison with the standard merit increase of 4 or 5 percent.

As a first step in implementing this concept, companies establish equity in the base salaries of their executives (a one-time salary adjustment may be necessary to achieve this). They then provide annual salary adjustments to all executives equal to the average annual increase (if any) in executive salary ranges.

Other companies have eliminated annual base pay increases alto-
gether and added their equivalent value to the targeted or potential
amount of the annual incentive. These companies will provide a
general adjustment to base salaries, but this will be a discretionary
amount every two to three years.

Q 3:12 How can companies reduce the inflationary impact of annual base salary increases?

Most companies do not like to be perceived as average in the way
they pay executives. Thus a number of companies pay at the 75th
percentile of labor market competitors (see Q 3:9). This compensation strategy creates two significant problems. One obvious problem
is that many companies are paying more than is necessary. The
second problem is less obvious: as more companies pay at the 75th
percentile, the median salary increases, and companies chase an
ever-increasing target. This can be circumvented by the following
actions:

1. Pay below the 75th percentile of competitors.
2. Pay all executives an "economic" increase approximately equal
   to the average salary range adjustment and then allow for a
   "merit" increase to 20 percent of the executive population (one
   of five employees, i.e., high performers).
3. Use "lump sum" merit increases (that are not added to base
   salary but paid as a one-time bonus) periodically in lieu of
   regular merit increases.
4. Establish an "expected level of performance" for executives in
   the merit increase plan and communicate to them that the merit
   increase norm is that associated with the expected level of
   performance. Such terminology (normal increase rather than
   average increase) is easier to communicate and more flattering.

Salary Banding; Other Increases

Q 3:13 Are there alternatives to base salary ranges and merit pay for executives?

Yes. Two new ideas have been implemented in a number of large,
progressive companies: range banding and economic pay increases.

Range Banding. Range banding represents the combining of two or more salary ranges into a broader range or "band." The banding of executive job classifications produces fewer and broader salary ranges or bands. Bands are different from salary ranges in that they include a number of executive jobs and job families and they do not have a midpoint, only minimums and maximums.

Companies use banding to enhance the career mobility of executives. Banding allows for lateral job movement of executives within the company (thus supporting career development moves) and puts less emphasis on single incumbent job equity. Annual or group incentives, long-term incentives, and perquisites can also be the same for a given band, which may facilitate administration. Another advantage of banding is that executive teamwork is easier to achieve, because many executives are in the same salary range, rather than in different or competing salary ranges.

The disadvantage of banding is that it can be difficult to determine which executive jobs to assign to one band. Numerous jobs must be assigned, and labor market information on the value of an executive job to the company can frequently indicate that one job would be very low in one band or very high in another band. Another disadvantage to banding is that it requires strong performance management systems, because typical salary administration guides are not as meaningful (e.g., midpoints, merit increase guides).

Economic Pay Increases. Under this salary program, merit pay and salary ranges are eliminated. A job rate is established for each executive job. The concept and strategy is that executives should not be in training for their jobs, and therefore broad salary ranges are not necessary. The market rate for the executive job is the executive's job rate. Salary increases are given annually equal to some economic factor such as the average increase in the overall labor market. Executives are motivated and challenged to achieve company business objectives through other executive compensation programs such as short- and long-term incentives. The advantage of the economic pay increase is that executives can be more objective in determining budgets and salary increases for nonexecutive employees, since executives are not included in the merit increase program. Moreover, administrative effort by managers and human resource staff is significantly reduced. The disadvantage is that executive salaries have little upward movement under an economic pay increase system, other than promotions.

Q 3:14   What are some positive company experiences with salary banding?

This idea is becoming prevalent. Most surveys will indicate that 20 to 35 percent of surveyed companies are using broad banding. Positive experiences indicate that, where implemented, the concept results in greater employee focus on career development, and it encourages broader skill/managerial development by executives in order to enhance their salary growth within the band. Executives in particular respond to the less-structured environment and flexibility that surround the use of broad bands, in that they place more emphasis on performance measurement (i.e., goal setting and goal evaluation) within the annual bonus plan (variable pay), rather than merit pay (fixed pay). This is beneficial to both the executive and the company.

The banding concept seems to work best in organizations that are going through a cultural change, or a change in strategic direction, because this new approach to salary administration is a tool for the company to use in effecting change.

Example. Company A has consolidated three divisions into two divisions and has sold a fourth division. In addition, the company has offered all employees a one-time special early retirement program, which was accepted by some executives. A number of executive jobs have had significant changes in responsibilities. In response to these facts, the company has updated all executive job descriptions and has replaced current salary ranges with salary bands that group numerous executive jobs into the same band. The impact of this action will be to:

1. Reduce executive concern over whether new job responsibilities are higher or lower in the hierarchy of executive jobs
2. Increase the company's ability to modify executive job responsibilities after the restructuring (due to continuing changes in the strategic direction of the business) without affecting the status or hierarchy of executive job grades, since most future changes will not affect the executive's assigned salary band

Q 3:15 What are some negative company experiences with salary banding?

On the negative side, some organizations are not ready for the renewed focus on performance management that is associated with broad banding. The wider salary ranges associated with salary banding require new definitions of promotions and new merit increase guidelines. Executives therefore need to be trained in these new policies.

There is also a requirement for new methods for market pricing jobs (see Q 3:8), because many jobs are grouped into one salary band rather than individual salary ranges. Career paths for executives must be analyzed before companies determine the number of salary bands.

Salary bands have not faced any test of time; that is, banding has not yet been used over an extended period. One concern is that with fewer promotions (which means fewer base pay increases) and ongoing inflation (which keeps the bands increasing), executives will not be able to progress through the salary band. Some companies would not view this as a problem; however, their executives may not agree.

A final negative is the question of "if there is not any problem with current salary ranges, then why change to salary bands"?

Example. A company is going through a cultural change from a paternalistic environment to a risk-oriented environment. It decides to implement salary bands for its executive jobs.

After all jobs are assigned to a new salary band, the company finds the need to define future promotions. It separates each executive band into four segments; however, the previous number of salary ranges in each band equaled four. Each salary band segment is similar to one of the former salary ranges! Has the company really changed its salary ranges?

Q 3:16 What have been company experiences with economic pay increases?

This idea is not as prevalent as salary banding. Only a few companies have tried using economic increases, with some positive results:

1. When economic pay increases are used only for executives, and merit pay increases are used only for nonexecutives, the executives do a better job of administering merit pay systems for nonexecutives, simply because executives do not participate in the merit pay system.

2. Because economic pay systems do not require goals, the focus of each executive's effort is more clear, because the executive does not have merit pay goals and annual incentive plan goals.

On the negative side, where economic pay increases are used, human resource departments are "pressured" to establish higher job rates for executive positions, and to establish high annual economic pay increases.

Chapter 4

Annual Incentives

The vast majority of companies provide annual incentive opportunities to their executive management team. While base salary remains the largest fixed element of an executive compensation package, the value of annual incentives to the total cash compensation package is growing. Companies use annual incentives to reward executives when company and/or individual performance meets company expectations. Key issues in the development of an annual incentive plan include the degree to which executive, business unit, or company performance determine annual incentive payout and the measures used to evaluate individual executive, business unit, and/or company performance. This chapter provides a comprehensive overview of annual incentive plans and addresses the reasons companies use annual incentives, the types of incentive plans, the strengths and weaknesses of frequently used plans, and alternative solutions to the various incentive plan design issues.

General Considerations 4-2

Plan Design 4-10

Performance Measures 4-23

Performance Standards 4-29

Funding Incentive Plans 4-33

General Considerations

Q 4:1   How is short-term or annual incentive defined?

Annual incentive is a term that is frequently used interchangeably with short-term incentive. Short-term or annual incentive is usually defined as an incentive paid for performance over no more than one year. Short-term incentives can measure performance, and be paid over periods less than one year, e.g., quarterly or semi-monthly, depending upon company planning cycles. For example, the retail and advertising industries use short-term objectives of three to six months; however, short-term incentives (and total cash compensation) are usually measured over a fiscal year. Usually these programs pay out the earned amount in cash (some companies pay all or part in stock).

Short-term incentive plans can be formal or informal. If they are informal, there may be no written plan and no predetermined funding method or participant allocation rules. Some companies prefer not to establish a formal annual incentive plan and instead simply have a policy of paying out bonuses annually that are based on the company's performance, without any predetermined funding method or participant allocation rules. This allows a company, within the context of overall firm performance, to provide incentives and rewards to executives based on their own individual performance. The informal method is most often recommended for small companies where the cost of creating a formal program is not justified; however, an informal plan is also appropriate for any company that feels that flexibility is necessary to retain valued executives by increasing their proportionate reward, and by small companies that want to provide "contingent remuneration" (i.e., compensation that varies and is based on performance).

Most short-term incentive plans are designed to produce a payout for an executive that is either a specified percentage of base salary or a percentage of a total target amount to be paid if company objectives are met.

A typical annual incentive plan would provide incentive opportunities that vary by job level:

CEO	40–60%
VP	25–35%
Others	20%

The highest percentage potential is given to the highest ranking executive, who is assumed to have the most responsibility for ensuring that the company achieves its annual objectives. From a company perspective, it is desirable to have a higher amount of total cash compensation "at risk" and subject to performance achievement for the higher level executive. This is known as bonus progressivity (i.e., bonus amounts for executives progress higher as job responsibility increases). This is also desirable because higher level executives can make decisions that directly affect company success; therefore, their total cash compensation should be contingent upon the success of these decisions (i.e., pay for performance).

The payment for short-term incentives is usually made at the close of the plan cycle. Voluntary or mandatory deferral is, however, occasionally used for all or part of the earned amount.

Q 4:2 How prevalent are annual incentive plans?

The vast majority of companies (90 percent, according to industry surveys) have an annual incentive plan. Those few companies that do not have incentive plans believe that base salary (and performance-based salary adjustments) can effectively distinguish between levels of performance. Compensation surveys show that while base salaries are somewhat higher in nonbonus companies, the additional money does not compensate for the lack of an incentive opportunity.

Q 4:3 What is the rationale for having an annual incentive plan?

Most companies have an annual incentive plan in order to motivate executives to achieve annual company operating goals. A second reason for incentive pay, especially for companies with relatively small revenue, is that these plans make a part of the executive payroll a variable cost. The total cost of these payments can be a significant part of after-tax profits.

Another rationale for having annual incentive plans is that if executives can make decisions and judgments that affect company results for the year, then it makes sense for these executives to have a significant part of their current earnings dependent upon the achievement of these results.

A final, important, reason for having an annual incentive plan is to offer competitive compensation programs that can attract and retain executives. With over 90 percent of companies offering executives annual incentives, a company would be at a recruiting disadvantage without such a program. It is interesting to note, however, that while executives in the recruitment situation seem to be concerned about the existence of a program, they rarely question how much the plan paid out in the past, perhaps because of the expectation that such plans will pay off in the future.

Planning Tip. Because incentive plans can lose their effectiveness over time, plans should have a three-year expiration cycle. Every three years, participation, performance goals, and payout should be reviewed and the necessary modifications or revisions made. Otherwise, plans tend to continue without reassessment or revision.

Q 4:4   How is eligibility in annual incentive plans typically determined?

Participation should be limited to those individuals who can substantially affect the performance measures used in the annual incentive plan. Companies often use competitive market practice to determine annual incentive plan eligibility. If it is perceived that a position would be incentive-eligible in other competing companies, a company will often make it eligible for the incentive plan in order to establish annual incentive plan eligibility practices parallel to those in competitive organizations.

Incentive plan eligibility is typically expressed as a percentage of total employment. This percentage varies from 1 percent or less in very large companies, to up to 10 percent in very small companies. There is an inverse relationship with respect to annual incentive plan eligibility: As company size increases, the percentage of executives in an annual incentive plan decreases. For example, the number of executives (as a percentage of total employment) eligible for annual incentive payments in a company with $100 million of sales will be approximately 5 percent; however, the number of executives (as a percentage of total employment) with annual incentive plan eligibility in a company with $1 billion of sales would be approximately 1 percent. This is because the number of executives (as a percentage of total employment) who can influence annual business results is greater in a small company where there are fewer organizational levels, fewer business systems, and less overall structure.

Companies also use a number of other factors to determine eligibility in an annual incentive plan. These include: base salary, job level, reporting relationship, job title, or any combination of these.

More specific techniques used to establish eligibility include:

1. Requiring senior executives to recommend jobs that they judge to be "critical" to business success;

2. Establishing a targeted award level for all management positions and a maximum pool of target award dollars that can be utilized by each department executive, and requiring each department executive to recommend eligibility up to the maximum amount of the target award pool; and

3. Using one of the previous factors (e.g., job level, reporting relationship, title) and allowing each recommending executive to add up to an additional 10 percent to the initial eligibility list.

Whatever method is used for determining eligibility, one consequence is certain: Eligibility will increase over time. There are few, if any, documented instances of companies where annual incentive plan eligibility has gone down.

Q 4:5   Which forms of payment are typically used in an annual incentive plan?

Annual incentive awards are paid in cash, stock, or some combination of the two. Cash awards are the most common, although a number of small companies will use stock, particularly where cash is scarce.

The issue of deferral is an important consideration in determining the form of payout. There are voluntary and mandatory deferrals. Most mandatory deferrals are short term, while voluntary deferrals can be both short and long term. The following are examples of mandatory deferral:

Example 1. A $12,000 annual incentive award is earned by an executive, for whom one of two mandatory deferral schedules is arranged: $4,000 is paid in the year earned, $4,000 is paid after one year, and $4,000 after two years. This method allows the company to meet retention or "golden handcuff" objectives. Executives do not usually favor such a mandatory deferral method because they view the annual incentive as being "earned twice."

Example 2. In the second case, the deferral schedule calls for $6,000 to be paid in cash and $6,000 to be provided in the form of restricted stock, with one half of the shares vesting after one year and the other half vesting after two years. This alternative has the advantage of making the executive a stockholder; the arrangement could also call for 100 percent of the restricted shares to be vested upon any involuntary termination in order to avoid the inference that such an award must be earned twice.

Voluntary deferral can be arranged in any number of ways. For example, the executive might arrange for regular installment payments to commence after a designated deferral period. This could provide an excellent means of funding a known future expense such as a child's college education. An annual incentive award might also be deferred until retirement, allowing an executive to build supplemental retirement funds. Here are some examples of voluntary deferral:

Example 3. An executive wishes to defer an annual bonus earned during the upcoming fiscal year. An irrevocable election form is signed by the executive asking the company to defer any earned amounts for five years (which happens to be when the executive's oldest child will start college). A $12,000 bonus is earned, and the company advises the executive, then has the executive choose, from a number of alternatives, one or more funds where the deferred amount is invested during the deferral period.

Example 4. An executive wishes to defer an annual bonus earned during the upcoming year until retirement. The same procedure is followed as described in Example 1, except that the deferral period is until the executive's retirement. This is known as a voluntary long-term deferral. In contrast, Example 1 illustrates a voluntary short-term deferral.

When deferrals are permitted as part of any annual incentive plan, the form of payment and the method of deferral must be specified in accordance with the doctrine of constructive receipt, outlined in Qs 5:39 and 5:40. Most deferrals as described in this question represent unfunded liabilities for a company, meaning that the company acknowledges its obligation to pay the deferred amounts per the executive's deferral agreement. If the company goes into bankruptcy, these deferred funds are available to creditors. For this reason, some companies will establish secular trusts to secure the payment of deferred funds. (See Qs 9:30 and 9:31.)

A similar situation exists if a company is sold. The new owner may decide to cancel obligations to provide deferred funds. For this reason, many companies will establish an irrevocable rabbi trust to secure the promise to pay these funds in the future. (See Q 9:29.)

Q 4:6 Are annual incentive plan payments pensionable compensation?

Most surveys will show that at least two thirds of all companies, large or small, include annual incentive plan payments as pensionable compensation in qualified or nonqualified retirement plan packages. Total cash compensation (base salary plus annual incentive) tends to be used by executives to establish a basic standard of living; therefore, any pension amount should be a percentage of total cash compensation.

Q 4:7 What is the tax impact of annual incentive plans on the executive?

For a cash-basis company, annual cash incentive payments are deductible as and when the payments are actually made to the employee. For an accrual-basis company, amounts paid in cash to employees are deductible as and when the obligation to make the payments accrues (i.e., when the liability for payment is fixed and definite and not subject to indeterminable future events). An exception to this rule is made for the deduction of bonus payments by accrual-basis companies, if a full or partial payment is made up to two and one-half months prior to the end of the fiscal year. This is an important factor for a company to consider, particularly if substantial amounts of annual incentives are paid, because if a company can take a tax deduction in the year in which the annual incentive amounts have been accrued, it can not only reduce the amount of taxes paid in that year but it will further improve its cash flow position.

Executives recognize income from annual bonus payments in the year in which payment is received. For example, if an executive defers an annual incentive compensation plan, there is no taxable event until the deferral period has expired (provided the deferral was made in compliance with constructive receipt principles). Whenever an executive defers income under these circumstances, the company cannot take a tax deduction until the year in which the payment is received.

> **Planning Tip.** Companies need to consider the cost effect of allowing executives to defer annual incentive amounts earned. Accounting regulations require that annual incentives be booked as an expense when they are earned; however, for purposes of calculating the company's taxes, a deduction cannot be taken for these annual incentive amounts until they are paid.

Annual incentive compensation must also comply with Internal Revenue Service (IRS) regulations on reasonableness (see Qs 1:31 and 1:32). Companies cannot use annual incentive compensation as a disguised distribution of profits or they lose the deductibility of these payments.

Q 4:8   What is the accounting treatment for annual incentive plans?

Like salaries, cash incentive payments are typically accrued as expenses for the accounting period in which the related services are performed. For example, annual incentive compensation payment amounts are charged to the income statement in the year in which they are earned.

Any accrued but unpaid incentive payments are shown in the liability section of the balance sheet. For example, a company using an incentive compensation plan must accrue these expenses each year on the income statement and then transfer this future liability to the balance sheet, if not fully earned in one fiscal year.

> **Example.** An executive is provided with a short-term incentive compensation opportunity of $20,000 to be earned over a 12-month period. The company will be required to accrue one quarter of this targeted amount ($5,000) each quarter on the income statement. At the end of the year, $20,000 will have been accrued on its income statement. Any difference between what has been accrued and what is actually paid is reconciled. Had the incentive award period in this example been 15 months rather than 12 months, then the company would have accrued one fifth of the targeted award, or $4,000 each quarter. At the end of the fiscal year (four quarters), $16,000 would have been accrued, and this amount is then transferred to the liability section of the balance sheet. In Year 2, an additional $4,000 is charged to the income statement and the balance sheet. Upon payment of the incentive amount in Year 2, the actual payment is reconciled to the accruals, and the total amount of liability on the balance sheet is reversed.

While this is how accounting accruals are generally conducted for a short-term incentive compensation plan, the Financial Accounting Standards Board (FASB) has modified some accounting regulations. For example, amounts accrued each year can be adjusted based on the anticipated level of the final payment. For these reasons, human resource professionals dealing with incentive compensation plan design, whether annual or long term, should coordinate both accounting and tax implications with the company's financial department.

Q 4:9   Is shareholder approval required for annual incentive plans?

Shareholder approval is required for annual incentive plans only if the plan design or payment uses company stock; however, many

companies do seek shareholder approval in order to maintain positive relations with their shareholders.

Plan Design

Q 4:10 What are the key issues in the design of an annual incentive program?

There are many important issues to address in the design and/or
review of an annual incentive program. Some of these issues are:

1. What is the appropriate incentive plan payout level? What
   should the target payout be if the business objectives are
   achieved?

2. Which executives should be eligible for the annual incentive
   program? Where do executive incentive plans end and middle
   management incentive plans begin? What jobs have measurable performance goals? What jobs are critical to company
   success?

3. What is the appropriate measure of business performance?
   What financial measures, quantitative measures, or nonfinancial measures should be used to evaluate performance? What
   is the level of performance that should be established for
   payment of the standard or target incentive amount?

4. What is the appropriate leverage to be used in the payout
   schedule? How much should an executive receive for exceeding
   the established objectives, and how much should the executive
   be penalized for not achieving the established objectives?

5. What is the method of incentive fund accrual? What is the
   appropriate threshold level (minimum performance level) in
   both performance and amount of payment?

6. How should company performance, business unit performance, and individual performance be weighted when establishing performance measures (see Qs 4:34 and 4:40)?

7. What will be the form of payment? Will deferral of earned
   payments be permitted?

Q 4:11   What are the basic plan designs for annual incentive plans?

The basic plan designs for annual incentive plans are:

- Profit sharing plans
- Growth or improvement plans
- Target performance plans
- Peer company comparison plans
- Matrix plans
- Discretionary plans

Q 4:12   How does a profit sharing plan operate?

Under a profit sharing plan, the company pays a predetermined percentage of company or division profits as a cash bonus to selected participants. There usually is not a performance threshold level such as an earnings target or return on stockholder equity.

Example. Company A has a profit sharing plan. It allocates 7 percent of after-tax profits to a pool to be shared among its 12 executives. This amount is allocated among executives in the following manner:

CEO	25%
COO	13%
CFO	8%
Other 9 executives	6%

At the end of the fiscal year, sales were $36 million. After-tax profits were $5 million. The pool would be $350,000 ($5 million × 7%). The incentive would be distributed as follows:

CEO	25%
COO	13%
CFO	8%
Other 9 executives	6%

At the end of the fiscal year, sales were $36 million. After-tax profits were $5 million. The pool would be $350,000 ($5 million × 7%). The incentive would be distributed as follows:

CEO	0.25 × $350,000 = $87,500
COO	0.13 × $350,000 = $45,500
CFO	0.08 × $350,000 = $28,000
Other 9 executives	0.06 × $350,000 = $21,000

Q 4:13   What are the advantages of a profit sharing plan?

There are several distinct advantages to a profit sharing plan, including:

1. The plan is easily understood by participants.
2. No incentive plan payouts occur unless the company or division is profitable.
3. Incentive plan payouts increase in direct proportion to profits.

Q 4:14   What are the disadvantages of a profit sharing plan?

The primary disadvantage of the profit sharing plan is that incentive plan payouts are open-ended, which could possibly result in large windfalls.

Example. The facts are the same as in the example at Q 4:12 except that over time the plan was not changed but, through acquisition and growth, the company became a $120 million revenue company. Assume that there was $12 million in after-tax profits. The bonus pool would have increased to $840,000 (7% × $12 million). The incentive payments would have increased as follows:

CEO	0.25 × $840,000 = $210,000
COO	0.13 × $840,000 = $109,200
CFO	0.08 × $840,000 = $ 67,200
Other 9 executives	0.06 × $840,000 = $ 50,400

Bonuses would have increased more than 100 percent, but operating performance would have declined. The profit margin of $5 million compared to $36 million (from the example in Q 4:12) is approximately 14 percent; however, the profit margin of $12 million compared to $120 million is 10 percent, or a decline of approximately 30 percent.

The other disadvantage of a profit sharing plan is that the amount of capital needed to produce the profit does not play a role in measuring performance.

Q 4:15 How does a growth or improvement plan operate?

Typically a company selects one or more performance factors (net earnings, earnings per share (EPS) or sales growth are commonly used; see Q 4:37). The incentive pool is created based upon improvement over the prior year's results. The average of several prior years may be utilized to minimize year-to-year variations. A percentage of increased profits, revenues, or sales growth is typically used to create the pool.

Example. Company C has a growth or improvement plan in which its executives share as follows:

CEO	25%
COO	13%
CFO	8%
Other 9 executives	6%

Company C's after-tax profits during the prior three years averaged $5 million, and Company C decides to allocate to the pool 50 percent of its after-tax profits in excess of $5.5 million, an increase of 10 percent over the prior three-year averages. If profit is below $5.5 million, the incentive plan will not provide a payout. If Company C's after-tax return hits $6.2 million, the pool, therefore, is $350,000 (0.7 million × 0.50). The distribution would be:

CEO	$0.25 \times \$350,000 = \$87,500$
COO	$0.13 \times \$350,000 = \$45,500$
CFO	$0.08 \times \$350,000 = \$28,000$
Other 9 executives	$0.06 \times \$350,000 = \$21,000$

Q 4:16   What are the advantages of a growth or improvement plan?

The distinct strength of this type of plan is that it pays an incentive only if there is improvement. This plan is ideal if a company believes that base salary compensates an executive for managing the firm and incentive plans reward the executive for additional effort and improvement, in performance. Because the plan focuses on improvement there is no need for accurate forecasting of business conditions and performance targets.

Q 4:17   What are the disadvantages of a growth or improvement plan?

There are several drawbacks to these types of plans. Improvement over past results is not always an appropriate performance measure for the future. In some years, performance of a company can be outstanding if it maintains prior year profit levels.

Example. The facts are the same as in the example at Q 4:15 except that the economy fell into a major recession and Company C saw its product demand evaporate; however, through cost cutting and new products, Company C achieved a $5 million after-tax profit, even when its competitors were losing money. Under the growth or improvement plan, none of the executives would have received a bonus.

Conversely, in some years, improvement over past results may not indicate good management performance. For example, a company's 10 percent growth rate may indicate poor performance in a high-growth industry where demand is increasing at a 25 percent rate. Executives could be receiving a bonus even if they substantially underperformed against their competitors. In periods of cyclical or fluctuating profits, executives can be rewarded for the same improvement over and over.

Q 4:18   How does the target performance plan work?

Under the target performance plan, the company establishes "targeted" performance levels based on projected business results during the plan year. The company has the choice of setting aside either a fixed percentage of executive salaries (or range midpoints) or a fixed percentage of after-tax profits in the incentive pool for awards when the target is reached; it can also choose the results to measure for purposes of the plan (see Q 2:28). The incentive pool then increases to a maximum performance level or decreases to a minimum or threshold performance level. This approach is widely used and is easily adopted to individual business units.

Example. Company D has a target performance plan. The following performance goals are established to determine incentive payments (as a percentage of executive base salary):

After-Tax Returns

Position	Minimum Percentage (10%)	Target Percentage (14%)	Maximum Percentage (18%)
CEO	25	50	60
COO	20	40	48
CFO	15	30	36
Others	12.5	25	30

If the target of a 14 percent increase in the chosen performance factor is achieved, the payout would be as follows:

Title	Base Salary	Percentage	Payout
CEO	$200,000	50	$100,000
COO	160,000	40	64,000
CFO	125,000	30	37,500
Executive 1	110,000	25	27,500
Executive 2	88,000	25	22,000
Executive 3	88,000	25	22,000
Executive 4	76,000	25	19,000
Executive 5	75,000	25	18,750
Executive 6	70,000	25	17,500
Executive 7	68,000	25	17,000
Executive 8	68,000	25	17,000
Executive 9	65,000	25	16,250

If the performance level fell between the defined targets—for example, 12 percent—the incentive payments could be extrapolated or only the lower target amount paid out.

Q 4:19   What are the advantages of a target performance plan?

A target performance plan clearly establishes the criteria for generating the incentive pool based on the projected business results, and accrues incentive funds based on the level of performance achievement. If the pool is based upon participant salaries, it automatically increases in relation to new participants. Shareholder interest can be protected by the way the minimum performance level is established and how the maximum level is capped. The shareholder can be assured of a minimum performance before bonuses are paid.

Q 4:20   What are the disadvantages of a target performance plan?

The primary disadvantage of this type of plan is that it is difficult to estimate targeted performance accurately. Targets must be established each year, which requires accurate forecasting of company results, external business conditions, and competition in order to establish accurate target, minimum, and optimistic objective performance levels.

Q 4:21   How does a peer company performance plan operate?

The company selects one or more financial measures and a group of competitor companies to be compared against. A targeted incentive pool is created for these competitors. The targeted incentive pool for the company can be established by using a percentage of participant salaries/midpoints or of profits. At the end of the performance period, actual performance of the company is compared to the average performance of the peer group. An increasing pool is provided to company executives as relative performance of the company exceeds peer company performance.

Example. Hospital A has identified bed occupancy (the percentage of hospital beds that are utilized over the year) as the prime objective next year. During the current year, bed occupancy was 76 percent. In the geographic area in which Hospital A competes, the average bed occupancy is 78 percent. The following matrix determines the payout as a percentage of executive base salary:

Bed Occupancy

Position	Average Percentage	2% Above Average	4% Above Average
CEO	40	48	52
CFO	30	36	39
COO	20	22	26
Others	15	16.5	19.5

If, during the next year, bed occupancy for the region was again at 78 percent and Hospital A improved its bed occupancy to 78 percent, the incentive payout would be from the first column average. But, assume that average bed occupancy for the region dropped to 60 percent and Hospital A's bed occupancy dropped to 70 percent. Despite this drop in bed occupancy, Hospital A would pay the highest level of bonus (the third column) because Hospital A's bed occupancy was more than 4 percent above the average.

Q 4:22 What are the advantages of a peer company performance plan?

This plan is clearly performance-based. It insulates the company's performance from uncontrollable market conditions because these conditions should, in theory, affect all companies to the same degree. The need for accurate forecasting is therefore unnecessary. The peer company performance type of plan reinforces the shareholder interest. Investors who choose to invest in a given industry want to invest in the company that outperforms the other companies in that industry, the company that has the best returns in the industry.

Q 4:23 What are the disadvantages of a peer comparison plan?

The greatest difficulty with this plan is related to comparison factors. Data may not be available for all competitors. Peer comparison plans are most common among companies in industries that are easily defined and produce uniform and easily available financial data. Banking and hospitals are two industries that meet these criteria and frequently use peer comparison plans.

Q 4:24 What are the key features of a matrix plan?

With a matrix plan, the company establishes a two- or three-dimensional performance matrix for each group of executives covered, incorporating various performance measures and indicating the percentage of salary or after-tax profit payable at various performance levels. Frequently, these plans utilize two or more design features or two or more performance measures. Although primarily used in annual incentive plans, this plan design approach is also utilized in long-term incentive plans, such as performance unit plans (see Chapter 7).

Example. Company E has a matrix incentive plan. Its performance measures are sales growth and return on equity (ROE). The payout matrix for the corporate officers' position is shown in Chart 4-1, which shows that if the sales growth target of 14 percent and ROE target of 8 percent are achieved, the participants would receive 100 percent of their targeted annual incentive. Performance below 10 percent sales growth or below 6 percent ROE would result in no incentive payment. The incentive payment is capped so that performance above 10 percent of ROE or 18 percent sales growth would still provide a maximum incentive payment of 130 percent of targeted incentive. Performance between the established points (e.g., ROE of 7 percent and sales growth of 12 percent) would be 85 percent, per Chart 4-1.

Chart 4-1								
ROE *(%)*			SALES GROWTH (in Percentages)					
	10	*11*	*12*	*13*	*14*	*15*	*16*	*17*	*18*
6	70	75	80	85	90	95	100	105	110
7	75	80	85	90	95	100	105	110	115
8	80	85	90	95	100	105	110	115	120
9	85	90	95	100	105	110	115	120	125
10	90	95	100	105	110	115	120	125	130

Q 4:25 What are the advantages of a matrix plan?

A matrix plan focuses an executive on two or three significant performance measures. This approach also facilitates the weighting of performance levels. For example, an ROE of 6 percent (minimum performance) would earn a payment of 90 percent of the targeted incentive award if sales growth was 14 percent (targeted perform-ance). See Chart 4-1.

Q 4:26 What are the disadvantages of a matrix plan?

It is extremely difficult to estimate targeted performance of one performance measure, and even more difficult to do the same for two performance measures. Accurate forecasting is required of company results, competitive conditions, and economic conditions. In addi-tion, a matrix plan "documents" the payout schedule, and does not permit any discretionary judgment or flexibility of the payment decision.

Q 4:27 What is a discretionary plan?

A discretionary plan is one in which a chief executive officer (CEO) or other senior executive in a company determines individual incentive compensation payments on a purely discretionary basis at the end of a designated annual incentive compensation award period. No fixed goals or profit percentages drives this determination of incentive awards. The plan concept depends upon the fairness of the decision-making executive (or a committee of executives) to allocate incentive compensation awards on an equitable basis and in direct relation to the contributions of each eligible executive.

Q 4:28 What are the advantages of a discretionary plan?

The primary advantage of this type of plan is that the executive determining the individual bonus amounts can evaluate all events that occurred during the incentive award period, and the contribu-tions made by each individual, so that a fair and logical incentive award can be determined for each individual.

In addition, the award amount is discretionary: There are no cost parameters on the payments from the plan, nor are there any fixed business conditions or results that must be achieved or estimated.

Q 4:29 What are the disadvantages of a discretionary plan?

There is no level of expectation established with the incentive plan participant; therefore, there is no direct motivation for participants under this type of plan. The discretionary plan is also subject to any personal bias of the person or persons responsible for determining individual incentive amounts, and there is a tendency in the administration of these plans simply to increase the award payments during each new incentive award period, rather than varying incentive compensation payments based on measurable performance criteria.

Q 4:30 Are executives categorized as U.S. expatriates included in annual incentive compensation programs?

Yes. Most expatriate programs follow a policy of providing the U.S. expatriate on assignment overseas with the equivalent executive compensation program provided to counterparts working in the United States. Because the expatriate is part of an international business unit, this policy often requires modifications to plan performance measures and in some cases to the type of plan. Payment is also frequently arranged entirely or partially in the local currency. This is done as a convenience to the expatriate and also because local and U.S. tax laws make this cost-effective for both the company and the expatriate.

> **Example.** A U.S. expatriate executive is assigned to manage a company profit center in Europe. Typically, in the executive's newly assigned country, the amount of potential (targeted) annual bonus is 20 percent of base salary. This executive's current annual bonus potential is 25 percent. The company will normally keep the executive's total cash compensation "whole" by keeping the annual bonus potential at 25 percent. In addition, the company will typically pay a portion of any annual bonus earned in local currency. The amount paid in local currency will be equal to the

after-tax/take-home amount of annual bonus, assuming that the bonus will most likely be spent in local currency.

Q 4:31 Do companies with international operations include local national executives in incentive compensation plans?

Incentive compensation practices vary by country, but where they are typically part of a company's total compensation program in a specific country, incentives are provided to local nationals. As a general rule, the amount of incentive compensation provided in non-U.S. countries is less than that provided in the United States. Therefore, total compensation strategies (discussed in Chapter 11) for executives are particularly important because non-U.S. business objectives and total compensation practices vary significantly from those in the United States.

Q 4:32 Can incentive compensation plans be utilized in new ventures/start-up businesses?

Yes. New ventures or start-up businesses will typically establish incentive compensation plans that are tied to "milestone" accomplishments rather than to accomplishments during a specific annual or quarterly period. Because the business plans for these companies cannot always be established annually, incentive payments are tied to certain critical accomplishments (milestones) that must be achieved if the new venture is to be successful. The timing of these critical accomplishments or milestone events cannot always be predicted with great accuracy; therefore, the incentive compensation plan should be modified to meet the unique business characteristics of new venture organizations. Generally, the size of the incentive award will also vary in accordance with the length of a milestone. For example, if a milestone is expected in a year and a half, targeted incentive compensation would also be equal to the annual award multiplied by 1.5.

Q 4:33 How can annual incentives for executives be distinguished from those for mid-level managers?

Many companies adopt middle management annual incentive programs that are extensions of the executive annual incentive program. Other companies will design completely different programs. In this case, companies need to ensure that middle management executives do not receive a low or zero bonus when executives receive high bonus amounts, and vice-versa. Performance measures should be similar even if plan design differs.

Companies typically design executive incentive plans for those individuals or executives in the company who are eligible for both annual incentive plans and long-term incentive plans (stock awards). This eligibility criteria helps to distinguish executive annual incentive plan eligibility from that of middle management.

Another clear distinction is through the development of a company's total compensation strategy (see also Chapter 11). Companies can identify a specific business purpose for each element of compensation, such as a targeted labor market pay level to be achieved by the company. This can be done for both executive jobs and nonexecutive managerial jobs. This type of activity helps to ensure that plan design and performance measures are integrated between executive jobs and middle-management jobs.

Q 4:34 How can short-term incentive plans be integrated with executive compensation plans during a merger of two companies?

Upon the merger of two companies, a choice must be made as to which company compensation plan will continue. A transition to a new plan may be in order. If eligibility will not be continued for some executives after the transition, such executives will typically be provided with a plan buyout amount equal to the last incentive award or the average of the last two or three incentive awards paid. This can be done at any time during or shortly after the new incentive award period.

Any existing short-term incentive plans should also be reviewed after the merger to determine whether changes are necessary. In addition, the performance measures used in any plan generally require change after a merger. All other administrative provisions (i.e., form of payout, deferral, plan approvals) should also be reviewed after a merger. A task force of representatives from both companies should be given the responsibility of reviewing alternatives against an established total compensation strategy (see Chapter 11) and then presenting them to the new CEO or other approving authority for final approval.

The task force does not always conclude that the buying company's annual incentive plan should be adopted. The acquired company may have a better plan. Real experience in these situations is that the plan that has paid more to the executives over the past few years gets first priority by any reviewing committee.

Performance Measures

Q 4:35   What types of performance measures are commonly used in annual incentive plans?

Performance measures commonly used in annual incentive plans fall into three general categories: quantitative, financial, and nonfinancial.

Q 4:36   What are some examples of quantitative performance measures?

The most common types of quantitative performance measures are:

- Market share
- Sales units
- Inventory turns
- Productivity ratios
- Customer satisfaction surveys
- Production volume
- Shipping errors
- Budget/expense levels

Q 4:37   What financial performance measures are commonly used in annual incentive plans?

Most companies rely on financial measures for their annual incentive plans. The most frequently used financial performance measures are:

- Target earnings
- Target sales
- Increases in profits or earnings per share growth
- Increases in sales
- Profit margin
- Return on capital
- Return on assets
- Return on equity

Target earnings are frequently used even though this performance measure may not reflect the effects of inflation on the company's performance. Other companies use financial ratios such as return on assets and return on equity. The shortcoming of these ratios is that they reflect an accounting value of the investment base, rather than current market value. Some executives believe that these shortcomings can be overcome by using some measure of "shareholder value," which in its most simple form consists of increases in stock price plus stock dividends. Shareholder value can also be any other financial measure that will drive stock price up, such as a favorable "market to book value" ratio, or a favorable ratio of ROE to the cost of capital. A few companies also use similar measures of "economic value-added." This is defined as any increases in the net worth of the company. No matter what financial performance is chosen, there is still a requirement for accurate measuring and forecasting, so that annual incentive payments motivate executives and assist the company in meeting its business goals.

Q 4:38   What is earnings per share and how is it calculated?

Earnings per share is a frequently encountered measure of profitability. This ratio is computed by dividing net income attributable to common stock by the average number of common shares outstanding. There are two types of EPS: fully diluted and primary. Both include common shares outstanding and common stock equivalents such as securities, convertible preferred stock, unexercised stock options that have an increase in value over the option price, and any other security that will enable the owner to become a common shareholder. Primary EPS uses year-end shares outstanding, while fully diluted EPS uses the average of the beginning and year-end shares outstanding for the year.

Earnings per share has been criticized as a measure of profitability because it does not consider the amounts of assets or capital required to generate that level of earnings. Two firms with the same earnings per share will not be equally profitable if one of the firms requires twice the amount of assets or capital to generate those earnings than does the other firm. Despite this limitation, EPS is a commonly accepted management performance criterion, and many believe that EPS directly influences stock price.

Q 4:39   What is return on assets and how is it calculated?

Return on assets is an effective way to assess management's performance in using assets to generate earnings. This measure is often called the return on investment and is calculated by dividing net income, however defined (typically net/after-tax income), by average total assets.

This measure is frequently used in financial institutions, where earnings returns on assets (cash) is a critical indicator of business success.

Q 4:40   How is return on equity calculated?

Most shareholders are more interested in the rate of return on common shareholder's equity than the rate of return on assets. To compute this financial measure, divide earnings, however defined (typically after-tax earnings), by the average shareholder's equity. Equity includes par value of preferred stock, par value of common stock, capital contributed in excess of par value on common stock, and retained earnings.

Q 4:41   How is return on capital calculated?

Return on capital is generally measured by comparing earnings to the two primary sources of capital available for the company: long-term debt and equity issued in the form of company stock. Therefore, this formula has earnings plus interest on long-term debt in the numerator, with the sum of the company's long-term debt plus equity as the denominator.

Interest on long-term debt is added to the numerator to show the typical earnings number as a net income or after-tax earnings value, without any reduction for expenses (interest), incurred in obtaining the long-term debt. Because this value would already have built in a deduction of any expenses accrued and paid for the maintenance of long-term debt during that earnings period, it is only fair to add these earnings back to the numerator so that a fair return measure can be established against the two sources of capital in the denominator.

Q 4:42   What nonfinancial performance measures are commonly used in annual incentive plans?

Nonfinancial performance measures are also used by many companies, particularly in divisional business units. As with financial performance measures, quantitative measures are used most in large mature companies that have a great deal of historical information and computer systems support in order to gather and analyze the information required.

Nonfinancial performance measures include:

- Management development goals
- Equal employment opportunity/affirmative action goals
- Targeted completion of new facilities
- Organization consolidations
- Implementation of quality teams
- Achievement of product development goals
- Identification of acquisition candidates

The use of nonfinancial measures is increasing as a result of current business conditions that include mergers, acquisitions, divestitures, restructurings, and downsizing, all of which require a new focus of executive time and effort. Another reason for increased use of nonfinancial measures concerns current changes in the role of managers from directors of work to facilitators of work, a change that requires a corresponding change in executive behavior. Nonfinancial performance measures can be a tool in achieving this business objective. Companies using them need to be aware, however, that executives must exercise judgment on the degree of achievement. While some executives are not comfortable with this responsibility, many others welcome the challenge of evaluating the level of goal achievement—particularly because it offers the opportunity to look back on past achievements, rather than trying to look forward in times of uncertainty to estimate future performance.

Q 4:43 What is the difficulty of using performance measures in annual incentive plans?

Most companies use more than one performance measure, e.g., a financial performance measure and a nonfinancial performance measure, or two financial performance measures, in their annual incentive plans. This can increase the complexity and decrease the understanding of the plan. Multiple goals also make it more difficult to project targeted performance goals.

Companies cannot and should not attempt to direct all elements of the management function through the use of an annual incentive plan. To include all management performance measures in the annual incentive plan is an error because certain types of management performance do not correlate to an annual timetable. Examples of this are increasing shareholder value, or achieving other long-term business objectives that are best rewarded through the company's long-term incentive plan.

Q 4:44 How does a company decide whether the incentive programs should be based on group or individual performance?

The primary factor to consider is whether the company has the capability to measure corporate, division, department, or individual performance accurately. A company must also consider whether it is practical to establish performance targets for individual executives, given its culture (team versus individual) and management style. For example, a company that focuses on team performance may not want to use individual executive objectives in its annual incentive plan. Setting individual targets is time-consuming. Most companies initially establish incentives on group performance (corporate, divisional, or department) and use individual targets as an adjustment to group performance. This approach balances the organization's need for teamwork while recognizing the individual's contribution. Generally, this balancing is accomplished by calculating a portion of the incentive payout earned by formula, with the remainder based on the manager's evaluation of individual executive performance.

Performance measures are typically weighted. For example:

1. Organization goals 50 percent plus individual goals 50 percent; or

2. Corporate goals 50 percent plus divisional goals 25 percent plus individual goals 25 percent.

Q 4:45 How do performance measures vary by group or organizational level?

Corporate performance measures are typically financial—such as earnings per share, return on capital, return on equity, or net income. Divisions generally use quantitative measures such as sales volume, expense budgets, number of units sold, operating income, or market share. Individual performance measures are represented by such objective measures as completion of a complex project on time and within budget, identification of a significant number of potential customers, or customer satisfaction levels of 99.5 percent on all customer service calls. Performance measures should "build up the organization," so that individual goals contribute to divisional goals, which contribute to corporate goals.

Q 4:46 What performance measures work best for a manufacturing organization?

Most manufacturing companies are capital-intensive; thus, performance is commonly measured by some earnings return on capital. There are three primary sources of capital in a manufacturing company:

- Borrowed money (long-term debt)
- Money raised from stock sale (equity)
- Use of retained earnings (equity)

Long-term debt and equity are therefore factored into the earnings return measure. Return on capital is typically calculated as net earnings plus the after-tax interest on long-term debt, divided by long-term debt and equity.

Quantitative measures are also frequently utilized in manufacturing companies and include cost and expense issues such as reduction in operating expense or achievement of targeted cost of goods sold. Manufacturing companies sell products rather than services; therefore, sales units, market share, and net sales are also quantitative performance measures for such companies.

Q 4:47   What performance measures work best in financial institutions?

Financial institutions manage cash, which is an asset; therefore, return on assets is the most common performance measure, because it compares earnings to assets. Financial institutions also focus on net interest (interest received minus interest paid), total deposits, the percentage of nonperforming assets, and staff expenses as a percentage of total sales and general and administrative expenses (SG&A). These quantitative measures are used simply because success in each of these can drive success in the financial institution.

Q 4:48   Which performance measures are best for a service company?

Return on equity is the primary performance measure in a service company because increasing the net worth or equity of the company is a primary business goal. Service companies also use a number of quantitative and objective performance measures such as customer service ratings and quality of services ratings, because repeat business is critical to company success and quality measures drive repeat business.

Performance Standards

Q 4:49   What are the basic methods of comparing performance in annual incentive plans?

Once the performance measures have been chosen, the most critical aspect in the design of an annual incentive plan is the setting of performance standards. Although the specifics vary a great deal among types of companies and within industries, there are four main ways of establishing performance targets. They are:

- The look forward method
- The peer group method
- The look back method
- The percentage of profits approach

Q 4:50   How does the look forward approach to performance comparison work?

In a look forward plan, actual performance is measured against targets that are established each year based on business plans. This approach is most prevalent in annual plans. Its obvious advantage is that it focuses on the annual business plan.

Q 4:51   How does the peer group approach to performance comparison work?

In the peer group approach, actual performance is measured against performance of a group of competitor companies. This approach focuses on the firm's relative performance against competitor firms. It is appropriate only where timely and accurate competitor information is available. It is frequently used in banks, savings and loans, and utilities. The basic assumption in this plan is that outside forces will have had a similar effect on the performance of both the company and the comparison group. A company that has performed better than the comparison group is assumed to have demonstrated above average performance.

Q 4:52   How does the look back approach to performance comparison work?

The improvement or look back plan compares a company's current performance with its prior performance. Look back plans are most often established by young, growth-oriented companies, where accurate forecasting is difficult. One weakness of this plan design is that improvement over prior performance may not be an indicator of good performance.

Q 4:53 How does the percentage of profits approach to performance comparison work?

In this approach, a fixed percentage of income is used to fund a bonus pool. This fairly common approach results in a bonus pool funding without reference to a business plan or economic conditions. The drawback to this approach is that these fixed percentages tend to stay in place for many years, and thus are not responsive to economic conditions, competitive practice, and targeted total cash compensation.

Q 4:54 May performance maximums be set for annual incentive plans?

Because it is believed that company performance is ultimately driven by outside influences rather than by executive performance, maximum levels are generally determined for executive performance. For example, a natural disaster such as flood could create a boom in the construction industry, as could a competitor going out of business. In this case, the boom has nothing to do with executive performance. Surveys are readily available on this, and would indicate that these maximum levels are generally set at 150 to 250 percent over the targeted performance level.

Q 4:55 Do companies typically establish a threshold performance level in annual incentive award plans?

Most annual incentive plans are based on the achievement of certain performance levels that include a threshold or minimum performance level. If these threshold levels are not met, no incentive plan payments will be made. Some typical threshold levels used in incentive compensation plans are as follows:

1. *Competitor level.* Company performance must be above a minimum competitor performance level.

2. *Dividend payments.* Sufficient profits must be made to cover a targeted dividend payment to shareholders.

3. *Minimum return against an alternate investment.* The company's return on investment (e.g., return on equity, return on assets, return on capital) must be greater than alternate investment opportunities of shareholders such as short-term money market rates, certificates of deposit, or three-month treasury bills.

4. *Interest rate.* The company's return on investment must be at least equal to the prime interest rate level.

5. *Past performance.* Performance level must be at least equal to that of the previous year or the average of the last three years.

The appropriateness of threshold levels is a critical motivating factor in incentive plan design. Thresholds should not be so low as to guarantee regular incentive plan payments, nor should they be so high as to be unattainable.

Q 4:56   How can appropriate performance standards be determined?

If performance standards are too high and are never or rarely achieved, resulting in no incentive payments, executives will perceive these standards as being unattainable and the incentives actually will become disincentives. If performance standards are too low and are always achieved, the incentive plan becomes part of the salary program.

A rule of thumb in establishing performance standards is that in a ten-year period there would be one or two years in which there are no incentive payments and there would be one or two years where incentive payments would be at the maximum level.

While incentive payments do fluctuate in companies, it is becoming increasingly rare for an executive who is a participant in an annual incentive plan to receive no incentive payment. If an executive is eligible for an incentive payment of up to 40 percent of base salary, but over a prolonged time span is always earning between 20 to 40 percent and never earns less than 20 percent, it makes more sense to build that 20 percent into the base salary and offer the remainder as a true variable incentive payment.

Funding Incentive Plans

Q 4:57 How do companies determine the size of award appropriate in annual incentive compensation plans?

Companies will typically measure total cash compensation (annual salary plus annual bonus) provided in competitor companies and then establish their own targeted levels of base salary and annual bonus. In addition, companies will establish a total compensation strategy as outlined in Chapter 11, which provides a guideline on the size of annual incentive awards and long-term incentive awards.

The size of incentive awards is scope-sensitive, meaning that as company size increases, the amount of incentive award increases. For example, the controller in a company with $100 million in sales might have a target incentive award of 20 percent of base salary, while the same job in a company with $1 billion in sales might have a target incentive award of 30 percent.

Q 4:58 What factors drive the amount of annual incentive amounts paid to executives?

Four factors determine the amount of incentive pay an executive receives:

1. The amount of the executive's base salary or salary range midpoint;
2. The level the executive occupies within the organization;
3. The industry in which the executive works; and
4. The individual performance of the company.

Base Salary. Typically, the higher the base salary, the larger the incentive opportunity (both as a percentage of base and, of course, the amount). For example, a CEO earning $200,000 will probably be eligible for a larger incentive payment than a CEO earning $100,000.

This is partly explained by the fact that base salaries are significantly affected by the size of the corporation.

Organizational Level. The CEO normally is eligible for the largest incentive opportunity. Typically, his or her direct reports are eligible for 70 to 80 percent of the CEO bonus (expressed as a percentage). For example, if the CEO's bonus target is 50 percent of base salary, his or her direct reports will be eligible for between 35 to 40 percent of their base salaries. The next reporting level typically is eligible to receive between 50 and 60 percent of the CEO's percentage.

Industry. The manufacturing and service industries tend to pay larger incentive amounts then do industries such as health care or insurance.

Individual and Company Performance. One normally would assume that the better the company performance, the larger the amount the executive would receive as incentive payment. In most cases this holds true when analyzing individual company plans and payout. When looking at one specific company, incentive payments will typically be larger in those years where performance was better.

Because many companies establish annual incentive payment targets based on prior years' performance, poorly performing companies tend to establish lower performance targets. For example, a company that is losing money may see breaking even as excellent management performance, worthy of incentive payments; however, another company that historically has made a 20 percent return on investment may establish its targets at 22 percent return on investment. In the long run it will be easier for a poorly performing company to improve performance (break even and pay a bonus) than it will for a higher performing company to improve its performance.

Q 4:59 How does the pool method operate when used in determining incentive funds?

The pool method is a popular means of determining an incentive payout. An overall incentive pool is calculated for all participants or a group of participants, and each individual award is determined as a share of the pool. The following table demonstrates the pool method:

Participant	Total Annual Incentive Pool	Pro-Rata Share of Annual Incentive Pool (%)	Target Annual Incentive	Individual Pro-Rata Annual Incentive Award*
A		30	$ 30,000	$ 36,000
B		20	20,000	24,000
C		15	15,000	18,000
D		15	15,000	18,000
E		10	10,000	12,000
F		10	10,000	12,000
G	$100,000	100	$100,000	$120,000

*The actual total annual incentive award was 120 percent of the targeted amount.

Q 4:60   Are there advantages to the pool method?

Yes. The primary advantage to the pool method is that it correlates the aggregate payout and costs to the number of participants or level of performance. In addition, it allows the performance of the organization, business unit, or department to drive annual incentive plan payments.

Q 4:61   Are there disadvantages to the pool method?

Yes. The pool method has two basic disadvantages:

1. Superior performance by one or more persons cannot be rewarded.
2. An increase in the number of participants can dilute the available incentive payment of existing participants, unless the annual incentive pool increases as well.

Q 4:62   How is the participant method used in determining incentive pools?

Each participant has an incentive opportunity that is not affected by the performance of other participants, although the individual's own award may be adjusted based on his or her performance. The total payout is simply the sum of individual participant awards, after adjusting the target fund by company (or business unit) performance, as can be seen in the following table:

Participant	Annual Incentive	Target Performance Rating (%)	Adjusted Company Annual Incentive	Individual Target Performance Rating (%)	Individual Annual Incentive Award
A	$ 30,000	120	$ 36,000	100	$ 36,000
B	20,000	120	24,000	100	24,000
C	15,000	120	18,000	120	21,600
D	15,000	120	18,000	80	14,400
E	10,000	120	12,000	120	14,400
F	10,000	120	12,000	80	9,600
	$100,000		$120,000		$120,000

Q 4:63   Are there advantages to the participant method?

Yes. The participant method makes it much easier to communicate the incentive opportunity to participants. Moreover, because individual performance has a direct effect on individual incentive payments, each participant is motivated to achieve goals established in the annual incentive award plan.

Q 4:64   Are there disadvantages to the participant method?

Yes. The major disadvantage of the participant method is that it can make the amount of funds allocated for the annual incentive difficult to control. A recommending executive can rate individuals in a manner inconsistent with that of other departments. The best way to control this is to use the performance of the business unit or company to determine the incentive pool for each department or group of executives, and then to require that individual executive awards equal the pool generated by that performance.

Q 4:65   Do incentive plans have maximum or caps on incentive payments?

Most incentive plans do cap the potential payout opportunities so that managers would not benefit by events that are beyond the control of management. In the view of many companies, performance that substantially exceeds budgeted targets is more a reflection of poor budgeting or non–company-related economic conditions than excellent executive performance.

The arguments against capping incentive payout are twofold. First, if the goal is to tie performance to payout, then if performance exceeds all expectations, the incentive payment should exceed all expectations. Second, if the executive is at risk on the downside (i.e., he or she could receive less or nothing), the executive should have the upside potential uncapped.

A cap on incentive plan payouts may be expressed as an absolute dollar limitation (either on contributions to the pool or on individual awards) or as a percentage or multiple of the projected maximum payout.

Chapter 5

Long-Term Incentive Plans

Long-term incentive programs, frequently called capital accumulation plans, are offered to executives by a majority of companies. In fact, participation in these plans traditionally determined those employees considered executives. Three basic plan designs are utilized when implementing a long-term incentive plan. The first, the purchase plan, requires an executive to make an investment. The second, the appreciation plan, grants the executive the right to receive the value of the appreciation in the employer's stock. The third, the full-value plan, grants the executive the full value of the company stock plus any appreciation that may result over a period of years. This chapter discusses general design and administration issues for long-term incentive plans. Chapter 6 deals specifically with purchase plans; Chapter 7 covers appreciation and full-value plans; and Chapter 8 deals with the effects of combining two different long-term plans.

General Considerations 5-2
Plan Comparisons 5-12
Compensation Philosophy 5-21
Plan Design 5-23
Stock Options 5-26
Omnibus Plan 5-29
Tax Considerations 5-30
Stock Option Exercise 5-35
Plan Administration 5-40

General Considerations

Q 5:1   What are long-term incentive plans?

Long-term incentive plans or capital accumulation plans are long-term programs that give executives the opportunity to accumulate estate-building capital when the value of the company's stock increases or when long-term company objectives are met. Because stock options are the most prevalent type of capital accumulation plan, many individuals use the two terms interchangeably. Stock options are, however, only one approach to capital accumulation and long-term incentives.

Q 5:2   What are the characteristics of long-term incentive plans?

Long-term incentive plans usually are structured with a three- to five-year time frame; however, to provide continuous incentives, many companies make annual grants that may subsequently result in annual payments. Long-term plans are generally stock-based or use increases in stock prices as the basis for payout, because they are designed to create an interest in the executive that mirrors the interest of the company's shareholders. Payments are typically made in stock, cash, or a combination of the two, and if the combination approach is used, sufficient cash is paid out or withheld to cover the executive's tax obligation for the stock and/or cash received.

Q 5:3   How is eligibility for participation in long-term plans determined?

Only those executives who can make decisions that affect a company's long-term results usually participate in long-term incentive plans. When this criterion is used, participation in long-term plans is usually limited to a handful of executives. Survey information regarding Fortune 500 companies shows, however, that the trend is to extend eligibility for long-term incentive plans to middle managers at salary levels beginning at approximately $75,000 in large companies and $60,000 in small companies.

Emerging and growth companies that may have cost and cash flow problems tend to include larger numbers of executives in these programs to compensate for lower base salaries. They also use long-term plans, with their accompanying prospects of huge future payout, as a recruitment and retention tool. This offsets the fact that these same companies often provide total cash compensation that is less than that provided for similar positions in large companies. Surveys show that these small, entrepreneurial companies use three to four times the amount of stock, as a percentage of total common shares outstanding in the company, for their long-term incentive plans than do large companies. This is because long-term plans with stock do not require cash or a charge to earnings, as do short-term incentives.

Most companies use long-term plan participation as a motivator so that the executives selected for participation are given the message that they have been selected for membership in a special group. The criteria used in establishing eligibility for long-term incentive plans are the same as those used for short-term incentives. For example, typical criteria include base salary/salary midpoint, job grade, reporting relationship, and job title.

Q 5:4   How prevalent are long-term incentive plans?

The majority of publicly traded companies offer some form of long-term incentive for their executives. As shown in Chart 5-1, stock options are used more often than any other form of long-term incentive. During the past few years restricted stock has been the fastest growing long-term plan, particularly because it has the strongest retention value (see Q 5:5). Of greatest significance in Chart 5-1 is that the types of long-term income used by companies do not add up to 100 percent, indicating that most companies use more than one form of long-term incentive. (See Chapter 2 for a discussion of the prevalence of annual long-term incentives in private companies.)

Q 5:5   What is the rationale for having a long-term incentive plan?

Most companies provide long-term incentive plans primarily because they believe offering an executive an ownership position or the potential for one will effectively motivate that executive to achieve the long-term goals of the company. A second reason is retention, or

Chart 5-1. Prevalence of Long-Term Incentives in Public Companies

Stock Options	94%
Restricted Stock Options	45%
Performance Plans	40%
SAR	66%
Other	27%

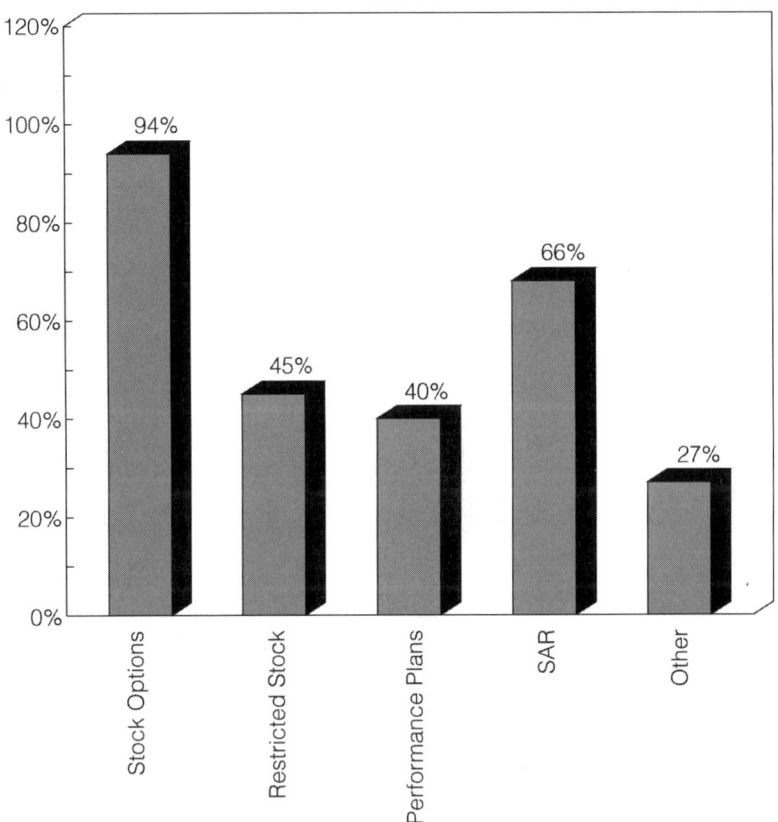

Source: Management Performance International, Inc.

keeping the executive employed by the company, particularly during a company restructuring. This is achieved by adding "vesting requirements" to long-term grants. For example, an executive is provided with the right to purchase 1,000 stock option shares at a fixed price. These rights might "vest" by 25 percent every four years, meaning that the executive can purchase 250 shares after Year 1, 500 shares after Year 2, 750 shares after Year 3, and 1,000 shares after Year 4. Given the fact that most stock option plans would have a total award period of ten years, this provides ample opportunity for the executive to exercise the right to purchase.

By providing annual grants of 1,000 shares as shown in the previous example, a number of vested and nonvested stock option grants will be ongoing, and any executive leaving the company would lose his nonvested shares.

A third reason for providing long-term incentive plans is to offer the executive a significant opportunity for capital accumulation. If stock prices increase, this can be a significant factor in total compensation.

Q 5:6 What should be considered in selecting a long-term incentive plan?

In reviewing the numerous alternatives, there are some basic questions that, if evaluated honestly, will help determine the type of plan design that most effectively meets the employer's strategic compensation goals. The following list of key issues in capital accumulation is designed to outline questions that should be considered:

1. *Executive Investment.* Will the executive be required to make an investment, or will the executive participate in the plan without an investment?

2. *Ownership.* Will the objective of the program be to create ownership of stock by the executive, or is the intent to reward the executive for improvement in stock price or some other financial measure?

3. *Company Impact.* What are the key long-term business factors in the company business plan? What company goals should a long-term incentive plan support? How will the company

change in the next three to five years, and what long-term incentive plan can best support this anticipated change?

4. *Performance Factors.* What performance factor is indicative of company success? Is it stock price, or is it some other measure such as earnings per share (EPS) or return on equity? Is it important for executives to be motivated and rewarded based on company performance measures that they can directly influence, rather than stock price, which is subject to outside factors such as stock market performance or the state of the economy?

5. *Accounting and Tax Impact.* What are the tax, accounting, and financial impacts on the company and/or the executive?

   - The impact of the plan's tax treatment:
     — When will the taxable event occur for the executive and entitle the company to a corresponding compensation deduction in calculating its taxes?
     — What is the plan's effect on the executive's individual tax situation? Will it be ordinary or capital gains tax?
     — Will the executive be subject to a potential alternative minimum tax?

   - The impact of the plan on financial issues:
     — Is the payout chargeable as an expense against the company's income statement?
     — Must the payout be accrued as a liability on the company's balance sheet?
     — How important are income statement costs to the company?
     — What percentage of the shares outstanding will be required for the plan, and how much dilutive effect will the plan have on EPS?

6. *Payout Levels.* What level of payout should the executive receive when long-term objectives are achieved? How much capital accumulation is appropriate and fair to the company, to the shareholders, and to the executive? What mix of short-term incentive and long-term incentive is desirable?

7. *Grant Frequency.* How often should long-term grants and/or awards be made?

8. *Corporate and Legal Restrictions.* What corporate and legal restrictions affect the company and/or the executive?

   • What is the impact of federal and state securities laws on the plan?

   • What considerations should be given to corporate insiders under SEC short-swing profit liability rules?

9. *Estate Building.* Is the long-term incentive plan intended to supplement retirement? How long will most participants be in the plan and how does this affect the amount of potential capital accumulation? If stock prices advance in the future as they have in the past, will the amount of capital accumulation be excessive?

10. *Eligibility.* Which executives have a direct effect on long-term performance? What is the eligibility in competitive companies? What will be the impact if eligibility is increased or decreased?

Q 5:7 What are the principal types of long-term incentive plans?

There are several variations on the long-term incentive plan, with stock options and stock appreciation rights (SARs) the most frequently utilized plan designs (see Qs 7:3–7:11; although SARs have recently lost much of their appeal as a compensation device). Performance share and performance unit plans are also commonly used, and restricted stock has recently had a resurgence in use. Most long-term incentive plans fall into four basic plan categories.

The first category includes plans that will provide the executive with stock provided that he or she makes an investment. These plans are the most common type of long-term incentive and are called purchase plans (see Chapter 6). Purchase plans include the following:

• Nonqualified stock options

• Incentive stock options (ISOs)

• Discounted nonqualified stock options

• Book value purchase plans

The second category includes plans that grant the executive the appreciation in the employer's stock over a certain period, but not the value of the stock itself. These plans, known as appreciation plans, include SARs, phantom shares, and book value appreciation rights.

The third category of plans provides the executive with the full value of the share over a specified period, and in some cases also provides the executive with the appreciation in the value of the shares over this period. These plans are called full-value plans because the executive receives all of the benefits of the grant without having to make an actual investment. The plans include restricted shares, performance shares, and performance units.

Both appreciation and full-value plans are covered in detail in Chapter 7. Finally, there are combination plans, which utilize two or more plan types. These are discussed in detail in Chapter 8.

Q 5:8   What new forms of long-term incentive are currently emerging?

Three new long-term incentive awards are being considered by a number of companies in addition to the other forms of long-term incentive outlined in Q 5:7. These are:

1. *Performance-Based Restricted Stock.* Under this plan, the executive is granted full-value restricted shares with a performance-based restriction that will accelerate the vesting of restricted shares from a designated maximum period to a shorter time frame. For example, an executive is granted 1,000 restricted shares with a four-year time lapse restriction. A performance-based restriction is added to the provisions of the grant, such that if company earnings per share increase 15 percent after the first year, the restrictions will lapse one year earlier (i.e., after three years). If a 15 percent earnings per share growth is achieved during Year 2, the restrictions will lapse one additional year earlier (i.e., after the second year).

2. *Leveraged Stock Options.* This concept encourages an executive to purchase shares of company stock with personal funds. For every one share of stock that is purchased by the executive, the executive will receive four or five stock option shares. These

stock option shares are above and beyond normal annual company stock awards. Thus the purchase of company shares by the executive is "leveraged" on behalf of the executive by the grant of the additional stock option shares. These leveraged stock options will typically carry the same plan provisions as the regular company stock option grants.

3. *Shareholder Value/Economic Value Plans.* These plans are based on the assumption that normal financial performance measures (e.g., earnings per share, return on capital, return on equity) do not accurately correlate with true shareholder value. True shareholder value is defined as increases in stock price plus dividends. Other performance measures should be used in long-term incentive plans, ones that will more accurately correlate with increases in shareholder value. A number of different shareholder value performance measures are being considered by companies. These shareholder value measures are not always found on company financial statements, but are defined by each company and utilized to motivate executives to achieve established goals in each of these areas, the theory being that such achievement will drive up company stock price.

Q 5:9 What is economic value-added?

Economic value-added (EVA) has many definitions. The most common ones are net earnings minus the cost of capital or return on capital divided by the cost of capital employed in the business. The earnings and return on capital numbers are easily identified in financial statements. The cost of capital is a little more difficult. Capital in a business is, of course, equity and borrowed money. Borrowed money has debt; long-term debt can also be identified on company financial statements. The cost of equity is more difficult to calculate. Most experts on this subject will say that this cost of equity is equal to what an investor could be earning elsewhere.

Therefore, to calculate cost of capital, companies need to add the value of all capital (e.g., buildings, equipment, investment in people and products or services), and apply a cost of capital to this value that is typically a hypothetical statistic determined by adding a typical investor return (e.g., T-bill interest of 6 to 7 percent) to a premium that is required to attract an investor to company stock (e.g., 5 to 6 percent). The total cost of capital (e.g., 11 to 13 percent) is then multiplied by total capital and compared to pre-tax operating profit. To the extent executives increase pre-tax operating profit in relation to the cost of capital, they are adding "economic value" to a company.

Q 5:10 How do EVA plans work?

The most common steps required for implementation of an EVA plan are:

1. *Select an EVA definition.* For example, when Coca-Cola established an EVA plan it used the following definition: NOPAT (net operating profit after tax) minus cash plus inventory plus [accounts receivable – accounts payable] plus noncurrent assets multiplied by cost of capital equals EVA. The current year's EVA minus the prior year's EVA equals the EVA that can be shared with all executives.

2. *Determine eligibility by evaluating who can have an effect on EVA.* In most companies this is the executives; however, some companies include many other managers and/or all exempt employees.

3. *Design a payout schedule.* There are two dimensions to this decision. The first is to establish the targeted amount of annual incentive or annual plus long-term incentive to be paid to each participant. The second is to analyze the company's business plans to determine potential growth in EVA. Analysis of the company's projected EVA based on business plans and targeted business performance in operating and/or strategic plans, plus a knowledge of competitive levels of annual/long-term incentive, are the two key facts required to develop the payout schedule. The potential increases in EVA, if business plans and targeted results are achieved, can be correlated to a company's targeted amounts of incentive to be provided to each executive, so that payout opportunities are properly estimated.

4. *Determine if EVA amounts earned will be paid in current cash and/or deferred.* In most EVA plans the executive participants will have a portion of earned awards paid currently (the amount that would parallel competitive levels of annual incentive) and

a portion deferred until termination or retirement. Deferred amounts are eligible for the same investment alternatives that exist in a company's retirement plan or something similar to these investment alternatives with some additional investment choices like split-dollar insurance or company-owned life insurance. Nonexecutive participants are typically paid entirely in current cash.

Planning Tip. A unique feature typically found in EVA plans is that payout schedules do not have any maximum. The logic for this is that the higher the EVA, the higher the shareholder value. Like many sales incentive plans there is no need to have a maximum because as targeted performance levels are exceeded, everyone wins.

Q 5:11   What is shareholder value?

These definitions, like EVA, also vary. The simplest one is stock price increases plus dividends equals shareholder value. The more sophisticated definition is return on capital divided by the cost of capital. The latter definition assumes that the correlation of these two measures will drive stock price and enhance shareholder value.

Q 5:12   How do shareholder value plans work?

Shareholder value plans work in the same way as performance plans, in that if an established goal is achieved, the executive will earn a long-term incentive and at the same time increase shareholder value.

Example. A company establishes a shareholder value measure of return on equity over the cost of equity. An increase in the ratio of these two measures will, it is believed, increase shareholder value. If return on equity is 16 percent and the cost of equity is 8 percent, the ratio is 2:0. If the company can increase this relationship to 2:1 or higher, investors will see that the true value of the company is increasing, and this factor will drive stock value up.

Shareholder value plans have the same advantages and disadvantages as other similar performance-based plans, and there are no guarantees that the stock market will react to the return on equity/cost of equity relationship, just as there is no guarantee that the stock market will relate to a favorable earnings per share or return on capital growth measure used in a performance plan. Some companies believe, however, that shareholder value plans provide a more accurate means of measuring executive performance and its correlation to stock price.

Q 5:13   What is a long-term performance plan?

A long-term performance plan provides incentives to an executive if long-term business objectives are achieved. It is similar in design to a short-term incentive plan except the performance cycle is typically three to five years. Common performance plans are performance shares and performance units. These plans pay in cash, stock, or a combination of cash and stock.

Q 5:14   What is a stock option plan?

A stock option plan grants an executive the right to purchase a fixed number of company common shares, at a fixed price, over a specified period, after some vesting schedule is met. For example: An executive is granted a stock option on 1,000 shares, at $20 per share, over ten years, and this right vests at a rate of 25 percent per year. After four years, the executive is fully vested, and if the stock price has a market value of $35 per share at that time, the executive may purchase up to 1,000 shares at $20 per share.

Plan Comparisons

Q 5:15   What is the advantage of a stock option plan over a long-term performance plan?

A stock option plan involves no out-of-pocket cost to the company, but it does provide the company with positive cash flow when the executive purchases the stock. In addition, there is no accounting charge to the income statement if the stock option is granted at full market value; that is, the option exercise price is equal to the then-market value of the shares of company stock provided by the stock option. If the option is a nonqualified option, the company receives a tax deduction upon exercise; however, this does not apply to an ISO. Stock options also have the advantage of tying the executive's reward to what shareholders care most about: the price of company stock.

On the other hand, long-term performance plans require a charge to the company earnings (even though the company receives a tax deduction for this amount). If the long-term performance plan is paid in cash, the company incurs negative cash flow (i.e., significant out-of-pocket cost). From a shareholder relations perspective, performance plans can pay out when stock price goes down.

Q 5:16 What are the advantages of a stock option plan over a restricted share plan?

The advantages stock option plans have over restricted share plans are the same as those outlined for stock option plans in Q 5:15. In contrast, restricted stock grants require an accounting charge to the income statement at the time of grant, based on the price of the share at that time. The company receives a tax deduction equal to the value of the restricted share at the time the restrictions lapse.

Restricted stock grants are not purchased by the executive. From a shareholder perspective, this can be a negative because executives can earn restricted shares during a time when the stock price has not changed.

Q 5:17 What is the disadvantage of stock options compared to long-term performance plans?

The major disadvantage of using stock options instead of long-term performance plans is that stock options have a dilutive effect on EPS. For example, if a company's earnings are $10 million and the number of shares outstanding is one million, then the company's EPS is calculated by dividing $10 million by one million, which equals $10 per share. If that company implements a new long-term stock option plan to add one million shares outstanding, the EPS calculation will, upon the exercise of all stock options (all other factors remaining the same), become $10 million divided by two million, which equals $5 per share. There has been significant dilutive effect on the EPS; this will be viewed negatively by both investment analysts and shareholders.

Other disadvantages of a stock option are that the executive must use personal funds to purchase the shares or borrow money to come up with the purchase price. If money is borrowed, the executive is at risk if the stock price goes down. Also, stock options are valuable only if share prices increase.

With respect to long-term performance plans, nothing is earned if goals are not achieved; however, the executive does not have to use personal funds or borrow money, because no purchase is required. Also, the performance plan is directly related to executive effort and to results as indicated by the company performance measure used in the plan. In contrast, stock options are subject to the vagaries of the stock market and do not necessarily correlate with executive performance.

Q 5:18   Are there disadvantages to using stock options as compared to restricted stock?

Stock options have a dilutive effect, as shown in Q 5:17, and they are only valuable to the executive if stock price increases. Executives must also purchase the stock option. In contrast, restricted shares require no executive investment and can have value to the executive even if the stock price goes down. While restricted shares also have a dilutive impact on the company's earnings per share, one can argue that executives are still motivated to raise company stock price so that the value of their restricted shares is higher at the time restrictions lapse. When this occurs, the company benefits from the tax deduction amount because this amount is equal to the value that the executive earns when the restrictions lapse, even though the company's accounting charge was equal to the lower value of the shares at the time of grant.

Q 5:19   Under what circumstances is a performance plan the best type of long-term incentive for a company to select?

In privately held companies, where ownership dilution is a concern, long-term performance plans are a good alternative to other incentive plans. Any public company that can measure long-term performance and wants to motivate executives to achieve long-term performance goals in the business plan would want to consider such a plan. In addition, any company whose stock is not traded very much and therefore has slow or erratic growth in stock price can also benefit from a performance plan.

Q 5:20   Under what circumstances are stock-based plans the best form of long-term incentive for a company to select?

The idea behind any long-term incentive plan is to motivate executives to do what is best for the company and its shareholders, and there is no better way to accomplish this than by making sure that the interests of both the executive and the shareholder are the same. This can be done by tying executive compensation to stock performance. In today's executive compensation environment, where public companies are under tremendous scrutiny by the media on potential excesses of executive compensation, stock plans, which directly align shareholder and executive interests, are an advantage. Consider the case of an executive who earns $10 million from a stock option over a five-year period. If the total increase in company stock price was $10 billion over that same period, media criticism of executive earnings can be completely neutralized.

Privately held corporations can also benefit from using stock-based plans as a way of gradually transferring ownership or voting control.

As a long-term incentive, the economic value to an executive of a stock-based plan can be duplicated through the use of a performance plan; however, stock options are less expensive to the company because they have no charge to the income statement. Restricted shares have a charge at the time of grant. Normally, this is better than when the restrictions lapse, provided that stock price increases.

Q 5:21   How can companies get executives to own stock?

The following alternatives are available:

1. Establish a minimum ownership requirement for executives. Companies using this alternative typically vary ownership

levels by job level. For example, minimums could be set at 3,000 shares for an executive vice president, 2,000 shares for a senior vice president, and 1,000 shares for a vice president. Executives are typically given three years or more to accumulate minimum ownership positions.

2. Use reload options (see Q 6:37). These provide an additional ownership opportunity for executives by offering them new (reloaded) stock options every time they exercise an existing stock option share and retain ownership of those shares.

3. Grant restricted stock shares (see Q 7:31). These provide immediate ownership to executives; however, the executive must meet the restriction before taking possession of the shares. In addition, companies can also require that executives continue ownership of restricted shares for a designated period after the restrictions lapse.

4. Provide leveraged stock options (see Q 5:8). Upon purchase of company shares the executive is given the right to purchase additional stock options in amounts equal to three to five times the number of shares purchased. Therefore the executive has "leveraged" the purchase of shares by obtaining the right to purchase a significant number of additional shares. Companies that use this alternative may also require the executive to retain ownership of the purchased shares for a designated period.

Q 5:22   What are the advantages of shareholder value/EVA plans over stock plans?

Advocates of shareholder value/EVA plans argue that these forms of long-term incentive motivate executives to increase the value of a company by meeting business goals that they control or significantly influence. The primary drivers of a company's stock price are shareholder value/economic value because if shareholders or potential shareholders see the company growing on these measures, they will continue to buy company shares and share price will respond by increasing as well. These measures are not subject to the vagaries of the stock market, and are therefore the best indicators of true value added to a company by executive performance.

Stock plan advocates argue that despite the vagaries of the stock market, it is the only true indicator of shareholder value, and therefore stock plans are the best form of long-term incentive. They produce a direct correlation between shareholders and executives because both own (or have the potential to own) shares. Measures of shareholder value/EVA cannot be exchanged for real dollars between owners/shareholders. Stock certificates can be exchanged for real dollars.

Q 5:23   What are the advantages of shareholder value/EVA plans over performance plans?

The advocates of shareholder value/EVA plans suggest that these plans use performance measures that cannot be manipulated by executives. Most traditional accounting measures can be manipulated by executives. For example, earnings per share goals can be easily met if executives buy back company shares, and thus lower the number of shares outstanding. Also, the traditional accounting measures in performance plans have goals that are negotiated between executives and the company chief executive officer (CEO) and/or board compensation committee. Executives are motivated to negotiate low goals that they are assured to meet so that incentive payments are earned. This is not the case with EVA plans where typically the payout schedule has a targeted amount but no maximum; therefore, executives are always motivated to maximize their performance.

Advocates of performance plans suggest that they motivate executive performance because the measures used in these plans are directly controlled or influenced by executives. In shareholder value/EVA plans, executives do not directly influence the cost of capital. Moreover, performance plans can be structured to pay out in company stock rather than cash and thus create more direct ties between executives and shareholders.

Q 5:24   What are the general rules regarding taxation of long-term incentive plans?

The company receives a federal income tax deduction at the time the executive incurs an ordinary income tax event. Plans that defer executive recognition of income will also defer the date on which a company may claim a tax deduction.

Capital gains tax applies to a corporate capital asset. Because stock is a capital asset, an executive who sells stock is subject to a capital gains tax. Companies receive no tax deductions for the capital gains tax. The only form of long-term incentive that offers executives capital gains on shares of stock before they are owned is the ISO (discussed in Chapter 6).

Q 5:25 What are the basic accounting issues for a long-term incentive plan?

The basic issue for accounting purposes is whether a given cost associated with a long-term capital accumulation plan will be expensed currently or whether it will be treated as a long-term capital expense that must be accrued as plan benefits are earned. Many believe that the Accounting Principles Board (APB) Rule 25 and Financial Accounting Standards Board (FASB) Rule 28 on long-term capital accumulation plan accounting treatment are contradictory and inconsistent.

APB Rule 25 specifically states:

> Compensation for services that a corporation receives as consideration for stock issued through employee stock option, purchase, and award plans should be measured by the quoted market price of the stock at the measurement date less the amount, if any, that the employee is required to pay . . . if a quoted market price is unavailable, the best estimate of the market value of the stock should be used to measure compensation. The Measurement Date for determining compensation cost in stock option, purchase, and award plans is the first date on which are known both (1) the number of shares an individual employee is entitled to receive and (2) the option or purchase price, if any.

In contrast, FASB 28 states that SARs and other "variable stock awards" as well as variable performance awards, where measurement dates cannot be established, will require that companies accrue cost over the period that the award is being earned.

Given these statements, consider for example that a stock option granted at market value has no charge to the company's income statement. The SAR produces a similar benefit to the executive but requires an accounting charge to the company's income statement.

The opposing point of view is that because an executive receives income from a stock option only after the executive sells the shares on the open market, the stock market, and not the company, is actually providing the executive with this income. In contrast, the SAR represents actual amounts paid to the executive by the company, and it is therefore appropriate that only this form and similar forms of long-term incentive require an accounting charge to the company's income statement.

Example 1. An executive is granted 1,000 stock option shares and at the time of grant the stock is trading at $20 per share, which is also the executive's option price. At the time of grant, under APB 25, the number of shares to be purchased by the executive and the purchase price are known. This amount is $20,000. Because the value of the option at the time of grant is $20,000, and the amount to be paid to the executive is $20,000, the company has zero charge to its income statement.

Example 2. An executive is granted 1,000 nonqualified stock option shares with an SAR on all the shares. At the time of grant, the stock is trading at $20 per share and the option price is also $20 per share. At the time of grant, the company must accrue during each quarter of the SAR award period the amount of stock appreciation per share, such that when the SAR is exercised the amount of actual compensation paid to the executive is equal to the amount that has been accrued on the company's income statement over the award period. If the executive received $15,000 in stock appreciation, then the company would have charged its income statement with $15,000.

Because of this debate, the FASB has been reviewing the accounting treatment of stock options for many years. In December 1995, the FASB issued a regulation that requires companies to select APB 25 accounting treatment for stock awards or select Financial Accounting Statement (FAS) 123 which requires companies to calculate a "fair value" to all stock awards and charge this fair value to earnings over the vesting period of the stock award. This fair value is measured by an option pricing model that meets criteria established by the FASB. If a company elects not to use FAS 123, it will be required to calculate the fair market value of any stock awards and show the EPS impact that would have occurred had this value been taken as a charge to earnings. This footnote must appear in the company's financial statements. For companies electing to continue the use of APB 25, the effective date of the regulation is any fiscal year starting after December 15, 1994. If companies elect to use FAS 123, the effective date is any fiscal year starting after December 15, 1996.

One acceptable option pricing method is the Black-Scholes option model.

Q 5:26   How does the Black-Scholes option pricing model work?

The Black-Scholes option model considers the following:

1. Current market price of the stock award
2. Expected life of the stock award
3. Volatility in the company stock over the expected life
4. Risk-free rate of return over the expected life of the stock award
5. Discounted present value of the amount that the executive will have to pay for the stock award
6. Expected dividend over the life of the stock award

A simplistic explanation of the Black-Scholes formula is that the value of a stock award can be determined by calculating the difference between the current market price and the discounted present value of the purchase price to the executive, recognizing that both are adjusted for stock price volatility and the value of dividends. Unfortunately, the actual Black-Scholes formula is considerably more complicated. The good news is, however, that computer discs available from human resource and CPA firms facilitate the use of Black-Scholes in determining the fair value of stock awards.

Critics of Black-Scholes suggest that the key assumption in this option model is that the variance in the rate of return from stock price appreciation and short-term interest rates is constant over the expected life of the stock award. This, they claim, is unrealistic because significant economic events may alter returns from stock price appreciation during the expected life of the stock award. Moreover, the stock market is not always an orderly process whose variance can be statistically measured. The stock market is driven by emotion. Despite this debate, many large companies have already started using the Black-Scholes method to project company stock price for purposes of meeting the FASB "fair value" earnings charge and to meet public company reporting requirements on stock awards established by the SEC.

A typical Black-Scholes calculation is shown below.

Example.

Current Market Value of the Stock Award	$40
Expected Life	10 Years
Volatility	1.25
Risk-Free Rate of Return	7%
Dividends	3% per year
Discounted Present Value of the Purchase Price on the Stock Award	$30
Fair Value	$10

Under FAS 123 the fair value calculated in the example would be accrued on the company income statement over the vesting period of the stock option.

Compensation Philosophy

Q 5:27 How should a corporate compensation philosophy be utilized in plan design?

A company's compensation philosophy or strategy statement should be the basis for designing any long-term incentive plan. These statements should provide a clear understanding of the organization's business and/or human resource goals so that the value and impact of its compensation programs can be established. The following information from the total compensation strategy statement (see Q 11:3) can provide guidance in the design of long-term incentive plans:

1. Competitive labor markets are defined and a targeted level of executive long-term incentive is established.

2. The company's culture and management style are defined. This helps determine whether long-term incentive plans should be decentralized for major company divisions or centralized at the corporate level. Information on the company culture can also determine the level of risk acceptable to the long-term incentive plan.

3. Key business performance measures are identified.

4. The statement identifies where changes in business goals should be supported by the long-term incentive compensation program, so that executive effort is focused on key business success factors.

5. The strategy statement states whether executive stock ownership is desirable within the company.

Planning Tip. Companies can no longer use the general philosophy of "to attract, retain, and motivate executives," or "to pay for performance." Total compensation strategy statements need to be very specific in today's business environment and should include a reference to the types of programs desired by the company (e.g., goal-based annual incentives, stock-based long-term incentives). These statements should also identify targeted compensation levels (e.g., 50th percentile, 70th percentile). Once established, these total compensation philosophy/strategy statements are useful guides in the design of executive compensation programs.

Q 5:28 What is the primary disadvantage of long-term performance plans?

Experience shows that many companies are unable to forecast accurately for a three- to four-year period. Strategic plans that typically run three to four periods are updated every year; however, long-term incentive plans that are objective-based cannot be adjusted every year. Therefore, companies must work to improve their accuracy in predicting business results to be achieved at the end of a three- to four-year period and then to tie compensation to these results. In addition, as market, financial, and other business conditions change over long-term performance periods, executives may become eligible for "windfall" bonuses or, conversely, become ineligible for bonuses because of unforeseen changes in the business environment.

Long-term performance plans can only be successful where management has a successful track record of long-term forecasting, or where management operates in a relatively stable business environment. For example, an aerospace company with large volume contracts every three to four years would not typically be affected by annual changes in cost-of-living or other measures of the economy. The same might also be true of a nonprofit organization. On the other hand, consumer product companies and advertising agencies typically must react immediately to changes in economic conditions, and in consumer habits or attitudes. Long-term forecasting is most difficult in these organizations.

Plan Design

Q 5:29 How do companies typically determine the amount of the long-term incentive payout or grant?

Two basic methods are used to establish the potential payout amount of the long-term plan. These two methods are the salary multiple approach (see Q 5:30) and the targeted income approach (see Q 5:31).

While these are the two most common methods used by companies to establish the payout or grant amount for long-term incentive plans, other companies choose to make their own decisions for each executive. In the absence of any predetermined formula or approach, companies make these individual decisions based typically on previous grant amounts and on current company performance. The advantage of this approach is that it gives the company total flexibility in providing long-term incentive awards while yearly grant increases satisfy the executive. The drawback to this approach is that companies focus their decisions on internal factors without regard to the realities of the competitive labor market. This could result in a significantly high or low reward to key executives.

Other companies use sophisticated computer modeling programs to predict stock price and/or company performance. The Black-

Scholes method (see Q 5:26) is an example of a sophisticated stock price projection method.

Q 5:30   How does the salary multiple approach work in determining the size of long-term incentive awards?

The salary multiple approach is the easiest to explain and is used by companies who provide stock option grants. This approach expresses the total value of the stock option (number of shares multiplied by the price per share) as a multiple of the participating executive's base salary. For example, companies can survey the option value provided by competitive companies over a four-year period, and if that option value for a given group of executives is four times their salary, the option value provided by the company to those executives over a four-year period would be four times their base salary or salary range midpoint.

> **Example.** An executive has a base salary of $100,000. The company stock price is $20 per share. The company has determined that, under the salary multiple approach, this executive should receive stock options that are four times the executive's base salary over the next four years. The total option value for this executive should be $400,000 ($100,000 × 4). If this company grants stock options every two years, then this executive should receive stock options with a value of $200,000 for each grant ($400,000 ÷ 2). With the stock trading at $20 per share, this executive would receive 10,000 stock option shares for each grant during the two-year period ($200,000 ÷ $20 = 10,000 shares).

The advantage of the salary multiple approach is that it provides a simple, easy to understand basis for determining the number of shares in a stock option grant. The drawback of this approach is that it measures option value (number of shares times stock price) rather than actual gain/income received by the executive. A second drawback is that the company stock price continuously changes, and as the stock price increases, the number of shares will decrease. For example, if the stock price in the example was $30 per share at the time the executive was to be granted the second stock option award, the number of shares provided to the executive would be 6,667 rather than 10,000 ($200,000 ÷ $30 = 6,667 shares).

Q 5:31   How does the targeted income approach work in determining the size of a long-term incentive award?

Under performance plans, companies simply determine a targeted income level for their long-term incentive (see Chapter 11, "Building a Total Compensation Strategy"). Under this approach, targeted income levels are established for each executive position.

This is a little more difficult under a stock option plan. Under these plans, companies project stock price appreciation, and based on this projection provide the executive with a number of shares that will deliver the targeted amounts of appreciation over the stock award period.

Example. To project stock price, a company can use the following stock price formula: Stock price equals stock multiple times EPS. Therefore companies can predict stock price appreciation as shown in the following table.

Year	Stock Multiple	Earnings Per Share	Stock Price
1999	5	$2.00	$10.00
2000	5	$2.10	$10.50
2001	5	$2.30	$11.50
2002	5	$2.50	$12.50
2003	5	$3.00	$15.00

Total Stock Appreciation = $5.

Given these stock price projections, which estimate stock appreciation to be $5 over the stock option award period of four years, the company would then take its targeted long-term income for this position and divide it by the estimated stock appreciation. If the targeted income was $10,000, then the company would want to give this executive 2,000 shares ($10,000 ÷ $5 = 2,000 shares).

The advantage of the targeted income approach is that it enables companies to determine grant levels for both stock options and other long-term incentive grants (i.e., performance plans). The drawback of this approach is that it requires companies to estimate stock price, and while there are many methods for doing this (such as in the previous example), no method can realistically factor in the vagaries of the stock market and the fact that the stock market does not always respond directly to company earnings performance.

Stock Options

Q 5:32 What are the different types of stock options?

The two primary types of stock options are the statutory stock option, also known as the ISO, and the nonstatutory stock option, known as the nonqualified stock option. The statutory regulations of the ISO are contained in Internal Revenue Code (the Code) Sections 421 and 422, while the tax treatment for nonstatutory (i.e., nonqualified) stock options is governed by Code Section 83.

Each of these types of stock options has a different tax treatment. The statutory option or ISO may qualify for the capital gains tax. All nonstatutory/nonqualified stock options subject the executive to ordinary income tax until the executive owns the shares, at which time the executive is in possession of a capital asset and will then be eligible for capital gains tax on future stock appreciation.

Q 5:33 What is the typical exercise period for a stock option?

The typical maximum exercise period for a nonqualified stock option is ten years. The typical exercise period for an ISO is five years, although statutory regulations allow for the ISO to run ten years. Because the ISO statutory requirements state that executives must exercise/purchase the ISO and then hold it for one year after exercise (two years after grant) before realizing capital gain on the entire appreciation, companies have typically opted to have a shorter exercise period. Another reason for this practice is that when the ISO was first authorized there was a sequential exercise requirement, meaning that each ISO grant had to be exercised (in total) sequentially. For example, if an executive had two ISO grants, one in 1998 at $30 per share and one in 1999 at $20 per share, the executive would have to exercise all of the 1998 grants at $30 (after meeting all required vesting periods) before the executive could exercise the 1999 shares granted at $20. This additional complexity prompted companies to shorten the exercise period. Survey data show that companies have continued this practice even though there is no longer a sequential requirement for ISO.

Companies should consider a number of good reasons for not following the typical practice of a ten-year exercise award period for nonqualified stock options. One reason is that the longer the option's term the greater the benefits to the executive holding the option, because the executive will have greater flexibility in determining when to exercise the stock option for tax and financial planning purposes as well as from a stock market timing point of view. Another reason is the benefits to the company: Executive retention is encouraged by the longer exercise period. Some companies have also elected to extend stock option exercise periods for those executives who reach retirement. Such an approach provides flexibility to the executive in determining when to exercise the stock option after retirement, when funds would typically be needed. The tax, financial planning, and market timing issues become extremely critical for an executive who has retired. An example of this is to allow an executive three years after retirement to exercise all vested stock options.

In contrast, there is a good reason for not shortening the exercise period. Most companies provide executives with multiple forms of long-term incentive (e.g., stock options, restricted stock, perform-ance plans). It is also typical for companies to make long-term incentive awards annually. Therefore, executives have numerous grants from numerous forms of long-term incentive at any given point of time. Extending the exercise period to ten years adds com-plexity to this issue. Shortening the exercise period is beneficial to executives as they try to manage these multiple forms of long-term incentive in their best interest.

Q 5:34   What is the rationale behind using stock-based plans?

It is much less expensive for the employer to use stock in compen-sating executives than it is to provide them with cash from a long-term incentive plan. While earnings are reduced whenever cash is provided, this is not true for stock. Stock does, however, have a dilution cost: Stock grants are common stock equivalents, thus dilut-ing shareholder equity. It is commonly believed, however, that the dilution cost has significantly less impact on the company than do charges to the income statement. A second logic for using stock-based plans is that if the company is achieving its goals, stock should be worth far more over time than its original grant value. The appreciation in the shares is not a "cost" to the company; the gain received by the executive is provided by the stock market at the time shares are sold. Therefore companies have good economic reason to use stock-based plans.

In addition, publicly traded corporations like to use stock-based plans because this enables them to place a large block of stock in "friendly hands," which makes takeover attempts more difficult. Privately held corporations can also benefit from using stock-based plans as a way of gradually transferring ownership or voting control.

Q 5:35   Under what conditions are stock options effective?

For a stock option plan to be effective, the company's stock must be consistently appreciating or have sufficient fluctuation from the grant price such that the executive is motivated to exercise the stock option when the market value is well above the option value. A stock option that has an option exercise price that is above the current market price is said to be "under water."

Q 5:36   In what cases are stock options ineffective?

Under certain circumstances, stock options may not be an effective executive incentive. Stock options in mature companies with poor stock price growth potential are effective neither as a retention nor as a motivational tool. Stock options in highly cyclical industries are not necessarily an effective motivational tool because much of the gain in the price of stock results from circumstances beyond the executive's control, although such stock options may be an effective retention factor during the growth portion of the cycle.

In addition, if executives do not have sufficient cash resources to purchase stock options, their interests may not be tied to those of shareholders. Stock options are also ineffective during a corporate restructuring, sale, or recapitalization because they are not owned shares and the executive may not benefit from the corporate restructuring, sale, or recapitalization.

Q 5:37   How do companies determine the number of shares to reserve for stock option plans?

There is no formula consistently used to determine the number of shares to reserve for long-term plans; practice has shown, however, that three factors affect this number: industry, company size, and the company's life cycle (i.e., growth versus maturity).

In general, companies reserve between 5 percent and 10 percent of their outstanding shares for executive stock option plans over a five-year period. This equals from 1 percent to 2 percent per year of the shares outstanding. Small growth companies in a high-risk, start-up situation will usually allocate higher percentages to their executive stock option plans. The percentage of shares outstanding in these cases is three to four times that of a typical company.

Omnibus Plan

Q 5:38   What is an omnibus plan?

An omnibus plan is a long-term incentive compensation plan submitted to company shareholders for approval that includes every conceivable form of long-term incentive, both stock-related plans and nonstock-related plans. A rationale for such a broad-based plan is that shareholder approval for a new long-term plan will not have to be sought as business conditions change. These plans generally authorize the issuance of a number of shares to be used for any or all stock award plans.

For example, an omnibus plan can provide grants for nonqualified stock options, ISOs, discounted stock options, SARs, restricted stock grants, performance shares, performance units, or reload stock options. Before any grant is made, a company's board compensation committee would review current business requirements and approve a recommendation from management on the right form of long-term incentive grant. At times, executives at different levels in the organization could receive different forms of long-term incentive.

One concern about omnibus plans is that they are too general and may not provide sufficient information to the shareholders who must approve them. This problem can be overcome if omnibus plans include limitations on the grants per executive and/or a minimum company performance that must be achieved before various long-term grants are provided. For example, an omnibus plan could include the following statement: "No executive can own more than 3 percent of the shares outstanding." The type of grant would not matter to the shareholders because the number of shares per executive is limited. Another example of a company protection statement in an omnibus plan might be: "No long-term incentive grant will be made in any given year unless shareholder dividends were paid in the previous year and company return on capital is at least 10 percent." This type of statement in the omnibus plan protects shareholder interests.

Tax Considerations

Q 5:39　How does the tax doctrine of constructive receipt affect a long-term incentive plan?

In Q 5:24, there is a general discussion of the taxation on long-term incentive plans. Under the doctrine of constructive receipt, an executive who has unrestricted control in determining income to be received will be subject to tax. For example, interest from a bank CD or savings account is taxable in the tax year it is credited to an individual's account, even though the individual does not take receipt of the money. Because the individual could have taken it, he or she is in constructive receipt, and an ordinary income tax is due in that tax year.

Compensation payments constitute income to the executive and a deduction to the company (assuming they are taxed as ordinary income) in the year they are actually or constructively received. With cash-based plans, the timing is relatively clear. With stock-based plans, the timing depends largely on the terms of the stock award. Generally, a stock award granted to an executive as compensation is not included in that employee's income because, under the doctrine of constructive receipt, it is subject to risk of forfeiture. Once an executive earns a stock award, or exercises a stock option, the executive no longer has any risk of forfeiture, and must report ordinary income that is equal to the difference between the fair market value of the stock and the amount, if any, paid for the stock. At this time, the company is entitled to a corresponding tax deduction.

Code Section 83 provides that property vests when it is not subject to a substantial risk of forfeiture. This vesting concept is not the same as vesting in a long-term incentive plan. For example, under stock option plan vesting, the executive simply earns the right to purchase the shares, but until the purchase occurs there is a risk of forfeiture.

Q 5:40 What are some of the conditions that create a substantial risk of forfeiture in a long-term incentive plan?

The most important condition that creates a substantial risk of forfeiture is that the company could be liquidated, and the executive would lose his or her stock award. Another condition might be that an executive's right to the stock is dependent upon future performance of the company. For example, under a performance plan grant an executive receives the opportunity to earn 1,000 shares of stock if company EPS increase 10 percent per year over the next four years. Because the executive may not earn the shares unless that goal is achieved, a risk of forfeiture clearly exists.

Q 5:41 What are some of the conditions that do not create a substantial risk of forfeiture in a long-term incentive plan?

Such conditions are extremely rare. For purposes of determining whether stock has substantially vested under Code Section 83, a substantial risk of forfeiture may not exist merely because the executive must forfeit the shares of stock or stock options, if the company liquidates, if the executive is convicted of a crime and terminated for cause, or because the executive may accept a job with a competing firm. Companies are quick to overcome these potential situations that would not create a substantial risk of forfeiture, by stating in their plan texts that any and all potential payments must be approved by the committee administering the plan. These committees are, in most cases, composed of outside members (nonemployees) of the board of directors, who have the authority under the plan to amend, modify, rescind, or change awards in any way.

Another example of a condition that may not create a risk of forfeiture is a restricted stock grant where the restriction is a clearly attainable performance restriction such as earnings growth of 1 percent per year for a company that has been historically earning 10 percent per year for the past ten years. The IRS could view this as a restriction that does not have any risk of forfeiture and thus declare that the executive is in constructive receipt and that the entire value of the shares is taxable.

Q 5:42 What is the general tax effect of a stock option?

There are three different times in the life of a stock option at which it may be taxable to the employee: (1) at the time it is granted, (2) at the time it is exercised, and (3) at the time the share of stock is sold.

Statutory Options. A statutory option is one that qualifies (as opposed to one that is "nonqualified") for special tax treatment (e.g., capital gains). An employee in compliance with the required statutory holding periods will incur no tax consequences upon the grant or exercise of the option under Code Sections 421 and 422 and will be taxed only when the stock is sold. This is the case for ISOs. An additional statutory requirement is that, upon exercise of the option, the share of stock must be held for one year after exercise (two years after grant), before it is sold. If this provision is met, the difference between the value of the share at the time it is sold and the option price is taxed as capital gains. If the holding period is not complied with, ordinary income tax treatment applies.

Nonstatutory Options. For a nonstatutory or nonqualified option, the employee is not taxed at the time of grant, but there is a taxable event at the time of exercise. When the employee sells the share, the gain recognized (the difference between market price of the stock at the time of exercise and the market value of the stock at the time of sale) will be taxed as long-term capital gain if the share was held one year after the exercise date. Because the executive incurred a taxable event at the time of exercise equal to the difference between the exercise price and the option price, the future tax base of that share is the market value of the share at the time of exercise.

Furthermore, an executive exercising an option must satisfy state and federal withholding requirements at the time of exercise. She cannot delay the taxable event until the end of the tax year in which the exercise occurs.

Q 5:43 What is the general tax effect of a stock appreciation right?

Stock appreciation rights (see Qs 7:3–7:7) are not taxed at the time they are awarded; there is no constructive receipt during the award period. At the time SARs are exercised, a taxable event has occurred and the executive must pay ordinary income tax. The company then receives a tax deduction because this income is taxed at ordinary income tax rates. An executive taking the SAR in cash must also satisfy federal and state withholding requirements. The same is true if the executive takes the stock appreciation right in shares of stock. This can be accomplished by having the company withhold the required amount for taxes from the value of the SAR and then delivering the remaining shares to the executive. These remaining shares would be subject to capital gains tax if held for one year from the date of exercise.

Q 5:44 What is the general tax effect of a restricted stock grant?

There is no tax at the time a restricted stock option is granted, and there is no constructive receipt during the restriction period because there is a clear risk of forfeiture. When the restrictions lapse, there is an ordinary income tax event to the executive equal to the number of shares multiplied by the market price of the shares at the time the restrictions lapse. The company gets a tax deduction equal to the same amount. Again, the executive must satisfy federal and state withholding requirements and may do so by having the company sell sufficient shares to meet withholding requirements.

Q 5:45 What is the general tax effect of a performance plan award?

There is no tax on either a performance share or a performance unit at the time of grant, nor is there any tax during the performance period, because the executive is not in constructive receipt of the performance grant. Once the performance grant is earned, there is an ordinary income tax event equal to the total value received by the executive (number of shares or units multiplied by the price per share or unit). The executive must satisfy both federal and state withholding requirements. Moreover, shares issued to the executive may be used to pay the withholding tax or the amount may be deducted from the cash award.

Q 5:46   How does the constructive receipt doctrine affect deferred compensation?

It is critical to structure deferred compensation plans so that the executive cannot be regarded as being in constructive receipt of the compensation before it is actually received as compensation. In designing deferred compensation plans, the following safeguards should be included:

1. If the executive's decision to defer compensation (rather than to receive it currently) is voluntary, then the executive should make the election before the services are rendered.

2. If the compensation is deferred to some specific or determinable future date, the executive should, as a general rule, not be given a unilateral election to defer it to a still later date once the services have been rendered. For example, if an executive has elected to defer compensation until age 65, the executive should not have a unilateral second election to defer its receipt until some age beyond age 65.

3. Most companies will require executives to provide an "irrevocable election" to defer future compensation prior to the performance period of the incentive compensation plan. For example, an executive makes an irrevocable election prior to the start of a three-year performance plan to defer for five years any income earned from the plan. In this case, the doctrine of constructive receipt has been met by virtue of the executive's signing an irrevocable election prior to the time that the compensation is earned.

Q 5:47   What is the economic benefit theory?

Under the economic benefit doctrine, when an economic benefit has been granted, the executive may be taxed currently. Economic value can be cash or anything equivalent to cash.

Example. Executive A earns $20,000 under a company's incentive compensation plan. In accordance with a doctrine of constructive receipt, the executive defers that amount for a five-year period.

During the third year of the deferral, the executive borrows $20,000 from the bank and uses the deferred income as collateral for the loan. This executive has received economic benefit from the $20,000, and under the economic benefit tax doctrine, the deferred amounts become taxable immediately.

Q 5:48   What is a Code Section 83(b) election?

Code Section 83(b) allows an employee to choose to be taxed immediately on the amounts received in connection with a substantially "nonvested" right, i.e., compensation that has not been constructively received (see Q 5:39). This is accomplished by having the executive file an election with the IRS stating that he or she will pay ordinary income on the value as measured at the time of grant. Any future appreciation in the stock property will be treated as capital gain when sold. This election must be made within 30 days after the stock is received.

The most significant drawback of the Code Section 83(b) election is that if the executive does not receive the stock, he forfeits taxes previously paid and cannot take a tax loss. Balancing this against the fact that stock price can go up or down, the election of Code Section 83(b) is not so compelling.

Example. An executive is given 1,000 restricted shares with a three-year restriction period at a time when the current stock price is $20. Within 30 days, the executive elects under Code Section 83(b) to pay tax on the $20,000 grant value. Upon completion of the three-year restriction period, the executive takes possession of the shares but has no taxable event. Upon the future sale of these shares, the difference between the sale price and $20 per share is subject to capital gains (if the shares are held for one year under the current tax laws).

Stock Option Exercise

Q 5:49   What are the different ways an employee can pay the exercise price of a stock option?

There are three primary ways for an employee to pay the exercise price of an option: (1) cash, (2) already-owned stock, i.e., a stock swap (see Q 5:53), and (3) "cashless exercise." Cash is the easiest method. Where an executive delivers shares of already-owned stock, the market value of the stock is applied toward the exercise price. As an example, Executive C has an option to purchase 1,000 shares of Company D stock at an exercise price of $10 per share (1,000 shares × $10 = $10,000). If the then-current market price is $25 per share, Executive C can pay the exercise price by delivering 400 shares of stock already owned (400 shares × $25 = $10,000). The cashless exercise is described in Q 5:51.

Q 5:50   How do the Section 16 rules of the SEC affect stock plans and the way employees can pay for stock?

Under Section 16 an insider is not allowed to purchase and sell shares of stock within a six-month period.

Section 16 of the 1934 Act provides that the exercise of an option is not considered a purchase, but the granting of the option is considered a purchase event. Under these rules insiders have the possibility of paying for their shares through a stock swap, a cashless exercise, or by immediately selling shares after the exercise. The Section 16 rules lessen the need for a stock appreciation right and other techniques designed to provide insiders with the cash required to exercise their stock options. An important provision of Section 16 is that stock options granted as Rule 16b-3 shares are not matchable with a purchase event created by the issue of different stock options under Rule 16b-3. This means that executives can sell previously exercised stock option shares as well as previously owned shares without being subject to the "matching" provision of Section 16.

Q 5:51   What is a cashless option exercise?

Federal Reserve Board Regulation T of the NASD rules (see Q 5:52) permits broker-dealers to treat an option exercise notice as if it were stock and, as a result, to advance funds to the executive in order to pay for the exercise of the option. This is called the cashless exercise of stock options. It is called "cashless" because the executive can pay the option exercise price for the stock with the proceeds of the sale from the underlying shares. The process involves the executive's giving the company an irrevocable exercise notice that instructs the company to deliver the stock subject to the option to the executive's broker. The executive signs a promissory note to pay the exercise price. The broker is then instructed to sell the shares and to deliver the proceeds to the company. The company is thus provided with the option exercise value, and the executive then receives the remaining value.

> **Example.** An executive has 1,000 stock option shares vested at an option price of $30. In order to exercise the option, the executive owes $30,000. The current market price of the stock is $50. The executive completes a request to the company to exercise these shares and instructs the company to provide the shares to the broker. The executive also completes a promissory note to pay the broker $30,000, and is liable to the broker for the payment of $30,000. The broker then sells the 1,000 shares at the $50 stock price. From the $50,000 proceeds, $30,000 is paid to the company; the executive then has $20,000 of taxable income. The company will deduct minimum required federal and state withholding taxes and appropriate broker fees from the executive's $20,000 and then return the net proceeds to the executive.

Q 5:52   What is Regulation T, and what is its effect on executive compensation?

Regulation T affects executive compensation because it affects how an executive can finance the exercise of options or sale of stock through a brokerage account. Specifically, the amount a customer must deposit in a margin account and the amount the broker may lend are prescribed by the Board of Governors of the Federal Reserve Board by authority of the Securities Exchange Act of 1934 under Regulation T. Regulation T permits the cashless stock option exercise (see Q 5:51).

Q 5:53   What is a stock swap?

A stock swap is another name for the method of allowing an executive to deliver already-owned stock, instead of paying cash, to exercise a stock option.

Example. An executive has the right to purchase 1,000 shares of stock at an option exercise price of $30. The executive also owns outright 600 other shares of company stock with a current market value of $50. The amount required to exercise the 1,000 stock option shares is $30,000 (1,000 × $30). The value of the shares owned by the executive is also $30,000 (600 shares × $50). The executive can swap 600 shares for the exercise of 1,000 shares, after which the executive will own 1,000 shares.

Q 5:54 What is a pyramiding stock swap exercise?

Pyramiding is an extension of a stock swap that involves a series of stock swaps enabling the executive continuously to exchange the value of stock owned to purchase a stock option.

Example. Executive A owns one share of stock with a market value of $50. The executive also has an option to buy 200 shares at an option price of $10 per share. The executive could turn in the one share worth $50 in order to exercise a portion of his option as to five shares at $10 per share. He would then surrender those five shares, valued at $250, to exercise his option as to 25 shares, which have a market value of $1,250 (25 shares at $50), and then surrender those 25 shares to exercise his option as to 125 shares, and then surrender nine shares to exercise his option as to the remaining 45 shares. At the end of the process, he would have 161 shares worth $8,050. (This example ignores for illustrative purposes the tax withholding requirement.)

Q 5:55 What is the tax treatment of a stock swap or pyramiding exercise?

The impact of a stock swap or pyramiding exercise depends on whether the stock option is nonqualified or a statutory/qualified option.

Nonqualified Option. With a nonqualified option, the exchange of already-owned shares for the same number of shares is a tax-free exchange, i.e., the owned shares keep their current tax basis. The fair market value of any additional shares received is taxable income to the executive, and the new shares have a tax basis equal to that fair market value.

> **Example 1.** An executive had the right to purchase a nonqualified stock option of 1,000 shares at $30 per share. The executive swaps 600 shares owned at a market price of $50 to exercise the right to purchase 1,000 shares. The 600 originally owned shares represent a tax-free exchange, and the tax basis on these shares remains the same. The 400 new shares with a current market value of $50 per share represent $20,000 (400 shares × $50) of taxable income, taxed at ordinary income tax rates. Therefore, the new tax basis for the 400 shares will be the current market price of $50.

Incentive Stock Option (Statutory Option). With a statutory stock option (incentive stock option) the exchange is tax free if the option meets all statutory requirements. The executive will not be taxed at the time of exercise on the amount by which the value of the newly acquired shares exceeds the value of the shares already owned. The shares that are swapped keep their same tax basis. The new shares have a tax basis of zero.

> **Example 2.** An executive is granted 1,000 incentive stock options at an option exercise price of $30. The executive swaps 600 shares at a market value of $50 to meet the exercise price of $30,000. The 600 original shares are a tax-free exchange, and the tax basis for these shares remains unchanged. The 400 new shares have a tax basis of zero. If those shares are held for the one-year holding period required of the incentive stock option and then sold, they will be subject to capital gains tax based on the sale price minus zero, their original tax basis.

Q 5:56   Are there drawbacks to a pyramiding exercise or stock swap?

Yes. Remember that any shares surrendered by an insider to the company to satisfy the exercise price are deemed to have been sold for purposes of Section 16 of the 1934 Act, and are therefore match-able against any other purchases by that insider during the preceding and succeeding six months. Furthermore, if the plan is already in place and does not permit payment by stock, then the plan would have to be amended and certain formalities would have to be followed (see Qs 5:57 and 5:58).

The other major drawback of pyramiding is the requirement that companies take an accounting charge when options are exercised with shares that are not mature.

Plan Administration

Q 5:57   What is needed to institute a long-term incentive plan?

A company's board of directors normally has the right to authorize the issuance of any authorized but unissued shares for purposes of a long-term incentive plan. The board of directors, through their compensation committee, may either make grants of stock or adopt a formal stock plan and grant full value shares or options up to the number of authorized but unissued shares available for use in executive compensation plans. Any company whose shares are traded on a listed stock exchange must have its executive compensation plan approved by shareholders if the plan involves awards or payments of executive compensation in the form of stock traded on that exchange.

Regardless of stock awards or stock payments, a publicly traded company may choose to obtain shareholder approval for a plan as a method to provide that grants under the plan will meet Section 16 (of the 1934 Act) requirements. A privately held company will often want to obtain shareholder approval as a courtesy to its owner-managers. Once a plan has been adopted and approved by shareholders, the board of directors (or a compensation committee of outside directors of the board in the case of public companies wishing to qualify for Rule 16b-3 exceptions to Section 16 (see Chapter 11)) will make grants under the plan periodically and as needed in order to compensate executives.

Special rules apply to statutory or incentive stock option plans because they must meet certain conditions so the executive can receive preferred tax treatment (see Q 6:6).

Q 5:58   What is needed to amend a long-term incentive plan?

In general, any requirement necessary to adopt a plan is necessary to amend it materially. The approval process for a Section 16 exemption under Rule 16b-3 is on a grant-by-grant basis. A material amendment would be considered to be a new grant requiring board or shareholder approval under Rule 16b-3 provisions.

Q 5:59   What information about a long-term incentive must be disclosed in a company's proxy statement?

Any new capital accumulation plan (short-term or long-term) that utilizes company stock must be approved by shareholders. This is a regulation of the stock exchanges where the stock is traded, although most companies would have these plans approved by shareholders anyway as a matter of good business principle and for purposes of protecting the plan administrators from potential lawsuits by unhappy shareholders who may simply not like the plan.

Any "material" amendment to a long-term plan would also be approved by shareholders. The term material is subject to prudent definitions but normally means any substantial change in the level or type of award, or the number of participants. Material changes that are submitted to shareholders would be described along with disclosures of the amounts of cash (or stock) that would have been set aside during the previous or current fiscal year, had the plan been in effect.

On an ongoing basis, the SEC requires a public company to report in its annual proxy statement the following information on its top five executives:

1. A summary chart of cash compensation earned during the last three years

2. A table on stock option grants made during the last fiscal year plus an estimate of the future value of these stock awards

3. A special table on the stock options of these executives and the number and value of those awarded and exercised during the last fiscal year, plus the unrealized value of unexercised options and stock appreciation rights

4. A table of estimated retirement benefits including special supplemental retirement benefits

5. The composition of the board compensation committee and a discussion by the committee of CEO compensation, its philosophy, and how levels of pay are determined

6. Two performance graphs that compare company performance to outside standards

7. A description of employment contracts and any special severance arrangements for the top five executives

8. Outside director compensation programs (fees, retainers, consulting contracts, retirement plans, etc.)

9. A detailed report on any stock options that were repriced during the last fiscal year

These provisions of the SEC are described in more detail in Qs 2:26 and 2:28. They are extremely comprehensive and were designed by the SEC to insure that all compensation of top officers and performance of the company were reported in one place and made available to shareholders (and to media personnel and other employees) so that any potential excessive total compensation would be clear.

Q 5:60   How should long-term incentive compensation plans be handled during a merger of two companies?

Companies that merge must first determine whether one of the existing long-term incentive plans will remain. Whether one of the plans is retained or a new plan developed, one or both of the companies will need to buy out existing long-term incentive awards. This is typically done by prorating existing awards based on the vested amount of any stock options or by using a prorated payment for any performance plans or restricted stock plans. For example, if the performance period or restriction period is four years and the merger occurs after Year 2, a 50 percent proration is applied to the plans and paid to the executive.

Key plan provisions should be reviewed in making a transition to a new long-term incentive plan after a merger. These include the following:

• Eligibility

- Size of awards
- Type of long-term incentive plan
- Frequency of grant
- Award period
- Vesting requirements
- Plan administration issues (e.g., approvals, administrating committee, form of payment)

A total compensation strategy, as discussed in Chapter 11, is also extremely valuable to develop during a merger.

Q 5:61   How should deferred compensation be integrated during a merger of two companies?

There are three key issues to be evaluated in deferred compensation plans during a merger. These are:

1. Investment alternatives available to participants
2. Analysis of whether the plans are funded or unfunded and/or secured with a rabbi trust, secular trust, or some form of insurance
3. Plan administration

Conclusions on these issues can be used to determine future deferral provisions. In most cases, the acquiring company practices prevail. A better approach is, however, to establish a task force of both acquiring and acquired company representatives to: (1) identify current practices, (2) select and evaluate alternative solutions, (3) recommend a solution and obtain approval, and (4) implement these approved provisions.

Rarely do two merged companies apply similar investment alternatives to deferred accounts, nor do they have similar wording in their plan documents on the maintenance and security of individual accounts. In some cases, the merger raises questions on the level of risk that deferred accounts will not be paid, because the merger modifies the new company's financial strength. Full payout of all deferred accounts may need to be considered.

Q 5:62   What is an example of integration of deferred accounts?

Say, for example, that Company *A* merges with Company *B*, and Company *A* is the surviving company. Company *A* has 60 deferred accounts that are invested in company stock units or have the T-bill interest rate applied quarterly. Company *B* has 40 deferred accounts that are invested in: (1) a real estate investment trust, (2) mutual funds, (3) stock/equities fund, (4) company-owned life insurance, and (5) prime rate. Plan administration is handled by each company's treasurer's department.

The companies form a joint committee to evaluate and recommend a future structure for all future deferred accounts. The committee concludes that because one company has only a few conservative investments and the other has numerous aggressive investments, a revised group of investment alternatives needs to be established by using a "middle of the road" strategy. They select the following:

- Quarterly T-bill interest
- The stock/equities fund
- The mutual fund
- Company stock units

All other former investment alternatives went through a "buyout" and conversion to one of these four alternatives. Each participant was provided with full information and asked to make revised selections by an established date in the future, otherwise all deferred accounts would be converted into company stock units.

Plan administration was placed in the acquiring company's treasurer's department, and the primary individual in the acquired company who administered deferrals was transferred to the acquiring company to assist in administering all deferred accounts.

Both companies had unfunded deferred accounts, which remained that way.

Chapter 6

Purchase Plans

Purchase plans are the most frequently used type of long-term incentive plan and come in many forms, eight of which are covered here: incentive stock options, nonstatutory stock options, discounted stock options, premium stock options, option reloads, book value purchase plans, convertible debentures, and junior stock plans. Such plans require executives to make an actual investment if they wish to own shares of the company. The chapter examines the tax, legal, and financial implications of purchase plans, as well as their relative strengths and weaknesses.

General Considerations 6-2
Incentive Stock Options 6-3
Nonstatutory Stock Options 6-10
Discounted Stock Options 6-16
Premium Stock Options 6-19
Option Reloads 6-22
Book Value Purchase Plans 6-24
Convertible Debentures 6-27
Junior Stock Plans 6-30
Performance-Based Stock Options 6-32

General Considerations

Q 6:1   What is a purchase plan?

Purchase plans are capital accumulation plans that give the executive the opportunity to purchase stock at a future date.

Q 6:2   What are the different types of purchase plans?

The eight main forms of purchase plans, all of which are discussed in this chapter, are as follows:

- Statutory (incentive) stock option plans
- Nonstatutory stock option plans
- Discounted stock option plans
- Premium stock option plans
- Option reload plans
- Book value purchase plans
- Convertible debenture plans
- Junior stock plans

Q 6:3   What are the fundamental differences between different types of purchase plans?

Purchase plans are similar in that they provide a way for a company to compensate employees with stock. Purchase plans differ primarily in how they compensate employees with stock, the tax treatment of the specific transaction, and the amount of investment required of the employee.

Q 6:4   How are stock option exercise prices set?

The most common approach is to set an option exercise price at the market value of the share of stock at the time of grant. In using this standard approach, companies take the average selling price of the stock at the beginning of the day and at the end of the day, and use this as the fair market value at the time of grant.

Companies that use discounted stock options, which are stock options with an option exercise price that is below the market value at the time of grant, will typically use the same approach of averaging stock price on the date of grant, and then discounting this amount by a fixed dollar per share amount or percentage amount. Upon grant of this stock the executive immediately realizes the appreciation potential, but may still be subject to specific vesting requirements in the stock option.

Companies can also grant premium stock options, which are options with an exercise price that is above the current market value at the time of grant. Along the same lines, companies will establish the fair market value at the time the premium stock option is granted and increase that amount by a fixed dollar amount, or by some specified percentage.

Example.

Regular Stock Option Grant:
    Average fair market value at the time of grant = $10
    Executive exercise price = $10

Discounted Stock Option:
    Fair market value at the time of grant = $10
    Executive exercise price = $5

Premium Stock Option:
    Fair market value at the time of grant = $10
    Executive exercise price = $15

Q 6:5 How long is the typical option exercise period?

Most surveys on this subject show that nonqualified options typically have a ten-year exercise period while ISOs typically have a five-year exercise period. Junior stock plans and book value purchase plans typically have an exercise period that is three to five years.

Incentive Stock Options

Q 6:6 What is an incentive stock option?

ISOs were created by the Economic Recovery Act of 1981, and the requirements that apply to them were modified by the Tax Reform Act of 1986. As a result, ISOs are required to meet the statutory requirements of Internal Revenue Code (Code) Section 422, which provides the following:

1. The ISO must be granted only to an employee of the issuing company, its parent, or a subsidiary of the issuing parent.

2. The ISO must be granted pursuant to a plan that specifies the total number of shares that may be issued under options and the employees or class of employees that are eligible to receive options. The plan must be approved by the company shareholders within 12 months before or after the date that the plan is adopted.

3. The maximum exercise period for the ISO cannot exceed ten years. The executive eligible for the plan cannot own more than 10 percent of the total combined voting class of stock in the company.

4. The ISO cannot be transferable by the optionee during the optionee's lifetime.

5. The exercise price of the ISO cannot be less then the fair market value of the stock on the date of the grant.

6. The executive cannot sell shares exercised under an ISO program within two years from the date the option is granted, or within one year from the date the option is exercised or purchased.

7. An executive cannot exercise ISOs that have an option value (number of shares multiplied by the option price at the time of grant) that exceeds $100,000 during any given calendar year. This $100,000 limitation is cumulative (i.e., if not used in one year, the following year it is $200,000).

8. The owner of an ISO who retires must exercise the option within three months of termination from active employment.

9. The terms of an ISO cannot be amended or changed in the future in a way that would serve to give the optionholder a material increase in benefits available; otherwise, the ISO will be considered a new grant under Code Section 422.

In obtaining shareholder approval for an ISO plan, companies will typically quote all or a portion of these Code Section 422 statutory requirements in the proxy statement provided to the shareholders so that it is clear that the shareholders are approving the ISO plan that meets all statutory requirements.

Q 6:7   What is the tax treatment of an ISO?

An executive does not recognize income upon the granting of the ISO. In addition, the executive does not recognize income or incur a taxable event upon the exercise (or purchase) of the stock option.

When an ISO share is sold by an executive who has held the share for one year after exercise (two years after the grant) per the statutory requirement, the executive will incur a capital gains tax liability on the entire spread, that is, the difference between the sale price and the option exercise price.

The company is allowed no tax deduction from the granting of an ISO, the exercise of an ISO, or the sale of ISO shares by the executive, because the executive has incurred capital gains tax rather than ordinary income tax. Companies will receive a tax deduction only when executives incur ordinary income tax.

If an executive sells or transfers shares that were acquired under the exercise/purchase of an ISO, but does so within two years after the ISO is granted or within one year after purchasing/exercising these shares, then the executive has incurred a disqualifying distribution. He has then disqualified the option as an ISO and loses the favorable tax treatment of capital gains. In that event, the executive will realize ordinary income in the year of the disqualification in an amount equal to the difference between the price of shares on the date of sale and the option price. The company can, of course, be entitled to a tax deduction on the amount of ordinary income taxed to the employee in the year in which the employee realizes the income from a disqualifying disposition; however, it is difficult for companies to keep track of these disqualifying dispositions. Some will track this via their transfer agent, while others will require employees to inform them of any disqualifying disposition of an ISO.

Example 1. On July 1, 1995, Executive A was granted an ISO for 1,000 shares of Gable Company stock. The exercise price is $20, the current value of the stock on the date of grant. On November 1, 1997 (two years later), A exercised her option to purchase the

1,000 ISO shares when the current fair market value was $24, by paying the full purchase price of $20,000 ($20 × 1,000 shares).

In December 1999, A sells her 1,000 shares when the current market value is $28, and receives $28,000 ($28 × 1,000 shares). Because she has satisfied the holding period requirements by not selling the stock within two years of the date of grant and one year of the date of exercise, she is entitled to capital gains treatment on the full amount of the spread between the date of grant and the date of the sale, or $8,000 ($28,000 – $20,000).

Gable Company does not receive a tax deduction when the option is granted, exercised, or sold.

Example 2. On July 1, 1997, Executive B is granted an ISO for 1,000 shares of Gable Company stock. The exercise price is $20, the current value of the shares on the date of grant. On November 1, 1999, B exercised his option to purchase the 1,000 shares when the current fair market value was $24, by paying $20,000 ($20 × 1,000 shares). In December 1999, B sells his 1,000 shares at a current market value of $28 per share and receives $28,000 ($28 × 1,000 shares). Executive B has met the two-year holding period by not selling the stock within two years of the date of grant; however, he has not met the one-year holding period from the date of exercise and will therefore be required to pay ordinary income tax on the $8,000 spread [(market price – option price) × number of shares].

Gable Company will receive a tax deduction in 1997 equal to the $8,000 of income received by Executive B.

Q 6:8   What is the effect of the alternative minimum tax on the tax treatment of an ISO?

The owner of an ISO may be subject to the alternative minimum tax (AMT) in the year the ISO is exercised because proceeds from the exercise are preference income as defined by the Code and are subject to an AMT calculation. AMT income on the ISO is equal to the difference between the fair market value of the stock at the date of exercise and the exercise price of the option, multiplied by the number of shares. The AMT calculation is made in the same tax year as the regular ordinary income tax calculation, and the executive is required to pay the greater amount of the AMT or the ordinary income tax. Rarely does the AMT calculation produce a tax that is greater then ordinary income; however, this can occur when an executive exercises many ISOs.

In addition, at the time the executive sells the ISO shares, the executive will (assuming the shares were held one year or more after exercise and at least two years after the grant) be required to pay capital gains tax on the difference between the sale price and the exercise price, regardless of whether the executive paid ordinary income tax or AMT during the year that the ISO was exercised.

Example.

	AMT Calculation	*Ordinary Income Tax Calculation*
Gross Income	$300,000	$300,000
Adjustments	$ 20,000	$ 20,000
Adjusted Gross Income	$280,000	$280,000
AMT Preference Income	$100,000	$ 0
Deductions	$ 25,000	$ 30,000
Exemptions	$ 0	$ 0
Taxable Income	$355,000	$250,000
Ordinary Income Tax (36%)		$ 90,000
AMT (28%)	$ 99,400	

The executive would pay a higher tax than the normal ordinary income tax, because the AMT was greater than the ordinary income tax. Also, when the shares from the ISO are sold, if held for one year from the date of exercise (two years from the date of grant), the executive would be subject to capital gains tax on the difference between the sale price and the exercise price. If the executive were to sell the shares in the same taxable year as the exercise without holding them for another year, then the spread or gain to the executive (difference between sale price and exercise price) would automatically be taxed at ordinary income tax rates.

Q 6:9 What is the accounting impact of an ISO?

A company must decide whether to follow APB 25 or FAS 123 in determining the accounting impact of an ISO (see Q 1:45).

If it follows APB 25, the company does not recognize any expense in connection with the granting of the ISO, either at the time of grant or upon the exercise of the ISO, because APB 25 states that any compensation expense for a stock option will be established at the "measurement date." The measurement date is that time when two variables are known: the number of shares that can be purchased by the executive, and the price per share to be paid by the executive. Compensation expense is the difference between the fair market value of the shares on the measurement date and the amount paid by the executive. Because all ISO grants must be at the fair market value per the statutory regulations that apply to these grants, there will never be a charge to earnings on an ISO under APB 25.

> **Example.** An executive is granted 1,000 shares under an ISO program at a time when the fair market price is $20. Because the executive has the right to purchase the 1,000 shares at $20, the provisions of the APB 25 measurement date have been met, and the company calculates its charge to earnings by taking the compensation value of $20,000 (1,000 × $20) and subtracts what the employee is required to pay, which is also $20,000 (1,000 × $20), thus resulting in an expense accrual against earnings of zero.

If the company selects FAS 123, the company under its provisions must calculate the "fair value" of the ISO at the time of grant and charge its earnings with this amount over the vesting period of the ISO. The fair value calculation is discussed in Q 1:49.

ISOs that have not been exercised are considered common stock equivalents and are factored into the determination of earnings per share (EPS) (see Q 6:16), and can have a dilutive cost impact on the company's EPS and balance sheet if the stock price appreciates.

Q 6:10 What approach is used in calculating the fully diluted earnings per share for an ISO?

The fully diluted earnings per share calculation method is discussed in Qs 1:49 and 1:52.

Q 6:11   How prevalent are ISOs?

ISOs exist in the majority of publicly traded companies. They are currently the only form of long-term incentive that offers executives the benefit of lower capital gains tax treatment (than ordinary income tax) on stock appreciation that occurs prior to stock ownership, i.e., the exercise of the stock option. Appreciation from nonqualified stock options is taxed at ordinary income tax rates; however, under the ISO the executive can purchase the shares, hold them for one year after exercise (two years after the grant), and receive capital gains tax treatment on the entire spread or difference between sale price and purchase price.

Most surveys of executive compensation will show that 90 percent or more of all companies, public or private, use stock options. Shown as follows, 98 percent of large companies and 93 percent of small companies use nonqualified stock options while 67 percent of large companies and 52 percent of small companies use ISOs.

Plan Type	Prevalence in Large Companies	Prevalence in Small Companies
Nonqualified Options	98%	93%
ISO	67%	52%
Restricted Stock	45%	28%
Performance Shares	34%	18%
Other	12%	22%

Source: Management Performance Int'l., Inc. survey data.

Q 6:12   What are the advantages of an ISO?

The ISO continues to make sense to the executive because of its financial planning feature: With the ISO, the executive chooses when the taxable event will occur, because the ISO generates taxable income only when it is sold. Nonqualified stock options, on the other hand, generate a taxable event when they are exercised/purchased; therefore, the ISO provides the executive with the opportunity to defer income without taxation, and possibly defer income and receive lower taxation at the same time.

ISOs also make sense from the company's perspective whenever the company is at a low or zero effective tax bracket, and does not need a tax deduction. When this is the case, the ISO's lack of tax deductibility (its primary disadvantage) is negated.

As ordinary income tax rates increase, capital gains tax will be much more attractive to executives. The ISO is the only form of long-term incentive that offers capital gains tax treatment on the full appreciation received by the executive from a stock plan.

Planning Tip. Companies with ISOs may want to encourage executives to notify them of any disqualifying dispositions of an ISO so that the company can receive a tax deduction in the amount of the gain received by the executive.

Q 6:13   What are the primary disadvantages of an ISO?

From a company's perspective, the primary disadvantage of an ISO is the lack of a company tax deduction when the executive exercises the option, which can make this an expensive compensation program for the company to offer.

From the executive's perspective, the ISO shares must be held for one year after exercise (two years after the grant) before they can be sold and capital gains tax treatment received. Company stock price could go down during this period, eliminating any possibility of gain for the executive. Of course the executive could sell the shares prior to the end of the holding period and disqualify the ISO, incurring ordinary income as an alternative to losing all of the appreciation that may have existed at the time of exercise. Another disadvantage of the ISO to the executive is the $100,000 limitation in option value (option price multiplied by number of shares) that can be exercised during any given year. Also, executives may be subject to an AMT (see Q 6:8), which could produce a higher tax than the normal ordinary income tax rates during the year that ISOs are sold.

Nonstatutory Stock Options

Q 6:14   What is a nonstatutory stock option?

A nonstatutory or nonqualified stock option is any option that has no statutory requirements like those of an ISO. On the one hand, this form of stock option offers significantly greater flexibility than does the ISO, but on the other hand nonstatutory stock options do not qualify for favorable tax treatment (i.e., capital gains).

Q 6:15 How prevalent are nonstatutory stock options?

As shown in Q 6:11, companies typically grant nonqualified stock options along with other forms of long-term incentive. No other form of long-term incentive is as popular or used as much as the nonquali-fied stock option because of its favorable accounting treatment (see Q 5:25 for current treatment, Q 1:43 for proposed treatment).

During recent years when ordinary income tax rates approximated capital gains tax rates, the qualified stock option (ISO) did not provide any substantial tax advantage to executives. Higher ordinary income tax rates should increase the popularity of ISOs, although the flexibility of the nonqualified stock option (no statutory require-ments, unlike the ISO) should keep it the most popular form of long-term incentive for years to come.

Q 6:16 What is the accounting treatment of a nonstatutory stock option?

A company must decide to follow APB 25 or FAS 123 in determin-ing the accounting impact of a nonqualified stock option (see Q 1:45).

Under APB 25, if a nonqualified stock option is granted at the current market price, the company has no charge to its earnings statement. APB 25 requires a "measurement date" when two things are known: the price per share to be paid by the executive and the number of shares that the executive can purchase. This measurement date exists at the date of grant. APB 25 goes on to state that any company earnings charge will be the difference between the compen-sation value of the stock option, to be measured by the number of shares multiplied by the fair market value per share, and employee value, which is the amount that the employee will pay for the shares, to be measured by the employee price per share multiplied by the number of shares. Because these values are equivalent for a non-qualified stock option granted at fair market value, there is no charge to the company's earnings.

In the case of a discounted stock option, the company must recognize a compensation expense equal to the compensation value at the time of grant minus the employee value. For example, if a nonqualified stock option is granted at $5 below fair market value, the difference between compensation value and employee value is $5, which must be charged to earnings.

If the company elects to follow FAS 123, under this accounting regulation it must take a charge to earnings based on the "fair value" of the option. For an example of the fair value calculation see Q 1:49. This charge must be accrued over the vesting period of the stock option.

Q 6:17   How does a company calculate dilution with a nonqualified stock option?

A company's EPS are diluted by both a nonqualified stock option and an incentive stock option. The fully diluted earnings per share calculation method is discussed in Qs 1:49 and 1:52.

Q 6:18   What is the tax treatment of a nonstatutory stock option?

Nonqualified stock options are not taxed at the time the shares are granted.

At the time the nonstatutory stock options are exercised, the executive is subject to ordinary income tax on the spread (i.e., the difference between the market price at the time of exercise and the exercise price paid by the executive). The company receives a tax deduction equal to the amount of income received by the executive (the spread). For example, if an executive exercises the right to purchase 1,000 shares at $20 per share when the current market value is $30, then the spread, or the amount of gain provided to the executive is $10,000 (1,000 shares × $10 stock appreciation). The executive is subject to ordinary income tax on the $10,000, and the company gets a tax deduction on the same amount of $10,000. Once the employee takes ownership of the shares, future gains will be taxed at capital gains tax rates if the employee holds the shares for one year or more. If the shares are held for less than one year, any subsequent appreciation in the shares between the time they were purchased and the time they were sold would be taxed at ordinary income tax rates.

Q 6:19 What are the advantages of nonqualified stock options?

Most companies find that the nonqualified stock option has significant appeal because of the great flexibility it provides in plan design. No statutory requirements need to be met, and the company sets the option price. Companies can also apply dividend equivalents to nonqualified stock options, providing dividend payments to executives who have nonqualified stock option shares even if they are not yet owners of these shares. Companies use dividend equivalents as a means of allowing the executive to build cash to use in purchasing the stock options. When used, dividends are typically on a one-for-one basis.

> **Example.** A company grants an executive a nonqualified stock option of 1,000 shares, which vests 25 percent per year. The award period is ten years. The company also assigns to the executive dividend rights for each share of stock. The company pays a $2.50 annual dividend on each share of stock, with $.65 per share to be paid each quarter ($2.50 ÷ 4), for a total of $650 each quarter (1,000 shares × $.65) or $2,500 ($650 × 4) per year.

Companies can also attach SARs to nonqualified stock options as another means of providing the executive with cash that can be used to purchase other stock options. These are typically in the form of tandem or parallel rights. Tandem SARs with a stock option are an "either/or alternative," i.e., the executive can exercise one or the other but not both. Parallel SARs with a stock option are mutually independent grants. The exercise of one has no impact on the exercise of the other.

> **Example 1: Tandem SAR with Nonqualified Stock Option.** An executive is granted 1,000 nonqualified stock options with tandem SARs on each stock option share. If the executive subsequently exercises 250 SARs, then 750 shares remain to exercise as either a stock option purchase or an SAR.

> **Example 2: Parallel SAR with Nonqualified Stock Option.** An executive is granted 1,000 nonqualified stock options with 1,000

SARs to parallel the stock option. If the executive subsequently exercises 250 SARs, there remain 1,000 nonqualified stock options and 750 SARs.

There is also a significant cost advantage to nonqualified stock options if the company elects APB 25 and grants the option at the current market value. In this case, there is no charge to the income statement. In addition, upon exercise of a nonqualified stock option, the company gets the benefit of a tax deduction on the total appreciation (compensation) realized by the executive. Under an ISO, unless the stock is sold prior to the end of the applicable holding period, there is no tax deduction for the company. If the ISO is held for one year after exercise (two years after grant), the executive receives capital gains tax treatment when the shares are sold. This is why nonqualified stock options are the most common form of long-term incentive.

Q 6:20　What are the disadvantages of the nonqualified stock option?

With a nonqualified stock option, the optionee is taxed at the time that the shares are exercised, so there is no deferral of the tax as there would be with an ISO. The corporation is required to withhold minimum federal tax amounts from the spread recognized by the executive at the time that the stock option is exercised. This can result in an additional burden to the executive, who must find the money to purchase the stock option and to pay the taxes on the spread to be realized upon purchase/exercise of that stock option.

Executives classified as insiders also have to consider the rules of Section 16(b) of the Securities Exchange Act of 1934 (the 1934 Act), which prohibit an insider from conducting any simultaneous buy/sell transaction within a six-month period (see Qs 2:18 and 2:19 for additional information on Section 16).

Q 6:21　Can features be added to nonstatutory stock options to offset the withholding burden?

Yes. The following three methods are most often used in dealing with the withholding and payment burdens:

1. The corporation can provide a cash bonus on exercise. (A variation on this method involves the use of a tandem stock option/SAR, discussed in Chapter 9.)

2. The corporation can withhold from the number of shares issuable upon exercise of the option that number of shares necessary to satisfy the withholding requirement, or can accept from the employee a larger number of shares of stock in a stock-for-stock exercise.

3. The company can offer a cashless exercise to the executive. These enable the executive to use the proceeds from a simultaneous purchase and sale of shares, to pay the purchase or exercise price.

Where an insider is involved, Section 16 of the 1934 Act will have an impact if one of these methods is chosen.

Q 6:22 How do ISOs compare with nonstatutory stock options?

The principal benefit of the ISO accrues to the executive, who is entitled to capital gains treatment on the full value of the spread (difference between sale price and option exercise price) at the time of sale. The other remaining advantage of the ISO is that the executive can defer the taxable event until the sale of the underlying shares.

From the company's perspective, the loss of a tax deduction on an ISO makes it a more costly form of stock option than the nonqualified stock option, which provides the company with a tax deduction based on the spread at the time of exercise (market value at exercise minus option price paid by the executive at exercise).

Example. An executive receives one nonqualified stock option share and one incentive stock option share with a grant price of $20. If these shares were exercised when the stock price was $30 and sold when the stock price was $35 after one year, then with the assumed tax rates shown on the table, the total tax on the incentive tax option share, at $4.20, is less than the total tax on the nonqualified share of $4.50.

	Tax on Nonqualified	Tax on ISO
Grant Price $20	0	0
Exercise Price $30	$3.10*	0
Sale Price $35	$1.40**	$4.20**
	$4.50	$4.20

---

*Ordinary income tax equals 31 percent (asset held for less than 18 months).

**Capital gains tax equals 28 percent (asset held for less than 18 months).

Discounted Stock Options

Q 6:23   What is a discounted stock option?

Although a discounted stock option (DSO) is technically any nonstatutory option with an exercise price that is lower than the fair market value of the stock at the time of grant, the term usually refers to an option with an exercise price that is fixed at a substantial discount from the fair market value on the date of grant. Frequently, these plans are utilized for compensating outside members of the Board of Directors (see Chapter 13).

Traditionally, a DSO has been used to encourage immediate ownership and to protect against drops in the market price. To reinforce the ownership element, the purchased stock is sometimes subject to some holding period and/or tenure restrictions. For example, the shares acquired under such a plan may not be sold for a certain period after the purchase or must be resold to the company at the discounted price if the executive terminates employment prior to a specified date.

Example. Executive A works for Gable Corporation, which grants her an option for 1,000 shares of its stock on August 18, 1996. The exercise price of the option is $5, which is one-half the market value of $10. On September 1, 1997, the current value of the stock is $14 and A decides to exercise her option and purchase 1,000 shares for $5,000. For 1997, A has $9,000 of reportable income, which is computed as follows:

Value of the stock ($14 × 1,000)	$14,000
Purchase price	(5,000)
Reportable Income	$ 9,000

Gable Corporation receives a corresponding $9,000 tax deduction. In October 1999, A sells the 1,000 shares at $20 per share and reports a $6,000 taxable capital gain; Gable is not entitled to a deduction for that gain.

The exercise price for DSOs is generally expressed as a fixed price, although it is more rarely expressed as a percentage of market value at the time of exercise. If the exercise price is allowed to vary with the market price, the executive is at a real disadvantage for purposes of the SEC Section 16 rules, as she will not be deemed to have acquired the shares until the option is actually exercised.

Q 6:24   How prevalent are DSO plans?

The DSO is not frequently used as a long-term incentive compensation program for executives. It is not viewed favorably by shareholders, who have to pay the full price for their shares.

Q 6:25   What is the tax treatment for a DSO?

The tax consequences resulting from the grant and exercise of a DSO are the same as those applicable to nonstatutory options in general. Absent a Code Section 83(b) election, the discounted option is not compensation to the executive when granted, but becomes income upon its exercise recognizable by the employee and deductible by the corporation.

Q 6:26   What is the accounting impact of a DSO?

A company must decide to follow APB 25 or FAS 123 in determining the accounting impact of a DSO. If it follows APB 25, the company must take an earnings charge equal to the amount of the discount. (See Q 1:42.) If it elects FAS 123, it must take an earnings charge equal to the "fair value" of the stock option. (See Q 1:49.)

Q 6:27　What are the advantages of a DSO plan?

The primary advantage of a discounted stock plan is the "cushion" provided an executive if the stock price falls and the built-in appreciation or gain the executive receives is diminished. A DSO is also a way to defer compensation effectively, as no taxable income will be generated to the executive (absent a Code Section 83(b) election) until the option is exercised. (See Chapter 13 for the advantages of the director's compensation deferral.)

Q 6:28　What are the disadvantages of a DSO plan?

The most often voiced criticism of a discounted stock plan is that the executive receives a reward even if the stock price does not appreciate or does not depreciate more than the discount.

Under a DSO plan, even decreasing stock prices can generate large rewards.

Example 1. Executive B received 10,000 DSOs as part of the recruitment process. The option price was $34 and the current stock price was $68. Three years later when B exercised the options, the stock price had declined to $52 per share. At that point, B still received $180,000 (($52 − $34) × 10,000) for "managing" the stock price down by $16 per share.

A second disadvantage is that the company must reflect the benefit provided to the executive in the discount of the exercise price at the time of grant of the option as compensation expense for accounting purposes even though the company is not entitled to the corresponding tax benefit until the option is exercised.

Another potential problem with DSOs is the depth of the discount, because at some point the grant of a deeply discounted option becomes the transfer of the underlying shares. Instead of granting an executive an option to purchase a small number of shares at a deeply discounted price, a company can give the same initial benefit to an executive by granting him an option to purchase a larger number of shares at a price that is not so deeply discounted.

Example 2. In the previous example, Executive B had received 10,000 DSOs with an exercise price of $34 versus the $68 market price; the value of the benefit granted to him at that time by the company was $340,000. If the company had granted him 25,000 options with an exercise price of $50, the immediate spread would have been $450,000. In that case, he would have received only $50,000 upon the sale of the underlying shares after the company's dismal performance during the three years he held them.

Q 6:29   How deeply can DSOs be discounted?

The Internal Revenue Service (IRS) has avoided issuing regulations on the point at which a deeply discounted option would be considered to be a "sham" option and recharacterized as a transfer of the underlying stock, taxable immediately as income to the recipient. [See Rev. Proc. 90-3, 1990-1 I.R.B. 54]

As a practical matter, discounts of more than 50 percent begin to expose the company and the executive to this kind of recharacterization. A company considering deeply discounted stock would be wise to consider getting a private letter ruling from the IRS on the appropriateness of the discount.

Premium Stock Options

Q 6:30   What is a premium stock option?

A premium stock option permits an executive to purchase company stock at a price that is above the current market value of the shares. The premium attached to the stock option above the current market price is typically in an amount equal to the normally expected minimum growth of the company stock price, to serve as a threshold amount that guarantees the company will perform at a minimum level. The stock price must increase before the executive can benefit from the stock option.

Example. Executive C works for the Cable Corporation and on July 1, 1997, when the market value of company shares is $10, she is granted an option to purchase 1,000 shares of stock at an exercise price of $15 per share. The stock option grant has 25 percent vesting per year over four years, and the stock award period is ten years. At the completion of the fourth year C is fully vested and can exercise the right to purchase 1,000 shares at $15 per share. The assumption is that during the four years of vesting, the company stock price will have gone well beyond $15 per share; therefore, shareholders, and the executive, will have benefited. In addition the company will have retained the services of the executive during the same period. In summary, everyone wins.

Q 6:31   How is the premium established on a premium stock option?

There are several ways to establish the premium. The most common methods are the treasury bill (T-bill) and the peer-group methods. The T-bill method is intended to reflect the cost of capital so that an executive may, for example, receive a ten-year option for 1,000 shares at a $47.75 exercise price when the current market value is $38. Assuming that the T-bill return is 7 percent, the $38 stock price might reach the $47.75 exercise price after five years, and the executive would have an additional five years to exercise the stock option. The rationale for this approach is that the executive should not profit unless the executive can make the company outperform a low-risk investment such as treasury bills.

The peer-group approach, which is most appropriate for publicly traded companies and those companies with easily identifiable competitors, focuses on relative performance against competitor firms. For example, consider an airline company stock that is traded at $80 that wants to establish the price at which an option would be exercisable after five years. It would multiply $80 (the current price) by the industry average stock price appreciation. If the industry average stock growth rate was 10 percent over five years, the exercise price would then be established at $88. The peer-group approach emphasizes that an executive should not be rewarded if her company's stock price does not at least outperform the average rate of performance within its industry peer groups. As a result, in this example, if the company's stock price moved 20 percent upward to $96, which exceeds the predetermined average, the executive would exercise that option at $88 and would profit $8 per option. If the company stock price moved only 10 percent (the industry average), the executive could still exercise the option and purchase shares, although she would receive no immediate reward or gain.

Q 6:32   How prevalent are premium stock options?

Premium stock options are not common among companies, although several large companies have implemented these plans.

Q 6:33   What is the accounting impact of a premium stock option?

A company must decide to follow APB 25 or FAS 123 in determining the accounting impact of a premium stock option. If it follows APB 25, the company must take an earnings charge equal to the difference, if any, between the current fair market value at grant and the executive's option price. The executive's exercise price is typically greater than the current market value at the time of grant under a premium stock option; therefore, there will be no charge to earnings under APB 25. (See Q 1:45.)

If the company elects FAS 123, it must take an earnings charge equal to the "fair value" of the stock option at the time of grant. (See Q 1:49.)

Q 6:34   What is the tax treatment of a premium stock option?

There is no tax effect to the corporation or to the executive at the time a premium stock option is granted. The corporation is, however, entitled to a deduction equal to the amount that is taxable when the executive receives ordinary income equal to the spread between the option exercise price and the fair market value of the shares. Because the spread is taxable as ordinary income, the company is required to withhold taxes.

Q 6:35   What is the advantage of a premium stock option?

This type of plan appeals to companies that believe that an executive should only be rewarded if the company stock appreciates more than a certain amount, and/or if they believe that an increase in company stock should be achieved before a stock option has value to the executive. A premium stock option plan will pay out only if there is either an active market for the stock and the stock appreciates or company performance drives the stock price up.

Q 6:36   What is the disadvantage of a premium stock option?

From the executive's perspective, the premium stock option requires stock appreciation, and the stock market does not always respond to company performance; in fact, the vagaries of the stock market will, in some cases, drive the stock price down when company performance goes up.

On the other hand, an executive can use the performance characteristics of a premium stock option to justify higher than normal award levels (i.e., higher performance should equal a higher number of stock options).

From the company's perspective, the only disadvantage is that if the company stock price does not move or goes down when company performance goes up, then executives will not be motivated, and may leave the company.

Option Reloads

Q 6:37   What is an option reload plan?

Under an option reload plan, at exercise an executive will receive new options at the current market price for the same number of shares that were used to exercise the original option, and with the same terms as the original option.

Example. On July 1, 1997 an executive receives an option to purchase 1,000 shares of company stock at an option price of $25. In July 1999, 50 percent of the shares have vested, and the executive exercises the right to purchase 500 of these shares when the current market price is $45. When the executive takes possession of these 500 shares, the company will issue to the executive another 500 stock option shares with an option price at the current market value of $45, with the same vesting period and with the same stock award period as the shares just purchased.

Option reload plans are typically provided in addition to normal annual or biannual grants of stock options or other forms of long-term incentive. Most companies will require that executives hold the underlying shares that they have exercised for a minimum period of years in order to receive the reload stock options.

Option reload plans can be used in connection with both qualified and nonqualified stock option plans. Naturally, the reload options for a nonqualified plan would be nonqualified shares and for an ISO plan would be ISO shares.

Q 6:38   What is the accounting impact of a reload option?

A company must decide to follow APB 25 or FAS 123 in determining the accounting impact of a reload stock option (see Q 1:45). If it follows APB 25, the company must take an earnings charge equal to the difference, if any, between the current fair market value at grant and the executive's option price. If the company elects FAS 123, it must take an earnings charge equal to the "fair value" of the stock option at the time of grant (see Q 1:46).

The executive's reload option typically has the same terms as the option that triggered the exercise and subsequent "reloading" of the stock option; therefore, the accounting treatment of the reload option will be the same as the accounting treatment of the original option.

Q 6:39   What is the tax treatment of a reload option?

The tax consequences of the reload option would be the normal tax consequences of statutory or nonstatutory options, depending on the type of option the reload option is deemed to be.

Q 6:40   What are the advantages of an option reload provision?

This feature can encourage stock ownership, particularly if the company requires an executive to keep the exercised shares that trigger the reload event.

A reload feature makes sense for virtually all companies with stock option plans (see Q 6:41 for a caveat where ISOs are involved).

Although allowing an executive to pay an option exercise price with already-owned shares allows him or her to end up with a larger number of shares after the exercise, he or she does not end up with the ownership level that the company wished to give him or her. Adding an option reload feature rectifies this situation.

Planning Tip. A reload plan could include a requirement that the shares received upon the exercise of the original option be held for a certain period in order for the reload option to vest.

Q 6:41   What are the disadvantages of an option reload plan?

A company must be careful in granting a reload option in connection with the exercise of an ISO. If the ISO was not developed to include a reload feature, adding the reload option could modify the terms of the ISO, disqualifying it for the preferred capital gains tax treatment. Companies must also be sure to establish limits on the use of the reload feature; otherwise, they can easily run out of authorized shares.

Planning Tip. Companies should establish a "sunset" provision to any reload option, indicating how long the reload feature will be in effect. A never-ending reload feature could be a significant drain on authorized shares and can dilute EPS.

Book Value Purchase Plans

Q 6:42   What is a book value purchase plan?

A book value purchase plan grants an executive the right to purchase a fixed number of company book value shares at its current book value price, over a fixed period, after meeting a specified vesting provision. Book value is determined by dividing company equity by the number of shares outstanding, to get a book value price per share.

Example. On July 1, 1994, an executive is granted the right to purchase 1,000 book value shares at a price of $100, over a ten-year period. This right vests at 25 percent per year. The executive buys the shares six years later, when company book value is $140, thus receiving a $40,000 gain (1,000 shares × ($140 − $100)).

Obviously, these plans will typically require the executive to sell the book value shares immediately back to the company (because there is no market other than the company to sell the shares). Therefore, the company must accrue cash in order to buy the shares back from the executive. This is significantly different from the case of stock option shares used by a public company where the shares are traded on a stock market. In this case, the public company does not have to accrue cash to buy the shares back from the executive.

Q 6:43   What is the accounting impact of a book value purchase plan?

The accounting treatment for a book value purchase plan is the same as that for a stock option. A company must decide to follow APB 25 or FAS 123 in determining the accounting impact of a book value purchase grant. If it follows APB 25, the company must take an earnings charge equal to the difference, if any, between the current fair market value at grant and the executive's option/exercise price on the book value share. Because the executive's exercise price is typically the same as the current fair market value at the time of grant under a book value purchase grant, there will typically be no charge to earnings under APB 25. (See Q 1:42.)

If the company elects FAS 123, it must take an earnings charge equal to the "fair value" of the book value share at the time of grant. (See Q 1:46.)

Q 6:44   What is the tax treatment of a book value purchase plan?

The tax treatment of a book value purchase plan is similar to that of an incentive stock option. There is no tax at the time of grant, to either the company or the executive. When the company repurchases the stock from the executive, it is not entitled to a tax deduction for the "loss" it has incurred by selling shares at a lower price than the repurchased price, nor for the conceptual compensatory element resulting from the increase in the value of the shares. The appreciation that the executive receives is taxed at the capital gains tax rate at the time the book value shares are sold back to the company; therefore, the company receives no tax deduction.

Q 6:45 What are the advantages of a book value plan?

Many publicly traded companies feel that compensating the executive on the actual increase in the company's book value rather than as a result of the vagaries of the stock market constitutes the primary advantage of book value plans. Privately held companies benefit from not having to perform costly and often inaccurate appraisals of their stock, as is the case with stock options.

Q 6:46 What are the disadvantages of a book value plan?

From the company's perspective, a book value plan achieves much the same compensatory goal as a phantom stock arrangement, yet is less advantageous from a tax point of view because the company is entitled neither to a deduction at the time of grant nor to any deduction, either for compensation or for a loss, at the time it repurchases the shares.

From the executive's perspective, while he or she is not penalized if the stock market value of the stock declines despite an increase in the company's book value, he or she receives no benefit from the market value of the shares.

Q 6:47 For what type of companies does a book value plan make sense?

Book value plans are helpful for privately held companies whose stock does not have an easily ascertainable market value, but want to achieve the goals usually associated with stock-based plans. Although valuation of the stock can be obtained through the use of a professional appraiser, such a procedure involves additional expense for the company, and the results of the appraisal may not satisfy either the company or the executive.

A publicly traded company can benefit from a book value plan in that it can give an equity interest in the company to its executives yet tie their reward to the company's performance rather than the vagaries of the stock market.

Many companies use a separate, nonvoting class of stock for use in their book value plans, and those who base the repurchase price on a multiple of earnings use a nondividend class of stock for their book value plans. These approaches would not, however, be appropriate for an S corporation because of the one-class-of-stock restriction.

Convertible Debentures

Q 6:48   What is a convertible debenture?

A convertible debenture is a fixed income debt security that is sold at a fixed price to an employee. The debenture has a face value on which periodic interest is paid to the executive, and it is typically convertible into stock of the company at a later date such as after the executive has completed a specified period of employment or specific performance goals have been met. Most companies have traditionally included a provision in the plan that the conversion right will be terminated if the debenture is transferred in order to discourage executives from transferring the debentures.

Convertible debentures involve securities that have to be registered under federal and most state laws unless an available exemption exists and the availability of an exemption depends on the details of each offer or offering.

Example. On February 3, 1994, Executive A purchased a convertible debenture from Altoona Corporation that had a ten-year maturity, a face value of $10,000, and paid an annualized interest rate of 8 percent. The current market value of the stock was $25. The debenture allowed a conversion to Altoona stock if, after five years, A was still employed and the return on investment over the five-year period was at least 9 percent. The conversion ratio was 40 shares for each $1,000 face value of the debenture equivalent to a purchase price of $25 per share. Each year, A was to receive $800 interest on the debenture, which would be taxable income to A and deductible to Altoona Corporation.

In March 1999, Altoona Corporation achieved or exceeded its 9 percent target rate of return and A was still an executive with the company. A's debenture therefore became convertible to 400 shares of stock. A elected to convert the debentures at the point when the market value of the stock was $36 per share. At the time of this conversion, neither A nor the company experienced any tax consequences.

In April 2000, A decided to sell his 400 shares of stock for the then-current market price of $39 per share. He had a gain of $5,600, which is computed as follows:

Proceeds from sale ($39 × 400 shares)	$15,600
Purchase price or basis	(10,000)
Gain	$ 5,600

The sale of the stock has no impact on the company.

Q 6:49 Is shareholder approval required to issue convertible debentures?

Although shareholder approval is not generally required to issue convertible debentures, approval of the board of directors is required when a company issues a debt obligation; however, it is prudent to obtain shareholder approval to avoid the possibility of a shareholder lawsuit challenging the appropriateness of the debt issuance.

Q 6:50 What is the accounting impact of a convertible debenture?

The accounting treatment for a convertible debenture plan is the same as that for other stock awards. A company must decide to follow APB 25 or FAS 123 in determining the accounting impact of a convertible debenture grant. If it follows APB 25, the company must take an earnings charge equal to the difference, if any, between the current fair market value at grant and the executive's conversion price of the debenture share. Because the conversion of the debenture to company shares is typically a lateral and nontaxable event there is typically no accounting impact at that time. When the executive sells company shares (after holding for one year), the executive would pay capital gains tax.

If the company elects FAS 123, it must take an earnings charge equal to the "fair value" of the common share equivalent convertible debenture share at the time of grant. (See Q 1:46.)

Q 6:51   What is the tax treatment of a convertible debenture?

If the convertible debenture is purchased by the employee at its fair market value, no tax event occurs at that time. If the market value of the debenture is greater than the amount paid by the executive, then that excess is included in the executive's income, and deducted by the corporation as a compensation expense, in the year of purchase. There is no taxable event to the company or the employee when the debenture is converted; however, upon the sale of the underlying shares, the employee is taxed on the gain he or she is deemed to have incurred, which is the sale price of the shares minus the amount he or she paid for the converted debenture.

Interest paid on the debenture prior to its conversion will be interest income to the executive and an interest deduction to the company. (For an example of how a convertible debenture works, see Q 6:48.)

Q 6:52   What is the EPS impact of a convertible debenture?

If the debenture's cash yield at the date of issuance is two thirds of the bank prime interest rate, then the debentures are treated as common stock cash equivalents. As a result, EPS are affected not only as a result of the compensation expense but also as a result of the additional number of outstanding shares.

Q 6:53   What are the advantages of a convertible debenture program?

The principal advantage of using a convertible debenture is that the executive invests money in the company, which closely ties the interests of the executive and the shareholders. A convertible debenture program also minimizes the executive's downside risk by providing a fixed obligation of the company to pay both principal and interest to the executive and, if the stock price declines, the executive would still receive his or her principal back at the time the debenture matures. Furthermore, because interest at the prevailing interest rate is typically paid on the amount invested in the debenture, if the executive chooses not to convert, that executive will get his or her money back with interest, so the executive does not suffer a lost opportunity cost.

Q 6:54　What are the disadvantages of a convertible debenture program?

The primary disadvantage of a convertible debenture is that in most states it has to be registered under both federal and state securities laws, and the time and expense involved in this process may make the program prohibitive. Another disadvantage is the lack of executive involvement in the company stock's down side. Finally, the requirement that the executive make a substantial capital investment in order to participate in the program may be a problem because interest on any debt used to finance the purchase of the debenture is not deductible to the executive.

Q 6:55　For what type of company does a convertible debenture plan make sense?

A convertible debenture plan makes sense for those companies whose compensation philosophy includes the belief that an executive should make a substantial investment in the company's future, but who also recognize that because of the substantial investment required of the executive, his or her participation in the company stock's down side should be minimized.

Junior Stock Plans

Q 6:56　What is a junior stock plan?

Junior stock is a class of stock having lesser voting, dividend, and liquidation rights than ordinary common stock. Under a junior common stock plan, an executive receives junior stock that becomes convertible at a favorable rate into common stock. Junior stock plans were popular in the 1970s until the SEC and the Financial Accounting Standards Board (FASB) proposed a rule that would require the full spread at conversion to be treated as an expense item to be reflected in the profit and loss statement and chargeable against earnings. This change eliminated the effectiveness of junior common stock, and most organizations dropped their existing plans.

> **Example.** Executive E is an executive of Altoona Corporation. On January 1, 1994, she was granted and exercised an option to acquire 1,000 shares of Altoona's junior common stock at $1 per share. The junior stock converts to common stock if EPS reaches $12 by December 31, 1997. The current market value of Altoona Corporation shares is $10. On January 1, 1998, Altoona Corporation's EPS is $14 and E is still an executive with the company. The junior common stock converts to regular common stock.

Q 6:57   What are the advantages of a junior stock plan?

The primary advantage of a junior stock plan, prior to the SEC and FASB changes, was that it provided the executive with capital gains treatment not only on the future growth in value of the common stock, but also on the initial spread between the acquisition cost of the junior common stock and the common stock value at the date of purchase of the junior common stock. This offered substantial leverage in providing low cost equity participation to executives. Tax reform changes coupled with the SEC and FASB rulings stripped junior stock plans of these advantages.

Q 6:58   What are the disadvantages of a junior stock plan?

In addition to the lack of tax deductibility, three disadvantages of junior stock result from its use of a separate class of stock. First, the device is unavailable to the S corporation. Second, shareholder approval is likely to be required in order to authorize the new class of stock, unless such a class already exists. Lastly, the value to public companies of a second class of stock that would in all likelihood not be registered is limited, as the executive's ability to resell his or her shares is limited.

Q 6:59 How prevalent are junior common stock plans?

Junior stock plans were previously adopted by many high technology companies and other companies that anticipated high stock price appreciation. Since FASB ruled that a charge to earning is required at the time of exchange, these plans have all but disappeared.

Performance-Based Stock Options

Q 6:60 What are performance-based stock options?

Performance-based stock options are regular nonqualified or ISOs granted to executives at typical option award levels and award periods, except that the vesting of the option is dependent upon or affected by the achievement of specified performance goals of the company.

Example. An executive is given the right to purchase 1,000 shares of company stock at $20 per share (current fair market value). The vesting in this grant occurs when company EPS increase from $3 to $4 per share.

Q 6:61 What are the advantages of performance-based stock options?

The primary advantage to the company is that the company performance goal must be achieved before the executive can realize any value from the stock option. Board compensation committee members have favorable opinions of this form of long-term incentive because it is performance-driven. Moreover, if stock price is the performance measure, then the executive will receive value from the stock option only if shareholders also receive the same value from stock appreciation.

From an executive's point of view, the performance measure is simply another "hurdle" or "qualifier" that must be met in order to exercise the stock option. Most companies will, however, use a performance measure that the executive can influence or directly control so that executive motivation and retention is realized from the performance-based option.

Q 6:62   What are the disadvantages of performance-based stock options?

There can be disadvantages to the executive and to the company if the performance measure is not achieved.

Example 1. A company establishes 10 percent average annual EPS growth as the performance measure that must be achieved before vesting occurs on a stock option grant. An executive is given the right to purchase 1,000 shares at $20 per share (current fair market value). During the award period, the company does not achieve the EPS goal, but company stock price increases to $25 per share. The executive cannot exercise the stock option because the performance measure was not met.

In this example, the EPS goal may have been realistic or unrealistic. In either case, the executive would be dissatisfied. This could be a disadvantage to the company if the executive loses motivation to perform or resigns. The company objectives of motivating the executive to achieve EPS growth and of retaining key executives were not achieved.

Example 2. A company establishes $5 stock price appreciation as the performance measure that must be achieved before vesting occurs on a stock option grant. An executive is given the right to purchase 1,000 shares of stock at $20 per share (current fair market value). During the award period the company stock increases to $24 per share. The executive cannot exercise the stock option because the performance measure was not met. The disadvantage to the company and the executive is the same in this example as in Example 1.

Planning Tip. Company performance goals in a performance-based stock option should be realistic and should not be structured to result in a go or no-go situation. It is better to have various levels of performance achievement so that executives can accrue eligibility to exercise a portion of the stock option as they meet the established performance levels.

Q 6:63 What are the tax consequences of performance-based stock options?

The tax impact to the company and to the individual executive for performance-based stock options depends upon whether the option is nonqualified or whether it is an ISO. Nonqualified stock options have no taxable event at grant, and the executive is taxed at ordinary income rates on any stock appreciation at the time of exercise. The company receives a tax deduction equal to the amount of stock appreciation received by the executive.

With an ISO, there is no taxable event at the time of grant, and, upon exercise, the executive defers tax until sale. If the stock is held for one year or more before a sale (two years from grant date), the executive is taxed at the capital gains tax rate. In this event, the company receives no tax deduction. If the stock is sold by the executive after less than one year, then the executive is taxed at ordinary income tax rates and the company does not receive a tax deduction. (See Qs 6:7 and 6:18.)

Q 6:64 What is the accounting treatment of a performance-based stock option?

Determining the accounting treatment for this form of long-term incentive can be challenging. In most cases, the company accountants and CPA firm will conclude that the award is "variable," in which case FASB 28 applies, and the company must accrue the anticipated value over the award period. The anticipated value means that any stock price appreciation is calculated and multiplied by the percentage of vesting that has occurred at that point. The company will anticipate that the performance measure will be met.

It is possible, but unlikely, that company accountants and their CPA firm will conclude that the performance measures will be met without question, and the award is therefore not variable. In this case the company must decide to follow APB 25 or FAS 123 in determining the accounting impact. If it follows APB 25, the company must take an earnings charge equal to the difference, if any, between the current fair market value at grant and the executive's option price (when the performance goal is met). Because the executive's exercise price is typically greater than the current market value at the time of grant under a performance-based stock option, there will be no charge to earnings under APB 25. (See Q 1:42.)

If the company elects FAS 123, it must take an earnings charge equal to the "fair value" of the stock option at the time of grant. (See Q 1:46.)

Example. An executive is granted 1,000 stock options at $20 per share with a performance measure that requires an average annual increase in EPS of 10 percent over the next four years before vesting can occur. After one year the stock price increases to $25 per share.

This is a variable award plan, and the company will anticipate that the EPS goal will be achieved, charging its earnings with that $5 per share increase multiplied by 250 shares (one fourth of the shares, because this is the first year of the four-year vesting period).

Q 6:65   What is an indexed stock option?

This is a form of performance stock option that has the option price "indexed" to some performance measure.

Example. An executive is given the right to purchase 1,000 shares of company stock at $20 per share (current fair market value). The vesting in this grant occurs in accordance with the following:

25 percent vesting when the stock price increases to $22
50 percent vesting when the stock price increases to $24
75 percent vesting when the stock price increases to $26
100 percent vesting when the stock price increases to $28

The accounting and tax treatment is the same as with a performance-based stock option.

Chapter 7

Appreciation and Full-Value Plans

Appreciation and full-value plans are long-term incentive plans that provide the executive with a benefit interest that does not require any actual investment by the executive. The two most common types of appreciation plan are the stock appreciation right plan and the book value appreciation right plan. The two most common types of full-value plans are restricted stock grants and performance plans. This chapter addresses the tax, legal, and financial implications of appreciation and full-value plans, including the circumstances where these types of plans work best and their relative strengths and weaknesses.

Appreciation Plans   7-2
Stock Appreciation Rights   7-2
Book Value Appreciation Rights   7-10
Full-Value Plans   7-12
Phantom Stock Plans   7-13
Restricted Stock Grants   7-18
Performance Unit Plans   7-21
Performance Share Plans   7-23

Appreciation Plans

Q 7:1   What are appreciation plans?

Appreciation plans provide opportunities for capital accumulation over a long term (at least three to five years) by granting the eligible executive the right to receive the value of share appreciation. Appreciation is typically based on changes in either the fair market value of shares of stock traded by public companies, or the appraised price of shares in private companies. Another approach is to measure appreciation based on changes in the book value of the company. These plans do not require the executive to make an investment.

Q 7:2   What are examples of appreciation plans?

The most prevalent types of appreciation plans are the stock appreciation right (SAR) and the book value appreciation right. SARs provide long-term income as company stock price increases while book value appreciation rights provide long-term income as company equity (book value) increases.

Stock Appreciation Rights

Q 7:3   What is a stock appreciation right?

An SAR is the right to receive the value of the appreciation of a specified number of shares of a company's capital stock over a specified period of time. An SAR plan can provide that the SAR be exercised by the employee after a specified vesting period, or it may be structured with a specified maturity date. Payment of any applicable stock appreciation is determined at maturity if the executive is still employed by the company at that date.

Upon exercise or maturity of an SAR, the executive will receive the full appreciated value in any combination of cash, stock, or other consideration, as specified in the SAR agreement. Most companies using the SAR will pay some of the appreciated value in cash so that the executive's tax liability can be offset.

SARs may be issued as "stand alone" rights to the executive or they can be linked with other forms of long-term income, usually stock options. An SAR may be granted "in tandem" with a stock option or "parallel" to a stock option. In tandem stock options (see Q 8:19) the exercise of one stock appreciation share cancels one stock option share, and vice-versa. Under parallel SAR/stock option plans, the executive receives an award of both forms of long-term income and the exercise of one is separate from the exercise of the other.

Example 1: Tandem Stock Option/SAR. Executive A works for Alpha Corporation. She receives a nonqualified stock option of 1,000 shares and SARs in tandem with a stock option also equal to 1,000 shares. The option price at the time of grant is $20 per share, which represents the current market price of the stock. There is a one-year vesting provision, and the award period is ten years. After five years, the stock has increased to $40 per share. A exercises her right to the stock appreciation in 500 shares and receives $10,000 (500 shares × $20 per share stock appreciation). A has 500 shares remaining, which she can exercise as either a stock option or an SAR. A could use the $10,000 she received from exercising the SAR to purchase 500 nonqualified stock option shares, because the cost to exercise is also equal to $10,000 (500 shares × $20 option price).

The income to A for exercising 500 SARs and 500 nonqualified option rights is as follows:

Event	500 Shares Stock Option	500 Shares SAR
Exercise value	$20,000[1]	$10,000[2]
Amount paid	$10,000	0
Income	$10,000	$10,000

[1] $40 × 500 shares = $20,000.

[2] ($40 − $20) × 500 shares = $10,000.

Example 2: Parallel Stock Option/SAR. Executive B is an executive with Bravo Corporation. He is granted a nonqualified stock option of 1,000 shares and a parallel SAR of 1,000 shares. The option price for both the stock option and the SAR at grant is $20 per share, which represents the current market price of the stock.

There is a one-year vesting period, and the award period is ten years. After five years the stock price has increased to $40 per share. B exercises his right to 500 stock appreciation shares that have a value of $10,000 (500 shares × ($40 − $20) = $10,000), and he exercises his right to purchase 500 nonqualified stock options, which also have an exercise price of $10,000 ($20 × 500 shares). The amount of income in the example is the same as in the previous example; however, B still has 500 remaining SARs and 500 remaining nonqualified stock option shares.

Q 7:4 How do the SEC Section 16 rules affect SARs?

An SAR is considered to be a derivative security subject to the reporting requirements set forth under Section 16(a) of the Securities Exchange Act of 1934 (the 1934 Act). Under Section 16(b) of the 1934 Act, an SAR grant is an exempt transaction if Board committee or shareholder approval is obtained within certain time frames (using the same guidelines as for stock options, explained in Q 2:19). SAR grants are also considered to be exempt transactions under Rule 16b-3 if the SARs were held, or if any shares issued upon exercise of the SAR were not sold, for six months following the grant date. If the executive controls the exercise of the SAR, any such exercise for shares is treated the same as the exercise of a stock option (i.e., exercise is not a matchable purchase or sale for Section 16(b) purposes). If the SAR is exercised for a cash payment, such cash settlement is also an exempt transaction under Section 16(b) if Board committee or shareholder approval is obtained (see Q 2:19) within the guidelines of Rule 16b-3. For Section 16(a) reporting purposes, an exercise of the SAR for shares will be reportable currently on a Form 4, while an exercise of the SAR for cash is reportable on a Form 5 after the end of the year.

For purposes of registration requirements under the Securities Act of 1933, an SAR needs to be registered if it can be exercised for shares at a time determined by the executive (i.e., the executive is making an investment decision). If registration is required under the 1933 Act, it must be done before the SAR can be exercised. Companies with publicly traded stock may use a Form S-8 registration statement. Private companies may be able to rely on the "private placement" exemption from registration under Rule 701 (see Q 2:15).

Q 7:5   How prevalent are SARs?

The SAR is most commonly granted in tandem with a stock option plan (normally, a nonqualified stock option plan, because if an SAR were granted with an incentive stock option (ISO), the exercise of the SAR would disqualify the ISO and prevent the executive from receiving any of its favorable tax treatment; see Q 6:7). Most surveys will show that the use of SARs within large publicly traded companies has decreased. This is because the cashless exercise (see Q 5:51) provides the same benefit as an SAR without the same accounting impact (see Q 7:7).

Q 7:6   Should the SAR be eliminated now that the cashless exercise is possible?

Under the cashless option exercise (see Q 5:51) the company and executive receive the benefit equal to that of an SAR without the company having to accrue expenses for this amount of compensation on its income statement. Appreciation payments from an SAR must be accrued on the company's income statement. Therefore, there is no reason for public companies to use SARs, except possibly for insiders, and key executives as defined in Q 2:19. For purposes of Section 16 of the 1934 Act, cashless exercise involves a sale of securities. Thus, it is "matchable" with any nonexempt purchase within a six-month period. Insiders are subject to a six-month holding period between the purchase and sale (or sale and purchase) of stock. Private companies may still find SARs to be valuable in situations where it is not desirable to give employees the right to receive actual shares of company stock.

Q 7:7   What is the accounting impact of an SAR plan?

The SAR is considered to be a "variable plan award" in accounting terminology. The number of shares to be granted and or purchased by the executive, as well as the price of such shares, cannot be determined until the date of exercise; therefore the Accounting Principles Board (APB) Ruling 25, which is used for stock options (see Qs 6:9 and 6:16), does not apply to the SAR.

Companies can elect to use either FAS 28 or FAS 123 to establish the accounting treatment of SARs. Under FAS 28, any company that grants an SAR must accrue the anticipated compensation during the award period on its earnings statement. This accrual is calculated by measuring the amount by which the company's current stock price exceeds the SAR grant price, multiplied by the number of shares that are vested. Changes in the market value of SARs between the date of grant and the date of exercise can thus create significant costs.

Example 1. 1,000 SARs are granted to an executive at $20 per share, with a four-year vesting period (25 percent per year). After Year 1 the price per share has increased to $25. The company would have to charge its income statement with $1,250, which is the first year's stock appreciation ($5) multiplied by 250 shares (1,000 shares × 25% vesting). The same calculation would be done for all subsequent years that the SAR is outstanding.

Under FAS 28, accruals for an SAR will go up and down over the award period. A final cost accrual is always calculated by the company when the SAR is exercised such that the total accrual over the SAR award period is equal to the amount paid to the executive. Accruals are entered into the income statement each year and then shown in the balance sheet as accrued liabilities.

Example 2.

Assumptions: 1,000 SARs at $20/share.
Stock price after Year 1 = $25
Stock price after Year 2 = $20
Stock price after Year 3 = $25
Stock price after Year 4 = $30
SAR exercised after Year 4 at $30/share

	Year 1	Year 2	Year 3	Year 4
Income Statement	$5,000	($5,000)	$5,000	$ 5,000
Balance Sheet	$5,000	($5,000)	$5,000	$10,000
At Exercise				($10,000)

Under FAS 123, a company must calculate the "fair value" of the SAR at the time of grant and charge its earnings statement with this amount over the vesting period. Fair value calculations are discussed in Q 1:49.

Q 7:8   What is the tax treatment of an SAR plan?

The grant of an SAR is not a taxable event because the executive has no constructive receipt at that time. The exercise of the SAR is, however, taxable because the executive recognizes income in an amount equal to the appreciation per share multiplied by the total number of shares exercised. For example, if an executive exercises 1,000 SARs that have appreciated $20 per share, that executive will incur a taxable income of $20,000.

Amounts received by an executive from an SAR are taxed at ordinary income tax rates, and are subject to federal and state withholding regardless of whether payments are in cash or in stock. If the total value of the SAR is paid in stock, then the cost basis for the shares will be the fair market value on the date of exercise of the SAR.

As noted in Q 7:7, the company charges the compensatory value of an SAR against its quarterly and annual income statements when an SAR is exercised (whether for cash or for stock). The company is also entitled to a compensation deduction equal to the total appreciation value received by the executive.

The tax consequences of an SAR are compared to those of a stock option in the following example:

Example. An executive exercises 500 SARs and 500 nonqualified stock options, both having a grant price of $20 and a fair market value upon exercise of $40.

Event		*500 SARs, 500 Stock Options*
Exercise value:	SARs:	$10,000 (500 × ($40 $20))
	Options:	$10,000 (500 × ($40 – $20))
Taxes @ 40%:	SARs:	$4,000 ($10,000 × 40%)
	Options:	$4,000 ($10,000 × 40%)
Amount paid for stock options:		$10,000 (500 × $20)
Amount received if stock is sold:		$20,000 (500 × $40)
Net income:		$12,000 ($20,000 + $10,000 – $10,000 – $8,000)

Note. If this executive used the net proceeds from the SAR ($10,000) to exercise 500 stock option shares (-$10,000), he would still have $20,000 remaining to use for taxes. Using a tax rate of 40 percent, the executive's total tax is $8,000, leaving a net gain of $12,000.

Q 7:9   When do SARs typically vest?

Typically, the vesting requirements of an SAR will be similar to those of other stock option grants. In the case of an SAR granted in tandem to a nonqualified stock option, the vesting of the SAR will mirror that of the stock option to which it is attached. The most common vesting provision for nonqualified stock options is 25 percent per year, or full vesting after four years. The most common vesting period for an ISO is 100 percent after one year. The reason for this difference is that the statutory requirements of ISOs (i.e., one-year holding period after exercise) drive companies into using shorter vesting periods for ISOs.

Q 7:10   What are the advantages of an SAR plan?

From the executive's point of view, SARs provide a cashless way to receive the benefits of stock appreciation without having to purchase the stock, as would be the case with a stock option. For insiders, subject to SEC Section 16 rules, the SAR can provide a way to ensure the cash necessary to exercise stock options. However, since cashless exercises can be exempt transactions under the Section 16 (of the 1934 Act) rules, the use of SARs has declined. Private companies may also find the use of SARs to be advantageous where the company prefers to avoid the purchase of actual shares by its executives.

SARs that are not attached to stock options (stand-alone SARs) are also used by many companies with international operations. Companies use the SAR for key foreign national executives as a means of providing a long-term incentive in the total executive compensation package. The tax laws of many non-U.S. countries are, of course, different from those of the United States, and in some cases, the granting of a stock option can result in a taxable event outside of the

United States. Appreciation received from the stand-alone SAR is taxed at normal income tax rates for the specific country where the executive is located, the taxable event occurring when the SAR is exercised (i.e., whenever the value is received).

> **Example.** A non-U.S. executive is given appreciation rights to 1,000 shares of company common stock. These rights vest 25 percent per year until there is full vesting after four years. The executive has ten years to exercise these rights. If the grant price of the shares was $20 per share, and if the executive exercises the right to the appreciation in all shares after six years when the stock price is $50 per share, then the company provides the international executive with $30,000 (1,000 shares × $30 ($50 – $20)).

Q 7:11   Are there disadvantages to using SARs?

Yes. The primary disadvantage of an SAR plan is its negative accounting consequence, which is that the company must take a charge to earnings during each quarter/year in which the SAR is outstanding. Thus the SAR is a costly form of long-term income. In reality the SAR provides the same net benefit to the executive as a stock option plan; however, with a stock option, the appreciation is "free" to the company (the company does not have to take a charge to earnings) and the executive also receives the money once the stock is sold. With the SAR, the company must pay the appreciation itself.

SARs do not normally fill company goals of encouraging stock ownership for executives. Most surveys will indicate executives exercise SARs for cash approximately 90 percent of the time, meaning that only 10 percent of the SARs result in stock ownership. Also, because they do not encourage stock ownership, SARs do not provide voting rights, dividends, or other rights associated with stock ownership.

A final disadvantage is that SARs have an "uncapped liability." If the company stock price continues to increase, then the accounting accrual for the appreciated value in the SAR will grow each year. In large companies this can amount to millions of dollars of expense that the company has accrued on both its income statement and balance sheet.

Q 7:12   For what type of company does an SAR make sense?

With the current SEC Section 16 rules, which give insiders much greater flexibility in the exercise of stock options and associated SARs, there is virtually little reason for a company to use an SAR plan unless there is a significant need to deliver cash to executives so that they can (or are required to) use it to purchase company stock. This would typically apply only to a young company whose executives have low tenure with the organization and have not had an opportunity to build capital accumulation and or a stock ownership position.

Book Value Appreciation Rights

Q 7:13   What is a book value appreciation right?

A book value appreciation right is the right to receive the value of the appreciation in a specified number of book value shares. Book value is defined as equity divided by company shares outstanding. For example, if company equity is $10 million and the number of shares outstanding is two million, then the book value is $5 per share. Book value share appreciation rights are normally "stand-alone" rights granted to an executive and are not normally granted in tandem or parallel to stock options. They are particularly useful for private companies without publicly traded shares of stock. Some public companies also use book value appreciation units along with another form of stand-alone long-term incentive (such as a performance plan).

> **Example.** Executive A works for a private company. She is granted 1,000 book value appreciation rights at a time when the book value per share in the company is $5. The vesting period for these rights is one year, and the award period is five years. At the completion of the five-year period, the company's book value is $12 per share. A can then exercise her right to the book value appreciation shares, and in this case would receive $7,000 ($12 – $5 = $7 book value appreciation × 1,000 shares).

Few companies use book value appreciation rights. Surveys indicate that less than 5 percent of public companies and less than 10 percent of private companies use this form of long-term incentive.

Q 7:14 What is the accounting impact of a book value appreciation right?

A book value appreciation right is also considered to be a "variable plan award" in accounting terminology, meaning that this plan is governed by FAS 28. A company must measure the appreciation in book value shares during each period for which it issues an income statement, and the amount by which the shares have increased must be accrued to the income statement. Changes in the book value of the shares between the date of grant and the exercise date of the book value right will continue to accrue on the company's income statement during the entire award period.

In summary, a book value appreciation right has the same accounting treatment as an SAR. Therefore the compensation expense of the book value appreciation right will fluctuate along with the company's book value per share.

Q 7:15 What is the tax treatment of a book value appreciation right?

There is no taxation upon the granting of a book value appreciation, because the executive is not in constructive receipt of any value at that time. Upon exercise of a book value share appreciation right, the executive would recognize ordinary income equal to the total amount of book value appreciation received (book value at exercise minus book value at grant). The book value appreciation share therefore has the same tax treatment as the SAR.

Again, payment of the book value appreciation share is a compensation deduction for the company in its calculation of taxable income. Any book value appreciation share payment to an executive is subject to federal and state withholding.

Q 7:16 What are the advantages of book value appreciation rights?

To the executive in a company that has significant potential for growth in net worth/equity, the book value appreciation right provides a cashless way to receive income as the book value share appreciates in value. Like the SAR, this form of long-term incentive offers the executive the opportunity for substantial capital accumulation without the need to raise money to purchase any book value shares.

Book value appreciation rights can be advantageous to executives in private companies in that they provide long-term income opportunities without diluting the private company stock holdings of current owners.

Q 7:17   Are there disadvantages to book value appreciation rights?

Yes. As with the SAR, the book value appreciation right is a costly form of long-term incentive in that it requires a charge to the income statement and can be an "uncapped liability" to the company. The book value right does not represent a true ownership position in private companies that do not have any publicly traded shares because book value shares do not carry voting rights and similar rights associated with stock ownership.

Full-Value Plans

Q 7:18   What are full-value plans?

Full-value plans are capital accumulation plans that grant the executive the full value of a company's stock over a long term (three to five years). Full-value plans can provide executives with the full value of a company share and/or the appreciation from a full-value company share. It is significant to note that full-value plans do not require the executive to make an investment.

There are three primary forms of full-value plans: phantom shares, restricted shares, and performance plans.

Q 7:19   Why would a company choose to implement a full-value plan rather than a purchase plan?

It is important for companies to consider full-value and purchase plans in full recognition of their current business needs. Both full-value and purchase plans can permit the executive to gain from the appreciation in the price of a company's stock; however, while a full-value plan gives the executive the value of the underlying stock, the purchase plan requires the executive actually to purchase the value of the underlying stock. The prospect of a full-value long-term incentive award would more strongly motivate an executive to remain with the company. For this reason many companies going through restructuring, with much uncertainty about the future, will choose full-value plans to retain their executives. In contrast, companies in significant growth periods may believe that an executive should make more of an investment in the organization. In such a case, purchase plans would typically be chosen over full-value plans. Increased media focus on the subject of executive compensation has further encouraged a company attitude that executives should make some amount of investment in the company with purchase plans, just as shareholders do.

Still other companies blend both perspectives and provide executives with stand-alone full-value grants in addition to stand-alone purchase plan grants. This practice of multiple long-term incentive grants (i.e., two different grants from two different plans) is occurring in well over 60 percent of all large publicly traded companies. As shown in Chart 5-1, in fact, many companies use three different types of long-term incentive plan grants.

Phantom Stock Plans

Q 7:20　What is a phantom stock plan?

A phantom stock plan is a plan in which executives are granted "pretend" (or "phantom") shares of stock rather than real shares. Phantom stock is a right to the increase in value of "phantom" (rather than real) shares of a corporation's common stock or book value stock, over a specified period of time. The bonus is typically an amount equal to the difference between the fair market value of the shares of common stock on the date of grant and the fair market value of the stock at the later specified date, although the difference can be measured using book value or some other performance measure. Phantom stock plans are similar to SAR plans, except that participants often have no choice with respect to the specified date of exercise in the typical phantom stock plan. The award when the phantom stock is converted may be paid out in either cash or stock.

Example. Executive C is an executive with Gable Corporation. On August 28, 1991, C is granted 1,000 shares of phantom stock that have a book value at the time of grant of $10 per share. The plan will vest in five years. During the five years, Gable Corporation declares an 8 percent dividend. The plan credits additional shares to C's account for the dividend payments as follows:

Year	Book Value	Beginning Year	Additions From Dividends	End of Year
1994	$10.00	$1,000.00	$ 80.00	$1,080.00
1995	10.60	1,080.00	86.40	1,166.40
1996	11.30	1,166.40	93.31	1,259.71
1997	12.00	1.259.71	100.77	1,360.48
1998	12.80	1,360.48	108.84	1,469.32
1999	13.60	1,469.32	117.55	1,586.87

On August 29, 1999, C is credited with 1,586.87 shares. The appreciation value from the initial date of grant is $3.60, and C receives $5,712.73. Gable Corporation is entitled to a deduction of $5,712.73, which represents that amount that C reports as taxable income.

A phantom stock plan, like an SAR plan, is subject to 1934 Act Section 16(a) reporting and Section 16(b) liability (see Qs 2:17–2:19), and should therefore fully comply with the Rule 16b-3 provisions so that grants under the plan will be exempt transactions. Even if rewards are payable only in cash, the phantom stock will, however, be deemed to be a derivative security and treated like an option for purposes of the Section 16 rules, if its value is "derived from the value of an equity security." If the value of the phantom stock is determined from a formula based on earnings per share and return on equity, it will be a derivative security because it derives its value from the components of an equity security.

From the company's perspective, the use of phantom stock achieves the goals of increasing the executive's economic interest in the company and permitting him to participate in its growth, and yet permits the existing shareholders to retain all voting and liquidation rights associated with their ownership of shares. From the executive's perspective, he or she can acquire these interests without laying out funds or being subject to an immediate tax.

Phantom stock plans are sometimes utilized as a mechanism for a deferred compensation arrangement. Under this scenario, the executive elects to have his or her deferred compensation expressed in phantom shares of a company's stock. This sort of phantom stock plan is discussed more in depth in Chapter 9.

Q 7:21   Are dividends paid on phantom stock?

Dividends may, but need not, be paid on phantom stock. Some companies choose to pay dividends based on the philosophy that they have provided the executive with an interest that mirrors the interest of a shareholder. Other companies focus on the increased compensation expense that they must recognize for financial accounting purposes and choose not to pay or accrue phantom dividends.

Dividends may either be accrued or actually paid on phantom stock. If dividends are to be paid out, they result in income to the executive without deduction to the corporation. If dividends are accrued, they may be either allocated to the executive and eventually paid out when the phantom stock is paid out, or they may be converted into phantom stock themselves. This latter method results in a compounding of the benefit, and provides a far greater benefit from holding phantom stock than actual shares of stock.

Q 7:22   How prevalent are phantom stock plans?

Phantom stock plans are not used frequently by publicly held corporations: Fewer than 5 percent of public companies utilize this capital accumulation method for rewarding their executives. Private companies use this method much more frequently, although it is impossible to gather any statistics because of the unavailability of public information.

Q 7:23   What is the accounting impact of a phantom stock plan?

Appreciation in the value of the units and any dividends paid or credited during the period are reported as a compensation expense to the company. A public company will accrue the expense and charge it against earnings on a quarterly basis.

Because no stock is typically issued, the only impact on earnings per share in any period is the amount of compensation expense recognized by the company for financial reporting purposes.

Q 7:24   What is the tax treatment of a phantom stock plan?

The executive has no income, and the corporation receives no tax deduction upon the grant of phantom stock units.

As long as the executive does not have the right to any distribution from his phantom stock, other than dividends payable on the stock, the executive will not be taxed on his or her phantom stock until the units are converted to actual cash or stock. Whether he or she receives cash or stock, the executive will be taxed at ordinary income rates. The company is entitled to a deduction for the amount it pays to the executive, including the value of the stock distributed, as and when the executive realizes income, even if that amount includes phantom dividends accrued on the phantom stock.

If the executive is entitled to draw upon his phantom stock units, he or she will be deemed to be in constructive receipt of the units and taxed immediately on their value; therefore, the company should make sure that the units are not set apart for him or her or otherwise made available so that he or she may draw upon them.

If the executive receives stock as a result of the conversion, the appreciation in those shares will be taxed as a capital gain at the time he or she sells the shares, if held for one year.

Q 7:25   What are the advantages of a phantom stock plan?

A phantom stock plan allows the executive to participate in the growth of the value of the company without actually making him or her a shareholder and diluting the value of issued stock.

The executive receives the same value as with a grant of stock, and yet is not required to make an investment, so that he or she is not at risk if the company's performance falters. Furthermore, he or she is able to defer being taxed on the benefit, which he or she could not avoid with a grant of stock. From the company's perspective, unless the granted stock is restricted, phantom stock may have more of a "retaining" incentive as the executive receives no benefit unless he or she continues with the company.

Q 7:26   Are there disadvantages to a phantom stock plan?

Yes. The principal disadvantage is that the costs are fully charge-able for financial accounting purposes as expenses as and when accrued. For smaller companies, or companies in cyclical businesses, this may be especially troubling.

Phantom stock that is converted into cash can be a severe drain on the company's cash, and many companies may not have sufficient cash flow to meet this potentially large expense. Therefore many companies prefer to convert phantom shares into real shares of stock.

Q 7:27   When do phantom stock units typically vest?

The typical vesting period for phantom stock units is five years.

Q 7:28   For what type of company does a phantom stock plan make sense?

In a privately held corporation, there is more of an incentive to use phantom stock rather than a true stock-based compensation technique in order to avoid dilution to current shareholders, as well as more of a reason to pay out phantom stock conversions in cash rather than in stock (although this may not apply to a cash-poor privately held company). Privately held companies will prefer to use phantom stock plans based on the book value of the stock, which will generally be much more easily ascertainable than the market value for the same stock.

Q 7:29 What is a shadow stock plan?

A shadow stock plan is another name for a phantom stock plan.

Restricted Stock Grants

Q 7:30 What is a restricted stock grant?

Under a restricted stock grant (RSG), an executive is granted shares of stock that are subject to forfeiture unless certain conditions are met. The shares become available to the executive as the restrictions lapse, usually on the completion of a period of employment or based on the performance of the company. The executive receives dividends and has full voting rights on his or her shares of restricted stock.

> **Example.** On January 1, 1995, Executive A, an executive at Gable Corporation, receives at no cost an award of 1,000 restricted shares of Gable Corporation. The restrictions will lapse on January 1, 1999, as long as A is an employee of Gable Corporation at that time. If she leaves the company prior to that time, the shares revert back to Gable Corporation. At the time of the award, the shares are worth $10 each and the $10,000 total cost must be amortized as a compensation expense over the five-year period. On January 1, 1999, A is still employed by Gable Corporation and the restrictions lapse. At this time the shares are worth $18 each. Assuming that she had not made a Code Section 83(b) election, A would recognize $18,000 as income on January 1, 1999, and Gable Corporation will be entitled to the corresponding $18,000 tax deduction, even though this amount differs from the $10,000 compensation expense it had accrued on its books.

Q 7:31 How prevalent are restricted stock grants?

The volatility of the stock market makes restricted stock a popular capital accumulation device because the executive receives value even if the stock price falls—without having to make any personal investment under this type of plan. As a result, approximately half of the large publicly traded companies utilize RSGs.

Privately held companies that offer RSGs usually attach two conditions to the grant. The first condition is that the executive receives the stock after all restrictions lapse, and the second condition mandates that the company has the right of first refusal if and when the executive wants to dispose of the stock.

Q 7:32   What is the accounting impact of a restricted stock grant?

Accounting regulations FAS 123 and APB 25 apply to an RSG. A company must select one of these regulations to calculate the earnings charge. Under APB 25, the compensation value at the time of grant is accrued as an expense to the company. This expense is determined by measuring the value of the shares at the time of grant (number of shares multiplied by stock price), minus the amount to be paid by the executive (typically zero on most RSGs).

If a service requirement is the "restriction" or condition for vesting of the restricted stock, then the compensation value is accrued over the applicable service or restriction period; however, if the stock is forfeited, the compensation expense recorded in previous financial reporting periods can be reversed to reflect the amount of the forfeiture. Under accounting regulations, the appreciation in the value of the restricted shares from the date of grant to the date of vesting is not recognized as a compensation expense for accounting purposes even though the full value of the shares at vesting is a tax deduction to the company. The reason for the tax deduction to the company is that the tax regulations allow a company an expense deduction for compensation and the release of restrictions on an RSG represents taxable compensation to the executive.

On a company's earnings per share calculations, the earnings and the number of outstanding shares of the company's stock are diluted because, under an RSG, shares have been issued and earnings have been charged with an expense.

Q 7:33   What is the tax treatment of a restricted stock grant?

The value of restricted stock granted to the executive will be taxable to the executive and deductible by the company in the year in which it is no longer subject to a substantial risk of forfeiture (i.e., when the restrictions lapse).

As long as no Code Section 83(b) election has been filed, dividends paid on restricted stock prior to the time the executive's rights become substantially vested can be deducted by the company as a compensation expense.

Q 7:34   How does a Code Section 83(b) election affect a restricted stock grant?

If an executive makes a Code Section 83(b) election on a grant or restricted stock, he or she will be taxed immediately on the fair market value of the restricted stock at the time of grant. Dividends paid on the shares will be normal dividend income to the executive, which is not subject to withholding and not deductible by the company. In the event that the executive elects Section 83(b) treatment and later forfeits the subject stock, he or she will not be entitled to any refund for the taxes paid; however, he or she will be entitled to treat the forfeiture as a sale of the stock at a loss (i.e., capital loss).

Q 7:35   What is the typical vesting period for a restricted stock grant?

Restrictions on RSGs generally lapse in three to five years. Restrictions may lapse all at once at the end of the vesting period or in annual installments during the vesting period.

Q 7:36   What are the advantages of a restricted stock grant?

An RSG program is attractive from the company's perspective, fulfilling the goals of turning management into stockholders, yet retaining them through the restrictions on transferability. Most companies believe that restricted stock is a strong motivation and retention mechanism for executives.

Q 7:37   Are there disadvantages to a restricted stock grant?

Yes. Restricted stock is often criticized as a "freebie" for management because most companies condition the vesting of the stock only on service and do not impose any additional performance requirements. The executive is rewarded even when there is no improvement in a company's performance. This is not the type of situation where a reward seems appropriate. Existing share value is diluted as a result of the grant of stock for which no purchase price—or only a nominal one—has been paid.

Q 7:38   For what types of companies do restricted stock grants make sense?

Restricted stock may be most useful and defensible as grants to high-potential middle managers and professional employees in order to recognize those individuals with unique skills and contributions who are not normally eligible to receive stock options. Furthermore, a company with difficulty recruiting or retaining key contributors can use RSGs as a recruitment bonus. Finally, RSGs are especially attractive to private companies as the transfer restrictions ensure that outsiders will not be able to acquire shares of the company's stock.

Performance Unit Plans

Q 7:39   What is a performance unit plan?

A performance unit plan (PUP) grants the executive performance units, which can be earned based on the attainment of company performance targets over a specified period, generally three to five years. The plan will set goals for the company and establish a fixed value for the units. The reward for the executive is equal to the number of units earned multiplied by the fixed value of the performance unit. The reward may be paid in cash or stock or a combination of both.

Q 7:40   How are performance measures established for a performance unit plan?

The company must determine the goals to be used for a PUP, generally an earnings per share (EPS) goal, return on capital, return on equity, or some combination of these financial measures. The company must also decide what compensation amount should be provided if goals are met, exceeded, or not met. The performance measure is generally determined based on the performance of a group rather than of an individual, and the members of the group share in the reward relative to their contributions. Many companies will establish a percentage midpoint as the target award for a performance unit grant.

> **Example.** Company A decides that it will allocate 100 performance units to an executive. It establishes a value of $50 for the performance units. Company A will pay out 100 of the performance units if EPS growth averages 10 percent over a three-year period. Company A will pay 75 units if EPS growth is 8 percent over the award period, and it will pay 125 units if EPS growth is 12 percent over the award period.
>
> Assuming that the 10 percent EPS growth is reached, the executive will receive 100 performance units at a value of $5,000 (100 units × $50 per unit).

Q 7:41   What is the accounting impact of a performance unit plan?

For financial accounting purposes, PUPs are treated as "variable plan awards" and thus are subject to the same accounting treatment as the SARs. Therefore, the company will have to accrue the estimated compensation expense proportionately over the award period.

Q 7:42   What is the tax treatment of a performance unit plan?

The executive recognizes no taxable income at the time of grant of the performance units. Once performance units are earned, the executive has a taxable event at the ordinary income tax rates, and the company will receive a tax deduction equal to the value received by the executive.

Q 7:43   What is the typical award period for a performance unit plan?

A typical PUP award period will be equal to the period covered by the company's strategic plan, which is generally three to five years.

Q 7:44   What are the advantages of a performance unit plan?

The principal advantage of a PUP is that it provides an opportunity for long-term capital accumulation to the executive based on company performance on which the executive can have a direct effect, rather than on stock market performance, which the executive cannot directly influence. Performance unit grants are often provided in addition to stock options or other market-based forms of long-term income so that the executive is rewarded for both stock performance and the achievement of key company long-term business goals.

Q 7:45   Are there disadvantages to instituting a performance unit plan?

Yes. The primary disadvantage of PUPs is the difficulty of accurately establishing performance goals for a period of three years or more. Also, because these plans typically pay in cash, a substantial charge to earnings occurs when goals are achieved. This represents a negative accounting consequence, and this charge to earnings occurs throughout the entire award period.

Performance Share Plans

Q 7:46   What is a performance share plan?

A performance share plan operates similarly to a PUP, except that the value of each performance share is tied to the value of a company's share of stock. A performance share plan therefore provides a dual incentive to the executive to achieve the earnings goal established under the plan and to further influence company stock price, because the higher the stock price the higher the value of the shares earned at the end of the award period.

> **Example.** Company B decides to provide 100 performance shares to an executive. Company B will pay out the 100 shares if company EPS growth is 10 percent over the next three years. It will pay out 75 shares if company EPS growth is 8 percent, and it will pay 125 shares if company EPS growth is 12 percent over the period. Assume that the stock price at the time of grant is $50 per share. At the end of the award period, if the company achieved its target EPS growth of 10 percent, then the executive would receive 100 performance shares. If the stock price at the end of the award period is $70, then the value received by the executive is $7,000 (100 shares × $70 per share). The compensation expense to the company's income statement will also be $7,000, accrued over the three-year award period. The executive will be taxed on ordinary income tax rates based on the $7,000 of income, and the company will receive a $7,000 tax deduction.

Q 7:47   What is the tax treatment of a performance share grant?

The executive recognizes no income at the time of grant of the performance shares. Once a performance share is earned, the executive has a taxable event at the ordinary income tax rates, and the company will receive a tax deduction equal to the value received by the executive in the year payment is received.

Q 7:48   What is the accounting treatment of a performance share?

Companies can elect to use either FAS 28 or FAS 123.

Under FAS 28, any company that grants a performance share must accrue the anticipated compensation during the award period on its earnings statement. This accrual is calculated by measuring the amount by which the company's current stock price exceeds the SAR grant price, multiplied by the number of shares that would be earned at 100 percent payout of the performance share, multiplied by a prorated number of years of the award period. Companies can assume a payout that is greater or less than 100 percent if this represents the most likely payout level. Changes in both the payout level and the market value of performance shares between the date of grant and the date of exercise can thus create significant costs.

Under FAS 123, a company must calculate the "fair value" of the performance share at the time of grant and charge its earnings statement with this amount over the award period. Fair value calculations are discussed in Q 1:49.

Chapter 8

Combination Long-Term Plans

Tandem plans utilize more than one type of long-term incentive plan. Usually, tandem plans provide executives with a choice between two types of options or awards. Once the executive chooses one alternative, the other is canceled. Two of the most common tandem plan combinations are the phantom stock/stock option plan and the restricted stock/stock option plan. A third variation of the tandem plan is the contingent stock award plan, which requires the executive to purchase and hold one option before obtaining access to a second option or other award. This chapter covers the requirements for implementing tandem plans as well as suggestions on maximizing their effectiveness.

General Considerations 8-1
Performance Share/Stock Option Plans 8-3
Restricted Stock/Stock Option Plans 8-7
SAR/Stock Option Plans 8-11

General Considerations

Q 8:1   What is a tandem plan?

A tandem plan grants an executive a choice between two types of capital accumulation plans. By choosing or exercising one alternative the other is canceled. For example, an executive can be granted 1,000 stock option shares and 1,000 stock appreciation rights (SARs) attached to each of the nonqualified stock options. If the executive exercises 250 of the SARs, then the executive has 750 remaining of either nonqualified stock options or SARs.

Q 8:2 What is a parallel plan?

A parallel plan grants the executive two types of capital accumulation plans that are mutually exclusive and stand-alone. The choice or exercise of one alternative has no effect on the other type of grant. For example, an executive could be granted 1,000 stock option shares and 1,000 SARs under a parallel plan. If the executive exercises 500 SARs, then the executive still has 500 SARs and 1,000 nonqualified stock options remaining.

Q 8:3 Are there advantages to creating tandem or parallel combination plans?

Yes. For example, combining a nonqualified stock option with an SAR results in a long-term incentive plan that does not require an executive to invest funds, and at the same time provides the executive with an opportunity to use cash from the SAR to purchase a nonqualified stock option.

Other combination plans can provide the executive with opportunities for stock appreciation and capital accumulation from a performance-based plan that is not subject to the vagaries of the stock market. From the company's point of view, combination plans offer the opportunity for a dual incentive, that is, incentive for the executive to increase stock price and achieve long-term company performance goals.

Q 8:4 Are there disadvantages to tandem and parallel combination plans?

Yes. The primary credo of the tandem and parallel plans is that they provide downside protection to the executive, which is a protection that the average shareholder does not receive. For example, if an executive is provided with 1,000 nonqualified stock option shares and 1,000 long-term performance shares, the executive could earn the performance share grants based on achieving long-term performance goals even if, at the same time, the stock price is flat. On the other hand, the executive could exercise the stock option grants if the stock price went up even if the long-term performance goals in the performance share plan were not met. Thus the executive is protected in a way that other investors are not. From the investors' perspective, this represents an "unlevel playing field": The executive can win when the investor loses.

Q 8:5   What compensation combinations are the most common in combination long-term plans?

Three combinations are used most frequently:

1. Stock options and performance plans (performance shares or performance units);

2. Restricted stock and stock options; and

3. SARs and stock options.

Performance Share/Stock Option Plans

Q 8:6   What are combination stock option and performance plans?

These plans grant the executive stock options and either a performance share plan or performance unit plan (see Qs 7:46 and 7:39, respectively). The stock option plan would normally have a vesting period equal to the performance award period in the performance plan (e.g., four years). Under a tandem plan, upon conclusion of the vesting and performance award period, the executive would choose one award or the other. Under a parallel plan, the executive would then have the right to purchase the stock options and would receive the performance plan award if earned. Under either tandem or parallel arrangements, the stock option plan would typically have an award period of ten years, meaning that after completion of vesting (e.g., during the fourth year), the executive would have an additional period of time (e.g., six years) to exercise the stock option.

> **Example 1: Tandem Plan.** An executive is granted 1,000 perform-ance shares and 1,000 stock option shares. The performance shares have a four-year award period, during which time specific earnings per share growth is to be achieved. The stock option award has a four-year vesting period and following the 100 percent vesting after four years the executive may exercise the right to purchase the option any time up to ten years from the date of grant.
>
> If, at the end of the four years, the executive elects to take the performance shares (if earned), then the stock options are can-celed. If at the end of the four years the executive has not earned the performance shares or elects the stock option for other reasons, the performance shares are canceled.
>
> **Example 2: Parallel Plan.** An executive is provided with 1,000 performance shares to be earned over a four-year period if specific earnings per share goals are achieved. The executive is also provided with a 1,000 share stock option award, with four-year vesting and a ten-year award period. These grants are mutually exclusive: The exercise of any number of stock options has no effect on the performance shares, and any performance shares earned have no effect on the stock options.

Q 8:7   What is the accounting impact of combination performance share and stock option plans?

The accounting treatment is different for performance shares and stock options, which should affect plan consideration. Under a par-allel plan, the grants stand alone and the stock options and perform-ance shares each receive their regular accounting treatment. For a stock option, the company must select the use of either FAS 123 or APB 25. (See Q 1:45.)

Under a tandem plan, the accounting treatment of the perform-ance share would prevail. A performance share plan is a "variable plan award" and the company would have to elect the use of account-ing regulation FAS 28 or FAS 123.

Under FAS 28, a company is required to accrue the estimated compensation expense proportionately over the performance share award period, with adjustments made for any increases or decreases in the market value per share of stock. At the time the executive earns the performance shares a final accounting for expenses would occur, and the total amount earned by the executive would equal the total amount accrued by the company as an expense. If the executive chose the stock option in lieu of the performance share, at the end of the vesting period, then no additional compensation expense would be accrued for the remaining period of the stock option award. Liabilities accrued for the performance share during its award period would be reversed from the liability portion of the balance sheet once the stock option was elected.

Under FAS 123, the company is required to calculate a "fair value" of the performance share at the time of grant and accrue this cost over the award period. The fair value calculation is discussed in Q 1:49.

Example: Tandem Performance Share and Stock Option Grant. A company provides an executive with a combination grant of 1,000 performance shares at $20 per share and 1,000 nonqualified stock option shares, also at $20 per share, the current fair market value. The performance shares have an earnings per share growth objective of 20 percent over four years. The nonqualified stock options vest at 25 percent per year or 100 percent after four years. These grants are tandem, meaning that the executive must choose one or the other after the four-year period.

The accounting treatment for the nonqualified stock option would be to use either FAS 123 or APB 25; however, because this is a tandem grant, the accounting treatment of the performance shares would prevail, because the executive is most likely to choose them. Therefore, for each of the four years, the company would calculate its earnings charge by multiplying the number of vested shares in the performance share grant by any stock appreciation during the financial period being measured, minus any earnings charge to date. If in Year 1 the per-share appreciation was $5 and in Year 2 the per-share appreciation was $12, the accounting accrual on the company's income statement would be $1,250 in Year 1 and $4,750 in Year 2, calculated as follows:

Year 1: 1,000 shares $\times$ 25% (1 year $\div$ 4 years) = $250 $\times$ $5 = $1,250

Year 2: 1,000 shares $\times$ 50% (2 years $\div$ 4 years) = $500 \times $12
= \$6,000 – \$1,250 = \$4,750

Q 8:8 What is the tax treatment of combination performance share and stock option plans?

The executive recognizes no taxable event at the time of grant for either a tandem or parallel combination plan of performance shares and stock options. If, under either plan, a performance share plan is earned, the value of the performance share award is taxable income to the executive at ordinary income tax rates. The company receives a tax deduction equal to the amount of income received by the executive. If the executive should have elected to defer income from the performance share, then the taxable event and the company tax deduction would be deferred as well. On the other hand, if the stock option is exercised under either tandem or parallel grants, then the executive is taxed at ordinary income tax rates on the spread in value between the option price and the exercise price, if the stock option is nonqualified. The company is eligible for a tax deduction in the same amount as the spread. If an incentive stock option (ISO) is used, the tax may be deferred until sale, and if held for one year after exercise (two years after the grant), the executive would pay capital gains tax. The company would not be eligible for a tax deduction if the gain is subject to the capital gains tax.

Q 8:9 Are there advantages to a combination plan of performance shares and stock options?

Yes. The primary advantage is that such a combination allows the executive to make choices that are financially advantageous. A parallel plan offers greater flexibility to the executive: The executive determines when to exercise the stock option and influences company performance in achieving the earnings goal and subsequent payment of the performance share. Under a tandem plan, the executive has the opportunity to choose one plan or the other at the end of the award/vesting period.

From the company's point of view, these plans assist in retaining key executives and can provide a "dual incentive" for the executive to increase stock price as well as achieve company performance goals.

Q 8:10 Are there disadvantages to the combination performance share and stock option plan?

Yes. An accounting charge is required for the performance share, which can be costly for the company. Under the tandem plan, this may be reversed at the end of the award period if the executive chooses the stock option; however, during the award period earnings have been reduced because of the accruals required for the performance share.

Executives must utilize their own cash to exercise stock options. Under a tandem plan, it is unlikely that the executive would elect the stock option if a performance share has been earned. Under a parallel plan, the executive can utilize cash earned from a performance share award to purchase the stock option.

These types of plans can be criticized by the media and by shareholders for giving the executive downside protection (i.e., potential earnings from the performance share even if the stock price remains constant), which shareholders do not have.

Q 8:11 For what type of company does a combination performance share and stock option plan make sense?

A parallel grant of these forms of long-term incentive makes great sense to both the company and the executive in that the performance plan can generate cash to purchase the stock options. Any company wishing to build executive stock ownership can require its executives to use the cash earned from a performance share plan to purchase stock under a stock option plan.

Restricted Stock/Stock Option Plans

Q 8:12 What is a tandem restricted stock/stock option plan?

A tandem restricted stock/stock option plan grants both restricted stock awards and nonqualified stock options. Under this type of plan, the participant is allowed to choose whether to keep the restricted stock or to exercise the options, which cancels the restricted stock award. Furthermore, vesting of the restricted stock would also cancel the related stock option.

Example. Gable Corporation provides its directors with an annual retainer fee of $36,000. One half of the fee, or $18,000, is paid in cash and the remaining $18,000 is paid-in to a tandem restricted stock/stock option plan at a ratio of three restricted stock to one stock option. One director receives 720 shares of restricted stock ($18,000/$25, the current market value) and 2,160 nonqualified stock options with an exercise price of $25. She receives annual dividends on the restricted stock until the restrictions lapse in five years, at which point she will receive the stock and the corresponding nonqualified options will be canceled. In the alternative, the director can exercise her options at any time before the restrictions lapse and forfeit the restricted stock.

The following table shows how much the stock price moves, thereby determining whether the restricted stock or nonqualified stock option is a more advantageous alternative.

Stock Price Appreciation (in %)	Value of One Restricted Share	Gain on Three Option Shares Above the Exercise Price	Excess Value of Options
0	$25.00	0.00	$(25)
20	30.00	15.00	(15)
30	32.50	22.50	(10)
40	35.00	30.00	(5)
50	37.50	37.50	0
60	40.00	45.00	5
70	42.50	52.50	10
80	45.00	60.00	15

Assuming a three-to-one ratio, the crossover point is at a 50 percent stock appreciation level. Above this point, the director should exercise her options, which cancel the restricted stock ownership.

Q 8:13 Can a parallel grant be made of restricted shares and stock option shares?

Yes. As a parallel grant, each form of long-term incentive stands on its own, and a company must follow all applicable tax and accounting regulations for each.

Example. A company grants an executive 1,000 restricted shares when the stock price is $20 per share, and provides the same executive with 3,000 stock option shares at $20 per share, the current fair market value. The restricted shares have a four-year restriction period, and the stock option shares vest at 25 percent per year. With respect to the restricted stock, the company would be required to take a charge to earnings equal to $5,000 per year for four years (1,000 shares × $20 per share divided by four years). The stock options would have no charge to earnings because they were granted at the current market value.

Q 8:14   What is the accounting impact of a combination restricted stock/stock option plan?

The accounting treatment is the same for restricted shares and stock options, so it is not a plan design consideration. Under a parallel plan, the grants stand alone and the stock options and restricted shares each receive their regular accounting treatment. For a stock option, the company must select the use of either FAS 123 or APB 25. (See Q 1:45.)

Under a tandem plan, the accounting treatment of the most likely event would prevail. Because the executive is more likely to choose restricted stock, the company would elect to use accounting regulation APB 25 or FAS 123.

APB 25 requires the company to determine the earnings charge at the time of grant. This calculation is done by multiplying the number of shares by the price per share and then accruing this amount over the restriction period.

FAS 123 would require the company to determine the "fair value" of the restricted shares and charge its earnings over the restriction period.

Q 8:15   What is the tax treatment of a combination restricted stock/stock option plan?

The tax treatment at the time of grant is similar for both forms of long-term incentive. The executive would not recognize income on either the restricted shares or the stock options at that time. If the nonqualified stock option is exercised, a taxable event would occur to the executive, and the executive would have to pay ordinary income tax on the spread between the option price and the exercise price. If the restricted stock award is exercised, the executive would also be required to pay ordinary income tax on the total value of the restricted shares at the time the restriction has lapsed. The company would also receive a tax deduction equal to the taxable income incurred by the executive. Once the executive takes possession of shares, future taxation would be at the capital gains tax rate. If held for one year, the shares would be eligible for capital gains tax once sold.

> **Example.** An executive takes possession of 1,000 restricted shares when the price per share is $40. The executive has $40,000 taxable income at ordinary income tax rates. The company has a $40,000 tax deduction in the same year.
>
> If the executive's tax rate was 30 percent, then the ordinary income tax would be $12,000 ($40,000 × 30%). In this case, the executive could sell 300 shares to fulfill the tax obligation (300 shares × $40 = $12,000). The remaining 700 shares would be subject to capital gains tax and if held for one year or more would be subject to a maximum tax rate of 28 percent on any additional appreciation beyond the current value of $40 per share. If sold before one year, any share appreciation beyond $40 would be subject to the executive's current ordinary income tax rate (in this case 30 percent).

Q 8:16 What are the advantages of a combination restricted stock/stock option plan?

The primary advantage of this type of plan is that it gives executives an immediate ownership position through the restricted stock so that the participant can vote and receive dividends, but can also take advantage of appreciation in the company stock.

Q 8:17 What are the disadvantages of the combination restricted stock/stock option plan?

This type of plan is criticized because the restricted stock component is not available to the average company shareholder. At a minimum, if it has a typical time lapse restriction, this component rewards the executive for tenure, regardless of stock market performance. The executive would not be likely to invest in the stock option component if the stock price appreciates, because the restricted shares receive the share appreciation without any investment by the executive.

Q 8:18 For what type of company does a restricted stock/stock option plan make sense?

A company that wants to give immediate ownership to the executive while encouraging the executive to make an investment should consider a restricted stock/stock option plan. Also, a company that expects and/or wants to motivate executives to work toward significant growth in its stock price would want to consider this type of combination plan.

SAR/Stock Option Plans

Q 8:19 What is a tandem SAR/stock option plan?

This type of tandem plan grants the executive SARs that are attached to nonqualified stock options. Most companies grant one SAR for each stock option granted. The exercise of one SAR cancels out one stock option. The real value of this type of tandem plan is the opportunity it offers the executive to exercise SARs to raise the cash necessary to then exercise/purchase stock options and pay the required income tax. With this plan, even insiders are allowed to pay the option exercise price by using the increase in the value of the company shares, which decreases the amount of personnel investment required.

Under Section 16 of the 1934 Act, the SAR for insiders is subject to the requirement of Section 16(b), which requires insiders to avoid any combination of purchase or sale for a six-month period.

Some companies set the option price of the tandem SAR higher than the exercise price of the stock option to encourage the executive to exercise the option rather than the SAR.

Example 1. Executive A is an executive of Altoona Corporation and participates in their long-term incentive plan. On January 15, 1994, he receives 1,000 SARs with a $10 base price, attached to 1,000 nonqualified stock options with a $10 option price. The current market value of the stock is $10. Five years later in January 1999, the current market value of Altoona stock has risen to $30. If A takes all of the SARs, he will receive $20,000 ($20 in stock appreciation × 1,000 SARs). If he were to exercise all of his stock options he would also receive $20,000 ($20 in appreciation × 1,000 shares).

Example 2. Executive B is an executive of Altoona Corporation and also participates in their long-term incentive plan. On January 15, 1994 she receives 1,000 SARs with a $10 base price attached to 1,000 nonqualified stock options with a $10 option price. The current market value of the stock is $10. Five years later in January 1999, the current market value of Altoona stock has risen to $30. If B exercises 500 of the SARs, she would receive $10,000 ($20 in appreciation × 500 shares). She can then use the $10,000 in cash to exercise the remaining 500 nonqualified stock option shares which have an option price of $5,000 ($10 × 500 shares). B still has $5,000 remaining in cash to use for meeting her ordinary income tax obligations.

Q 8:20   What is a parallel SAR/stock option plan?

This type of plan grants the executive a fixed number of SARs and a separate number of nonqualified stock options. The exercise of one form of long-term incentive does not cancel any shares in the other because these are stand-alone grants.

Q 8:21   How prevalent are SAR/stock option plans?

These plans have historically appeared as tandem plans, with almost one third of the publicly traded companies using them during the 1980s. These plans have not been as popular in the 1990s because of the significant changes in the SEC Section 16 rules. Specifically, insiders have considerably more flexibility to exercise stock options and then immediately to sell the underlying securities without violating the short-swing liability rules of Section 16(b) of the 1934 Act. SEC regulations provide for the stock option grant to be a purchase event; therefore, once the insider exercises the shares, typically three to four years after grant, there is no requirement at that time for the insider to hold the shares. Companies are also not using these combination plans as frequently because, in practice, executives were exercising the SARs and letting the stock option rights expire. Thus company objectives of stock ownership were not being achieved. The plans were becoming long-term cash plans.

Q 8:22 What is the accounting impact of combination SAR/stock option plans?

The accounting requirements of the SAR will prevail with respect to tandem SAR/stock option plans, and there would be an accounting charge throughout the award period. A company can select either FAS 28 or FAS 123 treatment. If FAS 28 is selected, the earnings charge is equal to the number of vested shares of the SAR multiplied by the stock appreciation per share. If FAS 123 is selected, the earnings charge is determined at the time of grant and is equal to the "fair value" of the SAR, which is then accrued over the vesting period. For an explanation of fair value calculations, see Q 1:49.

With a parallel SAR/stock option plan, the same is true in that the SAR is subject to an accounting charge as just described. The stock option is subject to either FAS 123 or APB 25 treatment. (See Q 1:45.) The company must select one of these; however, if it has already selected FAS 123 for the SAR, it must also use it to calculate the earnings charge for the stock option.

Q 8:23 What is the tax treatment of combination SAR/stock option plans?

There is no tax impact to the company or to the executive at the time of the grant. When the executive receives income from either the SAR or the stock option, the executive will be taxed at ordinary income rates and the company will receive a tax deduction equal to the value or appreciation received by the executive.

If the SAR is payable in stock, then the executive would receive capital gains treatment on future appreciation after the exercise of the SAR. If the shares are held for at least one year, then the capital gains tax rate would apply. The same would be true upon the exercise and purchase of the nonqualified stock option.

Chapter 9

Executive Benefit Plans

Various tax rules serve to severely limit the tax-favored treatment of certain employer-provided retirement benefits and perquisites. In response, companies are implementing specialized executive programs to compensate for regulatory limitations and to respond to competitive recruiting pressures. Nonqualified retirement plans allow executive retirement benefits to be provided on a selective confidential basis up to virtually any level of compensation commensurate with the contributions of the executive to the company. The plan might be designed to resemble a defined benefit, defined contribution, or 401(k) type of benefit that incorporates executive pre-tax income deferrals and matching contributions at the employer's option. Split-dollar life insurance plans provide life insurance benefits, executive cash value accumulation, and postretirement paid-up insurance at little or no cost to the executive. The life insurance benefit is particularly attractive to senior executives seeking ways to protect wealth (generated by stock options or other equity incentives) from high estate tax rates. Group insurance disadvantages, such as inflated cost for life insurance coverage exceeding $50,000, lack of permanence, and non-portability are primary reasons that executive split-dollar plans are so widely accepted today. Executive disability insurance plans are being used to provide higher coverage levels than typical group long-term disability coverage limits, offering tax advantages to the company and the executive alike. Employers are thus able to provide benefit plans for top management that are competitive with peer companies. This chapter covers the ERISA and general tax issues of executive benefit plans, as well as plan design and competitive practices.

General Considerations 9-2
Qualified Retirement Plans 9-3
Nonqualified Retirement Plans 9-5
Tax Considerations 9-13
Funding Arrangements 9-21
Insurance-related Nonqualified Deferred Compensation Plans 9-24
Split-Dollar Life Insurance 9-27
Executive Disability Income Insurance 9-30
ERISA Considerations 9-32
Other Considerations 9-38

General Considerations

Q 9:1   Why are executive benefit plans so important?

Recruiting and retaining uniquely skilled executives is a vital component of corporate management. In today's business environment it is commonplace for competitors to seek valuable people with years of training and experience from peer companies. The seniority and abilities of a key executive represent an immeasurable investment of someone's time and money. It is no secret that meaningful retirement, death, and disability benefits, along with traditional compensation items, tied to continuous employment are crucial elements in attracting and retaining key executives. As a matter of fact, executives today expect and require these benefits as a condition of continued employment. If these benefits were not provided by the employer, the executive would need additional cash compensation to purchase them.

Q 9:2   How do traditional benefit programs fail executives?

Unfortunately, traditional benefit programs such as 401(k) and other qualified retirement plans, group life insurance, and group disability income protection have been restricted and severely limited by federal legislation. Numerous statistical studies indicate that executives typically need approximately 60 to 70 percent of final pay in order to maintain their standard of living after retirement. Without company benefits and tax-advantaged methods to accumulate funds, this goal is typically unattainable.

Q 9:3 How do these executive benefit programs fit into overall compensation?

Executive benefit programs are usually considered to be long-term incentives. Instead of cash, the company provides insurance, investment, or retirement benefits to relieve the executive of having to acquire the benefits personally with after-tax dollars. The flexibility and confidentiality of these plans present an excellent opportunity to replace benefit packages that would be lost by individuals that the company wishes to recruit.

Executive benefit plans are also a tool used by companies to retain recruited executives. Such plans are often designed so that the executive who terminates employment stands to lose all or part of the plan benefits.

Qualified Retirement Plans

Q 9:4 What makes a retirement plan *qualified*?

Qualified retirement plans are retirement plans that (1) are either a stock bonus plan, a pension plan, or a profit-sharing plan, and (2) meet the qualification requirements contained in Section 401(a) of the Internal Revenue Code (Code).

Q 9:5 Why is *qualification* of a retirement plan desirable?

The advantages in a retirement plan being *qualified* are the following:

1. Employees are not currently taxed when contributions are made; such taxation is postponed until distribution.
2. Employer contributions are currently deductible to the company.

3. Earnings and income are not currently taxed to the trust or the participants; taxation of the participant occurs when plan distributions are made.

4. Certain favorable tax treatment may be available to participants for plan distributions, such as the ability to rollover certain amounts to an IRA or another qualified plan and continue tax deferred treatment.

Q 9:6   Are there limits on contributions and benefits under a qualified retirement plan?

Yes. Code Section 401(a)(17) limits the amount of annual compensation that may be taken into account for a participant under a qualified retirement plan. Prior to the Omnibus Budget Reconciliation Act of 1993 (OBRA), such limit was $200,000, as adjusted for inflation. OBRA reduced this maximum limitation to $150,000, as adjusted for inflation (the limit for 1999 is $160,000).

Code Section 415 serves to limit *annual additions* to qualified retirement plans. *Annual additions* to a plan include employer contributions, employee contributions, and forfeitures (rollovers from another qualified plan are not counted as annual additions). For defined benefit plans, the plan's annual benefit provided to a participant at Social Security retirement age cannot exceed the lesser of (1) $90,000, as adjusted for inflation (for 1999, $130,000) or (2) 100 percent of the participant's average compensation for his or her highest consecutive three years. For defined contribution plans, annual contributions cannot exceed the lesser of (1) $30,000 or (2) 25 percent of the participant's compensation.

With respect to 401(k) plans, Code Section 402(g) limits the annual amount of elective pre-tax deferrals of a participant to $7,000, as adjusted for inflation (for 1999, the limit is $10,000).

Code Section 401(k) nondiscrimination rules provide that the average deferral percentage of the *highly compensated* employees (as defined under Section 414(q) of the Code to include, generally, any employee who was a five percent owner at any time during the year or the prior year, or, for the prior year, had compensation from the employer in excess of $80,000) as a group cannot exceed the average deferral percentage of the *nonhighly compensated employees* as a group by a pre-determined percentage amount. Similar nondiscrimination rules apply to employer matching contributions under Code Section 401(m). It should be noted that the Small Business Job Protection Act of 1996 (SBJPA) added new Sections 401(k)(12) and 401(m)(11) to the Code, effective for plan years beginning on or after January 1, 1999. These provisions provide a *safe harbor* design alternative for satisfying the nondiscrimination tests for 401(k) and 401(m) contributions. Essentially, in order to avoid the nondiscrimination tests, a plan must provide either a minimum matching contribution or a minimum nonelective contribution. Details regarding these safe-harbors and related notice and amendment requirements are described in IRS Notice 98-52.

Prior to 1997, Code Section 4980A imposed a 15 percent excise tax on any *excess distributions* from a qualified retirement plan. *Excess distributions* were defined as the aggregate amount of retirement plan distributions made to a participant during any calendar year to the extent that the amount distributed exceeded the greater of (1) $150,000 or (2) $112,500, as adjusted for inflation (for 1997, this adjusted amount was $160,000). The Taxpayer Relief Act of 1997 (TRA '97) repealed this 15 percent excise tax, effective with respect to excess distributions received after December 31, 1996.

All of these limitations produce a form of reverse discrimination because they cap a benefit or the accrual of a benefit for primarily highly compensated employees. Although companies will still want to maximize the use of qualified retirement plans, due to these limits, many companies have been spurred to develop alternative nonqualified deferred compensation plans that could be used to ensure that executives who were adversely affected by these provisions would be made whole.

Nonqualified Retirement Plans

Q 9:7 Can compensation and benefits be deferred outside of a qualified retirement plan?

Yes, through nonqualified deferred compensation arrangements. Such arrangements may be provided through group plans or in individual employment or other agreements and serve to delay receipt of income and its taxation until a later date.

Q 9:8   What are the primary approaches for deferring compensation?

One approach involves an agreement between the executive and the company for the executive to give up some portion of his current compensation in exchange for the company's promise to make a deferred payment sometime in the future. Typically the executive defers some portion of his annual compensation. To encourage the executive to make this deferral, many companies have offered a guaranteed investment return that is higher than the executive can hope to obtain on his own, in recent years it has become more common to offer investment options that mirror a company's 401(k) plan investments. In addition, a company may choose to match any compensation the executive elects to defer. Under this approach, the investment options and the match level also typically mirror the company's 401(k) plan.

Another approach is for the company to provide an additional benefit to the executive. This second approach does not involve any real income deferral on the part of the executive but does involve the company's promise to make additional payments to the executive at some time in the future.

Deferred compensation as used herein refers to either of these somewhat different approaches.

Q 9:9   What is a nonqualified deferred compensation plan?

A nonqualified deferred compensation plan is a plan that is not subject to most of ERISA and does not receive the same favorable tax treatment under the Code as does a qualified retirement plan. However, because these plans are not subject to the restrictive provisions of ERISA or the Code, they can be designed to cover selected executives. In general, these plans cannot be made available to the rank and file employees without subjecting the plan to stringent ERISA requirements regarding participation, vesting, funding, and fiduciary responsibility. The trade-off for this flexibility is that nonqualified benefit plans result in income recognition for the participant when the employee's right to the benefit is no longer subject to a substantial risk of forfeiture and the company does not receive a deduction until the time when the compensation is actually paid to the employee.

Q 9:10   How does a nonqualified deferred compensation plan differ from a qualified plan?

Nonqualified plans do not qualify for the special tax treatment afforded to plans that meet the qualification requirements contained in Code Section 401(a).

Q 9:11   What do nonqualified deferred compensation plans typically provide?

Because a nonqualified deferred compensation plan is usually tailored to one executive or a small group of executives, these plans vary greatly in what they provide. Typically, these plans provide for postretirement payments to the executive, postretirement and preretirement death benefits, and preretirement disability payments. Some of the plans provide for payments prior to retirement. Except in the case of Code Section 457 plans, there is no restriction on the amount to be deferred. And because a nonqualified plan is not attempting to satisfy Internal Revenue Service (IRS) regulations, the plan can be highly discriminatory as to who is covered and what benefits are provided.

Q 9:12   What is the rationale for creating nonqualified deferred compensation plans for executives?

A nonqualified deferred compensation plan can be used, among other things, to supplement an executive's retirement benefits, to make up for any reduction in retirement benefits under the company's qualified retirement plans, to aid an executive in deferring taxable income to a future date (when presumably tax rates will be reduced), to provide early retirement incentives, to replace lost benefits that an executive can suffer when switching from one employer to another, or to "handcuff" the executive by providing deferred compensation which can be forfeited if the executive leaves the company earlier than a specified time.

Q 9:13 What are the typical objectives of the executive in deferring income under a nonqualified deferred compensation plan?

The executive typically defers compensation to provide for future financial commitments and to lower current taxable income. Deferral of compensation is a method of systematic tax-deferred savings. This may make sense for a highly paid employee, who is at the highest marginal tax rate to defer income, particularly in today's business environment.

Q 9:14 What are the typical objectives of the company in providing a deferral program?

The primary reasons for providing deferred compensation plans to executives is the need for companies to attract and retain executives. Competition for executives forces companies to try to develop compensation plans that will be attractive to executives; as qualified plans become more and more restricted as to how much an executive can receive in benefits, executives are asking for plans that will supplement the companies' retirement plans. Companies also need these plans to attract the key executives they wish to hire away from other companies. These plans can be used to replace qualified plan benefits that a desired executive must give up if he leaves before vesting.

Q 9:15 Who can generally benefit under a nonqualified deferred compensation plan?

Typically, nonqualified deferred compensation plans are designed to benefit the following:

1. Key executives;

2. A select group of management or highly compensated employees; and

3. Employees whose qualified retirement plan benefits ordinarily would be limited under Code Section 415 (see Q 9:6).

A nonqualified deferred compensation plan may also be designed to benefit employees who do not satisfy the requirements for participating in a qualified plan or to reward employees for their services. However, the use of a nonqualified deferred compensation plan for a broad cross-section of employees could cause the plan to come under the requirements of certain pension plan provisions of ERISA.

Q 9:16   Are there different types of nonqualified deferred compensation plans?

Yes, there are several types of nonqualified deferred compensation plans. These include:

Supplemental executive retirement plan (SERP). A SERP is generally an unfunded plan maintained by an employer primarily to provide additional retirement benefits for a select group of management or highly compensated employees.

> **Example.** Company A needs to attract a number of new executives who will give up retirement benefits from their current employers in order to join Company A. Therefore, Company A offers a SERP that provides these executives with a minimum benefit from a combination of the company's defined pension benefit plan and the nonqualified deferred compensation plan of 60 percent of final average pay (as defined in the plan), if the executive stays employed with the company until age 62 or after.

Excess benefit plan. This is a plan maintained by an employer solely for the purpose of providing benefits for select employees in excess of the limitations on contributions and benefits imposed by Code Section 415 on qualified retirement plans, without regard to whether the plan is funded.

Because an excess benefit plan is not generally governed by a strict statutory or regulatory framework (although funded excess benefit plans must meet certain ERISA requirements), an excess benefit plan offers flexibility because it can be drafted to meet the specific needs of the employer.

The major limitations in establishing an unfunded excess benefit plan relate to the tenuous position of the participant. The participant holds the status of a general, unsecured creditor with regard to the excess benefit plan benefits; as a result, the participant may not have any comfort that he or she will ever receive any benefits under the plan, especially if the employer is not well-capitalized.

A second limitation relating to an unfunded excess benefit plan is that, unlike a qualified retirement plan, the employer who establishes such an excess benefit plan generally does not receive an income tax deduction for its contributions until the contributions are actually distributed or made available to the participants, which can often be years in the future.

A third major limitation on the use of an excess benefit plan is that an excess benefit plan is expressly limited to a plan maintained *solely* for providing benefits to the plan participants in excess of the limitations imposed by Code Section 415. The term *solely* has not been clearly defined. As a result, the employer must make certain that the sole purpose for establishing the excess benefit plan is to provide benefits in excess of the limitations contained in Code Section 415 to protect the status of the plan as an excess benefit plan. If the plan ceases to be considered an excess benefit plan, it may be considered a top-hat plan under ERISA.

Benefit restoration plan. This type of deferred compensation plan is sometimes referred to as a *benefit equalization plan* or *wrap plan*. It is designed to restore to the executive the benefits "lost" to him or her under the company's qualified retirement plans due to the restrictions on the amount of compensation that can be counted under Code Section 401(a)(17) and/or the deferrals and related matching contributions that were not allowed to be contributed to the company's 401(k) plan due to the Code Section 401(k) and (m) nondiscrimination rules.

IRS private letter ruling (PLR) 9530038 has approved the linking of a nonqualified deferred compensation plan to a qualified 401(k) plan provided that, in the year prior to the year that the compensation is earned (year 1), the executive elects to defer a fixed amount of his year 2 compensation. During year 2, the entire elected deferral amount is withheld on a pre-tax basis. Immediately after the commencement of year 3, a determination is made as to the portion of the pre-tax deferrals that can be contributed to the employer's qualified 401(k) plan (as a year 2 contribution) after consideration of the nondiscrimination rules. That portion is then credited to the 401(k) plan and the remaining portion of the deferral remains in the nonqualified deferred compensation plan. The PLR also specifies that at the time of the initial deferral election in year 1, the participant must acknowledge that he has a right to receive compensation in an amount equal to the actual 401(k) deferral permitted for year 2.

The IRS has addressed 401(k) wrap plans in other rulings, including PLRs 9807027 and 9807010. These rulings describe the need for the dual election in year 1 (i.e., an election to defer an amount of year 2 compensation and a second election to defer the maximum amount permitted under the 401(k) plan for year 2). Under these rulings, the maximum 401(k) deferral was determined in January of year 3 and the appropriate portion of the elected deferrals was transferred and credited to the 401(k) plan.

A plan for governmental or tax-exempt employers under Code Section 457. An *eligible* deferred compensation plan under Code Section 457 is an unfunded plan that provides for annual deferrals of the lesser of (1) $7,500, as adjusted for inflation (for 1999, $8,000) or (2) one-third of includible compensation (unless a special $15,000 catch-up provision applies). An *ineligible* deferred compensation plan under Code Section 457(f) is an unfunded deferred compensation plan that does not meet the requirements of an *eligible* Code Section 457 plan. Under an *ineligible* Code Section 457 plan, deferrals are included in taxable income of the participant in the first taxable year in which there is no substantial risk of forfeiture. Special trust requirements apply to plans maintained by a state or local government employer.

Individual deferred compensation arrangements and plans. An executive may choose to enter into a deferral agreement with his or her employer, or be designated by the employer as being eligible to participate in the employer's nonqualified deferred compensation plan, which permits the executive to elect to defer payment of compensation. The executive has until the year before the year in which services are rendered in connection with the compensation being deferred to elect the deferral. The IRS has stated in Revenue Procedure 92-65 that it will only issue rulings on unfunded deferred compensation arrangements if

1. The election to defer is made before the beginning of the taxable year in which the compensation is payable (however, for the first tax year of implementation of a nonqualified deferred compensation plan, or the first taxable year in which a participant in such a plan first becomes eligible to participate, the deferral election can be made up to 30 days after the effective date of the plan or the initial eligibility date);

2. The plan must define the time of payment of the deferred amounts and the method of distribution (i.e., lump sum, installments, etc.);

3. The plan may provide for early distributions only for "unforseeable emergencies";

4. The participants have the status of unsecured general creditors of the employer;

5. Any grantor trust used must conform to the model issued under IRS Revenue Procedure 92-64 (see Appendix A); and

6. The participant's rights to benefits are not subject to alienation, pledge, or garnishment.

Q 9:17   What factors must be considered by a company in determining the appropriateness of a deferred compensation plan?

Deferred compensation is not always an appropriate ingredient in an executive compensation program because deferred compensation is not suited for every executive. In determining whether a deferred compensation plan is appropriate for a given situation, the following questions need to be answered:

1. Is it possible that a qualified plan is more valuable to the company as a tool for retaining middle level employees?

2. Do the requirements of ERISA burden the plan with so many details that a nonqualified plan is more suitable?

3. Does the executive for whose benefit the plan is being considered have a competitive current level of compensation?

4. Do the requirements of the Code lessen the tax benefits of a qualified plan or burden the plan with so many restrictions that a nonqualified plan is more beneficial?

5. Will the anticipated tax benefit be offset by loss of Social Security income?

6. What is the level of executive confidence regarding the company's ability or future willingness to pay?

7. Does the company have a need to provide a better retirement plan or a "golden handcuff"?

8. Is the executive in question a major stockholder?

Tax Considerations

Q 9:18   How are nonqualified plans treated for tax purposes?

A nonqualified deferred compensation plan does not satisfy the requirements contained in Code Section 401(a) and, as a result, does not receive the favorable tax treatment afforded plans that do satisfy those requirements. Generally, an employer contributing to a nonqualified plan will be entitled to a deduction in the year in which the amount attributable to the contribution is includible in the gross income of the participating employees, which may not be until some future date.

Q 9:19   What is an example of the tax treatment on company contributions to a nonqualified plan?

Say, for example, that Company A implements a nonqualified benefit restoration plan for its senior executives. The plan is intended to make up for limitations imposed by Code regulations on company matching contributions to a 401(k) plan. Any amount that the company contributes to the plan, in any given year, will be a charge or deduction to the income statement for purposes of financial reporting; however, in calculating earnings for purposes of determining the company's tax obligation that same year, the company contribution to the plan cannot be taken as a deduction or charge to the income statement. This is shown in Chart 9-1.

Chart 9-1

Assumptions: Company *A* contributes $10,000 to an executive's SERP account in 1995 and in three additional years (1996 through 1998). The executive retires in 1999.

Accounting Income Statement

	1995–98	1999
Company income	$100,000	$100,000
SERP contribution	$ 10,000	–0–
Company taxable income	$ 90,000	$100,000

Tax Income Statement

	1995–98	1999
Company income	$100,000	$100,000
SERP contributions	–0–	$ 40,000
Company taxable income	$100,000	$ 60,000

Comparison to tax treatment under a qualified retirement plan:

Company B implements a qualified 401(k) retirement plan for its senior executives and other employees. The plan is intended to provide all employees with an opportunity to establish retirement income from both their own contributions and from company contributions. Any amount that the company matches/contributes to the plan, in any given year, will be a charge or deduction to the income statement for purposes of financial reporting, and for purposes of determining the company's tax obligation that same year, the company contribution to the plan can also be taken as a deduction or charge to the income statement. This is shown in Chart 9-2.

Chart 9-2

Assumptions: Company *B* contributes $10,000 to an executive's 401(k) account in 1995 and in three additional years (1996 through 1998). The executive retires in 1999.

Accounting Income Statement

	1995–98	1999
Company income	$100,000	$100,000
401(k) contribution	$ 10,000	–0–
Company taxable income	$ 90,000	$100,000

Tax Income Statement

	1995–98	1999
Company income	$100,000	$100,000
401(k) contributions	$ 10,000	–0–
Company taxable income	$ 90,000	$100,000

Q 9:20 Are contributions to a funded plan treated differently than contributions to an unfunded plan?

Yes. Generally, contributions to an unfunded plan are not deduct-ible by an employer and are not includible in an employee's income until some future date when the benefits are distributed or made available to the employee. A contribution to a funded plan is gener-ally deductible by the employer and is included in an employee's income not in the year the contribution is made, but in the year it is not subject to substantial risk of forfeiture.

Q 9:21 How are employers who establish funded excess benefit plans treated for tax purposes?

The employer generally is entitled to deduct contributions made pursuant to the provisions of a funded plan in the year in which the contributions are made. In an unfunded plan, the employer cannot deduct contributions until they are included in the participating employee's income (i.e., when paid).

In addition, the employer must maintain separate accounts for funded plans covering more than one participant in order to be entitled to a deduction.

Q 9:22   How are employees who benefit from excess benefit plans treated for tax purposes?

The tax treatment to the employee depends upon whether the excess benefit plan is unfunded or funded. If unfunded, no tax liability occurs to the employee until payments are received. If funded, there is tax liability to the employee to the extent vesting in future benefits occurs each taxable year.

Q 9:23   Are contributions made pursuant to a nonqualified deferred compensation plan includible in an employee's income under the constructive receipt doctrine?

Generally no. If the employee's control over the contributions is subject to substantial limitations, then contributions to a nonqualified deferred compensation plan should not be subject to the constructive receipt doctrine. Generally, a taxpayer includes the amount of any item of gross income in his gross income for the taxable year in which he receives it, unless, under the taxpayer's method of accounting, it is properly included in a different period. Generally, the employee, as a cash method taxpayer, includes amounts in gross income when they are actually or constructively received. The constructive receipt doctrine is set forth in Treas. Reg. Section 1.451-2(a).

Q 9:24   Are contributions made pursuant to a nonqualified deferred compensation plan includible in the employee's income under the economic benefit doctrine?

Generally no. If contributions are made, or amounts set aside in accordance with a nonqualified deferred compensation plan are subject to the claims of the employer's general creditors, then such contributions or amounts should not be subject to the economic benefit doctrine. If, on the other hand, contributions to the plan are protected from the employer's creditors and the rights of the participating employees to the benefits provided under the plan are nonforfeitable, the economic benefit doctrine should apply and the contributions should be includible in the participating employee's income. The economic benefit doctrine is set forth in Code Section 83 and Treas. Reg. 1.83-3.

Q 9:25   How does Code Section 83 apply to property transfers to an employee in exchange for the performance of services?

In general, Code Section 83 provides rules for the taxation of property transferred to an employee in connection with the performance of services. This property is generally not taxable to an employee until it has been transferred to, or becomes substantially vested in, the employee. The application of Code Section 83 can be broken down as follows:

- What is a transfer of property? A transfer of property occurs when a person acquires a beneficial ownership interest in the property. [Treas. Reg. Section 1.83-3(a)]

- When is property substantially vested? Property is substantially vested for purposes of Code Section 83 when it is either transferable or not subject to a substantial risk of forfeiture. A substantial risk of forfeiture exists when rights in property that are transferred are conditioned either upon the future performance, or nonperformance, of substantial services by any person, or the occurrence of a condition related to a purpose of the transfer. [Treas. Reg. Section 1.83-3(c)]

- When are property rights transferable? The rights of an employee in property are transferable if the employee can transfer any interest in the property to any person other than the transferor of the property, but only if the transferee's rights in the property are not subject to a substantial risk of forfeiture. [Treas. Reg. Section 1.83-3(d)]

- What is property? The term *property* includes real and personal property other than money or an unfunded and unsecured promise to pay money in the future. The term also includes a beneficial interest in assets, including money, that are transferred or set aside from the claims of creditors of the transferor. [Treas. Reg. Section 1.83-3(e)]

If the contributions under a nonqualified deferred compensation plan are subject to the claims of the employer's general creditors, then such contributions do not meet the definition of property. Therefore, there can be no transfer of property within the meaning of Code Section 83. If, on the other hand, contributions under a nonqualified deferred compensation plan are not available either to the employer or the employer's general creditors, and the participating employees are fully vested in the contributions, then there is a transfer of property within the meaning of Code Section 83, and the employee is subject to tax on the transferred amount.

Q 9:26   What are the tax consequences under a Code Section 457 plan?

If the plan is an *eligible* Code Section 457 plan, then participants are taxed when amounts are actually or constructively received. If the plan is an *ineligible* Code Section 457 plan (i.e., a Code Section 457(f) plan), then the participant is taxed in the first taxable year in which there is no *substantial risk of forfeiture* of the right to receive the deferred benefit. *Substantial risk of forfeiture* is defined in Code Section 457(f)(3)(B) in a manner similar to Code Section 83 terms.

Q 9:27   When are deferred compensation arrangements subject to FICA and FUTA taxes?

Amounts deferred under a nonqualified deferred compensation plan are subject to Federal Insurance Contributions Act (FICA) tax. Section 3121(v)(2) of the Code provides guidance as to when amounts deferred under or paid from a nonqualified deferred compensation plan are taken into account as wages for purposes of FICA taxes. A *special timing rule* applies to nonqualified deferred compensation requiring that such compensation be subject to FICA tax (including the hospital insurance portion of Medicare) on the later of (1) the date the services are performed that create a right to the deferred compensation amount or (2) the date that the deferred compensation is no longer subject to a substantial risk of forfeiture (i.e., is vested). Final regulations became effective January 29, 1999 and apply on and after January 1, 2000. Prior to such time, employers are permitted to use a reasonable, good faith interpretation of the provisions of the Code (which would include following the final regulations). Special transition rules are provided under the final regulations.

Under the final regulations, if deferred compensation is subject to FICA before the year in which the compensation is actually paid to the employee, no FICA tax will be applicable at the time of payment of such compensation or any earnings thereon (provided that the interest credited is based on a reasonable rate of interest or rate of return). Typically, at the time that the deferred compensation is *credited*, the affected executives are earning compensation in excess of the taxable wage base for the year (for 1999, $ 72,600). Currently, there is no dollar limit on wages subject to the hospital insurance (HI) portion of Medicare tax. As a result, the deferred compensation *credited* for the year usually will only be subject to the HI portion of FICA tax. If an employee is completely vested in the plan, any amounts contributed to the plan for the year on the employee's behalf will be subject to the HI tax. An employee who is not 100 percent vested in the plan will be taxed on the incremental increased vested portion of his or her plan account balance during the year.

For *account balance* deferred compensation plans, the amount taken into account as FICA wages equals the principal amount credited to the employee's account for the year, increased or decreased by any income attributable to such amount through the date that such amount is taken into account as FICA wages.

If the amount credited is not readily known for a given year by December 31, there are two methods for withholding the HI tax. The *estimated method* permits an employer to reasonably estimate an amount as wages paid on the last day of the calendar year. There are rules set forth in the regulations for handling any shortfall. The *lag method* allows an employer to determine the amount credited for the year on any date in the first quarter of the next calendar year. The amount credited will then be treated as wages on that date and must be increased by interest at a fixed rate that is not less than the applicable federal rate (the AFR is the mid-term applicable federal rate for January 1 of the calendar year, compounded annually) until it is included in wages.

An employer can withhold the employee's portion of the amount of the HI tax due from the employee's paycheck. An employer might consider paying the employee's portion of such tax itself and seek reimbursement from the executive at a later date. Where the amount of HI tax owed is relatively small and where the cost of communicating with the executives equals or exceeds the amount of the tax, the employer might consider paying employee's portion of the HI tax itself without reimbursement. However, if the employer pays such tax on behalf of its executives, each affected executive would be subject to income tax and additional HI tax on the employer's payment of the employee's portion of the tax.

> **Example.** An employer established a nonqualified deferred compensation plan for certain executives under which a percentage of annual compensation is credited annually on behalf of eligible employees (e.g., an employee earned $200,000 in compensation for the year and the employer credited 10 percent of such amount, or $20,000, to the plan as nonqualified deferred compensation for the year). In addition, a reasonable rate of interest is credited annually on the balance credited to each employee's account as of the last day of the preceding plan year. All amounts credited under the plan are 100 percent vested. The plan provides that any amount deferred under the plan for the plan year will be taken into account as wages on the last day of the year.
>
> The amount deferred to each employee's account for the plan year (in the example, the $20,000) is taken into account for FICA tax purposes as of the last day of the calendar year. As no earnings have yet been credited on such amount, none are taken into account. Any future earnings on such deferred amount are ignored for FICA tax purposes as well.
>
> The employee in the example has total wages for FICA tax purposes for the year of $220,000. The wage base limit that applies for the OASDI portion of FICA results in no additional OASDI tax being due on the $20,000. However, because there is no wage base limit on the HI portion of FICA, additional HI tax liability results from the $20,000 amount deferred.
>
> For nonaccount balance plans (i.e., SERPs with defined benefit formulas), FICA tax is due at the time the present value of the future payment or payments in which the employee has become vested under the plan during that period becomes "reasonably ascertainable." This calculation will require actuarial assistance.
>
> It should be noted that the grant of stock options, stock appreciation rights, or other stock value rights is not considered a "deferral of compensation" under the Code Section 3121(v) regulations for

purposes of treatment as wages for FICA taxation. FICA tax generally applies at the time of exercise.

The rules concerning withholding under the Federal Unemployment Tax Act (FUTA) are similar to those under FICA.

Funding Arrangements

Q 9:28   What is a rabbi escrow agreement?

A rabbi escrow agreement or an escrow account is another informal way of funding unfunded deferred compensation plans. Under this approach, a company guarantees deferred compensation amounts by creating an escrow fund with a financial institution as escrow agent. The company makes contributions to the account in an amount determined to be adequate to fund the benefits provided in the deferred compensation plan. As long as the assets in the account remain subject to the claims of the company's general creditors, the contributions to the account will not be includible in the executive's income. Income earned from the investment of the escrow fund can either be paid to the company or be applied toward the company's obligation. The income is taxable to the company. In all other respects, this arrangement has the same general provisions and tax consequences as the rabbi trust (see Q 9:29).

Q 9:29   What is a rabbi trust?

A rabbi trust is an irrevocable trust into which assets earmarked for benefit liabilities are contributed. Trust assets typically are protected for use in meeting the benefit liabilities, but they must remain accessible to the company's general creditors in the event of bankruptcy or insolvency. The contributions and earnings are not taxable to the executives, and the company does not get a deduction for its contributions. The earnings from the trust's investments are taxable to the company.

The general creditors' access to the trust assets in the event of bankruptcy or insolvency creates an element of risk for the executives. This uncertainty is the biggest drawback of rabbi trusts. However, companies that have installed rabbi trusts tend to view the bankruptcy and insolvency risk as minimal and to consider the rabbi trust as a safety net for benefits in the case of a takeover.

The primary use of rabbi trusts continues to be to fund nonqualified retirement programs, although they can be used for voluntary deferred arrangements. The appeal of the rabbi trust as a funding vehicle is that when properly structured, it will successfully defer income for the executive while protecting the benefit from all but general creditors. However, if the trust is not designed in accordance with provisions accepted by the IRS, it runs the risk that the executives may be deemed in constructive receipt of trust assets at the time the trust is funded.

The IRS initially approved the concept in a 1980 private letter ruling. [PLR 8113107] Under this ruling, a congregation contributed amounts into an irrevocable trust it established for the benefit of its rabbi (hence the term rabbi trust). The IRS ruled that because the assets were subject to the general creditors of the congregation, the rabbi was not in constructive receipt of the contributions to the trust. Additional private letter rulings reinforced this concept. Because private letter rulings are meant to apply to specific situations, it is prudent, however, for a company to request a private letter ruling that will ensure the validity of the arrangement.

In summary, the advantage of a rabbi trust is that it secures the promise to pay deferred compensation and, therefore, insures that a new company owner and/or new company management cannot change the company's obligation to pay the vested deferred amounts. If the company goes into bankruptcy, the company creditors can use deferred funds in a rabbi trust to pay company debts. The disadvantage of the rabbi trust is that it does not guarantee the payment of deferred funds, but it does postpone the executive's payment of income tax on the deferred funds. Companies that use rabbi trusts do so to protect deferred compensation during a merger, restructuring, or acquisition when there can be changes in company ownership and company management.

In 1992, the IRS issued Revenue Procedure 92-64, which provides a model form of rabbi trust document (see Appendix A). The model trust document permits the trust to be irrevocable or revocable (or to become irrevocable upon a "change in control") and to invest in employer stock.

Q 9:30 What is a secular trust?

Secular trusts or Code Section 402(b) trusts fund benefit obligations on a current basis; assets are secured until the time of distribution to the beneficiary. Because the assets are not available to general creditors, the funds in the secular trust are taxable income to the beneficiaries. When properly structured, the secular trust can provide the same after-tax benefit as a rabbi trust while costing the company less. This is due to the generally lower tax rates to which individuals are subject and the fact that the company can gross-up an executive's income to pay the tax liability attributable to the annual funding requirement. (The gross-up process is described in Q 10:31 for excise taxes.)

In summary, the advantage of a secular trust is that it secures the payment of deferred compensation, as well as the promise to pay deferred compensation. However, this benefit carries a significant disadvantage in that the secular trust is taxable income to the executive. The amount of taxable income to the executive each year is determined by the extent to which the executive is vested in any amounts in the trust each year. For example, if the executive is vested in 10 percent of the deferred compensation of $100,000 in a secular trust in the first year of deferral, then that executive has taxable income of $10,000 that year.

Q 9:31 What are the major distinctions between a secular trust and a rabbi trust?

The major differences between a secular trust and a rabbi trust are that (1) while creditors can claim assets held in a rabbi trust, money held in a secular trust cannot be reached by creditors and (2) assets in a rabbi trust are not taxable income to the participants while in the trust, whereas assets in a secular trust are taxed to the participant when contributed and as income is earned.

Q 9:32   Can life insurance also be used by an employer to fulfill its promise to an employee?

Yes, a company may purchase insurance policies to fund its promise. These policies are referred to as corporate-owned life insurance (COLI). A COLI contract generally covers the lives of several employees, and the financial interest that the employer seeks to "insure" generally is determined by the contracted benefits the corporation is obligated to pay on the death of the covered employee. A corporation can in many cases reduce the cost of the plan by using properly designed and priced life insurance contracts.

Insurance-related Nonqualified Deferred Compensation Plans

Q 9:33   How is life insurance used by an employer to fulfill its promise to an employee?

A corporation will generally purchase specially designed cash value (universal or variable) life insurance policies on individual employees. The cash value in these life insurance policies generates an investment income that is generally exempt from current income tax (i.e., the inside buildup). The ability of a corporation to borrow against the cash value to pay future premiums and deduct the interest has been eliminated for all future contracts and is being phased out for all policies in force as of the end of 1996.

The employer is the owner and beneficiary of the policies and pays the premiums. The employer may pay benefits to the employee with funds obtained from withdrawing up to their basis in the policies and then if necessary borrowing against the cash value of the policies. Since 1996, interest on loans from an insurance policy is not deductible on loans over $50,000.

The employer must accrue for the future liabilities of plan, but can offset these liabilities with the increases in the cash value and the accruals for the future tax deductions. The employer may not take a current tax deduction for the contributions made to the plan but can accrue for the projected tax deductions that will be available when the benefits are paid.

If the policies are structured correctly and the performance of the policies' investment accounts meets or exceeds the plan assumptions, the policies will have sufficient cash value to fund the benefit payments and the interest on the loans and maintain the policies for the life of the insured.

The policies must be kept in force for the life of the insured to prevent a taxable event to the company. If the policy is surrendered before the death of the insured, all cash value in excess of the basis in the policy, including loans, will be taxable income to the owner of the policy. If the policy is held until the death of the insured, all proceeds of the policy will be received free of income tax, including the cancellation of the loans, by the owner of the policy.

Q 9:34   Can life insurance other than COLI be utilized to fund nonqualified deferred compensation programs?

Yes, it is possible to use the same concept without the company owning the insurance contract. The executive can own an insurance contract such that the benefit at retirement will be equal to a targeted amount of supplemental retirement income. Under this concept, there are two ways to provide these benefits.

1. The executive would reach an agreement with the company to have the company pay the premium by providing the executive with taxable income (grossed-up for taxes if desirable; see Q 10:31) in an amount equal to the required premium on the insurance contract.

2. The executive would enter into a slightly different agreement. The executive and the company would split the life insurance policy. This is called a *split-dollar* plan. The company would agree to pay the premium in return for a collateral assignment of a portion of the cash value equal to the company's premium payments. The employee would pay the term cost of the life insurance (PS-58 costs) annually. Upon retirement or death of the insured the company could bonus out the portion of the cash value it owns if it so chooses.

In either case contributions would continue during the executive's career. If the executive terminates employment either voluntarily or involuntarily, the company no longer has any obligation to pay the premium. The executive can, however, continue premium payments on his own or can structure arrangements with a subsequent employer to cover the premium cost. Therefore, these methods have portability for the executive.

Q 9:35 What is the difference between COLI and *retail* life insurance contracts?

COLI is a specially designed life insurance contract designed for use in funding unfunded nonqualified deferred compensation plans and keyman insurance coverage. COLI will generally have more liberal underwriting requirements and may even have guaranteed issue provisions if the group is large enough. Unlike "retail" cash value life insurance policies, COLI will generally have significant amounts of cash value in the first year and will always have more cash value than a retail policy with the same investment provisions.

Q 9:36 What are the advantages of using employee-owned life insurance to fund nonqualified deferred compensation benefits?

From the company's perspective, the advantages are as follows:

1. The company incurs no annual accrual on its balance sheet. Therefore, the deferred compensation obligation is neither an asset nor a liability to the company.

2. The company either receives a tax deduction for the amount of the premium since this amount is accounted for as taxable income to the executive, or, if a split-dollar plan is used, the company will get a refund of all of the premium payments it has made upon termination of employment or death of the employee.

3. If the executive terminates, the executive could continue any premium payments on his or her own. Thus, the executive is motivated to remain with the company.

Advantages to the executive are as follows:

1. The deferred compensation plan is *secured* through the insurance contract without the complexity of a rabbi or secular trust.

2. The perquisite is *portable* to the executive: The executive can continue paying premiums on his or her own or make arrangements with a new employer to cover the premium cost.

3. Because an insurance contract is the funding mechanism, some of the deferred compensation payments to the executive from the insurance contract are received income tax free.

Split-Dollar Life Insurance

Q 9:37   What is split-dollar life insurance?

It is not a unique kind of life insurance policy, but an arrangement by two parties jointly to purchase a permanent, cash-value life insurance policy: someone who needs the permanent life insurance benefit and someone with the means of paying the premiums. Split-dollar is utilized by most business entities today. This traditionally means an executive will enjoy the benefits and the employer will pay the premiums, although there are differing variations. For purposes of this chapter, we describe the arrangement most typically used.

Q 9:38   How is split-dollar treated under ERISA?

Split-dollar may be provided for any employee, shareholder, or director of the company. It is considered a welfare benefit plan under ERISA, but is not subject to participation, reporting, or funding requirements. The benefit may be fully discriminatory and confidential.

Q 9:39   How does the policy splitting occur?

The components of the policy are its premium, cash value, and death benefit. Premiums are split with the executive paying the *term insurance cost* of the insurance death benefit provided (as described by Revenue Ruling 64-328) and the employer paying the remainder. The death benefit and cash value are first allocated to the employer, up to the amount of its cumulative premium outlay, with the balance allocated to the executive or the executive's designated beneficiary.

Q 9:40   Must the executive pay his part of the premium?

Either the executive directly pays the term cost of the coverage or this amount must be included on the executive's W-2 as additional taxable income. Employers often "gross up" this added income so the executive has zero net out-of-pocket cost for the coverage.

Q 9:41   How is the policy split accomplished?

With *collateral assignment split-dollar*, the policy is owned by the executive and an assignment is executed in favor of the employer, entitling it to a death benefit or cash value allocation equal to its cumulative premium outlay. All excess death benefits and cash values belong to the executive or his beneficiary by virtue of his ownership rights in the policy.

With *endorsement split-dollar*, the policy is owned by the employer and the death benefit is allocated to the executive through an endorsement agreement. All cash values are owned by the employer. Tax authority for split-dollar rests primarily in Revenue Rulings 64-328 and 66-110.

Q 9:42   What happens when the executive retires?

The policy is typically *rolled out* from the employer to the executive. The executive may receive a paid-up life insurance benefit, cash values, or retirement benefit. The amount of postretirement benefit depends on whether the employer elects to recover its premium outlay or to award its share of the policy to the executive, which would be taxable as bonus compensation and deductible to the company. Policy values are typically withdrawn to cover tax costs.

Q 9:43   What are common split-dollar applications?

Split-dollar plans are often used to replace or supplement group term life insurance plans on a more tax-efficient basis, to provide large amounts of coverage for estate tax protection and to reduce asset risk in nonqualified retirement plans.

Q 9:44 What problems do executives experience in group term life insurance plans?

Although the first $50,000 of noncontributory group term life insurance is not income taxable to the employee or estate taxable to his estate, many employers want to provide higher noncontributory coverage amounts to executives. However, the excess coverage over $50,000 is income taxed to the executive, regardless of the actual cost to the employer, at an inflated rate determined by IRS Group Term Table I. For example, the employer might pay $100 per month for $500,000 coverage for an executive. However, the executive is forced to pay income tax on $150 per month of additional income, resulting in $648 additional tax liability per year for this benefit (assuming an individual tax rate of 36 percent). Group term coverage also typically terminates at retirement, is not portable, and provides no cash values.

Note that the IRS issued new Group Term Table I rates in early 1999 (effective for coverage provided on or after July 1, 1999). The new rates serve to reduce the amount of taxable income imputed to employees for excess coverage when compared to prior years. However, the new rates also serve to create potential imputed taxable income for employee-paid premium plans, including supplemental group insurance plans.

Q 9:45 Why is split-dollar effective in replacing group term coverage?

Split-dollar coverage provides significant amounts of coverage to executives at a fraction of the income tax cost of group term. The coverage is portable if the executive decides to terminate prior to normal retirement age (split-dollar agreements typically provide for a buyout of the policy from the employer under such circumstances). At retirement, the executive typically has coverage paid up for life with cash values.

Q 9:46 Why is split-dollar useful in estate planning?

When an executive forms an irrevocable life insurance trust to purchase an insurance policy on himself or jointly on himself and his spouse (second-to-die coverage), amounts must be gifted to the trust each year that may far exceed the executive's annual gift exclusion ($10,000 per beneficiary per spouse). Split-dollar allows large amounts of coverage to be owned by the trust with the annual gifts valued at the *term costs* of the coverage instead of the entire policy premium. This greatly enhances the already considerable leverage afforded by life insurance trust.

Planning Note: IRS Notice 99-36 provides that contributions made with the intent to have a charity enter into a split-dollar life insurance arrangement with a donor's trust will not qualify for a charitable deduction.

Q 9:47 How can split-dollar enhance a nonqualified retirement plan?

Under most circumstances, nonqualified plans are informally funded with an asset, perhaps corporate-owned life insurance, that may be held by a rabbi trust for enhanced security. The asset is still subject to confiscation by corporate creditors in the event of bankruptcy of the employer. Split dollar allows the executive to own the policy and the cash value exceeding the premiums paid by the employer so that the asset risk is more balanced. Only the premiums, that portion of cash value representing *principal* assigned to the employer, are subject to credit risk instead of the entire cash value.

Executive Disability Income Insurance

Q 9:48 How does an executive disability income insurance plan work?

Group long-term disability (LTD) plans typically cap benefits at a percentage of income, usually 50 to 60 percent, and a dollar limit, usually $5,000 per month. Many plans insure only salary and exclude bonuses. This causes highly compensated executives to be underinsured. Executive disability income plans consist of individual policies issued on the executives in addition to the LTD plan. This builds insurance to an appropriate percentage level, usually 80 percent of compensation.

Q 9:49   What legal framework should exist to minimize taxation of executive disability plans?

If the employer does not establish a *sick pay plan*, the benefits paid to the executive could be considered *ad hoc* compensation to the executive and taxed as a dividend. This is easily avoidable by incorporating a written plan authorizing payments to disabled executives. Many experts consider the existence of an insurance policy sufficient precedent for a sick pay plan.

Q 9:50   How are benefits taxed to the executive?

Taxation of executive disability income benefits depend on whether premiums are paid by the employer or the executive. If the employer pays premiums, the benefits will be taxable as ordinary income to the executive when received. If the executive pays the premiums, the benefits will be income tax free.

Q 9:51   How are premiums taxed to the executive and the employer?

If the employer pays disability insurance premiums, they may be tax-deducted by the employer as an ordinary business expense but not taxed to the executive. This results in taxable income benefits. If the employer pays premiums and includes them in the executive's taxable income, they are taxable to the executive but benefits are tax-free.

Q 9:52   Are executive disability premiums more expensive than LTD?

Individual executive disability insurance policies are typically noncancelable and guaranteed renewable to age 65. In other words, the premiums may not be increased and the policy has to be renewed as long as premiums are paid. Policies typically offer extra features not available in LTD plans and, depending on the number of executives in a plan, may be eligible for significant discounts.

Q 9:53 Do executive disability income plan have to be funded by the employer?

Typically, senior management plans are funded by the employer. Many plans being installed today on second and third tier management groups are offered on a contributory basis through payroll deduction, sometimes with a partial employer contribution.

ERISA Considerations

Q 9:54 What are the general ERISA requirements for a nonqualified deferred compensation plan?

The ERISA (Title I) rules covering participation, vesting, funding, reporting, and disclosure and fiduciary requirements apply to pension benefit plans, which are maintained by an employer and provide retirement income or deferral of compensation to termination of employment or beyond. This definition would encompass most nonqualified deferred compensation plans. However, ERISA exempts certain arrangements from the vast majority of these requirements. Specifically, an unfunded arrangement maintained "primarily for the purpose of providing deferred compensation for a select group of management or highly compensated employees" (often referred to as a *top hat plan*) will not be subject to ERISA rules regarding participation, vesting, funding and fiduciary responsibilities. In addition, governmental plans, church plans, and unfunded excess benefit plans are exempt from the ERISA rules.

To date, the Department of Labor has not provided definitive regulatory guidance on the top hat plan exemption. However, in DOL Advisory Opinion 90-14A, the DOL does offer the view that a top hat plan must cover only employees who, by virtue of their position or compensation level, have the power to meaningfully negotiate the design and operation of the deferred compensation plan as it affects them.

Unfunded deferred compensation plans maintained by a company primarily to provide deferred compensation for a select group of management or highly compensated employees must comply with the reporting and disclosure and administrative and enforcement provisions of Title 1 of ERISA. Note, however, that *funded* deferred compensation plans must meet all the requirements of Title 1.

For top hat plans, ERISA regulations provide that the plan administrator may satisfy the reporting and disclosure requirements by filing a statement with the Secretary of Labor which includes the following:

1. The name and address of the employer;

2. The employer identification number assigned by the IRS;

3. A statement that the plan is maintained primarily for the purpose of providing benefits for a select group of management or highly compensated employees; and

4. A statement of the number of such plans and the number of employees in each such plan. Only one identifying statement need be filed for each employer maintaining such plan or plans. The statement must be filed within 120 days after the plan becomes subject to Title I of ERISA by mailing such statement to the Pension and Welfare Benefits Administration.

Sample Statement:

Top Hat Plan Exemption
Pension and Welfare Benefits Administration
Room N-5638
U. S. Department of Labor
200 Constitution Avenue, N.W.
Washington, D.C. 20210

Re: Alternative Method of Compliance for Pension Plans for Selected Employees

To Whom It May Concern:

This report is being filed by _____ (the "Employer"), _____ [insert Employer address] pursuant to Department of Labor regulation 29 C.F.R. Section 2520.104-23 to comply with the reporting and disclosure requirements of Part 1 of Title I of the Employee Retirement Income Security Act of 1974, as amended (ERISA), for the following unfunded pension plan(s) (the "Plan(s)") maintained by the Employer for a select group of management or highly compensated employees:

[Insert Name of Plan(s)]

Employer's Tax Identification Number: [insert EIN]

Number of Employees covered by the Plan(s) : [insert number]

The Employer maintains the Plan(s) primarily for the purpose of providing deferred compensation for a select group of management or highly compensated employees.

Sincerely Yours,

The Secretary of Labor has the authority to request additional documentation.

ERISA also requires each deferred compensation plan to provide a claims procedure for participants and beneficiaries. This should be contained in the applicable plan documents.

Q 9:55 What are the general participation, vesting, and funding requirements for a nonqualified deferred compensation plan?

Unfunded deferred compensation plans maintained by a company for the purpose of providing deferred compensation for a select group of management or highly compensated employees are excluded from the participation, vesting, and funding requirements of ERISA.

Q 9:56 What are the general fiduciary issues for a nonqualified deferred compensation plan?

Unfunded deferred compensation plans maintained by the company primarily for the purpose of providing deferred compensation for a select group of management or highly compensated employees are excluded from the fiduciary responsibilities provisions of ERISA.

Q 9:57 Is plan termination insurance needed for a nonqualified plan?

Unfunded deferred compensation plans maintained by the company primarily for the purpose of providing deferred compensation for a select group of management or highly compensated employees are excluded from ERISA provisions covering plan termination insurance.

Q 9:58 For purposes of ERISA Title I, is a nonqualified deferred compensation plan generally considered funded or unfunded?

Nonqualified deferred compensation plans generally are *unfunded* plans because they are merely promises by the employer to pay the employee compensation at some future date. However, a nonqualified deferred compensation plan may also be a *funded* plan. This occurs when a separate fund is created by an employer who irrevocably sets aside an amount with a third party for the benefit of an employee.

Q 9:59 What is the difference between a funded and an unfunded plan?

Whether or not a plan is funded or unfunded generally requires an examination of the surrounding facts and circumstances.

Funded plans. A plan usually will be considered funded if an amount is irrevocably placed with a third party for the benefit of an employee and neither the employer nor its creditors has any interest in this amount.

Unfunded plans. An unfunded plan is merely an unsecured promise by an employer to pay compensation to an employee at some future date. The employer may set aside assets in order to fulfill its promise to the employee, but the set-aside assets must remain part of the employer's general assets and subject to the claims of the employer's creditors. The employer's promise may not be secured in any way. The participant may rely only on the credit of the employer and generally has no rights to the assets other than as a general unsecured creditor.

Q 9:60 For purposes of ERISA Title I, are plans affected by whether or not they are considered funded or unfunded?

Yes. If a plan is funded, the plan will have to satisfy the requirements contained in Title I of ERISA, which pertains to participation and vesting, funding, and fiduciary requirements. If a plan is unfunded, the plan may be exempt from these requirements.

Q 9:61   Does an employer inadvertently create a top hat plan that is subject to ERISA requirements when it provides benefits to one executive under an employment contract?

Generally no. Benefits provided to one executive under an individual employment contract will ordinarily not be considered a top-hat plan. In several DOL advisory opinions, the DOL ruled that contractual arrangements with individual executives were merely employment contracts and not "employee pension benefit plans" as defined by ERISA and, therefore, not subject to the requirements of ERISA.

Q 9:62   How does the employer pay the benefits provided by a top hat plan?

An employer generally pays the benefits provided under a top hat plan out of its general assets at the time the payments become due pursuant to the terms of the plan. The executive must rely solely on the employer's promise to pay these benefits and assumes the risk that these benefits may not be paid if there is an unfriendly change in the management of the employer or a change in the employer's financial situation. For example, if the employer becomes insolvent, the participating employees may not receive any benefits. In addition, if the employer is acquired in a hostile takeover, the new management team may terminate the plan and limit the benefits to be paid to the accrued or vested benefits.

Q 9:63   Can employer assurances be made that future benefits will be paid without subjecting employees to current taxation?

Yes. Top hat plans have adopted a number of informal funding arrangements to address the issue of employer assurances. (See Qs 9:28 through Q 9:47.)

Q 9:64 Is a top hat plan a funded or unfunded plan for purposes of Title I of ERISA?

A top hat plan is generally defined as an unfunded plan under ERISA Sections 201(2), 301(a)(3), and 401(a)(1), and generally will be unfunded if plan benefits are payable out of the employer's general assets and any participant in the plan has no greater rights in these assets than a general unsecured creditor.

Conversely, a plan will generally be considered funded if the assets are segregated or otherwise set aside and are identified as a source to which participants may look for the payment of their benefits.

Q 9:65 Are contributions to an unfunded top hat plan treated differently than contributions to a funded top hat plan?

Yes. Contributions to an unfunded top hat plan are generally not deductible by an employer and are not includible in an employee's income until the benefits are actually distributed or made available to the employee. Employer contributions to a funded top hat plan are, however, generally deductible by the employer and includible in the employee's income in the year the contribution is made. Note that contributions made to a funded top-hat plan that are subject to a substantial risk of forfeiture will generally not be deductible to an employer or includible in the employee's income until the benefits vest and are not subject to a substantial risk of forfeiture.

Q 9:66 Is an excess benefit plan subject to the ERISA Title I requirements?

An excess benefit plan may be subject to certain requirements under Title I of ERISA depending upon whether the plan is funded or unfunded. An excess benefit plan is defined in ERISA Section 3(36) as a plan maintained by an employer solely for the purpose of providing benefits for certain employees in excess of the limitations on contributions and benefits imposed by Code Section 415, without regard to whether the plan is funded. If the plan is unfunded, the plan is exempt from the requirements under Title I of ERISA. If the plan is funded, the plan is subject to certain requirements under ERISA.

Q 9:67 Is an excess benefit plan subject to the participation, vesting, and funding requirements imposed by Title I of ERISA?

No. An excess benefit plan, whether funded or unfunded, is not subject to the participation and vesting rules of Part 2 of Title I of ERISA and the funding rules of Part 3 of Title I.

Q 9:68 Is an excess benefit plan subject to the reporting and disclosure requirements imposed by Title I of ERISA?

It depends on whether the plan is funded or unfunded. A funded excess benefit plan will be subject to the reporting and disclosure requirements under Part 1 of Title I of ERISA; an unfunded excess benefit plan will not.

Other Considerations

Q 9:69 Is a nonqualified deferred compensation plan a security subject to SEC registration?

Prior to 1995 the SEC was granting no-action letters permitting nonqualified deferred compensation plans to be implemented without registration under the 1933 Securities Act. The staff never gave out the supporting rationale, but it was generally understood that either these plans were not securities or there was no offer of sale involved in their establishment.

The SEC has departed from its prior informal position and is no longer issuing no-action letters on the subject. In addition, at a host of conferences and seminars over the last few years the SEC has indicated that it considers all nonqualified deferred compensation plans as potentially registrable, subject to certain exemptions.

In general, the Securities Act of 1933 prohibits the offer or sale of securities unless a registration has been filed or an exemption is available. The current registration exemptions are as follows:

1. Section 3(a)(2), for qualified plans (unless employee contributions, including 401(k) contributions, are allocated to investment in employer securities);

2. Section 3(a)(4), exemption for not-for-profit corporations;

3. Section 3(a)(11), for securities offered and sold only to persons resident within a single state (the so-called intrastate exemption);

4. Section 3(b), for certain small offerings (up to $5 million);

5. Regulation D (Rules 501 through 508) (the so-called *private placement rules*); and

6. Section 4(2), for transactions not involving a public offer (Rule 701) (subject to certain volume limits).

Regulation D would appear to provide a safe harbor for most nonqualified deferred compensation plans. This set of rules generally limits sales of securities to specific numbers of purchasers (no more than 35 offerees can fail to qualify as *accredited investors*). A participant will be an accredited investor if he or she is either a director or executive officer of the employer, or has a net worth of more than $1 million, or has income in excess of $200,000 in each of the two most recent years (or joint spousal income for such period in excess of $300,000) and will likely be expected to earn the same income level in the current year.

Most small nonqualified deferred compensation plans will satisfy the statutory and regulatory exemptions and will not therefore be subject to registration. However, it remains to be seen whether the plans provided in larger organizations would be subject to registration and therefore would have to be analyzed carefully to determine if statutory exemption would be available.

If a plan should have registered but did not do so, and there was no fraud involved, the penalty, if any, would be slight; the main penalty would be to trigger a one-year recision right in the hands of participants. This would largely be an academic exercise: participants in the nonqualified deferred compensation plans are voluntary participants, and it would not serve for them to cancel their participation in the plan. There is one problem with this: the IRS may construe that the right of recision may trigger a constructive receipt problem for income tax purposes for the plan participants. The other area of concern would be that regardless of how slight the penalties may be, if any, for the failure to register a plan that the SEC finds should have been registered, the corporation would have to report that there has been a securities violation. This may negatively influence investors, since they would not understand the real details of what was involved. This situation appears to be reaching a critical stage; therefore, employers should be cautious in implementing these plans and should review plans that are currently in place to determine the consequences of non-registration versus registration.

Chapter 10

Perquisites and Other Benefits

Executive perquisites are special reward programs made available to executives only on a select basis. They entitle an executive either to special status such as via a country club membership or to a special benefit such as a luxury car.

Most companies provide executives with other benefits such as employment or severance contracts.

This chapter defines perquisites and other benefits, providing information on a number of program design issues and discussing the relevant tax and accounting considerations.

General Considerations 10-1
Tax and Accounting Impact 10-11
Contracts 10-16

General Considerations

Q 10:1   What is an executive perquisite?

An executive perquisite is any program or right provided only to designated executive positions, picking up where benefit programs end and providing the executive with additional benefits. These additional benefits can either make up for lost qualified benefits (e.g., a supplemental retirement benefit replacing the benefit an executive would otherwise lose because of the Employee Retirement Income Security Act of 1974 (ERISA) and Internal Revenue Code regulatory limitations), or provide benefits beyond those in a company's regular benefit plans (e.g., a supplemental retirement benefit that gives an executive a retirement of 60 percent final average pay rather than the 40 percent final average pay provided in the company's regular retirement plan).

The additional benefits provided by perquisite programs also serve to assist the executive in conducting job responsibilities. For example, a luncheon or country club membership can facilitate customer contact and conducting business with a customer.

Generally, an executive perquisite has intrinsic or status value that far exceeds its extrinsic or economic value. For example, a special parking place for an executive's car or a larger and more luxurious office has high intrinsic value to an executive but little if any economic value.

Q 10:2   What are examples of executive perquisites?

Common perquisites are:

- Cellular phone
- Company car
- Country and/or luncheon club memberships
- Estate, financial, or tax planning
- Expense accounts for customer entertainment
- First-class air travel and/or company planes
- Laptop computer
- Larger, more luxurious office; executive secretary/assistant
- Limousine service when traveling
- Severance contract
- Supplemental disability and life insurance
- Supplemental retirement benefit

Other popular perquisites are:

- Employment contracts
- Free use of company products/services
- Home offices
- Special deferred compensation programs
- Spouse travel
- Supplemental health reimbursements
- Time off for business and/or community relationships

Q 10:3 How are cellular phone perquisites typically provided?

Companies contract with a vendor to provide, under favorable pricing, either portable or car-installed cell phones for selected executives. The company will select the model of phone and the monthly billing plan.

The monthly bill, with the monthly fee and all toll calls, will be sent to the executive, who will then expense the monthly fee and all monthly business calls. At the end of the year, the company will have the executive complete a form indicating the percentage of personal use of the phone. The total amount of monthly fees paid by the company will be multiplied by the personal use percentage and that amount added to the executive's W-2 as imputed income.

Q 10:4 How do companies structure company car programs for executives?

Some organizations will simply provide a car allowance. Others will select a car leasing company and determine one lease amount or monthly lease amounts for eligible executives. For example, the position of chief executive officer might have a lease value of $800 (Jaguar or comparable), executive vice presidents $650 (luxury car), senior vice presidents $500 (full-size car), and vice presidents $450 (mid-size automobile). The company also selects a tenure for the lease (three years is common), and documents those expenses associated with car maintenance that will be paid by the company, such as for gas, servicing, and car-wash expenses. In some cases sales force car maintenance contracts with companies like Firestone or Goodyear will be made available to executives as well.

The executive is then free to select any car in that lease value category. Monthly lease bills are paid directly by the company, and the executive submits monthly expenses for all other covered expenses. At year-end the company will have the executive complete a form indicating the percentage of personal use of the company car. All expenses paid by the company will then be multiplied by the personal use percentage and this amount added to the executive's W-2 form as imputed income.

Q 10:5 How do companies provide country club/luncheon club perquisites?

This perquisite is declining in use because the Internal Revenue Service (IRS) does not allow a company to take a tax deduction for the reimbursement of club dues, initiation fees, etc. Company response to this is to reduce the availability of the perquisite, not to eliminate the perquisite for everyone.

Where the membership perquisite is provided, the executive joins a country club or luncheon club and any initiation fees and ongoing monthly fees are paid by the company. With respect to country clubs this reimbursement will also typically include special assessments (if any), locker fees, club storage fees, and minimum dining fees. All amounts paid by the company for the privilege of membership are imputed income to the executive.

When a country club or luncheon club is used for entertainment, all fees are also reimbursed by the company and the company is able to take a tax deduction for 50 percent of these costs, per IRS regulations. There is no imputed income for these costs to the executive.

Q 10:6 How are financial planning programs provided to executives?

This perquisite is gaining in popularity because executive total compensation programs can be so complex that executives need help in determining how best to use the programs to meet their personal financial goals and to lower their taxes. Companies will either select financial planning firms that the executive can use and then have the executive interview specific financial planning consultants in the firm, or simply tell the executive to select the financial planning consultant of his or her choice. In either case there should be a clear company policy that defines the services that are included in this perquisite. There are typically three service elements to this perquisite:

1. *Estate planning.* Helping the executive structure the estate so that wealth is passed on to the heirs in the most tax-advantageous way.

2. *Investment planning.* Developing personal financial objectives with the executive and establishing an investment strategy that will best achieve those goals.

3. *Tax planning.* Showing the executive how to avoid taxes (not evade taxes, which is illegal).

Estate planning starts with the preparation of wills for the executive. Federal estate tax regulations, which enable an executive who dies to pass on his or her estate to the spouse, must be accounted for in the will. When both executive and spouse die, the estate goes to heirs, often children, who must then pay an estate tax immediately of 20 percent on the portion of the estate that exceeds $1.2 million in value. This amount is escalating each year under tax legislation passed in 1997, so that by the year 2006 the amount of the estate tax exclusion will increase from $1.2 million to $2 million. There are many ways to avoid estate tax, and consultants can help executives determine how they may want to achieve this.

In order to determine the appropriate investment strategy, a consultant must understand many personal facts about the executive, such as future purchases he or she is saving for, the desired retirement date, any plans to leave the company, existing or anticipated children, or how long the executive plans to stay married. Obviously a consultant must have good "chemistry" with the executive and there must be strong trust and confidence in the relationship. The consultant must also thoroughly understand company benefit plans and executive incentive and stock award plans so that a strategy can be recommended to the executive on how best to use these plans to meet all personal financial objectives. For example, when should an executive exercise a stock option? Or, should an executive take annual incentive pay in cash or defer?

Tax planning relates to both estate and investment planning in that the consultant reviews the executive's current tax forms and payments, considers these with regard to both estate and investment plans, and recommends ways to reduce the executive's tax obligation.

Financial planner fees are typically paid by the company and the amount is added to the executive's W-2 statement at year-end. Tax advice is deductible to the extent that fees exceed 2 percent of the executive's adjusted gross income, but this rarely occurs.

Q 10:7 Do expense accounts for entertainment purposes have maximums?

In some cases entertainment expense accounts have maximum limits; however, this perquisite is normally provided as part of a company's regular business expense policy, and in that policy there is a statement that officers (or other designated executives) are authorized to entertain customers and/or suppliers. Also, outside the policy, a company will often provide executives a perquisite of box seats or special seats at sporting, cultural, or entertainment events. Executives may also entertain at eating establishments or at luncheon or country clubs. These business occasions must be documented with the date, event, business purpose, persons attending, etc. The amounts are not imputed income to the executive, and the company can deduct 50 percent of the costs for tax calculation purposes.

Q 10:8 What is the typical amount of severance in a severance contract for an executive?

This perquisite has also been gaining in popularity since the numerous corporate restructurings of the late 1980s and 1990s. Executives simply want some protection if their jobs are eliminated, and the severance contract bridges the gap of income and benefit eligibility whenever an executive must find another job. The most common salary continuation period in these contracts is six months. Some such contracts go for one year or more, particularly if there is a change of control during a merger, acquisition, etc., and the executive loses employment as the result of this event. These are called "golden parachutes" (see Q 10:29).

Q 10:9　What are typical amounts of supplemental life insurance for executives?

Supplemental life insurance typically starts at a minimum of one times base salary and goes up to three times salary. The company will typically pay the premiums related to one times salary and the executive will pay premiums for any life insurance greater than one times salary.

If disability insurance is provided by the company, the maximum is often set by the insurance company at a monthly income level that is well below the monthly salary of senior executives. Most companies will pay the cost to increase the maximum salary in a disability case or they will take out a separate policy just for executives.

Q 10:10　What are typical supplemental executive retirement plan benefit amounts?

The amounts vary considerably. Companies with a defined benefit plan typically use the same approach for their supplemental executive retirement plan (SERP). For example, a company might state in its SERP contract that an executive will receive 50 percent of final average pay upon retirement at age 62 with at least 20 years of service. The supplemental retirement benefit is calculated by determining the total retirement amount in the SERP contract, and subtracting from that amount the retirement income paid to the executive from the company's qualified defined benefit retirement plan. Any remaining amount will be paid separately by the company. Most companies offer a SERP benefit of 50 percent to 70 percent in a defined benefit SERP.

In a company with a 401(k) plan (defined contribution plan), the supplemental retirement benefit is typically a fixed amount of annual company contribution to an executive's retirement account, designed to supplement the executive's actual retirement, and will range from 5 percent of base salary to 15 percent of cash compensation (salary plus annual bonus). When the defined contribution plan is used, projections are made of retirement income for each executive using assumptions of investment performance and retirement account growth along with similar projections of retirement benefit to be realized from the company's 401(k) plan. The overall objective is the same: to insure that the executive can retire with adequate ongoing income given his or her income at the time he or she retires.

Q 10:11 How do companies conduct an analysis of executive perquisites provided in competitive companies?

The first activity is to define the companies that are competitors. This is normally done as part of a company's total compensation strategy. Competitors may be national, regional, local, and/or industry-specific. One of the best ways to define competitive companies is based on a review of where their executives are hired from, and where executives go when they leave the company.

The next activity is to identify the information to be surveyed in these competitive companies. The most important facts are:

1. *Perquisite program eligibility.* What executives (by title) are eligible for what perquisite.
2. *Benefit level.* A specific description of each level of benefit provided for each perquisite.
3. *The value of the perquisite to the executive.* This can be determined by either asking for the amount of company contribution/payment made to the executive and/or to an organization on behalf of the executive, or providing a specific basis or formula for calculating value.

Calculating the value of perquisites is important if a company is to evaluate the level of competitiveness of its programs; however, this can be difficult for a perquisite like special deferred compensation where a competitor provides enhanced investment opportunities to executives (see Q 10:12).

Q 10:12 How are executive perquisites valued?

The following techniques are used for common and other popular perquisites:

Perquisite	*Valuation Method*
Cellular phone	Annual amount paid by company
Company car	Annual lease value and operational costs added to executive's W-2
Country/luncheon club	Annual amount paid by company (initiation fees are either eliminated from the analysis or amortized over a fixed period)
Financial and/or tax planning	Annual amount added to executive's W-2
Expense accounts	Annual amount paid by company
First-class air travel	Not valued in competitive analysis, or a fixed number is selected and used by a company if the competitor provides the perquisite
Laptop computer	Amount paid by company
Luxurious office and/or executive secretary/assistant	Not valued in competitive analysis, or a fixed number is selected and used by a company if the competitor provides the perquisite
Limousine service	Not valued in competitive analysis as a perquisite, but when traveling considered a normal business expense
Severance contract	Either not valued in competitive analysis or amortized over a fixed period, e.g., if severance is two years' salary plus bonus, plus buyout of all stock options vested and unvested, then value is determined by taking current salary plus last bonus times two plus a Black Scholes value of all outstanding stock options (if Black Scholes not available, use $33\frac{1}{3}$ percent of current stock option price times number of shares at that price)
Supplemental insurance	Annual amount of premium paid by company
Supplemental retirement	Annual amount of company contribution
Employment contracts	Not valued in competitive analysis, or a fixed number is selected and used by a company if the competitor provides the perquisite

Perquisite	Valuation Method
Free use of company products/ services	Not valued in competitive analysis, or a fixed number is selected and used by a company if the competitor provides the perquisite
Home offices	Annual amount paid by company
Special deferred compensation programs	Not valued in competitive analysis, or a fixed number is selected and used by a company if the competitor provides the perquisite
Spouse travel	Annual amount paid by company
Supplemental health reimbursements	Annual amount paid by company
Time off for business or community relationships	Not valued in competitive analysis, or a fixed number is selected and used by a company if the competitor provides the perquisite

Q 10:13   How do companies select executive perquisites?

Executive perquisites are part of a company's total compensation strategy. (See Chapter 11.) The most common factors considered in determining a company's perquisite strategy are:

1. *Mix of total direct compensation.* Once a company decides how much total pay it is willing to provide an executive position, it then decides the mix of total pay. Typically, perquisites compose a small part of the total pay package (see Q 11:11), e.g., 5 percent of total pay. The decision on perquisite mix can be driven by company culture, the attitudes and value systems of the chief executive officer, opinions of board members, industry visibility or status in the community, the company's strategy, level and competitive position of salary, annual bonus, and stock or other long-term award.

2. *Community relationships.* Some companies want certain executives to promote the company at business and community associations. Also, most companies receive numerous requests to donate money to local civic associations, universities, etc. One way for companies to respond to community demands is

to contribute only to those organizations whose board of directors includes an officer of that company. This is an excellent way to control charitable giving; however, the company must be willing to give officers time off to participate in the organization's board meetings.

3. *Business relationships.* Executives can promote the company's products/services or image by participating in business associations or in organizations/facilities frequented by business people. Many perquisites can be provided that meet these business objectives, e.g., club memberships, spousal travel, use of company products/services, expense accounts, and time off for community board of director participation.

4. *Executive retention.* Executives like perquisites, so companies use them to retain key people. A company's strategy could be to provide something to these key people that other competitors do not provide. This suggests competitive advantage as opposed to meeting competitive practice. Both are potential company strategies for executive perquisites.

5. *Executive productivity.* Many companies do not want their executives to lose productivity because of travel or personal financial concerns. They want the executive to focus on business/job issues during the working day. This objective is served by perquisites such as financial planning, special deferred compensation plans, severance contracts, supplemental health reimbursements, use of limousines when traveling, or company planes.

Each company must evaluate the importance of these strategy considerations and develop a strategy statement that will guide the selection and level of executive perquisites.

Tax and Accounting Impact

Q 10:14 What are the tax regulations on the reimbursement of travel expenses?

In order to be fully deductible by the company and not included in the compensation of executives, travel expenses must be incurred while the executive is away from home in pursuit of company business. When this occurs, all transportation costs, meals and lodging, and expenses directly related to the travel are deductible. Entertainment expenses (see Qs 10:7 and 10:15) are not deductible. Travel expenses must be documented by the executive and maintained by the company in specific terms. For example, for each expense, the company must be able to identify the specific category of expense, the amount of the expense, the date and place, and the overall business purpose of the trip. Travel by the executive's spouse is not a business expense unless the spouse is an employee or unless the spouse is expected to fulfill a business purpose during the travel.

Q 10:15 What are the tax regulations on the reimbursement of entertainment expenses?

Since 1997, a company's deductible portion of business expenses is limited to 50 percent, unless the entertainment was a company picnic, Christmas party, or sporting event organized to benefit a tax-exempt organization, in which case the deduction is 100 percent.

Like travel expenses, entertainment expenses must be thoroughly documented. The company must be able to identify the date, time, and place the expense occurred, the type of entertainment, the person(s) being entertained, the nature of business discussions, and the relationship to company business. The entertainment expense must be "directly related to" or "associated with" the company's business if it is to be a tax deduction to the company and excluded from compensation of the executive. An expense is directly related to a company's business if it involved an active discussion aimed at obtaining immediate revenue (as opposed to mere goodwill), or occurred in a clear business setting such as a hospitality room. An expense is associated with a company's business if it is associated with the active conduct of the company's business and precedes or follows a substantial and bona fide business discussion.

Q 10:16 What are the tax regulations on the reimbursement of club memberships?

Under current tax regulations, the payments made for club memberships are not tax deductible to the company. Specific business expenses that occur at a club location, such as luncheon or meeting costs, are deductible to the company if they are documented. Such a business expense must have a business purpose and the documentation must include the date, time, and place, the person(s) attending, and the nature of the business discussions. As a regular business expense, these costs are not taxable to the executive.

Amounts paid by a company for club initiation fees, monthly fees, assessments, etc., are imputed income to the executive and are included in that executive's W-2 tax form. As noted previously, the company does not receive a tax deduction in this case.

Q 10:17   What are the tax regulations on company cars?

Company car costs are a tax deduction to the company. For the executive, the amount of payment made by the company is not taxable to the extent that the car is used for business purposes; however, personal use of the company car, which includes commuting, does constitute taxable income to the executive and is imputed on the executive's W-2 tax form. Each year, the executive must maintain records of business and personal use of the company car, and is responsible for advising the company of this information each year. In the event of a tax audit of the executive, it is the executive who is responsible for satisfying the questions of tax auditors.

> **Example.** A company provides its executives with leased cars of their choice, up to a maximum monthly amount of $500. Executive A leases a car for $500 and drives the car 20,000 miles in one year. The executive advises the company that 70 percent of the mileage is personal use of the car. The company imputes $4,200 to the executive's W-2 at year-end, calculated as follows: $500 × 12 months = $6,000; $6,000 × 70% = $4,200.
>
> The company also pays operating and maintenance costs for the car (gasoline, repairs, car washes, etc.). The amount paid by the company in that year was $1,200. Additional imputed income of $840 would be added to the executive's W-2 at year-end. The amount is calculated as follows: $1,200 × 70% = $840.

Sample company car provisions in executive employment agreements are provided in Appendix D at the back of this book.

Q 10:18   What are the tax regulations on company payments of car/cellular phones and laptop computers?

The company typically pays for the cost of these perquisites and the intent is that they will be used primarily for business purposes. Accordingly, the cost is a tax deduction to the company and is not taxable to the executive. Any personal calls are imputed income to the executive along with a prorated portion of the monthly service fee. The executive is responsible for advising the company of any personal use and the company adds this to the executive's W-2 at year-end.

> **Example.** A company provides an executive with a laptop computer and a cellular phone. The company phone is installed in the executive's company car. All are primarily used for business purposes. At year-end, Executive A advises the company that the laptop computer was used 100 percent for business, but that 10 percent of the car phone use was personal use. The monthly fee for the car phone is $20. The executive in this case will have $24 of imputed income, calculated as follows: $20 × 12 months = $240; $240 × 10% = $24.

Q 10:19   What are the tax regulations on company payments of supplemental life insurance for executives?

The cost of company-provided supplemental life insurance is taxable income to the executive unless the insurance is provided under a group-term policy. Under a group-term policy, the benefit is tax-free to the executive up to the first $50,000 of life insurance coverage. The cost of additional insurance is taxable income to the executive, and the amount of this taxable income is not the amount the company actually pays in premiums, but it is the amount based on an IRS table of coverage or "uniform premiums." The IRS has revised the Uniform Premium Table (Table I) used to calculate the cost of group-term life insurance which must be included in the employee's gross income. [64 Fed Reg 29788 (June 3, 1999)] Under the revised table, premiums are lower, which has the effect of treating employees with certain amounts of life insurance coverage as though they had less taxable income as a result of that coverage. Generally, the revised uniform premiums are effective July 1, 1999; however, employers have until the last pay period of 1999 to make any needed adjustments on the amounts withheld. Under these new regulations, employee-pay-all supplemental group term life insurance programs may be affected.

Q 10:20 What are the tax regulations on the executive perquisites of company planes and first-class travel?

In most cases these expenses are business-related and are a tax deduction to the company. They are not considered taxable income to the executive.

With respect to company planes, a log is maintained on the date and travel destination, passengers, and the business purpose of the flight. If an executive decides to take a company plane to a vacation destination, then the company is required to impute income to the executive's W-2 at year-end because the use of the company plane was personal, not business-related.

First-class air travel is documented on company expense reports and the fact that a company elects to provide certain officers with first-class versus coach travel is an internal company decision and has no impact on the business purpose of the travel, nor on the taxation.

Q 10:21 What are the tax regulations on the executive financial planning perquisite?

Financial planning can include estate planning, tax planning, investment strategy planning, and general financial advice and counsel. With this perquisite, the company agrees to pay an outside consultant a specified fee or maximum fee, for most types of financial planning advice (described in the company's policy statement) other than advice on what investments the executive should select. This perquisite requires that the planner be very familiar with the executive's financial objectives and personal situation and the company benefit programs and long-term/stock awards and their terms and provisions.

All amounts paid by the company are taxable income to the executive and represent a tax deduction to the company. The amounts are imputed onto the executive's W-2 at year-end. Fees paid by the company for tax counsel and tax preparation may be deducted by the executive to the extent they exceed 2 percent of the executive's adjusted gross income. This rarely occurs, so for practical purposes all financial planning fees are taxable income to the executive.

Q 10:22   What is the accounting treatment of executive perquisites?

Where executive perquisites are treated as compensation expense to the executive, the company can deduct the cost as a compensation expense under selling, general, and administrative expenses (SG&A) on the income statement. Companies can also deduct business expenses paid for an executive as expenses under SG&A.

Contracts

Q 10:23   What are the types of executive contracts?

There are several types of executive contracts:

1. *Employment contract.* Identifies a term of employment, the services to be provided by the executive during this term, and the compensation to be provided by the company.

2. *Retirement contract.* Establishes a fixed retirement benefit for an executive. Typically the benefit is offset by any retirement benefits that the executive will receive from the company's qualified plans and the contract promises to pay the difference if the executive meets specified tenure and/or age requirements.

3. *Severance contract.* Provides for specified compensation in the event the executive is involuntarily terminated (other than for cause). A severance contract can be a golden parachute or non-golden parachute contract. The golden parachute applies to change-of-control situations and has either a single trigger (change of control only) or a double trigger (loss of job and change of control).

4. *Combination contract.* Any combination of the previous three contracts.

Q 10:24   How does a company select the type of executive contract?

Company business objectives will be the primary factor driving the decision on executive contracts. Competitive practice can also be a secondary consideration.

If a company has a group of executives who are all age 50 or older, or if it needs to attract mid-career executives to the business, then retirement contracts can be an effective tool for attracting and retaining key executives. If a company is in an industry that is subject to acquisition or divestiture, or subject to extensive restructuring or reorganization, then a severance contract can be an effective tool for retaining key executives. Employment contracts can be a valuable tool for retaining executives in many different business environments. In summary, business necessity will determine the type of employment contract that best fits the business.

Q 10:25   What are the advantages of an employment agreement?

Employment agreements are considered a perquisite because, from the executive's perspective, they guarantee employment during the term of the contract. They can also benefit the company in the retention of executives, because they make it difficult for the executive to leave the company. The agreement also provides the company with an opportunity to add to the contract a restrictive covenant that prohibits the executive from working for a competitor.

Q 10:26   What are the disadvantages of an employment agreement?

The contract limits the executive's freedom to seek a better job opportunity, particularly if the agreement prohibits work for a competitor. A disadvantage to the company is that an executive with an employment agreement cannot be terminated unless the remaining terms of the contract are paid. So even if the executive's performance deteriorates during the term of the contract, the company still has to employ the executive until the end of the contract term.

Q 10:27   Are noncompete clauses enforceable?

Generally, yes, particularly if the company agrees to pay the executive during the time that he or she is prohibited from working. Court cases have shown that a company cannot prohibit an executive from seeking any type of work; however, companies can pay executives who possess company secrets on future products, patents, etc., for a fixed period, and generally stop them from going to work for a competitor. The broader the restrictions (e.g., geographic restrictions, type of work) the less likely the enforceability under varying state courts.

Q 10:28   Are employment agreements enforceable?

It is difficult for a company to enforce an employment agreement against an executive who terminates, because if the company takes the executive to court, cases have shown that the courts will not require executives to provide services against their will. Court opinions have said that the executive simply ceased rendering services under the contract and the contract is therefore void. In such a case, the company will, however, be able to cease payments to the executive, and will be able to enforce the return of confidential company material. If there is a noncompete agreement, it will be enforceable under the conditions described in Q 10:27.

It is much easier for an executive to enforce an employment agreement, because if the company elects to cease making payments to the executive, the courts will see this as a breach of contract by the company and will typically require the company to continue payment of compensation under the terms of the contract. Any desire of the company to terminate involuntarily an executive under contract will not be successful unless the reason for termination is for "cause," such as theft or embezzlement.

An example of a definition of termination for "cause" is as follows:

Cause shall be defined as but not limited to:

1. Refusal or failure to implement reasonable directives of the company.

2. Willful misconduct or gross negligence in the performance of job duties.

3. Irresponsible conduct that has an adverse impact on the company's reputation or standing in the community or with customers.

4. Conviction of a crime involving moral turpitude to include fraud, theft, or embezzlement.

5. Conduct that is in violation of the executive's common law duty of loyalty to the company.

6. Fraudulent conduct in connection with the business affairs of the company.

7. Willful or persistent failure to attend to job duties.

8. Breach of any material terms or provisions of the executive's employment agreement.

Planning Tip. Employers and employees may wish to consider an employment contract that allows either party to cancel the contract within a specified notice period, such as 90 days or 120 days. It can also be beneficial for both parties to have in the employment contract an involuntary termination (severance) provision that allows the company to make this decision provided it guarantees the executive some minimum severance, such as six months' salary.

Sample employment termination provisions in employment agreements are provided in Appendix D at the back of the book.

Q 10:29   What is a golden parachute?

A golden parachute is an agreement that provides a generous severance package to top executives in the event of a change of control of the company (e.g., acquisition, merger). A golden parachute can have a "single trigger" or "double trigger." A single-trigger agreement allows the executive to receive the stated severance benefits when the change of control occurs, even though the executive keeps his or her job. A double-trigger agreement allows the executive to receive the stated severance benefits when both a change of control and a loss of job occur.

Q 10:30   What is a silver parachute?

A silver parachute is the same as a golden parachute except it applies to management-level positions rather than officer-level positions. It too is triggered by a single event (change of control) or a double event (change of control plus loss of job). The severance benefits of a silver parachute are typically not as good as those found in the golden parachute.

Q 10:31   What is a tin parachute?

A tin parachute is the same as a silver parachute except that it applies to nonmanagement positions rather than to management positions. It is triggered by either a change of control or a change of control plus a loss of job. The severance benefits of a tin parachute are not typically as good as those found in a silver parachute.

Q 10:32   How is a change of control defined?

A change of control is typically defined to include the following types of events:

1. Any sale, merger, or consolidation of the company with another company that involves all or substantially all of the company's assets;
2. The passing of a resolution by the board of directors or the shareholders to liquidate the assets of the company in one or more transactions;
3. Any takeover of all or substantially all of the assets of the company by any person or persons other than the current shareholders; or
4. A sale of a majority of the voting securities of the company by the existing shareholders.

Q 10:33   What are the advantages and disadvantages of golden parachutes?

Among the many positive and negative arguments for and against golden parachutes are the following:

Positives	*Negatives*
1. Assistance in retaining key executives during a time of restructuring in the business.	1. Help in keeping management in control and not selling the business even though such a sale would be in the best interest of the shareholders.
2. Motivation for executives to negotiate the best deal possible for shareholders because the executives already have their deal.	2. Encouragement to leave after a merger/takeover, the time key executives are needed most.
3. Executive jobs are the most likely jobs to be eliminated during a takeover, and a special severance helps to bridge the earnings gap while the executive looks for another position.	3. Parachute payments go to the highly compensated people who already have substantial compensation levels. It is unfair to give these payments only to highly paid individuals when nonexecutives also lose their jobs.

Q 10:34 What government regulations impact golden parachute payments?

Internal Revenue Code Section 280G and the proposed regulations issued thereunder contain the rules on golden parachute payments. These rules apply to payments "in the nature of compensation" to a "disqualified individual" if such payments are contingent upon change in ownership or effective control of a company or are contingent upon a change in ownership of substantially all of the assets of a company. Under Code Section 280G, a company is denied a tax deduction for any "excess parachute payment." Under Code Section 4999, a tax penalty is imposed on the individual who receives a parachute payment equal to 20 percent of any "excess parachute payment."

Q 10:35 What are payments "in the nature of compensation"?

Basically, all wages and salary, bonuses, severance pay, fringe benefits, pension benefits, and other deferred compensation arising out of an employment relationship are treated as compensation payments. Transfers of property, such as stock options, are also treated as compensation payments.

Q 10:36 Who is a "disqualified individual"?

Any employee or independent contractor of the company who is, at any time during the 12-month period immediately prior to a change of control, a shareholder (owner of more than 1 percent of the company, or, if less, owner of stock valued at more than $1 million), an officer, or a highly compensated individual (among the highest paid 1 percent of employees, or, if less, one of the highest paid 250 employees) is a disqualified individual under Code Section 280G.

Q 10:37 When do the golden parachute tax rules apply?

A payment to an officer, director, or highly compensated individual will be deemed to be a parachute payment if it is contingent upon a change of control of the company and the total present value of all such contingent compensation exceeds 299 percent of the "base amount," that is, the individual's average annual compensation during the five tax years immediately prior to the change of control.

Once it has been established that a parachute payment exists, the corporation will not be entitled to deduct the part of the payment that constitutes an "excess parachute payment," and the individual receiving the payment will be subject to a 20 percent excise tax on the excess, in addition to all other ordinary income tax obligations.

The parachute provisions do not apply to certain "small business corporations," which are corporations that have only one class of stock and no more than 75 shareholders (all individuals, none of whom are non-resident aliens), i.e., have elected Subchapter S status or are eligible to do so. The parachute rules also do not apply to non-publicly traded corporations if the stockholders have approved the change of control payments by more than a 75 percent vote with "adequate disclosure" of all material facts. For the nonpublic corporation, the reason for adopting parachute agreements is not as compelling because management generally controls more than a majority of the stock and it is unlikely that the company will find itself in a hostile takeover situation.

Q 10:38 What is an "excess parachute payment"?

An excess parachute payment is any payment that exceeds the "base amount." The distinction between a parachute payment and an "excess parachute payment" is an important one because when a parachute payment exists, it could become an "excess parachute payment" if payments aggregate to three times the base amount or more. When this occurs, all payments beyond the base amount are deemed to be excess.

Q 10:39 Are there certain types of payments not considered to be parachute payments?

Yes. The following types of payments are exempt from being considered a parachute payment:

1. Any payment that is "reasonable compensation" for services actually performed for the company on or after the date of the change of control. Note that annual compensation after the change of control cannot be significantly more than compensation received prior to the change of control and that severance payments are not considered "reasonable compensation."

2. Payments to or from a qualified retirement plan. Such amounts are not taken into account in applying the "3 times base amount" parachute test.

Q 10:40 What are payments "contingent" on a change of control?

Payments specifically conditioned upon a change of control include those payments (1) made under a contract providing for specific payments upon a change of control and (2) contingent upon an event closely associated with a change of control, such as a tender offer, termination of employment, or significant reduction in employment duties and responsibilities. Payments made with respect to an event that occurs within the 12-month period prior to or after a change of control are presumed to be "contingent" payments. If an employment contract is entered into or amended within the 12-month period before a change of control, all benefits under that contract are deemed to be contingent on a change of control (such a presumption can be rebutted). In some cases, only the nonvested portion of a payment that is accelerated upon a change of control will be treated as a parachute payment (e.g., stock options that are partially vested become fully vested upon a change of control and only part of the "transferred" value is treated as a parachute payment).

Q 10:41 How is the "excess parachute payment" calculated?

First, the individual's "base amount" is determined. The base amount is the average annual compensation over the most recent five taxable years ending before the date of the change of control. If an individual has less than five full years of compensation, the average is based on the number of years for which the individual receives any compensation and the compensation for any partial year is annualized. Next the value of payments contingent upon the change of control is determined. If the aggregate present value of these change-of-control benefits equals or exceeds three times the base amount, then the change-of-control payments are "parachute" payments. If the aggregate present value of the change-of-control payments is less than three times the base amount, then none of the payments are "parachute payments."

The proposed regulations provide that for purposes of determining "present value," a discount rate equal to 120 percent of the applicable federal long-term rate (under Code Section 1274(d)), compounded semi-annually, is used.

The "excess parachute payment" is the excess of the parachute amount over an amount equal to one times the average annual compensation of the individual.

The amount of the excess parachute payment may be reduced by the portion of the payment that is considered "reasonable compensation" for services actually performed by the individual before the date of the change of control. The proposed regulations provide that factors to be examined in determining whether a payment is in the nature of reasonable compensation include the following:

1. The nature of the services performed;

2. Historical compensation for performance of such services; and

3. Compensation of persons performing similar services in situations where there is no change of control.

Severance payments are not considered to be reasonable compensation for purposes of reducing the excess parachute amount.

Q 10:42   Are certain types of payments not subject to a change of control but still considered as parachute payments?

Yes. Any compensation payment made pursuant to an agreement that violates any generally enforced federal or state securities laws or regulations and made in connection with a potential or actual change in ownership or control will be considered a parachute payment.

Q 10:43   How are stock options treated for parachute purposes?

The proposed regulations under Code Section 280G specify that, for purposes of determining when the "property is transferred" (thus, treated as payments "in the nature of compensation"), transfer of nonqualified stock options is deemed to occur at the time that the options become vested. The value of the "transfer" is determined by examining the difference between the exercise price and the value at the time of vesting, the probability the option will increase or decrease in value, and the length of the option exercise period. The proposed regulations do not address the treatment of incentive stock options.

Q 10:44   Are parachute payments subject to tax withholding rules?

Yes. Parachute payments are treated as wages subject to tax withholding and are reported (for employees) on the individual's IRS Form W-2. FICA and FUTA tax withholding rules also apply. The company should also withhold the 20 percent excise tax on the excess parachute amount.

Q 10:45   Is there a way to avoid the 20 percent excise tax on excess parachute payments?

The best way to avoid the excise tax is to provide that if any change of control payment is considered to be an "excess parachute payment," that payment will not be made (i.e., limit parachute payments to 299 percent of the base amount).

Another alternative is for a company to agree to pay the executive's extra tax burden by "grossing up" the executive's parachute excise tax. In the gross-up process, the company pays the amount of the excise tax to the executive, calculates the ordinary income tax burden created by the extra payment, and pays that amount to the executive as well. In some cases, the company grosses up the tax on the tax.

Q 10:46   What is an example of a golden parachute payment?

A company provides executives with a "change of control" golden parachute payment such that if control of the company changes and if the executive is involuntarily terminated within two years of the change of control (double-trigger provision), then the executive will be provided with the following severance payments and benefits:

1. An amount equaling one year's base salary, calculated by taking the higher of the current annual salary in effect at the time of the involuntary termination or the highest annual salary in effect during the four previous years;

2. The higher of the previous year's incentive award or the highest incentive award paid during the previous four years;

3. An amount equal to the number of vested and unvested shares from each long-term stock option award multiplied by the "spread" calculated by subtracting the option price minus the company stock price under the terms of the sale or merger;

4. An amount equal to the target award level of each long-term performance plan in effect at the time of the company sale or merger;

5. Payment of one year's country club dues and one additional personal financial plan review with the executive's financial planning consultant;

6. Payment of the lease on the executive's company car for a period of one year with an option for the executive to purchase the car at the end of one year at the wholesale bluebook value; and

7. Provision of an office and payment of monthly secretarial services for a period of one year.

Assume that the total aggregate present value of the severance package is $500,000. The company would then calculate the "base amount" compensation (average W-2 pay during the last five years). If this amount were $200,000, then the executive would not be subject to any excess parachute payment excise tax because the amount of the parachute payment ($500,000) would not exceed 299 percent of the base amount (299% × $200,000 = $598,000).

If the base period amount were $150,000, an excess parachute payment would result because the amount of the parachute payment ($500,000) would exceed 299 percent of the base amount ($150,000 × 299% = $448,500). In this case the executive would owe a 20 percent excise tax, and it would be based on the amount of the parachute payment over the base amount, which would equal $350,000 ($500,000 − $150,000 = $350,000). The excise tax would be $70,000 (20% × $350,000 = $70,000), and this would be in addition to the executive's ordinary income tax on the $500,000.

Q 10:47   What are typical provisions in a retirement contract?

A retirement contract establishes a retirement benefit for an executive in the future if certain age and/or tenure requirements are met by the executive. Two concepts are typically used in these contracts:

1. A specific benefit level is established. Any retirement benefits from the company's qualified retirement plan that the executive is entitled to at the time of retirement are deducted from the specified benefit level. The company would then pay the executive the additional amount upon retirement.

2. A specific benefit level is established and paid upon retirement.

Both of these alternatives could include a social security payment offset as well. Alternative 1 could also include an offset from any other company's retirement plan that will pay retirement income benefits to the executive. The primary objective of this concept is simply to guarantee the executive a fixed retirement benefit, typically expressed as a percentage of final average pay.

The second alternative is simpler, but requires accurate forecasting of an executive's retirement income and retirement age to insure that the supplemental benefit provided by the contract will, when added to other sources of retirement income available to the executive, provide the desired level of total retirement income for the executive.

Q 10:48   Why do companies use retirement contracts for executives?

The primary reason for these contracts is to attract and retain executive talent in the organization. On the one hand, when a company has an excellent group of experienced executives, one way to keep them in the company is to provide them with adequate retirement benefits. Many companies also need to hire additional executives from outside the business. When this is done, it is common for that executive to give up or lose retirement credits or benefits from his or her former employer. One way to attract an executive to a company is to provide that executive with a retirement contract.

Another important reason for retirement contracts is that, in most cases, executives do not receive adequate retirement income from a qualified retirement plan, because ERISA and Internal Revenue Code regulations tend to discriminate against higher-paid employees. The limitations on qualified retirement plan contributions and benefit levels simply do not allow an executive to receive retirement income, measured as a percentage of final average pay, that is equal to that of nonexecutives.

Q 10:49   What are the advantages and disadvantages of retirement contracts?

Some of the advantages and disadvantages of retirement contracts include:

Advantages	*Disadvantages*
1. Help to retain executives who are subject to Internal Revenue Code limitations on benefits and who would therefore receive less retirement benefits than earned.	1. Can be difficult to establish equitable eligibility for this contract. These contracts can be discriminatory with respect to eligibility.
2. Help to attract mid-career people who would typically lose retirement benefits when they leave their former employer.	2. Require additional administration time and cost. Executives with this contractual benefit will require statements on the status of invested funds and potential benefit levels, etc.
3. Can be structured to encourage executives to use some of their own funds to improve future retirement benefits.	3. Could be viewed by nonexecutive employees as inequitable and unfair.

Q 10:50 What is an example of an executive retirement contract?

Retirement contracts will vary depending on the benefit level to be provided. Most professional financial planners will suggest that executives plan on a total retirement benefit of 50 percent to 70 percent of final average pay. In addition these same consultants will suggest that Social Security benefits will equal 10 percent to 20 percent of final average pay. Using a 60 percent targeted benefit and assumptions that Social Security payments will equal 15 percent of the executive's final average pay and that the company's qualified retirement plan will provide a retirement benefit of 25 percent of final average pay (15% + 25% = 40%, or 20 percent short of the targeted benefit), an executive's retirement contract might read as follows:

> You will be eligible for the company's supplemental retirement program, which will provide you with 20 percent of your final average pay if you reach age 60 with at least 20 years of company service. This is in addition to benefits you will receive from the company's qualified 401(k) retirement plan and from Social Security.

Another more sophisticated way to structure benefits in a retirement contract that does not use targeted benefit levels is as follows:

> You will be eligible for the company's supplemental retirement program. Depending on company pre-tax earnings performance each year, the company will contribute 0 to 10 percent of your annual salary, provided you have contributed (deferred) at least 5 percent of your base salary to the supplemental retirement fund each year. You will be fully vested in all amounts you contribute to the retirement fund; however, company contributions to the retirement fund will vest as follows: 50 percent at age 55, 75 percent at age 58, and 100 percent at age 62.

Chapter 11

Building a Total Compensation Strategy

There are five elements to executive compensation: base salary, benefits, short-term incentives, long-term incentives, and perquisites. Each of these elements has complex tax, accounting, and regulatory considerations. In addition, companies change, as do the purposes of these elements of executive compensation. For these reasons, companies find that they need to develop a strategy on how each of these elements should be used. This chapter provides information on the compensation, benefit, and other factors to be considered in developing the appropriate mix of executive compensation and on the overall total compensation strategy for a company. The chapter also identifies specific subjects that should be included under each element of executive compensation discussed in a strategy statement, and provides examples of strategy statements

General Considerations 11-2
Compensation Factors 11-3
Benefit Factors 11-6
Other Factors 11-9
Determining the Mix 11-10
Developing a Total Strategy 11-14
Approval and Implementation 11-15
Examples of Strategy Statements 11-17

General Considerations

Q 11:1 What is a total compensation strategy?

A total compensation strategy serves as a statement of the business value of and philosophy behind a company's compensation and benefit programs. The statement identifies the purpose of all executive compensation programs and establishes parameters that guide the utilization of those programs within the organization (see Q 1:1).

Q 11:2 What elements of executive compensation are included in a total compensation strategy statement?

The five elements of executive compensation are base salary, short-term incentives, long-term incentives, benefits, and perquisites (see Q 1:1). Total compensation strategy statements address all of these executive compensation elements.

Q 11:3 What are the business purposes of a total compensation strategy?

Total compensation strategies give organizations the opportunity to accomplish the following:

1. Evaluate the cost of executive compensation programs to the company versus the value of executive compensation to company executives;

2. Compare executive compensation costs in the company with similar costs in other companies;

3. Identify how executive compensation programs are supporting business goals;

4. Identify how executive compensation programs are supporting human resource goals;

5. Define competitive labor markets and establish a targeted competitive level of executive pay appropriate for the company;

6. Identify where changes or enhancements to executive compensation programs are required in support of changing business and human resources objectives;

7. Determine measures of key performance (for use in executive compensation programs) that drive business success;

8. Identify primary areas of executive activity and behavior that are required for business success;

9. Identify where executive compensation programs may need to differ by company business unit; and

10. Determine all communication necessary to convey to executives (and non-executives) the company's executive compensation philosophy, executive compensation program roles and purposes, and individual plan objectives.

Compensation Factors

Q 11:4   What factors determine a total compensation strategy?

In building a total compensation strategy, the company should review the following factors: its basic philosophy; mission and vision; business plans; life cycle; internal factors such as organizational structure, business processes and systems, and work force demographics; external factors such as tax and accounting regulations, industry regulations, and competitive environment.

Q 11:5   How does a company's philosophy affect its total compensation strategy?

A company's business philosophy encompasses its basic values and beliefs. It defines the environment in which a total compensation strategy will be administered. For example, a management style that focuses on short-term gains needs a total compensation strategy that emphasizes short-term incentives. Companies with a highly delegative and informal management style need a total compensation strategy that emphasizes team performance from short-term and long-term incentive compensation programs. Companies with a paternalistic philosophy might place a heavier emphasis on salary and benefits.

Q 11:6   How can a company's mission or vision statement affect its total compensation strategy?

A company's mission statement identifies the purpose of the organization, while a vision statement is best described as a tangible image that should guide the company's executives as they implement the company mission. These terms will frequently set the company's philosophy and culture as well as its total compensation strategy. For example, a well-known consumer products company has a statement that its vision is to be the number one consumer products company in the world. In contrast, another leading U.S. company has a mission statement of service to humanity. These mission statements affect both company culture and total compensation strategy as follows:

Mission	*Culture*	*Total Compensation Strategy*
Best consumer product company in the world	Risk-taking, aggressive, and high degree of change	Heavy emphasis on incentive compensation and high pay levels
Service to humanity	Paternalistic, heavy emphasis on planning and controlled, profitable growth	Typical mix of incentive compensation elements, high base salary and benefits

Q 11:7   How can a company's business plan affect a total compensation strategy?

The business strategies and plans of any company will directly affect a total compensation strategy. For example, a company that has short-term concerns such as cash flow, short-term debt, or reorganization following a merger would likely place significant emphasis on short-term incentives in its total compensation strategy. In contrast, a company that has just made a major capital investment would likely emphasize long-term incentives in its total compensation strategy. Another example is a company that is planning a number of mergers and company reorganizations that could result in significant employee turnover. This company would likely focus its total compensation strategy on benefits and perquisites.

Business plans also contain key performance measures that should be utilized in executive compensation plans and total compensation strategies (see Qs 4:29–4:34).

Q 11:8 How can a company's life cycle affect its total compensation strategy?

A company life cycle is commonly expressed as one of three stages: growth, maturity, and decline. A small growth company without a lot of cash might establish a total compensation strategy that emphasizes long-term income in the form of stock options, because from a cost perspective, stock options are not charged to a company's earnings. A mature company with sufficient cash that has applied more extensive and varied performance measures might establish a total compensation strategy that emphasizes performance-based short-term or long-term incentives. Similarly, a company in a cycle of decline would probably emphasize benefits and perquisites.

Q 11:9 How do internal factors affect a company's total compensation strategy?

Like business plans, internal factors have a direct impact on the development of a total compensation strategy. Organizational structure is one such factor: A decentralized company with various strategic business units must decide if these units should have similar or different total compensation strategies.

Quality management programs (e.g., quality circles) are a major internal factor for many companies. The teamwork and team building required in these organizations will frequently drive a total compensation strategy that emphasizes profit sharing in both short- and long-term incentive plans.

Other internal factors are the number of policies and procedures in an organization, and the sophistication of its financial reporting methods. When these internal factors are present in an organization, they will usually drive performance-based incentive plans (both short- and long-term).

The demographics of a company's executive work force can also drive a total compensation strategy. For example, if there is a shortage of executives in the labor market, long-term incentive plans (like restricted stock) could be a major element of executive compensation in the total compensation strategy. If many executives are approaching retirement age, this factor could drive the use of benefit or perquisite enhancements as the major emphasis of the total compensation strategy.

Q 11:10 How do external factors affect a company's total compensation strategy?

Highly regulated industries such as utility companies, transportation companies, and nonprofit organizations typically have not adopted a total compensation strategy with a heavy emphasis on incentive compensation (both short- and long-term). These companies would typically adopt a total compensation strategy that emphasizes salary and benefits.

On the other hand, companies under heavy external competitive threat can use total compensation strategy statements to emphasize the achievement of immediate short-term business goals.

Another external factor is the constant change in tax and accounting regulations, which can direct total compensation strategies, particularly with respect to long-term income. For example, major tax law changes historically have caused companies to restructure long-term income in the form of stock awards that emphasize either capital gains or ordinary income tax, whichever is most favorable at the time.

Benefit Factors

Q 11:11 What benefit programs should be included in a total compensation strategy statement?

Total compensation strategy statements should include provisions for health care benefits and costs, retirement, capital accumulation plans, and life and disability insurance. These four benefit programs are affected by changing business conditions and thus can affect a company's total compensation strategy. Other benefits, such as holidays, vacations, and time off with pay, usually do not vary with business conditions and business priorities and therefore are not included in a total compensation strategy statement.

Q 11:12   How can health care plan benefits and costs affect a total compensation strategy statement?

The decade of the 1990s has already seen an unparalleled focus on health care cost containment. The current 20 percent annual growth in health costs represents an excellent reason for companies to develop a total compensation strategy. One such health care strategy may be to maintain the current employer/employee cost responsibility ratio at 60 percent for employer and 40 percent for employee during the next three years. Another example would be for a company to establish employer health care cost levels such that benefits are at or below 10 percent of the average monthly payroll costs for full-time active employees.

Self-insurance is another key strategy with respect to health care plans. While many companies have adopted this strategy as a means of cost control, this may not be appropriate for companies with low cash flow amounts. Therefore, any self-insurance strategy should also be included in a company's total compensation strategy statement as a means of establishing both direction and cost parameters for this important element of health care.

Q 11:13   How can retirement benefits affect a company's total compensation strategy statement?

Retirement benefits for executives include those from a defined benefit or defined contribution pension plan plus those retirement benefits from any nonqualified plan or supplemental executive retirement plan (see Q 9:31). A total compensation strategy statement should identify the desired level of executive retirement benefit, in recognition of required costs. For example, the total retirement benefit for executives from a qualified and nonqualified plan can be targeted for 20 percent of final average pay, if retirement occurs at age 60, after 20 years of service.

There are other important dimensions of a retirement benefit strategy. Prior retirement benefits from another employer should be considered for inclusion in the targeted retirement benefit for executives. The integration of targeted retirement benefits with those provided by the government (in the form of social security) should also be referenced in a total compensation strategy statement.

Q 11:14 How can life insurance and disability insurance affect a company's total compensation strategy statement?

Any consideration of life insurance in a total compensation strategy should be focused primarily on the level of supplemental life insurance to be either provided to executives by the company or purchased by the executive. For example, a company may provide life insurance for non-executives in an amount equal to base salary and for executives in an amount double that of base salary, since the surviving spouse of an executive will generally require greater income replacement upon the executive's death. A similar issue exists for disability insurance; however, in most companies the executive benefit involves a higher maximum dollar amount of disability income protection provided by the company's disability plan rather than the provision of additional disability insurance. This is accomplished by establishing a minimum percentage of income protection for executives so that they can receive a similar value from the disability plan. For example, a typical disability plan might provide 50 percent of base salary up to $1,500 per month. For executives, the total compensation strategy may be to provide 50 percent of base salary with no maximum, or with a maximum of $3,000 per month rather than $1,500 per month.

Q 11:15 How can capital accumulation plans affect a company's total compensation strategy statement?

Like retirement benefits, capital accumulation plans include any tax qualified plan benefit (e.g., a 401(k) plan with a company matching 50 percent of the employee contribution up to a maximum of 6 percent of base salary), plus any nonqualified plan benefit, including plans known as Internal Revenue Code (the Code) Section 415 excess plans (see Q 9:16). The U.S. government, through the Internal Revenue Code requirements, sets the maximum contribution that companies can make to a qualified plan. Companies can use their total compensation strategy statement to identify and evaluate the amount and cost of any excess benefit plan that can generally restore the company contributions or matching amounts to the level prescribed by the qualified plan but restricted by Code Section 415. This same strategy issue applies to capital accumulation plans such as profit sharing plans or ESOPs. As with other benefit plan issues, the inclusion of company strategies in a total compensation strategy statement disciplines a company to deal with both the benefit and cost implications appropriate for its business.

Other Factors

Q 11:16   Can total compensation strategies vary by company business unit?

Yes. This can be most appropriate in large companies that are in more than one business. The factors that determine a total compensation strategy (see Q 11:4) will indicate whether strategies should differ among company business units. For example, a parent company may establish a business strategy of growth in another industry. The business characteristics, level of risk taking, and the time span for product/service development may differ significantly between the existing and contemplated industries; thus, total compensation strategies will differ as well.

> **Example.** A regional utility company wants to expand its business into other states so that it can purchase additional power from these states for use during peak usage periods. The department responsible for this expansion has business characteristics similar to the real estate industry in that it has an aggressive and deal-oriented environment, quite unlike the utility industry, which is more stable, cautiously aggressive, and highly regulated. These different business characteristics will drive different total compensation strategies. The expanded department may have a total compensa-

tion strategy that uses incentive compensation extensively while the parent company may have a total compensation strategy that focuses more on long-term income programs.

Q 11:17 Can total compensation strategies be developed for international businesses?

Yes. The integration of compensation and benefits is most critical in companies with international operations because government-mandated benefits differ significantly from country to country. Business strategies for international companies or business units of a multinational company can also vary significantly from those in the United States. Companies should consider comparing (1) the total compensation levels among countries where they have international operations and (2) the competitiveness of total compensation levels within each of those countries.

Measuring international compensation and benefit levels is considerably more difficult for the following reasons: (1) many different programs exist; (2) ability to measure total compensation varies between countries; (3) a greater knowledge of benefit accounting and tax laws is required for the measurement of total compensation (e.g., benefit cost determination can vary significantly depending on who pays what and how); (4) compensation cost analysis can vary depending on the evaluation methods used for stock-related plans. While these factors can also apply in a comparison of U.S. companies, the complexity is multiplied when conducting total compensation analyses for international businesses.

Determining the Mix

Q 11:18 How can a company determine the proper mix of executive compensation elements in a total compensation strategy statement?

After reviewing the factors determining a total compensation strategy (see Qs 11:4–11:10) companies will typically identify target amounts for each element of executive compensation and express them as a percentage of base salary.

For example:

Compensation Element	Percentage of Base Salary
Annual incentive award	30
Long-term incentive award	35
Benefits	40
Perquisites	5
TOTAL	110%

Under this example, an additional 110 percent of base salary can be earned from other elements of executive compensation. This percentage will vary by position in an organization. Higher-level jobs will typically have a higher percentage of annual incentive and long-term incentive award potential plus perquisites, while benefits will remain relatively constant. The logic behind higher amounts of incentive is that higher-level jobs with greater responsibility should have greater total compensation dependent upon performance. Companies typically believe, as well, that higher-level positions with greater responsibility require more perquisites such as complex financial planning assistance and greater use of business clubs.

Q 11:19 How should companies define competitive labor markets?

Many companies will develop a list of labor market competitors who are either in the same or similar businesses or who represent companies from which employees can be recruited. An important factor in this determination is to ensure that competitor companies are not necessarily limited to those organizations that market the same product or service. For instance, human resources talent can be found outside of the direct competition; therefore, a total compensation strategy needs to be flexible.

Labor markets for executive positions are national. Surveys show very little total compensation differences based on location. Thus, geography should not be a primary factor in defining competitive labor markets (see Q 1:16).

Q 11:20   Should all companies establish a total compensation strategy to pay at the 50th percentile of labor market competitors?

No, but companies should start at this point. If a company's business environment is high growth, and a number of new employees are being recruited from outside the company, then a company's total compensation strategy might appropriately be to pay above the 50th percentile of competitors. This strategy should be applied equally to current as well as new employees.

A company's total compensation strategy may be to pay below the 50th percentile in certain situations: if the supply of executives may exceed the demand; actual pay levels of executives may be well above the market median; or company performance may be far below expected levels and profit may be threatened. This decision should be reviewed annually to determine whether it remains appropriate.

Q 11:21   How can a company decide on the type of short-term incentive?

A simple method to determine the best type of short-term incentive for a company is to compare the six types of short-term incentive (discretionary, percentage of profit, growth, performance target, peer comparison, and matrix plan) described in Chapter 4 to the factors that determine a total compensation strategy as described in Q 11:4. Once a company has evaluated the factors that determine a total compensation strategy, it can use this information to decide on the type of short-term incentive. An example of this is shown in Chart 11-1, which first lists the six types of short-term incentive (horizontally) and then lists (vertically) the factors that determine the total compensation strategy (in this example, only the life cycle factor is shown). In the first example, a decision is made concerning the application of a discretionary plan to the small company that is in the growth life cycle. In this case, where there is little sophistication in measuring performance, the discretionary plan fits the growth company's life cycle very well and a YES is entered into that column. The same conclusion is reached with respect to the percentage of profit plan type, and the growth plan type. On the other hand, the performance target, peer company comparison, and matrix plan concepts all require the use of sophisticated performance measures, and a NO is entered into these categories to indicate that they are not the best plan type given this company's growth life cycle characteristics. The second example in Chart 11-1 is a large company in a mature life cycle, with stable cash flow and a high ability to measure performance. In this case, the growth, performance target, peer company, and matrix plan types are assigned a YES, indicating that these concepts would work well in this business environment. The discretionary and percentage of profit plan types are assigned a NO.

If companies will prepare a similar analysis to that shown in Chart 11-1 for all six factors that determine a total compensation strategy, then the best plan type can emerge from this analysis and guide the company in its selection process.

Chart 11-1. Short-Term Incentive Selection

	Discretionary	Percentage of Profit	Growth	Performance Target	Peer Comparison	Matrix Plan
Growth Life Cycle	YES	YES	YES	NO	NO	NO
Mature Life Cycle	NO	NO	YES	YES	YES	YES

Q 11:22 How can companies decide on the best type of long-term incentive?

A similar analysis as that described in Question 11:21 for short-term incentives can be used in selecting the long-term incentives. The various types of long-term incentives described in Chapters 5 through 8 can be compared to the factors that determine a total compensation strategy, so that a judgment can be made for the plan type that best fits each strategy factor. An example of this is shown in Chart 11-2, which compares three long-term stock award alternatives (nonqualified stock options, restricted stock, and stock appreciation rights) to three specific business objectives (low cost, executive ownership, and long-term stock appreciation). From this specific comparison, the nonqualified stock option, which does not have any charge to the company's income statement, emerges as the best form of long-term income if the primary business objective is low cost. With respect to achieving executive ownership, the restricted stock alternative emerges as the best alternative because it is the only one of the three that provides for immediate ownership at the time of grant. With respect to the third business objective of long-term stock appreciation, the chart indicates that the nonqualified stock option and the stock appreciation right are the best alternatives since the value of both is dependent upon stock appreciation.

Chart 11-2. Long-Term Incentive Selection

Business Objective	Nonqualified Stock Option	Restricted Stock	Stock Appreciation Right
Low cost	YES	NO	NO
Executive ownership	NO	YES	NO
Stock appreciation	YES	NO	YES

Any method used to determine the best type of long-term incentive requires a judgment call and follows a two-step process: (1) identifying business concerns that need to be supported with a total compensation strategy, and (2) identifying the plan types that can be utilized in a total compensation strategy in direct support of business objectives.

Developing a Total Strategy

Q 11:23   What should be included in a total compensation strategy statement?

A total compensation strategy should include statements that address the following:

1. A description of the company's total compensation philosophy as it applies to each element of total compensation. For example, will compensation plans be "pay for performance," or will they remain relatively constant from year to year; will benefit plans be "cost sharing" or will the employer pay most costs?

2. The purpose of each element of total compensation (base salary, annual bonus, long-term incentive, perquisites, and

benefits), and, where possible, a specific reference as to how the element(s) support company business and/or human resource objectives.

3. The structure of each element of executive compensation. For example, will long-term plans be stock-based or performance-based; will health care plans be self-insured?

4. The targeted levels of labor market competitiveness for each element of total compensation by strategic business unit or major department, as appropriate. For example, maintain salary and bonus levels that are at the 50th percentile for a select group of competitive companies.

5. The criteria for communication of the company's executive compensation program, to include what should be communicated, and to whom communication should occur (e.g., executives, non-executives, members of the Board of Directors).

Approval and Implementation

Q 11:24   Who should approve a total compensation strategy?

Companies with a board compensation committee should use these directors to approve a compensation strategy (see Q 2:23). Outside directors on a board compensation committee will typically have the responsibility of approving the design of executive compensation programs and strategies, and of approving individual stock plans for officers. Companies without a board compensation committee would typically have the CEO approve a total compensation strategy.

Q 11:25   How should a total compensation strategy be communicated to executives?

There are two key events related to the communication of a total compensation strategy to executives. The first of these is the full communication of the strategy statement itself through group or individual meetings. Simple discussion of the entire total compensation strategy document is the most simple and effective way to accomplish this communication. Elaborate video or slide presentations are not necessary. Each executive should be given a copy of the strategy statement for reference throughout the year. The value that can be realized from communicating a total compensation strategy is as follows:

1. A certain level of expectation is established with respect to the purpose of each element of executive compensation.
2. The priorities of each element of executive compensation are clarified, which helps bring focus to the individual activities and efforts of each executive.
3. The value of the amount of total compensation (both financial and nonfinancial) to the individual executive is established, along with the contributions that are required of each executive.

The second event in communicating total compensation strategies is to inform each executive at the end of each year of her major accomplishments and actual earnings for that year. This can be accomplished with an individual executive compensation statement showing the following information:

1. Base salary earned.
2. Annual incentive amounts paid.
3. Long-term income awards granted that year, plus the number of shares and the value of all shares that have vested from previous year grants.
4. Perquisite values expressed as either amounts actually used and added to the executive's W-2 or expressed as typical executive usage (e.g., club memberships, first-class air travel, and company car expenses paid).
5. Benefit program values—typically, a summary from a company's benefit statement. If a company does not use a benefit statement, the value of company payments for health care, retirement plans, life/disability insurance, and capital accumulation should be added to the individual executive compensation statement.

Many companies develop excellent total compensation strategy statements but do not realize their full value because they fail to communicate the objectives of the programs as well as the results.

Ongoing communication of a company's total compensation strategy enables it to receive a full value from this business activity.

Another dimension in communicating total compensation strategy is that other constituencies—for example, shareholders and non-executives—could benefit from knowledge of the company's total compensation strategy. However, communication to these other constituencies can be a double-edged sword. On the one hand, any communication is subject to criticism, and on the other hand, the absence of communication can sometimes create incorrect conclusions about company executive compensation programs. Any communication to shareholders or non-executives should therefore be conducted only if the value far exceeds the potential for criticism.

Examples of Strategy Statements

Q 11:26 What is an example of a total compensation strategy statement for a small company?

A small company might have the following total compensation strategy statement:

1. Our company's total compensation philosophy for executive positions will be performance-driven. We believe that individual executive performance can have a direct impact on company success. We will therefore emphasize incentive compensation opportunities as we provide executives with the following elements of total compensation:

    - Base salary in payment for the performance of ongoing job responsibilities

    - Short-term incentives, annual reward opportunities for accomplishing specific, key objectives in the annual business plan

    - A long-term income plan in the form of stock options

    - Perquisites that overcome the limits imposed by the government

    - A level of benefit programs equal to those provided by competitors.

2. Base salary and benefits will be established at or below the 50th percentile of the general industry. Benefit costs will be shared by employer and employee, with 60 percent paid by the employer, 40 percent by the employee. Incentive compensation will be established at the 75th percentile of the general industry.

3. Stock awards will be approximately double those of general industries. This is critical if we are to attract the new executives required by our company to achieve growth objectives.

4. Perquisites will be significantly below competitive practice and will be limited to supplemental retirement and supplemental life insurance for officers.

5. All executives will receive copies of this total compensation strategy statement.

Q 11:27   What is an example of a total compensation strategy statement for a large company?

A large company total compensation strategy statement might look like the following:

1. The foundation of our corporate executive compensation philosophy will be to pay above labor market averages if company performance is above labor market averages. Each company division will also develop its own strategy statement, consistent with the concepts in this corporate philosophy statement.

2. Total cash compensation (base salary plus annual bonus) will be targeted for the 50th percentile of selected peer companies in the outside labor market, with incentive compensation opportunities having significant upside potential such that high performance could bring total cash compensation to the 75th percentile of selected peer companies. The annual incentive award will be based on both company and individual performance.

3. Long-term income will be in the form of:

   • Competitive stock option grants, giving executives the same opportunity as our shareholders to purchase company shares. Incentive stock options will be utilized to the maximum extent possible, as long as the capital gains tax remains favorable. The level of stock option grants will be at the 50th percentile of our selected peer company group.

- Performance share grants, annually rewarding executives for accomplishing results in the three-year strategic plan. All goals in this plan will be approved by the board compensation committee. The combined value of stock options and performance shares are intended to place our total compensation between the 60th and 75th percentile if all performance goals are achieved.

4. Perquisites will be provided if they accomplish the following:

- Allow executives to allocate more time to the job and less to conducting personal affairs

- Assist executives in accomplishing job responsibilities

- Make up benefits lost due to regulatory limits on qualified benefits. The following perquisites meet this criteria: club memberships, financial planning assistance, first-class air travel, supplemental retirement plan, and Code Section 415 excess plan benefits associated with our savings and thrift plan.

5. Benefits will be the same as those typical of our selected peer company group. We will self-insure health care, disability, and life insurance up to a maximum amount, and insure above that point. Our retirement plan will be a defined contribution plan and will be integrated into our 401(k) savings plan.

6. The company will conduct annual meetings with executives to communicate the total compensation strategy. An annual statement will also be provided to each executive indicating their individual value from our total compensation programs.

7. Each company division will use this corporate total compensation strategy to prepare its own strategy statement and submit it to the CEO for approval.

Q 11:28   What is an example of a total compensation strategy statement in an entrepreneurial, high-growth company?

Entrepreneurial companies would typically have a total compensation strategy statement similar to the following:

1. The overall strategy of our company's executive compensation is that individual wealth can be created when company growth occurs. We will achieve this by providing our executives with three to four times the amount of stock ownership that is provided to similar jobs in other businesses. The factors that drive success of this company are growth in customers and revenue and growth in earnings. When this occurs, stock price will increase significantly and executive compensation will increase significantly.

2. Base salary and annual bonus levels will be below the 50th percentile of the labor market until pre-tax income exceeds $1 million. Our strategy will then be to increase our total cash compensation toward but not over the 50th percentile.

3. Long-term income will have no maximum or targeted labor market position, because executives will be treated like entrepreneurs and share in the capital created by stock growth, just like the original company shareholders.

4. Perquisites will be kept at a minimum except where they have a direct business value. Policies that fit this definition are first-class air travel, club memberships and fees (grossed-up for tax purposes), customer outings, meals, and entertainment.

5. Benefits will focus on protecting the executive and family from catastrophic events. Therefore, we will have competitive in-hospital coverage, disability insurance, and life insurance. Coverage of occasional doctor visits, dental exams, retirement, etc. will be below competitive averages.

6. Formal communication programs of our executive compensation strategy are unnecessary because of the informal culture of our organization and the free access of all executives to compensation data. We do expect, however, that our executives will respect the need for the confidentiality of compensation information on non-executive people.

Chapter 12

Small Company Considerations

Small companies typically have quite different executive compensation plans from those of large companies. One reason is that they often have less cash to spend on plan funding. Small companies therefore use different types of long-term incentives—specifically, stock option plans—to overcome their limited cash flow. This chapter provides specific information on how small companies, particularly family-owned businesses, structure their executive compensation to support the unique characteristics of their environment.

General Considerations 12-1
New Venture Businesses 12-9

General Considerations

Q 12:1 How does the mix of executive compensation elements differ in small companies?

Small companies tend to allocate more total compensation dollars to long-term incentives than do large companies. This is because unlike base salary and bonuses, which require cash flow and are a business expense, long-term incentives (specifically stock options) presently require neither company cash flow nor a charge to company earnings (if stock options are granted at fair market value at the time of grant).

As a result, small companies incur less compensation expense by using stock options (see Chart 12-1). In fact, surveys show that small companies provide three to four times the number of shares to executive compensation plans, as a percentage of total shares outstanding, than do large companies (15 percent versus 5 percent of total shares outstanding over five years, according to a survey by Management Performance Int'l Inc.).

Charts and discussions in Chapter 1 provide more survey information on the differences in the mix of total compensation between small companies and large companies.

Chart 12-1. Compensation Expenses of Executive Pay

Form of Compensation	Business Expense	Cash Flow Required
Base salary	Yes	Yes
Cash bonus	Yes	Yes
Bonus deferred or paid in stock	Yes	No
Stock options	No	No
Restricted stock	Yes	No
Performance plan	Yes	No

Q 12:2 How do small companies with less sophisticated business performance measures establish annual incentives?

Target performance plans (see Q 4:15) use financial and nonfinancial goal achievement as the basis for the annual incentive plan payment. Since small companies do not always have sophisticated business performance measures, and if performance fluctuates significantly from year to year, they will find other types of annual incentive plans more suitable.

Growth improvement plans (see Q 4:12) are often chosen because annual incentive payments can logically be tied to growth in factors such as the number of customers, accounts, sales, or assets. The plan assumption is that as growth occurs on these factors, earnings (however defined) will also improve. Discretionary bonus plans (see Q 4:24) are also most commonly used because under these plans the company chief executive officer (CEO) can determine the appropriate bonus award given the performance of each individual executive as well as the company's overall ability to pay.

Q 12:3 How can small companies with a small human resources staff determine appropriate compensation levels?

Two sources provide general information on actual compensation levels. *The Officer Compensation Report* (Panel Publishers, 2000) provides multi-industry total cash compensation (salary plus bonus) and long-term income compensation levels for more than 12 key executive positions. Large consulting firms also publish executive compensation surveys.

Q 12:4 What form of long-term incentive is most appropriate for small companies?

From a cost perspective, stock options (see Qs 6:9 and 6:11) are best for small companies, because they require no charge to the company's income statement and bring cash to the company when the executive purchases the shares. Private companies can use phantom shares (see Q 7:28) or book value shares to avoid dilution of stock.

A number of long-term incentive plans are useful motivators, and can further company business objectives. Company net worth (equity) can best be built by a plan that measures increases in book value (earnings divided by equity). If the objective is to build executive stock ownership, restricted stock (see Q 7:30) can provide this immediately while motivating executives to remain with the company until the restrictions have been met. A performance plan (see 7:46) is best used to reward executives for the achievement of long-term business goals under their direct control.

The most motivating long-term incentive plan is one that provides immediate value in terms of growth and personal net worth to the executive, has a high potential value, and requires little or no cost to the executive. The restricted stock plan comes closest to all of these objectives.

As shown in Chart 12-2, stock options are the most popular form of long-term incentive in small companies, as they are in large companies. This parallels a similar survey shown in Chart 6-1. Book value plans are widely used in the small company because they reward executives for building the net worth of the company, while phantom stock plans are also used extensively in the small company because they motivate the executive to build company stock price without having to use actual shares and thus dilute the stock holdings of current shareholders.

Chart 12-2. Popular Forms of Long-Term Incentive

Plan type	Prevalence*
Stock options	87%
Restricted stock	22%
Performance plans	14%
Phantom stock plans	43%
Book value plans	28%

*Totals are greater than 100% because companies use more than one form of long-term incentive.

Source: HR Management, Inc. Survey on the Prevalence of Long-Term Incentive Plans in the Small Company.

Q 12:5   How can small companies attract high-quality people without offering competitive base salary and bonus amounts?

By providing significantly greater amounts of long-term incentives in the form of stock options, small companies can offer a competitive total compensation package. Chart 12-3 contrasts small and large company compensation packages.

As shown in Chart 12-3, this small company offers considerably less base salary and benefits but significantly greater long-term incentive potential via 150,000 shares rather than 15,000 shares.

The other attractive recruitment tool for small companies is the typically greater scope of accountability offered the executive. For example, a chief financial officer (CFO) in a small company may also be responsible for the human resources and public relations areas. In a large company the CFO would be a separate position from that of chief personnel officer and chief public relations officer.

Chart 12-3. Sample Small and Large Company Employment Offers

Executive Compensation	Company with Sales at $50 million	Company with Sales at $5 billion
Base salary	$100,000	$400,000
Annual incentive	$ 25,000	$200,000
Long-term incentive	$150,000 s/o shares at $3 per share	15,000 s/o shares at $30 per share
Benefits	25% of base salary	35% of base salary
Perquisites	Company car	Car + club membership + financial planning

While the breadth of knowledge and accountability is higher in small company executive jobs, the complexity of business operations in a large company requires a greater depth of knowledge and accountability. Depending upon how this issue is presented to the executive, it can be a good recruiting tool.

Another attractive recruitment tool for small companies is often found in the nonprofit sector. Many nonprofit organizations emphasize the job satisfaction realized from doing a job that also enables one to fulfill a social responsibility. For example, a position in a YMCA or a day care facility for the elderly can provide a double reward to the executive (i.e., both job satisfaction and the satisfaction of answering a societal need). The well-known for-profit ice cream company Ben & Jerry's highlighted the same issue in recruiting a new chief executive officer.

Q 12:6 How can small companies offer competitive executive retirement plans without incurring significant costs?

Several types of nonqualified plans for executives, such as the nonqualified supplemental executive retirement plan discussed in Q 9:16, 401(k) benefit restoration plans discussed in Q 9:16, and Internal Revenue Code (Code) Section 457 plans for nonprofit companies discussed in Q 14:13 are useful for small companies. Because these plans need not be provided to non-executive employees, they can keep costs down.

Another advantage of these nonqualified plans is that benefits can be tied to the achievement of specified company performance goals. For example, an arrangement that mirrors the characteristics of a 401(k)-type plan may provide matching funds to the executive subject to that executive's achieving a 10 percent increase in company earnings during the fiscal year. Nonfinancial goals can be used for this same purpose.

Q 12:7   When and how do family-owned companies provide stock to non-family members?

During a successful start-up or threshold phase of business growth, many entrepreneurial family-owned companies decide to provide additional stock ownership to family and non-family executives. This serves primarily to retain key executives to lead the company into future successful growth and development phases. There are six key ways to deliver stock ownership:

- Book value (Q 6:41)
- Phantom shares (Q 7:20)
- Restricted stock (Q 7:30)
- Stock options (Q 6:6, 6:14)
- Performance shares (Q 7:46)
- Nonqualified profit sharing (Q 4:9)

Individual awards are determined as a percentage of a predetermined target award or as a predetermined pro rata share of incremental profit.

Q 12:8   What total compensation strategies are used in small companies?

As discussed in Qs 12:4 and 12:6, small companies tend to use a higher number of stock option shares (as a percentage of the total shares outstanding) and lower levels of base salary and annual bonus than is the case in large companies. This concept is shown in the following table, which shows how company size can drive total compensation strategy.

Compensation Element	Small Companies	Medium Companies	Large Companies
Base salary	Low	Low	Average
Annual bonus	Low	Average	Average
Long-term/stock plans	Very high	High	Average
Benefits/perquisites	Average	Average	Average

Small companies use a strategy weighted in favor of long-term incentives because they can offer generous levels of potential award without any negative impact on the company income statement. Then if the small company goes public, executives can exercise the stock options and sell them on the stock market, where there is no negative impact on company cash flow. If the company remains private, most plans will require the executive to sell the shares back to the company. When this occurs, the company is, hopefully, in a better cash flow position than it was at the time the stock option was granted. Many private companies will structure plans so that they can control when the executive is allowed to sell shares back to the company.

Q 12:9   How do small, high-growth companies establish competitive values on executives when their companies are doubling in size every one or two years?

As discussed in Q 12:8, companies offer generous levels of stock options to reward executives for the rapid growth of an organization. With respect to total cash compensation, however, small companies are at a disadvantage if they establish targeted levels based on current revenues, because executive pay levels are scope-sensitive. As company sales increase, compensation also increases.

Example. A company has current sales of $20 million, but projects sales at $60 million in three years. The company needs to hire a new executive. If it establishes targeted total cash compensation at the $20 million sales level, then the executive could be paid below median market levels when the company reaches $60 million, unless pay increases were significant. The 2000 *Officer Compensation Report* (Panel Publishers/Aspen Publishers, Inc.) shows that the median base salary of a chief executive officer in a company with sales of $20 million is $168,000, while the same job in a company with sales of $60 million is $231,000, a difference of 37.5 percent.

Companies can overcome this problem by using projected sales when establishing targeted total cash compensation levels in high-growth companies.

Planning Tip. A good standard to use in establishing pay levels for the small, high-growth company is to use company sales that are projected for up to three years beyond the current date. For example, the company described in the Example above could use the three-year projected sales of $60 million to establish the targeted base salary level of its chief executive officer.

Q 12:10   Are design issues for annual incentive compensation plans different in the small company?

No, the design issues are the same, but the solutions to these design issues may be different.

Eligibility. In a large company, the number of executives that are offered participation in the annual incentive plan is approximately 0.5 percent to 1.0 percent of total employment. In a small company, the number of executives offered participation in the annual incentive plan is 5-10 percent of total employment.

Performance measures. Most medium and large companies use annual performance goals that are contained in the annual business plan (i.e., a performance-based plan that uses projected results at year-end). Most small companies review performance by looking back and making a judgment on what actually happened versus what should have happened (i.e., a discretionary plan).

Q 12:11   How are executive benefits and perquisites different in the small company?

Panel Publishers' *2000 Executive Compensation Report* provides survey data on the prevalence of benefits and perquisites in small companies. The most frequent perquisites are a supplemental executive retirement plan and a company car, in addition to regular benefits of health, dental, life, and disability insurance, plus a 401(k) plan. Regulatory maximums on the amount of pre-tax employee contributions and tax-deductible company contributions to a 401(k) plan generally limits the value of such a plan to executives; therefore, the supplemental executive retirement plan (SERP) or excess plan may have significant value (see Q 9:16).

New Venture Businesses

Q 12:12   How is incentive compensation structured in new venture businesses?

The most common definition of a new venture business is that it is a division or wholly owned subsidiary of a larger company, and that it operates in an industry that is not the same as the core business of the parent/owner. The financing for the new venture typically comes from the parent company or primary shareholder/owner. An example was the General Mills restaurant business, which was a separate venture from its core business of cereal and other store-bought foods. In this case, the restaurant venture became very successful and grew into a second core business for the company.

In new venture businesses, executive compensation can be structured in the same manner as in all other businesses, or the annual and long-term incentives can be combined and targeted payouts linked to the accomplishment of "milestone" objectives.

Example. A manufacturing company has a new venture into computer software. The software division has a new product that it wants to put into a regional test market and then market nationally. The test market phase will take two to two and one-half years (Milestone 1). The rollout nationally will take an additional three years (Milestone 2). The company can combine targeted income for each executive position from the short-term incentive plans and the long-term incentive plan and provide payment when and if each milestone is achieved. The company can also develop a payout schedule so that if one or both of the milestones are achieved in advance of the scheduled date, then a greater amount of incentive compensation is paid. Correspondingly, if one or both of the milestones are achieved, but well after the scheduled date, then less than the target incentive is paid.

Q 12:13   How are base salary and benefits structured in new venture businesses?

New venture companies typically have base salary, benefits, and perquisites that parallel parent company or general industry norms. In some situations, these companies must employ executives who can manage a business that will be five to ten times its current size in a short time (i.e., two to three years). New venture companies use two techniques to attract and retain key executives into this type of dynamic business environment:

1. Follow small company practices and project sales for the next three years, then establish base salary under the assumption that those sales will be achieved (see Q 12:9).

2. Link base salary increases to the successful accomplishment of the milestones.

Chapter 13

Board of Directors' Compensation

Public attention has intensified on the roles, responsibilities, and performance of company boards of directors. Director positions are becoming more difficult to fill, given the increased liability and time demands associated with corporate governance. This in turn has increased the importance of director compensation. Both the amounts and forms of compensation have changed significantly over the past several years. Amounts paid for the most common forms of director compensation—meeting fees and annual retainers—are increasing, as is the prevalence of stock-based plans and retirement plans for directors. This chapter covers current trends and issues in board compensation.

General Considerations 13-2
Outside vs. Inside Directors 13-3
Compensation Methods 13-6
Other Benefits 13-8

General Considerations

Q 13:1 How does a company choose the members of its board of directors?

Directors of a company do not apply; they are asked to serve. When they agree, they are then elected by the stockholders of that company. In private companies, the major stockholders usually function as executive officers and directors. In public companies, stock ownership plays a much smaller factor in the election of officers and there are a number of "outside" directors, as well as "inside" directors.

Q 13:2 What is the role of a company board of directors?

Members of a company board of directors share responsibilities such as the following:

1. Representing shareholders in ensuring that the activities of the business properly fulfill the company's objectives of providing a product or service to society, providing employment, and providing appropriate financial returns to shareholders.

2. Providing the chief executive officer (CEO) with advice and counsel on the strategic direction of the corporation.

3. Within their areas of expertise, providing other senior executives of the company with advice on specific company programs and activities (for example, financial statements, public relations activities, legal advice and counsel, employment relations).

4. Overseeing the activities of the company's auditors and financial department and the board audit committee. In this capacity, directors would typically review and endorse company investment policy, payment of dividends, and general utilization of financial resources.

5. Through a board compensation committee, approving the design of executive compensation programs, the appointment of key officers, specific compensation increases, stock awards, and other forms of remuneration for top executives.

6. Evaluating company products and services.

As policy makers and strategic planners, members of a company's board of directors play an extremely critical role in today's business environment. They are no longer "rubber stamps" to internal management policies. The number of organizational changes such as reorganizations, mergers, restructurings, and recapitalizations that have occurred in recent years has significantly increased the role of directors, as well as their compensation.

Outside vs. Inside Directors

Q 13:3 Why would a company choose to have outside directors?

As discussed in Chapter 2, an employee benefit plan must be approved by a committee of outside directors in order to take advantage of the Securities Exchange Commission (SEC) Rule 16b-3 exemption, which provides that grants of stock options and other securities under a plan to insiders will not be deemed to be purchases of those securities for purposes of determining Section 16(b) liability. For purposes of Section 16, such outside directors must be "nonemployee" directors, which term does not include former company officers who become outside directors, consultants, lawyers, bankers, and others who earn more than $60,000 from the company or any person employed by the company who earns more than 5 percent of the gross revenue. Therefore, a company will ask people who do not work for the company—well-qualified "outsiders"—to sit on its board of directors and will pay them a special retainer and per-meeting fees.

Even for privately held companies for whom the Section 16 exemption is not relevant, outside directors are useful as a mechanism to insulate the company against shareholder derivative challenges to the amounts or types of executive compensation paid because courts apply the business judgment rule to the compensation decisions made by disinterested directors. Specifically, courts will assume that the disinterested directors used their best business judgment in deciding on the compensation paid.

Q 13:4   What are the typical compensation elements for directors?

Most companies compensate their directors with some combination of annual retainers for their services and additional fees for their attendance at actual committee meetings and meetings of the board. Many companies have also established certain special stock plans for their directors, and others give directors retirement benefits after a minimum period of service. Few provide directors with other benefits merely for serving as directors. For example:

Outside Director Compensation in a Small Company:

Annual retainer	$ 5,000
Committee fees ($500 per meeting × 10 meetings)	$ 5,000
TOTAL	$10,000*

*Plus reimbursement of all necessary expenses for meeting attendance.

Outside Director Compensation in a Large Company:

Annual retainer	$20,000
Committee fee ($1,000 per meeting × 10 meetings)	$10,000
TOTAL	$30,000*

*Plus some or all of the following benefits:

1. Retirement benefit equal to the amount of the annual retainer to be paid for the lesser of ten years or the total number of years of board service, upon reaching the retirement age of 70;

2. A one-time stock option grant of 1,000 shares of company stock with the same plan provisions (e.g., vesting, award period) as that provided to key executives; and

3. Reimbursement of all necessary expenses for attendance at company board meetings and committee meetings.

Q 13:5   Are inside directors compensated specifically for their activities as directors?

Directors who are also executive officers of a corporation are usually not given additional compensation such as annual retainers or meeting fees for acting as directors, although many companies adjust the base salaries of their executives who also serve on the board.

Q 13:6   How much do outside directors receive for their services?

The size of retainer and meeting fees paid to "outside" directors varies greatly from company to company. Unfortunately, it is statistically impossible to isolate the factors that determine the level of compensation accorded to directors, although the size of the company in question is one indicator. The average retainer in a small company is between $1,000 and $5,000, while the average retainer in a large company is $15,000 to $20,000. Typical board meeting fees range from $250 to $500 per meeting in a small company and $1,000 to $1,500 per meeting in a large company. Statistically, this means that the average director receives less than 5 percent of the compensation paid to a CEO of a Fortune 500 company. However, directors spend considerably less time on company matters than the CEO. A key factor in determining compensation can be the hourly rate of the director versus the hourly rate of the CEO. In most companies the hourly rate of the CEO would be higher because the responsibility of the job is greater than that of any individual director.

Most large companies also provide an additional retainer and/or meeting fees for service on a committee of the board. A typical committee retainer ranges between $2,000 and $5,000, while typical committee meeting fees run between $1,000 and $1,500 per meeting.

Note that the director may elect to defer receipt of these fees until a future date as agreed with the company. Similarly, the company may wish to pay the outside director his retainer in the form of stock options or restricted stock. If an outside director desires to defer payment of any portion of these fees to a future year, the director will need to make the deferral election prior to the start of the year in which the fees would have been paid.

Compensation Methods

Q 13:7   How is director income taxed?

Directors are taxed on the amounts paid to them by the company, as on all other income. Outside directors are not, however, considered employees of the company; therefore, the company need not withhold taxes and social security payments from their fees. Instead, a director's income is considered self-employment income. This is the case regardless of whether she receives a retainer or fees for attending meetings or serving on committees.

Q 13:8   What methods are used in deferring compensation for directors?

There are two principal methods a company will use in deferring compensation of its board members. The most common method is simply to defer payment of the retainer and annual fees—as well as the taxes on such compensation—until a future date, which is typically retirement from the board or some other event. Another method is to allow a director to invest his deferred compensation in units of phantom stock, with the dividends credited on the purchased units being reinvested in additional units.

Q 13:9   In what types of performance-based plans do directors participate?

Under the Section 16 rules, a director's disinterested status will not be affected by her (1) merely being eligible to participate in a plan, (2) participation in a nondiscretionary plan, (3) participation in a participant-directed exempt plan, or (4) election to receive the annual retainer fee in securities.

A growing number of companies are offering their directors the opportunity to participate in capital accumulation plans. The company's rationale for doing this is similar to its motives for adopting plans for its officers and employees, which is to provide incentives to people who are performing services for the company by giving them the chance to participate in the growth that their performance and decisions may cause.

Stock options granted to outside directors are subject to the same tax rules as options granted to regular employees.

Q 13:10 How are stock options used in compensating directors?

Some companies offer directors the option to receive their annual retainer in the form of stock. In such a case, the fee is equal to the amount of the "spread" of a discounted stock option, the anticipated spread of an option granted at fair market value, or the grant value of restricted stock shares. For example, instead of paying a $10,000 fee to a director, a company could grant that director options to purchase 500 shares of stock with a market value of $12,500 ($25 per share) at a discount of $5 per share ($20 per share purchase price × 500 shares = $10,000), or grant the director 400 restricted shares (typically a three- to five-year restriction) also with a value of $10,000 (400 × $25 per share market value).

There are several significant benefits to using discounted stock options. The director is taxed on the compensation element (the amount of the spread), yet that director has effectively invested in stock using pre-tax dollars. Using the example above, assume that the director involved is in the 31 percent federal income tax bracket and a 10 percent state income tax bracket. If that director receives the $10,000 retainer in cash, only $5,900 would remain after taxes. Taking that $5,900 plus the additional $2,500 paid to exercise the options, the director would be able to purchase a total of only $8,400 in company stock. On the other hand, by choosing to receive discounted stock options, the director receives $12,500 in stock, for which a total of $6,600 (the $2,500 exercise price plus taxes of $4,100) is paid. As for the company, it has not only saved the cash it would have had to pay the director but it will also receive cash when the director exercises the option. In addition, the company has succeeded in giving the director a personal interest in the company that is more closely aligned with the interests of the company's stockholders.

Q 13:11   How do the Section 16 rules apply to directors' options?

Directors are insiders. The decision to receive the annual fee or retainer in the form of options is considered a purchase for purposes of Section 16 of the 1934 Act and is matchable against any sale by that director of company securities within the six months before or after that purchase.

Q 13:12   Do companies provide "regular" stock plans for directors?

Yes. Many companies allow their directors to participate in restricted stock plans and tie the vesting of the stock to years of service on the board.

Q 13:13   Can tandem SARs/stock options be granted to directors?

Yes. Tandem SARs/stock options may be granted to directors; the SARs will be taxed in the same manner as if they were granted to company executives.

Other Benefits

Q 13:14   What other benefits are typically provided to directors?

Most publicly traded companies will provide outside directors with liability insurance and expense reimbursement, while others may also provide additional benefits such as medical insurance, life insurance, or retirement plans. The rationale for providing limited benefits, simply stated, is that the outside directors are not employees of the company but were asked to be directors as a result of their corporate expertise in their primary jobs, which provide them with the coverage they require.

Q 13:15   Do companies provide retirement benefits for their directors?

Many companies choose to provide directors with a special retirement plan. Companies usually make the benefit payable at age 65 or the normal retirement date, which is often later than age 65.

A typical retirement plan for an outside director would include provisions such as:

- A minimum service requirement for eligibility
- Increasing benefit levels based on the number of years, over the minimum number, served as a director
- A maximum benefit level equal to a specified percentage, often approaching 100 percent, of the retainer
- Forfeiture of rights if the director competes with or otherwise harms the company

Q 13:16   Can Keogh plans be utilized by outside board members?

Outside directors are considered to be self-employed, independent contractors and therefore are eligible to create a tax-qualified retirement plan (i.e., Keogh plan). They can contribute a portion of their fees to the plan. Larger deductions are available in some cases. Investment income on the amount contributed builds up tax-deferred with the director paying tax only as she receives payment.

Q 13:17   Can Keogh plans be utilized by insider board members?

Even where a company chooses to pay its inside directors special fees for serving as directors, Internal Revenue Code regulations prevent an insider board member (who is not considered a self-employed individual) from participating in a Keogh plan.

Q 13:18   What are some new trends in board of director compensation?

The most significant new trend for outside directors (other than those included in this chapter, such as retirement benefits and stock awards) is a benefit called the "legacy" grant. Legacy grants involve the promise of the company to pay, on the outside director's behalf, upon his death a substantial amount to a charitable organization specified by that director. The legacy grant is funded via the life insurance benefit concept, with the intent being that all or part of the legacy amount is funded by the cash value of the life insurance. For example, a company may offer an outside director the opportunity to provide a legacy grant of $250,000 to an educational institution or a nonprofit charity of her own choice, upon death. The company would then take out a life insurance policy on the executive, with the charity as the beneficiary, and fund payments/premiums with the cash value of the policy. Upon payment, the company and the former director would receive a rather significant public relations value from the activity.

The legacy grant concept is a significant recruiting tool for companies, helping them attract high quality directors to their organization.

Q 13:19   Do outside directors get perquisites?

Yes, many of the programs previously described in this chapter are good examples: legacy grants, life insurance, retirement, access to deferred compensation investments used by the company, and so forth. In addition, these directors often can travel first class or in company planes, are given liberal expense accounts, can use company products or services (if applicable), receive the same Christmas gifts that the company provides to its customers, and can be invited to company outings at various resorts or sporting events with all expenses paid.

Chapter 14

Executive Compensation in the Not-For-Profit Organization

There are a number of differences in the structure of executive compensation programs at the not-for-profit (or nonprofit) organization. The purpose of these organizations differs from that of the for-profit company, so it follows that the purposes and methods used to establish executive pay can also vary significantly.

General Considerations 14-1
Base Salary 14-5
Annual Incentives 14-6
Long-Term Incentives 14-10
Perquisites 14-11

General Considerations

Q 14:1   What is a not-for-profit company?

Not-for-profit companies are organizations that do not exist for the purpose of creating profit or "value for shareholders" and are defined in the various Internal Revenue Code (Code) sections as generally including the following:

501(c)(3) Organizations: Hospitals, religious and charitable organizations

501 (c)(4) Organizations: Civic leagues or associations

501 (c)(5) Organizations: Labor or agricultural organizations

501 (c)(6) Organizations: Chambers of commerce, boards of trade, and business associations

501 (c)(14) Organizations: Credit unions

Q 14:2   How does the mix of executive compensation elements differ in a not-for-profit company?

Executives of not-for-profit companies receive quite different compensation packages than do their counterparts in for-profit companies. Following are some of the compensation elements for nonprofit company executives:

1. Base salary: Typically, higher levels
2. Annual incentive: Typically, lower levels
3. Long-term incentive programs: Few if any such programs
4. Perquisites: Not as common
5. Benefits: Equal to or greater than those in for-profit companies

The reason for these differences in the mix of total compensation is threefold: Not-for-profits (1) are more regulated; (2) operate a personal service business where their purpose is to meet human needs rather than produce a product for profit; and (3) focus primarily on quality of service, not financial return to shareholders.

Q 14:3   How do the business objectives of executive compensation plans differ in a not-for-profit company?

Chart 14-1 shows how the different business objectives of non-profit and for-profit companies can affect their determination of executive compensation elements. Although base salary and benefits tend to serve the same purposes in both organizations, annual incentive plans, long-term incentive plans, and perquisites can be very different. As can be seen from Chart 14-1, annual incentive plans typically have completely different performance measures in not-for-profit and for-profit organizations. While long-term incentive plans are not typically used in the not-for-profit company, they could have a useful business purpose and should be considered.

Chart 14-1

	For-Profit Company	Not-for-Profit Company
Base salary	Established by labor market, based on job value	Same
Annual incentive	Rewards for achieving additional profit	Rewards for achieving expense control
Long-term incentive	Additional rewards for achieving additional profit or stock growth	Rarely used because most organizations are not publicly owned
Benefits	Protection against financial hardship due to illness	Same
Perquisites	Convey status to senior executives	Not needed (e.g., country clubs rarely used to conduct business)

Example. A YMCA has a building campaign with two phases: Phase I is to raise money, and Phase II is the actual construction. Goals are established for both phases. A long-term incentive plan is established using the goals for Phase II:

1. Minimum goal: Meet building schedule with costs exceeding estimates by up to 5 percent.
2. Target goal: Meet building schedule within cost estimates.
3. Maximum goal: Meet building schedule under cost estimates.

If any of these goals is met, an incentive payout will be made as follows: $5,000 for achieving the minimum goal, $10,000 for the target goal, and $15,000 for the maximum.

Q 14:4   Does the size of the organization affect executive compensation in a not-for-profit organization?

Yes, two not-for-profit executives with the same position account-ability but in different size organizations will likely have different total compensation. For example, a hospital administrator in a 100-bed hospital will make less total compensation than a hospital ad-ministrator with similar job responsibilities in a 1,000-bed hospital. The reason is a belief that the position in the 1,000-bed hospital has more complexity and a greater magnitude of accountability and impact on the organization. The same is true of an executive director in a YMCA with a $1 million budget versus the same job with a budget of $10 million. The director with the $10 million budget will make more total compensation.

Q 14:5   Does the type of not-for-profit organization affect the level of executive compensation?

Yes. For example, the executive director of a United Way agency will typically have a higher level of total compensation than the executive director of another similar organization. The reasons for this are size (see Q 14:4) and the fact that the primary comparisons of executive compensation in a not-for-profit organization are against other similar not-for-profits. In this example, executive compensation in other non-United Way agencies is not as relevant. The same is true when reviewing total compensation of a hospital administrator ver-sus an executive director of a United Way agency. The primary labor market comparisons for the hospital administrator will be to other hospital administrators.

Another factor is that in for-profit companies, profit margins drive varying levels of executive compensation; that is, the industries with a higher profit margin tend to have higher levels of executive com-pensation. Profit margins do not drive executive compensation in not-for-profits because there is no profit. Of course, fundraising could be substituted for profit in driving executive pay levels in nonprofit organizations. (The higher the amount of funds raised, the higher the level of executive pay.)

Q 14:6   Does geographical location affect executive compensation in the not-for-profit company?

In contrast to the for-profit company, where geographical differences are rare, the not-for-profit organization will find that executive compensation is affected by geography. A not-for-profit executive does not typically transfer at the request of the organization, so there is no reason for these organizations to establish executive pay on the basis of a national labor market. A not-for-profit executive tends to be employed from the local labor market; therefore, local pay levels are a major factor in executive compensation along with size of the not-for-profit organization. (See Q 14:4.)

Base Salary

Q 14:7   How are base salary ranges established in not-for-profit companies?

The number of labor market surveys continues to increase in the not-for-profit industry, and these surveys serve as the primary basis for establishing competitive base salary ranges on executive as well as non-executive positions. Survey data are reported as averages (weighted averages) or in trend lines that compare total cash compensation (base salary plus annual incentive, if any) to a measure of scope such as annual budget or number of hospital beds.

Not-for-profit organizations use a second technique of internal job evaluation to drive decisions on base salary ranges. (See Q 3:3 for a description of internal job evaluation methods.) As is the case with the for-profit companies, the not-for-profits encounter discrepancies between results from internal job evaluation and results from the use of external labor market surveys. When this occurs, the first step is to review all assumptions to ensure that they are correct, then either to use broad salary ranges to accommodate different results on job values or to recognize that the ultimate criterion for valuing any job is its worth on the labor market.

Q 14:8   Are merit increases to base salary used in not-for-profit companies?

Yes. Merit increases are an important issue for executive and non-executive positions in a not-for-profit company because base salary is frequently the primary form of direct compensation. Also, merit increases can drive the value of indirect compensation plans like life or disability, which have benefits determined as a multiple of base salary. As discussed in Q 14:2, not-for-profit organizations tend to have lower annual incentive compensation and little long-term incentive compensation; thus, merit increases are a primary way to motivate executives.

Annual Incentives

Q 14:9   What is the prevalence of annual incentive plans in not-for-profit companies?

Annual incentive plans are not as prevalent in nonprofits as in for-profit companies. When such plans are provided, the amount of incentive is typically less in the not-for-profit organization. As shown in Chart 14-2, approximately 65 percent of nonprofits surveyed used some form of annual incentive plan in 1994; compare this to the 96 percent used in for-profit companies. It is relevant to note, however, that the 65 percent usage of annual incentive plans in nonprofits represents a 13 percent increase during the last three years.

Chart 14-2. Prevalence of Annual Incentive Compensation Plans

	Percentage of Companies with Annual Incentive Compensation Plans	
	1991	*1994*
For-profit companies	92	96
Not-for-profit companies	52	65

Q 14:10 Does the size of the annual incentive award in the not-for-profit company differ from that in the for-profit company?

Yes. As shown on Chart 14-3, the award for a chief executive officer in a for-profit company will typically be 20-25 percent higher than the similar position in a not-for-profit company. The same is true for other executive positions.

Chart 14-3. Average Size of Annual Incentive Awards

	Targeted annual incentive for CEO
For-profit companies	50% of base salary
Not-for-profit companies	40% of base salary

As indicated in Q 14:7, more not-for-profit organizations are surveying total cash compensation (base salary plus annual incentive). As a result, the current trend toward increased usage of this executive compensation element is expected to continue. As more not-for-profits observe that annual incentive plans are the norm, more new plans will be implemented.

Q 14:11 What performance measures are typically used in the annual incentive plans of not-for-profit companies?

Performance measures are qualitative and quantitative. The most common qualitative measure is patient/user service evaluations or ratings, while the most common quantitative measure is budget/expense control. Other performance measures in not-for-profit companies are similar to those in for-profit companies. These are discussed in Qs 4:36, 4:37, and 4:42.

Q 14:12 How is eligibility determined for annual incentive plans in not-for-profit companies?

Typically, eligibility is granted only to the chief executive officer or executive director and key department heads or officers who report directly to the senior executive.

Q 14:13   What regulations guide incentive compensation plans for the not-for-profit company?

Code Section 403(b) Plans. Code Section 501(c)(3) organizations (non-profit organizations organized exclusively for religious, charitable, scientific, public safety, literary, or educational purposes, including charities, social welfare agencies, private hospitals and health care organizations, private schools, religious institutions and research facilities), which are exempt from tax under Code Section 501(a) and certain public educational institutions may offer employees a tax-sheltered annuity plan under Code Section 403(b). Contributions to a Code Section 403(b) plan may consist of salary deferrals, employee after-tax contributions, employer matching contributions, and other nonelective employer contributions. Suitable funding vehicles for a Code Section 403(b) plan are limited to annuity contracts issued by insurance companies and custodial accounts which are invested in shares of regulated investment companies (certain church-related organizations may use retirement income accounts as described in Code Section 403(b)(9)).

Code Section 403(b) plans generally are not subject to ERISA, provided that participation is voluntary, there are no matching or other nonelective employer contributions, there is limited employer involvement and all rights under the funding vehicles are enforceable solely by the employee. In addition, Code Section 403(b) plans of public education institutions and church plans are exempt from ERISA. All other Code Section 403(b) plans are considered to be "pension plans" under ERISA.

Pre-tax salary deferrals under Code Section 403(b) plans and earnings on these contributions are tax-deferred until distributed from the plan. At that time, such amounts are taxed as ordinary income. However, such salary deferrals are subject to FICA and FUTA taxes at the time of contribution. Salary deferrals under Code Section 403(b) plans are subject to certain contribution limits, including the Code Section 402(g) limit on elective deferrals (for 1999, $10,000), the Code Section 415(c) annual addition limit and the Code Section 403(b)(2) maximum exclusion allowance. For employees with at least 15 years of service, the limit on elective deferrals may be increased under Code Section 402(g). Salary deferral contributions are also subject to the "universal availability" nondiscrimination test.

This test provides that if any employee participates in the Code Section 403(b) plan, then all eligible employees must be given the opportunity to participate (can apply a $200 minimum deferral amount). Employees who participate in an eligible Code Section 457 plan, a 401(k) plan, or another 403(b) plan may be excluded. In general, most of the Internal Revenue Code rules relating to tax-qualified retirement plans also apply to Code Section 403(b) plans, including the annual includible compensation limit (for 1999, $160,000), the minimum required distribution rules and certain restrictions on distributions before age 59 $\frac{1}{2}$. If the 403(b) plan is subject to ERISA, vesting requirements, funding requirements, survivor annuity distribution requirements, and reporting and disclosure and fiduciary requirements are also applicable.

Code Section 401(k) Plans. The Small Business Job Protection Act of 1996 amended the Internal Revenue Code to permit private, non-profit organizations to offer Code Section 401(k) plans to employees for plan years beginning on or after January 1, 1997. Code Section 501(c)(3) organizations may also continue to offer 403(b) plans.

Code Section 457 Plans. Code Section 457 applies to deferred compensation plans maintained by a state, political subdivision of a state, any agency or instrumentality of a state or political subdivision of a state, rural electric cooperatives, and any other tax-exempt organization. An *eligible* deferred compensation plan under Code Section 457(b) is an unfunded plan that provides for annual deferrals of the lesser of (1) $7,500, as adjusted for inflation (for 1999, $8,000) or (2) one-third of includible compensation (unless a special $125,000 catch-up provision applies). Under an *eligible* Code Section 457 plan, amounts deferred, plus any earnings, are taxable when distributed (or otherwise made available to the participant, i.e., the "constructive receipt" concept). For tax-exempt employers (non-governmental plans), the plan must provide that all amounts of compensation deferred, plus all investments and earning attributable to such amounts, remain the sole property of the employer, subject to the claims of general creditors, until such time as the deferred compensation (plus earnings) is made available to the participant.

Ineligible Code Section 457 plans (Code Section 457(f) plans) are deferred compensation plans that do not meet the requirements of an eligible Code Section 457 plan. Code Section 457(f) requires that all deferred amounts, plus earnings, remain general assets of the employer, subject to the claims of general creditors. Therefore, a tax-exempt organization may not maintain a Code Section 457(f) plan for employees unless the plan is exempt from ERISA's funding requirements (i.e., it is a government plan, a church plan, a foreign plan, an excess benefit plan or a "top hat" plan). The deferred compensation amounts are taxable to participants in the first tax year in which there is no substantial risk of forfeiture (defined in Code Section 457(f)(3) in a way that is closely related to the definition of the same term under Code Section 83). There is a "substantial risk of forfeiture" if the participant's right to receive the amounts deferred (plus earnings) are conditioned on the future performance of substantial services. In PLR 9815039, the IRS found that a plan design which requires forfeiture of the participant's account upon termination by the employer "for cause" met the substantial risk of forfeiture standard. In PLRs 9823014 and 9815039, the IRS ruled that a two-year deferral period was sufficient to meet the substantial risk of forfeiture standard. Benefits under a Code Section 457(f) plan may not be distributed before separation from service, or, if earlier, ago 70 $\frac{1}{2}$ (or in the event of certain unforeseen emergencies). Taxation of distribution from *ineligible* Code Section 457 plans are governed by Code Section 72 (relating to annuities).

Certain "bona fide vacation leave, sick leave, compensatory time, severance pay, disability pay or death benefit plan" maintained for employees of tax-exempt organizations are not subject to the Code Section 457 rules. (See Q 14:16.)

Long-Term Incentives

Q 14:14   What types of long-term incentive plans are prevalent in not-for-profit companies?

As with for-profit companies, the most common form of long-term incentive in not-for-profit companies is the stock option. The phantom equity plan is the second most common form of long-term incentive plan. As shown in Chart 14-4, few not-for-profit companies use any form of long-term incentive.

Chart 14-4. Long-Term Incentives in Not-for-Profit Companies

Form of Long-Term Incentive	Prevalence in Not-for-Profit Companies
Stock options	34%
Phantom stock	26%
Performance shares	18%

Perquisites

Q 14:15   What types of perquisites are prevalent in not-for-profit companies?

Few, if any, perquisites are used in not-for-profit companies. For this reason, the subject is rarely included in a survey. Favorable parking, full payment at association meetings, free attendance at fund-raising events such as dinners or golf outings, and free or preferential use of the not-for-profit company facilities are common. Typical perquisites in a for-profit company, such as a company car, club memberships, first-class air travel, or financial planning, are not needed in not-for-profits, since in most cases their facilities are local.

The one perquisite that is used by a small number of not-for-profits is the Section 457 plan referenced in Q 14:13. In addition, the organization may choose to establish a "bona fide severance plan." Such a severance pay plan is not subject to the Section 457 prescribed limitations on company contributions.

Q 14:16   What are the requirements for establishing a "bona fide severance plan" in a not-for-profit organization?

Code Section 457 governs the income tax treatment of nonqualified deferred compensation plans maintained by tax-exempt organizations and state and local government entities. All Code Section 457 plans are "unfunded." Unless a plan is exempt from Code Section 457 treatment (for example, a "bona fide severance plan") the deferred compensation plan must satisfy the requirements of Code Section 457(b) or Code Section 457(f). (See Q 14:13.)

A "bona fide severance plan," under Code Section 457(e)(11), is not treated as a deferred compensation plan. Therefore, such a severance plan may provide benefits in excess of the Code Section 457 limits and such benefits are not required to be subject to a substantial risk of forfeiture. However, if the IRS decides that an employer's "severance plan" is really a deferred compensation plan subject to Code Section 457(f), then any amounts not subject to a substantial risk of forfeiture would be immediately taxable to the participant.

No regulations or other guidance under Code Section 457(e)(11) has been issued yet by the IRS with respect to a "bona fide severance plan." Other Code sections, ERISA rules, and case law do provide some guidance. Particularly helpful are the ERISA rules that describe a severance pay plan. Remembering that a "pension plan" under ERISA is a plan that provides for the deferral of income by employees for periods extending to the termination of employment or beyond, tax-exempt employers wanting to take advantage of the "severance plan" exception to the Code Section 457 rules would be wise to follow the criteria for severance plans that are considered to be "welfare plans" under ERISA. Specifically, DOL Regulations Section 2510.3-2(b) provides that a severance pay arrangement which provides benefits upon the termination of employment will not be treated as a "pension plan" for ERISA purposes as long as (1) the payments are not contingent, directly or indirectly on the employee's retirement, (2) the total payments do not exceed twice the employee's annual compensation for the year prior to the termination of employment and (3) the payments are completed within two years of termination of employment.

When implementing a "bona fide severance plan," the employer must determine whether the plan simply permits the deferral of compensation until retirement, or whether the severance benefits truly result from an unanticipated termination of employment (i.e., not just based upon the passage of time).

Chapter 15

Special Early Retirement Programs

A company that needs to reduce staff or reorganize may wish to offer certain employees the opportunity to retire early. Frequently, special early retirement "window" programs are made available under an existing retirement plan for those employees who meet specified age and service requirements (such as age 55 with 20 years of service). An employer may also wish to consider the implementation of a special retirement incentive program outside of an existing retirement plan. These types of programs typically provide for severance payments and, in many cases, employer-paid continued health benefits during the severance period. This chapter discusses early retirement window arrangements, explaining their rationale and detailing associated benefits, agreements by employees in exchange for early retirement, consequences for company and employee, and ERISA implications.

Overview 15-2
Severance Programs 15-3
Planning Early Retirement Programs 15-4

Overview

Q 15:1   How does a special early retirement window program work under an existing retirement plan?

Also known as early retirement "window periods," early retirement programs are one-time opportunities for employees to elect retirement at a younger age than normally specified in a company's pension plan. The employee must make this election during a designated period (window period) and is typically eligible for enhanced retirement benefits under the plan. The special election will also typically allow for the retirement benefit to be initiated at a time that is earlier than the normal retirement age in the plan (e.g., age 50 rather than age 60).

> **Example 1.** A company offers employees an opportunity to retire early under the company's pension plan at age 55 (rather than age 60) if they have 20 years of service. Retirement benefits are started immediately based on the pension plan's normal formula.

> **Example 2.** A company offers an enhanced early retirement benefit to any employee who elects early retirement under existing plan provisions at age 55 with 20 years of service. The enhanced benefit is that no actuarial reduction will be applied to the employee's retirement calculation if payments commence prior to age 65, as normally would be the case under the plan.

These programs can be applied to qualified pension plans or to nonqualified special executive retirement plans (SERPs).

Q 15:2   Why do companies offer special early retirement window programs?

Typically, such plans are offered because of a reorganization and/or downsizing of the company's operations, which creates the need for fewer employees. The automation of work processes or the discontinuation of company products/services can also create the need for companies to use these programs.

As competition increases, companies are finding that they need to conduct their business in different and more efficient ways. Sometimes this results in the need for fewer employees. Rather than lay off or terminate employees, companies offer special early retirement programs, so that longer service employees can pursue other employment or nonemployment interests.

Severance Programs

Q 15:3   Do companies offer special severance programs along with special early retirement programs?

Yes. Companies may choose to do this as encouragement and motivation for employees to accept the program, particularly if the purpose of the program is to downsize the work force. In many early retirements, the employee is required to find another position or adjust to a new career or lifestyle. There is a need to help the employee bridge this gap by providing him with the time and financial support to make the adjustment. Most employees who accept these programs decide either to look for another position or to start their own businesses.

Example. An eligible executive is provided with a one-year continuation of base salary if a special early retirement program is accepted.

Q 15:4   What are the typical severance benefits used along with a special early retirement program?

A review of numerous early retirement program provisions shows that companies will normally provide special early retirement program participants with one of the following two special benefits whenever severance is provided as part of an early retirement program:

1. Additional eligibility for the company's regular severance program (severance is not normally given to retirees); or

2. An enhanced severance program that is a one-time program with more favorable benefits than the company's regular severance program.

However, ERISA issues need to be examined anytime a special retirement program is implemented as explained in Qs 15:8 and 15:11.

Planning Early Retirement Programs

Q 15:5   How do companies fund special early retirement programs?

A company will take a one-time charge to earnings in the year that the special program is provided. This charge is then shown on the company's balance sheet as an accrued liability. Estimates are required on the number of employees who will accept the program, and actual acceptance is then reviewed after the fact to ensure that accrued funds are sufficient. Adjustments could be required after final costs are calculated.

Q 15:6   What, if any, are the negative consequences to companies that implement special early retirement programs, and how can these consequences be handled?

One important consideration is the possibility that the company will lose a large number of executives or nonexecutives who have crucial skills, or will lose all or most of its managers in a given department because they are offered and accept the program.

> **Example.** A company offers a special early retirement program to employees age 55 or older who have 20 or more years of service. The finance department has five executives eligible for the program: the chief financial officer, the treasurer, the controller, the tax executive, and the information services executive. All accept the program.

It should be noted that at least one federal court has held that a company did not violate ERISA's fiduciary duty or nondiscrimination provisions by preventing "valuable" employees from taking early retirement. In *McNab v. General Motors Corp.* [162 F. 3d 959 (7th Cir. 1998), *cert. denied*, 119 S. Ct. 1762 (1999)], the company adopted a special early retirement plan that allowed eligible employees to retire at age 50. Under the terms of the plan, management could offer participation to select employees. A management committee was given the discretion to make final eligibility decisions based on the "best interests" of the company.

Companies should carefully evaluate the potential consequences of special early retirement programs before they offer them in order to avoid a negative impact on company operations. A company can offset this potential negative impact either by evaluating the qualifications of replacement candidates within the organization or by structuring the special program so that there is time to find replacement candidates from outside the company. It is also possible that a reorganization or downsizing will result in the elimination of certain executive positions; these executives can be given eligibility in the program.

Another possible situation is that certain jobs, vacated by the acceptance of a special early retirement program, could be combined or even eliminated after the company knows which executives accept the program. These pivotal issues should all be evaluated before a program is offered.

Q 15:7 Are there any negative consequences to employees who accept a special early retirement program?

Yes. An employee, especially an executive, might have a pension plan that pays a lump-sum benefit. Such an individual who wishes to accept early retirement must also consider whether current investments and investment strategy need to be revised. The risk for growth of these funds into continued or future retirement income would be transferred to the individual at early retirement.

Another factor is that these early retirement programs rarely provide individuals with their full amount of required retirement income, particularly when there is no eligibility for Social Security benefits. Thus, executives will typically need to develop supplemental retirement income and/or secure another job until they begin full retirement. These programs require a great deal of personal financial planning before an individual can decide whether to accept or reject early retirement.

Q 15:8   What are the ERISA and Internal Revenue Code implications of a special early retirement program under a qualified pension plan?

A company will want to maintain the tax-qualified status of its employee retirement plan under Section 401(a) of the Code and thereby take a tax deduction in the year that it makes a contribution to the employee pension plan. The company will also want its pension plan to continue to meet ERISA requirements. A number of issues must be considered by companies who are considering a special early retirement program within their qualified pension plan.

Plan amendment. Typically, companies will need to amend their qualified plans in order to offer a special early retirement program, because under regular plan provisions the special program is not authorized. The amendment will simply allow for a subsidized benefit during the early retirement period.

> **Example 1.** A qualified defined benefit plan offers early retirement benefits for participants who have attained age 55 and have completed at least 15 years of service. The company desires to offer a special early retirement window program that would provide an enhanced benefit to those participants otherwise eligible for early retirement under the plan by tacking on an additional five years of credited service to the benefit calculation. An amendment is required to the plan.

> **Example 2.** A qualified defined benefit plan allows for an early retirement at age 55 with an actuarial reduction in retirement benefits for commencement of benefit payments prior to age 65. A special early retirement window program offers early retirement at age 55 with no actuarial reduction for early commencement of benefit payments. This requires a plan amendment.

Any plan amendment would be subject to certain nondiscrimination testing. It should also be noted that a pattern of repeated window programs may be deemed to create a permanent feature of the plan subject to certain "anti-cutback" rules contained in Section 411(d)(6) of the Code. Plan amendments adding special early retirement window benefits to a qualified pension plan that normally provides a retirement benefit that is integrated with Social Security benefits should be carefully reviewed by the plan's actuary to determine whether the amendment could have a discriminatory effect on the non-highly compensated participants.

Discrimination as to benefits. A tax-qualified pension plan may not discriminate with respect to highly compensated employees (as defined in Section 414(q) of the Code) versus lower-paid employees. If most of the employees who are eligible for a special early retirement window program are highly paid executives, then the special program could be offering benefits that discriminate in favor of the executives. This would jeopardize the tax-qualified status of the plan.

Window programs implemented under tax-qualified pension plans must meet certain requirements under Code Sections 401(a)(4) and 410(b), including the requirement that the timing of the plan amendment cannot have a discriminatory effect and the requirement that the group of employees to whom the special early retirement window benefit is currently available must satisfy certain minimum coverage tests.

Partial termination of a plan. Another qualified pension plan issue that can be triggered by a special early retirement window program is that if too many participants accept early retirement, then the plan may experience a *partial termination*, and those *affected participants* (who accept the early retirement) must be 100 percent vested in their accrued benefits under the qualified pension plan. Since most early retirement window programs set eligibility standards at ten or more years of service and since, under Code provisions, the maximum number of years of service that can be required for a participant to become 100 percent vested in his or her accrued benefits under a tax-qualified plan is less than such number, this issue would most likely be moot.

Disclosure. The plan amendment that provides for a special early retirement window opportunity must be communicated to all plan participants. This does not present a problem prospectively; however, it can be a problem retrospectively.

Example. An executive decides to take early retirement with actuarial reduction under normal plan provisions at age 55 with 20 years of service in March of a given year. The company announces a special enhanced early retirement benefit with no actuarial reduction in September of the same year. The employee may claim that the company was "considering" the enhancement in March, but failed to communicate this to the employee. The employee could bring a lawsuit against the retirement plan administrators claiming that they did not fulfill their obligation of communicating planned changes in the early retirement provision of the qualified pension plan. Although most federal courts have held that plan amendment decisions are "settlor" functions, not "fiduciary" functions, many of the same courts have held that communication to participants is a plan administrative function subject to ERISA's fiduciary rules. Courts have held that participants should not be "affirmatively misled" with respect to future plan changes under consideration by senior management of the company. Some courts take the view that an employer must disclose to participants an early retirement incentive plan that was under internal discussion if such discussion was being given "serious consideration" by the employer. [Fischer v. Philadelphia Elec. Co., 96 F. 3d 1533 (3d Cir. 1996), *cert. denied*, 117 S. Ct. 1247 (1997)]

Q 15:9   Do companies require employees who elect a special early retirement benefit to sign noncompete and/or nonlitigation agreements?

Yes, in return for special retirement and/or special severance benefits, employees will typically be asked to sign an agreement that prohibits them from taking a similar position with direct competitors and using any company confidential information that the employee had access to during employment. These agreements will also include a release/waiver provision that prohibits the employee from filing a lawsuit against the company for any reason. The rationale for these agreements is simply that companies believe they are giving the employee some special consideration/benefit and expect some special consideration in return.

Care should be taken to draft a plan amendment containing special early retirement benefits to include in the eligibility provision a requirement for the participant to execute such types of agreements/releases as a condition to receipt of the special benefit. The form of agreement/release will need to meet the requirements of applicable laws in addition to ERISA. For example, under the Older

Workers Benefit Protection Act of 1990 (OWBPA) amendments to the Age Discrimination in Employment Act (ADEA), certain requirements must be met in order for a release of claims to be valid. Such requirements include the following:

1. The release must be contained in a written agreement, understandable by the individual executing the agreement.

2. The release must specifically refer to rights or claims under ADEA.

3. The individual can only waive claims that arise up to the time that the release is signed.

4. Valuable consideration must be provided in return for the signed release, in addition to anything of value to which the individual is already entitled.

5. The individual must be advised, in writing, to consult an attorney prior to execution of the release.

6. An individual must be given at least 21 days (45 days if it is a "group" termination) to consider the release agreement.

7. The release agreement must provide that the individual has at least seven days after execution of the release to revoke the agreement (the agreement should provide that the release will not be effective and the related special benefits will not be paid until such revocation period has expired).

8. If a group termination is involved (e.g., an early retirement incentive program or reduction in force program), remember that a 45-day consideration period applies and the employer must inform the individuals in writing as to the group of employees covered by the program (including eligibility factors and window time limits) and as to the job titles and ages of all employees eligible for the program and of the individuals in the same job class or unit who are not eligible.

Q 15:10 Do companies provide medical benefits along with a special early retirement program?

The company's existing group health plan language on the availability of benefits to retirees will typically be used for any special program. In other words, an early retiree is a retiree and is eligible for any retiree medical benefits.

If severance pay is provided as part of a special early retirement program, then the company may wish to consider continuing to pay, during the severance period, its share of applicable premiums under its group health plan as part of the cost of continuation of group health coverage benefits (if elected by the terminated employee) under the Consolidated Omnibus Budget Reconciliation Act of 1985, as amended (COBRA).

Q 15:11 Are there special ERISA rules to consider if the company wishes to provide an early retirement incentive program outside of a qualified retirement plan?

Yes. A company should design its severance arrangement to fall into the category of a *welfare plan* for ERISA purposes, not a *pension plan*. In order for a severance program to be considered a welfare plan under ERISA:

1. The total severance amount cannot exceed twice the employee's annual compensation for the year prior to the termination of service;

2. Payments must be completed within 24 months after the termination of service; and

3. The payments cannot be contingent directly or indirectly upon the employee's retirement, i.e., a company must be sure that eligibility requirements do not track eligibility requirements for retirement benefits too closely. For example, a program should identify the eligible group by job function or location and be careful of setting eligibility by age and years of service. A company may consider having an open eligibility class with benefit amounts keyed to length of service.

Example. The company establishes an early retirement incentive program that provides that a severance payment will be made for all employees who terminate employment within a specified window period. Such severance amount is determined based on years of service.

Years of Service	Severance Amount
Fewer than 10	4 weeks' pay
10 to 15	8 weeks' pay
16 to 20	12 weeks' pay
More than 20	16 weeks' pay

If the severance plan is deemed to be an ERISA *welfare plan,* it is subject to ERISA's reporting and disclosure requirements and fiduciary requirements. However, unlike a *pension plan* under ERISA, an ERISA *welfare plan* is not subject to ERISA's funding, vesting, and joint and survivor annuity form of payment requirements.

Chapter 16

U. S. Executives Working Overseas

This chapter defines and shows sample policies of the various types of executive expatriate compensation pro grams to include foreign service premiums; housing, cost of living, relocation, and education allowances; language training; home leave; company cars; and other perquisites typical for executives on overseas assignment. The critical issue of tax equalization is described, including definitions of hypothetical home country tax and home country tax withholding, and how these programs help the executive cope with double taxation (home country and foreign country) while working overseas. The final section of the chapter discusses questions on special compensation to include protection from currency fluctuation, stock appreciation rights, and other forms of long-term income while on overseas assignment, and "net-to-net" compensation plans.

General Considerations 16-2
Tax Considerations 16-9
Special Compensation 16-16

General Considerations

Q 16:1   What is an executive expatriate?

The term "expatriate" refers to an individual who is assigned to a position located outside of his home country. Home country typically refers to the country of natural (by birth) citizenship, and is typically the current place of residence for the individual. An executive expatriate is considered an officer or key manager within a company and will normally be provided with special allowance or benefits/perquisites that are equal to or greater than those provided to non-executive expatriates. For example, the executive expatriate may be given a higher housing allowance or better company car than the non-executive expatriate.

Q 16:2   What are the typical elements of an executive expatriate compensation package?

Executive compensation packages vary by company size and company culture. Typically, the larger the company the more structured the expatriate package. The smaller the company the more expatriate benefits are determined by negotiation. Company culture is a factor because it will drive the level of expatriate benefit. For example, a paternalistic company with a "family" environment will tend to ensure that the executive expatriate is reimbursed dollar for dollar for any extra costs, while a large company will establish expatriate allowances from tables and not try to achieve any dollar-for-dollar reimbursement. The most common strategy is to "keep the executive expatriate whole" in comparison to other similar executives who are not on overseas assignment.

A good definition of the term "keep whole" is that the executive expatriate will "neither gain nor lose total compensation because of the overseas assignment."

Given these general parameters, the most common elements in an executive expatriate program are as follows:

- Foreign service premium (and, on occasion, a hardship allowance)
- Cost of living allowance

- Housing allowance
- Relocation allowance
- Education allowance
- Language training
- Home leave
- Tax equalization
- Company car
- Club membership
- Supplemental medical

Q 16:3   What is a foreign service premium?

A foreign service premium is a percentage of base salary, 5 to 15 percent, that is provided to the executive expatriate during the duration of the overseas assignment, but it does not continue after repatriation back to the home country. It is intended to motivate the executive to accept the relocation to the foreign country (particularly if there is a "career risk" of being out-of-sight, out-of-mind of the top officers in the company), and to help the executive maintain a higher standard of living in the foreign country—typically the overseas executive will need to increase the amount of customer and/or employee entertaining.

Q 16:4   What is a hardship allowance?

A hardship allowance is provided in addition to a foreign service premium in those countries where the standard of living is considerably below that of the home country. The hardship premium is typically 10 to 15 percent of base salary and is provided for the duration of the overseas assignment. Like the foreign service premium, the hardship allowance discontinues upon repatriation back to the home country.

Q 16:5   What is a cost of living allowance?

A cost of living allowance (COLA) is designed to offset additional costs incurred by the executive expatriate in the overseas country.

The allowance is determined from published tables (e.g., ORC in New York City, AIRINC in Washington, D.C., Runzheimer in Rochester, Wisconsin, and similar organizations). The tables measure "spendable income," which includes goods and services such as food, clothing, recreation, insurance, and transportation. Spendable income does not include income that the executive expatriate uses for such things as housing, education, or taxes.

Spendable income tables compare the price of goods and services in the executive's home country versus those in the overseas country and establishes the difference, which is then provided to the executive tax-free in a monthly allowance. If the tables show that the price of goods and services is lower in the overseas country, then there is no allowance.

Because prices continually change, these tables are updated monthly; it is possible that the allowance could vary from month to month. For example, the costs of food and clothing could be increasing more rapidly in the executive's home country than in the overseas country, which could cause the tables to show a smaller difference in spendable income, which then lowers the cost-of-living allowance. Employee relations problems can, however, result if the executive suddenly has a lower allowance and less money to spend on goods and services; therefore, most companies will not implement monthly table changes until there is a significant difference (i.e., 4 to 5 percent), and they will give the expatriate two to three months' advance notice. Another common practice is to review the cost of living tables quarterly or semi-annually and make adjustments only two to four times a year, again with significant notice.

The term "tax free" means that if a cost-of-living allowance results in additional taxable income to the executive (which it typically does), any increase in tax owed by the executive (in either the home country or the overseas country) is paid for by the company. This calculation is included in the company's tax equalization policy (see Q 16:12).

Cost-of-living allowances are typically calculated in home company currency but paid in the overseas country's local currency since the allowance is normally spent at the overseas location. This can present a problem to the executive expatriate if the currency exchange rate between the home country and the overseas country becomes unfavorable (i.e., the home country currency exchange rate produces less of a cost-of-living allowance simply due to the fluctuating values of currency). Companies may therefore have exchange rate protection if the COLA tables are only published in home country currency (see Q 16:14).

Q 16:6   What is a housing allowance?

The concept of the housing allowance is to reimburse the executive expatriate for the difference between "assumed monthly housing costs at the home country" (monthly mortgage payment), and the actual monthly housing costs at the overseas country, with a maximum established for the overseas housing costs. Tables are published by firms like ORC, AIRINC, and Runzheimer (see Q 16:5). There is the obvious potential of a debate between the executive expatriate and the company on what the maximum housing costs should be at the overseas country. Companies need to establish a policy on this issue before they offer the overseas assignment to the executive expatriate.

The assumed monthly housing costs at the home country are established in the tables by analyzing the executive's level of income, home country location, and number of persons in the family who live in the current home. This number will often be close to the amount of foreign service premium.

Example. An executive with a base salary of $150,000 from the United States is given an overseas assignment in England. The executive is told she will receive a 10% foreign service premium ($15,000 annually or $1,250 per month). In addition, the executive is provided with a housing allowance at the overseas location in the amount of 50,000 pounds sterling per year or 4,167 pounds sterling per month minus assumed monthly housing costs in the home country of $1,200 (determined from tables). Under current currency exchange rates, the $1,200 is equal to approximately 720 pounds sterling. Therefore, the executive's housing allowance is 3,447 pounds sterling (4,167 − 720 = 3447).

In this example, the executive expatriate would probably use the 3,447 pounds sterling housing allowance and most of the foreign service premium to pay for housing at the overseas location. Note that the hypothetical housing cost of $1,200 is approximately equal to the foreign service premium of $1,250.

Thus, an alternative approach to the combination of foreign service premium and housing allowance is simply to combine the two and provide the executive expatriate with free housing at the overseas location, but with a maximum.

Example. An executive with a base salary of $150,000 from the United States is given an overseas assignment in England. The executive is told he will receive free housing at the new assignment but that the maximum payment by the company for this housing will be 50,000 pounds sterling per year, or 4,167 pounds sterling per month. The company pays no foreign service premium, but reimburses the executive the full amount of the monthly housing allowance of 4,167 pounds sterling. The result is free housing at the overseas location.

Q 16:7 Do executive expatriates receive reimbursement of any home sale or other relocation costs when they take an overseas assignment?

Yes, home sale benefits are typically the same as that provided for relocations with home sale within the home country, plus there are some additional reimbursements provided for expenses that are unique to international relocations.

Companies with a relocation policy that includes home sales will typically reimburse employees for costs associated with the home sale, such as real estate costs and closing costs, and in some large companies will even have loss-on-sale protection programs. For example, if the appraised value of the home is less than the amount that the employee paid for the home, the company will reimburse the difference or some percentage of the difference.

Other typical reimbursements in company relocation policies include:

- Home-finding trip for executive and spouse to the overseas location
- Shipment costs of all household belongings

- Business class air travel for the family to the overseas location
- Storage of some furniture during the overseas assignment
- Temporary living expenses for the employee and family prior to arrival of household goods
- Shipment of pets and/or other special handling items (e.g., art work, statues)
- Miscellaneous expense allowance (e.g., one month's salary for use in fixing up the new home)

In the case of an executive expatriate who leases an apartment, the company would pay for any fees associated with lease termination.

Companies that do not have a relocation policy will need to determine whether they will provide (or negotiate) the reimbursement of these standard relocation costs.

Other typical reimbursements unique to international relocations are:

1. *Protection against capital gains tax upon sale of home.* The typical criteria for this reimbursement are:
   a. The protection only applies on the difference between the purchase price and sale price of the executive's current home.
   b. The minimum waiting period applicable to the sale of capital assets is met.
   c. The home is the executive expatriate's primary residence.

2. *Costs/fees associated with the rental of the executive's principal residence during the overseas assignment.* This is normally in lieu of any other home sale assistance from the company.

3. *Appliance allowance for the new home at the overseas location.* This is frequently necessary because the electric systems at the overseas location are different from those in the executive's home country; therefore, the executive's current appliances will not work at the new location.

4. *Costs/fees associated with passports, visa, work permits, etc.* Such costs are normally a business expense.

All of the reimbursements under a home sale/relocation for executive expatriates are part of the tax equalization program provided by the company.

Q 16:8   What is a home rental program?

An executive expatriate who decides not to sell his primary residence may either leave the home unoccupied or rent it. If it is left unoccupied, he may want to pay someone to maintain the home (e.g., cutting the grass, providing pest control, periodic inside-home inspections, and repairs). Most companies will reimburse the executive for these costs.

In the case of home rental, the executive expatriate will contract with a home management firm to rent the home, and would be reimbursed for rental fees, outside maintenance, and inside repairs. There is normally a limit for these costs such as one or two months' rent value per year.

Q 16:9   What is an education allowance?

When an executive expatriate relocates her family to an overseas location, the children need to be enrolled in a school with an educational curriculum similar to that in the home country. These schools may be private and have tuition fees or similar fees for books, labs, etc. Any cost associated with maintaining the child's educational advancement as it would have been in the home country are reimbursed by the company under an education allowance program.

Q 16:10   What is language training?

This is a common reimbursement to an executive expatriate for all costs incurred while learning the language at the new overseas location. It applies to the executive and his family as well. Costs for the executive are a business expense, while costs for the family can either be business (particularly if the spouse is expected to entertain local customers or employees) or part of the relocation program, which is designed to help the family adapt to the new culture and environment.

Q 16:11   What is home leave?

Home leave is intended to allow the executive expatriate and family to reunite ties with family and friends back at the home country. It is normally provided in conjunction with vacation, and reimburses the executive for all travel costs (business class airfare), plus car rental and hotel and meals for any non-vacation days. When home leave is taken, there is frequently a business day or two to visit the company home office in the home country. One trip per year is the norm, and all expatriate allowances are maintained during the home leave.

Some expatriates have children attending college while the executive is on overseas assignment. In these situations, companies will allow three or four return trips home for the student-child at major holidays and semester breaks.

Executive expatriates will often wish to combine tour packages with their home leave (e.g., one week at an island resort that is on the way back to the home country). In these cases, companies will provide reimbursement up to the cost of a round-trip business class airline ticket for the executive and family.

Example. The round-trip business class airfare for an executive expatriate and family is $4,000. The executive wishes to have the family take a resort island tour package in combination with round-trip coach airfare while on home leave. The cost for executive and family is $5,000. The company would reimburse the executive for $4,000.

Home leave may subject the executive to additional tax liability. If this is the case, most companies will assume this additional tax liability.

Tax Considerations

Q 16:12   What is tax equalization?

The objective of a tax equalization policy is to insure that the executive expatriate will pay the same federal and state tax while on overseas assignment as would have been paid if the executive had been paid the same direct compensation (excluding expatriate program allowances) and stayed working in the home country (i.e., the executive expatriate will neither gain nor lose as the result of the overseas assignment). Companies will use international CPA firms to calculate the following:

1. *Hypothetical home country income.* The amount of income that the executive expatriate would have had if he or she had worked and lived in the home country during the previous tax year. It includes the following:

   - Base salary

   - Annual incentive

   - Long-term incentives/stock awards that were an ordinary income tax event to the executive that year

   - Imputed income on home country perquisites, supplemental life insurance, etc.

   - Capital gains and capital losses incurred by the executive that year in the home country

   - Exemptions allowed by home country tax laws

   - Itemized or standard deduction amounts allowed under home country tax laws

   - Any other income or deduction normally taken by the executive under home country tax laws (e.g., gains or losses from rental of a second home, dividends)

   Any allowances or reimbursements provided by the company under the executive expatriate program are excluded.

2. *Hypothetical home country tax.* This calculation represents the amount of federal and state tax that the executive expatriate would have paid had she lived in the home country during each year of the overseas assignment. The hypothetical tax does not include any allowances or reimbursements provided under the expatriate compensation program.

3. *Hypothetical home country withholding tax.* An estimate of the deductions to the executive expatriate's income that would be required to offset the hypothetical tax calculated from the hypothetical income, this is based on the withholding allowances outlined in the home country tax law.

The amount of hypothetical withholding tax is made equal to the hypothetical tax, which then becomes the actual tax obligation of the executive expatriate each year of the overseas assignment. Any actual tax obligations beyond this amount will be reimbursed to the executive.

4. *Foreign taxes.* Foreign taxes levied on the executive expatriate in the overseas country (or any other country where business is conducted by the executive) will also be paid by the company. Executive expatriates may be subject to "double taxation" from both home country and overseas country on the same income. Companies will typically pay any foreign country tax assessed to the executive expatriate.

One way to summarize is as follows:

Actual U.S. tax to be paid by executive
Actual foreign tax to be paid by executive
= Amount company reimburses or pays for executive

The company is taking on significant financial support for the executive; therefore, it will require the executive to maintain adequate and accurate financial records. Home country or overseas country tax obligations incurred by the spouse are typically the responsibility of the executive and spouse.

Q 16:13   What is tax-free income?

This refers to the company practice of tax gross-up, and is designed to insure that the executive does not pay any additional taxes due to the allowances and reimbursements provided by the expatriate program.

For example, if an executive is provided with a $2,000 per month housing allowance, she will have $24,000 added to annual income and will be required to pay taxes (federal and state if applicable) on this amount. Under a tax gross-up (or tax-free) policy, the company will calculate the amount of this tax given the executive (e.g., adjusted gross income, exemptions, deductions) and pay this amount to tax authorities on behalf of the executive. This tax gross-up amount also becomes additional income to the executive, and the company will perform the same calculation on this amount and pay the tax on behalf of the executive (also known as the tax on the tax). In some cases there is a tax gross-up on a tax gross-up. Most companies will have to limit the tax gross-up calculation to two or three times. The overall effect of the tax gross-up is that allowances or reimbursements under the expatriate program are tax free.

Q 16:14   What is spendable income?

These are items that an expatriate purchases with disposable income or income that is left after paying/allocating income to federal and state taxes, housing costs, benefits, and personal savings. It is used to establish a cost-of-living allowance for the executive expatriate. Spendable income includes the following:

- Food—both at home and away from home
- Clothing
- Recreation
- Personal care
- Commuting and transportation
- Household furnishings and maintenance
- Alcohol/tobacco
- Medical expenses outside of insured plan reimbursement

The process used to measure these items is as follows:

1. Spendable income is identified by level of base salary.
2. On-site surveys are taken at the home country and the overseas country by pricing a "market basket" of representative items in each of the above categories.
3. An index is developed, typically with the home country location considered 100% and the overseas country as some percentage of 100%, e.g., 110%.
4. The index is multiplied by the amount of spendable income to determine the executive expatriate's cost of living allowance.
5. The allowance is then converted to local currency used in the overseas country.

Where the index is less in the overseas country, there is simply no supplemental allowance given to the expatriate (see Q 16:5).

Q 16:15   What are foreign earned income exclusions?

A U.S. resident must pay an income tax on payments made for services rendered in the United States and, if a non-resident, on payments made for performing services outside of the United States. If the foreign country where the services are performed also levies an income tax, then there is double taxation; however, the United States allows taxpayers to elect and claim a credit or deduction on their U.S. income tax form for foreign earned income paid or accrued during the tax year if they meet certain criteria:

1. The taxpayer is a U.S. citizen who has a foreign tax home, defined as a principal place of employment.

2. The U.S. citizen is a bona fide resident of the foreign country, generally meaning that the executive must reside in the foreign country for an entire taxable year.

Example. A U.S. executive moves to Germany in July 1996. Can she claim a deduction for foreign earned income in 1996? The answer is no, but if the executive remains in Germany through 1997, she can file an amended return for 1996 to claim a deduction, because she became a bona fide resident during 1997. The executive was also a bona fide resident during 1997 and can claim a deduction for foreign earned income for this year as well.

The maximum amount of this foreign earned income deduction is $70,000 per taxable year. The term "earned income" refers to salaries, bonuses, overseas premiums and allowances, home leave payments, and tax equalization payments.

In addition, executive expatriates can deduct "reasonable" housing allowances, up to $30,000 per year, that exceed a base housing amount equal to 16 percent of the salary of a U.S. government employee, GS-14, step 1.

The amount of foreign earned income excluded from an executive expatriate's U.S. income cannot exceed the total foreign income earned.

Example. An executive expatriate has foreign earned income as follows:

Base salary	$100,000
Bonus	$ 25,000
Housing allowance	$ 40,000
COLA allowance	$ 10,000
Other allowances	$ 10,000
Total foreign earned income	$185,000
Foreign earned income exclusion	($70,000)
Housing exclusion ($40,000 minus base housing amount of $10,000)	($30,000)
Total foreign income exclusion	($100,000)

Q 16:16   How can executive expatriates avoid taxes when on overseas assignment?

Tax evasion is against the law, but tax avoidance is not. There are three primary methods used by expatriates to avoid taxation:

1. Reclassifying executive expatriate allowances;

2. Changing the country that pays income to the executive expatriate; and

3. Deferring executive expatriate income.

Reclassifying allowances. These actions have the effect of providing the executive expatriate with the same benefit or allowance, but in a different form that is allowed by the local country. Some experts in this field have said that it simply means "calling it something different," but in fact the benefit received is coming from a completely different source.

Example 1. Companies can own or lease housing, and then provide it to the executive expatriate, rather than a housing allowance. In many countries this action results in preferential or lower taxation from the overseas country and the United States.

Example 2. In some overseas countries, allowances for things such as education or home leave are not taxable by the overseas country if paid directly by the company rather than as an allowance to the executive.

Changing the country that pays the income. Many overseas countries determine taxation on the basis of the number of days spent working in their country. This leads to a practice of paying the executive expatriate in Country *A*, only for the time he worked in Country *A*. Other names for these payments are "offshore payments" or "dual contracts."

Example 1. An executive expatriate with an overseas residence in Japan spends 25 percent of his working days in other southeast Asian countries. The home country of the executive expatriate provides 75 percent of all compensation to the executive while he is located in Japan, and 25 percent of all compensation is paid "offshore" or outside of Japan. Therefore, 25 percent of this income is not taxed in Japan.

Example 2. An executive expatriate has two employment contracts with her company. Under these dual contracts, one provides payment for all employment services provided in the United Kingdom and the other provides payment for all services worked in European countries.

Deferring income. The timing of compensation provided to executive expatriates can have significant impact on taxation costs. In particular, annual bonus and long-term stock payments, if deferred, can save company costs on tax equalization.

Example 1. An executive expatriate defers annual bonus earned during a three-year assignment overseas. The company saves significant tax gross-up expenses.

Example 2. An executive borrows funds needed to pay foreign taxes while on an overseas assignment. Under this loan-bonus plan, the executive is given a bonus to pay back the loan after she returns to the United States. The bonus includes interest charges on the loan. The company has again saved significant tax gross-up expenses.

Note: Specific tax laws of the United States and the overseas countries (and related tax treaties) must be carefully analyzed before these ideas are implemented. It is recommended that CPA firms or tax attorneys be used for counsel and advice.

Q 16:17   Can an executive expatriate avoid capital gains tax on the sale of a home while on overseas assignment?

Yes, an exemption or "suspension" of capital gains is available for the period the executive is overseas, if certain conditions are met:

1. The home was the executive's primary residence.

2. Reinvestment of the capital gain from the sale occurs within the required time period after the executive returns to the United States.

3. Occupancy of a new home occurs within the required time period after the executive returns to the United States.

4. The total time period from sale to repurchase does not exceed the maximum time period for the exemption.

Vacation homes do not qualify under these provisions.

Special Compensation

Q 16:18   Are executive expatriates protected against currency fluctuations?

This is one of the most volatile issues for executive expatriate programs. An executive receiving additional income as the result of currency fluctuation tends to view this as a natural right; however, if currency fluctuation results in less income, the executive will complain loudly and tell the company that there is an obligation to make up the loss.

The many allowances available to executive expatriates (e.g., housing, cost of living, education) can all be paid in the foreign currency of the overseas country. But if any portion is paid in U.S. currency, the problem begins.

Companies take one of three positions on this issue:

1. Limit currency fluctuations to a specific percentage change each month or quarter (e.g., 1 percent).

2. Establish a fixed exchange formula at the beginning of the overseas assignment and keep it throughout the assignment.

3. Explain to the executive expatriate at the beginning of the overseas assignment that fluctuation will occur, and that no action will be taken by the company.

Alternative 1 seems the most reasonable to both the company and the executive expatriate, especially if it is also agreed that all allowances will be reviewed and reestablished each year if currency fluctuations change total direct compensation by more than 5 percent in any given year. This establishes a level playing field and maintains the balance sheet concept of having the executive expatriate neither gain nor lose in total compensation due to the overseas assignment.

Q 16:19   What is a completion bonus?

This is a bonus paid to an executive expatriate after he completes the overseas assignment and has returned to the United States. This is frequently used when the executive expatriate is asked to take a lateral career move to an overseas assignment that will broaden his knowledge and experience, or situations when the executive expatriate is asked to take an assignment in an undesirable area, which might also provide a hardship allowance. (A completion bonus can also be used in lieu of a hardship allowance.)

Q 16:20   Can stock options be granted to executive expatriate?

Yes, however, some foreign countries tax these transactions at the time of grant, even though no stock ownership has occurred. (A stock option is the right to purchase shares of company stock in the future.)

Another problem with stock options is that if the expatriate exercises them while overseas, there is the possibility of double taxation (foreign tax on the proceeds plus U.S. tax) and the potential cost of tax equalization. The exercise terms of existing stock option grants held by an executive expatriate are an important consideration prior to the move overseas. Most companies will let the executive exercise any existing stock options while overseas; however, they will issue stock appreciation rights during the period of the overseas assignment.

Surveys by large CPA firms and large compensation consulting firms indicate that the majority of companies in the United States use stock appreciation rights for expatriates and foreign national executives.

Q 16:21   What are free-standing stock appreciation rights?

Stock appreciation rights (SARs) are the rights to stock appreciation over a base price, during a fixed number of years, after some vesting period has been met. The term "free standing" means that the SARs are not attached to a stock option, but stand alone.

> **Example: Free-Standing SAR.** An executive expatriate on a four-year overseas assignment is given rights to the stock appreciation of 1,000 shares of company stock during the four-year period. The executive must hold the rights for one year prior to exercise. The base price at the time of grant is $20.

> Three years later, the stock has a value of $50 and the executive exercises the right to the stock appreciation. The executive is paid $30,000 minus appropriate taxes ($50 – $20 = $30; $30 × 1,000 shares = $30,000)

> **Example: SAR Attached to Stock Option.** An executive expatriate on a four-year overseas assignment is given 1,000 stock option shares with 1,000 stock appreciation rights attached to these shares. They are in tandem, in that the executive can exercise either the stock option or the stock appreciation right. There is a one-year holding or vesting period. The base price at the time of grant is $20.

> Three years later, the stock has a value of $50, and the executive exercises 600 of the stock appreciation rights. The executive is paid $18,000 ($50 – $20 = $30; $30 × 600 = $18,000). The executive has 400 remaining shares of stock options or stock appreciation rights.

Q 16:22   Can long-term bonus plans be used for executive expatriates?

Yes, and they would be structured in the same way as similar plans for U.S.-based executives (see Q 7:39 and Q 7:46). The only difference is that performance measures would be based on the overseas business unit objectives rather than U.S. business unit objectives. Some companies will also require the executive to defer any amounts earned from the long-term plan until the executive returns to the United States from the overseas assignment, so that the company can save significant costs on tax equalization and duplicate taxes (foreign and United States).

Q 16:23   Can annual incentive plans be used for executive expatriates?

Yes, and they would be structured in the same way as similar plans for U.S.-based executives except with respect to the form of payment. The earned bonus can be paid in (1) local currency, (2) home country currency, or (3) a split payment of local and home country currency.

The tax implications of any "split payment" should be evaluated before a decision is made to use this alternative. Some companies will give the executive the choice of the form of currency, so that the executive can take advantage of current currency exchange rates.

Q 16:24   What kind of medical benefits are provided to executive expatriates?

Most companies will maintain the executive's eligibility in the home country medical plan, although care must be taken to make sure that the definition of "eligible employee" in the plan documents and insurance contracts is drafted to include such persons. Under the balance sheet concept, the executive expatriate should neither gain nor lose in compensation during the overseas assignment; however, many overseas countries will have statutory benefits that the executive expatriate must be granted. If this is the case, the home country medical plan is the "floor," or the minimum coverage provided. The executive selects the medical coverage used, and the company coordinates benefits so that there is no duplication of benefits paid.

Another alternative to accommodate statutory benefits at the overseas location is for the country to provide local private medical care that "clones" the company's medical plan. This will also achieve the concept of equality of medical care for the executive expatriate while overseas.

Large companies will often join an international medical plan that has member health facilities in multiple cities throughout the world.

Executive expatriates can then use these facilities while living or traveling overseas.

Q 16:25 What happens to an executive expatriate's pension plan while on overseas assignment?

Companies typically will continue making contributions to an executive's pension plan on the same basis as if the executive were still in the home country.

Many overseas countries have statutory retirement plans that require a company or executive contribution. Companies will make these contributions, and most will ensure that the total amount contributed by the executive while overseas is the same as if the executive were in the home country. This element of company cost is an important part of the decision on using expatriates.

If the executive should be overseas long enough to have qualified for a pension payment at retirement age from the overseas statutory pension plan, then companies will coordinate benefits with the home country pension plan so that the executive neither gains nor loses in the amount of pension due.

Q 16:26 How are life insurance and disability established for executive expatriates?

These benefits are kept at the same level that would exist if the executive were still in the home country. For example, if an executive has a disability plan that provides 60 percent payment of base salary upon disability, then this same benefit would apply to an overseas disability. The more important issue to the company is the length of the disability. The company is still providing allowances to an executive expatriate and, hopefully, the executive will be returning to work very soon. If not, the executive will probably be repatriated.

Q 16:27 What perquisites are provided to executive expatriates?

This varies by the level of executive as well as the overseas country where the executive is assigned. The one rule of thumb that applies is simply that, all factors being equal, the executive in the overseas assignment will have greater perquisites than if he were in the home country, particularly if the home country is the United States. This is the one exception to the balance sheet concept. For example, it is standard practice for an executive in most overseas countries to be given a company car, while this is not the case in the United States. In addition, the overseas executive is frequently there to develop business and, therefore, is given a more liberal expense account than in the home country.

This issue must be determined on an individual case basis, taking into account the local norms and the level and business purpose of the overseas assignment.

Q 16:28   What is done for executive expatriates upon repatriation?

Typically, companies will bring executives back to their home country and provide them with similar relocation benefits as they had when taking the expatriate assignment. These include:

- Home-finding trip for the executive and spouse
- Shipment of all household belongings
- Business class air travel for executive and family
- Temporary living expenses for executive and family prior to arrival of household goods; this also includes extended rental of an automobile, since cars are normally shipped separately from household goods and take longer on an international relocation
- Delivery/shipment of any household goods kept in storage
- Shipment of any special handling items like pets or art work
- Miscellaneous expense allowance (typically one month's base salary)

For executives who seek an apartment, many companies will also pay for any security deposits or up-front fees required of a new lease. Executives who purchase a new home will also receive reimbursement of any closing costs on the purchase.

Q 16:29   What special compensation is provided to an executive expatriate who takes a second overseas assignment?

The first issue that must be addressed in these situations is whether the executive should be reclassified from expatriate to international employee. General practice is for a company to classify all employees as "international" if they have been working outside of their home country for five years and if there is no future plan to repatriate the employee.

An executive who takes a second assignment as an expatriate would be provided with the same program in the new overseas location as was provided in the first location. Housing, COLA, and education allowances may be different in the new location, but the executive is still given the same expatriate support programs

If an executive is reclassified as an international employee, then the common practice is to provide one of two compensation methods: the "net to net" compensation program and the "modified home country balance sheet program." (These concepts may have different names in some companies, but the theory is the same.)

The modified home country balance sheet approach is a first step in "disconnecting" the executive expatriate from a full expatriate compensation program. As foreign service assignments of the executive continue, the second step is adoption by the company of a net to net compensation program.

Q 16:30   What are the elements of a net to net compensation program?

The following eight elements are normally found in a net to net compensation program:

1. Base salary is in local currency and is established by awarding the executive an actual base salary equal to the same salary range position previously held by the executive in the home country. For example, an executive with a 110 percent compensation ratio in the home country would have a 100 percent compensation ratio in the new overseas country's salary range assigned to their position. The compensation ratio is the per-

centage relationship of actual base salary to the salary range midpoint, with the midpoint equalling 100 percent.

2. No foreign service premium would be paid.

3. A fixed housing allowance would be provided. (Said another way, free housing up to a maximum.)

4. A COLA would be provided based on a comparison of the old location to the new location. (Published tables are typically used from ORC, AIRINC, etc.)

5. Tax protection (not tax equalization) is provided. Tax protection means that the company will compare net income after deducting taxes and add the housing and COLA allowances in the home country or country where the executive was previously assigned, to net income in the new country after the same deductions and additions. (Hence the basis of the term "net to net.") The executive is responsible for her own taxes but may receive a reimbursement from the tax protection program if taxes in the new overseas country would result in a substantial reduction of net income.

6. Educational and language allowances are negotiable and depend on the individual situation of the executive. There is no reliable survey data on company practices in this area.

7. Companies may maintain a "phantom home country base salary" for pension plan purposes, and, if so, ongoing company contributions would be made to this retirement benefit. In these cases, upon retirement, any retirement income earned in a foreign country would be deducted from the retirement income that the executive earns from the home country. Some large companies have an "offshore pension plan" that clones the home country pension plan and is specifically for international employees who may have multiple overseas assignments during their career, and multiple pensions. The offshore plan establishes a minimum retirement, typically tied to final average pay and years of service, and then consolidates all executive pension amounts to avoid duplication of payments.

8. Medical, insurance, and disability are normally provided to the executive expatriate per normal practice of the new overseas country. Large companies may develop offshore medical plans or use an international medical plan with numerous facilities

around the world in order to provide the executive with a minimum benefit level.

Q 16:31   What are the typical elements of a modified home country balance sheet compensation program?

Six elements typically constitute a modified home country balance sheet compensation program:

1. Base salary is paid in local currency and is established using compensation ratio comparisons of former location to new location, as described in the net to net compensation program.

2. No foreign service premium is paid.

3. A fixed housing allowance is provided (i.e., free housing as with the net to net compensation program).

4. A COLA is provided (from tables) based on a comparison of living costs in the executive expatriate's home country vs. current overseas location.

5. Tax equalization is provided to the executive expatriate.

6. All other allowances and benefits/pension are per the company's regular executive expatriate compensation program.

Q 16:32   Is there a checklist of issues that should be considered by a company and/or executive in developing an executive expatriate compensation program?

This is a useful tool, and such a list would include the following:

Pre-Assignment

- Education regarding the history, government, language, weather, economy, living standard, location, and culture of the overseas country
- Compensation program of similar executive positions in the overseas country or in similar countries
- Term of overseas assignment
- Business objective of executive expatriate position and repatriation plans

- Legal documents required, for example, passports, visa, work permits, drivers license, letters of credit, letters of competency
- Medical requirements, for example, vaccinations and statutory medical/pension plans in the new country
- Compensation and allowances, and the source (i.e., ORC COLA tables)
- Pre-assignment visit by executive and spouse to examine housing, appliances, food/sanitation standards, clothing styles, availability of personal services, medical facilities, educational facilities, recreational facilities, religious and social opportunities, and servants
- Local transportation, shopping, telephone service, currency, and miscellaneous issues like spousal employment or anything specific to the individual executive and family

Starting the Overseas Assignment

- Decision and implementation of home sale vs. home rental
- Language training
- Children's education registration at new location
- Full documentation of pay, allowance, benefits, vacations, home leave, tax equalization, special short-term or long-term incentive plans, automobile purchase or shipment, and perquisites
- Necessary documents such as visas, business cards, change of address notices, revised wills
- Relocation plan to include shipment of household goods, family travel, temporary living location, and home sale
- Development of new banking relationships and enrollment into new medical facilities
- Purchase of new appliances
- Assimilation plan at work and in the home so that all the family gets acclimated to the new environment in a satisfactory manner.

International assignments are challenging but they can also be exciting, educational, and rewarding for all executives.

Chapter 17

Executive Compensation in the Public Sector

Executive compensation programs in public sector organizations (e.g., schools, governments) are being reviewed at many locations as the result of board of director interest in improving the organization while, at the same time, controlling executive compensation costs. Tenure-based pay systems are being replaced by performance-based pay systems. Annual incentive plans and supplemental retirement plans are new ideas to public sector organizations and can be useful tools in attracting, retaining, and motivating executives. This chapter answers questions on current differences between public and private sector base salary, performance management, incentives, benefits, and perquisites.

Q 17:1   What is the driving philosophy behind executive compensation in the public sector versus that in the private sector?

In the private sector, the driving philosophy is pay for performance. Additionally, executives have a significant amount of compensation at risk or subject to the achievement of performance goals. There are varying opinions on how well this is done, but the philosophy and intent of executive pay is clear.

In the public sector, the driving philosophy is tenure-based; that is, the longer you occupy a position, the higher the pay.

This is the cause of great debate. Merit pay systems have been tried in both government and schools, but are still not widely used, except in the federal government where some higher level civilian employees are under merit pay. Critics claim that the absence of performance-based pay for executives results in an absence of accountability, which leads to mediocrity and poor quality.

The opposing argument is that public sector executives are clearly accountable to school boards, or elected officials, and the public will not stand for poor quality.

Q 17:2   How is base salary different in the public sector organization than in the private sector organization?

Many jobs in the public sector have no counterpart in the private sector that can be used for comparison (e.g., director–road maintenance, superintendent of schools); however, there are many jobs in the public sector that are similar to others in the private sector, such as director of accounting or personnel.

When jobs are similar, the base salary levels in the public sector tend to be different from the private sector for two reasons:

1. The labor market definition is typically more limited in the public sector than in the private sector.
2. The salary ranges used in the public sector are broader than those in the private sector.

Labor Market Definition. Government organizations tend to market price their jobs against other government organizations. Schools tend to market price their jobs by comparing to other schools. Public sector organizations use a more limited labor market because not all labor market organizations have jobs that are similar to their own. This tends to perpetuate industry practice or, as some would say, makes it incestuous, because labor market pricing of jobs is only conducted within the industry.

Salary Ranges. The tenure-based pay philosophy in the public sector results in automatic step increases each year (based on tenure). These step increases require a broad salary range because there are so many steps (in some cases 15 or 20 steps with a 3 to 4 percent pay increase per step). The result is broader salary ranges. A recent survey by the human resource consulting firm of HR Management, Inc. showed a typical public sector organization salary range for executive positions to be 70 percent. The same number in the private sector, per the American Compensation Association, is 40 to 50 percent (see Q 17:5).

This factor produces an interesting characteristic of public sector base salary levels. At the low end of the salary range, actual base salary rates are significantly lower than those in the total labor market (although they parallel those of other organizations in the public sector labor market). At the high end of the salary range, actual base salary levels are significantly above those in the total labor market (although they parallel those of other organizations in the public sector labor market).

Q 17:3   Are job evaluation systems used for executive positions in public sector organizations?

Yes, the same job evaluations used in the private sector are adopted/modified for public sector organizations. The descriptions used in each job evaluation factor are simply modified. For example, the descriptions in a common job evaluation factor of "interactions with others" are compared for a private corporation and public sector (school) organization in the following chart:

Level	Private Sector Description	Public Sector Description
1	Other employees	Department employees
2	Vendors & suppliers	Professional associations
3	Customers	Students
4	Directors & officers	County administrators
5	Board of directors	Members of school board

Q 17:4   Can merit increases to base salary work for executive positions in public sector organizations?

Yes, but such merit increases are rare because, in most cases, public sector jobs are unique and hard to measure. Take, for example, a superintendent of curriculum development or a county sheriff. What performance measures are appropriate for curriculum development? Measures like student grades or SAT scores are affected by other variables, and there are few if any national evaluations on the quality of curriculums. The same is true for a county sheriff. Most performance measures selected will also be affected by many other factors.

Most public sector positions have been granted "tenure-based" salary increases for years. Public organizations have little experience with performance evaluation programs, which are the basis for merit pay increases. For these reasons merit pay has little use.

The few public sector organizations that have tried merit pay have used performance measures like the following:

Position Title	Performance Measure
School Teacher	1. Teaching skills (measured by observation)
	2. Student test scores (national tests)
	3. Peer ratings by other teachers
	4. Teacher scores on continuous education courses
Police Officer	1. Knowledge of the law (measured via tests)
	2. Number of crime prevention programs in department/geographic area
	3. Opinion survey of public safety in department/geographic area
	4. Crime rate in department/geographic area

The disadvantages of a tenure-based pay increase (discussed in Q 17:5) can be overcome with a merit increase system; however, a new set of challenges must be met if merit pay is to be more effective. The major challenge is the selection of performance measures.

Q 17:5   What are the advantages and disadvantages of tenure-based pay increase systems?

Tenure-based pay increase systems use tenure as the basis for an annual pay increase. An example follows:

Position: Director of Accounting

Years of Experience	1	2	3	4	5	6	7	8
Compensation (in $ thousands)	$40.0	$41.6	$43.3	$45.0	$46.8	$48.7	$50.6	$52.6

Years of Experience	9	10	11	12	13	14	15	16
Compensation (in $ thousands)	$54.7	$56.9	$59.2	$61.6	$64.1	$66.7	$69.4	$72.2

The difference between the rate at Year 1 and Year 16 is 80 percent. This is unusually broad versus typical private sector practice, which, according to the American Compensation Association, would be 30 to 40 percent for non-executive positions and 50 percent for executive positions. (See Q 17:2.) This quantitative analysis shows the first disadvantage of tenure-based pay systems, as shown in the following chart:

Tenure-Based Pay Increase Systems

Advantages	*Disadvantages*
1. Retention of executives.	1. At the higher steps, pay is well above the labor market, resulting in higher annual costs.
2. Costs are predictable.	2. Pay levels and cost escalate each year regardless of performance.
3. Less administrative time and cost without the need to measure performance.	3. Executives have less motivation to perform because there is no financial incentive tied to the achievement of work results.

Q 17:6 Why do public sector organizations prefer a tenure-based pay increase system?

Many executive positions in the public sector report to an elected official, and elected officials frequently change. Whenever there is change, new attitudes and opinions on compensation can occur, resulting in an irregular pay system. To avoid this, the tenure-based pay system was developed. It has eliminated discretionary judgments on pay increase by the elected executives (who come and go) and was intended to stabilize the compensation of the non-elected executive.

Most would agree that this objective has been achieved; however, because of the disadvantages suggested in Q 17:5 (i.e., high pay levels vs. the labor market, automatic escalating costs each year, and the absence of any focus on performance achievement), many school boards and county/state officials have been prompted to look for alternative solutions. The few government organizations and school districts that have implemented merit pay for higher level executives (with modest success) have found that they require significant time to train executives in goal setting, coaching/counseling, completing the performance evaluation form, and discussing performance results with employees. Private sector corporations have reached the same conclusion.

The question becomes: Does the extra training effort make merit pay increase systems more effective than tenure-based pay increase systems? The answer simply depends on the level of achievement of the organization. If an organization (public or private) is experiencing high performance, a change in pay increase systems will probably have little value to the organization. If the organization, however, is experiencing mediocre or below average performance, then a change in pay increase systems can have a positive effect on the organization.

Q 17:7   Are salary ranges used in the public sector?

Yes, but salary ranges found in the public sector are typically different from those found in the private sector. They contain numerous steps and are, therefore, broader in length.

Example. Assume that the labor market value for the executive position of chief financial officer in a $100 million sales company is $75,000 per year. In a private sector company the salary range would typically be as follows:

Private Sector Salary Range

Minimum	Midpoint	Maximum
$60,000	$75,000	$90,000

Assume as well that the labor market value for the executive position of chief financial officer in a county school district is $75,000. In this public sector organization, the salary range would typically be as follows:

Public Sector Salary Range

Step 1	Step 2	Step 3	Step 4	Step 5
$54,100	$56,300	$58,600	$60,900	$63,300

Step 6	Step 7	Step 8	Step 9	Step 10
$65,800	$68,400	$71,100	$73,900	$76,900

Step 11	Step 12	Step 13	Step 14	Step 15
$80,000	$83,200	$86,500	$90,000	$93,600

Q 17:8 Are annual incentives used in public sector organizations?

Generally, no. There are some special award programs that pay a lump-sum bonus for some extraordinary/outstanding performance, but the public sector does not make use of incentive compensation for executives. Many believe that, like many not-for-profit organizations, the public sector is missing a great opportunity to motivate executives with an annual incentive plan; however, since these organizations rarely have a merit increase system on which to base pay, they also have no performance measures or performance evaluation system within the organization. Performance measures are an essential requirement of any incentive compensation plan.

Q 17:9 Are long-term performance plans or stock award plans used in public organizations?

There is no stock, nor are there stockholders, in public sector organizations. As discussed in previous questions, because there is rarely any ability to measure performance in these organizations annually or over the long term, these plans rarely exist. The significant payments from stock plans (and other forms of long-term compensation) to private sector executives are certainly a big advantage with respect to total compensation for these executives.

Q 17:10 Are insured benefits in the public sector better than those in private companies?

HR Management, Inc. analyzed the benefit plans in 25 public sector organizations and 25 private sector organizations. There were no significant differences in the level of benefit coverage. With respect to executive cost, the public sector organizations charged their executives less than the private sector organization for approximately the same level of insured benefit coverage.

This is not surprising, since private corporations have been more aggressive in passing on insured benefit plan cost increases to all employees. This has been accomplished through cafeteria benefit plans that allow employees to select the level of benefit and associated cost, and by more aggressive use of managed care organizations like HMOs and PPOs (health maintenance organizations and preferred provider organizations).

Private companies have also been experiencing more downsizing and merger acquisition activity than public sector organizations. Thus the public sector has maintained a higher level of "career employment" and "status quo" than private companies, where organization tenure and loyalty have changed significantly. The organization and the executive in the private sector are more independent in today's business environment. This facilitates a different strategy on benefit costs.

Q 17:11 Are retirement plans in the public sector better than those in private companies?

The same survey mentioned in Q 17:10 also reviewed retirement plans. There were no significant differences in eligible retirement benefits between public and private sector organizations; however, public sector executives had an average tenure greater than that for private company executives. This is consistent with the tenure-driven compensation systems used in the public organization.

A significantly greater number of executives in private companies had eligibility for supplemental retirement plans than in the public sector where these plans are rarely used.

Q 17:12   Can supplemental retirement plans be used in public sector organizations?

Yes, but they rarely are used for the following reasons:

1. Public sector executives are not paid compensation at the level of many billion-dollar private companies (i.e., $250,000 to $1,000,000); therefore, the regulatory maximum in retirement plans rarely affects the public sector executive as it can affect the private sector executive.

2. Private companies are not tenure-driven. In addition, they frequently want executives to retire early so that they can get new ideas into the organization. For executives of such companies there is a business need for a SERP, which is not the case in most public sector organizations.

One can easily conclude that in public sector organizations there is an organizational and motivational value to executives in considering performance-driven base pay and annual incentive plans; however, this is not the case with SERPs. They are rare in public sector organizations because there is little need for them.

Q 17:13   Are public sector organizations subject to Title VII of the Civil Rights Act of 1964, the Fair Labor Standards Act, Americans with Disabilities Act, Age Discrimination in Employment Act, or other such regulations?

Yes, but over the years such regulations have had little impact on public sector executives. Equal pay is rarely an issue because of the tenure-driven nature of public sector pay systems. All executives are automatically treated equally. The tenure-driven philosophy also results in many older executives in the public sector. Public sector organizations also have shown over the years that they do an excellent job in adhering to the race, sex, and national origin provisions of Title VII.

Q 17:14   Do public sector executives have perquisites?

Yes, but not anywhere close to the level of the private company executive. The most popular perquisites in the private sector are first-class air travel, cellular phones, company cars, club memberships, financial planning, and supplemental executive retirement plans, all of which are rarely provided to any public sector executive. The absence of SERPs for public sector executives is discussed in Q 17:12.

Q 17:15   How can compensation plans be used to attract high-quality executives into the public sector?

The downsizing and restructuring that have occurred in private companies during the past 10 years has resulted in the availability of a number of high-quality executives who could make valuable contributions in public sector organizations. But these executives typically have been trained in, and have developed, work methods in performance-driven organizations rather than in tenure-driven organizations; therefore, they rarely consider the public sector.

A change in the compensation plans of public sector organizations can attract these executives. These changes are:

1. Smaller salary ranges with fewer automatic step increases

2. The use of performance-based pay increases in lieu of step increases once a median labor market base pay rate is reached (or immediately used at the time of initial employment)

3. Annual incentive compensation that is determined from achievement of annual performance goals

These compensation plan changes could also have an extremely positive impact on current executives in the public sector, since the changes can motivate them to achieve goals that are critical to a high-quality public organization.

Chapter 18

Compensation for Temporary Executives

As a result of numerous corporate restructuring, downsizing, mergers/divestitures, and other such changes in today's business environment, we have available an ever-growing number of unemployed executives with extensive knowledge and ability who are over age 50. At the same time, companies are showing more interest in using independent contractors to fulfill short-term and/or project work at the executive and non-executive level. These factors have contributed to a significant increase in the use of temporary executives at both public and private companies, and the emergence of recruiting firms that deal exclusively with the placement of temporary executives. This chapter explains the various legal and practical issues relevant to this expanding executive labor market and the creative compensation packages that are being offered to participating executives.

In recent years a number of companies have come under increased scrutiny for the use of independent contractors to avoid having to pay for benefits such as health insurance or retirement plans.

General Considerations 18-2
Incentives and Benefits 18-7
Federal Protection 18-9

Conversion to Full-Time Status   18-9
Current Litigation   18-10

General Considerations

Q 18:1   What is a temporary executive?

A temporary executive is an executive whose employment consists of temporary assignments from a temporary employment firm. The executive is an employee of the temporary employment firm, and has FICA and other tax withheld from his paycheck. The temporary employment firm finds suitable temporary work for the executive, billing the company that uses the executive. A portion of this billing is kept by the temporary employment firm, and a portion is given to the executive.

Most temporary executives are employed in offices rather than in production/operations or technical support positions, shown as follows:

Types of Employment for Temporary Executives

1.	Office Work: (Includes management, advisory board, financial, legal, MIS, human resources, public, and government relations projects)	60%
2.	Production and Operations Work: (Includes traffic, inventory, warehousing, distribution, and scheduling projects)	5%
3.	Technical Work: (Includes sales, marketing, engineering, research, and similar occupations)	35%

Source: HR Management, Inc.

Q 18:2   Are temporary executives independent contractors?

No, not as long as they are on the payroll of the temporary employment firm. An independent contractor is self-employed and is responsible for his or her own FICA and tax withholding. Independent contractors must estimate their earnings, and file quarterly tax payments on IRS Form 1040ES and other appropriate state tax forms. Independent contractors may or may not be incorporated.

The independent contractor will bill the company directly for his or her employment services and will receive a Form 1099 annually from the company which summarizes taxable income paid to the executive.

Q 18:3   What are the advantages and disadvantages of being an independent contractor to the executive?

An independent contractor will perform project- or task-oriented services in his or her area of expertise for any employer. Advantages and disadvantages are as follows:

Advantages	*Disadvantages*
1. There is no "middleman," so the independent contractor can charge less, and earn more.	1. The independent contractor must take all of the legal and financial risk of being an employer.
2. There is the security of a job during the contract period and help in finding the next temporary assignment.	2. All taxes and office costs must be absorbed by the independent contractor, as well as health insurance costs.
3. Most firms will provide benefits after a minimum service period.	3. The independent contractor finds it difficult to sell and perform services.
4. The independent contractor can turn down undesirable work.	4. The independent contractor has irregular needs because of unpredictable staff work load demands.

Q 18:4   What are the advantages and disadvantages of independent contractors to a company?

More and more companies are benefiting from contacts with temporary executives, whether as independent contractors or as staff members of a temporary employment firm. The advantages and disadvantages are as follows:

Advantages	*Disadvantages*
1. Can add or subtract to payroll as dictated by business need.	1. Temporary executives are not familiar with company procedures.
2. Company can avoid severance during a downsizing.	2. Temporary executives do not understand the company's culture and decision making process.
3. There is access to multiskilled executives.	3. Loyalty may not be as high as with a permanent executive who has long tenure with the company.
4. Hiring and training costs lower.	
5. Costs (including benefits) are not any greater for the temporary executive.	
6. Temporary executives can bring fresh ideas to company problems.	

Q 18:5   What is the difference between a short-term and long-term temporary assignment?

A short-term assignment is typically for one month to one year. A long-term assignment is typically for one year or more.

Q 18:6   What is outsourcing?

Outsourcing is the use of an outside firm or non-employees to accomplish the types of projects formerly performed in-house by employees. Executive responsibilities can be outsourced. For this purpose, a company may decide to use a temporary executive who is either an independent contractor or an employee of a temporary employment firm, for an employment period that may be short- or long-term.

Outsourcing can also involve the use of leased executives. Leased executives are full-time employees of a leased employee company, but are dedicated to, who work for, another client company. The leased employee receives all benefits from the leased employee company, which also administers all the employee's FICA and tax withholding. In this regard the leased employee firm is similar to a temporary employee firm except that leased employees tend to be on permanent assignment to the client company.

Q 18:7   What are other alternatives to outsourcing?

Companies may use their own employees on a part-time or flextime basis. Part-time refers to the use of an executive for a fixed number of hours per day or week that is well under the normal 40-hour work week. For example, a part-time executive may work from 1 to 5 p.m. every day, or the same hours only on the last week of the month to assist in the preparation of month-end financial reports.

Flextime executives tend to work longer hours than a part-time executive but typically the hours will be either before or after the normal business hours. For example, a flextime executive may work from 2 to 8 p.m. or 6 a.m. to 12 p.m.

Q 18:8   How do temporary executives obtain an assignment?

If the executive is with a temporary firm, the firm will normally have an assignment manager who is responsible for understanding the executive's experience and abilities, and for finding a company that needs these abilities.

A temporary executive who is an independent contractor must rely on reputation and personal contacts to find a use for her services. Many such executives will develop "referral representatives," that is, people in the business community who are aware of the executive's abilities or who have known the executive for a long time, and can refer the executive's name to companies in the business community, whether it be local, national, or international.

Q 18:9 Can temporary executives be placed on an overseas assignment?

Yes. If this occurs, the executive would typically be on a short-term assignment and would receive reimbursement of all travel and living costs. It would be rare for a temporary executive to be an expatriate, as discussed in Chapter 16.

Q 18:10 How is base salary determined for temporary executives?

This will depend on the number of hours that the executive is asked to work per day. If the executive is working normal daily hours, the base salary could be expressed as a monthly rate and would be similar to the monthly rate that the executive would be paid if he or she were a permanent employee of the company. If the executive is not working normal hours and is an independent contractor who is hired to perform a specific project, the base salary will typically be expressed as an hourly rate.

Another factor affecting the base salary is whether the executive is an independent contractor or an employee of a temporary employee firm. If an employee, the firm will charge a base salary plus a fee to cover its costs. If an independent contractor, the executive could also add selling and administrative costs to the fee.

Example 1. An executive who was previously making $12,000 per month ($120,000 per year) takes early retirement. He decides to do consulting as an independent contractor. Soon after, he is hired by another company as a temporary employee for a period of six months to fill in for an executive who is having surgery. The temporary executive will be using his primary skills in his area of expertise, and will be working normal work hours during the period of employment. The executive charges the company $14,400 per month. He determines this fee by adding 20 percent to his competitive labor value of $12,000 ($12,000 × 1.2 = $14,400).

Example 2. An executive who was previously making $12,000 per month ($120,000 per year) takes early retirement. She decides to work for a temporary employment firm. Soon after, she gets an assignment as a temporary employee for a period of six months to fill in for an executive who is having surgery. The temporary executive will be using her primary skills in her area of expertise, and will be working normal hours during this period. The executive's temporary firm charges the company $15,000 and pays the executive $12,000. The remaining $3,000 is retained by the temporary employment firm to cover its costs.

In both of the previous examples the fees included a base salary that paralleled the temporary executive's former rate and labor market value. Additional costs to the executive and/or temporary employment firm were passed on to the company; however, the company did not incur any more costs than it would have if the executive were its own employee because the company is not paying for, or contributing to, the executive's benefit costs.

Another example of base salary costs is the executive who is on project work or an hourly fee structure. Hourly rates are essentially established by supply and demand and labor market factors. Executive hourly rates could parallel business consultant rates, which vary from $200 to $1,000 per hour in most cases, or they could be less, depending on the nature of the work.

Example 3. An executive who is an independent contractor is hired by a company to help it implement a new product inventory system. The executive has already done this kind of work for other companies and can estimate the number of hours to do the task with reasonable accuracy. The executive's fees are $200 per hour, with the estimated number of hours at 120. If the executive accomplishes the project after the 120 hours, the total fees would be $24,000 ($200 × 120 hours = $24,000).

It is common for compensation to be defined in a contract between the company and the temporary executive or his or her temporary employment firm.

Incentives and Benefits

Q 18:11   Are temporary executives provided with incentive compensation?

They can be. If incentive compensation is provided, it is normally defined in the temporary executive's contract, along with the performance goals (if any) that will be used to determine payment. Most temporary executives receive incentive compensation while employed full-time by a company, which can be a basis for determining the potential size of an incentive award for temporary executives.

An alternative is to obtain labor market compensation surveys and identify competitive amounts of incentive compensation paid to similar positions. If the nature of the temporary work is project work, incentive compensation would typically be built into the hourly fee or be defined as an add-on, particularly if it was based on the work being performed in advance of the estimated time or on some quality standard.

Another type of incentive compensation provided to executives as well as non-executives who perform temporary work is the longevity or tenure bonus. Such bonuses are normally given by a temporary employment firm. For example, if an executive stays with the temporary employment firm for one year, the firm may grant the executive a lump-sum bonus in order to retain his or her services in the future.

Some temporary employment firms will also give "merit increases" to executives if they stay for a fixed period of time (e.g., one year). The motivation is simply retention of that executive's service.

Q 18:12   Are temporary executives provided with stock awards?

It would be rare for a temporary executive to receive any stock or other long-term award. "Long term" in most businesses is defined as three to four years, and it would be rare for any company to have a temporary executive in place for this long.

Q 18:13   Are temporary executives provided with perquisites?

No, these are not part of the compensation of a temporary executive.

Q 18:14   What insured benefits are provided to temporary executives?

Independent contractors must provide their own benefits. An executive employee with a temporary employment firm will typically be given a low level of medical benefits (e.g., reimbursement of 50 to 60 percent of costs after a high deductible, for example, $1,000, has been met), provided that a minimum number of hours have been worked (e.g., 1,000 hours). Temporary employment firms are not obligated to give benefits, but this is a tool for them to retain good employees.

In all cases there will be a coordination of benefits with other benefit coverage that the executive or spouse is eligible to receive.

Q 18:15 Are temporary executives provided with retirement benefits?

It is rare for a temporary employment firm to provide executives with retirement plan eligibility. If the temporary employment firm does maintain a qualified retirement plan, then employees who complete 1,000 or more of service per year would generally be provided with benefits.

Federal Protection

Q 18:16 Are temporary executives subject to federal regulations on equal pay, age, etc.?

Yes, the provisions of Title VII of the Civil Rights Act of 1964, the Americans with Disabilities Act, and other antidiscrimination laws all apply to temporary employees.

Conversion to Full-Time Status

Q 18:17 Can temporary executives be converted to full-time status?

Yes, this occurs often, and the executive's compensation will need to be converted into the company's ongoing total compensation programs. A temporary employment firm will normally require that the executive be employed with it and with the client company for a minimum employment period before it will agree to converting the executive to full-time status with the client company.

Q 18:18   If a temporary executive converts to a full-time employee, are there benefit issues that arise?

Yes. If a temporary employee converts to full-time status with the employer, the following benefit issues must be considered:

1. *Eligibility for qualified retirement plans.* Most qualified retirement plans have waiting periods before eligibility begins. If the temporary executive is a "leased employee" (within the meaning of Code Section 414(n)) prior to conversion to full-time employee status, as long as the gap period between the two periods of employment does not exceed five years, then, generally, the period of service for the employer as a leased employee must be counted under the qualified retirement plan for eligibility purposes.

   Example. Employee A works as a leased employee for Company Z from January 1995 until December 1998. In January 1999, Employee A becomes a full-time employee of Company Z. Company Z's 401(k) plan requires completion of one year of service before an employee is eligible to participate in the plan. Under the IRS qualified plan rules (Code Section 414(n)(4)), Employee A is eligible for plan participation on the first plan entry date on or after his date of hire as a full-time employee of Company Z, because prior service as a leased employee must be taken into account.

2. *Vesting service under qualified retirement plans.* Prior service as a leased employee must generally be counted for vesting purposes pursuant to the IRS qualified plan rules. [IRC § 414(n)(3), (4)]

It should be noted that qualified retirement plans can be drafted to minimize the impact of these rules.

Current Litigation

Q 18:19   How does the *Microsoft* case affect the temporary employee arena?

Vizcaino v. Microsoft [173 F3d 713 (9th Cir 1999)] is basically a case of worker misclassification. The courts have ruled that Microsoft misclassified certain "independent contractors," "freelancers," and "temporary" workers. Such workers should have been covered under IRS tax withholding rules and under benefit plans such as the employee stock-purchase plan that covered all other common law employees.

Since the May 1999 decision of the Ninth Circuit in *Microsoft,* other groups of temporary workers have filed lawsuits against other companies for retroactive benefits, and further litigation is bound to occur. Companies need to examine their staffing practices closely and evaluate the status of their workers. The more control that the company has over a worker, the more likely that such worker will be considered a common law employee of the company, and, as such, possibly eligible for certain company benefits.

Chapter 19

Economic Profit-Based Incentive Plans

The economic profit-based incentive plan is one of the most popular new ideas in executive compensation. Large human resources consulting firms report that one company in five is considering this new performance measure and one company out of every ten has implemented an executive compensation plan that uses economic profit or some similar measure. As a performance-based alternative to traditional accounting measures, both large and small companies are adopting this type of plan.

The term *economic profit* was derived from the term *economic value added,* which is now a trademark term of the consulting firm Stern Stewart, which is given credit for creating the idea for this performance measure. Many variations of this concept are being used. It is not derived from financial ratios that are part of traditional general accounting principles and, therefore, it is viewed as a performance measure that is not as easy to manipulate and is more closely related to shareholder interests.

This chapter discusses a number of economic profit definitions and implementation issues.

Overview 19-2
Implementation 19-8

Case Studies   19-16

Overview

Q 19:1   What is economic profit?

There are multiple definitions of economic profit. They all relate to some measure of company profitability that exceeds a company's cost of capital. In its most basic form, the cost of capital is a company's annual payment of debt and its payment to shareholders in the form of dividends. Profit is annual net profit after taxes. If a company is earning $10 million and it is paying $6 million in long-term debt and $3 million in dividends to shareholders, then it is earning $1 million in excess of its cost of capital. To advocates of this concept, this is true economic profit rather than the profit reported in financial statements, which may not have any relationship to the true economic health of the company. The reason for this is that the profit in financial statements includes such factors as nonrecurring gains, business write-offs, expenses that are postponed, and other one-time special accounting entries that do not present an accurate picture of company and executive performance in any given fiscal year.

The concept of economic profit can be much more sophisticated than this basic definition. The most common method of calculating economic profit involves comparing net or operating profit to a fixed cost of capital multiplied by capital employed in the business and under the control and direct influence of a group of executives. The capital under the control and direct influence of a group of executives includes the following:

- Cash
- Inventory
- Accounts receivable
- Accounts payable
- Equipment

Example. A division of Company A has operating profit in the amount of $5 million. The total amount of capital is $30 million and the cost of using the capital is 10 percent, or $3 million. The economic profit equals $2 million.

operating profit − (capital × percentage cost of capital) = economic profit

$5,000,000 − ($30,000,000 × 10%) = $2,000,000

Q 19:2   What is economic value-added?

Like economic profit, there are multiple definitions of economic value added (EVA). The consulting firm Stern Stewart typically defines EVA as being similar to economic profit but much more sophisticated. It will use some measure of profit and compare it to capital employed multiplied by a cost of capital, but the cost of capital is not a fixed number. One method used to calculate cost of capital is to take an expected investor return and add to it a premium investment return that a potential shareholder would expect in order to invest in the company rather than seek the investment that provides the normal return, and then multiply this percentage by a beta factor that is determined by analyzing the company's stock performance in comparison to the stock market. If a company's stock performance is the same as the stock market, the beta factor is 1.0. If the company's stock performance is more volatile than the stock market, the beta factor is *greater than* 1.0; and if the company's stock performance is less volatile than the stock market, the beta factor is *less than* 1.0. Obviously, a great deal of analysis is involved in this process. Since it is a more sophisticated measure, a company may need to take additional steps to ensure that its executives understand the measure.

Q 19:3   How is economic profit used in executive compensation plans?

In most companies, economic profit is the performance measure that drives both annual and long-term incentives for eligible executives. The amount of incremental economic profit achieved is pro-rated to the eligible executive group using a percentage of the incremental economic profit. In this regard, economic profit plans are similar to profit sharing plans.

Economic profit plans differ from profit sharing and other incentive plans in that they typically require a mandatory deferral for some portion of the incentive earned. The mandatory deferral is applied to the long-term or deferred portion of the payment.

Example. Company B has the following economic profit-based incentive plan:

Incremental Economic Profit:	$2,000,000
Executive A's Prorated Share:	10% or $200,000
Amount Paid Currently:	40% or $80,000
Amount Deferred:	60% or $120,000

The amount deferred can be a short- or long-term deferral. Long-term deferrals are typically until retirement. Thus, the economic profit plan can be a form of supplemental retirement benefit. Short-term deferrals would typically have a vesting provision. For example, a plan may provide for 20 percent vesting per year with a total payment of deferred amounts after five years. The deferred amount would be subject to some investment interest and appreciation potential. Most companies establish investment alternatives and the executive then selects the investment of his or her choice. If the executive voluntarily resigns or is involuntarily terminated for reasons other than cause, the executive is paid the amount of deferred compensation that is vested.

Example. Company B has the following vesting provision:

Amount Deferred:	$120,000
Vesting Provision:	20 percent per year
Actual Annual Appreciation:	10 percent per year
Voluntary Termination after 3 Years	
Amount Paid:	$96,000
$120,000 × 10% for 3 Years =	$160,000
$160,000 × 20% × 3 Years =	$96,000

Q 19:4 What are the advantages of economic profit plans?

First, economic profit plans focus executives on performance factors that drive increases in the value of the company. Traditional executive incentive plans use accounting measures that may or may not drive increases in the value of the company.

Second, executive gains are typically uncapped percentages of economic profit. Therefore, the need for estimating levels of performance against accounting-based performance measures is eliminated. Many noneconomic profit performance measures use goals that are in the company's annual budget, and as such may or may not be realistically achieved. Human judgment on the appropriate level of goal achievement is always better at the end of the fiscal year than at the beginning. Moreover, when executives figure out that their incentive compensation is dependent upon the goals that they are to establish, they may set goals that are artificially low. This problem does not exist with economic profit plans.

Third, economic profit is a tool for strategic business decision making. For example, when a company is evaluating possible acquisition, merger, divestiture, or spin-off actions, it can calculate the estimated change in economic value after the action to see if company value will be improved as a result of the action. If not, the action should be changed or dropped from consideration.

Fourth, large consulting firms have conducted studies that show that EVA and economic profit plans are better drivers of company stock price than traditional accounting measures. Therefore, shareholder value, the primary focus of many corporations, can be directly improved with these plans. These studies show that companies that use the economic profit measure produce greater profit from the capital they employ and that this attracts investors and drives stock price up.

Q 19:5 What are the disadvantages of economic profit plans?

Many compensation experts dispute the fact that economic profit or EVA plans have a stronger correlation to shareholder value. They point to historical evidence of successful companies that have used traditional accounting measures in their executive incentive plans for years, which drive shareholder value along with many other factors, such as the quality of the company's products, its reputation with consumers, etc. They further state that all performance measures are subject to the vagaries of the stock market and shareholder value is driven by stock market performance as well as measures of company performance.

In addition, few executives have impact on the cost of capital. Moreover, it is difficult for a large company to change its capital structure. Even if it were able to do so, only a few people would be involved in that decision, including the chief executive officer, the chief financial officer, and one or two others.

Furthermore, there are some highly publicized examples of EVA plans that have not worked. One of these is AT&T's plan. In September 1993, *Fortune* magazine stated that the company was a leading example of the success of EVA plans, and shortly thereafter the company announced a major downsizing and cost reduction program because its stock price and overall financial performance were well below projections and previous levels of company performance.

Finally, the concept of economic profit and in particular cost of capital are very complicated, and many executives do not understand them. Many cost-of-capital calculations use a beta factor that assumes a rational stock market when the history of stock market performance is clearly not rational.

Q 19:6   What impact do executives have on economic profit?

There are two primary ways in which executives have an impact on economic profit. The first is profit itself. Executive jobs affect the amount of operating profit in a company and some further influence the net profit through their job performance. All functional areas of the business, such as advertising, sales, marketing, manufacturing/operations, research and development, financial management, and human resources, have an impact on the success of a company and its ability to make profit. Another major factor of executive performance that affects profit is payments on long-term debt. If a company borrows money, it incurs interest payments on the debt, which have a negative impact on profitability unless the borrowed money must produce additional income very quickly. Simply put, the higher the operating profit or net profit in a company (whichever is used in the economic profit formula), the higher the economic profit will be.

The use of capital is the other primary way that executives influence economic profit. For example, cash, equipment, the relationship of receivables and payables, and the use of other assets have an impact on capital. In addition, borrowed money may be considered part of cash assets or some other category of capital that is used to develop future profit. Since the cost of capital is some percentage of capital, the lower the amount of capital, the higher the economic profit will be.

Q 19:7 Can executives affect the cost of capital?

More and more companies that use economic profit have adopted a fixed cost of capital because they believe that executives neither understand nor affect the cost of capital. Cost-of-capital calculations are developed from capital asset pricing models that use sophisticated calculations such as interests rates, stock performance of peer companies, expected rates of return, premium rates of return, discounted cash flow, and beta factors (the extent to which a company's stock price changes with the stock market). As discussed in Q 19:6, the primary concern for executives in an economic profit plan is operating profit or net profit, whichever is used in the formula, not cost of capital. Another consideration is that the cost of capital does not change very much from year to year.

Q 19:8 Can economic profit be used in divisions or strategic business units?

Yes, some companies using economic profit apply it only to certain divisions or strategic business units. Operating profit is the typical numerator and capital that the division executive directly affects is used in the cost-of-capital calculation. A constant cost-of-capital percentage is used.

Example. A manufacturing company identifies cash, equipment, raw materials, and inventory as the factors of capital in a given division. The total amount of these factors is $80 million. The company uses a fixed percentage of 10 percent in calculating the cost of capital. The cost of capital is, therefore, $8 million ($80,000,000 × 10%). The division makes $10 million in operating profit. The economic profit is $10 million minus $8 million, or $2 million.

operating profit – cost of capital = economic profit

$10,000,000 – ($80,000,000 × 10%) = $2,000,000

The division executives in this example must either increase the operating profit or decrease the value of capital used in operating the business.

Q 19:9 Can economic profit plans be used with other annual or long-term incentive plans?

Yes, a company can have both an annual incentive plan that uses financial and nonfinancial goals as the basis for payment and a long-term incentive plan based on an economic profit performance measure. It is also possible to do the reverse and have an annual incentive based on economic profit and have a traditional long-term incentive plan like a stock option plan. There is no limit to the creativity that can be applied to the design of executive compensation plans.

Implementation

Q 19:10 What steps are necessary to implement an economic profit plan?

To implement an economic profit plan, the following six steps are necessary:

1. *Define profit.* In most cases the measure used is operating profit, pretax profit, or profit after taxes (net profit). In a

division organization, operating profit is most commonly used; in a corporate organization both pretax profit and net profit are used. Most corporate organizations use pretax profit because it includes factors that executives can directly control or influence. Other than a chief executive officer, financial officer, and tax officer, few executives impact net profit.

2. *Define capital.* Capital has multiple definitions. For a corporate organization, the simplest definition is shareholder equity and long-term debt. For a division organization, it is cash, equipment, receivables, and inventory. Any variation of these basics may be found in an economic profit plan.

3. *Define the cost of capital.* A fixed percentage can be used to define the cost of capital. Many companies use 10 percent because the consulting firm Stern Stewart recently reported that an analysis of 1,000 companies showed that the median cost of capital was 10 percent, with a range of between 7 percent and 15 percent. Other companies desire a more sophisticated approach that uses a beta factor (the extent to which a company's stock price changes with the stock market) and many other variables such as normal interest rates expected by an investor and premium interest rates expected by an investor.

4. *Calculate current economic profit.* This establishes the base economic profit, and is typically accomplished in two steps: (1) multiply the cost of capital (a percentage) by capital resulting in a total dollar amount; and (2) select the amount of operating profit (or other profit measure). This amount might be the previous year's operating profit or an average of the previous two or three years' operating profit. The base economic profit is the amount by which operating profit exceeds the cost of capital. It is possible that could result in a negative number. If this occurs, the payment will not typically begin until there is a positive economic profit.

5. *Determine eligibility and payment potential.* Eligibility is normally limited to a few top executives. Each executive who is eligible to participate in the plan is assigned a percentage of the amount of economic profit that exceeds the base amount. Some plans have broader eligibility and

when this occurs, each person will be assigned a percentage of salary that is a targeted amount of incentive that corresponds to the expected level of improvement in economic profit. If that expected level of improvement is achieved, then the targeted incentive amount is paid. If that expected level of improvement is not achieved, then the targeted amount is reduced. If the expected level of improvement is exceeded, the targeted amount is increased. This type of plan does not normally have a cap or minimum. If economic profit improves, there is a payment to the executive. If there is no improvement, there is no payment. The final decision in this area is to decide if any amount of payment should be deferred (see Q 19:3).

6. *Assign plan administration accountabilities.* Since senior executives are included in these plans, the company's board compensation committee will almost always be the plan administrator and approve all plan provisions, plan eligibility, plan calculations and definitions, plan payments, etc. The actual implementation of these activities will be delegated to a company officer (e.g., the chief financial officer or chief human resources officer).

Q 19:11   How is economic profit performance correlated to compensation?

The first consideration in a strategic compensation plan is whether economic profit will be a performance measure for both the annual *and* long-term incentive plans or for just one of the plans. A second consideration is the amount of the increase in economic profit that will be available as incentive payment to executives.

Example. Economic profit in Company Q is $48.3 million. Company Q is willing to pay 30 percent of any improvement as executive incentive pay. The expectation is that economic profit will increase 10 percent per year. The company has decided that economic profit should drive both the annual and long-term incentive. Therefore, if economic profit reaches the 10 percent increase, the amount of incentive in the first year of the plans would be $1.45 million ($48,300,000 × 10% improvement × 30% payment to all executives).

There are 11 executives selected for eligibility in the plan. Their targeted incentive is as follows:

Title	No. of Executives	Targeted Annual Incentive	Targeted Long-term Incentive
Chief Executive	1	$150,000	$150,000
Senior Vice President	3*	$225,000	$225,000
Vice President	7**	$350,000	$350,000
Totals:	11	$725,000	$725,000

*$75,000 each times 3 executives equals $225,000

**$50,000 each times 7 executives equals $350,000

In this example, the total of $1.45 million in targeted payments is equal to the expected improvement in economic profit of $1.45 million. If the amounts are not equal, the company might want to use economic profit as the basis for either the annual or the long-term incentive rather than for both plans. For example, a company might use economic profit as the basis for its annual incentive plan and stock options as the basis for its long-term incentive plan.

Q 19:12   How are payments made for economic profit awards that are earned as part of a long-term incentive plan?

The final decision in building the plan is to decide on the provisions for paying the long-term incentive amount. Most companies would defer the payments using one of the following methods for paying deferred amounts:

Vesting (Short-Term Deferral)

Amount Earned Each Year: $150,000
Vesting Period for Each Award: 5 Years

Year	1995	1996	1997	1998	1999	2000	2001	2002	2003	2004
Amount Earned ($000)	$150	$150	$150	$150	$150	$150	$150	$150	$150	$150

Paid: ($000)

Year:	1995	1996	1997	1998	1999	2000	2001	2002	2003	2004
1995	$30	$30	$30	$30	$30					
1996		$30	$30	$30	$30	$30				
1997			$30	$30	$30	$30	$30			
1998				$30	$30	$30	$30	$30		
1999					$30	$30	$30	$30	$30	
2000						$30	$30	$30	$30	$30
2001							$30	$30	$30	$30
2002								$30	$30	$30
2003									$30	$30
2004										$30

As shown in this example, the executive always has some amount of vested payment in each future year, if some amount is earned in each current year. This accomplishes a retention objective for the company. If the executive voluntarily leaves, he or she will forfeit some amount of unvested money.

In addition, companies will typically add appreciation to any unvested amounts each year. This adds a great deal of complexity to the administration of long-term deferred plans, so some organizations will add appreciation only if amounts are not taken when vested and deferred until some specific time after the end of the vesting period. For example, assume that an executive has earned $150,000 from an economic profit plan and is eligible for payment of the $150,000 over a five-year period. The executive, prior to earning the amount, elects to defer for seven years after the end of the vesting period. A company might only add appreciation on the seven years after the end of the vesting period but not add any appreciation during the five years that the $150,000 was vesting.

Banking Amounts Earned (Long-Term Deferral)

Amount Earned Each Year:	$150,000
Vesting Period for Each Award:	5 Years

Year	1995	1996	1997	1998	1999	2000	2001	2002	2003	2004
Amount Earned ($000)	$150	$150	$150	$150	$150	$150	$150	$150	$150	$150

Banked: ($000)

Year:										
1995	$150									
1996		$150								
1997			$150							
1998				$150						
1999					$150					
2000						$150				
2001							$150			
2002								$150		
2003									$150	
2004										$150

Paid: 2005 or at retirement

In the case of long-term deferrals, there are always appreciation opportunities for deferred amounts. The primary reason for banking payments is to provide a supplemental retirement benefit to the executive; therefore, the deferral is until retirement. Another advantage is that payments are never as equal as shown in the example. Therefore, with the banking concept, the executive simply has an account that he or she can add to as economic profit is improved and payments are made.

It is also possible to have a combination plan that uses the banking concept whereby a payment of some percentage of the total amount banked is paid to the executive during his or her working years. Using the above example, the executive could have been paid 20 percent of the total amount accumulated over five years. Because of this, the amount paid upon retirement is reduced. From the executive's viewpoint, it is valuable to have access to these funds during working years when certain major expenses (e.g., a child's college education, purchase of second home, etc.) occur. From the company's viewpoint, an interim payment is a good reminder of how valuable the plan is and that the executive should remain with the organization. Furthermore, payments from an economic profit plan are not subject to the uncertainties of the stock market.

Q 19:13   How are economic profit plans communicated to executives?

Like any other executive compensation plan, they are communicated when initiated, when progress reports are provided, at least annually, and when an annual statement of the status of any plan accounts in the executive's name is issued. The success of the plan is dependent upon the effectiveness of the company's communication to the executive. The executive must understand the desired performance goal to be achieved and the reward opportunity.

Companies need to provide eligible executives with a statement of the plan's purpose, the definition of economic profit and how it will be calculated, and examples of potential compensation that may be earned at various levels of improvement in economic profit. Executives should also understand payment procedures, potential payments (if any) in the event of termination (voluntary and involuntary), disability provisions, and plan administration account-abilities.

Q 19:14   May nonexecutives participate in economic profit plans?

Yes, but it is best to implement plans with broad eligibility in phases. For example, a company might grant eligibility to executives in phase one and, if the plan is successful, add eligibility for managers in phase two. If the plan proves successful again, additional eligibility may be offered to nonmanagers in a third phase. By using such phases, an organization can manage the plan's success and effectiveness.

Another important step that should be accomplished in phase one is to estimate future improvements in economic profit to ensure that as participants are added, future payments are not diluted for those already in the plan. The cost of additional eligibility should be funded with higher levels of improvement in economic profit. For example, if a company consistently has been improving economic profit by 10 percent annually, the 10 percent increase is on a larger base amount every year and the amount of dollars available for distribution will increase to cover the additional rewards to additional participants.

Example. Economic profit in Company G is $50 million. The plan pays 10 percent of any improvement in economic profit. The company achieves a 10 percent improvement each year for five years. Amounts of economic improvement are as follows:

	Year 1	Year 2	Year 3	Year 4	Year 5
Base Amount	$50 M	$55 M	$60.5 M	$66.6 M	$73.3 M
Improvement	$5 M	$5.5 M	$6.1 M	$6.7 M	$7.3 M

The amount of economic profit to be awarded increased from an initial $5 million to $7.3 million five years later.

Q 19:15   Should economic profit plans have a fixed term?

Yes, economic profit plans should have a fixed term, also known as a "sunset provision." Although this factor is often overlooked in plan design, it is important to the success of a plan. Most compensation experts agree that consistent improvements in this measure cannot be achieved indefinitely. Rather than wait for a plan to become ineffective, it is better to limit its term.

One possibility is to alternate an economic profit plan with an incentive plan that uses other performance measures. At this point, few companies have used such an alternation, but it is a worthwhile idea because executives will respond to whatever performance measure is used and companies go through different business conditions that require different performance measures.

Case Studies

Q 19:16   What are some examples of companies that have used economic profit or EVA plans?

In addition to AT&T's plan, which is discussed in Q 19:5, the Coca-Cola Company is one of the largest companies to use an economic profit plan. Coca-Cola's definition of profit is net operating profit after tax (NOPAT), and its capital definition includes cash, inventory, nonperforming assets, and the amount of accounts receivable in excess of accounts payable. The company communicates a cost-of-capital percentage using sophisticated calculations, and it uses a beta factor. NOPAT must exceed the capital value times the cost of capital in order to have any economic profit.

An example of a smaller company that uses an economic profit plan is Valmont Industries in Valley, Nebraska. Valmont has an economic profit performance measure that also uses net operating profit after tax, but it uses a fixed amount of 10 percent for cost of capital.

SPX Corporation, an auto supplier, has an EVA plan that the company claims has helped it go from a net income loss to a positive net income. The company has publicly stated that its EVA plan has been a "change accelerator." Its plan extends to over 4,000 employees and the chief executive officer recently earned nearly $2 million from the plan.

In 1996, the chief executive officer earned an annual bonus of $920,000 and he "banked" another $1.05 million in deferred compensation due to the significant increases in net income and the fact that the EVA plan focused employees on finding ways to increase net income without spending additional capital.

The SPX EVA formula is a standard operating profit after taxes minus selected amounts of capital times a cost of capital that is designed to "mirror" the kind of return investors would expect from alternate investments. The plan was communicated to all company personnel, who were told that if profits increased, they would all share in the success. From a strategy perspective, the incentive plan was designed to provide above average competitive compensation for nonexecutive positions, if earned, and to be part of competitive compensation, if earned, for executive positions.

An example of an unsuccessful economic profit plan is at CSX Corporation, a major transportation company. CSX implemented a plan with detailed communication to managers on how improvements in net income could bring substantial compensation rewards. Unfortunately, the division managers did a fantastic job of increasing sales and net income by increasing business, but at a cost of neglecting service to some major current customers and these customers went elsewhere for their transportation needs.

There was no deferred compensation to the CSX plan, only current compensation. The plan has since been changed. This is a good example of how an economic profit plan could have been used as a long-term incentive plan instead of an annual plan. The annual plan could have focused on nonfinancial performance measures like customer service.

Q 19:17   How can economic profit plans be used to help a company accomplish a business turnaround?

The following is a case study on the use of an economic profit plan in a company that is planning to go through a restructuring and possible downsizing.

Case Study: Company T

Current situation: Company T had declines in sales for three consecutive years from 1994 through 1996. The company kept profits the same during this period by putting a freeze on hiring and through some forced attrition, but eventually reached a point at which more significant steps had to be taken to turn the business around.

Company T is a service company that has seen its market share decline because of increased competition. When the company recognized this issue, it started a development project in 1995 that would provide significant computerized enhancements to its service capabilities. While these new capabilities will provide Company T with a competitive edge, the development is not expected to be complete until the year 2000.

Other efficiencies had to be realized if the current level of profitability was to be retained. A new incentive plan was implemented in 1997 that uses economic profit as the performance measure. The incentive plan was intended to be used as the annual incentive plan. By the end of 1998, the economic profit-based plan was in operation for two years.

Economic profit incentive plan design: This plan is intended to be the annual incentive plan for selected executives who will continue to receive stock options. If the company's financial results can be improved, it is believed that company stock will immediately increase.

The plan uses operating profit in comparison to the cost of capital. Capital is defined as equipment, cash, nonperforming assets, and the sum of receivables over payables. A fixed percentage of 10 percent is used in calculating the cost of capital. The plan has a five-year term. Fourteen executives are eligible, and have the opportunity to share in 20 percent of the increases to economic profit over the base amount, which is calculated at the beginning of each fiscal year. The amounts allotted for each executive position are prorated as follows:

Title	Number	Individual Percentage	Cumulative Percentage
Chief Executive Officer	1	20%	20%
Senior Vice President	3	10%	30%
Vice President	10	5%	50%
			100%

The plan motivates executives to achieve the following goals:

1. *Improve operating profit.* The company must sell more and maintain profit levels by keeping operating costs down. Operating costs cannot be reduced by eliminating employee positions because this has already been done, but operating costs may be reduced by evaluating ways to reduce office and general administrative costs.

2. *Reduce the use of capital.* In particular, the company must improve the relationship of receivables and payables, in an effort to always owe exactly what the company is owed.

3. *Get the new computer equipment in quickly.* The goal is for old equipment to be taken off the books and thereby make the capital definition go down.

Current Results. As of the end of 1998, economic profit had improved significantly and the company had earned $5 million in the first year and $4 million in the second year. These amounts were allocated as follows:

Year 1 Economic Profit: $5,000,000 × 20% = $1,000,000

Year 1 Awards:

Position	Economic Profit	Allocation %	Award
Chief Executive Officer	$1,000,000	20%	$200,000
Senior Vice President	$1,000,000	10%	$100,000
Vice President	$1,000,000	5%	$50,000

Year 2 Economic Profit: $4,000,000 × 20% = $800,000

Year 2 Awards:

Position	Economic Profit	Allocation %	Award
Chief Executive Officer	$800,000	20%	$160,000
Senior Vice President	$800,000	10%	$80,000
Vice President	$800,000	5%	$40,000

Company T's plan has obviously been successful. The primary reason is that a number of savings have been realized in the office environment such as "just in time" delivery of office supplies, turning down HVAC systems on weekends, improved management of receivables and payables, and aggressive selling and placement of new accounts.

It is not expected that this kind of improvement can continue. If the economic profit plan is going to provide any payments in the next three years, the new computerized equipment must provide the efficiencies. Executive focus has been on this issue, and the new equipment will be implemented some time in 1999.

The executives in Company T have focused on specific activities that can bring greater success to the company and avoid downsizing. All too often, executives believe that cost cutting is best achieved by reducing headcount. At times this is correct, but the economic profit plan in Company T opens up thinking to broader opportunities to save money and increase operating profit while reducing capital.

Q 19:18   How can economic profit plans be used to help a company overcome significant competitive pressure?

The following case study demonstrates the use of an economic profit plan in a company that must find a way to continue its success in a business environment that is becoming more competitive. Similar businesses seem to be popping up overnight and everyone is looking for a piece of the market.

Case Study: Company C

Current situation. Company C has been one of the industry leaders for the last ten years. But competitive pressure is growing every year. The competitors do not have a better product, but there are many of them vying for customers in a limited market. Significant steps have to be taken to maintain market share in the future.

Company C is in the medical service/computer business. It provides a computerized office management system for medical offices. There has been a need for this product for many years and the efficiencies that it provides are well received by all customers. Because so many similar companies have emerged in the past two years, Company C is finding that market leadership is harder to maintain each year.

A new incentive plan was implemented in 1997 that uses economic profit as the performance measure. The incentive plan was intended to be used as both the annual and long-term executive plans. By the end of 1998, the economic profit-based plan had been in operation for two years.

Economic profit incentive plan design. The strategy is for this plan to be the catalyst for increasing sales and profitability, which will be rewarded in annual incentive plan payments, and to be the catalyst for new product development, which will be rewarded in long-term incentive plan payments.

The plan uses operating profit in comparison to the cost of capital. Capital is defined as cash, inventory, equipment, and the sum of receivables over payables. A fixed amount of 10 percent is used in calculating cost of capital. The plan has a five-year term. Six executives are eligible, and have the opportunity to share in 50 percent of the increases to economic profit over the base amount, which is calculated at the beginning of each fiscal year. Half of the 50 percent, or 25 percent, is paid in current cash, and the other half is deferred. Deferred amounts are subject to vesting at 25 percent per year. This coincides with the previous stock option plan, which also allowed for vesting at 25 percent per year. Deferred amounts are invested and each executive can select from alternatives offered by the company. Once vesting occurs, payments will be made unless the executive further defers on a voluntary basis.

The target award for the annual and the long-term portions of the plan are as follows:

Title	Number	Individual Percentage	Cumulative Percentage
Chief Executive Officer	1	35 %	35%
Senior Vice President	2	12.5%	25%
Vice President	8	5 %	40%
			100%

The plan motivates executives to achieve the following goals:

1. *Increase sales.* With greater sales, profit will increase and this is the opportunity to earn annual incentive during the next two to three years. After this period, higher sales should come from an expansion of the company's product line.

2. *Reduce the use of capital.* In particular, the company must focus the use of cash on product development. The company believes that current products have applications in business environments other than the medical field, and that this will require minor adjustments to the system.

3. *Current results.* As of the end of 1998, economic profit had improved and annual incentive payments were about the same as they were under the previous plan. An equal amount has been booked and deferred into long-term accounts.

The plan has been successful to date, but the real test is whether it is a motivator in expanding company products to other markets. If this business goal is accomplished, the plan offers substantial incentive award to all participants. All participants see the plan as an opportunity to receive substantial reward if the company is successful. The company is quick to point out to its executives that they stand to gain a great deal of additional compensation without having to invest any of their own money. Once this plan has operated for five years, the company expects to implement a completely different type of both annual and long-term incentive plan, based on business conditions at that time. As in the case study in Q 19:17, the executives in this company are focused on specific activities that can bring greater success to the company in the future.

Q 19:19   What is an example of an economic profit plan that was unsuccessful?

The following case study demonstrates the use of an economic profit plan that was unsuccessful. The plan was discontinued after two years. It was implemented in a company that had just retired its entrepreneurial chief executive officer. There were also numerous company practices and organizations that needed to be modified if the company was to be successful in the future.

Case Study: Company I

Current situation. Company I has been in the insurance industry for many years. It became successful because of an outstanding sales force. Currently, sales are down, and the company is simply trying to service its customer base. Competitive pressure is growing every year.

The new chief executive officer is a young person who inherited the company and wants to bring some new ideas to the organization. A new incentive plan was implemented in 1995 that used economic profit as the performance measure. The incentive plan was intended to be used as both the annual and long-term executive plans. By the end of 1997, the economic profit-based plan had been in operation for two years and no payments had been made.

Economic profit incentive plan design. The strategy was for this plan to be the catalyst for increasing sales and profitability. The plan used operating profit in comparison to the cost of capital. Capital was composed primarily of those assets on the balance sheet. All stock was private and there are little retained earnings. A fixed amount of 10 percent was used in calculating cost of capital. The plan had a five-year term. All employees were eligible and had the opportunity to share in 50 percent of the increases to economic profit once economic profit was a positive amount. (It was at a negative at the plan's inception.) All of the amounts earned were to be deferred. Deferred amounts were paid after a vesting schedule was met. Vesting was at 25 percent per year, and all deferred amounts were "banked" by the company and invested by the company.

The plan was intended to motivate executives to achieve the following goals:

1. Increase sales and profit;

2. Eliminate redundancies in the organization; and

3. Change and streamline organizational structure and jobs.

Current results. As of the end of 1998, economic profit was still in the negative and the plan was cancelled. The company now has the problem of determining a replacement plan that all employees can participate in. Profit sharing is currently under consideration.

Unlike the other case studies discussed in this chapter, Company I implemented an economic profit plan in the hope that it would be a cure for all its problems. In addition to implementing the plan, it is essential that executives in any economic profit incentive plan understand specifically what goals must be achieved and what they must do to achieve those goals and, in turn, earn incentives under the plan.

Chapter 20

Trends in Executive Compensation

This chapter describes new ideas and trends in the field of executive compensation. The selection of topics is determined by media issues, facts in public company proxies, subjects discussed at executive compensation forums and conferences, and observations of executive compensation administration in public and private companies.

Total Cash Compensation 20-1
Long-Term Compensation 20-10
Regulatory Issues 20-18
Outside Directors 20-25

Total Cash Compensation

Q 20:1 How are base salary levels changing for executive positions in large companies?

During 1998, salaries for chief executive officer (CEO) positions increased 7.5 percent for those receiving increases, and for all CEO positions, including those not receiving increases, the average increase was 4.5 percent. These figures are based on a survey of 100 proxies of large public companies. For other executives in the top five positions, 1998 salary increases were 7.4 percent for those receiving increases, and for all other top executive positions, including those not receiving increases, the average increase was 6.3 percent. These increases are consistent with executive salary increases reported in surveys conducted by the large human resource consulting firms, which reported salary increases of 7 to 8 percent for CEO positions in 1998. For other top executive positions, the typical survey reported a broader range of increase of 5 to 8 percent in 1998.

For 1999, base salary levels for large-company executives are expected to increase at least 5 percent, as suggested in large human resource consulting firm surveys. It is more realistic, however, to expect increases closer to the rate of increase during the previous five years, i.e., 7 to 8 percent.

A new idea being studied by many large companies is budgeting executive salary increases at the same level as projected increases in company pretax profit. Chart 20-1 shows corporate profits in relation to CEO salary increases.

Chart 20-1. CEO Salary Increases

Year	CEO Salary Increase	Corporate Profit Increase
1994	8%	25%
1995	8%	15%
1996	7%	10%
1997	7.5%	7%
1998	7.5%	7%

Source: Selected company proxies.

The information in Chart 20-1 suggests that salary increases for CEOs are constant and not necessarily related to corporate profits. However, a company might more effectively use salary increases to motivate executives by budgeting the increases in relation to projected corporate profit increases. In the example in Chart 20-1, in 1997 and 1998, if a company's profits were projected to be 7 percent, a budgeted 7 percent salary increase for corporate officers would make sense. In 1999, if a company's profits were projected to increase 20 percent, a budgeted salary increase of more than 7 percent (e.g., 10 percent) would make sense for corporate officers. Actual corporate profit performance will automatically be reflected in measures of executive total cash compensation. Chart 20-2 demonstrates increases in total cash compensation for CEO positions in relation to corporate profit increases.

Chart 20-2. CEO Total Cash Compensation Increases

Year	CEO Total Cash Compensation Increase	Corporate Profit Increase
1994	20%	25%
1995	17.5%	15%
1996	12%	10%
1997	10%	7%
1998	10%	7%

Source: Selected company proxies.

Chart 20-2 verifies that total cash compensation increases as corporate profits increase. This is not surprising, since most annual incentive plans are driven by corporate profit (and other performance measures in most cases). In addition, total cash compensation increases exceed percentage increases in base salary. This is consistent with the pay for performance concept found in most company annual incentive plans.

The idea of basing executive salary increase on projected increase in company profits is worthy of consideration in 1999 and beyond.

Q 20:2 How are base salary levels changing for executive positions in small companies?

During 1998, the average increase in base salary for executives in small companies was 5 percent, for those who received increases. Because there are so many small companies that did not give salary increases to executives, particularly CEOs, a calculation of the average salary increase for all companies would be misleading. The data on small company executive salary increases are based on a survey of 100 proxies of small public companies. This average salary increase is similar to base salary increases for the previous five years and is expected to continue in 1999.

Planning Tip. A useful rule of thumb on projecting salary increases for executives is that as company size doubles, executive salaries increase 20 percent. Chart 20-3 illustrates this norm.

Chart 20-3. Executive Salary Levels by Company Size

Position	Median Salary at $100M Sales	Median Salary at $200M Sales	Median Salary at $400M Sales	Median Salary at $800M Sales	Median Salary at $1 Billion Sales
CEO	$300,000	$360,000	$430,000	$520,000	$625,000
Chief Operating Officer	$240,000	$290,000	$350,000	$420,000	$500,000
Chief Mktg. Officer	$150,000	$180,000	$220,000	$260,000	$315,000
CFO	$150,000	$180,000	$220,000	$260,000	$310,000
Chief HR Officer	$125,000	$150,000	$180,000	$210,000	$240,000

Source: Economic Research Institute Executive Compensation Assessor.

Executive salary levels can also vary by industry, as shown in Chart 20-4.

Chart 20-4. Executive Salary Levels by Industry

Position	Median Salary in a Mid-sized Pharmaceutical Firm	Median Salary in a Mid-sized Retail Firm
CEO	$525,000	$425,000
Chief Operating Officer	$400,000	$340,000
Chief Mktg. Officer	$225,000	$190,000
CFO	$225,000	$190,000
Chief HR Officer	$175,000	$150,000

Source: Economic Research Institute Executive Compensation Assessor.

Q 20:3 Is the $1 million cap on the deductibility of executive pay in public companies having any influence on executive base salary levels?

No. A review of public company proxies shows numerous top executives with base salary levels over $1 million. Examples are shown in Chart 20-5.

Chart 20-5. Executive Base Salary Levels Over $1 Million

Company	Position	Base Salary
Allied Signal	CEO	$2,000,000
General Electric	Senior Vice President, Finance	$1,025,000
Hewlett Packard	CEO	$1,700,000
UNISYS	CEO	$1,200,000

Section 162(m) of the Internal Revenue Code (Code) requires that any executive pay above $1 million be performance-based; otherwise, the amount over $1 million cannot be taken as a tax deduction by the company. Code Section 162(m) gives clear guidelines on how companies can meet this requirement for performance-based pay. Annual incentives, stock options, and most other forms of long-term incentive are all exempt from the cap. Because the loss of a company tax deduction applies only to the amount of salary over $1 million, the cost consequences to a company are very small.

Example. The Eli Lilly Corporation CEO has a salary of $1.2 million. Therefore, $200,000 is not a tax deduction to the company. If the company is in the top corporate tax bracket of 35 percent, the loss of a $200,000 tax deduction increases its taxes by $70,000 ($200,000 × 35% = $70,000). As a percentage of Eli Lilly's corporate profits, $70,000 is less than 0.1 percent.

Public corporations are, however, mindful of Code Section 162(m), as evidenced by the comment of compliance they are required to make. For example, the W. R. Grace proxy has, like all public company proxies, a statement on Code Section 162(m). It reads:

Section 162(m) of the Internal Revenue Code prohibits the Company from deducting annual compensation in excess of $1 million paid to the executive officers named in the Summary

Compensation Table of the Proxy Statement, unless such compensation is performance-based and satisfies certain other conditions. It is the [Compensation] Committee's view that, with the exception of base salaries and any discretionary annual incentive compensation payments or non-performance-based payments provided for under Mr. Costello's [the chief executive officer] employment agreement, amounts awarded under the Company's executive compensation program qualify as performance-based compensation and are therefore expected to be fully deductible.

Q 20:4 How are annual bonus levels changing in large companies?

Annual bonus awards to executives continue to increase significantly as a percentage of base salary. Examples are shown in Chart 20-6.

**Chart 20-6. Executive Bonus Percentages
in Relation to Base Salary**

Company	Position	Bonus Percentage of Base Salary
Corning	CEO	150%
General Motors	CEO	140%
Quaker Oats	CFO	119%
Rockwell	CEO	225%

It follows that the dollar amount of annual incentive awards is also increasing significantly. Cash compensation during the second half of the 1990s has almost doubled. The typical annual target incentive award for a large-company CEO in 1993 was 60 percent; in 1998 it was 75 percent. The average actual incentive award for a large-company CEO in 1993 was 75 percent (versus a target of 60 percent); in 1998 it was 100 percent of base salary (versus a target of 75 percent).

The most unusual annual incentive award was paid to Stephen Ruzika, the chief financial officer (CFO) of Tyco International. He received an annual incentive award of $3,225,000, which was based on the performance of company stock price. This exceeded the annual incentive award received by his bosses; the prior CEO, who received no annual incentive award; and the current CEO, who received an annual incentive award of $2,544,260.

One of the largest annual incentive payments went to Jack Welch, the CEO of General Electric, who received $5.5 million.

Annual incentive amounts of $1 million are quite common in large companies.

Q 20:5 How are annual bonus levels changing in small companies?

These organizations have a much wider spread in actual bonus awards to CEOs and other top executives. Most of it can be explained by the fact that these companies are highly entrepreneurial and top executives may go three to four years with a modest bonus or no bonus and then receive a substantial payment when the company reaches financial success and can afford to pay an annual incentive award. The spread of actual awards in 50 small companies surveyed was 0 to 100 percent of base salary; the average was 67 percent of base salary.

Another characteristic of annual incentive awards in small companies is that the actual incentive paid as a percentage of base salary is typically lower than that paid in large companies (even though the range of payments is broader than it is in large companies). The actual bonus award as a percentage of base salary in small companies typically falls between 50 and 75 percent versus 75 to 150 percent in large companies.

Q 20:6 How are annual incentive practices changing?

There is greater leverage in today's annual incentive plan payout schedules than in previous payout schedules, with more gradual accrual of incentive funds when company performance is below target, and much steeper payout accrual when targeted company performance is exceeded.

An example of greater leverage in a company's annual incentive plan is the Rockwell International annual incentive plan, under which senior executive positions are subject to multiple performance measures that are used to determine actual individual incentive awards. These measures are earnings per share, return on equity, cash flow, total shareholder return (stock price appreciation plus dividends), interbusiness sharing of competencies, and development of strategic alliances. Both company performance and individual performance are reviewed, and the range of actual executive awards was 73 percent of target to 158 percent of target, with an average of 132 percent.

Another way that annual incentive practices are changing is the increasing use of discretionary award criteria by board compensation committees. The 1997 Rockwell International plan again provides an example. Under that plan, the compensation committee awarded the CEO an incentive award of $2.25 million (225 percent of his base salary of $1 million) plus an additional discretionary award of $1.25 million "in recognition of his pivotal role as Chief Executive Officer from February 1988 through September 1997 in guiding the transformation of the Corporation from a broadly diversified concern into an enterprise sharply focused on commercial electronics markets."

Per proxy regulations of the Securities and Exchange Commission (SEC), public companies are required to state the executive compensation philosophy of the company and to provide specific comments on the rationale for the compensation of the CEO. Information on executive pay in company proxies is constantly increasing as board compensation committees fulfill their obligation of explaining executive pay to shareholders and/or potential investors.

Annual bonus practices in small companies are also changing and becoming more creative. One small company, Caraustar, Inc., has both annual stock option awards and annual bonus awards driven by economic profit. This creative plan results in performance-based awards that increase as the company's economic profit increases. An economic profit target is established each year and a targeted incentive and stock option award is established. The company determines the economic profit actually achieved and that drives the actual award. This kind of idea in executive compensation can truly impact the behavior and work priorities of executives as well as benefit company shareholders.

Q 20:7 What changes are occurring in the mix of base salary and annual incentive for executive positions?

A greater percentage of total cash compensation is being earned from the company's annual incentive plan, partially because of the greater leverage in incentive plan payout schedules as discussed in Q 20:6. When incentives are earned, they are higher than in previous years, both in percentage terms and in real dollars.

The other reason is that board compensation committees are enforcing a higher level of pay for performance. Larger numbers of executives are receiving an incentive payment that is the same as or less than that received in the previous year because company performance goals were only partially achieved or not achieved. Correspondingly, when incentive payments are made, they are much higher. For example, in a study of 100 company proxies from 1997, 42 percent of the CEOs either did not receive an annual incentive payment or received an annual incentive payment that was the same as or less than the previous year's. This is double the number from the previous year, which was 20 percent. For those in the study group who received a higher incentive payment than they received in the previous year (58 percent), the average award as a percentage of base salary was 135 percent and the average increase in award level from the previous year was 38 percent.

Examples of executive positions that received no bonus increase in 1998 are shown in Chart 20-7.

Chart 20-7. Executives with No Annual Bonus Increase

Company	Position	Annual Bonus	Percentage Increase Over Prior Year
FMC Corp.	CEO	$ 190,000	0%
Emerson Electric	CEO	1,100,000	0%
Weyerhaeuser	CEO	95,000	0%
Tyco Ltd.	CEO	0	0%
Navistar Int'l	CEO	480,000	0%
Johnson & Johnson	CFO	332,000	0%

Chart 20-7 (*cont'd*)

Company	Position	Annual Bonus	Percentage Increase Over Prior Year
Cooper Industries	CFO	230,000	0%
Apple Computer	CFO	0	0%
Ethly Corp.	CFO	50,000	0%

It is not surprising that the financial performance of most companies shown in Chart 20-7 did not meet company expectations, thus proving that their annual executive incentives are working as performance-based plans, i.e., lower company performance than planned means lower bonus, no bonus, or no increase in bonus.

Long-Term Compensation

Q 20:8   How are stock award levels changing for executive positions?

The size of stock option and other stock awards continues to increase significantly. The average stock option award value (defined as stock price times number of shares) granted to CEOs in large companies during 1998 was approximately $10 million, more than double the value granted two years ago. For example, in 1997 the CEO of Hewlett Packard received 150,000 stock options (the same as the number received the previous two years on average), which had an option value of $7,875,000 (150,000 multiplied by the option price of $52.50). This option represents a 4.6 multiple of base salary. Large human resource consulting firms report in their surveys that typical option values for CEO positions in large companies are approximately 4.5 times base salary per year. This is double the similar statistic of four years earlier. The CEO of Hewlett Packard also has $38.5 million in unexercised in-the-money options at the end of the fiscal year. The in-the-money option value was calculated based on the difference between the exercise price of each outstanding stock option and the average company stock price in October 1997.

Some examples of stock option multiples of base salary in 1998 proxies are as shown in Chart 20-8.

Chart 20-8. Executive Stock Option Multiples of Salary

Company	Position	Salary	Option Multiple of Salary
WR Grace	CEO	$ 900,000	4.4
Dana Corp.	CEO	945,000	3.7
Navistar Int'l	CEO	650,000	1.0*
AMOCO	CEO	997,000	12.6
Rockwell Int'l	CEO	1,000,000	14.1
Coca Cola	Sr. VP	452,000	18.1*
Deere & Co.	Sr. VP	373,000	2.0
American Home Products	Sr. VP	440,000	7.2
Corning	Sr. VP	500,000	2.3
Sara Lee	EVP	553,000	8.5*

*Also had another form of long-term incentive award.

As shown in Chart 20-8, there is a wide range of option values in large corporate organizations. This factor is even greater in mid-sized and small, entrepreneurial companies.

The number of jumbo stock option grants also continues to increase. For example, the CEO of Sara Lee Corporation received 604,591 stock options in 1997 with an option value of $22.3 million. This option value is 24 times salary. This CEO has $8.3 million in unexercised in-the-money options at the end of the company's fiscal year.

The size and number of other stock awards, namely restricted stock awards, also continue to increase significantly. Five years ago the large human resource consulting firms reported that approximately 25 percent of large companies used restricted stock. In 1997 the number was 40 to 45 percent. These used to be one-time awards, but that is no longer the case. For example, the CEO of UNOCAL Corporation received a restricted stock award in 1997 of $569,473.

This is in addition to restricted stock awards made during the two previous years. This same executive also received stock option shares in 1997 (88,000 shares with an option value of $2,887,500) and a long-term incentive plan payout in 1997 of $578,050.

Many of the restricted stock awards are also jumbo grants. For example, the new CEO of Coca-Cola Company has restricted shares with a year-end value of $113,368,750. Grants of this nature tend to have a longer restriction period, i.e., ten or more years or until the executive's retirement.

Typical stock option award levels are shown in Chart 20-9.

Chart 20-9. Typical Stock Option Award Levels

Salary	Option Multiple of Salary for Companies With Only Stock Options	Option Multiple of Salary for Companies With Stock Options & Other Forms of Grants
$1,000,000	5.0	4.0
$ 750,000	4.0	3.5
$ 500,000	3.5	3.0
$ 250,000	2.5	2.0
$ 100,000	1.0	0.75

Source: Company proxies.

The option values in Chart 20-9 are at the median level. At the 75th percentile, there is significant leverage in option values. For example, at the $500,000 base salary level, the 75th percentile option value is 7.0.

Typical restricted stock award levels for senior executive positions are one to two times annual salary. This statistic is developed by looking at one-time restricted stock awards and is not from ongoing annual restricted stock awards. Jumbo restricted stock grants are typically done only for a CEO and are at least ten times base salary with a long restriction period, i.e., ten years rather than the normal three to five years.

Q 20:9   Does the use of performance-based stock options continue as a trend?

Yes. For example, in 1977 Dupont created the bicentennial stock option, which was made in lieu of the normal annual option grant. As stated in the Dupont proxy, "[T]his grant was designed to encourage greater management innovation and creativity to accelerate revenue growth and thus shareholder value." Dupont accomplished this by stating in the stock option terms that half would be exercisable when the stock price reached $75 and half when the stock price reached $90. These amounts were 145 percent and 170 percent of the grant price. If these hurdles were not achieved within five years of the date of grant, the stock options would be forfeited. Clearly the Dupont executives had a performance-based option that put their total compensation at a higher level of risk. Because of this, larger-than-normal grants were made. This is a common practice with performance-based stock options.

A different type of performance-based plan is used by the Fort James Corporation. It is a type of performance accelerated restricted stock award plan (PARSAP). Under this plan, performance-based shares are granted with a vesting period of eight years, at which time the shares are awarded; however, if performance goals are met during the vesting period, the performance shares may be earned. The performance measure is that the company must be in the top quartile of a peer group as measured by total shareholder return (TSR). The significance of this type of performance-based plan is that the accounting treatment can be that of restricted stock rather than that of a variable award, because the award will ultimately vest regardless of actual performance achieved. With restricted stock the charge to earnings is fixed at the time of grant as stated in Accounting Principles Board (APB) Ruling 25 and Financial Accounting Standards Board (FASB) Ruling 123 (APB is the predecessor organization of FASB—see Q 7:32). When the performance-based measure makes the award variable, as is the case with the Dupont bicentennial stock option, the accounting treatment will be that of a variable award requiring accrual on the income statement during the award period as stated in FASB Ruling 28 (see Qs 7:7, 7:41).

Disney was one of the early trend setters in performance-based long-term grants a few years ago. More recently their CEO was granted 3 million performance-based stock options and 5 million non-performance-based stock options. A member of the Disney board estimated that if the stock price increased 15 percent, the CEO would have an option gain of over $1 billion.

Q 20:10 Have noncompete clauses been used in stock award plans?

Yes. IBM is the high-profile example of this concept. It required a former executive to give back the gain from a stock option that was exercised just before the executive voluntarily resigned to take a position with Digital Equipment Corporation. The executive had signed a noncompete agreement that stipulated if a stock option was exercised within six months of a voluntary termination, the executive would have to return the gain to the company. This case was settled out of court but no details have been released.

Generally, noncompete agreements are hard to enforce unless a company pays a terminated executive during the period that he or she cannot work for a competitor. Of course, this payment will probably be cash compensation (not long-term); however, noncompete agreements with stock options have a real potential to protect company confidential information and to deter an executive from quickly leaving to join a competitor.

Q 20:11 Are economic value-added (EVA) plans continuing as a trend?

Yes (see Chapter 19). EVA plans continue to be one of the hottest ideas in executive compensation. Compaq Computer Corporation made the following quarterly press release in 1997: "Compaq's first quarter earnings increase 66 percent: EVA more than triples." At SPX Corporation, the CEO credits EVA as an important part of his turnaround strategy. He publicly stated in the *Wall Street Journal,* "When linked to compensation EVA is a change accelerator."

There are many different definitions of EVA, but advocates believe that this performance measure produces a more direct link between company and executive performance and shareholder value. To advocates, traditional accounting measures are not as effective as EVA because achievement of the accounting measures does not correlate with shareholder value; however, the prevalence of EVA is about 33 percent in most surveys. This indicates that most companies still use accounting-based performance measures.

Surveys do not really tell the whole story in that many companies (more than 33 percent) are considering EVA, and this does not show up in surveys. This is true for private and public companies. A private company considering EVA is Rich & Company in Buffalo, New York.

Economic value added, as well as the acronym EVA, are registered trademarks of Stern Stewart, the creator of the term. Many companies use other terms such as *economic profit* or *value added*. For example, Transamerica Corporation has a value added plan that

> rewards management for improving operating results and efficiently employing the Corporation's capital. Awards under the Value Added Plan are based on the Corporation's actual Value Added, which is defined as the Corporation's Adjusted Net Income minus an equity charge, expressed as a percentage of the Corporation's Average Adjusted Equity, all as defined in the Value Added Plan.

Eli Lilly and Company has an EVA bonus plan, which is contained in Appendix I.

Q 20:12 Are reload stock features continuing as a trend?

Yes, they are. These plans are designed to increase executive stock ownership. In most of these plans, once an executive exercises a previously granted stock option, provided that the exercised stock option is held for a specified time period, that executive becomes eligible for another stock option grant (in addition to the company's regular annual stock option grant). An example is the Dupont plan, which requires an executive to hold the exercised option for five years. The grant reloads a nonqualified stock option at fair market value at the time of grant and these options have a term equal to the remaining term of the original option.

Q 20:13 Do many companies use stock ownership guidelines for executives?

Yes, most surveys of large companies show that 33 percent of the companies have some stock ownership guideline for executives. For example, at Johnson Controls all officers and senior managers in each business group are required to hold one to three times their annual salary in company stock. The CEO holds three times, senior officers hold two times, and other officers and senior managers hold one times their annual salaries. The company has a stock purchase plan that facilitates the acquisition of common stock by executives by allowing them to deduct up to $2,500 per month to purchase shares of company stock through the plan. The price of each share is 100 percent of fair market value at the time of purchase and no brokerage fees or commissions are charged to the executive. The company also bears the expense of administering the plan.

Some other companies that use stock ownership guidelines for executives are shown in Chart 20-10.

Chart 20-10. Stock Ownership Guidelines for Executives

Company	CEO Guideline (% of Salary)	SVP/VP Guideline (% of Salary)
Brunswick Corp.	500%	150% +
Campbell Soup	300%	100% +
Coca-Cola	700%	200% +
Dial Corporation	500%	100% +
Ford Motor Company	500%	100% +
IBM	400%	200% +
Motorola	400%	300%
General Motors	350%	100% +
Pfizer	300%	100%

Q 20:14 Are any executive loans still used in long-term plans?

A few companies still provide executive loans. These are not typically used because of the cashless exercise provision, which allows executives to execute a buy and sell transaction when exercising a stock option. The cashless exercise is normally done through a third party like Charles Schwab or a local bank. The executive technically borrows the money from the third party, who then buys the shares from the company and instantly sells the shares, keeping the purchase price (the amount borrowed) and some small fee or commission. The executive receives the proceeds, minus any re-quired minimum income tax withholding. The cashless exercise gives the executive the same value as a stock appreciation right (SAR) but the company takes no charge to earnings with the cashless exercise right as it would with an SAR.

Obviously the cashless exercise is not a vehicle to promote stock ownership; therefore, in companies where executive stock ownership is a priority, stock loans can be used. An example of such a provision is the Illinois Tool Works plan, under which executives can borrow money to finance the purchase of stock options at favorable interest rates. In that company, the interest rate is 5.9 percent. The amount borrowed is payable in five years; however, the note is repayable in 180 days following termination of employment with the company (or immediately if the termination is for cause or because the executive dies).

Company loans at favorable interest rates require imputed income to the executive to the extent that the loan is below market rates. In the case of Illinois Tool Works, the imputed rate of interest on loans is 7.34 percent per year.

Q 20:15 Are stock cancel and reissue plans still used?

These are rare, but a few companies still use them. One example is Apple Computer, which in July 1997 implemented a stock option exchange program. Under this cancel and reissue plan, executives were allowed to exchange all of their outstanding stock options for new options on a one-for-one basis. The new options had an exercise price of $13.25, and the former stock options had exercise prices that generally ranged from $16.50 to $29.75.

These plans can obviously be viewed negatively by shareholders because the company does not cancel and reissue the shares the shareholders have already purchased, so the shareholders suffer a sizable capital loss. For example, if a shareholder at Apple Computer purchased 1,000 company shares at $29.75 and the stock is now trading at $13.25, the shareholder has a $16.50 per share loss, or $16,500 total loss.

The purpose of cancel and reissue is simply to retain key execu-tives so that they can turn a business around.

Q 20:16   What are other trends in long-term incentives?

Two other trends deserve mention:

1. *Certificates of extra compensation.* One company, Johnson & Johnson, uses certificates of extra compensation. These are performance units that measure the company's value by adding half of the company's net asset value and half of its earnings power value, and dividing the sum by the number of shares of Johnson & Johnson common stock outstanding. Earnings power value is calculated by taking the capitalized value of earnings averaged over the previous five years. These performance units are essentially deferred compensation and are paid at the end of the executive's career with the company. The units vest over a five-year period from date of grant, with the final value being determined on retirement or termination.

   Certainly if executives understand the potential value of this extra compensation, these certificates can have significant potential for retaining key executives in the company until retirement or involuntary termination (other than for cause).

2. *Performance-based stock awards.* This new long-term compensation plan is used by Harnischfeger Industries. Similar to performance-based stock options, these awards are, however, performance-based stock awards. If the company's stock price goes up to a specified price, a specified number of shares are awarded to the participating executives. An interesting feature of this plan is that the executives in the plan give up their annual stock option grants. In the Harnischfeger plan, the stock price must increase 30 percent over the base price within three years. More shares are granted if the stock price increases 50 percent or 70 percent.

Regulatory Issues

Q 20:17   What has been the reaction to FAS 123 on the accounting for stock options?

The reaction has been as expected: Companies are electing not to use FAS 123, which results in a charge to earnings. Rather, companies are following APB 25, which does not create a charge to earnings for stock options granted at 100 percent of fair market value at the time of grant (provided there is no performance criteria on the stock option that would make it a variable award and subject it to accounting accrual as stated in FAS 28). One exception to this rule has been Berkshire Hathaway, the leader of which, Warren Buffett, has stated that his company will elect to take a charge to earnings (under FAS 123) for executive stock options.

FAS 123 does not require companies that use APB 25 to take an earnings charge, but these companies are required to show in their financial statements the impact on earnings per share of any stock awards that the company subjects to APB 25. Companies are responding to this FASB requirement, a response almost always shown as a footnote in the financial statements of the company's annual report.

An example is the annual report of Ethyl Corporation, which states that "the Company continues to apply APB Opinion No. 25 and related interpretations in accounting for the stock option plan. Accordingly no compensation cost has been recognized for the stock option plan." The company goes on to explain that it used the Black-Scholes option pricing model to calculate the earnings per share impact of its stock option plan as prescribed in FAS 123. It provides the Black-Scholes assumptions on dividend yield, expected volatility of company stock price, the risk-free interest rate assumption, and the expected life of the stock option. The company further states:

> Had compensation cost for the Company stock option plan been determined based on the fair value at the grant date consistent with the fair-value method prescribed by FASB Statement No. 123, the Company's 1997 and 1996 net income would have been reduced on a pro forma basis from $77,530,000 to $77,355,000 and from $92,972,000 to $92,881,000, respectively. Basic and diluted earnings per share in 1997 would have decreased from $.71 to $.70. Basic and diluted earnings per share in 1996 would have been unchanged at $.78.

Q 20:18   Have the SEC regulations on the reporting of public company performance comparisons in annual proxies had an impact on executive compensation?

Although it is difficult to identify any direct correlation between the SEC regulations and company pay and performance practices, most executive compensation consultants believe that these comparisons (company performance graphs to executive compensation as reported in company proxies) do have an impact on how board compensation committee members view executive pay. Both senior company executives and compensation committee members want to see a comparison of company performance and company pay, as it is required to be reported in their company proxies. The analysis of these two variables is a major activity in public companies. The difference between company performance criteria on the company performance graphs and company performance measures used by board compensation committees in determining executive pay is analyzed by corporate boards as they report in their company proxies.

The SEC requires company performance graphs in public company proxies to compare the five-year (or in some cases, ten-year) cumulative return of an investment in that company's stock to investment returns using the Standard & Poor's 500 Index (S&P 500) and some other peer company composite selected by the company. Although this is not the most common performance measure used in determining executive pay, it serves as a valuable check and balance for board compensation committees.

Chart 20-11. Correlations of Company Performance Graphs in Proxies to Changes in Executive Pay—Survey of 100 Large Public Companies

Executive Pay Up	*Executive Pay Down*
Company Performance Up	Company Performance Down
56%	20%

Executive Pay Up	*Executive Pay Down*
Company Performance Down	Company Performance Down
20%	4%

Chart 20-11 suggests that there are some companies (24 percent) where performance (as measured by company stock price) and pay do not correlate. On further examination of the proxies, however, it becomes clear that board compensation committees use performance measures other than total shareholder return.

An example is the proxy of Corning, Inc. Company performance on the proxy graph showed investment in Corning stock was down from the previous year, while S&P 500 and peer group investment went up; however, in its report on CEO compensation, the board compensation committee stated that the company "met or exceeded" goals that were referenced in the proxy. Examples of these goals included "an increase in earnings per share of 28% . . . distribution to Corporation's shareholders of the common stock of both Quest Diagnostics Incorporated and Covance Inc. . . . achieving net profit after tax equivalent to 175% of the target opportunity set by the Committee."

This issue—how to measure corporate performance and correlate it to executive pay—provokes ongoing debate in corporate board rooms. The SEC regulations have certainly increased the focus on the issue.

Q 20:19   Has the capital gains tax rate decrease to 20 percent had any effect on executive pay?

Yes. A survey of 100 large companies showed a modest gain of 2 percent in the use of incentive stock options (ISOs), from 90 percent in 1996 to 92 percent in 1998. The ISO provides the opportunity for gains to be taxed at capital gains tax rates if the option is held after exercise and not sold for 12 months, in which case a capital gains tax of 28 percent applies, or not sold after exercise for 18 months, in which case a 20 percent capital gains tax applies. When either of these events occurs, the full appreciation is taxed at the capital gains tax rate.

Example. Assume that an executive has 10,000 ISOs granted in July 1995 at a price of $20. The executive exercises the right to purchase in 1997 when the market price is $35. The executive holds the stock until July 1999 and sells when the price is $50, for a total gain of $30 ($50 – $20 = $30) multiplied by 10,000, or $300,000, which is taxed at a capital gains tax rate of 20 percent, or $60,000 ($300,000 × 20% = $60,000), for a net gain of $240,000.

Had the executive been granted a nonqualified stock option, the executive would have been taxed at ordinary income tax rates at the time of exercise. If the executive was in the 39.6 percent marginal ordinary income tax bracket, the tax at exercise would have been $59,400 ($35 – $20 = $15; $15 × 10,000 = $150,000; $150,000 × 39.6% = $59,400). In addition, when the executive sold the nonqualified shares, there would have been an additional capital gains tax of $30,000 ($50 – $35 = $15; $15 × 10,000 = $150,000; $150,000 × 20% = $30,000). The total tax paid with the nonqualified stock option would have been $89,400 ($59,400 + $30,000 = $89,400), for a net gain of $210,600 instead of the $240,000 gain with the ISO.

There are some disadvantages to ISOs. First, there is no tax deduction to the company when the executive is subject to capital gains tax. Second, statutory requirements limit the annual vesting to $100,000 (i.e., the option value of the stock price multiplied by the number of shares cannot exceed $100,000); therefore, an executive cannot be made eligible to exercise more than $100,000 in ISO value in any given year. This vesting limit is cumulative. For example, an executive who vests $100,000 per year over five years and does not exercise during this period has $500,000 of ISO value that can be exercised at the end of the fifth year.

There are other ways to take advantage of the lower capital gains tax rates, as follows:

1. Pay the executive's annual bonus in stock. When paid, the executive has a capital asset subject to capital gains tax. If the stock is held for at least one year, the tax rate is 28 percent; if it is held for 18 months, the tax rate is 20 percent.

2. Use the reload feature on stock awards, both stock options and restricted stock. The reload feature gives the executive another grant of options when he or she exercises any given number of stock option shares, or another grant of restricted stock whenever the restrictions lapse on the current restricted stock grant, provided the executive does not sell any of the exercised option shares or the former restricted shares.

Q 20:20   Will more executives be subject to the alternative minimum tax (AMT) if the use of ISOs increases in response to a lower capital gains tax?

Probably yes, because the AMT applies to preference income, and the paper gain from the exercise of an ISO is preference income. The

AMT was designed to close a loophole created by tax shelters and other activities that offered preferential treatment under the Code. The AMT requires taxpayers to calculate ordinary income tax and the AMT and pay the higher of the two taxes (see Q 6:8). The *Wall Street Journal* conducted a study of this issue and reported in early 1998 that the number of executives subject to the AMT will increase from approximately 600,000 to 6 million by 2000.

Q 20:21   What new regulations are pending?

The Levin and McCain bill has gone nowhere in Congress. This bill would limit the company tax deduction on stock options to the amount that the company would charge its earnings. This would essentially take away the company tax deduction on nonqualified stock options at the time they are exercised. It would also eliminate the company tax deduction on an ISO that is disqualified (sold before the minimum holding period after exercise of one year). Currently, on any disqualification, the executive is subject to ordinary income tax and the company can take a tax deduction in the same amount.

The Employee Stock Option Act of 1997 was introduced in Congress by Representative Amo Houghton. It goes in the opposite direction of the Levin and McCain bill. It would give tax breaks to employees with no penalty to the employer that provides stock options to both nonexecutive and executive employees. The stock option discussed in this legislation parallels an ISO in that there would be no tax to the employee at exercise and capital gains on all appreciation if the stock is not sold for two years after grant of the option and one year after exercise (same as an ISO). The idea is to have broader use of ISO-type compensation so that all employees have opportunities for capital accumulation as company success and stock price increase. This bill has also gone nowhere.

There is no major change expected in SEC or FASB regulations until after the next presidential election.

Q 20:22   Do current regulations allow stock options to be transferred?

Yes, if they are nonqualified stock options. One approach is a direct transfer before the option is exercised, typically made by an executive to a family member. The executive must pay ordinary income tax on the gain when the option is ultimately exercised by the family member. The advantage is that the option value is excluded from the executive's estate and therefore not subject to estate tax. There may, however, be a gift tax, so this idea should be reviewed with a tax attorney or tax accountant.

Another idea is to establish a deferred stock unit account. Under this approach the executive elects, in advance of exercise, to defer the gain on a stock option. The executive then makes the exercise via a stock swap, i.e., the use of currently owned shares to satisfy the option price. FICA taxes, if any, would have to be paid at the time of exercise. All deferred accounts are of course unfunded.

Example. Shortly after receiving a stock option grant, an executive irrevocably elects to defer any future gains into a deferred stock account. The executive owns 5,000 shares of company stock that have a current market value of $60. Their value is $300,000 (5,000 × $60 = $300,000). The executive has a stock option for 10,000 shares at an option price of $30, the exercise of which would require $300,000 ($30 × 10,000 = $300,000). The executive therefore swaps 5,000 shares for 10,000 shares. Because the executive had no opportunity to take the gain, there is no taxable event at the time of exercise. The tax has been deferred until the shares are withdrawn, typically at retirement.

Q 20:23　　With greater use of stock plans, is dilution a new issue in executive compensation that needs to be regulated?

Dilution is an important issue, but, it is hoped, one that will not be regulated. Dilution is increasing in executive stock plans. A recent study by Pearl Myer & Associates showed that 13 percent of the outstanding shares in a large company are being allocated to executive compensation plans. This figure was 5 percent in 1993. The *Wall Street Journal* reported that executive stock plans involve at least 7 percent of a company's outstanding shares. In small companies this percentage varies from 1 percent to 25 percent depending on the mix of ownership.

Stock plans clearly have a dilutive impact, and the question is how much dilution is acceptable. The well-known executive compensation consultant Frederic W. Cook suggests that this is an important issue and a potential solution is for a company to define new ranges of acceptable dilution for executive compensation plans.

Outside Directors

Q 20:24   How are remuneration levels changing for outside directors?

Remuneration levels continue to increase. As shown in Charts 20-12 and 20-13, the median total cash compensation for outside directors in large companies is $57,500, a 7.5 percent increase over the previous year. The median total cash compensation for outside directors in small companies is $26,000, a 6 percent increase over the previous year.

Chart 20-12. Outside Director Compensation in Large Companies

Median Annual Retainer	Median Board Fee	Median Committee Fee	Median Total Cash Compensation
$38,500	$1,200	$1,200	$57,500

Chart 20-13. Outside Director Compensation in Small Companies

Median Annual Retainer	Median Board Fee	Median Committee Fee	Median Total Cash Compensation
$20,000	$750	$750	$26,000

In addition to these levels of cash compensation, outside directors also receive substantial amounts of compensation in the form of stock grants, both stock options and stock awards. Of large companies, 85 percent give outside directors some form of stock grant. The median value of these grants is $40,000, and this is in addition to cash compensation. Total remuneration of outside directors is close to $100,000.

Example. American Home Products Corporation pays outside directors an annual retainer of $42,500, a committee service retainer of $9,000, $1,050 for each board or committee meeting attended, and 400 shares of company stock. The total annual value is $97,100 calculated as follows:

Annual retainer	$42,500
Meeting retainer	$ 9,000
Board meetings (11 meetings × $1,050)	$11,550
Committee meetings (5 × $1,050)	$ 5,250
Restricted stock (400 shares × $72)	$28,800
Total compensation:	$97,100

These significant levels of compensation parallel the continuous increases in responsibility and time commitments required of today's outside director.

Q 20:25 Are retirement plans still commonly established for outside directors?

No, retirement plans for outside directors are decreasing in large numbers. This is a major trend in outside director remuneration. In 1963, 60 percent of all companies surveyed had some form of retirement plan for outside directors. In 1998, that number was 25 percent.

Many public companies are creating opportunities for outside directors to defer their income until retirement in lieu of providing retirement benefits. For example, the Eaton Corporation allows outside directors to defer their $30,000 annual retainer to the company's deferred compensation plan. The rate of interest is either at a higher than prevailing rate depending on the number of years until a director's retirement from board service, or at prime bank rate.

Another deferral mechanism is the stock grants that are typical for outside directors. For example, Eaton Corporation provides outside directors with 5,000 stock option shares on the first year of board service and another 1,000 shares each year thereafter. This could amount to 10,000 shares over five years. If company stock price appreciates a modest 5 percent per year, the stock appreciation during five years would be $20 per share, or $200,000. Annualized (divide by five years), this is $40,000 in value that the director has essentially deferred.

Coca-Cola Company is one of the few large companies that has retained its outside directors' retirement plan. It provides directors (or their surviving spouses) who have at least five years of service and are at least age 55 with an annual retirement benefit equal to the annual retainer then payable to the directors for a period of time equal to the total number of years of service on the board. The current annual retainer at Coca-Cola is $50,000.

Q 20:26   Are stock awards common for outside directors?

Yes, they are. This is another significant trend in outside director remuneration. In 1993, 40 percent of companies surveyed (large and small companies) had some form of stock award for outside directors. In 1997, the number was 75 percent in both large and small companies. Campbell Soup Company has one of the most powerful stock-based total remuneration plans. It provides an annual board retainer of 2,400 shares of company stock. With a stock price of $40, this is a $96,000 value. The company also provides an annual grant of 2,000 stock options.

Small companies have similar plans. Cryolife, Inc., a small publicly held biotechnology company, provides outside directors with a modest $500 fee for each board meeting. If the company has six board meetings a year, total fees are $3,000. In addition, the company provides each outside director with 4,000 stock option shares each year. During a recent 12-month period, the company's stock advanced $5 per share, which is a potential value of $20,000 (4,000 × $5 = $20,000) for each outside director.

The use of stock is a major remuneration program for outside directors because it aligns their interests with those of shareholders. Some companies also have outside director stock ownership guidelines similar to executive stock ownership guidelines. Examples of outside director stock awards are shown in Chart 20-14.

Chart 20-14. Representative Outside Director Stock Awards

Company	Annual Stock Award
Northrup Grumman	1,500 stock option shares
Int'l Paper	2,100 restricted shares on election or reelection
Caterpillar	4,000 stock option shares
Goodyear	$2,500 per quarter of stock options as replacement for former retirement plan
Johnson & Johnson	1,100 stock option shares

Q 20:27   Are outside directors typically provided with benefits?

It is rare for companies to provide outside directors with full benefit and other insurance coverages that would be provided to executives and other employees. Approximately one out of 12 companies offers benefits to outside directors.

Q 20:28   Do outside directors receive change-of-control benefits?

No. Outside directors rarely receive this protection because they participate in the decision to approve the change of control. With more deferred compensation plans appearing for outside directors, deferred compensation benefits could increase.

In addition to deferred compensation, there are some companies that have retirement plans for outside directors that they will want to protect during any change of control.

Chapter 21

Compensation for Division Executives

This chapter answers questions on the total compensation of executives who operate in a noncorporate environment that has profit accountability. Such an environment may be called a group, division, strategic business unit, etc., and typically has a full complement of business executives, i.e., general management, sales and marketing, operations, finance, and human resources.

Compensation for these executives can in some respects be similar to or different from that provided to the corporate executives, depending on the situation involved.

Base Salary 21-1
Annual Incentives 21-3
Long-Term Incentives 21-6
Benefits and Perquisites 21-15

Base Salary

Q 21:1   What is a division executive?

A division executive has managerial responsibility over a primary business function in one of the corporate organization's profit centers. These profit centers have many names, such as division, strategic business unit, group, department, team, plant, or office. Primary business functions include sales, marketing, operations, manufacturing, finance/accounting, human resources, safety, customer relations, quality control, purchasing, engineering, research, regulatory affairs, and public relations. Included in this definition is the division's general manager/executive position.

Division executives may or may not have an officer title. Where officer titles are used, there is typically a distinction between a corporate officer and a division officer. A corporate officer is elected by the company's board of directors. A division officer, including the division manager or division president, is appointed by a company's chief executive officer. Some organizations will also have appointed corporate officers, appointed by the chief executive officer, and these are typically called staff vice presidents.

The focus of this chapter is on any of the executive positions in divisions. Corporate executives are not the focus of this chapter.

Q 21:2   How is base salary different for division executives?

Division executives with the same title as corporate officers will in most cases have completely different levels of base salary. A primary reason for this is that there is normally a smaller scope of accountability in the division position. For example, a corporate controller in a company with sales of $1 billion will have a higher salary than the same position in one of the company's divisions, which might have sales of $250 million. Job scope drives base salary and other compensation levels in executive positions.

Now consider two positions in two different organizations: one at the corporate organization level and one at the division organization level. The job duties are the same and the scope of accountabilities is the same. As shown in Chart 21-1, the division positions are normally at a lower base salary because of their lower degree of freedom to act within their job accountabilities.

Chart 21-1. Base Salary Levels of Division vs. Corporate Executives

Title	Company Size	Median Salary for Corporate	Median Salary for Division
President/General Manager	$250 million	$300,000	$240,000
VP Sales & Marketing	$250 million	$175,000	$145,000
VP Operations	$250 million	$165,000	$130,000
Controller	$250 million	$105,000	$ 85,000
VP Human Resources	$250 million	$125,000	$105,000

As a rule of thumb, division executive positions will have a labor market value approximately 80 percent of that of a similar position at the corporate level.

Annual Incentives

Q 21:3 How are annual incentive amounts different for division executives?

The targeted annual incentive for division executives is approximately the same as that for other positions in the organization with the same base salary. As shown in Chart 21-2, there are some functional differences in annual bonus targets (sales/marketing is higher than operations and other functions), but few differences based on division versus corporate position in the organization.

Chart 21-2. Targeted Annual Incentive Amounts for Division and Corporate Positions

Title	Salary	Median Annual Bonus Target for Corporate	Median Annual Bonus Target for Division
President/General Manager	$250,000	45%	40%
VP Sales & Marketing	$150,000	35%	35%
VP Operations	$150,000	30%	30%
Controller	$150,000	30%	30%
VP Human Resources	$150,000	30%	30%

As established in Q 21:2, for similar positions at corporate and division organization levels, the corporate position will typically have a higher base salary; therefore, for two similar positions at corporate and division organization levels, the corporate position would have an annual bonus target that is equal to or higher than that for the similar division position, depending on the magnitude of difference in scope and base salary between the two positions.

Example. Company A has a corporate controller and a division controller. Company B has a corporate VP Human Resources for the corporate office (250 employees) and a division VP Human Resources (250 employees). The total cash compensation for both positions is as follows:

Title	Scope	Base Salary	Target Bonus
Company A			
Corporate Controller	$1 billion	$150,000	30%
Division Controller	$250 million	$100,000	25%
Company B			
VP HR, Corp. Office	250 employees	$100,000	25%
Division VP HR	250 employees	$100,000	25%

Q 21:4   Is the mix of total cash compensation changing for division executives?

Yes, it is changing in favor of annual bonus payments. The same is true for all other executive positions. Companies want to have more cash compensation at risk and dependent upon company and individual performance. They are also putting more leverage into annual incentive plans, so that as performance goals are exceeded, payouts become larger than in the past. Chart 21-3 shows how the mix of annual salary and bonus is changing for executive positions.

Chart 21-3. Mix of Total Cash for Division Positions

Title	1993 Base Salary	1993 Annual Bonus	1998 Base Salary	1998 Annual Bonus
Division President	$220,000	35%	$250,000	40%
Division Controller	$ 85,000	20%	$100,000	25%
Division Sales Executive	$100,000	25%	$125,000	30%
Division HR Executive	$ 85,000	20%	$100,000	25%

Q 21:5   Should division executives have their annual incentive determined from division or corporate results?

In most companies both division and corporate results are used in the determination of division executive annual incentive amounts. The weighting is always in favor of the division performance measures because division executives can influence these results more than overall corporate results. As with corporate incentive plans, the bonus pool is typically driven by organization performance and the individual awards are then determined from an evaluation of individual performance against individual goals.

Example. The performance measures and weighting for a division controller's annual incentive are as follows:

Performance measures in the division bonus pool:

Performance Measure	Weighting
Corporate operating profit	20%
Division operating profit	60%
Division unit sales	20%

Performance measures for the division controller:

Performance Measure	Weighting
Cash investment results	30%
Timeliness and accuracy of financial reports	30%
Computerization of revised expense categories	30%
Meeting division training schedule	10%

21-5

The use of and/or weighting of corporate performance measures are intended to insure that division executives do not make any business decisions that may represent a positive short-term result for the division but negative short- or long-term impact on the corporation. In many businesses, one division can help another division, and this can be emphasized and rewarded through the annual incentive plan.

Long-Term Incentives

Q 21:6 How are levels of long-term incentives different for division executives?

The level of long-term incentive for division executives is approximately the same as that for other positions in the organization with the same base salary. As shown in Chart 21-4, the target award levels in long-term incentives are driven by base salary level regardless of whether the position is a division or corporate position within the organization.

**Chart 21-4. Targeted Stock Option Award Levels
for Division and Corporate Positions**

Title	Salary	Median Annual Stock Option Award Level
Division President/General Manager	$250,000	50%
Corporate VP Sales & Marketing	$250,000	50%
Corporate Controller	$150,000	35%
Division Controller	$100,000	30%
VP HR, Corp. Office	$100,000	30%
Division VP Human Resources	$100,000	30%

Q 21:7 Should division executives have their long-term incentive determined from division or corporate results?

Most companies include division executives in their corporate long-term incentive plan(s), which are in most cases either stock-based plans or long-term performance plans. Division results are rarely used in a long-term incentive plan. The theory is that corporate results are driven by the sum of all parts, and because each division contributes to the success of the company, the division executives should be participants in plans that are based on corporate success.

There is one major problem with this longstanding theory. There are no individual or organization performance measures in stock option plans or in long-term performance plans that are based on a corporate performance measure like return on equity or earnings per share. Thus, a division that does not meet its long-term objectives still benefits from the successes created from other profit centers in the corporation, or as the other profit center executives would say, "We get pulled down by a poor-performing division."

Because of this disadvantage, a new trend is emerging for organizations to put division executives into division-based long-term incentives. If, for example, Division A does not perform, there is no payment. Correspondingly, if it does perform, and another division does not, then Division A is not pulled down in terms of reward level by the poor-performing division. Here are some additional advantages and disadvantages:

Division-Based Long-Term Incentive Plans

Advantages	*Disadvantages*
1. Division executives have a greater impact on division results than on corporate results.	1. Make it difficult to develop teamwork and cooperation between divisions.
2. Division executives are more motivated when long-term incentives are based on division results.	2. Create inequities when one division may receive a long-term payment while another division may not.
3. Help to get division executives focused on those key factors that produce business success.	3. Require the setting of multiple goals rather than one or two primary goals for the company.
4. Get division executives thinking like owners rather than employees.	4. Do not align division executives with the interests of shareholders.

Q 21:8   How can long-term incentives be changed from stock options to incentives based on division results?

Identify those business performance measures that drive success in the business. Human resource consultants who specialize in this area suggest that four common performance measures are applicable in most organizations:

1. Revenue, however obtained. In a not-for-profit organization this may be occupancy rate in the hospital. In a for-profit company it may be unit sales. The point is to understand how to get sales revenue in the business.

2. Profit, or in the case of a not-for-profit, the excess of income over expenses. In some for-profit companies this may be operating profit; in others it may be pretax profit or net income.

3. Growth, in revenue, profit, unit sales, number of accounts, quality ratings, market share, etc. This is another excellent quantitative measure that may or may not be financial.

4. Cash. A division can have a cash flow statement just as a corporation does. Business objectives in a division are not always revenue- or profit-oriented. An example is after a merger, restructuring, or recapitalization of a business, when debt payments may be significant for a few years. Cash pays off debt. When RJR Nabisco was purchased by KKR, there was a significant annual debt of approximately $1 billion per year. One of the divisions in that company was given a business objective to generate cash to pay this debt.

Note that these are all simple business performance measures, ones that division executives clearly understand.

Q 21:9   What is the best way to design a payout schedule for a long-term incentive plan that is based on division results?

There are two common concepts used to meet this need. The first is a "matrix schedule." Two performance measures are used in the vertical and horizontal matrix and a payout percentage is designated in the middle box. An example is shown in Chart 21-5:

Chart 21-5. Sample Matrix Payout Schedule

		Revenue Growth				
		4%	6%	8%	10%	12%
	$12mm	11%	12%	13%	15%	18%
	$11mm	10%	11%	12%	14%	16%
Pre-tax	$10mm	9%	10%	11%	12%	14%
Profit	$9mm	8%	9%	10%	11%	13%
	$8mm	7%	8%	9%	10%	12%

In this matrix example, last year's revenue would logically have been between 4 percent and 6 percent, while the pretax profit would have been around $7.5 million; therefore, minimum acceptable performance would be to exceed $7.5 million with a revenue growth of at least 4 percent. A high-leverage design principle is then shown in the payout percentages in that payout amounts increase significantly as performance exceeds the minimum expectation. As performance reaches that defined in the top right corner, payout percentages are increased even more. The payout percentage could be a percentage of base salary, or a percentage of a predetermined bonus pool for all division executives.

The second payout schedule concept is the "target schedule." This schedule compares targeted payment to targeted performance, and allows for a less than targeted actual payment if actual performance is less than targeted performance. Correspondingly, if actual performance exceeds target performance, then the actual payment exceeds the target payment. An example is shown in Chart 21-6.

Chart 21-6. Sample Targeted Payment Payout Schedule

Actual Performance as a Percentage of Target	*Payment as a Percentage of the Targeted Fund*
130%	160%
120%	140%
110%	120%
100%	100%
90%	95%
80%	90%

Note the leverage in the payout schedule as performance exceeds target. The payment increases geometrically, not arithmetically. This is intended to motivate division executives to exceed the target by making the reward much greater.

Q 21:10   Can value-added performance measures be used in long-term incentives?

Yes, this concept is gaining in popularity throughout corporate America. The concept is to identify performance measures that are not found in general accounting principles (GAP), something other than earnings per share, net income, and the many return measures, such as return on equity, return on capital, or return on assets. With a value-added performance measure, a division is typically asked to increase the amount earned in excess of its cost of capital. (This is similar to economic value added (EVA), which is a registered trademark of Stern Stewart, its creator. Companies use a similar concept called "economic profit" or "value added." The challenge is to design a value-added formula that includes business processes controlled or directly influenced by the division executive and that is simple enough for all to understand.

In division value-added plans, capital typically has a more simple definition than that used in corporate capital. Division executives rarely influence equity capital—stock or retained earnings. But they do influence assets and liabilities within their division. The key to a value-added division incentive compensation plan is to establish a definite measure of these "value drivers" to division business success.

Q 21:11   What is an example of a value-added performance measure in a division?

When value-added is used as a performance measure, there are three steps in the calculation. First, value-added for the base year must be calculated. Next, value-added for the current year must be calculated to identify any increase from the base year. Finally, the incentive award is defined as a percentage of the incremental increase in value-added.

The assumptions in this example are:

Definitions of Capital	Current Value
1. The ratio of accounts receivable over accounts payable	$ 300 mm
2. Cash	$ 800 mm
3. Inventory	$1,200 mm
4. The value of nonperforming assets	$ 200 mm
Total:	$2,500 mm

Value-added is defined as the amount by which operating profit exceeds the cost of capital, or operating profit minus cost of capital. The cost of capital is fixed at 12 percent of capital. Operating profit for the base year is $1 million. Base year capital is $2.5 million, so the cost of capital is $300,000 ($2,500,000 × 12% = $300,000). Base year value-added is $700,000 ($1,000,000 – $300,000 = $700,000).

For the current year, if the division achieves operating profit of $1.2 million and reduces capital by $300,000, then the current year value-added is $936,000, calculated as follows:

$2,500,000 – $300,000 = new capital of $2,200,000

$2,200,000 × 12% = $264,000

$1,200,000 – $264,000 = $936,000

The increase in value-added from the base year to the current year is calculated as follows:

$936,000 – $700,000 = $236,000

In this company, the division incentive fund is set at 10 percent of incremental (additional) value-added each year. The incentive is calculated as follows:

$236,000 × 10% = $23,600

In reviewing the value-added definitions and calculations, how can the division executive increase the amount of incentive?

1. By decreasing the capital factors of cash and inventory
2. By eliminating the capital factor of nonperforming assets
3. By keeping the ratio of accounts receivable over accounts payable at 1.0
4. By increasing operating profit

The theory of valued-added division incentives is that with clear objectives, like the ones shown in this example, each division executive can be motivated to contribute to division success.

Q 21:12   How do companies determine the cost of capital?

More and more companies that have valued-added concepts in division incentives are using a fixed percentage, and 12 percent seems very common. Other alternatives require sophisticated analysis. One concept is to take a normal rate of return expected by an investor, and add to this a premium rate of return expected by an investor in order to invest in the company's stock rather than another company's stock. Then multiply this by a beta factor that is the extent to which the company's stock price follows the market (a beta of 1.0) versus the fact that the company's stock price does not have as much variation as the market (a beta of less than 1.0), or the fact that the company's stock price has more variation than the market (a beta of greater than 1.0).

Example 1.

Normal rate of return (Quarterly T-bill interest rate):	6%
Premium rate of return:	+ 6%
Beta factor:	× 1.0
Equals:	12%

Another alternative for determining the cost of capital is to use actual debt payments of interest on any borrowed funds and dividends paid top shareholders.

Example 2.

Interest on long-term debt:	$1,400,000
Dividends paid:	$1,000,000
Total:	$2,400,000
Capital:	$20,000,000
Cost of capital:	12%
	($2,400,000 ÷ $20,000,000 = 12%)

Q 21:13   Can division-based incentive plans be the same for an executive's annual incentive and long-term incentive?

Yes, it is possible to use division-based performance measures for a combination short-term and long-term incentive plan. Any of the examples shown in Q 21:9 or Q 21:11 could be used for the combination plan. Companies typically structure these plans by dividing the potential reward into short-term and long-term, then pay the short-term immediately in cash and defer the long-term portion. The long-term amount is often subject to vesting, and payment occurs only after vesting has occurred, e.g., 25 percent per year. Once an executive starts accruing long-term plan awards, the vesting has quite a compounding effect and the executive is encouraged to remain with the organization and not give up future payments.

Example. A company has a combination short-term and long-term division-based incentive plan. In the long-term plan there is 25 percent vesting of all earned amounts and the executive may take payment once vested, or decide to defer the amounts until a designated date in the future. Assume that an executive earns payments from the long-term incentive as follows:

Incentive Amount Earned	Amounts Vested Each Year							
	1992	1993	1994	1995	1996	1997	1998	1999
1991: $20,000	$5,000	$5,000	$5,000	$5,000				
1992: $24,000		$6,000	$6,000	$6,000	$6,000			
1993: $28,000			$7,000	$7,000	$7,000	$7,000		
1994: $16,000				$4,000	$4,000	$4,000	$4,000	
1995: $24,000					$6,000	$6,000	$6,000	$6,000
1996: $30,000						$7,500	$7,500	$7,500
etc.							etc.	etc.

Note that starting in year 1995 the executive is receiving payments from amounts earned during four different years (1991 through 1994). This continues as long as the executive keeps accruing long-term incentives and becomes a barrier to his or her leaving the company in that he or she will not want to give up the amounts previously earned and to be vested in the future. This is a classic form of "golden handcuffs," meaning a way to structure long-term incentive compensation so that the company retains executive talent.

Q 21:14   Can division-based incentive plans be used in not-for-profit organizations?

Yes, the same concepts apply, except performance measures are different:

Performance Measures

Not-for-Profit Organization	*For-Profit Company*
Patient satisfaction	Customer satisfaction
Excess of revenue over expenses	Profit
Revenue growth	Sales growth
Membership/occupancy rate	Unit sales
Expense savings	Selling, general, and administrative (SG&A) reductions
Cash	Cash
Fund raising	Cost of capital

Q 21:15   Can division-based incentive plans be used in international organizations?

Yes, international businesses are excellent candidates for the concept of division-based incentive compensation. Typically international organizations are profit centers. Moreover, there are fewer issues of international equity between international organizations, as can be the case in multi-divisions that are based in the United States.

Q 21:16   What are the disadvantages of division-based incentive compensation plans?

The theory of division-based incentive plans is excellent, but it has the following disadvantages:

1. Division-based incentive plans require goal setting for multiple divisions. The setting of accurate goals at the beginning of the

fiscal year is difficult for one business unit and more difficult for more than one business unit.

2. Division-based incentive plans require more administration time and cost. Someone must track each of the division plans and administer all aspects of the plan. This often requires additional manpower.

3. Stock options are simple and less costly.

4. Division incentives can result in a major focus on the division and therefore weaken corporate bonds or interest in the success of other divisions.

5. Division incentives can weaken the synergies between divisions. For example, a sales executive who is only rewarded on the results of his or her division may miss an opportunity to refer business or a sales lead to another division because he or she gets no reward for this action.

These factors should be considered before a division-based incentive is developed.

Benefits and Perquisites

Q 21:17   What perquisites are typically provided to division executives?

The most common perquisites for division executives are company cars, financial planning, entertainment expense accounts, club memberships, supplemental retirement plans, first-class air travel, and cellular phones. As with corporate executives, financial planning and supplemental retirement are a function of income level in that the higher the income, the greater the need. All of the other perquisites have a direct business relationship and can enhance the productivity of the executive or facilitate customer relationships.

Q 21:18   Are division executives subject to the same regulatory constraints as corporate executives?

Yes, regulations make no distinction as to corporate or division. For example, if a division executive wants to defer income, the

Internal Revenue Service (IRS) regulations on constructive receipt must be met and the executive must irrevocably elect to defer before the income is earned. The same is true with respect to the Securities and Exchange Commission's (SEC's) prohibition on the trading of company stock based on insider knowledge, which applies to division executives and anyone with inside information.

Q 21:19   Is the compensation of division executives included in public company proxies if they are one of the five highest paid employees?

It is included only if the division executive is an elected officer and in charge of a major functional area of the business. For example, Executive A and Executive B are both division presidents in a company with profit accountability for major service areas of the company. Both executives have total compensation that is within the top five of all executives. Executive A is an elected corporate officer, while Executive B is an appointed division officer. Only Executive A would need to have compensation reported in the proxy.

Q 21:20   Are there differences in the total compensation of division executives based on degree of autonomy?

Yes, the division with greater autonomy and greater independence will be paid more; however, it is difficult to obtain data on these differences. Some companies use sophisticated job evaluation programs for executives that can result in compensation differences based on the different freedoms to act. The Hay System is one of these programs.

Some large consulting firms also provide data on this basis, like Sibson & Company, which has three categories of data. The first is a division that is a separate profit center within a company, but it only has one product line or major business function. This type of division is not fully integrated, that is, it does not contain all business processes necessary to produce a product or service. An example is a division that might be in charge of purchasing for the company but also allowed to do purchasing for other companies. An information technology division is another example.

The second type of division is one that has all business processes necessary to produce a product or service. It has a product or service completely different from any other profit center in the company. The division also will typically have separate staff functions, such as financial or human resources, because of the different industry practices that are unlike those of other company profit centers or divisions. It will also typically do its own strategic planning, for example, an oil and gas exploration division in a consumer products company.

The third is somewhere between the other two. It is typically in the same industry as other divisions of the company and will have all business processes necessary to produce a product or service; however, it will probably share some staff services with other divisions, or have administrative or operating-type people in its division as opposed to strategists. An example is an envelope division of a publishing company that might have other divisions in the same industry, such as book publishing or education publishing.

Chapter 22

Small-Company Versus Large-Company Practices

This chapter covers the key differences between small entrepreneurial company and large multi-billion dollar company executive compensation practices.

While the types of executive programs are quite similar in small and large companies, the administrative features and pure numbers are significantly different.

Total Cash Compensation   22-1
Long-Term Plans   22-8
Benefits and Perquisites   22-13

Total Cash Compensation

Q 22:1   How do small and large companies define executives?

Both large and small companies use the same criteria to define their executives:

1. *Reporting relationship.* Typically those who report to a chief executive officer of the corporation or a division in the corporation.

2. *Job grade.* This is an excellent criteria but it should not be used alone because it will put pressure on the company's job classification system.

3. *Title.* Typically, an officer.

4. *Impact on the organization.* This is an open criterion, but it forces comparisons of each position's impact on the organization, and this can be helpful and revealing. Reviewing an executive position's purpose, value, and impact is always a worthwhile activity.

5. *Some combination of the above.* Produces a good check and balance when used. When only one criterion is used, it becomes too easy and inequities can result.

A additional method of defining executives in a company is to look at the total executives as a percentage of total employment. In a small company, this percentage is 5 to 10 percent; in a large company, the percentage is 0.25 to 1.5 percent. Thus, there is an inverse relationship in that the percentage of executives in a small company is large, while the percentage of executives in a large company is small.

Q 22:2   How do base salary levels in a small company compare to those in a large company?

Compensation in all executive jobs is scope-driven, that is, the same job will be paid more in a larger company than in a smaller company. The logic is that errors in the larger company can have greater consequences, and there are more resources there that require management. The primary measure of scope is sales, not profit. Some industries are more profitable than others. For example, pharmaceutical companies have higher profit margins than most consumer product companies; however, the pay levels for executive positions with similar levels of accountabilities in both industries will be about the same. Charts 22-1 and 22-2 show specific examples for representative executive positions.

Chart 22-1. 1998 Base Salary Levels in Small Businesses

Title	Company Size	Median Base Salary
Chief Executive Officer	$50 million	$260,000
Chief Financial Officer	$50 million	$135,000
Top Sales & Marketing Officer	$50 million	$135,000
Top Operations Executive	$50 million	$115,000
Top Human Resource Officer	$50 million	$100,000

Sources: Economic Research Institute executive compensation data and HR Management, Inc. data.

Chart 22-2. 1998 Base Salary Levels in Large Businesses

Title	Company Size	Median Base Salary
Chief Executive Officer	$1 billion	$550,000
Chief Financial Officer	$1 billion	$250,000
Top Sales & Marketing Officer	$1 billion	$225,000
Top Operations Executive	$1 billion	$185,000
Top Human Resource Officer	$1 billion	$165,000

Sources: Economic Research Institute executive compensation data and HR Management, Inc. data.

Q 22:3   How do annual incentive amounts in a small company compare to those in a large company?

Annual incentive amounts are higher in the larger company because incentive amounts are "progressive," just like the tax structure, where the higher the taxable income the higher the tax. With executive incentive plans, the higher the base salary, the higher the annual incentive percentage and amount. The logic for this is that executive jobs with a higher base salary have greater accountability and impact on the organization, and companies want jobs at this level to have a large percentage of total cash compensation at risk, or subject to achievement of performance goals. Examples of annual incentives paid to representative positions are shown in Charts 22-3 and 22-4.

Chart 22-3. 1998 Annual Incentive Amounts in Small Businesses

Title	Company Size	Median Annual Incentive
Chief Executive Officer	$50 million	$140,000
Chief Financial Officer	$50 million	$ 50,000
Top Sales & Marketing Officer	$50 million	$ 65,000
Top Operations Executive	$50 million	$ 35,000
Top Human Resource Officer	$50 million	$ 25,000

Sources: Economic Research Institute executive compensation data and HR Management, Inc. data.

Chart 22-4. 1998 Annual Incentive Amounts in Large Businesses

Title	Company Size	Median Base Salary
Chief Executive Officer	$1 billion	$450,000
Chief Financial Officer	$1 billion	$125,000
Top Sales & Marketing Officer	$1 billion	$125,000
Top Operations Executive	$1 billion	$ 65,000
Top Human Resource Officer	$1 billion	$ 60,000

Sources: Economic Research Institute executive compensation data and HR Management, Inc. data.

The total cash compensation for these positions is as shown in Charts 22-5 and 22-6. The information in these charts, as well as the information in all previous charts, is median data. The array of actual amounts around this data is in most cases plus or minus 25 percent with respect to base salary. For example, a position with a median base salary of $125,000 would have actual salaries that range from $95,000 to $155,000, a plus or minus 25 percent.

With respect to annual incentives, the array of actual amounts around the median statistic is in most cases plus or minus 100 percent. For example, a median annual incentive of $50,000 would have actual incentives that range from $0 to $100,000.

Q 22:4 What are typical amounts of total cash compensation in small and large companies?

Total cash compensation is the sum of base salary and annual incentive. In surveys, the individual amounts of reported base salary, when added to the individual amounts of reported annual incentive, do not always equal the individual amounts of reported total cash compensation. In overcoming this survey inconsistency, company practices differ. Some will take the sum of individual base salary and incentive and average it with the total cash compensation. Others will use total cash compensation and base salary and calculate the annual incentive as the difference between total cash and base salary. Another technique is to average either of these approaches with the same statistic over the last three to five years to avoid unusual ups and downs in the data, which can be caused by unusually high annual incentives in any given year. This is called "smoothing out" the data. Labor market surveys require some interpretation in order to reach a logical conclusion.

Charts 22-5 and 22-6 show total cash compensation for representative positions in small and large companies.

Chart 22-5. 1998 Total Cash Compensation in Small Companies

Title	Median Base Salary	Median Annual Incentive	Median Total Cash Compensation
Chief Executive Officer	$260,000	$140,000	$400,000
Chief Financial Officer	$135,000	$ 50,000	$175,000
Top Sales & Marketing Officer	$135,000	$ 65,000	$200,000
Top Operations Executive	$115,000	$ 35,000	$150,000
Top Human Resource Officer	$100,000	$ 25,000	$125,000

Sources: Economic Research Institute executive compensation data and HR Management, Inc. data.

Chart 22-6. 1998 Total Cash Compensation in Large Companies

Title	Median Base Salary	Median Annual Incentive	Median Total Cash Compensation
Chief Executive Officer	$550,000	$450,000	$1,000,000
Chief Financial Officer	$250,000	$125,000	$ 375,000
Top Sales & Marketing Officer	$225,000	$125,000	$ 350,000
Top Operations Executive	$185,000	$ 65,000	$ 250,000
Top Human Resource Officer	$165,000	$ 60,000	$ 225,000

Sources: Economic Research Institute executive compensation data and HR Management, Inc. data.

There are numerous surveys that can be used in reaching conclusions on the labor market value of executive jobs in both small companies and large companies. The large national consulting firms all publish excellent surveys, and there are many other published surveys that can be purchased from survey organizations.

Q 22:5   What are typical annual incentive amounts as a percentage of base salary for both small and large companies?

As shown in Chart 22-7, these vary and are progressive; that is, the higher the base salary, the higher the annual incentive. The data in these charts is the same for both small and large companies. The only exception would be the small entrepreneurial company that cannot afford to make competitive cash compensation payments because cash is scarce as the company attempts to grow. In these environments, the lower levels of cash compensation are offset by higher than normal stock option grants. It can be said that many executives in the smaller, entrepreneurial company are "betting on the big payoff," giving up cash compensation for a few years in order to help a high-potential company grow, and possibly go public, so that the company's stock increases in value much more than the stock of a larger company that is paying normal levels of cash compensation and stock options.

**Chart 22-7. Typical Targeted Annual Incentives
as a Percentage of Base Salary**

Base Salary	Annual Incentive
$ 75,000	20%
$ 100,000	25%
$ 125,000	30%
$ 150,000	35%
$ 200,000	40%
$ 250,000	45%
$ 350,000	45%
$ 500,000	50%
$ 750,000	60%
$1,000,000	75%

The targeted levels of annual incentive are developed from actual amounts of incentive paid by competitive companies. Surveys might report both targeted and actual annual incentives. It is important to realize that the actual amounts paid are the proper ones to use in survey analysis, simply because the competitive companies may not ever actually pay the targeted amount, but they obviously pay the actual amount reported.

Q 22:6   How are annual incentive plans structured in small and large companies?

In the small company these are either discretionary or formula-driven/profit sharing plans. The emphasis in these companies is on growth and many environments lack the sophisticated business planning and/or reporting systems that are needed for a goal-based annual incentive plan.

Many small businesses have a chief executive officer who is in daily contact with all other officers, for whom a discretionary incentive can be effective. There is constant dialogue on priorities and a lot of mutual problem solving, so the chief executive officer has a comprehensive basis for making individual incentive decisions. The other positive characteristic of the discretionary incentive is that no goal setting is required, and it is easier to look back and judge performance than it is to look forward and accurately predict what good performance should be during the next fiscal year.

In the company that focuses on growth, a profit sharing plan that funds an annual incentive pool based on incremental profit can work well. The only problem with these plans is that the percentage used to calculate the incentive pool will need to be lower as company success and higher profits are realized. For example, the former chief executive officer of Reebok had a profit sharing plan and as company profits grew the annual incentive grew from $6 million to $8 million to $10 million to $12 million, etc. Then profits leveled off and growth became small, but the plan had the same percentage of growth and still paid a substantial bonus of over $6 million in a year when performance went down. Profit sharing plans need to be reviewed each year to maintain their effectiveness or they should have a "sunset provision," that is, a fixed term (e.g., three years), after which a new plan will automatically be developed.

Almost all large companies have goal-based annual incentive plans. Company goals are established and, if achieved, a targeted incentive fund is generated. A threshold level of performance is also identified and a lesser incentive fund is authorized if this level of performance is achieved. Correspondingly, if performance goals are exceeded, a larger than target incentive fund is authorized. These performance-based plans work well in the large company because such companies have sophisticated business planning processes and reporting systems that can estimate and measure executive and company performance.

Long-Term Plans

Q 22:7   How many shares as a percentage of the total shares outstanding are reserved for executive compensation plans?

This varies significantly between small and large companies. The smaller the company, the larger the percentage of shares outstanding that are used for executive compensation plans: To offset the fact that smaller companies cannot always afford to pay competitive levels of cash compensation, significantly more stock options are granted.

Proxy analysis in public companies over a five-year period showed that 20 percent of the total shares outstanding in a small company were reserved for executive compensation, whereas only 10 percent of shares outstanding were used in a large company.

These statistics are almost double those of the preceding five years. For many years, the large company norm was 5 percent of the shares outstanding over a five-year period, and for a small entrepreneurial company it was 10 to 15 percent.

Q 22:8   What are the typical targeted amounts of incentive used in long-term incentive plans for small and large companies?

Like annual incentives, these are expressed as a percentage of base salary and are the same in small and large companies. Chart 22-8 shows the median amounts of targeted long-term incentive.

Chart 22-8. Typical Targeted Amounts of Long-Term Incentive

Base Salary	Targeted Long-Term Incentive
$ 75,000	25%
$ 100,000	30%
$ 125,000	35%
$ 150,000	40%
$ 200,000	45%
$ 250,000	50%
$ 350,000	50%
$ 500,000	60%
$ 750,000	70%
$1,000,000	75%

As shown in the chart, these amounts of long-term incentive are slightly higher than the targeted amounts of annual incentive. This is because most companies want executives to focus more on the long-term success of the business and to avoid taking short-term actions that might be advantageous for annual incentives but contrary to long-term success. An example is to meet an annual net income goal when the company might be better off to invest some of that net income into product development for the future.

Q 22:9   What is the typical mix of executive compensation elements in small and large companies?

As suggested in Qs 22:5 and 22:6, the smaller company tends to have a greater portion of total compensation allocated to long-term stock award plans, and a smaller portion of total compensation allocated to base salary and annual incentive—the cash elements of executive pay. Charts 22-9 and 22-10 contrast the mix of total pay for small and large companies. As shown in these charts, the small company also has a higher portion of total compensation allocated to benefits and perquisites, simply because these have a similar dollar value in small and large company executive jobs, and in the small company, which has lower cash compensation, the percentage is higher.

**Chart 22-9. Typical Mix of Total Compensation
in the Small Company
(Chief Executive Officer Position)**

Element of Executive Compensation	Percentage of Total Compensation	Example for CEO Position
Base salary	20%	$200,000
Annual incentive	10%	$100,000
Annualized value of long-term incentive	60%	$600,000
Annualized value of benefits and perquisites	10%	$100,000

Source: HR Management, Inc. database.

Chart 22-10. Typical Mix of Total Compensation in the Large Company (Chief Executive Officer Position)

Element of Executive Compensation	Percentage of Total Compensation	Example for CEO Position
Base salary	17%	$ 500,000
Annual incentive	12%	$ 375,000
Annualized value of long-term incentive	67%	$2,000,000
Annualized value of benefits and perquisites	4%	$ 125,000

Source: HR Management, Inc. database.

Q 22:10   How do small and large companies calculate the value of stock options?

For purposes of strategic compensation planning, both types of companies use the "annualized value of long-term incentives" (see Q 22:9). This requires estimating the value of a stock option, because when stock options are granted, only an option value exists. Option value is determined by option price multiplied by the number of shares. The need is to identify exactly what the real value (and income) will be to the executive for any given stock option, for comparison against other real income statistics like base salary, annual incentive, restricted stock (value at grant), performance shares (targeted value), and annual contributions to benefit plans. Many surveys have competitive option values. Companies can use this information to determine the number of shares to grant; however, this information is not useful in the strategic planning of executive compensation.

The annualized value of stock options can be calculated in two ways. One is a Black Scholes calculation (see Q 1:50), which will typically result in an annualized value that is approximately 33 percent of the grant price. So if a company grants stock options at a price of $30, the Black Scholes option pricing model will produce a value of approximately $10. Another way is to:

1. Gather competitive data on stock option grants over a five-year period.

2. Calculate the actual gain in company stock price over the next five years.

3. Calculate the actual appreciation (value) of the stock option to the executive over the original five-year period by multiplying the stock price appreciation by the number of shares in each stock option.

Both of these methodologies will provide the annualized value of a stock option and permit comparisons of this number to other real income received by the executive. In addition, the annualized value can be used in strategic executive compensation planning.

Q 22:11   How are long-term performance plans structured in small and large companies?

The plans are structured similarly in both small and large companies; however, the performance measures are different. Some small businesses use typical financial and quantitative performance measures, such as net income, earnings per share, return on equity, unit sales, quality ratings, and customer ratings, the same measures that are found in large companies. Other small companies use performance measures that reflect how well the company is growing, such as earnings growth, growth in net worth, achievement of research and development goals or interim milestones, product development or introduction in a specified geographic area, or growth in distributors.

Where typical financial or quantitative performance measures are used, long-term incentive plan structure is similar to that in the annual incentive in that a targeted incentive amount is made available to executives if a targeted performance goal is achieved. Another alternative used in the small company is to provide executives with a percentage of the growth in some financial measure, such as a percentage of net worth growth as shown below.

Example. A team of three executives is provided with the opportunity to share in the growth of their company's net worth. A long-term incentive is established whereby growth in net income over a five-year period will be shared with each executive. The share of each will be 5 percent. Current net worth is $20 million.

After five years net worth is $32 million. Each executive has earned $360,000, calculated by multiplying the incremental net worth of $12 million by 3 percent, to equal $360,000.

The advantage of a long-term plan that allows executives to share in the incremental profit or net worth that they help to create is that it gets them to think and act like shareholders. This is desirable to the shareholders and a significant motivation to the executives. Where used, this concept will provide the executive with an uncapped long-term incentive. The greater the incremental net worth (or other performance measure), the greater the executive's payment.

This concept is similar to the design features of a value-added plan where executives receive a percentage of the value added they help to create. These plans need to have a fixed time period or "sunset provision" so that they do not go on forever. Business needs and environments change, and long-term incentives need to change correspondingly in both the small and large company.

Benefits and Perquisites

Q 22:12   How do executive perquisites differ between small and large companies?

Perquisites are quite similar in both small and large companies, as shown in Chart 22-11. The costs in the large company may be higher because total pay is higher. For example, with financial planning, the costs are based on compensation level and the complexity of company compensation, which tend to be higher in larger companies. The same would be true for supplemental retirement plans where company contributions are driven by the compensation level of the executive.

In Chart 22-11, the most common perquisites and their frequency are shown. Many other perquisites are used in these companies (see Q 10:2); however, the perquisites in Chart 22-11 have a 50 percent prevalence or greater in both small and large companies.

Chart 22-11. Typical Perquisites in Small and Large Companies (Senior Executives)

Perquisite	Frequency of Use: Small Company	Frequency of Use: Large Company
Cellular phones	75%	80%
Company car	65%	50%
Country/luncheon club	80%	90%
Financial planning	90%	80%
First-class air	75%	80%
Severance contract	50%	65%
Supplemental retirement	65%	75%

Q 22:13 How are supplemental retirement plans typically structured in small and large companies?

The tax-qualified 401(k) retirement plan (a defined contribution plan) is used by almost all small companies. These may or may not have a company match. Supplemental retirement plans (SERPs) for executives in these companies are therefore in the form of supplemental 401(k)-type plans. Such plans typically do more than just make up for any lost company contribution and/or any maximum executive contribution (for 1999, $10,000 may be deferred on a pretax basis under a 401(k) plan, subject to certain limits imposed by nondiscrimination testing rules) now $10,000 per year. Executives may contribute unlimited amounts to the SERP.

A new trend in SERP plan design is to make the company contribution dependent upon the company meeting some performance criteria. The threshold performance measures in the annual incentive plan serve as one example. This is particularly prevalent in small companies where the board compensation committees are not willing to make long-term commitments to SERP contributions when the future profitability of the company is still an unknown.

The fund investment alternatives in the supplemental 401(k) plan may be more sophisticated than in the regular 401(k). These supplemental plans are nonqualified, so there are no ongoing government reporting and discrimination tests or other ERISA requirements (as long as the plan is a "top hat" plan). In addition, the compensation level of the executives in these plans is high and these individuals normally have a lot more experience with investments. More aggressive investments are included in these supplemental retirement plans.

Large companies typically have either a 401(k) retirement plan or a defined benefit retirement plan. The supplemental 401(k)-type plans in these businesses are structured similarly to those in small companies. The SERPs for companies that use defined benefit retirement plans are normally fixed benefit plans. For example, a large company might have a fixed supplemental retirement plan benefit of 60 percent of final average pay, minus retirement benefits from the company's qualified plan and social security, provided the executive retires with company consent at age 60 or higher and has 20 years of service. There is a trend to lowering the service requirement to less than 20 years or to having a liberal early retirement provision, such as no reduction of benefit if after age 55 and again with company consent. Investment alternatives for the defined benefit plans are, like those for the supplemental 401(k)-type plans, more sophisticated and more aggressive.

Q 22:14   How are benefits different in small versus large companies?

Medical, life, and disability benefits are quite similar in both small and large companies. There are only minor differences in the design features of each.

Medical plans in the small companies are often placed by insurance representatives rather than experienced human resource executives. Many small companies do not have benefit managers or analysts on their staffs. As a result, their medical plans are not monitored closely and costs per employee are higher. In addition, many small companies do not have Internal Revenue Code Section 125 flexible spending accounts plans that allow for pretax dollars to be used to pay medical costs not covered by the company's regular insured plan. These factors encourage a number of small company chief executive officers to have supplemental benefit plans in greater numbers than are found in large companies. While the frequency of these supplemental medical plans is decreasing because of the increased use of managed care networks, they are still quite common in small companies.

Supplemental life insurance and disability insurance are generally higher in large companies. In the case of supplemental life insurance, the amount of life insurance available is greater and the cost less in the large company simply because of the leverage of large numbers. For example, a small company might have supplemental life insurance of an additional two to three times base salary, while a large company would have two to five times base salary.

Disability insurance in a small entrepreneurial company is often not used because the owner or chief executive officer appropriately believes that he or she does not need it given significant stock ownership and net worth. In larger companies this is not the case.

Chapter 23

Executive Compensation Practices During a Restructuring

Compensation and benefit planners face a number of special issues during any type of corporate restructuring. This chapter will identify those issues and provide answers to many of the unique questions that have direct impact on the success of the restructuring. Numerous examples demonstrate the practical application of the answers suggested in the text.

Overview 23-1
Base Salary 23-12
Short-term Incentives 23-15
Long-term Incentives 23-20
Benefits and Perquisites 23-25

Overview

Q 23:1   What is a restructuring?

The term *restructuring* includes mergers, acquisitions, divestitures, recapitalizations, leveraged buyouts, reorganizations, downsizings, and other types of restructuring of a corporation. During the 1980s, the value (i.e., prices paid or revenue impact) of these activities in corporate America was over $300 billion. Leveraged buyouts alone were over $80 billion. In a five-year period in the 1990s this value was equaled.

Q 23:2 What are some examples of companies that have undergone restructurings?

In some cases there have been mergers or acquisitions between companies in similar industries, such as Nabisco, Inc. and RJR Tobacco, two consumer product companies. There are numerous examples of similar industry mergers in banking and finance institutions and oil and gas companies. Mergers have also occurred between dissimilar companies such as DuPont and Conoco, a chemical/consumer product company and an oil company. With respect to other types of restructuring that normally occurred within a company, the industry has been varied. Examples include leveraged buyouts, reorganizations, recapitalizations, and downsizings.

Whatever the form of the restructuring, a number of changes are likely to be encountered, such as new management styles and company cultures, decision-making processes, and even changes in the products and services provided.

For example, when Nabisco merged with RJR Tobacco, the culture of the new company went from risk-adverse to risk-oriented. The change had substantial impact on executive compensation programs and particularly on the mix of base salary to incentive pay. In the new risk-oriented company, there was much greater compensation at risk in incentive plans than there was prior to the merger.

At the same time, company products changed as many low-profit product lines were discontinued and new brand extensions were quickly introduced. Decision-making at company meetings was more streamlined with less analytical activity.

There are numerous other examples of company restructurings during the 1990s in which company cultures went from an autocratic management style where managers determined and directed work to a management style where managers were work facilitators who used quality circles and profit improvement committees. All of these cultural changes have a direct impact on executive compensation programs.

These changes are to be expected whether a restructuring occurs overnight or occurs gradually as a company grows and moves from a single-product/service focus to a multi-product focus. Restructurings require a rethinking of policies and practices used in the executive compensation programs of the organization.

Q 23:3   What issues must be considered when reviewing executive pay strategy during a restructuring?

While there are countless situations that may arise from a restructuring, there are certain key considerations for any individual reviewing executive pay and benefits strategies in a restructured organization. The following topics form a kind of checklist that may be used to identify those critical executive compensation and benefits issues and to develop alternative solutions to the problems.

Define the company's revised benefits and compensation philosophy. When two organizations come together, or when one company redefines itself, the resulting strategic changes in the company's executive benefits and compensation philosophy must be identified. The top human resource officer, the top financial officer, and the chief executive officer usually handle this process. In accomplishing such a task, it is important to look at revised business objectives in the company to see where executive pay plans can be used to support the new objectives. The retention of key executives is often a primary objective and executive pay is a crucial tool for meeting the objective.

A company's executive compensation philosophy includes a strategic mix of executive elements. These elements include salary, annual incentives, long-term incentives, benefits and/or perquisites, pay opportunities compared with those offered by competitors, performance-based elements, executive stock ownership, and communication.

Compare compensation and benefit levels. The need is clear for a redefinition of the competitive labor market that the company finds relevant, i.e., where will we hire executives from, and where will our executives go if they leave us? Perquisites should also be included in this comparison. With this information plus a sense of the company's new pay philosophy it is possible to develop an integration strategy.

Develop an integration strategy. This is simply how a company accomplishes the goals it sets out for itself. A revised executive pay strategy statement will identify what current programs are to be retained and where new programs need to be designed and/or implemented. A plan needs to be established on how to make the conversion and it must identify areas that require new administrative procedures. It is essential to make these determinations in advance of implementing the pay strategy changes so that cost implications of this part of the restructuring can be identified.

Address change of control. Internal Revenue Code Section 280G addresses the loss of deduction for excess parachute payments (and corresponding Code Section 4999 imposes a penalty tax on the recipient of the parachute payment equal to 20 percent of the excess parachute amount). In the early stages of a restructuring involving outside purchase of all or part of a company, it is important to identify any existing change of control provisions and determine whether any parachute payments have or will be made. Parachute payments are defined as those payments triggered by a change of control of the company. If such payments are in excess of 2.99 times the executive's average W-2 compensation during the five years preceding the change of control, a 20 percent excise tax is due from the executive in addition to any regular ordinary income tax.

If parachute payments are a factor in the restructuring, it is a good idea to prepare "best case" and "worst case" worksheets to determine what the cost will be and whether the "golden parachute" excise tax applies. The best case scenario would be if most of the payments triggered by the change of control were exempt from the calculation, and a worst case would mean that all the payments would be included as payments triggered by the change of control. For example, vested stock options may or may not be included in the calculation of the parachute payments.

Another concern regarding change of control is that parachute payments could motivate key executives to leave the company. If so, the company might want to take some action to encourage those executives to stay.

Prepare a statement to executives on future compensation and benefit plans. This is another crucial step at the beginning of the restructuring. Executives become concerned about the future and it is often prudent to send out a company statement or weekly statements that give current information on the process of the restructuring. Some companies have stated that no reductions in salary, annual incentive plan targets, or executive benefits will occur for one year after the change of control. Another company practice has been to communicate the terms of the enhanced severance or early retirement programs provided executives stay until the restructuring is completed.

Amend current compensation and/or benefit plans. While this information is normally covered in each of the plan texts, if it is not, ensure that the board compensation committee (or the board, if necessary) approves changes in the plan to allow for special restructuring actions with respect to the executive pay plans.

Develop and implement new plans. Significant lead time is required to plan the design and implementation phases of new programs and to ensure that all new features reflect changing priorities in the business plan. Many organizations look for assistance outside the company in structuring revised executive compensation and benefits programs that will influence executive behavior at a critical time for the company, and that will assist in meeting new business objectives.

Determine administrative support systems needed in new plans. As part of the post-restructuring planning process, it is important to determine how administrative support systems need to be modified or what new systems will need to be developed for the revised executive compensation and benefit programs. In particular, the area of computerized support should be considered. The revised programs also will need new communication programs for executives. It is important to let executives know when the communications will occur so that the "grapevine" does not create false expectations prior to that time.

Identify critical positions. Another important aspect of the process is to quickly identify which positions and executives must be retained during the restructuring and after the restructuring if the company is to remain successful. Those executives should quickly be made eligible for new compensation and/or executive benefit plans, or be provided with special contracts, payments, or stock grants, if appropriate, to encourage them to remain with the organization.

Manage issues with a task force. No matter how well-prepared an organization is, critical issues will arise unexpectedly. Finding the best way to solve those issues requires the input of many knowledgeable people in the organization. The formation of a task force of financial experts, human resource professionals, and line executives is a good way to ensure that all dimensions of an problem are taken into consideration when solutions are developed and implemented.

Q 23:4   What issues are unique to a restructuring involving an acquisition?

The issues arising from an acquisition depend on the circumstances of the acquisition, for example, whether the acquisition was "friendly" and the compatibility of the two existing executive compensation strategies.

Example. Company T acquires Company U in a friendly acquisition. The resulting issues are handled in the following manner:

Issue	*Action*
Philosophy and strategy	No change. Both companies have similar cultures, pay strategies, and executive pay strategies.
Pay levels	No issues. Company U's practices are similar to Company T's salary ranges, targeted amounts of annual incentive, etc.
Integration strategy	Company T's plans are adopted per the acquisition agreement with the exception of Company U's supplemental retirement plan, which was adopted by Company T because it represented an improvement over current practice.

Change of control	Not applicable. This was a friendly acquisition. No downsizing or job redundancies existed.
Statement of future compensation and benefits	The acquisition agreement stated that no changes in executive pay would occur for 12 months after the closing date and that any changes would be "no less favorable" than current levels.
Amendment to current plans	Company U's executives received slightly higher life insurance.
Develop new plans	None required.
Administrative support systems	Due to increases in Company T's long-term incentive plan (from Company U), a new participant reporting system was purchased for the stock option plan.
Critical positions	Not an issue because of the friendly acquisition.
Managing issues with a task force	A task force of executives from Company T and Company U reviewed all issues.

Q 23:5 What issues are unique to a restructuring involving a merger?

The issues arising from a merger depend on the specific circumstances of the merger and the makeup of the two companies involved. If the two companies have widely varied cultures and compensation plans, the executives are likely to have different expectations with respect to compensation and benefits plans. The differences must be handled in such a way as to retain key executives from both companies and to meet the objectives of the newly restructured company.

Example. Company V merges with Company W. The two companies have significantly different cultures and compensation strategies. The resulting issues are handled in the following manner:

Issue	*Action*
Philosophy and strategy	Because Company V and Company W have different cultures and compensation strategies, the companies choose to decentralize the handling of the strategy issues. The first step is to select corporate officers for the new company. Those not selected are asked to stay and assist with the restructuring until new positions or special severance packages are established for them. The corporate human resource department provides three alternative pay strategies that cover salary and annual incentive plans, and each business unit is asked to choose from the three alternatives. The compensation plans of top executives are determined by the chief executive officer. The corporate human resources department determines all long-term incentive plans.
Pay levels	Again, there are significant differences between the two companies. The three alternative compensation strategies from which the heads of business units must choose include choices on pay levels, salary ranges, targeted amounts of annual incentive, etc.
Integration strategy	Each business unit in the new company forms a task force to select from the choices set out by the corporate human resources department and to identify job redundancies.

Change of control	A double trigger change of control is in effect at the time of the merger. There are numerous job redundancies and downsizing is planned. Part of the merger agreement includes an enhanced severance and early-out retirement plan. A parachute payment worksheet with instructions is prepared by legal professionals.
Statement of future compensation & benefits	The acquisition agreement states that future executive pay levels and benefits will be "no less favorable" than current levels. A weekly report is sent to all executives on progress to date on all issues.
Amendment to current plans	All qualified plans must be amended. The amendment process is handled by employee benefits legal counsel. Significant swings in both companies' stock prices creates the need to amend stock option plans so adjustments or supplemental grants can be made.
Develop new plans	In addition to the new pay strategies, a new long-term incentive plan must be developed. Corporate human resources handles this task as well. In addition, a revised supplemental retirement plan must be designed. The companies' current programs are completely different. A task force is formed to design the new supplement retirement plan.
Administrative support systems	Due to increases in the new merged company's long-term incentive plan, and due to the new annual incentive and salary range alternatives developed by corporate human resources, a new participant reporting system is required and a special task force is formed to handle this part of the process.

Critical positions	The new chief executive officer made restricted stock grants to numerous key executives to encourage them to stay with the company during the difficult transition months.
Using task forces	Numerous task forces of executives are used to review all compensation issues resulting from the merger. Inevitably, productivity goes down significantly until all issues are resolved satisfactorily.

This example and the example in Q 23:4 illustrate that restructurings may take place with little difficulty or they may be very complicated, depending on the nature of the restructuring and the process instituted for handling the resulting issues. In any case, identifying potential problems is the first step.

Q 23:6 How are levels of compensation established for executives in separate business units or departments within a restructured company?

Potential compensation, including such programs as incentive plans and stock options plans, as well as base salaries, must be set at equitable levels for executives performing similar functions to avoid inequities and, as a result, the loss of key executives. However, business factors such as industry differences, location, business function, and profitability may make some kinds of inequities acceptable.

Example 1. Company A mergers with Company B and one of these organizations has a pay strategy that establishes pay levels at the 50th percentile while the other sets pay levels at the 75th percentile. If the two companies are in the same industry, this will definitely lead to inequities and problems. If the two companies are not in the same industry, there may be a reason to retain the separate practices, particularly if the two companies are following their own industry pay levels.

Example 2. Company C goes through a culture change in which executives are expected to behave differently and focus more on risk-oriented business goals. The company must determine whether current pay potential should remain the same or differ to recognize the greater risk in their jobs. In most cases, the pay potential in the annual incentive plan will increase and base salary will remain the same.

Q 23:7 If the company requires executives to be transferable between business units or departments, how is the executive compensation strategy affected?

If a company wants to transfer or relocate executives between business units or departments after the restructuring, different executive compensation programs could be a deterrent to the transfer. Common executive compensation plans among the businesses or departments could support this business objective.

Q 23:8 How should supplemental benefits and perquisites be handled in a restructuring?

Although supplemental benefits and perquisites may seem like a less important concern, in some cases, they can be important for the smooth execution of the restructuring. Particularly in a merger or acquisition, if executives feel that they are losing something in the restructuring, they may be motivated to leave the company or may not perform their duties to their best ability.

Example. Company A merges with Company B. Company A's executives fly first class or business class on company business. Company B's executives fly coach. There is no compromise available on this issue. The company will have to choose and specify one policy for use in the future.

The same is true for supplement benefits like life insurance and retirement. If both merged companies have accrued liabilities for supplemental retirement, there is an additional question of how these funds are now invested and how they will be invested in the future. The same is true with respect to funds in the qualified retirement plans. Although these plans apply to a small number of executives, analysis of the potential value in each is most important. Unfortunately, these kinds of issues are rarely considered prior to the restructuring.

Base Salary

Q 23:9 How should executive positions be classified for base salary purposes following a restructuring?

In most environments, executive positions will be evaluated with a common methodology, the dominant one being direct market pricing. The one exception is the very large multi-billion dollar public company that might have hundreds of executive jobs, and a point scoring job evaluation program might be necessary. A common methodology insures that all executive jobs are valued in the same way, using the same job accountability or description form as the source of job responsibilities.

Large companies that have many executive jobs in multi-business units may centralize the classification of senior executive jobs, but then decentralize the classification of other executive jobs. In this case, job evaluation guidelines, benchmark positions, competitive survey selection, and training on the process are required to ensure equitable administration.

> **Example.** Company A and Company B merge. Senior executive positions are evaluated in the corporate human resources department using a direct market pricing process. The evaluation of all other executive positions in various divisions is decentralized. The corporate human resources department provides each division with a list of benchmark executive positions that have already been evaluated, and a manual that identifies the surveys to be used and the procedures for evaluating all other positions. The corporate human resources department conducts cross-company executive job evaluation reviews. It prepares a matrix as shown in Chart 23-1 that lists the company salary ranges on the vertical axis and each company division on the horizontal axis. All job titles are then shown inside the matrix. Job evaluation results can be compared, audited, and cross-checked by using this technique. The company also uses an outside consultant, with whom the company reviews

all evaluations annually, after providing all information on company job responsibilities and the results of the company job evaluations.

Chart 23-1. Job Evaluation Matrix

Job Grade	Salary Range Midpoint	Division #1	Division #2	Division #3	Corporate
10	$300,000				CEO
09	$250,000				
08	$200,000	SVP & Gen. Mgr.			SVP Finance SVP Marketing
07	$170,000		SVP & Gen. Mgr.	SVP & Gen. Mgr.	
06	$140,000	VP Marketing			SVP Legal SVP R&D
05	$125,000		VP Marketing	VP Marketing	
04	$112,500	VP Finance VP Operations			SVP HR SVP MIS SVP & Treasurer SVP & Controller
03	$ 92,500		VP Operations VP Finance	VP Operations VP Finance	
02	$ 78,000	VP Distribution			
01	$ 65,000		VP R&D	VP MIS	

The senior vice president positions in Chart 23-1 could all be evaluated by the corporate human resource department, while each of the vice president positions could be evaluated by the organizational unit to which they report.

The matrix provides the opportunity to compare key executive jobs that are in the same business function, e.g., vice president of Finance in Division A and Division B. It also allows for a comparison between key executive jobs that are unique to any given division, such as the vice president of Research and Development in Division B and the vice president of Management Information Services in Division C. The Division B position might reflect the fact that while research and product development are the primary drivers of business success, management information services in Division C is one of the primary drivers of business.

Q 23:10 Should salary ranges be dictated by industry practices, location, or job responsibilities?

This strategy issue can have impact on overall employee relations in executive positions. For example, what if two similar jobs in two different divisions located in the same city have different salaries? One job might be a vice president of sales of a pharmaceutical company in Denver, Colorado, with a scope of accountability that reaches $200 million, while the other might also be a vice president of sales in Denver, Colorado, for a food company with a scope of accountability of $200 million. If one is paid $100,000 salary and the other $125,000, there will likely be an employee relations issue. However, it is possible that the executive at $100,000 has an annual bonus potential of 50 percent, or $50,000, while the executive at $125,000 has a bonus potential of 20 percent, or $25,000, giving both position the similar total cash compensation *potential.* This would be equitable and would simply reflect different pay strategies in each division.

As shown in Chart 23-1, a common salary range tends to put all positions on an equal basis and is very useful in environments in which executive talent must be transferable between divisions.

Q 23:11 Should salary administration practices be the same or different after a corporate restructuring?

Salary increases and administration policies in most companies are integrated with performance evaluation programs. Therefore, restructured companies must decide whether to utilize one common performance evaluation process and one salary administration process or different ones. In autonomous business units or divisions, it is not normally necessary to have common practices in this area. However, in similar business units or divisions, common practices are necessary for equitable base salary administration.

> **Example.** Company C has gone through an internal restructuring and has decentralized many business functions. It has also changed its culture to one that is more risk-oriented. One of the new profit centers decides to change its salary increase program to provide higher salary increases. After two years, the profit center has higher salary levels in its executive positions compared to similar positions in other profit centers, and its life insurance, disability insurance, annual bonuses (which are calculated on the basis of base salary), qualified and nonqualified company contributions to retirement programs, and long-term stock options (which are also calculated on the basis of base salary) are all higher. Major employee relations inequities have been created.

As shown in this example, the consequences of these policy issues during a restructuring can be significant.

Short-term Incentives

Q 23:12 Should eligibility for annual incentives be affected by a restructuring?

The effect of a restructuring on annual incentives depends on the company's pay strategy, specifically the mix of total cash compensation (salary plus annual incentive). Within merged companies, the size, culture, and business processes can vary between departments or business units, thus supporting different eligibility levels. Typically, however, the same criteria are used throughout the organization, such as salary or salary grade, reporting relationship, title, and profit impact. During an internal restructuring such as a reorganization, different eligibility levels are utilized by a company to emphasize a change in executive focus, behavior, or job methodology.

Q 23:13   Should short-term incentive plans be the same between company businesses or should they be designed to support different business unit objectives?

Short-term incentives are the most useful tool of all executive compensation elements for motivating executives. The issue here is whether compensation strategies should vary according to business units' objectives, or should all short-term incentive plans be the same?

> **Example.** Company A merges with Company B. Company A is a mature company that has a short-term incentive plan that is performance-based. It uses company and individual goals as the basis of annual incentive payments. The targeted level of incentive is at the median competitive level. Company B is a high growth company that uses profit sharing as the basis for each year's annual incentive, and then individual awards are determined on a discretionary basis, recognizing the way in which each executive responded to unforeseen events during the year. The targeted level of incentive is at the 75th percentile of competitive practice. Since these practices are very different, the company's pay strategy may need to be redefined. If the companies are in different industries, there may be a basis for retaining different practices. If they are in the same industry, a review of total cash compensation (salary plus annual incentive) will need to be conducted to see if a compromise can be made between the strategies or one company's current practices should be adopted by the other company.

Q 23:14   After a restructuring, how are potential award levels determined for annual incentives?

The risk/reward strategy determines potential award levels in annual incentive plans. As a major element in motivating executives, short-term incentives offer a significant opportunity to match executive skill and effort with company need. The greater the contingent remuneration (pay based on achievement of performance goals), the greater the executive motivation will be. This theory is valid, but only if an organization has the capability to set performance goals. In addition to target goals, there also must be a capability to set threshold goals and maximum goals. A threshold goal is the minimum acceptable level of performance on any goal that will qualify for an incentive payment. A target goal is the expected level of executive performance on any given goal. A maximum goal is the maximum level of performance on any given goal. Performance above this point is presumed to be a result of factors beyond the executive's control, such as acts of God or competitors going out of business.

If a company can establish goals for each of these levels, then a performance-based plan can be the basis for annual incentive payments after a restructuring. Otherwise, a discretionary plan or some kind of profit sharing or single formula plan can be used to drive annual incentive awards.

Q 23:15 What performance measures are used by restructured companies?

Restructured companies use the same kinds of performance measures that are used by all other companies. The difference is that, following a restructuring, the performance measures may need to be structured differently.

Example. Company C goes through an internal reorganization to improve efficiency and increase executive motivation to take risk. Company C also acquires another company. The performance goals in its annual incentive plan are changed to reflect these two business conditions as shown below:

Annual Incentive Goals Before Reorganization and Acquisition	Annual Incentive Goals After Reorganization and Acquisition
1. Net earnings	1. Cash flow from operations
2. Return on capital	2. New product development

The focus of Company C's goals changed from earnings to cash flow to pay off the debt from the acquisition. In addition, a change was made from return on capital to new product development goals to emphasize the importance of getting new product ideas into the market. Both of these goal changes are a direct result of the restructuring and the new business issues that it created.

The same situation will typically occur after an external restructuring as well.

Example. Company A and Company B merge. They both have annual incentive plans based on business goals. In the new company, goals are used in the annual incentive plan to emphasize the need to integrate the new businesses.

Company A

Annual Incentive Goals Before Reorganization and Acquisition	*Annual Incentive Goals After Reorganization and Acquisition*
1. Net earnings	1. Cash flow from operations
2. Quality	2. Organization consolidation
	3. Quality

Company B

Annual Incentive Goals Before Reorganization and Acquisition	*Annual Incentive Goals After Reorganization and Acquisition*
1. Net earnings	1. Cash flow from operations
2. Quality	2. Organization consolidation
	3. Quality

In this case, both companies added a nonfinancial goal to emphasize the importance of executive effort in solving organization consolidations required by the merger. Cash flow was substituted for net income, as was the case in the previous example, to emphasize its importance after the merger in paying off debt. Quality continued to be a major business goal. The order of importance of the annual incentive goals was also changed following the merger.

Q 23:16   If different goals are used among business units after a restructuring, how can a company achieve equity in the annual incentive program?

Creating a fair incentive program is always a challenge even when there is no restructuring. The principle of "equal stretch" must be achieved, that is, the degree of difficulty in achieving goals must be the same between departments or business units. For example, if

Division A has a cash flow goal of $1.1 million (a 10 percent increase) and Division B has a cash flow goal of $2.2 million (a 10 percent increase), the goal is the same even though the dollar amounts are different because Division B is twice the size of Division A. At the same time, goal equality may also result in Division A having a cash flow goal of $1.5 million (a 50 percent increase because a new product is being introduced in that division that year), and Division B having a cash flow goal of $2 million, the same as last year, because it will be taking $300,000 in earnings charges to fund new product development activities that year.

Goal equality should be achieved by reviewing the specific conditions in each organization to determine targeted or expected performance and then threshold and maximum performance levels. Many companies will set goals for an incentive plan year in the previous October if they use a calendar fiscal year. Then a goal update will be done in April of the plan year to ensure that goal equality and the targeted goal levels are still equitable in light of any changes in the company's performance.

Q 23:17   Is it possible for one business unit to have a performance target plan and another business unit to have a discretionary plan?

Yes, this occurs when business units are in completely different stages of business maturity. For example, a new division with new products that are just being developed and introduced may not allow for accurate planning and, therefore, a performance target plan may not be feasible. Another division may be a mature business that has had stable growth for 50 years and very accurate planning systems. In these environments, the new division may use a discretionary plan so that it can look back on what occurred and grant annual incentive payments to its executives that reflect their performance during the year and that take into account how they responded to new business challenges. The mature division may use a typical goal-oriented performance plan that includes goals from the annual business plan.

Q 23:18   Who should approve annual incentive payments in a restructured company?

This is a simple but potentially volatile compensation strategy issue in a restructured company. Approval authority must be determined in accord with the management style of the organization. Someone must approve all plan design, plan interpretations, eligibility, goals, actual achievement of performance goals, awards levels, and plan payments and administration. Many companies that have gone through an external restructuring will have plan design, goal setting, goal assessments, and approval of incentive funds done at the corporate level, and have individual awards approved by the top officer in the business unit or department. Decentralized businesses often follow the same strategy.

Other organizations will delegate all of these decisions to the individual business unit, and let them set their own plan design and cash compensation levels. This will work well if the business units are autonomous and do not have any interchangeability of executive talent and little intercompany business interactions.

Long-term Incentives

Q 23:19   How are long-term incentive plans affected by a restructuring?

The most important decision concerning long-term incentive plans following a restructuring is whether to use a different plan type for each business unit. Different types of plans would only be an option if the company has business units that are autonomous or in completely different cycles of maturity.

In any company, the type of long-term incentive plan is based on the company's long-term objectives, which must be supported or reinforced by the long-term incentive plan. Some companies believe that shareholder value is the most important long-term business objective. In such companies, either economic profit plans (see chapter 19) are used, or some form of stock award is granted, such as stock options, restricted stock, or performance shares.

Other companies believe that long-term business performance measures such as return on equity, return on capital, and earnings per share should be the basis for long-term incentives. In these cases a performance-based plan is used, for example, cash performance target, performance unit, or book value. With this type of plan, because the executive group directly influences the performance goal, the plan is not subject to the vagaries of the stock market.

A useful analysis is to construct a matrix with long-term incentive plan types on the vertical axis and company (or executive) objectives on the horizontal axis. In the center of the matrix is a comment on the degree to which a plan type supports the stated company objective.

As shown in Chart 23-2, if a company places high priority on executive retention and executive stock ownership, a restricted stock award plan would be the logical choice. If a company wants the plan to be based on performance, a type of performance-based plan is the obvious choice. If a company wants a long-term plan to contribute to executive retention and to require the executive to invest in the company, a combination of restricted stock and stock options would be a natural combination.

Chart 23-2. Selecting a Long-term Incentive Plan

	Business Objectives			
Plan Type	Executive Retention #1	Executive Invest Own Money #2	Performance-Based #3	Stock Ownership #4
A. Stock Option	Medium	High	Medium	Medium
B. Restricted Stock	High	Low	Medium	High
C. Performance Plan	Medium	Low	High	Medium
D. Book Value Purchase	Medium	High	High	Low

Q 23:20 Should long-term incentive plans be the same between business units or departments?

Incentive plans should always support the long-term goals of the business. If a merger or acquisition has occurred, one of the companies probably has converted its stock, creating the need to review the company's long-term business goals to see how the long-term incentive plan should change. The same is true in an internal restructuring such as a reorganization in which the type of long-term incentive can be a major issue.

Example. Company C goes through a culture change in which executives are expected to behave differently and focus more on risk-oriented business goals. However, a number of current executives were involuntarily terminated as organizational structures changed. Current executives are concerned about the same action occurring again in the future. If the company's long-term incentive plan includes stock options or performance shares, it would probably consider restricted stock, since it has a business objective of retaining the remaining executives and restricted stock has the best retention capability of any long-term incentive.

Q 23:21   How do restructured companies determine the size of long-term incentive awards?

To answer this question, a company must begin with competitive analysis. For stock options, an *option value* can be identified for each executive position (option value equals stock price times number of shares). Option value is typically expressed as a percentage of base salary. For executives at a base salary of $250,000, for example, an option value might range from 75 percent to 125 percent, or $187,500 to $312,500. If a company stock price were $25 per share, at an option value of $250,000, the competitive number of shares is 10,000 ($250,000 ÷ $25 = 10,000).

Companies also use option pricing models to determine the number of shares. Black Scholes is the most popular model. Black Scholes looks at a number of variables, such as award term, interest rates, stock volatility, and dividends, and provides an estimate of the real value of company stock today based on future appreciation. Black Scholes values normally are 30 percent to 40 percent of the grant price.

Example. A company grants stock at $30 per share and the Black Scholes value is 30 percent. The expected value of the option is $9 ($30 × 30% = $9).

To determine the number of shares using a Black Scholes value, a company must also determine, through its executive pay strategy, the targeted value that the executive should receive from the grant. Assuming that this is $90,000 for a given executive position, $90,000 divided by the $9 actual value expected to be provided by each share equals 10,000 shares as the grant size ($90,000 ÷ $9 = 10,000).

With respect to performance plans or restricted stock grants, the targeted value that the executive should receive from a long-term award, determined from the company's executive pay strategy, is the basis for the grant size or target award.

Example. Company D intends for a given executive position to earn $90,000 from a long-term incentive plan, and therefore, the targeted value of a performance plan grant would be $90,000. With respect to restricted stock, the value at grant would be $90,000. In Company D, 3,000 shares are awarded at a stock price of $30 per share to equal a grant of $90,000 (3,000 × $30 = $90,000).

These analyses are typically done over a three- to five-year period, and then converted to an annual program for purposes of making annual grants. If, for example, a company wanted to provide $450,000 to a given executive position over a five-year period, the value of each long-term incentive grant would be $90,000.

Example. Company S chooses restricted stock and stock options as the two types of long-term incentives that will best support its long-term objectives. Company S conducts a competitive analysis and determines a total pay strategy for company vice president positions as follows:

Position	Targeted Base Salary	Targeted Annual Incentive	Targeted Annual Long-term Incentive
Vice President	$250,000	$125,000	$150,000

The company further uses the Black Scholes model and the result of the calculation is that the current company stock price of $30 has a current value of $10. The total pay strategy is $150,000 per year. If the company wants to provide 50 percent of this in restricted stock and 50 percent in stock options, the awards are as follows:

Restricted stock: 2,500 shares ($150,000 × 50% ÷ $30 = 2,500)

Stock options: 7,500 shares ($150,000 × 50% ÷ $10 = 7,500)

Q 23:22   Is the number of shares used in executive long-term plans, as a percentage of the total shares outstanding, greater in a restructured company?

Yes. In particular when there is an internal restructuring, stock price is often down and this is an excellent time to grant long-term stock awards. Moreover, the executives in such an organization often are concerned especially if there has been a downsizing, and many companies in this situation use restricted stock to retain key executives.

With respect to an external restructuring such as a merger or acquisition, some executives may recently have had some kind of stock buyout and a replacement plan is needed for them. Executives who did not have a buyout of their current stock may expect the newly restructured company to recognize their contributions to the restructuring. This requires a long-term grant for them as well.

Large human resources consulting firms survey this subject continuously, and their surveys show that restructured companies typically use 15 percent to 20 percent of the total shares outstanding for executive pay plans. In comparison, nonrestructured companies use 10 percent to 15 percent.

Q 23:23   Does a restructuring prompt changes in award frequency and terms in long-term incentive plans?

The frequency and terms of awards within existing long-term incentive plans do not normally change. However, if the restructuring results in new plan types, the award terms of the new plan will be different. Typically, there will be an extra grant of some type of long-term incentive as a result of the restructuring. For example, following a restructuring a company may offer a one-time stock option grant to all executives or a special restricted stock to all executives.

Benefits and Perquisites

Q 23:24   How do executive benefits and perquisites change during a restructuring?

During internal restructurings and restructurings such as acquisitions, divestitures, and recapitalizations, executive benefits or perquisites rarely change. However, mergers and leveraged buyouts often trigger many changes in benefits and perquisites.

For example, if one company in a merger provides executives with company cars and the other does not, this issue must be resolved in the restructured company. It may be that the two resulting businesses are very different and very autonomous. However, in most cases, any inequity in executive benefits and perquisites must be quickly reviewed and resolved. An emerging trend in this area is flexible perquisites. Similar to a flexible benefits program, this approach allows executives to select their own perquisites within certain financial parameters.

> **Example.** Company A merges with Company B. Company A provides executives with company cars, first-class air travel, computers, financial planning, cellular phones, company-paid attendance at sporting and cultural events, and supplemental life insurance. Company B provides its executives with financial planning and company-paid attendance at sporting and cultural events if executives are entertaining customers. Both companies have a nonqualified supplemental 401(k) plan for executives, but they have different rates of company contributions to the plans. The total annual cost per executive for perquisites in Company A is $20,000; at Company B it is $6,500.

To resolve the disparity, the merged company allows first-class air travel for all executives and it merges the two supplemental retirement plans into one plan with a common company contribution. It also adds a flexible executive perquisite program that allows an executive an annual account of $15,000 to use on perquisites and selection of the supplemental perquisites of his or her choice. Each of the supplemental perquisites is valued as follows:

Cellular phone	$250
Company car	$7,500
Company-paid attendance at sporting and cultural events	$2,500
Financial planning	$5,000
Laptop computer	$2,500
Supplemental disability insurance	$500
Supplemental life insurance	$250

Q 23:25 Does eligibility for executive benefits and/or perquisites change during a restructuring?

A merger is typically the only type of restructuring that prompts a change in eligibility, because the two merging companies often have different types of programs. The two companies' plans must be merged in a way that is fair and equitable to all executives.

Companies use one of the following three strategies to resolve the disparity:

1. *Each business unit sets its own eligibility standards.* Executive pay and benefits under this approach are the responsibility of the head of the business unit. The corporate office, however, would establish the executive pay and benefits of the head of the unit.

2. *A corporate organization, such as human resources, sets all policy and practice guidelines.* This approach allows for centralized control and administration.

3. *The two strategies in numbers 1 and 2 above are combined.* The combination involves designating some policies like eligibility to the business unit, with benefit levels established by the corporate organization. This concept of split accountability is an effective way for all of the company's organizational entities to take ownership of successful program policy and practice.

No single approach is right for all companies. The key is to find the strategy for this policy issue and all policy issues based on the needs of the individual company. Understanding the organization's decision-making processes, general personnel practices and precedents, human resource climate, and specific corporate and business unit objectives is critical. Knowledge of the organization plus a knowledge of the issues and their potential solutions enables the compensation and benefits executive to successfully develop and implement strategies that support the restructured company.

Q 23:26   What perquisites are most commonly added or improved during a restructuring?

The most commonly added or improved perquisites in a restructured company are executive severance and early retirement opportunities. The business need for enhanced retirement during an "early out" or "window" period can be high, especially if there is an overlap of executive talent. A typical enhancement is to provide a nonreduced early retirement if executives meet a given age requirement, such as age 55, or required age plus years of service, such as 75 (age 55 + 20 years of service).

For executives who are not eligible for early retirement, a restructured company will most often offer severance packages. Severance packages are usually structured as follows:

- Salary continuation for at least six months, but sometimes as long as two years.
- Company pays executive's COBRA premiums for six months.
- Access to an outplacement firm to assist in finding a new position.

These elements of severance pay are not always part of the company's ongoing program, but they can be added as a special one-time enhancement with no commitment to continue in the future.

Appendix A

IRS Model Rabbi Trust Arrangement

Revenue Procedure 92-64 [1992-2 CB 422] provides the following model rabbi trust investment for plan sponsors to use. Using this model agreement, or parts of it, may reduce the number of occasions when the plan sponsor finds it necessary to seek private letter rulings from the Internal Revenue Service.

Rev Proc 92-64, 1992-2 CB 422.—"Rabbi trust" arrangements

——Section 1. Purpose

This revenue procedure contains a model grantor trust for use in executive compensation arrangements that are popularly referred to as "rabbi trust" arrangements. This revenue procedure also provides guidance for requesting rulings on nonqualified deferred compensation plans that use such trusts.

——Section 2. Background

The Internal Revenue Service receives and responds to many requests for rulings on the federal income tax consequences of trusts established in connection with unfunded deferred compensation arrangements. In many of these requests, the trust instruments are very similar. Consequently, in order to aid taxpayers and to expedite the processing of ruling requests on these arrangements, this revenue procedure provides a model trust instrument that plan sponsors may use.

——Section 3. Scope and Objective

The model trust provided in this revenue procedure is intended to serve as a safe harbor for taxpayers that adopt and maintain grantor trusts in connection with unfunded deferred compensation arrangements. If the model trust is used in accordance with this revenue procedure, an employee will not be in constructive receipt of income or incur an economic benefit solely on account of the adaptation or maintenance of the trust. However, the desired tax effect will be achieved only if the nonqualified deferred compensation arrangement effectively defers compensation. Thus, no inference may be drawn by reason of adoption of the model trust concerning constructive receipt or economic benefit issues that may be present in the underlying nonqualified deferred compensation plan. In addition, the use of the model trust does not change the rules generally applicable under section 6321 of the Code with respect to the attachment of a federal tax lien to a taxpayer's property and rights to property.

The Service will continue to rule on unfunded deferred compensation plans that do not use a trust, on unfunded deferred compensation plans that use the model trust, and, where the model trust is used, generally, on the issue of whether a trust constitutes a grantor trust within the meaning of subpart E, part I, subchapter J, subtitle A of the Internal Revenue Code of 1986. However, rulings will not be issued on unfunded deferred compensation arrangements that use a trust other than the model trust, except in rare and unusual circumstances.

Taxpayers that adopt the model trust and wish to obtain a ruling on the underlying nonqualified deferred compensation plan, must include a representation that the plan, as amended, is not inconsistent with the terms of the trust and must follow the guidelines outlined in Section 4 of this revenue procedure and Revenue Procedure 92-65, this Bulletin. Rulings issued on such deferred compensation arrangements will continue to provide that the Service expresses no opinion as to the consequences of the arrangement under Title I of the Employee Retirement Income Security Act of 1974 ("ERISA"). The Department of Labor has advised that whether a "top hat" or excess benefit plan is funded or unfunded depends upon all of the facts and circumstances. However, it is the DOL's view that such plans will not fail to be "unfunded" for purposes of sections 4(b)(5), 201(2), 301(a)(3), and 401(a)(1) of ERISA solely because there is maintained in connection with such a plan a trust which conforms to the model trust described in Section 5 of this revenue procedure.

In addition, rulings issued on deferred compensation arrangements using the model trust will provide that the Service expresses no opinion on the consequences under subchapter C of chapter 1 of subtitle A of the Code or under sections 1501 through 1504 on the trust's acquisition, holding, sale or disposition of stock of the grantor.

——Section 4. Guidance Regarding Trusts

01.   A private letter ruling on a nonqualified deferred compensation arrangement using a grantor trust subject to the claims of the employer's creditors will be issued only if the trust conforms to the model language contained in Section 5 of this revenue procedure. The model language must be adopted verbatim, except where substitute language is expressly permitted.

The request for a ruling must be accompanied by a representation that the trust conforms to the model trust language contained in this revenue procedure, including the order in which sections of the model trust language appear, and that the trust adopted does not contain any inconsistent language, in substituted portions or elsewhere, that conflicts with the model trust language. Of course, provisions may be renumbered if appropriate, language in brackets may be omitted, and blanks may be completed. In addition, the taxpayer may add sections to the model language provided that such additions are not inconsistent with the model language. Finally, the submission must also include a copy of the trust on which all substituted or additional language is either underlined or otherwise clearly marked and on which the location of the required investment authority language is indicated.

02.   The request for a ruling must contain a representation that the trust is a valid trust under state law and that all of the material

terms and provisions of the trust, including the creditors' rights clause, are enforceable under the appropriate state laws.

03.   The trustee of the trust must be an independent third party that may be granted corporate trustee powers under state law, such as a bank trust department or other similar party.

——Section 5. Model Provisions

01.   The model trust language in this section contains all provisions necessary for operation of the trust except describing the trustee's investment powers. Provisions agreed to by the parties should be used to describe investment powers. The trustee must be given some investment discretion, such as the authority to invest within broad guidelines established by the parties (e.g., invest in government securities, bonds with specific ratings, or stocks of the Fortune 500 companies).

The model trust language contains a number of optional provisions, which are printed in italics and marked as "OPTIONAL." The taxpayer may substitute language of its choice for any optional provision, provided that the substituted language is not inconsistent with the language of the model trust. The model trust language also contains several alternative provisions, which are printed in italics and marked as "ALTERNATIVE." The taxpayer must choose one of these alternatives. Items in brackets are explanatory.

02.   The text of the model trust follows.

TRUST UNDER _____ PLAN

OPTIONAL

(a)   This Agreement made this _____ day of _____, by and between _____ Company) and _____ (Trustee);

OPTIONAL

(b)   WHEREAS, Company has adopted the nonqualified deferred compensation Plan(s) as listed in Appendix .

OPTIONAL

(c)   WHEREAS, Company has incurred or expects to incur liability under the terms of such Plan(s) with respect to the individuals participating such Plan(s);

(d)   WHEREAS, Company wishes to establish a trust (hereinafter called "Trust") and to contribute to the Trust assets that shall be held therein, subject to the claims of Company's creditors in the event of Company's Insolvency, as herein defined, until paid to Plan participants and their beneficiaries in such manner and at such times as specified in the Plan(s);

(e)   WHEREAS, it is the intention of the parties that this Trust shall constitute an unfunded arrangement and shall not affect the status of the Plan(s) as an unfunded plan maintained for the purpose of providing deferred compensation for a select group of management or highly compensated employees for purposes of Title I of the Employee Retirement Income Security Act of 1974;

(f)   WHEREAS, it is the intention of Company to make contributions to the Trust to provide itself with a source of funds to assist it in the meeting of its liabilities under the Plan(s);

NOW, THEREFORE, the parties do hereby establish the Trust and agree that the Trust shall be compromised, held and disposed of as follows:

Section 1.   *Establishment Of Trust*

(a)   Company hereby deposits with Trustee in trust _____ [insert amount deposited], which shall become the principal of the Trust to be held, administered and disposed of by Trustee as provided in this Trust Agreement.

ALTERNATIVES—Select one provision.

(b)   The Trust hereby established shall be revocable by Company.

(b)   The Trust hereby established shall be irrevocable.

(b)   The Trust hereby established is revocable by Company; it shall become irrevocable upon a Change of Control, as defined herein.

(b)   The Trust shall become irrevocable _____ [insert number] days following the issuance of a favorable private letter ruling regarding the Trust from the Internal Revenue Service.

(b)   The Trust shall become irrevocable upon approval by the Board of Directors.

(c)   The Trust is intended to be a grantor trust, of which Company is the grantor, within the meaning of subpart E, part I, subchapter J, chapter 1, subtitle A of the Internal Revenue Code of 1986, as amended, and shall be construed accordingly.

(d)   The principal of the Trust, and any earnings thereon shall be held separate and apart from other funds of Company and shall be used exclusively for the uses and purposes of Plan participants and general creditors as herein set forth. Plan participants and their beneficiaries shall have no preferred claim on, or any beneficial ownership interest in, any assets of the Trust. Any rights created under the Plan(s) and this Trust Agreement shall be mere unsecured contractual rights of Plan participants and their beneficiaries against Company. Any assets held by the Trust will be subject to the claims of Company's general creditors under federal and state law in the event of Insolvency, as defined in Section 3(a) herein.

ALTERNATIVES—Select one or more provisions, as appropriate.

(e)   Company, in its sole discretion, may at any time, or from time to time, make additional deposits of cash or other property in trust with Trustee to augment the principal to be held, administered and disposed of by Trustee as provided in this Trust Agreement. Neither Trustee nor any Plan participant or beneficiary shall have any right to compel such additional deposits.

(e)   Upon a Change of Control, Company shall, as soon as possible, but in no event longer than ____ [fill in blank] days following the Change of Control, as defined herein, make an irrevocable contribution to the Trust in an amount that is sufficient to pay each Plan participant or beneficiary the benefits to which Plan participants or their beneficiaries would be entitled pursuant to the terms of the Plan(s) as of the date on which the Change of Control occurred.

(e)   Within ____ [fill in blank] days following the end of the Plan year(s), ending after the Trust has become irrevocable pursuant to

Section 1(b) hereof, Company shall be required to irrevocably deposit additional cash or other property to the Trust in an amount sufficient to pay each Plan participant or beneficiary the benefits payable pursuant to the terms of the Plan(s) as of the close of the Plan year(s).

Section 2. *Payments to Plan Participants and Their Beneficiaries.*

(a) Company shall deliver to Trustee a schedule (the "Payment Schedule") that indicates the amounts payable in respect of each Plan participant (and his or her beneficiaries), that provides a formula or other instructions acceptable to Trustee for determining the amounts so payable, the form in which such amount is to be paid (as provided for or available under the Plan(s)), and the time of commencement for payment of such amounts. Except as otherwise provided herein, Trustee shall make payments to the Plan participants and their beneficiaries in accordance with such Payment Schedule. The Trustee shall make provisions for the reporting and withholding of any federal, state, or local taxes that may be required to be withheld with respect to the payment of benefits pursuant to the terms of the Plan(s) and shall pay amounts withheld to the appropriate taxing authorities or determine that such amounts have been reported, withheld and paid by Company.

(b) The entitlement of a Plan participant or his or her beneficiaries to benefits under the plan(s) shall be determined by Company or such party as it shall designate under the Plan(s), and any claim for such benefits shall be considered and reviewed under the procedures set out in the Plan(s).

(c) Company may make payment of benefits directly to Plan participants or their beneficiaries as they become due under the terms of the Plan(s). Company shall notify beneficiaries as they become due under the terms of the Plan(s). Company shall notify Trustee of its decision to make payment of benefits directly prior to the time amounts are payable to participants or their beneficiaries. In addition, if the principal of the Trust, and any earnings thereon, are not sufficient to make payments of benefits in accordance with the terms of the Plan(s), Company shall make the balance of each such payment as it falls due. Trustee shall notify company where principal and earnings are not sufficient.

Section 3. *Trustee Responsibility Regarding Payments to Trust Beneficiary When Company is Insolvent.*

(a)   Trustee shall cease payment of benefits to Plan participants and their beneficiaries if the Company is Insolvent. Company shall be considered "Insolvent" for purposes of this Trust Agreement if (i) Company is unable to pay its debts as they become due, or (ii) Company is subject to a pending proceeding as a debtor under the United States Bankruptcy Code.

OPTIONAL

, or (iii) Company is determined to be insolvent by _____ [insert names of applicable federal and/or state regulatory agency].

(b)   At all times during the continuance of this trust, as provided in Section 1 (d) hereof, the principal and income of the Trust shall be subject to claims of general creditors of Company under federal and state law as set forth below.

(1)   The Board of Directors and the Chief Executive Officer [or substitute the title of the highest ranking officer of the Company] of Company shall have the duty to inform Trustee in writing of Company's Insolvency. If a person claiming to be a creditor of Company alleges in writing to Trustee that Company has become Insolvent, Trustee shall determine whether Company is Insolvent and, pending such determination, Trustee shall discontinue payment of benefits to Plan participants or their beneficiaries.

(2)   Unless Trustee has actual knowledge of Company's Insolvency, or has received notice from Company or a person claiming to be a creditor alleging that company is Insolvent, Trustee shall have no duty to inquire whether Company Is Insolvent. Trustee may in all events rely on such evidence concerning Company's solvency as may be furnished to Trustee and that provides Trustee with a reasonable basis for making a determination concerning Company's solvency.

(3)   If at any time Trustee has determined that Company is Insolvent, Trustee shall discontinue payments to Plan participants or their beneficiaries and shall hold the assets of the Trust for the benefit of Company's general creditors. Nothing in this Trust Agreement shall in any way diminish any rights of Plan participants or their

beneficiaries to pursue their rights as general creditors of Company with respect to benefits due under the Plan(s) or otherwise.

(4)   Trustee shall resume the payment of benefits to Plan participants or their beneficiaries in accordance with Section 2 of this Trust Agreement only after Trustee has determined that Company is not Insolvent (or is no longer Insolvent).

(c)   Provided that there are sufficient assets, if trustee discontinues the payment of benefits from the Trust pursuant to Section 3(b) hereof and subsequently resumes such payments, the first payment following such discontinuance shall include the aggregate amount of all payments due to Plan participants or their beneficiaries under the terms of the Plan(s) for the period of such discontinuance, less the aggregate amount of any payments made to Plan participants or their beneficiaries by Company in lieu of the payments provided for hereunder during any such period of discontinuance.

Section 4.   *Payments to Company.*

[The following need not be included if the first alternative under 1(b) is selected.]

Except as provided in Section 3 hereof, after the Trust has become irrevocable, Company shall have no right or power to direct Trustee to return to Company or to divert to others any of the Trust assets before all payment of benefits have been made to Plan participants and their beneficiaries pursuant to the terms of the Plan(s).

Section 5.   *Investment Authority.*

ALTERNATIVES—Select one provision, as appropriate

(a)   In no event may Trustee invest in securities (including stock or rights to acquire stock) or obligations issued by Company, other than a de minimis amount held in common investment vehicles in which Trustee invests. All rights associated with assets of the Trust shall be exercised by Trustee or the person designated by Trustee, and shall in no event be exercisable by or rest with Plan participants.

(a)   Trustee may invest in securities (including stock or rights to acquire stock) or obligations issued by Company. All rights associated

with assets of the Trust shall be exercised by Trustee or the person designated by Trustee, and shall in no event be exercisable by or rest with Plan participants.

OPTIONAL

except that voting rights with respect to Trust assets will be exercised by Company.

OPTIONAL

, except that dividend rights with respect to Trust assets will rest with Company.

OPTIONAL

Company shall have the right, at anytime, and from time to time in its sole discretion, to substitute assets of equal fair market value for any asset held by the Trust.

[If the second Alternative 5(a) is selected, the trust must provide either (1) that the trust is revocable under Alternative 1(b), or (2) the following provision must be included in the Trust]:

"Company shall have the right at anytime, and from time to time in its sole discretion, to substitute assets of equal fair market value for any asset held by the Trust. This right is exercisable by Company in a nonfiduciary capacity without the approval or consent of any person in a fiduciary capacity."

Section 6. *Disposition of Income.*

ALTERNATIVES—Select one provision.

(a)   During the term of this Trust, all income received by the Trust, net of expenses and taxes, shall be accumulated and reinvested.

(a)   During the term of this trust, or ___ [insert amount] part of the income received by the Trust, net of expenses and taxes, shall be returned to Company.

Section 7.   *Accounting by Trustee.*

OPTIONAL

Trustee shall keep accurate and detailed records of all investments, receipts, disbursements, and all other transactions required to be made, including such specific records as shall be agreed upon in writing between Company and Trustee. Within ___ [insert number] days following the close of each calendar year and within ___ [insert number] days after the removal or resignation of Trustee, Trustee shall deliver to Company a written account of its administration of the Trust during such year or during the period from the close of the last preceding year to the date of such removal or resignation, setting forth all investments, receipts, disbursements and other transactions effected by it, including a description of all securities and investments purchased and sold with the cost or net proceeds of such purchases or sales (accrued interest paid or receivable being separate), and showing all cash, securities and other property held in the Trust at the end of such year or as of the date of such removal or resignation, as the case may be.

Section 8.   *Responsibility of Trustee.*

OPTIONAL

(a)   Trustee shall act with the care, skill, prudence and diligence under the circumstances then prevailing that a prudent person acting in like capacity and familiar with such matters would use in the conduct of an enterprise of a like character and with like aims, provided, however, that Trustee shall incur no liability to any person for any action taken pursuant to a direction, request or approval given by Company which is contemplated by and in conformity with, the terms of the Plan(s) or this Trust and is given in writing by Company. In the event of a dispute between Company and a party, Trustee may apply to a court of competent jurisdiction to resolve the dispute.

OPTIONAL

(b)   If Trustee undertakes or defends any litigation arising in connection with this Trust, Company agrees to indemnify Trustee against Trustee's costs, expenses and liabilities (including, without

limitation, attorneys' fees and expenses) relating thereto and to be primarily liable for such payments. If company does not pay such costs, expenses and liabilities in a reasonably timely manner, Trustee may obtain payment from the Trust.

OPTIONAL

(c)   Trustee may consult with legal counsel (who may also be counsel for Company generally) with respect to any of its duties or obligations hereunder.

OPTIONAL

(d)   Trustee may hire agents, accountants, actuaries, investment advisors, financial consultants or other professionals to assist it in performing any of its duties or obligations hereunder.

(e)   Trustee shall have, without exclusion, all powers conferred on Trustees by applicable law, unless expressly provided otherwise herein, provided, however, that if an insurance policy is held as an asset of the Trust, Trustee shall have no power to name a beneficiary of the policy other than the Trust, to assign the policy (as distinct from conversion of the policy to a different form) other than to a successor Trustee, or to loan to any person the proceeds of any borrowing against such policy.

OPTIONAL

(f)   However, notwithstanding the provisions of Section 8(e) above, Trustee may loan to Company the proceeds of any borrowing against an insurance policy held as an asset of the Trust.

(g)   Notwithstanding any powers granted to Trustee pursuant to this Trust Agreement or to applicable law, Trustee shall not have any power that could give this Trust the objective of carrying on a business and dividing the gains therefrom, within the meaning of section 301.7701-2 of the Procedure and Administrative Regulations promulgated pursuant to the Internal Revenue Code.

Section 9.   *Compensation and Expenses of Trustee.*

OPTIONAL

Company shall pay all administrative and Trustee's fees and expenses. If not so paid, the fees and expenses shall be paid from the Trust.

Section 10.   *Resignation and Removal of Trustee.*

(a)   Trustee may resign at any time by written notice to Company, which shall be effective ___ [insert number] days after receipt of such notice unless Company and Trustee agree otherwise.

OPTIONAL

(b)   Trustee may be removed by Company on ___ [insert number] days notice or upon shorter notice accepted by Trustee.

OPTIONAL

(c)   Upon a Change of Control, as defined herein, Trustee may not be removed by Company for ___ [insert number] year(s).

OPTIONAL

(d)   If Trustee resigns within ___ [insert number] year(s) after a Change of Control, as defined herein, Company shall apply to a court of competent jurisdiction for the appointment of a successor Trustee or for instructions.

OPTIONAL

(e)   If Trustee resigns or is removed within ___ [insert number] year(s) of a Change of Control, as defined herein, Trustee shall select a successor Trustee in accordance with the provisions of Section 11(b) hereof prior to the effective date of Trustee's resignation or removal.

(f)   Upon resignation or removal of Trustee and appointment of a successor Trustee, all assets shall subsequently be transferred to the successor Trustee. The transfer shall be completed within ___ [insert number days after receipt of notice of resignation, removal or transfer, unless Company extends the time limit.

(g) If Trustee resigns or is removed, a successor shall be appointed, in accordance with Section 11 hereof, by the effective date of resignation or removal under paragraph(s) (a) [or (b)] of this section. If no such appointment has been made, Trustee may apply to a court of competent jurisdiction for appointment of a successor or for instructions. All expenses of Trustee in connection with the proceeding shall be allowed as administrative expenses of the Trust.

Section 11. *Appointment of Successor.*

OPTIONAL

(a) If Trustee resigns [or is removed] in accordance with Section 10(a) [or (b)] hereof, Company may appoint any third party, such as a bank trust department or other party that may be granted corporate trustee powers under state law, as a successor to replace Trustee upon resignation or removal. The appointment shall be effective when accepted in writing by the new Trustee, who shall have all of the rights and powers of the former Trustee, including ownership rights in the Trust assets. The former Trustee shall execute any instrument necessary or reasonably requested by Company or the successor Trustee to evidence the transfer.

OPTIONAL

(b) If Trustee resigns or is removed pursuant to the provisions of Section 10(e) hereof and selects a successor Trustee, Trustee may appoint any third party such as a bank trust department or other party that may be granted corporate trustee powers under state law. The appointment of a successor Trustee shall be effective when accepted in writing by the new Trustee. The new Trustee shall have all rights and powers of the former Trustee, including ownership rights in Trust assets. The former Trustee shall execute any instrument necessary or reasonably requested by the successor Trustee to evidence the transfer.

OPTIONAL

(c) The successor Trustee need not examine the records and acts of any prior Trustee and may retain or dispose of existing Trust assets, subject to Sections 7 and 8 hereof. The successor Trustee shall not be responsible for and Company shall indemnify and defend the succes-

sor Trustee from any claim or liability resulting from any action or inaction or any prior Trustee or from any other past event, or any condition existing at the time it becomes successor Trustee.

Section 12. *Amendment or Termination.*

(a) This Trust Agreement may be amended by a written instrument executed by Trustee and Company. [Unless the first alternative under 1(b) is selected, the following sentence must be included.] Notwithstanding the foregoing, no such amendment shall conflict with the terms of the Plan(s) or shall make the Trust revocable after it has become irrevocable in accordance with Section 1(b) hereof.

(b) The Trust shall not terminate until the date on which Plan participants and their beneficiaries are no longer entitled to benefits pursuant to the terms of the Plan(s) [unless the second alternative under 1(b) is selected, the following must be included:], "unless sooner revoked in accordance with Section 1(b) hereof." Upon termination of the Trust any assets remaining in the Trust shall be returned to Company.

OPTIONAL

(c) Upon written approval of participants or beneficiaries entitled to payment of benefits pursuant to the terms of the Plan(s), Company may terminate this Trust prior to the time all benefit payments under the Plan(s) have been made. All assets in the Trust at termination shall be returned to Company.

OPTIONAL

(d) Section(s) ___ [insert number(s)] of this Trust Agreement may not be amended by Company for ___ [insert number] year(s) following a Change of Control, as defined herein.

Section 13. *Miscellaneous.*

(a) Any provisions of this Trust Agreement prohibited by law shall be ineffective to the extent of any such prohibition, without invalidating the remaining provisions hereof.

(b) Benefits payable to Plan participants and their beneficiaries under this Trust Agreement may not be anticipated, assigned (either at law or in equity), alienated, pledged, encumbered or subjected to attachment, garnishment, levy, execution or other legal or equitable process.

(c) This Trust Agreement shall be governed by and construed in accordance with the laws of _____ .

OPTIONAL

(d) For purposes of this Trust, Change of Control shall mean; [insert objective definition such as: "the purchase or other acquisition by any person, entity or group of persons, within the meaning of section 13(d) or 14(d) of the Securities Exchange Act of 1934 ("Act"), or any comparable successor provisions, of beneficial ownership (within the meaning of Rule 13d-3 promulgated under the Act) of 30 percent or more of either the outstanding shares of common stock or the combined voting power of Company's then outstanding voting securities entitled to vote generally, or the approval by the stockholders of Company of a reorganization, merger, or consolidation, in each case, with respect to which persons who were stockholders of Company immediately prior to such reorganization, merger or consolidation do not, immediately thereafter, own more than 50 percent of the combined voting power entitled to vote generally in the election of directors of the reorganized, merged or consolidated Company's then outstanding securities, or a liquidation or dissolution of Company or of the sale of all or substantially all of Company's assets"].

Section 14. *Effective Date.*

The effective date of this Trust Agreement shall be _____, 19__ .

——Section 6. Effective Date

01.   This revenue procedure is effective on July 28, 1992.

02.   Ruling requests with respect to grantor trusts used in executive compensation arrangements and subject of the claims of the employer's creditors that are submitted to the Service subsequent to

the effective date of this revenue procedure must comply with the terms of this revenue procedure.

03. This revenue procedure does not affect any private letter rulings that were issued prior to the effective date. If a plan or trust that was the subject of such a ruling is amended, and such amendments affect the rights of participants or other creditors, such ruling will generally not remain in effect.

——Section 7. Public Comment

Written comments, including suggested language, concerning the model trust provision contained in this revenue procedure may be sent to the Internal Revenue Service, Office of the Associate Chief Counsel (Employee Benefits and Exempt Organizations), Attention: CC:EE:1:1, Room 5201, P.O. 7604, Ben Franklin Station, Washington, D.C. 20044.

Drafting Information

The principal author of this revenue procedure is Catherine Livingston Fernandez of the Office of the Associate Chief Counsel (Employee Benefits and Exempt Organizations). For further information regarding this revenue procedure, contact Ms. Fernandez at (202) 622-6030 (not a toll-free number).

Rev Proc 92-65, 1992-33 IRB 16—Rulings on unfunded deferred compensation arrangements. [Rev Proc 71-19, 1971-1 CB 698, amplified.]

——Section 1. Purpose

01. The purpose of the Revenue Procedure is to set forth the conditions, or circumstances, under which the Internal Revenue Service will issue advance rulings concerning the application of the doctrine of constructive receipt to unfunded deferred compensation arrangements and to amplify Rev. Proc. 71-19, 1971-1 C.B. 698.

——**Section 2. Background**

In 1960, the Service issued Rev. Rul 60-31, 1960-1 C.B. 174, concerning the application of the doctrine of constructive receipt to certain deferred compensation arrangements. Rev. Rul. 60-31, was modified by Rev. Rul. 64-279, 1964-2 C.B. 121, and Rev. Rul. 70-435, 1970-2 C.B. 100. The conditions under which the Service would issue advance rulings on unfunded deferred compensation arrangements, were originally published in Rev. Proc. 71-19, 1971-1 C.B. 698.

——**Section 3. Scope and Objective**

01.   In each request for a ruling involving the deferral of compensation, the Service will determine whether the doctrine of constructive receipt is applicable on a case by case basis. The Service will ordinarily issue rulings regarding unfunded deferred compensation arrangements only if the requirements of Rev. Proc. 71-19 are met and, in addition, the arrangement meets the following guidelines.

(a)   Section 3.01 of Rev. Proc. 71-19 states that, if the plan provides for an election to defer payment of compensation, such election must be made before the beginning of the period of service for which the compensation is payable, regardless of the existence in the plan of forfeiture provisions. The period of service for purposes of this requirement generally has been regarded by the Service as the employee's taxable year for cash basis, calendar year taxpayers. Rev. Rul. 68-86, 1968-1 C.B. 184; Rev. Rul. 69-650, 1969-2 C.B. 106; Rev. Rul. 71-419, 1971-2 C.B. 220. There are two exceptions to this general requirement, as follows:

(1)   In the year in which the plan is first implemented, the eligible participant may make an election to defer compensation for services to be performed subsequent to the election within 30 days after the date the plan is effective for eligible employees.

(2)   In the first year in which a participant becomes eligible to participate in the plan, the newly eligible participant may make an election to defer compensation for services to be performed subsequent to the election within 30 days after the date the employee becomes eligible.

(b)   The plan must define the time and method for payment of deferred compensation for each event (such as termination of employment, regular retirement, disability retirement or death) that entitles a participant to receive benefits. The plan may specify the date of payment or provide that payments will begin within 30 days after the occurrence of a stated event.

(c)   The plan may provide for payment of benefits in the case of an "unforeseeable emergency." "Unforeseeable emergency" must be defined in the plan as an unanticipated emergency that is caused by an event beyond the control of the participant or beneficiary and that would result in severe financial hardship to the individual if early withdrawal were not permitted. The plan must further provide that any early withdrawal approved by the employer is limited to the amount necessary to meet the emergency. Language similar to that described in section 1.457-2(h)(4) and (5) of the Income Tax Regulations may be used.

(d)   The plan must provide that participants have the status of general unsecured creditors of the employer and that the plan constitutes a mere promise by the employer to make any benefit payments in the future. If the plan refers to a trust, the plan must also provide that any trust created by the employer and any assets held by the trust to assist it in meeting its obligations under the plan will conform to the terms of the model trust as described in Revenue Procedure 92-64, this Bulletin. Finally, the plan must state that it is the intention of the parties that the arrangements be unfunded for tax purposes and for purposes of Title I of ERISA.

(e)   The plan must provide that a participant's rights to benefit payments under the plan are not subject in any manner to anticipation, alienation, sale, transfer, assignment, pledge, encumbrance, attachment, or garnishment by creditors of the participant or the participant's beneficiary.

——Section 4. Procedure

The general procedures of Rev. Proc. 92-1, 1992-1 I.R.B. 9, relating to the issuance of ruling and determination letters, and Rev. Proc. 71-19, 1971-1 C.B. 698, apply to requests relating to unfunded deferred compensation arrangements to the extent they are not covered by this revenue procedure.

——Section 5. Effect On Other Revenue Procedures

Rev. Proc. 71-19, 1971-1 C.B. 698, is hereby amplified to set forth the conditions under which the Service will issue advance rulings on unfunded deferred compensation plans.

——Section 6. Effective Date

The revenue procedure is effective on July 28, 1992.

Drafting Information

The principal author of this revenue procedure is Catherine Livingston Fernandez of the Office of the Assistant Chief Counsel, (Employee Benefits and Exempt Organizations). For further information regarding this revenue procedure contact Ms. Fernandez at (202) 622-6030 (not a toll-free call).

Appendix B

Sample Compensation Agreements

Three sample compensation plans, presented for consideration at a recent meeting of shareholders of Eastman Kodak Company and included in the proxy statement, are provided for your information, and to bring to life some of the related issues covered in this book. The first plan is a long-term compensation plan; the second plan is a management variable compensation plan; and the third plan is a wage dividend plan. Attachment 1 to this appendix provides two good examples of actual proxy disclosure provisions for executive compensation items.

PLAN 1: 1995 OMNIBUS LONG-TERM COMPENSATION PLAN

ARTICLE 1—PURPOSE AND TERM OF PLAN

1.1 Purpose

The purpose of the Plan is to provide motivation to selected Employees of the Company to put forth maximum efforts toward the continued growth, profitability, and success of the Company by providing incentives to such Employees through the ownership and performance of the Common Stock of Kodak. Toward this objective, the Committee may grant stock options, stock appreciation rights,

Stock Awards, performance units, performance shares, Performance Awards, Common Stock and/or other incentive Awards to Employees of the Company on the terms and subject to the conditions set forth in the Plan.

1.2   Term

The plan shall become effective as of February 1, 1995, subject to its approval by Kodak's shareholders at the 1995 Annual Meeting of the Shareholders. No Awards shall be exercisable or payable before approval of the Plan has been obtained from Kodak's shareholders. Awards shall not be granted pursuant to the Plan after December 31, 1999; except that the Committee may grant Awards after such date in recognition of performance for Performance Cycles commencing prior to such date.

ARTICLE 2—DEFINITIONS

2.1   Approved Reason

"Approved Reason" means a reason for terminating employment with the Company which, in the opinion of the Committee, is in the best interest of the Company.

2.2   Award

"Award" means any form of stock option, stock appreciation right, Stock Award, performance unit, performance share, Performance Award, shares of Common Stock under the Performance Stock Program, or other incentive Award granted under the Plan, whether singly, in combination, or in tandem, to a Participant by the Committee pursuant to such terms, conditions, restrictions and/or limitations, if any, as the Committee may establish by the Award Notice or otherwise.

2.3   Award Notice

"Award Notice" means a written notice from the Company to a Participant that establishes the terms, conditions, restrictions, and/or limitations applicable to an Award in addition to those established by this Plan and by the Committee's exercise of its administrative powers.

2.4   Award Payment Date

"Award Payment Date" means, for a Performance Cycle, the date the Awards for such Performance Cycle shall be paid to Participants. The Award Payment Date for a Performance Cycle shall occur as soon as administratively possible following the completion of the certification required pursuant to Subsection 13.5(c).

2.5   Board

"Board" means the Board of Directors of Kodak.

2.6   Cause

"Cause" means (a) the willful and continued failure by an Employee to substantially perform his or her duties with his or her employer after written warnings identifying the lack of substantial performance are delivered to the Employee by his or her employer to specifically identify the manner in which the employer believes that the Employee has not substantially performed his or her duties, or (b) the willful engaging by an Employee in illegal conduct which is materially and demonstrably injurious to Kodak or a Subsidiary.

2.7   CEO

"CEO" means the Chief Executive Officer of Kodak.

2.8   Change In Control

"Change In Control" means a Change In Control of Kodak of a nature that would be required to be reported (assuming such event has not been "previously reported") in response to Item 1(a) of the Current Report on Form 8-K, as in effect on August 1, 1989, pursuant to Section 13 or 15(d) of the Exchange Act; provided that, without limitation, a Change In Control shall be deemed to have occurred at such time as (i) any "person" within the meaning of Section 14(d) of the Exchange Act, other than Kodak, a Subsidiary, or any employee benefit plan(s) sponsored by Kodak or any Subsidiary, is or has become the "beneficial owner," as defined in Rule 13d-3 under the Exchange Act, directly or indirectly, of 25% or more of the combined voting power of the outstanding securities of Kodak ordinarily having the right to vote at the election of directors, or (ii) individuals who constitute the Board on January 1, 1995 (the "Incumbent Board") have ceased for any reason to constitute at least a majority thereof, provided that any person becoming a director subsequent to January 1, 1995 whose election, or nomination for election by Kodak's shareholders, was approved by a vote of at least three quarters (3/4) of the directors comprising the incumbent Board (either by a specific vote or by approval of the proxy statement of Kodak in which such person is named as a nominee for director without objection to such nomination) shall be, for purposes of this Plan, considered as though such person were a member of the Incumbent Board.

2.9 Change In Control Price

"Change In Control Price" means the highest closing price per share paid for the purchase of Common Stock on the New York Stock Exchange during the ninety (90) day period ending on the date the Change In Control occurs.

2.10 Change In Ownership

"Change In Ownership" means a Change In Control which results directly or indirectly in Kodak's Common Stock ceasing to be actively traded on the New York Stock Exchange.

2.11 Code

"Code" means the Internal Revenue Code of 1986, as amended from time to time, including regulations thereunder and successor provisions and regulations thereto.

2.12 Committee

"Committee" means the Executive Compensation and Development Committee of the Board, or such other Board committee as may be designated by the Board to administer the Plan; provided that the Committee shall consist of three or more directors, all of whom are both a "disinterested person" within the meaning of Rule 16b-3 under the Exchange Act and an "outside director" within the meaning of the definition of such term as contained in Proposed Treasury Regulations Section 1.162-27(e)(3), or any successor definition adopted.

2.13 Common Stock

"Common Stock" means Common Stock, $2.50 par value share, of Kodak which may be newly issued or treasury stock.

2.14 Company

"Company" means Kodak and its Subsidiaries.

2.15 Covered Employee

"Covered Employee" means an Employee who is a "Covered Employee" within the meaning of Section 162(m) of the Code.

2.16 Disability

"Disability" means a disability under the terms of any long-term disability plan maintained by the Company.

2.17 Effective Date

"Effective Date" means the date an Award is determined to be effective by the Committee upon its grant of such Award.

2.18 Employee

"Employee" means either: (a) a salaried employee of Kodak; or (b) a salaried employee of a Subsidiary.

2.19 Exchange Act

"Exchange Act" means the Securities and Exchange Act of 1934, as amended from time to time, including rules thereunder and successor provisions and rules thereto.

2.20 Key Employee

"Key Employee" means a senior level Employee who holds a position of responsibility in a managerial, administrative, or professional capacity.

2.21 Kodak

"Kodak" means Eastman Kodak Company.

2.22 Negative Discretion

"Negative Discretion" means the discretion authorized by the Plan to be applied by the Committee in determining the size of an Award for a Performance Period or Performance Cycle if, in the Committee's sole judgment, such application is appropriate. Negative Discretion may only be used by the Committee to eliminate or reduce the size of an Award. By way of example and not by way of limitation, in no event shall any discretionary authority granted to the Committee by the Plan, including, but not limited to Negative Discretion, be used to: (a) grant Awards for a Performance Period or Performance Cycle if the Performance Goals for such Performance Period or Performance Cycle have not been attained; or (b) increase an Award above the maximum amount payable under Sections 7.5, 8.6, 9.6, or 13.6 of the Plan.

2.23 Participant

"Participant" means either any Employee to whom an Award has been granted by the Committee under the Plan or a Key Employee who, for a Performance Cycle, has been selected to participate in the Performance Stock Program.

2.24 Performance Award

"Performance Award" means the Stock Awards, Performance units and Performance Shares granted to Covered Employees pursuant to Article 7. All Performance Awards are intended to qualify as "Performance-Based Compensation" under Section 162(m) of the Code.

2.25 Performance Criteria

"Performance Criteria" means the one or more criteria that the Committee shall select for purposes of establishing the Performance Goal(s) for a Performance Period or Performance Cycle. The Performance Criteria that will be used to established such Performance Goal(s) shall be limited to the following: return on assets, return on capital, shareholders returns, profit margin, earnings per share, net earnings, operating earnings, Common Stock price per share, and sales or market share. To the extent required by Section 162(m) of the Code, the Committee shall, within the first 90 days of a Performance Period or Performance Cycle (or, if longer, within the maximum period allowed under Section 162(m) of the Code), define in an objective fashion the manner of calculating the Performance Criteria it selects to use for such Performance Period or Performance Cycle.

2.26 Performance Cycle

"Performance Cycle" means the one or more periods of time, which may be of varying and overlapping durations, as the Committee may select, over which the attainment of one or more Performance Goals will be measured for the purpose of determining a Participant's right to and the payment of an Award under the Performance Stock Program.

2.27 Performance Formula

"Performance Formula" means, for a Performance Period or Performance Cycle, the one or more objective formulas applied against the relevant Performance Goals to determine, with regards to the Award of a particular Participant, whether all, some portion but less than all, or none of the Award has been earned for the Performance Period or Performance Cycle. In the case of an Award under the Performance Stock Program, in the event the Performance Goals for a Performance Cycle are achieved, the Performance Formula shall determine what percentage of the Participant's Target Award for the Performance Cycle will be earned.

2.28 Performance Goals

"Performance Goals" means, for a Performance Period or Performance Cycle, the one or more goals established by the Committee for the Performance Period or Performance Cycle based upon the Performance Criteria. The Committee is authorized at any time during the first 90 days of a Performance Period or Performance Cycle, or at any time thereafter (but only to the extent the exercise of such authority after the first 90 days of a Performance Period or Performance Cycle wold not cause the Awards granted to the Covered Employees for the Performance Period or Performance Cycle to fail to qualify as "Performance-Based Compensation" under Section 162(m) of the Code), in its sole and absolute discretion, to adjust or modify the calculation of a Performance Goal for such Performance

Cycle in order to prevent the dilution or enlargement of the rights of Participants, (a) in the event of, or in anticipation of, any unusual or extraordinary corporate item, transaction, event or development; (b) in recognition of, or in anticipation of, any other unusual or nonrecurring events affecting the Company, or the financial statements of the Company, or in response to, or in anticipation of, changes in applicable laws, regulations, accounting principles, or business conditions; and (c) in view of the Committee's assessment of the business strategy of the Company, performance of comparable organizations, economic and business conditions, and any other circumstances deemed relevant.

2.29 Performance Period

"Performance Period" means the one or more periods of time, which may be of varying and overlapping durations, as the Committee may select, over which the attainment of one or more Performance Goals will be measured for the purpose of determining a Participant's right to and the payment of a Performance Award.

2.30 Performance Stock Program

"Performance Stock Program" means the program established under Article 13 of the Plan pursuant to which selected Key Employees receive Awards for a Performance Cycle in the form of shares of Common Stock based upon attainment of Performance Goals for such Performance Cycle. All awards granted to Covered Employees under the Performance Stock Program are intended to qualify as "Performance-Based Compensation" under Section 162(m) of the Code.

2.31 Plan

"Plan" means the Eastman Kodak Company 1995 Omnibus Long-Term Compensation Plan.

2.32 Retirement

"Retirement" means, for all Plan purposes other than Article 18, a termination of employment from the Company on or after attainment of age 60 which constitutes a retirement under any defined benefit pension plan maintained by the Company which is either a tax-qualified plan under Section 401(a) of the Code or is identified in writing by the Committee as a defined benefit pension plan. For purposes of Article 18, "Retirement" means retirement under any defined benefit pension plan maintained by the Company which is either a tax-qualified plan under Section 401(a) of the Code or is identified in writing by the Committee as a defined benefit pension plan.

2.33   Stock Award

"Stock Award" means an Award granted pursuant to Article 10 in the form of shares of Common Stock, restricted shares of Common Stock, and/or Units of Common Stock.

2.34   Subsidiary

"Subsidiary" means a corporation or other business entity in which Kodak directly or indirectly has an ownership interest of 80 percent or more.

2.35   Target Award

"Target Award" means, for a Performance Cycle, the target Award amount, expressed as a number of shares of Common Stock, established for each wage grade by the Committee for the Performance Cycle. The fact, however, that a Target Award is established for a Participant's wage grade shall not in any manner entitle the Participant to receive an Award for such Performance Cycle.

2.36   Unit

"Unit" means a bookkeeping entry used by the Company to record and account for the grant of the following Awards until such time as the Award is paid, canceled, forfeited or terminated, as the case may be: Units of Common Stock, performance units, and performance shares which are expressed in terms of Units of Common Stock.

ARTICLE 3—ELIGIBILITY

3.1   In General

Subject to Section 3.2, all Employees are eligible to participate in the Plan. The Committee shall select, from time to time, Participants from those Employees who, in the opinion of the Committee, can further the Plan's purposes. Once a Participant is so selected, the Committee shall determine the type or types of Awards to be made to the Participant and shall establish in the related Award Notices the terms, conditions, restrictions and/or limitations, if any, applicable to the Awards in addition to those set forth in this Plan and the administrative rules and regulations issued by the Committee.

3.2   Performance Stock Program

Only Key Employees shall be eligible to participate in the Performance Stock Program.

ARTICLE 4—PLAN ADMINISTRATOR

4.1   Responsibility

The Committee shall have total and exclusive responsibility to control, operate, manage and administer the Plan in accordance with its terms.

4.2   Authority of the Committee

The Committee shall have all the authority that may be necessary or helpful to enable it to discharge its responsibilities with respect to the Plan. Without limiting the generality of the preceding sentence, the Committee shall have the exclusive right to: (a) interpret the Plan; (b) determine eligibility for participation in the Plan; (c) decide all questions concerning eligibility for and the amount of Awards payable under the Plan; (d) construe any ambiguous provision of the Plan; (e) correct any default; (f) supply any omission; (g) reconcile any inconsistency; (h) issue administrative guidelines as an aid to administer the Plan and make changes in such guidelines as it from time to time deems proper; (i) make regulations for carrying out the Plan and make changes in such regulations as it from time to time deems proper; (j) determine whether Awards should be granted singly, in combination or in tandem; (k) to the extent permitted under the Plan, grant waivers of Plan terms, conditions, restrictions, and limitations; (l) accelerate the vesting, exercise, or payment of an Award or the Common Stock of an Award when such action or actions would be in the best interest of the Company; (m) establish such other types of Awards, besides those specifically enumerated in Article 5 hereof, which the Committee determines are consistent with the Plan's purpose; (n) subject to Section 8.2, grant Awards in replacement of Awards previously granted under this Plan or any other executive compensation plan of the Company; (o) establish and administer the Performance Goals and certify whether, and to what extent, they have been attained; and (p) take any and all other action it deems necessary or advisable for the proper operation or administration of the Plan.

4.3 Discretionary Authority

The Committee shall have full discretionary authority in all matters related to the discharge of its responsibilities and the exercise of its authority under the Plan including, without limitation, its construction of the terms of the Plan and its determination of eligibility for participation and Awards under the Plan. It is the intent of the Plan that the decisions of the Committee and its action with respect to the Plan shall be final, binding and conclusive upon all persons having or claiming to have any right or interest in or under the Plan.

4.4 Section 162(m) of the Code

With regards to all Covered Employees, the Plan shall, for all purposes, be interpreted and construed in accordance with Section 162(m) of the Code.

4.5 Action by the Committee

The Committee may act only by a majority of its members. Any determination of the Committee may be made, without a meeting, by a writing or writings signed by all of the members of the Committee. In addition, the Committee may authorize any one or more of its number to execute and deliver documents on behalf of the Committee.

4.6 Delegation of Authority

The Committee may delegate some or all of its authority under the Plan to any person or persons provided that any such delegation be in writing; provided, however, that only the Committee may select and grant Awards to Participants who are subject to Section 16 of the Exchange Act or are Covered Employees.

ARTICLE 5—FORM OF AWARDS

5.1 In General

Awards may, at the Committee's sole discretion, be paid in the form of Performance Awards pursuant to Article 7, stock options pursuant to Article 8, stock appreciation rights pursuant to Article 9, Stock Awards pursuant to Article 10, performance units pursuant to Article 11, performance shares pursuant to Article 12, shares of Common Stock pursuant to Article 13, any form established by the Committee pursuant to Subsection 4.2(m), or a combination thereof. All Awards shall be subject to the terms, conditions, restrictions and limitations of the Plan. The Committee may, in its sole judgment, subject an Award to such other terms, conditions, restrictions and/or limitations (including, but not limited to, the time and conditions of exercise and restrictions on transferability and vesting), provided they are not inconsistent with the terms of the Plan. Awards under a particular Article of the Plan need not be uniform and Awards under two or more Articles may be combined into a single Award Notice. Any combination of Awards may be granted at one time and on more than one occasion to the same Employee. For purposes of the Plan, the value of any Award granted in the form of Common Stock shall be the mean between the high and low at which the Common Stock trades on the New York Stock Exchange as of the date of the grant's Effective Date.

5.2 Foreign Jurisdictions

Awards may be granted, without amending the Plan, to Participants who are foreign nationals or employed outside the United States or both, on such terms and conditions different from those specified in the Plan as may, in the judgment of the Committee, be necessary or desirable to further the purposes of the Plan or to accommodate differences in local law, tax policy or custom. Moreover, the Committee may approve such supplements to or alternative versions of the Plan as it may consider necessary or appropriate for such purposes without thereby affecting the terms of the Plan as in effect for any other purpose; provided, however, no such supplement or alternative version shall: (a) increase the limitations contained in Sections 7.5, 8.6, 9.6, and 13.6; (b) increase the number of available shares under Section 6.1; or (c) cause the Plan to cease to satisfy any conditions of Rule 16b-3 under the Exchange Act or, with respect to Covered Employees, Section 162(m) of the Code.

ARTICLE 6—SHARES SUBJECT TO PLAN

6.1   Available Shares

The maximum number of shares of Common Stock, $2.50 par value per share, of Kodak which shall be available for grant of Awards under the Plan (including incentive stock options) during its term shall not exceed 16,000,000. (Such amount shall be subject to adjustment as provided in Section 6.2.) Any shares of Common Stock related to Awards which terminate by expiration, forfeiture, cancellation or otherwise without the issuance of such shares, are settled in cash in lieu of Common Stock, or are exchanged with the Committee's permission for Awards not involving Common Stock, shall not be available again for grant under the Plan. Moreover, shares of Common Stock with respect to which an SAR has been exercised and paid in cash shall not again be eligible for grant under the Plan. The maximum number of shares available for issuance under the Plan shall not be reduced to reflect any dividends or dividend equivalents that are reinvested into additional shares of Common Stock or credited as additional performance shares. The shares of Common Stock available for issuance under the Plan may be authorized and unissued shares or treasury shares.

6.2   Adjustment to Shares

(a) In General. The provisions of this Subsection 6.2(a) are subject to the limitation contained in Subsection 6.2(b). If there is any change in the number of outstanding shares of Common Stock through the declaration of stock dividends, stock splits or the like, the number of shares available for Awards, the shares subject to any Award and the option prices or exercise prices of Awards shall be automatically adjusted. If there is any change in the number of outstanding shares of Common Stock through any change in the capital account of Kodak, or through a merger, consolidation, separation (including a spin-off or other distribution of stock or property), reorganization (whether or not such reorganization comes within the meaning of such term in Section 368(a) of the Code) or partial or complete liquidation, the Committee shall make appropriate adjustments in the maximum number of shares of Common Stock which may be issued under the Plan and any adjustments and/or modifications to outstanding Awards as it, in its sole discretion, deems appropriate. In the event of any other change in the capital structure or in the Common Stock of Kodak, the Committee shall also be authorized to make such appropriate adjustments in the maximum number of shares of Common Stock available for issuance under the Plan and any adjustments and/or modifications to outstanding Awards as it, in its sole discretion, deems appropriate. The maximum number of shares available for issuance under the Plan shall be automatically adjusted to the extent necessary to reflect any dividend equivalents paid in the form of Common Stock.

(b) Covered Employees. In no event shall the Award of any Participant who is a Covered Employee be adjusted pursuant to Subsection 6.2(a) to the extent it would cause such Award to fail to qualify as "Performance-Based Compensation" under Section 162(m) of the Code.

6.3 Maximum Number of Shares for Stock Awards, Performance Units, and Performance Shares

From the maximum number of shares available for issuance under the Plan under Section 6.1, the maximum number of shares of Common Stock, $2.50 par value per share, which shall be available for Awards granted in the form of Stock Awards, performance units or performance shares (including those issued in the form of Performance Awards) under the Plan during its term shall be 5,000,000.

ARTICLE 7—PERFORMANCE AWARDS

7.1 Purpose

For purposes of grants issued to Covered Employees, the provisions of this Article 7 shall apply in addition to and, where necessary, in lieu of the provisions of Articles 10, 11, and 12. The purpose of this Article is to provide the Committee the ability to qualify the Stock Awards authorized under Article 10, the performance units under

Article 11, and the performance shares under Article 12 as "Perform-ance-Based Compensation" under Section 162(m) of the Code. The provisions of this Article 7 shall have control over any contrary provision contained in Articles 10, 11, or 12.

7.2 Eligibility

Only Covered Employees shall be eligible to receive Performance Awards. The Committee will, in its sole discretion, designate within the first 90 days of a Performance Period (or, if longer, within the maximum period allowed under Section 162(m) of the Code) which Covered Employees will be Participants for such period. However, designation of a Covered Employee as a Participant for a Performance Period shall not in any manner entitle the Participant to receive an Award for the period. The determination as to whether or not such Participant becomes entitled to an Award for such Performance Period shall be decided solely in accordance with the provisions of this Article 7. Moreover, designation of a Covered Employee as a Participant for a particular Performance Period shall not require designation of such Covered Employee as a Participant in any sub-sequent Performance Period and designation of one Covered Em-ployee as a Participant shall not require designation of any other Covered Employee as a Participant in such period or in any other period.

7.3 Discretion of Committee with Respect to Performance Awards

With regards to a particular Performance Period, the Committee shall have full discretion to select the length of such Performance Period, the type(s) of Performance Awards to be issued, the Perform-ance Criteria that will be used to establish the Performance Goal(s), the kind(s) and/or level(s) of the Performance Goal(s), whether the Performance Goal(s) is (are) to apply to the Company, Kodak, a Subsidiary, or any one or more subunits of the foregoing, and the Performance Formula. Within the first 90 days of a Performance Period (or, if longer, within the maximum period allowed under Section 162(m) of the Code), the Committee shall, with regards to the Performance Awards to be issued for such Performance Period, exercise its discretion with respect to each of the matters enumerated in the immediately preceding sentence of this Section 7.3 and record the same in writing.

7.4   Payment of Performance Awards

(a) Condition to Receipt of Performance Award. Unless otherwise provided in the relevant Award Notice, a Participant must be employed by the Company on the last day of a Performance Period to be eligible for a Performance Award for such Performance Period.

(b) Limitation. A Participant shall be eligible to receive a Performance Award for a Performance Period only to the extent that: (1) the Performance Goals for such Period are achieved; and (2) the Performance Formula as applied against such Performance Goals determines that all or some portion of such Participant's Performance Award has been earned for the Performance Period.

(c) Certification. Following the completion of a Performance Period, the Committee shall meet to review and certify in writing whether, and to what extent, the Performance Goals for the Performance Period have been achieved and, if so, to also calculate and certify in writing the amount of the Performance Awards earned for the period based upon the Performance Formula. The Committee shall then determine the actual size of each Participant's Performance Award for the Performance Period and, in so doing, shall apply Negative Discretion, if and when it deems appropriate.

(d) Negative Discretion. In determining the actual size of an individual Performance Award for a Performance Period, the Committee may reduce or eliminate the amount of the Performance Award earned under the Performance Formula for the Performance Period through the use of Negative Discretion, if in its sole judgment, such reduction or elimination is appropriate.

(e) Timing of Award Payments. The Awards granted for a Performance Period shall be paid to Participants as soon as administratively possible following completion of the certifications required by Subsection 7.4(c).

(f) Noncompetition. No Participant shall receive payment for an Award if, subsequent to the commencement of a Performance Period and prior to the date the Awards for such period are paid, the

Participant engages in any of the conduct prohibited under Section 14.3.

7.5   Maximum Award Payable

Notwithstanding any provision contained in the Plan to the contrary, the maximum Performance Award payable to any one Participant under the Plan for a Performance Period is 50,000 shares of Common Stock or, in the event the Performance Award is paid in cash, the equivalent cash value thereof on the Performance Award's Effective Date.

ARTICLE 8—STOCK OPTIONS

8.1   In General

Awards may be granted to Employees in the form of stock options. These stock options may be incentive stock options within the meaning of Section 422 of the Code or nonqualified stock options (i.e., stock options which are not incentive stock options), or a combination of both. All Awards under the Plan issued to Covered Employees in the form of stock options shall qualify as "Performance-Based Compensation" under Section 162(m) of the Code.

8.2   Terms and Conditions of Stock Options

An option shall be exercisable in whole or in such installments and at such times as may be determined by the Committee. The price at which Common Stock may be purchased upon exercise of a stock option shall be not less than 100% of the fair market value of the Common Stock, as determined by the Committee, on the Effective Date of the option's grant. Moreover, all options shall not expire later than 10 years from the Effective Date of the Option's grant. Stock options shall not be repriced, i.e., there shall be no grant of a stock option(s) to a Participant in exchange for a Participant's agreement to cancellation of a higher-priced stock option(s) that was previously granted to such Participant.

8.3   Restrictions Relating to Incentive Stock Options

Stock options issued in the form of incentive stock options shall, in addition to being subject to the terms and conditions of Section

8.2, comply with Section 422 of the Code. Accordingly, the aggregate fair market value (determined at the time the option was granted) of the Common Stock with respect to which incentive stock options are exercisable for the first time by a Participant during any calendar year (under this Plan or any other plan of the Company) shall not exceed $100,000 (or such other limit as may be required by the Code). From the maximum number of shares available for issuance under the Plan under Section 6.1, the number of shares of Common Stock that shall be available for incentive stock options granted under the Plan is 16,000,000.

8.4   Additional Terms and Conditions

The Committee may, by way of the Award Notice or otherwise, establish such other terms, conditions, restrictions and/or limitations, if any, of any stock option Award, provided they are not inconsistent with the Plan.

8.5   Exercise

Upon exercise, the option price of a stock option may be paid in cash, shares of Common Stock, a combination of the foregoing, or such other consideration as the Committee may deem appropriate. The Committee shall establish appropriate methods for accepting Common Stock, whether restricted or unrestricted, and may impose such conditions as it deems appropriate on the use of such Common Stock to exercise a stock option. Subject to Section 19.9, stock options Awarded under the Plan may be exercised by way of the Company's broker-assisted stock option exercise program, provided such program is available at the time of the option exercise. The Committee may permit a Participant to satisfy any amounts required to be withheld under applicable Federal, state and local tax laws, in effect from time to time, by electing to have the Company withhold a portion of the shares of Common Stock to be delivered for the payment of such taxes.

8.6   Maximum Award Payable

Notwithstanding any provision contained in the Plan to the contrary, the maximum number of shares for which stock options may be granted under the Plan to any one Participant for a Performance Period is 200,000 shares of Common Stock.

ARTICLE 9—STOCK APPRECIATION RIGHTS

9.1   In General

Awards may be granted to Employees in the form of stock appreciation rights ("SARs"). An SAR may be granted in tandem with all or a portion of a related stock option under the Plan ("Tandem SARs"), or may be granted separately ("Freestanding SARs"). A Tandem SAR may be granted either at the time of the grant of the related stock option or at any time thereafter during the term of the stock option. SARs shall entitle the recipient to receive a payment equal to the appreciation in market value of a stated number of shares of Common Stock from the exercise price to the market value on the date of exercise. All Awards under the Plan issued to Covered Employees in the form of an SAR shall qualify as "Performance-Based Compensation" under Section 162(m) of the Code.

9.2   Terms and Conditions of Tandem SARs

A Tandem SAR shall be exercisable to the extent, and only to the extent, that the related stock option is exercisable, and the "exercisable price" of such an SAR (the base from which the value of the SAR is measured at its exercise) shall be the option price under the related stock option. However, at no time shall a Tandem SAR be issued if the option price of its related stock option is less than the fair market value of the Common Stock, as determined by the Committee, on the Effective Date of the Tandem SAR's grant. If a related stock option is exercised as to some or all of the shares covered by the Award, the related Tandem SAR, if any, shall be canceled automatically to the extent of the number of shares covered by the stock option exercise. Upon exercise of a Tandem SAR as to some or all of the shares covered by the Award, the related stock option shall be canceled automatically to the extent of the number of shares covered by such exercise, and such shares shall not again be eligible for grant in accordance with Section 6.1. Moreover, all Tandem SARs shall not expire later than 10 years from the Effective Date of the SARs grant.

9.3   Terms and Conditions of Freestanding SARs

Freestanding SARs shall be exercisable in whole or in such installments and at such times as may be determined by the Committee. The exercise price of a Freestanding SAR shall be not less than 100% of the fair market value of the Common Stock, as determined by the Committee, on the Effective Date of the Freestanding SAR's grant. Moreover, all Freestanding SARs shall expire no later than 10 years from the Effective Date of the Freestanding SAR's grant.

9.4   Deemed Exercise

The Committee may provide that an SAR shall be deemed to be exercised at the close of business on the scheduled expiration date of such SAR if at such time the SAR by its terms remains exercisable and, if so exercised, would result in a payment to the holder of such SAR.

9.5   Additional Terms and Conditions

The Committee may, by way of the Award Notice or otherwise, determine such other terms, conditions, restrictions and/or limitations, if any, of any SAR Award, provided they are not inconsistent with the Plan.

9.6   Maximum Award Payable

Notwithstanding any provision contained in the Plan to the contrary, the maximum number of shares for which SARs may be granted under the Plan to any one Participant for a Performance Period is 200,000 shares of Common Stock.

ARTICLE 10—STOCK AWARDS

10.1   Grants

Awards may be granted in the form of Stock Awards. Stock Awards shall be Awarded in such numbers and at such times during the term of the Plan as the Committee shall determine.

10.2   Award Restrictions

Stock Awards shall be subject to such terms, conditions, restrictions, and/or limitations, if any, as the Committee deems appropriate including, but not by way of limitation, restrictions on transferability and continued employment; provided, however, they are not inconsistent with the Plan. The Committee may modify or accelerate the delivery of a Stock Award under such circumstances as it deems appropriate.

10.3   Rights as Shareholders

During the period in which any restricted shares of Common Stock are subject to the restrictions imposed under Section 10.2, the Committee may, in its sole discretion, grant to the Participant to whom such restricted shares have been Awarded all or any of the rights of a shareholder with respect to such shares, including, but not by way of limitation, the right to vote such shares and, pursuant to Article 15, the right to receive dividends.

10.4   Evidence of Award

Any Stock Award granted under the Plan may be evidenced in such manner as the Committee deems appropriate, including, without limitation, book-entry registration or issuance of a stock certificate or certificates.

ARTICLE 11—PERFORMANCE UNITS

11.1   Grants

Awards may be granted in the form of performance units. Performance units, as that term is used in this Plan, shall refer to Units valued by reference to designated criteria established by the Committee, other than Common Stock.

11.2   Performance Criteria

Performance units shall be contingent on the attainment during a Common Stock of certain performance objectives. The length of the Common Stock, the performance objectives to be achieved during the Common Stock, and the measure of whether and to what degree such objectives have been attained shall be conclusively determined by the Committee in the exercise of its absolute discretion. Performance objectives may be revised by the Committee, at such times as it deems appropriate during the Common Stock, in order to take into consideration any unforeseen events or changes in circumstances.

11.3 Additional Terms and Conditions

The Committee may, by way of the Award Notice or otherwise, determine such other terms, conditions, restrictions, and/or limitations, if any, of any Award of performance units, provided they are not inconsistent with the Plan.

ARTICLE 12—PERFORMANCE SHARES

12.1 Grants

Awards may be granted in the form of performance shares. Performance shares, as that term is used in this Plan, shall refer to shares of Common Stock or Units which are expressed in terms of Common Stock.

12.2 Performance Criteria

Performance units shall be contingent on the attainment during a Common Stock of certain performance objectives. The length of the Common Stock, the performance objectives to be achieved during the Common Stock, and the measure of whether and to what degree such objectives have been attained shall be conclusively determined by the Committee in the exercise of its absolute discretion. Performance objectives may be revised by the Committee, at such times as it deems appropriate during the Common Stock, in order to take into consideration any unforeseen events or changes in circumstances.

12.3 Additional Terms and Conditions

The Committee may, by way of the Award Notice or otherwise, determine such other terms, conditions, restrictions, and/or limitations, if any, of any Award of performance units, provided they are not inconsistent with the Plan.

ARTICLE 13—PERFORMANCE STOCK PROGRAM

13.1 Purpose

The purposes of the Performance Stock Program are: (a) to promote the interests of the Company and its shareholders by providing a means to acquire a proprietary interest in the Company to selected Key Employees who are in a position to make a substantial contribution to the continued progress and success of the Company; (b) to attract and retain qualified individuals to serve as Employees in those positions; (c) to enhance long-term performance of the Company by linking a meaningful portion of the compensation of selected Key Employees to the achievement of specific long-term financial objectives of the Company; and (d) to motivate and reward selected Key Employees to undertake actions to increase the price of the Common Stock.

13.2 Eligibility

Any Key Employee is eligible to participate in the Performance Stock Program. Within the first 90 days of a Performance Cycle (or, if longer, within the maximum period allowed under Section 162(m) of the Code), the CEO will recommend to the Committee, and from such recommendations the Committee will select, those Key Employees who will be Participants for such Performance Cycle. However, designation of a Key Employee as a Participant for a Performance Cycle shall not in any manner entitle the Participant to receive payment of an Award for the cycle. The determination as to whether or not such Participant becomes entitled to payment of an Award for such Performance Cycle shall be decided solely in accordance with the provisions of this Article 13. Moreover, designation of a Key Employee as a Participant for a particular Performance Cycle shall not require designation of such Key Employee as a Participant in any subsequent Performance Cycle and designation of one Key Employee as a Participant shall not require designation of any other Key Employee as a Participant in such Performance Cycle or in any other Performance Cycle.

13.3 Description of Awards

Awards granted under the Performance Stock Program provide Participants with the opportunity to earn shares of Common Stock, subject to the terms and conditions of Section 13.8 below. Each Award granted under the Plan for a Performance Cycle shall consist of a Target Award expressed as fixed number of shares of Common Stock. In the event the Performance Goals for the Performance Cycle are achieved, the Performance Formula shall determine, with regards to a particular Participant, what percentage of the Participant's Target Award for the Performance Cycle will be earned. All of the Awards issued under the Performance Stock Program to Covered Employees are intended to qualify as "Performance-Based Compensation" under Section 162(m) of the Code.

13.4   Procedure for Determining Awards

Within the first 90 days of a Performance Cycle (or, if longer, within the maximum period allowed under Section 162(m) of the Code), the Committee shall establish in writing for such Performance Cycle the following: the specific Performance Criteria that will be used to establish the Performance Goal(s), the kind(s) and/or level(s) of the Performance Goal(s), whether the Performance Goal(s) is (are) to apply to the Company, Kodak, a Subsidiary, or any one or more subunits of the foregoing, the amount of the Target Awards, and the Performance Formula.

13.5   Payment of Awards

(a) Condition to Receipt of Awards. Except as provided in Section 13.7, a Participant must be employed by the Company on the Performance Cycle's Award Payment Date to be eligible for an award for such Performance Cycle.

(b) Limitation. A Participant shall be eligible to receive an Award for a Performance Cycle only if: (1) the Performance Goals for such cycle are achieved; and (2) the Performance Formula as applied against such Performance Goals determines that all or some portion of the Participant's Target Award has been earned for the Performance Period.

(c) Certification. Following the completion of a Performance Cycle, the Committee shall meet to review and certify in writing whether, and to what extent, the Performance Goals for the Performance Cycle have been achieved. If the Committee certifies that the Performance Goals have been achieved, it shall, based upon application of the Performance Formula to the Performance Goals for such cycle, also calculate and certify in writing for each Participant what percentage of the Participant's Target Award has been earned for the cycle. The Committee shall then determine the actual size of each Participant's Award for the Performance Cycle and, in so doing, shall apply Negative Discretion, if and when it deems appropriate.

(d) Negative Discretion. In determining the actual size of an individual Award to be paid for a Performance Cycle, the Committee may, through the use of Negative Discretion, reduce or eliminate the amount of the Award earned under the Performance Formula for the Performance Cycle, if in its sole judgment, such reduction or elimination is appropriate.

(e) Timing of Award Payments. The Awards granted by the Committee for a Performance Cycle shall be paid to Participants on the Award Payment Date for such Performance Cycle.

(f) New Participants. Participants who are employed by the Company after the Committee's selection of Participants for the Performance Cycle, as well as Key Employees who are selected by the Committee to be Participants after such date, shall, in the event Awards are paid for the Performance Cycle, only be entitled to a pro rata Award. The amount of the pro rata Award shall be determined by multiplying the Award the Participant would have otherwise been paid if he or she had been a Participant for the entire Performance Cycle by a fraction the numerator of which is the number of full months he or she was eligible to participate in the Performance Stock Program during the Performance Cycle over the total number of full months in the Performance Cycle. For purposes of this calculation, a partial month of participation shall: (1) be treated as a full month of participation to the extent a Participant participates in the Performance Stock Program on 15 or more days of such month; and (2) not to be taken into consideration to the extent the Participant participates in the Performance Stock Program for less than 15 days of such month.

(g) Noncompetition. No Participant shall receive payment for an Award if, subsequent to the commencement of the Performance Cycle and prior to the Award Payment Date for such cycle, the Participant engages in the conduct prohibited under Section 14.3.

13.6 Maximum Award Payable

Notwithstanding any provision contained in the Plan to the contrary, the maximum Award payable to any one Participant under the Plan for a Performance Cycle is 50,000 shares of Common Stock.

13.7 Termination of Employment During Performance Cycle

In the event a Participant terminates employment due to Death, Disability, Retirement or Termination of Employment for an Approved Reason prior to the Award Payment Date for a Performance Cycle, the Participant shall receive, if Awards are paid for such Performance Cycle and if he or she complies with the requirements of Subsection 13.5(g) through the Award Payment Date, a pro rata Award. The amount of the pro rata Award shall be determined by multiplying the Award the Participant would have otherwise been paid if he or she had been a Participant through the Award Payment Date for the Performance Cycle by a fraction, the numerator of which is the number of full months he or she was a Participant during such Performance Cycle over the total number of full months in the Performance Cycle. For purposes of this calculation, a partial month of participation shall: (1) be treated as a full month of participation to the extent a Participant participates in the Performance Stock Program on 15 or more days of such month; and (2) not be taken into consideration to the extent the Participant participates in the Performance Stock Program for less than 15 days of such month. Such pro rata Award shall be paid in the form of shares of Common Stock, not subject to any restrictions, limitations or escrow requirements. In the event of Disability, Retirement or Termination for an Approved Reason, the pro rata Award shall be paid directly to the Participant and, in the event of death, to the Participant's estate.

13.8 Awards

On the Award Payment Date for a Performance Cycle, the Committee shall issue to each Participant the Award, in the form of shares of Common Stock, he or she has earned for such Performance Cycle. Such shares of Common Stock shall be subject to such terms, conditions, limitations and restrictions as the Committee, in its sole judgment, determines.

ARTICLE 14—PAYMENT OF AWARDS

14.1　In General

Absent a Plan provision to the contrary, payment of Awards may, at the discretion of the Committee, be made in cash, Common Stock, a combination of cash and Common Stock, or any other form of property as the Committee shall determine. In addition, payment of Awards may include such terms, conditions, restrictions and/or limitations, if any, as the Committee deems appropriate, including, in the case of Awards paid in the form of Common Stock, restrictions on transfer and forfeiture provisions; provided, however, such terms, conditions, restrictions and/or limitations are not inconsistent with the Plan. Further, payment of Awards may be made in the form of a lump sum or installments, as determined by the Committee.

14.2　Termination of Employment

If a participant's employment with the Company terminates for a reason other than death, Disability, Retirement, or any Approved Reason, all unexercised, unearned, and/or unpaid Awards, including but not by way of limitation, Awards earned but not yet paid, all unpaid dividends and dividend equivalents, and all interest accrued on the foregoing shall be canceled or forfeited, as the case may be, unless the Participant's Award Notice provides otherwise. The Committee shall, notwithstanding Sections 4.4 and 19.11 to the contrary, have the authority to promulgate rules and regulations to determine the treatment of an Award under the Plan in the event of the Participant's death, Disability, Retirement or Termination for an Approved Reason, provided, however, in the case of Awards issued under the Restricted Stock Program, such rules and regulations are consistent with Section 13.7.

14.3　Noncompetition

Unless the Award Notice specifies otherwise, a Participant shall forfeit all unexercised, unearned, and/or unpaid Awards, including, but not by way of limitation, Awards earned but not yet paid, all unpaid dividends and dividend equivalents, and all interest, if any, accrued on the foregoing if, (i) in the opinion of the Committee, the Participant, without the prior written consent of Kodak, engages directly or indirectly in any manner or capacity as principal, agent, partner, officer, director, stockholder, employee or otherwise, in any business or activity competitive with the business conducted by Kodak or any Subsidiary; (ii) the Participant at any time divulges to any person or any entity other than the Company any trade secrets, methods, processes or the proprietary or confidential information of the Company; or (iii) the Participant performs any act or engages in any activity which in the opinion of the CEO is inimical to the best interests of the Company. For purposes of this Section 14.3, a Participant shall not be deemed a stockholder if the Participant's record and beneficial ownership amount to not more than 1% of the outstanding capital stock of any company subject to the periodic and other reporting requirements of the Exchange Act.

ARTICLE 15—DIVIDEND AND DIVIDEND EQUIVALENT

If an Award is granted in the form of a Stock Award, stock option, or performance share, or in the form of any other stock-based grant, the Committee may choose, at the time of the grant of the Award or any time thereafter up to the time of the Award's payment, to include as part of such Award an entitlement to receive dividends or dividend equivalents, subject to such terms, conditions, restrictions and/or limitations, if any, as the Committee may establish. Dividends and dividend equivalents shall be paid in such form and manner (i.e., lump sum or installments), and at such time(s) as the Committee shall determine. All dividends or dividend equivalents which are not paid currently may, at the Committee's discretion, accrue interest, be reinvested into additional shares of Common Stock or, in the case of dividends or dividend equivalents credited in connection with performance shares, be credited as additional performance shares and paid to the Participant if and when, and to the extent that, payment is made pursuant to such Award. The total number of shares available for grant under Section 6.1 shall not be reduced to reflect any dividends or dividend equivalents that are reinvested into additional shares of Common Stock or credited as additional performance shares.

ARTICLE 16—DEFERRAL OF AWARDS

At the discretion of the Committee, payment of any Award, dividend, or dividend equivalent, or any portion thereof, may be deferred by a Participant until such time as the Committee may establish. All such deferrals shall be accomplished by the delivery of a written, irrevocable election by the Participant prior to the time established by the Committee for such purpose, on a form provided by the Company. Further, all deferrals shall be made in accordance with administrative guidelines established by the Committee to ensure that such deferrals comply with all applicable requirements of the Code. Deferred payments shall be paid in a lump sum or installments, as determined by the Committee. Deferred Awards may also be credited with interest, at such rates to be determined by the Committee, and, with respect to those deferred Awards denominated in the form of Common Stock, with dividends or dividend equivalents.

ARTICLE 17—CHANGE IN OWNERSHIP

17.1   Background

Notwithstanding any provision contained in the Plan, including, but not limited to, Sections 4.4 and 19.11, the provisions of this Article 17 shall control over any contrary provision. Upon a Change In Ownership: (i) the terms of this Article 17 shall immediately become operative, without further action or consent by any person or entity; (ii) all terms, conditions, restrictions, and limitations in effect on any unexercised, unearned, unpaid, and/or deferred Award, or any other outstanding Award, shall immediately lapse as of the date of such event; (iii) no other terms, conditions, restrictions and/or limitations shall be imposed upon any Awards on or after such date, and in no circumstance shall an Award be forfeited on or after such date; and (iv) except in those instances where a prorated Award is required to be paid under this Article 17, all unexercised, unvested, unearned, and/or unpaid Awards or any other outstanding Awards shall automatically become one hundred percent (100%) vested immediately.

17.2   Dividends and Dividend Equivalents

Upon a Change In Ownership, all unpaid dividends and dividend equivalents and all interest accrued thereon, if any, shall be treated and paid under this Article 17 in the identical manner and time as the Award under which such dividends or dividend equivalents have been credited. For example, if upon a Change In Ownership, an

Award under this Article 17 is to be paid in a prorated fashion, all unpaid dividends and dividend equivalents with respect to such Award shall be paid according to the same formula used to determine the amount of such prorated Award.

17.3 Treatment of Performance Units and Performance Shares

If a Change In Ownership occurs during the term of one or more Common Stocks for which the Committee has granted performance units and/or performance shares (including those issued as Performance Awards under Article 7), the term of each such Common Stock (hereinafter a "current Common Stock") and each completed Common Stock for which the Committee has not on or before such date made a determination as to whether and to what degree the performance objectives for such period have been attained (hereinafter a "completed Common Stock"), it shall be assumed that the performance objectives have been attained at a level of one hundred percent (100%) or the equivalent thereof.

A Participant in one or more "current Common Stocks" shall be considered to have earned and, therefore, be entitled to receive a prorated portion of the Awards previously granted to him for each such Common Stock. Such prorated portion shall be determined by multiplying the number of performance shares or performance units, as the case may be, granted to the Participant by a fraction, the numerator of which is the total number of whole months that have elapsed since the beginning of the Common Stock, and the denominator of which is the total number of full months in such Common Stock. For purposes of this calculation, a partial month shall be treated as a full month to the extent 15 or more days in such month have elapsed.

A Participant in one or more "completed Common Stocks" shall be considered to have earned and, therefore, be entitled to receive all the performance shares or performance units, as the case may be, previously granted to him during each such Common Stock.

17.4 Treatment of Awards under Performance Stock Program

Upon a Change In Ownership, any Participant of the Performance Stock Program, whether or not he or she is still employed by the Company, shall be paid, as soon as practicable but in no event later than 90 days after the Change In Ownership, a pro rata Award for each Performance Cycle in which the Participant was selected to participate and during which the Change in Ownership occurs. The amount of the pro rata Award shall be determined by multiplying the Target Award for such Performance Cycle for Participants in the same wage grade as the Participant by a fraction, the numerator of which shall be the number of full months in the Performance Cycle prior to the date of the Change In Ownership and the denominator of which shall be the total number of full months in the Performance Cycle. For purpose of this calculation, a partial month shall be treated as a full month to the extent 15 or more days in such month have elapsed. To the extent Target Awards have not yet been established for the Performance Cycle, the Target Award for the immediately preceding Performance Cycle shall be used.

17.5   Valuation of Awards

Upon a Change In Ownership, all outstanding Units of Common Stock, Freestanding SARs, stock options (including incentive stock options), Stock Awards (including those issued as Performance Awards under Article 7), performance shares (including those earned as a result of the application of Section 17.3), and all other outstanding stock-based Awards (including those earned as a result of the application of Section 17.4 and those granted by the Committee pursuant to its authority under Subsection 4.2(m) hereof), shall be valued and cashed out on the basis of the Change In Control Price.

17.6   Payment of Awards

Upon a Change In Ownership, any Participant, whether or not he or she is still employed by the Company, shall be paid, in a single lump-sum cash payment, as soon as practicable, but no later than 90 days after the Change In Ownership, all of his or her Units of Common Stock, Freestanding SARs, stock options (including incentive stock options), Stock Awards (including those issued as Performance Awards under Article 7), performance units and shares (including those earned as a result of the application of Section 17.3), all other outstanding stock-based Awards (including those earned as a result of the application of Section 17.4 and those granted by the Committee pursuant to its authority under Subsection 4.2(m) hereof), and all other outstanding Awards.

17.7 Deferred Awards

Upon a Change In Ownership, all Awards deferred by a Participant under Article 16 hereof, but for which he or she has not received payment as of such date, shall be paid in a single lump-sum cash payment as soon as practicable, but in no event later than 90 days after the Change In Ownership. For purposes of making such payment, the value of all Awards which are stock based shall be determined by the Change In Control Price.

17.8 Section 16 of Exchange Act

Notwithstanding anything contained in this Article 17 to the contrary, any Participant who, on the date of the Change In Ownership, holds any stock options or Freestanding SARs that have not been outstanding for a period of at least six months from their date of grant and who on such date is required to report under Section 16 of the Exchange Act shall not be paid such Award until the first day next following the end of such six-month period.

17.9 Miscellaneous

Upon a Change In Ownership, (i) the provisions of Sections 14.2, 14.3, and 19.3 hereof shall become null and void and of no further force and effect; and (ii) no action, including, but not by way of limitation, the amendment, suspension, or termination of the Plan, shall be taken which would affect the rights of any Participant or the operation of the Plan with respect to any Award to which the Participant may have become entitled hereunder on or prior to the date of such action or as a result of such Change In Ownership.

ARTICLE 18—CHANGE IN CONTROL

18.1 Background

Notwithstanding any provisions contained in the Plan, including, but not limited to, Sections 4.4 and 19.11, the provisions of this Article 18 shall control over any contrary provision. All Participants shall be eligible for the treatment afforded by this Article if their employment terminated within two years following a Change In Control, unless the termination is due to (i) Death, (ii) Disability, (iii) Cause, (iv) Resignation other than (A) resignation from a declined reassignment to a job that is not reasonably equivalent in responsibility or compensation (as defined in Kodak's Termination Allowance Plan), or that is not in the same geographic area (as defined in Kodak's Termination Allowance Plan), or (B) resignation within 30 days following a reduction in base pay, or (v) Retirement.

18.2 Vesting and Lapse of Restrictions

If a participant is eligible for treatment under this Article 18, (i) all of the terms, conditions, restrictions, and limitations in effect on any of his or her unexercised, unearned, unpaid and/or deferred Awards shall immediately lapse as of the date of his or her termination of employment; (ii) no other terms, conditions, restrictions and/or limitations shall be imposed upon any of his or her Awards on or after such date, and in no event shall any of his or her Awards be forfeited on or after such date; and (iii) except in those instances where a prorated Award is required to be paid under this Article 18, all of his or her unexercised, unvested, unearned and/or unpaid Awards shall automatically become one hundred percent (100%) vested immediately upon his or her termination of employment.

18.3 Dividends and Dividend Equivalents

If a Participant is eligible for treatment under this Article 18, all of his or her unpaid dividends and dividend equivalents and all interest accrued thereon, if any, shall be treated and paid under this Article 18 in the identical manner and time as the Award under which such dividends or dividend equivalents have been credited.

18.4 Treatment of Performance Units and Performance Shares

If a Participant holding either performance units or performance shares (including those issued as Performance Awards under Article 7) is terminated under the conditions described in Section 18.1 above, the provisions of this Section 18.4 shall determine the manner in which such performance units and/or performance shares shall be paid to the Participant. For purposes of making such payment, each "current Common Stock," as that term is defined in Section 17.3, shall be treated as terminating upon the date of the Participant's termination of employment, and for each such "current Common Stock" and each "completed Common Stock," as the term is defined in Section 17.3, it shall be assumed that the performance objectives have been attained at a level of one hundred percent (100%) or the equivalent thereof. If the Participant is participating in one or more "current Common Stocks," he or she shall be considered to have earned and, therefore, be entitled to receive that prorated portion of the Awards previously granted to him for each such performance period, as determined in accordance with the formula established in Section 17.3 hereof. A Participant in one or more "completed Common Stocks" shall be considered to have earned and, therefore, be entitled to receive all the performance shares and performance units previously granted to him during each Common Stock.

18.5   Treatment of Awards under Performance Stock Program

If a Participant of the Performance Stock Program is eligible for treatment under this Article 18, he or she shall be paid, as soon as practicable but in no event later than 90 days after the date of his or her termination of employment, a pro rata Award for each Performance Cycle in which the Participant was selected to participate and during which the Change In Ownership occurs. The amount of the pro rata Award shall be determined by multiplying the Target Award for such Performance Cycle for Participants in the same wage grade as the Participant by a fraction, the numerator of which shall be the number of full months in the Performance Cycle prior to the date of his of her termination of employment and the denominator of which shall be the total number of full months in the Performance Cycle. For purposes of this calculation, a partial month shall be treated as a full month to the extent 15 or more days in such month have elapsed. To the extent Target Awards have not yet been established for the Performance Cycle, the Target Awards for the immediately preceding Performance Cycle shall be used.

18.6   Valuation of Awards

If a Participant is eligible for treatment under this Article 18, his or her Awards shall be valued and cashed out in accordance with the provisions of Section 17.5.

18.7   Payment of Awards

If a Participant is eligible for treatment under this Article 18, he or she shall be paid, in a single lump-sum cash payment, as soon as practicable but in no event later than 90 days after the date of his or her termination of employment, all of his or her Units of Common Stock, Freestanding SARs, stock options (including incentive stock options), Stock Awards (including those issued as Performance Awards under Article 7), performance units and shares (including those earned as a result of the application of Section 18.4 above), all other outstanding stock-based Awards (including those earned as a result of the application of Section 18.5 above and those granted by the Committee pursuant to its authority under Subsection 4.2(m) hereof), and all other outstanding Awards.

18.8   Deferred Awards

If a Participant is eligible for treatment under this Article 18, all of his or her deferred Awards for which payment has not been received as of the date of his or her termination of employment shall be paid to the Participant in a single lump-sum cash payment as soon as practicable, but in no event later than 90 days after the date of the Participant's termination. For purposes of making such payment, the value of all Awards which are stock based shall be determined by the Change In Control Price.

18.9   Section 16 of Exchange Act

Notwithstanding anything contained in this Article 18 to the contrary, any Participant who, on the date of his or her termination of employment under the conditions described in Section 18.1, holds any stock options or Freestanding SARs that have been outstanding for a period of at least six months from their date of grant and who on the date of such termination is required to report under Section 16 of the Exchange Act shall not be paid such Award until the first business day next following the end of such six-month period.

18.10   Miscellaneous

Upon a Change In Control (i) the provision of Sections 14.2, 14.3, and 19.3 hereof shall become null and void and of no force and effect insofar as they apply to a Participant who has been terminated under the conditions described in Section 18.1 above; and (ii) no action, including, but not by way of limitation, the amendment, suspension or termination of the Plan, shall be taken which would affect the rights of any Participant or the operation of the Plan with respect to any Award to which the Participant may have become entitled hereunder on or prior to the date of the Change In Control or to which he or she may become entitled as a result of such Change In Control.

18.11   Legal Fees

Kodak shall pay all legal fees and related expenses incurred by a Participant in seeking to obtain or enforce any payment benefit of right he or she may be entitled to under the Plan after a Change In Control; provided, however, the Participant shall be required to repay any such amounts to Kodak to the extent a court of competent jurisdiction issues a final and non-appealable order setting forth the determination that the position taken by the Participant was frivolous or advanced in bad faith.

ARTICLE 19—MISCELLANEOUS

19.1   Nonassignability

No Awards or any other payment under the Plan shall be subject in any manner to alienation, anticipation, sale, transfer (except by will or the laws of descent and distribution), assignment, pledge, or encumbrance, nor shall any Award be payable to or exercisable by anyone other than the Participant to whom it was granted.

19.2   Withholding Taxes

The Company shall be entitled to deduct from any payment under the Plan, regardless of the form of such payment, the amount of all applicable income and employment taxes required by law to be withheld with respect to such payment or may require the Participant to pay to it such tax prior to and as a condition of the making of such payment. In accordance with any applicable administrative guidelines it establishes, the Committee may allow a Participant to pay the amount of taxes required by law to be withheld from an Award by withholding from any payment of Common Stock due as a result of such Award, or by permitting the Participant to deliver to the Company, shares of Common Stock having a fair market value, as determined by the Committee, equal to the amount of such required withholding taxes.

19.3 Amendments to Awards

The Committee may at any time unilaterally amend any unexercised, unearned, or unpaid Award, including, but not by way of limitation, Awards earned but not yet paid, to the extent it deems appropriate; provided, however, that any such amendment which, in the opinion of the Committee, is adverse to the Participant shall require the Participant's consent.

19.4 Regulatory Approvals and Listings

Notwithstanding anything contained in this Plan to the contrary, the Company shall have no obligation to issue or deliver certificates of Common Stock evidencing Stock Awards or any other Award resulting in the payment of Common Stock prior to (i) the obtaining of any approval from any governmental agency which the Company shall, in its sole discretion, determine to be necessary or advisable, (ii) the admission of such shares to listing on the stock exchange on which the Common Stock may be listed, and (iii) the completion of any registration or other qualification of said shares under any state or Federal law or ruling of any governmental body which the Company shall, in its sole discretion, determine to be necessary or advisable.

19.5 No Right to Continued Employment or Grants

Participation in the Plan shall not give any Employee any right to remain in the employ of Kodak or any Subsidiary. Kodak or, in the case of employment with a Subsidiary, the Subsidiary, reserves the right to terminate any Employee at any time. Further, the adoption of this Plan shall not be deemed to give any Employee or any other individual any right to be selected as a Participant or to be granted an Award.

19.6 Amendment/Termination

The Committee may suspend or terminate the Plan at any time with or without prior notice. In addition, the Committee may, from time to time and with or without prior notice, amend the Plan in any manner, but may not without shareholder approval adopt any amendment which would require the vote of the shareholders of Kodak pursuant to Section 16 of the Exchange Act or Section 162(m) of the Code, but only insofar as such amendment affects Covered Employees.

19.7 Governing Law

The Plan shall be governed by and construed in accordance with the laws of the State of New York, except as superseded by applicable Federal Law.

19.8 No Right, Title, or Interest in Company Assets

No Participant shall have any rights as a shareholder as a result of participation in the Plan until the date of issuance of a stock certificate in his or her name, and, in the case of restricted shares of Common Stock, such rights are granted to the Participant under the Plan. To the extent any person acquires a right to receive payments from the Company under the Plan, such rights shall be no greater than the rights in or against any specific assets of the Company. All of the Awards granted under the Plan shall be unfunded.

19.9 Section 16 of the Exchange Act

In order to avoid any Exchange Act violations, the Committee may, from time to time, impose additional restrictions upon an Award, including but not limited to, restrictions regarding tax withholdings and restrictions regarding the Participant's ability to exercise Awards under the company's broker-assisted exercise program.

19.10 No Guarantee of Tax Consequences

No person connected with the Plan in any capacity, including but not limited to, Kodak and its Subsidiaries and their directors, officers, agents and employees makes any representation, commitment, or guarantee that any tax treatment, including, but not limited to, Federal, state and local income, estate and gift tax treatment, will be applicable with respect to amounts deferred under the Plan, or paid to or for the benefit of a Participant under the Plan, or that such tax treatment will apply to or be available to a Participant on account of participation in the Plan.

19.11   Compliance with Section 162(m)

If any provision of the Plan, other than the application of those contained in Articles 17 and 18 hereof, would cause the Awards granted to a Covered Person not to qualify as "Performance-Based Compensation" under Section 162(m) of the Code, that provision, insofar as it pertains to the Covered Person, shall be severed from, and shall be deemed not to be a part of, this Plan, but the other provisions hereof shall remain in full force and effect.

19.12   Other Benefits

No Award granted under the Plan shall be considered compensation for purposes of computing benefits under any retirement plan of the Company nor affect any benefits or compensation under any other benefit or compensation plan of the Company now or subsequently in effect.

PLAN 2: MANAGEMENT VARIABLE COMPENSATION PLAN

ARTICLE 1—PURPOSE, EFFECTIVE DATE, AND TERM OF PLAN

1.1   Purpose

The purposes of the Plan are to provide an annual incentive to Key Employees of the Company to put forth maximum efforts toward the continued growth and success of the Company, to encourage such Key Employees to remain in the employ of the Company, to assist the Company in attracting and motivating new Key Employees on a competitive basis, and to endeavor to qualify the Awards granted to Covered Employees under the Plan as "Performance-Based Compensation" as defined in Section 162(m) of the Code. The Plan is intended to apply to Key Employees of the Company in the United States and throughout the world.

1.2   Effective Date

The Plan shall be effective as of January 1, 1995, subject to approval by Kodak's shareholders at the 1995 Annual Meeting of the Shareholders of Kodak.

1.3 Term

Awards shall not be granted pursuant to the Plan after December 31, 1999; provided, however, the Committee may grant Awards after such date in recognition of performance for a Performance Period completed on or prior to such date.

ARTICLE 2—DEFINITIONS

2.1 Actual Award Pool

"Actual Award Pool" means, for a Performance Period, the amount determined in accordance with Section 6.4.

2.2 Average Net Assets

"Average Net Assets" means, for the Performance Period, the simple average of the Company's Net Assets for each of the following five fiscal quarters of the Company: the four fiscal quarters of the Performance Period and the fiscal quarter immediately preceding the Performance Period. For purposes of this calculation, Net Assets for a fiscal quarter shall be determined as of the end of such quarter.

2.3 Award

"Award" means the compensation granted to a Participant by the Committee for a Performance Period pursuant to Articles 6 and 7 or the compensation granted to a Key Employee by the Committee pursuant to Article 9. All Awards shall be issued in the form(s) specified by Article 5.

2.4 Award Payment Date

"Award Payment Date" means, for each Performance Period, the date that the amount of the Award for that Performance Period shall be paid to the Participant under Article 7, without regard to any election to defer receipt of the Award made by the Participant under Article 8 of the Plan.

2.5 Board

"Board" means the Board of Directors of Kodak.

2.6 Carryforward Amount

"Carryforward Amount" means, for a Performance Period, that portion, if any, or all of the difference, if any, between the Maximum Award for such Performance Period and the sum of all Awards paid under the Plan for such Performance Period, which the Committee elects to add to the Carryforward Amount.

2.7 Cause

"Cause" means (a) the willful and continued failure by a Key Employee to substantially perform his or her duties with his or her employer after written warnings identifying the lack of substantial performance are delivered to the Key Employee by his or her employer to specifically identify the manner in which the employer believes that the Key Employee has not substantially performed his or her duties; or (b) the willful engaging by a Key employee in illegal conduct which is materially and demonstrably injurious to the Company.

2.8 CEO

"CEO" means the Chief Executive Officer of Kodak.

2.9 Change In Control

"Change In Control" means a Change In Control of Kodak of a nature that would be required to be reported (assuming such event has not been "previously reported") in response to Item 1(a) of the Current Report on Form 8-K, as in effect on August 1, 1989, pursuant to Section 12 or 15(d) of the Exchange Act; provided that, without limitation, a Change In Control shall be deemed to have occurred at such time as (i) any "person" within the meaning of Section 13(d) of the Exchange Act, other than Kodak, a Subsidiary, or any employee benefit plan(s) sponsored by Kodak or any Subsidiary, is or has become the "beneficial owner," as defined in Rule 12d-3 under the Exchange Act, directly or indirectly, of 25% or more of the combined voting power of the outstanding securities of Kodak ordinarily having the right to vote at the election of directors, or (ii) individuals who constitute the Board on January 1, 1995 (the "Incumbent Board") have ceased for any reason to constitute at least a majority thereof, provided that any person becoming a director subsequent to January

1, 1995 whose election, or nomination for election by Kodak's share-holders, was approved by a vote of at least three-quarters (3/4) of the directors comprising the Incumbent Board (either by a specific vote or by approval of the proxy statement of Kodak in which such person is named as a nominee for director without objection to such nomination) shall be, for purposes of this Plan, considered as though such person were a member of the Incumbent Board.

2.10   Change In Ownership

"Change In Ownership" means a Change In Control which results directly or indirectly in Kodak's Common Stock ceasing to be actively traded on the New York Stock Exchange.

2.11   Code

"Code" means the Internal Revenue Code of 1986, as amended from time to time, including regulations thereunder and successor provisions and regulations thereto.

2.12   Committee

"Committee" means the Executive Compensation and Development Committee of the Board, or such other Board committee as may be designated by the Board to administer the Plan; provided that the Committee shall consist of three or more directors, all of whom are both a "disinterested person" within the meaning of Rule 16b-3 under the Exchange Act and an "outside director" within the meaning of the definition of such term as contained in Proposed Treasury Regulations Section 1.162-27(e)(3), or any successor definition adopted.

2.13   Common Stock

"Common Stock" means the Common Stock, $2.50 par value per share, of Kodak which may be newly issued or treasury stock.

2.14   Company

"Company" means Kodak and its Subsidiaries.

2.15 Covered Employee

"Covered Employee" means a Key Employee who is a "Covered Employee" within the meaning of Section 162(m) of the Code.

2.16 Disability

"Disability" means a disability under the terms of any long-term disability plan maintained by the Company.

2.17 Effective Date

"Effective Date" means the date an Award is determined to be effective by the Committee upon its grant of such Award.

2.18 Exchange Act

"Exchange Act" means the Securities Exchange Act of 1934, as amended form time to time, including rules thereunder and successor provisions and rules thereto.

2.19 Key Employee

"Key Employee" means either: (1) a salaried employee of the Company in wage grade 48 or above, or the equivalent thereof; or (2) a salaried employee of the Company who holds a position of responsibility in a managerial, administrative, or professional capacity and is in wage grade 43 or above.

2.20 Kodak

"Kodak" means Eastman Kodak Company.

2.21 Maximum Award

"Maximum Award" means, for a Performance Period, the dollar amount calculated in accordance with Section 6.2 by applying the Performance Formula for such Performance Period against the Performance Goals for the same Performance Period.

2.22 Maximum Award Pool

"Maximum Award Pool" means, for a Performance Period, the dollar amount calculated in accordance with Section 6.3(b) by adding the Maximum Award for the Performance Period with the Carryforward Amount.

2.23 Negative Discretion

"Negative Discretion" means the discretion granted to the Committee pursuant to Section 6.3(e) to reduce or eliminate the Maximum Award Pool or a portion of the Maximum Award Pool Allocated to a Covered Employee.

2.24 Net Assets

"Net Assets" means the Company's consolidated Total Shareholders' Equity and Borrowings (both short-term and long-term) as reported in its audited consolidated financial statements. The Committee is authorized at any time during the first 90 days of a Performance Period, or at any time thereafter in its sole and absolute discretion, to adjust or modify the calculation of Net Assets for such Performance Period in order to prevent the dilution or enlargement of the rights of Participants (a) in the event of, or in anticipation of, any unusual or extraordinary corporate time, transaction, event or development; (b) in recognition of, or in anticipation of, any other unusual or nonrecurring events affecting the Company, or the financial statements of the Company, or in response to, or in anticipation of, changes in applicable laws, regulations, accounting principles, or business conditions; and (c) in view of the Committee's assessment of the business strategy of the Company, performance of comparable organizations, economic and business conditions, and any other circumstances deemed relevant. However, if and to the extent the exercise of such authority after the first 90 days of a Performance Period would cause the Awards granted to the Covered Employees for the Performance Period to fail to qualify as "Performance-Based Compensation" under Section 162(m) of the Code, then such authority shall only be exercised with respect to those Participants who are not Covered Employees.

2.25 Net Income

"Net Income" means, for a Performance Period, the Company's consolidated Net Earnings (Loss) before Cumulative Effect of Changes in Accounting Principle for the Performance Period as reported in its audited consolidated financial statements. The Committee is authorized at any time during the first 90 days of a Performance Period, or at any time thereafter in its sole and absolute discretion, to adjust or modify the calculation of Net Income for such Performance Period in order to prevent the dilution or enlargement of the rights of Participants (a) in the event of, or in anticipation of, any dividend or other distribution (whether in the form of cash, securities or other property), recapitalization, restructuring, reorganization, merger, consolidation, spin-off, combination, repurchase, share exchange, liquidation, dissolution, or other similar corporate transaction, event or development; (b) in recognition of, or in anticipation of, any other unusual or nonrecurring event affecting the Company, or the financial statements of the Company, or in response to, or in anticipation of, changes in applicable laws, regulations, accounting principles, or business conditions; (c) in recognition of, or in anticipation of, any other extraordinary gains or losses; and (d) in view of the Committee's assessment of the business strategy of the Company, performance of comparable organizations, economic and business conditions, and any other circumstances deemed relevant. However, if and to the extent the exercise of such authority after the first 90 days of a Performance Period would cause the Awards granted to the Covered Employees for the Performance Period to fail to qualify as "Performance-Based Compensation" under Section 162(m) of the Code, then such authority shall only be exercised with respect to those Participants who are not Covered Employees.

2.26 Participant

"Participant" means either (a) for a Performance Period, a Key Employee who is designated to participate in the Plan for the Performance Period pursuant to Article 3; or (b) for purposes of Article 9, a Key Employee who is granted an Award pursuant to such Article.

2.27 Performance Criterion

"Performance Criterion" means the stated business criterion upon which the Performance Goals for a Performance Period are based as required pursuant to Proposed Treasury Regulations Section 1.162-27(e)(4)(iii). For purposes of the Plan, RONA shall be the Performance Criterion.

2.28 Performance Formula

"Performance Formula" means, for a Performance Period, the one or more objective formulas applied against the Performance Goals to determine whether all, some portion but less than all, or none of the Awards have been earned for the Performance Period. The dollar amount obtained through application of the Performance Formula shall be the Maximum Award. The Performance Formula for a Performance Period shall be established in writing by the Committee within the first 90 days of the Performance Period (or, if later, within the maximum period allowed pursuant to Section 162(m) of the Code).

2.29 Performance Goals

"Performance Goals" means, for a Performance Period, the one or more goals for the Performance Period established by the Committee in writing within the first 90 days of the Performance Period (or, if longer, within the maximum period allowed pursuant to Section 162(m) of the Code) based upon the Performance Criterion. The Committee is authorized at any time during the first 90 days of a Performance Period, or at any time thereafter in its sole and absolute discretion, to adjust or modify the calculation of a Performance Goal for such Performance Period in order to prevent the dilution or enlargement of the rights of Participants (a) in the event of, or in anticipation of, any unusual or extraordinary corporate item, transaction, event, or development; (b) in recognition of, or in anticipation of, any other unusual or nonrecurring events affecting the Company, or the financial statements of the Company, or in response to, or in anticipation of, changes in applicable laws, regulations, accounting principles, or business conditions; and (c) in view of the Committee's assessment of the business strategy of the Company, performance of comparable organizations, economic and business conditions, and any other circumstances deemed relevant. However, to the extent the exercise of such authority after the first 90 days of a Performance Period would cause the Awards granted to the Covered Employees for the Performance Period to fail to qualify as "Performance-Based Compensation" under Section 162(m) of the Code, then such authority shall only be exercised with respect to those Participants who are not Covered Employees.

2.30   Performance Period

"Performance Period" means Kodak's fiscal year or any other period designated by the Committee with respect to which an Award may be granted.

2.31   Plan

"Plan" means the Management Variable Compensation Plan.

2.32   Retirement

"Retirement" means retirement under any defined benefit pension plan maintained by the Company which is either a tax-qualified plan under Section 401(a) of the Code or is identified in writing by the Committee as a defined benefit pension plan.

2.33   RONA

"RONA" means, for a Performance Period, Return on Net Assets for the Performance Period. RONA shall be calculated by dividing Net Income for the Performance Period by Average Net Assets for the same period.

2.34   Subsidiary

"Subsidiary" means a subsidiary which is majority owned by Kodak and reported in Kodak's audited consolidated financial statements.

2.35   Target Award

"Target Award" means, for a Performance Period, the target Award amounts established for each wage grade by the Committee for the Performance Period. The Target Awards shall serve only as a guideline in making Awards under the Plan. Depending upon the Committee's exercise of its discretion pursuant to Section 6.4(c), but subject to Section 6.5, a Participant may receive an Award for a Performance Period which may be more or less than the Target Award for his or her wage grade for that Performance Period. Moreover, the fact that a Target Award is established for a Participant's wage grade for a Performance Period shall not in any manner entitle the Participant to receive an Award for such period.

ARTICLE 3—ELIGIBILITY

All Key Employees are eligible to participate in the Plan. the Committee will, in its sole discretion, designate within the first 90 days of a Performance Period which Key Employees will be Participants for such Performance Period. However, the fact that a Key Employee is a Participant for a Performance Period shall not in any manner entitle such Participant to receive an Award for the period. The determination as to whether or not such Participant shall be paid an Award for such Performance Period shall be decided solely in accordance with the provisions of Articles 6 and 7 hereof.

ARTICLE 4—PLAN ADMINISTRATION

4.1 Responsibility

The Committee shall have total and exclusive responsibility to control, operate, manage, and administer the Plan in accordance with its terms.

4.2 Authority of the Committee

The Committee shall have all the authority that may be necessary or helpful to enable it to discharge its responsibilities with respect to the Plan. Without limiting the generality of the preceding sentence, the Committee shall have the exclusive right: to interpret the Plan, to determine eligibility for participation in the Plan, to decide all questions concerning eligibility for and the amount of Awards payable under the Plan, to establish and administer the Performance Goals and certify whether, and to what extent, they are attained, to construe any ambiguous provision of the Plan, to correct any default, to supply any omission, to reconcile any inconsistency, to issue administrative guidelines as an aid to administer the Plan, to make regulations for carrying out the Plan and to make changes in such regulations as they from time to time deem proper, and to decide any and all questions arising in the administration, interpretation, and application of the Plan. In addition, in order to enable Key Employees who are foreign nationals or are employed outside the United States or both to receive Awards under the Plan, the Committee may adopt such amendments, procedures, regulations, subplans, and the like as are necessary or advisable, in the opinion of the Committee, to effectuate the purposes of the Plan.

4.3 Discretionary Authority

The Committee shall have full discretionary authority in all matters related to the discharge of its responsibilities and the exercise of its authority under the Plan including, without limitation, its construction of the terms of the Plan and its determination of eligibility for participation and Awards under the Plan. It is the intent of the Plan that the decisions of the Committee and its action with respect to the Plan shall be final, binding, and conclusive upon all persons having or claiming to have any right or interest in or under the Plan.

4.4 Section 162(m) of the Code

With regard to all Covered Employees, the Plan shall for all purposes be interpreted and construed in accordance with Section 162(m) of the Code.

4.5 Delegation of Authority

Except to the extent prohibited by law, the Committee may delegate some or all of its authority under the Plan to any person or persons provided that any such delegation be in writing; provided, however, only the Committee may select and grant Awards to Participants who are Covered Employees.

ARTICLE 5—FORM OF AWARDS

Awards may at the Committee's sole discretion be paid in cash, Common Stock, or a combination thereof. The Committee may, in its sole judgment, subject an Award to such terms, conditions, restrictions and/or limitations (including, but not limited to, restrictions on transferability and vesting), provided they are not inconsistent with the terms of the Plan. For purposes of the Plan, the value of any Award granted in the form of Common Stock shall be the mean between the high and low at which the Common Stock trades on the New York Stock Exchange as of the date of the grant's Effective Date.

ARTICLE 6—DETERMINATION OF AWARDS FOR A PERFORMANCE PERIOD

6.1 Procedure for Determining Awards

As detailed below in the succeeding Sections of this Article 6, the procedure for determining Awards for a Performance Period entails the following: (a) determination of Maximum Award; (b) determination of Maximum Award Pool; (c) determination of Actual Award Pool; and (d) allocation of Actual Award Pool among individual Participants. Upon completion of this process, any Awards earned for the Performance Period shall be paid in accordance with Article 7.

6.2 Determination of Maximum Award

(a) Purpose of Maximum Award. The Maximum Award for a Performance Period is an addend in the calculation of the Maximum Award Pool for such Performance Period.

(b) Calculation of Maximum Award. The Maximum Award for a Performance Period is the dollar amount obtained by applying the Performance Formula for such Performance Period against the Performance Goals for the same Performance Period.

6.3 Determination of Maximum Award Pool

(a) Purpose of Maximum Award Pool. The Maximum Award Pool, for a Performance Period, serves as the basis for calculating the maximum amount of Awards that may be granted to all Participants for such Performance Period.

(b) Calculation of Maximum Award Pool. The Maximum Award Pool for a Performance Period shall be calculated by adding the Maximum Award for such Performance Period with the Carryforward Amount.

(c) Limitation. The total of all Awards granted for a Performance Period shall not exceed the amount of the Maximum Award Pool for such Performance Period.

(d) Allocation of Maximum Award Pool to Covered Employees. Within the first 90 days of a Performance Period (or, if longer, within the maximum period allowed under Section 162(m) of the Code), the Committee shall allocate in writing, or establish in writing an objective means of allocating, on behalf of each Covered Person, a portion of the Maximum Award Pool (not to exceed the amount set forth in Section 6.5(a)) to be granted for such Performance Period in the event the Performance Goals for such period are attained.

(e) Negative Discretion. The Committee is authorized at any time during or after a Performance Period, in its sole and absolute discretion, to reduce or eliminate the Maximum Award Pool for the Performance Period, for any reason, based on such factors, indicia, standards, goals, and/or measures it determines in the exercise of its sole discretion. Similarly, the Committee is authorized at any time during or after a Performance Period, in its sole and absolute discretion, to reduce or eliminate the portion of the Maximum Award Pool allocated to any Covered Employee for the Performance Period, for any reason.

6.4   Determination of Actual Award Pool

(a) Purpose of Actual Award Pool. The Actual Award Pool for a Performance Period determines the aggregate amount of all the Awards that are to be issued under the Plan for such Performance Period.

(b) Establishment of Actual Award Pool. The Actual Award Pool for a Performance Period shall be the Maximum Award Pool for such period after adjustment, if any, by the Committee through Negative Discretion. Thus, to the extent the Committee elects for a Performance Period not to exercise Negative Discretion with respect to the Maximum Award Pool, the Actual Award Pool for the Performance Period shall be the Maximum Award Pool for such period.

(c) Allocation of Actual Award Pool to Individual Participants. The portion of the Actual Award Pool that will be Awarded to any individual Participant will be determined by the Committee, in its sole and absolute discretion, based on such factors, indicia, standards, goals, and measures which it determines in the exercise of its sole discretion. By way of illustration, and not by way of limitation, the Committee may, but shall not be required to, consider: (1) the Participant's position and level of responsibility, individual merit, contribution to the success of the Company and Target Award; (2) the performance of the Company or the organizational unit of the Participant based upon attainment of financial and other performance criteria and goals; and (3) business unit, division or department achievements.

(d) Adjustment to Carryforward Amount. To the extent the sum of all Awards paid for a Performance Period exceeds the Maximum Award for such period, the Carryforward Amount shall be reduced by an amount equal to such difference.

6.5   Limitations on Awards to Covered Employees

The provisions of this Section 6.5 shall have control over any Plan provision to the contrary.

(a) Maximum Award Payable to Covered Employees. The maximum Award payable to any Covered Employee under the Plan for a Performance Period shall be $4,000,000.

(b) Attainment of Performance Goals. The Performance Goals for a Performance Period must be achieved in order for a Covered Employee to receive an Award for such Performance Period.

(c) Allocation of Actual Award Pool. The portion of the Actual Award Pool allocated to a Covered Employee by the Committee pursuant to Section 6.4(c) shall not exceed the portion of the Maximum Award Pool allocated to such Covered Employee under Section 6.3(d).

ARTICLE 7—PAYMENT OF AWARDS FOR A PERFORMANCE PERIOD

7.1   Certification

(a) In General. Following the completion of each Performance Period, the Committee shall meet to review and certify in writing whether, and to what extent, the Performance Goals for the Performance Period have been achieved.

(b) Performance Goals Achieved. If the Committee certifies that the Performance Goals have been achieved, it shall, based upon application of the Performance Formula to the Performance Goals for such period, calculate and certify in writing the amount of: (i) the Maximum Award; (ii) the Maximum Award Pool; and (iii) the Maximum Award Pool to be allocated to each Covered Employee in accordance with Section 6.3(d). Upon completion of these written certifications, the Committee shall determine the amount of the Actual Award Pool for the Performance Period.

(c) Performance Goals Not Achieved. In the event the Performance Goals for a Performance Period are not achieved, the limitation contained in Section 6.5(b) shall apply to the Covered Employees. Further, any Awards granted for the Performance Period must be paid from the Carryforward Amount which shall be reduced to reflect the amount of such Awards.

7.2   Election of Form of Award

Prior to or coincident with its calculation of the amount of the Actual Award Pool for a Performance Period, the Committee shall, in its sole discretion, determine the form(s) in which to grant Awards under the Plan for such period.

7.3   Timing of Award Payments

Unless deferred pursuant to Article 8 hereof, the Awards granted for a Performance Period shall be paid to Participants on the Award Payment Date for such Performance Period, which date shall occur as soon as administratively practicable following the completion of the procedure described in Section 7.1.

ARTICLE 8—DEFERRAL OF AWARDS

At the discretion of the Committee, a Participant may, subject to such terms and conditions as the Committee may determine, elect to defer payment of all or any part of any Award which the Participant might earn with respect to a Performance Period by complying with such procedures as the Committee may prescribe. Any Award, or portion thereof, upon which such an election is made shall be deferred into, and subject to the terms, conditions and requirements of, the Eastman Kodak Employees' Savings and Investment Plan, 1982 Eastman Kodak Company Executive Deferred Compensation Plan or such other applicable deferred compensation plan of the Company.

ARTICLE 9—ADDITIONAL AWARDS

9.1 In General

In addition to the Awards that are authorized to be granted under Article 6 and paid under Article 7 for a Performance Period, the Committee may, in its sole judgment, from time to time grant Awards under the Plan from the Carryforward Amount.

9.2 Eligibility

All Key Employees, other than those who are Covered Employees, are eligible to receive the Awards authorized to be granted under this Article 9.

9.3 Form of Awards

Any Award granted by the Committee pursuant to the provisions of this Article 9 shall be issued in one or more of the forms permitted under Article 5 of the Plan.

9.4 Terms and Conditions

The Committee shall, by way of an Award notice or otherwise, establish the terms, conditions, restrictions and/or limitations that will apply to an Award issued pursuant to this Article 9; provided, however, such terms, conditions, restrictions and limitations are not inconsistent with the terms of the Plan.

9.5 Carryforward Amount

Upon the issuance of any Award under this Article 9, the Carryforward Amount shall be immediately reduced by an amount equal to the value of such Award.

ARTICLE 10—CHANGE IN OWNERSHIP

10.1 Background

Notwithstanding any provision contained in the Plan, including but not limited to Sections 1.1, 4.4, and 13.10, the provisions of this Article 10 shall have control over any contrary provision. Upon a Change In Ownership: (a) the terms of this Article 10 shall immediately become operative, without further action or consent by any person or entity; (b) all terms, conditions, restrictions and limitations in effect on any unpaid and/or deferred Award shall immediately lapse as of the date of such event; (c) no other terms, conditions, restrictions and/or limitations shall be imposed upon any Awards on or after such date, and in no event shall an Award be forfeited on or after such date; and (d) except where a prorated Award is required to be paid under this Article 10, all unvested and/or unpaid Awards or any other outstanding Awards shall automatically become one hundred percent (100%) vested immediately.

10.2 Payment of Awards

Upon a Change In Ownership, any Key Employee, whether or not he or she is still employed by the Company, shall be paid, as soon as practicable but in no event later than 90 days after the Change In Ownership, the Awards set forth in (a) and (b) below:

(a) All of the Key Employee's unpaid and/or deferred Awards; and

(b) A pro rata Award for the Performance Period in which the Change In Ownership occurs. The amount of the pro rata Award shall be determined by multiplying the Target Award for such Performance Period for Participants in the same wage grade as the Key Employee by a fraction, the numerator of which shall be the number of full months in the Performance Period prior to the date of the Change In Ownership and the denominator of which shall be the total number of full months in the Performance Period. For purposes of this calculation, a partial month shall be treated as a full month to the extent 15 or more days in such month have elapsed. To the extent Target Awards have not yet been established for the Performance Period, the Target Awards for the immediately preceding Performance Period shall be used. The pro rata Awards shall be paid to the Key Employee in the form of a lump-sum cash payment.

10.3 Miscellaneous

Upon a Change In Ownership, no action, including, but not by way of limitation, the amendment, suspension, or termination of the Plan, shall be taken which would affect the rights of any Key Employee or the operation of the Plan with respect to any Award to which the Key Employee may have become entitled hereunder on or prior to the date of such action or as a result of such Change In Ownership.

ARTICLE 11—CHANGE IN CONTROL

11.1 Background

Notwithstanding any provision contained in the Plan, including, but not limited to, Sections 1.1, 4.4, and 13.10, the provisions of this Article 11 shall control over any contrary provision. All Key Employees shall be eligible for the treatment afforded by this Article 11 if their employment with the Company terminates within two years following a Change In Control, unless the termination is due to (a) death; (b) Disability; (c) Cause; (d) resignation other than (1) resignation from a declined reassignment to a job that is not reasonably equivalent in responsibility or compensation (as defined in Kodak's Termination Allowance Plan), or that is not in the same geographic area (as defined in Kodak's Termination Allowance Plan), or (2) resignation within thirty days of a reduction in base pay; or (e) Retirement.

11.2 Vesting and Lapse of Restrictions

If a Key Employee qualifies for treatment under Section 11.1, his or her Awards shall be treated in the manner described in Subsections 10.1(b) and (c). Further, except where a prorated Award is required to be paid under this Article 11, all of the Key Employee's unvested and/or unpaid Awards shall automatically become one hundred percent (100%) vested immediately.

11.3 Payment of Awards

If a Key Employee qualifies for treatment under Section 11.1, he or she shall be paid, as soon as practicable but in no event later than 90 days after his or her termination of employment, the Awards set forth in (a) and (b) below:

(a) All of the Key Employee's unpaid and/or deferred Awards; and

(b) A pro rata Award for the Performance Period in which his or her termination of employment occurs. The amount of the pro rata Award shall be determined by multiplying the Target Award for such

Performance Period for Participants in the same wage grade as the Key Employee by a fraction, the numerator of which shall be the number of full months in the Performance Period prior to the date of the Key Employee's termination of employment and the denominator of which shall be the total number of full months in the Performance Period. For purposes of this calculation, a partial month shall be treated as a full month to the extent 15 or more days in such month have elapsed. To the extent Target Awards have not yet been established for the Performance Period, the Target Awards for the immediately preceding Performance Period shall be used. The pro rata Awards shall be paid to the Key Employee in the form of a lump-sum cash payment.

11.4   Miscellaneous

Upon a Change In Control, no action, including, but not by way of limitation, the amendment, suspension, or termination of the Plan, shall be taken which would affect the rights of any Key Employee or the operation of the Plan with respect to any Award to which the Key Employee may have become entitled hereunder prior to the date of the Change In Control or to which he or she may become entitled as a result of such Change In Control.

ARTICLE 12—SHARES SUBJECT TO THE PLAN

12.1   Available Shares

Subject to adjustment as provided in Subsection 12.2 below, the maximum number of shares of Common Stock, $2.50 par value per share, of the Company which shall be available for grant of Awards under the Plan during its term shall not exceed 1,000,000. Any shares of Common Stock related to Awards which terminate by expiration, forfeiture, cancellation or otherwise without the issuance of such shares, are settled in cash in lieu of Common Stock, or are exchanged with the Committee's permission for Awards not involving Common Stock, shall not be available again for grant under the Plan. The shares of Common Stock available for issuance under the Plan may be authorized and unissued shares or treasury shares.

12.2 Adjustment of Shares Available

(a) In General. The provisions of this Subsection 12.2 (a) are subject to the limitation contained in Subsection 12.2(b). If there is any change in the number of outstanding shares of Common Stock through the declaration of stock dividends, stock splits or the like, the number of shares available for Awards and the shares subject to any Award shall be automatically adjusted. If there is any change in the number of outstanding shares of Common Stock through any change in the capital account of Kodak, or through a merger, consolidation, separation (including a spin-off or other distribution of stock or property), reorganization (whether or not such reorganization comes within the definition of such term in Section 368(a) of the Code) or partial or complete liquidation, the Committee shall make appropriate adjustments in the maximum number of shares of Common Stock which may be issued under the Plan and any adjustments and/or modifications to outstanding Awards as it, in its sole discretion, deems appropriate. In the event of any other change in the capital structure or in the Common Stock of the Company, the Committee shall also be authorized to make such appropriate adjustments in the maximum number of shares of Common Stock available for issuance under the Plan and any adjustments and/or modifications to outstanding Awards as it, in its sole discretion, deems appropriate.

(b) Covered Employees. In no event shall the Award of any Participant who is a Covered Employee be adjusted pursuant to Subsection 12.2(a) to the extent it would cause such Award to fail to qualify as "Performance-Based Compensation" under Section 162(m) of the Code.

ARTICLE 13—MISCELLANEOUS

13.1 Nonassignability

No Awards under the Plan shall be subject in any manner to alienation, anticipation, sale, transfer (except by will or the laws of descent and distribution), assignment, pledge, or encumbrance, nor shall any Award be payable to anyone other than the Participant to whom it was granted.

13.2   Withholding Taxes

The Company shall be entitled to deduct from any payment under the Plan, regardless of the form of such payment, the amount of all applicable income and employment taxes required by law to be withheld with respect to such payment or may require the Participant to pay to it such tax prior to and as a condition of the making of such payment. In accordance with any applicable administrative guidelines it establishes, the Committee may allow a Participant to pay the amount of taxes required by law to be withheld from an Award by withholding from any payment of Common Stock due as a result of such Award, or by permitting the Participant to deliver to the Company, shares of Common Stock having a fair market value, as determined by the Committee, equal to the amount of such required withholding taxes.

13.3   Amendments to Awards

The Committee may at any time unilaterally amend any unearned, deferred or unpaid Award, including, but not by way of limitation, Awards earned but not yet paid, to the extent it deems appropriate; provided, however, that any such amendment which, in the opinion of the Committee, is adverse to the Participant shall require the Participant's consent.

13.4   Regulatory Approvals and Listings

Notwithstanding anything contained in this Plan to the contrary, the Company shall have no obligation to issue or deliver certificates of Common Stock evidencing Awards or any other Award resulting in the payment of Common Stock prior to (a) the obtaining of any approval from any governmental agency which the Company shall, in its sole discretion, determine to be necessary or advisable, (b) the admission of such shares to listing on the stock exchange on which the Common Stock may be listed, and (c) the completion of any registration or other qualification of said shares under any state or Federal law or ruling of any governmental body which the Company shall, in its sole discretion, determine to be necessary or advisable.

13.5 No Right to Continued Employment or Grants

Participation in the Plan shall not give any Key Employee any right to remain in the employ of the Company. Kodak or, in the case of employment with a Subsidiary, the Subsidiary, reserves the right to terminate any Key Employee at any time. Further, the adoption of this Plan shall not be deemed to give any Key Employee or any other individual any right to be selected as a Participant or to be granted an Award.

13.6 Amendment/Termination

The Committee may suspend or terminate the Plan at any time with or without prior notice. In addition, the Committee may, from time to time and with or without prior notice, amend the Plan in any manner, but may not without shareholder approval adopt any amendment which would require the vote of the shareholders of Kodak pursuant to Section 16 of the Exchange Act or Section 162(m) of the Code, but only insofar as such amendment affects Covered Employees.

13.7 Governing Law

The Plan shall be governed by and construed in accordance with the laws of the State of New York, except as superseded by applicable Federal Law.

13.8 No Right, Title, or Interest in Company Assets

No Participant shall have any rights as a shareholder as a result of participation in the Plan until the date of issuance of a stock certificate in his or her name, and, in the case of restricted shares of Common Stock, such rights are granted to the Participant under the Plan. To the extent any person acquires a right to receive payments from the Company under this Plan, such rights shall be no greater than the rights of an unsecured creditor of the Company and the Participant shall not have any rights in or against any specific assets of the Company. All of the Awards granted under the Plan shall be unfunded.

13.9   No Guarantee of Tax Consequences

No person connected with the Plan in any capacity, including, but not limited to, Kodak and its Subsidiaries and their directors, officers, agents and employees, makes any representation, commitment, or guarantee that any tax treatment, including, but not limited to, Federal, state and local income, estate and gift tax treatment, will be applicable with respect to amounts deferred under the Plan, or paid to or for the benefit of a Participant under the Plan, or that such tax treatment will apply to or be available to a Participant on account of participation in the Plan.

13.10   Compliance with Section 162(m)

If any provision of the Plan would cause the Awards granted to a Covered Person not to constitute qualified "Performance-Based Compensation" under Section 162(m) of the Code, that provision, insofar as it pertains to the Covered Person, shall be severed from, and shall be deemed not to be part of, this Plan, but the other provisions hereof shall remain in full force and effort.

PLAN 3: WAGE DIVIDEND PLAN

ARTICLE 1—PURPOSE, EFFECTIVE DATE, AND TERM OF PLAN

1.1   Purpose

The purpose of the Plan is to assist the Company in attracting, motivating and retaining its Employees by rewarding Employees for their contributions to the Company's growth and success, provided Company performance meets or exceeds established Performance Goals, and to endeavor to qualify the Awards granted to Covered Employees under the Plan as "Performance-Based Compensation" as defined in Section 162(m) of the Code.

1.2   Effective Date

The Plan shall be effective as of January 1, 1995, subject to approval by Kodak's shareholders at the 1995 Annual Meeting of the Shareholders of Kodak.

1.3   Term

Awards shall not be granted pursuant to the Plan after December 31, 1999; provided, however, the Committee may grant Awards after such date in recognition of performance for a Performance Period completed on or prior to such date.

ARTICLE 2—DEFINITIONS

2.1   Average Net Assets

"Average Net Assets" means, for the Performance Period, the simple average of the Company's Net Assets for each of the following five fiscal quarters of the Company: the four fiscal quarters of the Performance Period and the fiscal quarter immediately preceding the Performance Period. For purposes of this calculation, Net Assets for a fiscal quarter shall be determined as of the end of such quarter.

2.2   Award

"Award" means the compensation payable to a Participant by the Committee for a Performance Period pursuant to Article 7. All Awards shall be issued in one or more of the forms specified by Article 5.

2.3   Award Payment Date

"Award Payment Date" means, for each Performance Period, the date that the Awards, if any, for the Performance Period shall be paid to Participants pursuant to Article 7, without regard to any election to defer receipt of an Award made under Article 8 of the Plan.

2.4   Board

"Board" means the Board of Directors of Kodak.

2.5   Code

"Code" means the Internal Revenue Code of 1986, as amended from time to time, including regulations thereunder and successor provisions and regulations thereto.

2.6 Committee

"Committee" means the Executive Compensation and Development Committee of the Board, or such other Board committee as may be designated by the Board to administer the Plan, provided, however, that the Committee shall consist of three or more directors, all of whom are both a "disinterested person" within the meaning of Rule 16b-3 under the Exchange Act and an "outside director" within the meaning of the definition of such term as contained in Proposed Treasury Regulations Section 1.162-27(e)(3), or any successor definition subsequently adopted.

2.7 Common Stock

"Common Stock" means the Common Stock, $2.50 par value per share, of Kodak which may be newly issued or treasury stock.

2.8 Company

"Company" means Kodak and its Subsidiaries.

2.9 Covered Employee

"Covered Employee" means an Employee who is a "Covered Employee" within the meaning of Section 162(m) of the Code.

2.10 Effective Date

"Effective Date" means the date an Award is determined to be effective by the Committee upon its grant of such Award.

2.11 Employee

"Employee" means, for a Performance Period, any person employed by the Company during such Performance Period and compensated for services in the form of an hourly wage or salary, provided, however, that Limited Service Employees are not Employees.

By the way of example, and not by way of limitation, the term "Employee" does not include independent contractors or leased employees (within the meaning of Section 414(n) of the Code).

2.12 Exchange Act

"Exchange Act" means the Securities Exchange Act of 1934, as amended from time to time, including rules thereunder and successor provisions and rules thereto.

2.13 Kodak

"Kodak" means Eastman Kodak Company.

2.14 Limited Service Employee

"Limited Service Employee" means a person who is hired by the Company for the specific purpose of meeting short-term needs of 900 hours or less in any consecutive 12 month period and who is designated as a Limited Service Employee when hired.

2.15 Negative Discretion

"Negative Discretion" means the discretion authorized by the Plan to be applied by the Committee in determining the size of the Award to be paid to a Covered Employee for a Performance Period if, in the Committee's sole judgment, such application is appropriate. Negative Discretion may only be used by the Committee to eliminate or reduce the size of the Award earned by a Covered Employee pursuant to the Performance Formula. By way of example, and not by way of limitation, in no event shall any discretionary authority granted to the Committee by the Plan, including, but not limited to Negative Discretion, be used to (a) grant an Award to a Covered Employee for a Performance Period if the Performance Goals for such Performance Period have not been attained; or (b) increase an Award to a Covered Employee above the maximum payable under Section 6.2(b) of the Plan.

2.16 Net Assets

"Net Assets" means the Company's consolidated Total Shareholders' Equity and Borrowings (both short-term and long-term) as reported in its audited consolidated financial statements. The Committee is authorized at any time during the first 90 days of a Performance Period, or at any time thereafter in its sole and absolute discretion, to adjust or modify the calculation of Net Assets for such

Performance Period in order to prevent the dilution or enlargement of the rights of Participants, (a) in the event of, or in anticipation of, any unusual or extraordinary corporate item, transaction, event or development; (b) in recognition of, or in anticipation of, any other unusual or nonrecurring events affecting the Company, or the financial statements of the Company, or in response to, or in anticipation of, changes in applicable laws, regulations, accounting principles, or business conditions; and (c) in view of the Committee's assessment of the business strategy of the Company, performance of comparable organizations, economic and business conditions, and any other circumstances deemed relevant. However, if and to the extent the exercise of such authority after the first 90 days of a Performance Period would cause the Awards granted to the Covered Employees for the Performance Period to fail to qualify as "Performance-Based Compensation" under Section 162(m) of the Code, then such authority shall only be exercised with respect to those Participants who are not Covered Employees.

2.17   Net Income

"Net Income" means, for a Performance Period, the Company's consolidated Net Earnings (Loss) before Cumulative Effect of Changes in Accounting Principle for the Performance Period as reported in its audited consolidated financial statements. The Committee is authorized at any time during the first 90 days of a Performance Period, or at any time thereafter in its sole and absolute discretion, to adjust or modify the calculation of Net Income for such Performance Period in order to prevent the dilution or enlargement of the rights of Participants (a) in the event of, or in anticipation of, any dividend or other distribution (whether in the form of cash, securities or other property), recapitalization, restructuring, reorganization, merger, consolidation, spin-off, combination, repurchase, shares exchange, liquidation, dissolution, or other similar corporate transaction, event or development; (b) in recognition of, or in anticipation of, any other unusual or nonrecurring event affecting the Company, or the financial statements of the Company, or in response to, or in anticipation of, changes in applicable laws, regulations, accounting principles, or business conditions, (c) in recognition of, or in anticipation of, any other extraordinary gains or losses; and (d) in view of the Committee's assessment of the business strategy of the Company, performance of comparable organizations, economic and business conditions, and any other circumstances deemed relevant. However, if and to the extent the exercise of such authority after the first 90 days of a Performance Period would cause the Awards granted to the Covered Employees for the Performance Period to fail to qualify as "Performance-Based Compensation" under Section 162(m) of the Code, then such authority shall only be exercised with respect to those Participants who are not Covered Employees.

2.18 Participant

"Participant" means, for a Performance Period, an Employee who is designated to participate in the Plan pursuant to Section 3.2.

2.19 Participation Rules

"Participation Rules" means, for a Performance Period, the rules established by the Committee in accordance with Section 3.2 pursuant to which the Committee shall determine which Employees will be Participants for such Performance Period.

2.20 Performance Criterion

"Performance Criterion" means the stated business criterion upon which the Performance Goals for a Performance Period are based as required pursuant to Proposed Treasury Regulation Section 1.162-27(e)(4)(iii). For purposes of the Plan, RONA shall be the Performance Criterion.

2.21 Performance Formula

"Performance Formula" means, for a Performance Period, the one or more objective formulas applied against the Performance Goals to determine which Awards have been earned for the Performance Period and, if so, the amount of such Awards. The Performance Formula for a Performance Period shall be established in writing by the Committee within the first 90 days of the Performance Period (or, if later, within the maximum period allowed pursuant to Section 162(m) of the Code).

2.22 Performance Goals

"Performance Goals" means, for a Performance Period, the one or more goals for the Performance Period established by the Committee in writing within the first 90 days of the Performance Period (or, if later, within the maximum period allowed pursuant to Section 162(m) of the Code) based upon the Performance Criterion. The Committee is authorized at any time during the first 90 days of a Performance Period, or at any time thereafter in its sole and absolute discretion, to adjust or modify the calculation of a Performance Goal for such Performance Period in order to prevent the dilution or enlargement of the rights of Participants (a) in the event of, or in anticipation of, any unusual or extraordinary corporate item, transaction, event or development; (b) in recognition of, or in anticipation of, any other unusual or nonrecurring events affecting the Company, or the financial statements of the Company, or in response to, or in anticipation of, changes in applicable laws, regulations, accounting principles, or business conditions; and (c) in view of the Committee's assessment of the business strategy of the Company, performance of comparable organizations, economic and business conditions, and any other circumstances deemed relevant. However, if and to the extent the exercise of such authority after the first 90 days of a Performance Period would cause the Awards granted to the Covered Employees for the Performance Period to fail to qualify as "Performance-Based Compensation" under Section 162(m) of the Code, such authority shall only be exercised with respect to those Participants who are not Covered Employees.

2.23 Performance Period

"Performance Period" means Kodak's fiscal year.

2.24 Plan

"Plan" means the Wage Dividend Plan.

2.25 RONA

"RONA" means, for a Performance Period, Return on Net Assets for the Performance Period. RONA shall be calculated by dividing Net Income for the Performance Period by Average Net Assets for the same period.

2.26 Stock Equivalent

"Stock Equivalent" means an Award under Article 5 that is valued in whole or in part by reference to, or is payable in or is otherwise based on Common Stock.

2.27 Subsidiary

"Subsidiary" means a subsidiary which is majority owned by Kodak and reported in Kodak's audited consolidated financial statements.

ARTICLE 3—ELIGIBILITY AND PARTICIPATION

3.1 Eligibility

All Employees are eligible to participate in the Plan. However, the fact that a person is an Employee for a Performance Period shall not in any manner entitle such Employee to be eligible for an Award for the Performance Period. In order to be eligible for an Award for a Performance Period, the Employee must be designated as a Participant for such Performance Period by the Committee in accordance with Section 3.2 below.

3.2 Participation

Through the adoption of written Participation Rules within the first 90 days of a Performance Period, the Committee will, in its sole discretion, designate those Employees who will be Participants for such Performance Period. Pursuant to the Participation Rules for a Performance Period, the Committee may condition the receipt of Awards upon satisfaction of such preconditions and/or requirements as it, in its sole discretion, determines. The fact that an Employee is a Participant for a Performance Period shall not in any manner entitle such Participant to receive an Award for the Performance Period. The determination as to whether or not such Participant shall be paid an Award for such Performance Period shall be decided solely in accordance with the provisions of Article 7 hereof.

ARTICLE 4—PLAN ADMINISTRATION

4.1 Responsibility

The Committee shall have total and exclusive responsibility to control, operate, manage, and administer the Plan in accordance with its terms.

4.2 Authority of the Committee

The Committee shall have all the authority that may be necessary or helpful to enable it to discharge its responsibilities with respect to the Plan. Without limiting the generality of the preceding sentence, the Committee shall have the exclusive right: to interpret the Plan, to determine eligibility for participation in the Plan, to decide all questions concerning eligibility for and the amount of Awards payable under the Plan, to establish and administer the Performance Goals and certify whether, and to what extent, they are attained, to construe any ambiguous provision of the Plan, to correct any default, to supply any omission, to reconcile any inconsistency, to issue administrative guidelines as an aid to administer the Plan, to make regulations for carrying out the Plan and to make changes in such regulations as they from time to time deem proper, and to decide any and all questions arising in the administration, interpretation, and application of the Plan. In addition, in order to enable Employees who are foreign nationals or are employed outside the United States or both to receive Awards under the Plan, the Committee may adopt such amendments, procedures, regulations, subplans, and the like as are necessary or advisable, in the opinion of the Committee, to effectuate the purposes of the Plan.

4.3 Discretionary Authority

The Committee shall have full discretionary authority in all matters related to the discharge of its responsibilities and the exercise of its authority under the Plan including, without limitation, its construction of the terms of the Plan and its determination of eligibility for participation and Awards under the Plan. It is the intent of Kodak that the decisions of the Committee and its action with respect to the Plan shall be final, binding, and conclusive upon all persons having or claiming to have any right or interest in or under the Plan.

4.4   Section 162(m) of the Code

With regard to all Covered Employees, the Plan shall for all purposes be interpreted and construed in accordance with Section 162(m) of the Code.

4.5   Delegation of Authority

Except to the extent prohibited by law, the Committee may delegate some or all of its authority under the Plan to any person or persons provided that any such delegation be in writing.

ARTICLE 5—FORM OF AWARDS

Awards may at the Committee's sole discretion be issued and paid in cash, Common Stock, Stock Equivalents, or a combination thereof. Awards paid in the form of Common Stock or Stock Equivalents shall be issued for no consideration. The Committee may, in its sole judgment, subject an Award to such terms, conditions, restrictions and/or limitations (including, but not limited to, restrictions on transferability and vesting), provided they are not inconsistent with the terms of the Plan. For purposes of the Plan, the value of any Award granted in the form of Common Stock shall be the mean between the high and low at which the Common Stock trades on the New York Stock Exchange as of the date of the grant's Effective Date. To the extent Awards are granted in Common Stock or Stock Equivalents, such payments shall count against the number of available shares reserved under Section 9.1.

ARTICLE 6—DETERMINATION OF AWARDS FOR A PERFORMANCE PERIOD

6.1   Procedure for Determining Awards

Within the first 90 days of a Performance Period (or, if later, within the maximum period allowed under Section 162(m) of the Code), the Committee shall establish in writing for such Performance Period: (a) the Participation Rules; (b) the Performance Goal(s); and (c) the Performance Formula.

6.2 Limitations on Awards

The provisions of this Section 6.2 shall control over any Plan provision to the contrary.

(a) General Limitation. Participants in the Plan for a Performance Period shall be eligible to receive Awards for such Performance Period only if: (1) the Performance Goals for such Performance Period are achieved; and (2) the Performance Formula as applied against such Performance Goals determines that Awards have been earned for the Performance Period.

(b) Maximum Award Payable to Covered Employees. The maximum Award payable to any Covered Employee under the Plan for a Performance Period shall be $700,000.

ARTICLE 7—PAYMENT OF AWARDS FOR A PERFORMANCE PERIOD

7.1 Certification

Following the completion of each Performance Period, the Committee shall meet to review and certify in writing whether, and to what extent, the Performance Goals for the Performance Period have been achieved. If the Committee certifies that such Performance Goals have been achieved, it shall, based upon the Performance Formula, (i) calculate and certify in writing the amount of the Award earned by each Covered Employee; (ii) determine the actual size of the Award to be paid to each Covered Employee for the Performance Period by applying Negative Discretion, if and when it deems appropriate; and (iii) calculate the size of the Awards to be paid for the Performance Period to all other Participants.

7.2 Election of Form of Award

Prior to or coincident with its performance of the certifications required by Section 7.1, the Committee shall, in its sole discretion, determine the form(s) in which to grant Awards under the Plan for such period.

7.3   Negative Discretion

In determining the actual size of the Award to be paid to a Covered Employee for a Performance Period, the Committee may, through the use of Negative Discretion, reduce or eliminate the amount of the Award earned under the Performance Formula for the Performance Period, if, in its sole judgment, such reduction or elimination is appropriate.

7.4   Timing of Award Payments

Unless deferred pursuant to Article 8 hereof, the Award granted for a Performance Period shall be paid to Participants on the Award Payment Date for such Performance Period, which date shall occur as soon as administratively practicable following the completion of the procedure described in Section 7.1.

ARTICLE 8—DEFERRAL OF AWARDS

At the discretion of the Committee, a Participant may, subject to such terms, conditions, and limitations as the Committee may determine, elect to defer payment of all or a portion of the Award that would otherwise be paid to the Participant with respect to a Performance Period by complying with such procedures as the Committee may prescribe. Any award, or portion thereof, upon which such an election is made shall be deferred into, and subject to the terms, conditions, and requirements of the Eastman Kodak Employees' Savings and Investment Plan, the 1982 Eastman Kodak Company Executive Deferred Compensation Plan, or successor plans thereto.

ARTICLE 9—SHARES SUBJECT TO THE PLAN

9.1   Available Shares

Subject to adjustment as provided in Section 9.2 below, the maximum number of shares of Common Stock, $2.50 par value per share, of the Company shall be available for grant of Awards under the Plan during its term and shall not exceed 4,000,000. Any shares of Common Stock related to Awards which are terminated by expiration, forfeiture, cancellation or otherwise without the issuance of such shares, or are settled in cash in lieu of Common Stock, or are exchanged with the Committee's permission for Awards not involving Common Stock, shall not be available again for grant under the Plan. The shares of Common Stock available for issuance under the Plan may be authorized and unissued shares or treasury shares.

9.2   Adjustment of Shares Available

(a) In General. The provisions of this Subsection 9.2(a) are subject to the limitation contained in Subsection 9.2(b). If there is any change in the number of outstanding shares of Common Stock through the declaration of stock dividends, stock splits or the like, the number of shares available for Awards and the shares subject to any Award shall be automatically adjusted. If there is any change in the number of outstanding shares of Common Stock through any change in the capital account of Kodak, or through merger, consolidation, separation (including a spin-off or other distribution of stock or property), reorganization (whether or not such reorganization comes within the definition of such term in Section 368(a) of the Code), or partial or complete liquidation, the Committee shall make appropriate adjustments in the maximum number of shares of Common Stock which may be issued under the Plan and any adjustment and/or modifications to outstanding Awards as it, in its sole discretion, deems appropriate. In the event of any other change in the capital structure or in the Common Stock of the Company, the Committee shall also be authorized to make such appropriate adjustments in the maximum number of shares of Common Stock available for issuance under the Plan and any adjustments and/or modifications to outstanding Awards as it, in its sole discretion, deems appropriate.

(b) Covered Employees. In no event shall the Award of any Participant who is a Covered Employee be adjusted pursuant to Subsection 9.2(a) to the extent it would cause such Award to fail to qualify as "Performance-Based Compensation" under Section 162(m) of the Code.

ARTICLE 10—MISCELLANEOUS

10.1   Nonassignability

No Awards under the Plan shall be subject in any manner to alienation, anticipation, sale, transfer (except by will or the laws of descent and distribution), assignment, pledge, or encumbrance. Further, except in the case of an Award payable to a deceased Participant, no Award shall be payable to anyone other than the Participant to whom it was granted. In the case of an Award payable to a deceased Participant, the Committee shall, in the exercise of its sole and absolute discretion, determine the party to whom such Award shall be paid.

10.2 Withholding Taxes

The Company shall be entitled to deduct from any payment under the Plan, regardless of the form of such payment, the amount of all applicable income and employment taxes required by law to be withheld with respect to such payment or may require the Participant to pay to it such tax prior to and as a condition of the making of such payment. In accordance with any applicable administrative guidelines it establishes, the Committee may allow a Participant to pay the amount of taxes required by law to be withheld from an Award by withholding from any payment of Common Stock due as a result of such Award, or by permitting the Participant to deliver to the Company, shares of Common Stock having a fair market value, as determined by the Committee, equal to the amount of such required withholding taxes.

10.3 Regulatory Approvals and Listings

Notwithstanding anything contained in this Plan to the contrary, the Company shall have no obligation to issue, deliver, pay, credit or otherwise acknowledge any Award resulting in the payment of Common Stock prior to (a) the obtaining of any approval from any governmental agency which the Company shall, in its sole discretion, determine to be necessary or advisable, (b) the admission of such shares to listing on the stock exchange on which the Common Stock may be listed, and (c) the completion of any registration or other qualification of said shares under any state or Federal law or ruling of any governmental body which the Company shall, in its sole discretion, determine to be necessary or advisable.

10.4 No Right to Continued Employment or Grants

Participation in the Plan shall not give any Employee any right to remain in the employ of the Company. Kodak or, in the case of employment with a Subsidiary, the Subsidiary, reserves the right to terminate any Employee at any time. Further, the adoption of this Plan shall not be deemed to give any Employee any right to be selected as a Participant or to be granted an Award.

10.5 Amendment/Termination

The Committee may suspend or terminate the Plan at any time with or without prior notice. In addition, the Committee may, from time to time and with or without prior notice, amend the Plan in any manner, but may not without shareholder approval adopt any amendment which would require the vote of the shareholders of Kodak pursuant to Section 16 of the Exchange Act or Section 162(m) of the Code, but only insofar as such amendment affects Covered Employees.

10.6 Governing Law

The Plan shall be governed by and construed in accordance with the laws of the State of New York, except as superseded by applicable Federal Law.

10.7 No Right, Title, or Interest in Company Assets

In the case of Awards payable in the form of Common Stock or Awards resulting in the payment of Common Stock, no Participant shall have any rights as a shareholder as a result of participation in the Plan until the date of issuance of a stock certificate in his or her name or, in the event such Common Stock is issued in book entry form, until Kodak's transfer agent provides valid written notification thereof to the Participant, and, in the case of restricted shares of Common Stock, such rights are granted to the Participant under the Plan. To the extent any person acquires a right to receive payments from the Company under this Plan, such rights shall be no greater than the rights of an unsecured creditor of the Company and the Participant shall not have any rights in or against any specific assets of the Company. All of the Awards granted under the Plan shall be unfunded.

10.8   No Guarantee of Tax Consequences

No person connected with the Plan in any capacity, including, but not limited to, Kodak and its Subsidiaries and their directors, officers, agents and employees makes any representation, commitment, or guarantee that any tax treatment, including, but not limited to, Federal, state and local income, estate and gift tax treatment, will be applicable with respect to amounts deferred under the Plan, or paid to or for the benefit of a Participant under the Plan, or that such tax treatment will apply to or be available to a Participant on account of participation in the Plan.

10.9   Compliance with Section 162(m)

If any provision of the Plan would cause the Awards granted to a Covered Person not to constitute qualified "Performance-Based Compensation" under Section 162(m) of the Code, that provision, insofar as it pertains to the Covered Person, shall be severed from, and shall be deemed not to be a part of, this Plan, but the other provisions hereof shall remain in full force and effect.

10.10   Compliance with Exchange Act

With respect to Participants who are subject to Section 16 of the Exchange Act, transactions under this Plan are intended to comply with applicable conditions of Rule 16b-3 or its successors under the Exchange Act. To the extent any provision of the Plan or action by the Committee fails to so comply, it shall, but only insofar as it pertains to Participants who are subject to Section 16 of the Exchange Act, be deemed null and void, to the extent permitted by law and deemed advisable by the Committee.

DEFINITIVE COPY

(CORPORATE LOGO OMITTED)

EASTMAN KODAK COMPANY

This Proxy is Solicited on behalf of the Board of Directors.

Attachment 1

Sample Proxy Disclosure

Sample provisions of language describing executive compensation items contained in the 1999 proxy statements of Ford Motor Co. and Sprint Corp. are provided for your information. Each proxy statement contains a good example of a detailed explanation of the reasoning behind the executive compensation programs implemented by these companies.

Ford Motor Co.

1999 Proxy Statement

Section 16(A)

Beneficial Ownership Reporting Compliance

Based on Company records and other information, Ford believes that all SEC filing requirements applicable to its directors and officers were complied with for 1998 and prior years except that, due to a clerical oversight by the Company, [name omitted] had one late report of three transactions, and [name omitted] and [name omitted] each had one late report of one transaction. Each of these transactions was exempt under Section 16(b) of the Securities Exchange Act of 1934, as amended.

Compensation of Directors

Goal. Ford wants the directors' compensation to be tied to your interests as stockholders. Accordingly, 25% ($10,000) of a director's annual Board membership fee is deferred in the form of common stock units. This deferral, together with the restricted stock given to directors and director stock ownership goals, is part of Ford's commitment to link director and stockholder interests. These compensation programs are described below.

Fees. The following fees are paid to directors, other than the Chairman of the Board, who are not Ford employees:

Annual Board membership fee	$40,000
Annual Committee membership fee	$10,000
Attendance fee for each Board meeting	$ 1,000

The Chairman of the Board is paid a Chairman fee for each calendar quarter of $375,000, paid in restricted shares of common stock. These shares cannot be sold for one year and are subject to the conditions of the 1998 Long-Term Incentive Plan.

Deferred Compensation Plan. Under this plan, 25% of a director's annual Board membership fee must be deferred in common stock units. Directors also can choose to have the payment of all or some of the remainder of their fees deferred in the form of cash and/or common stock units. Each common stock unit is equal in value to a share of common stock and is ultimately paid in cash. These common stock units generate Dividend Equivalents in the form of additional common stock units. These units are credited to the directors' accounts on the date common stock cash dividends are paid. Any fees deferred in cash are held in the general funds of the Company. Interest on fees deferred in cash is credited semiannually to the directors' accounts at the then-current U.S. Treasury Bill rate plus 0.75%. In general, deferred amounts are not paid until after the director retires from the Board. The amounts are then paid, at the director's option, either in a lump sum or in annual installments over a period of up to ten years.

Restricted Stock Plan. Nonemployee directors also receive restricted shares of common stock. Each nonemployee director who has served for at least six months receives 2,000 shares of common stock subject to restrictions on sale. In general, the restrictions expire for 20% of the shares each year following the year of the grant. Each nonemployee director receives an additional 2,000 shares on the same terms when the restrictions on all of the prior 2,000 shares end.

Stock Ownership Goals. To further link director and stockholder interests, Ford established stock ownership goals for nonemployee directors in 1995. Each nonemployee director has a goal to own common stock equal in value to five times the sum of the director's annual Board and Committee fees within five years.

Life Insurance. Ford provides nonemployee directors with $200,000 of life insurance and $500,000 of accidental death or dismemberment coverage. The life insurance coverage continues after the director retires from the Board if the director is at least age 55 and has served for at least five years. A director who retires from the Board after age 70, or, with Board approval, after age 55, and who has served for at least five years may elect to have the life insurance reduced to $100,000 and receive $15,000 a year for life. The accidental death or dismemberment coverage may, at the director's expense, be supplemented up to an additional $500,000 and ends when the director retires from the Board.

Matching Gift Program. Nonemployee directors may give up to $25,000 per year to certain tax-exempt organizations under the Ford Fund Matching Gift Program. For each dollar given, the Ford Motor Company Fund contributes two dollars.

Certain Relationships And Related Transactions

Since January 1993, Ford has had a consulting agreement with [name omitted]. Under this agreement, [name omitted] is available for consultation, representation, and other duties (including service as a director). For these services, Ford pays him $100,000 per year and provides facilities (including office space), an administrative assistant, and security arrangements. This agreement will continue until either party ends it with 30 days' notice.

Since January 1999, Ford has had a similar consulting agreement with [name omitted]. Under this agreement, the consulting fee is $125,000 per calendar quarter, payable in restricted shares of common stock. The shares cannot be sold for one year and are subject to the conditions of the 1998 Long-Term Incentive Plan. The other terms of the agreement are substantially similar to those described in the paragraph above.

[Name omitted]'s husband owns a Ford-franchised dealership and a Lincoln Mercury-franchised dealership. In 1998, the dealerships paid Ford about $74.2 million for products and services in the ordinary course of business. In turn, Ford paid the dealerships about $9.1 million for services in the ordinary course of business. Also in 1998, Ford Motor Credit Company, a wholly-owned subsidiary of Ford, provided about $82.4 million of financing to the dealerships and paid about $7.5 million to them in the ordinary course of business. The dealerships paid Ford Credit about $74.6 million in the ordinary course of business.

[Name omitted] is a partner of Goldman, Sachs & Co. Goldman, Sachs has provided Ford with investment banking services for many years. Ford expects Goldman, Sachs to continue providing similar services in the future.

Compensation And Option Committee Report On Executive Compensation

(How Ford Determines Executive Compensation)

Purposes

Ford's executive compensation program aims to:

- Link managers' goals with your interests as stockholders.
- Support business plans and long-term Company goals.
- Tie executive compensation to Company performance.
- Attract and retain talented management.

Types Of Compensation

There are two main types of compensation:

(1) *Annual compensation.* This includes salary and bonus. Ford awards bonuses only when a year's profits and other performance criteria meet a certain level required under the bonus plan.

(2) *Long-term compensation.* This includes stock options and other long-term incentive awards based on common stock. The value of these awards depends on Company performance and future stock value.

Factors Considered In Determining Compensation

The Compensation Committee wants the compensation of Ford executives to be competitive in the worldwide auto industry and with major U.S. companies. Each year, the committee reviews a report from an outside consultant on Ford's compensation program for executives. The report discusses all aspects of compensation as well as how Ford's program compares with those of other large companies. Based on this report, its own review of various parts of the program, and its assessment of the skills, experience, and achievements of individual executives, the Committee decides the compensation of executives.

The consultant develops compensation data using a survey of several leading companies picked by the consultant and Ford. General Motors and the former Chrysler Corporation were included in the survey. Eighteen leading companies in other industries also were included because the job market for executives goes beyond the auto industry. Companies were picked based on size, reputation, and business complexity.

The Committee looks at the size and success of the companies and the types of jobs covered by the survey in determining executive compensation. One goal of Ford's compensation program is to approximate the survey group's average compensation, adjusted for company size and performance. In 1998, Ford's executive salaries and long-term incentive awards generally were at this average. Data on bonuses for the surveyed companies are not yet available, but the Committee expects Ford's 1998 bonuses to be above the average of the survey group.

The Committee also considers the tax deductibility of compensation paid to the Named Executives. In 1998, you approved the terms of the new Annual Incentive Compensation Plan so that certain compensation paid to these individuals would be deductible by the Company under federal tax law. In 1995, you approved the terms of the 1990 Long-Term Incentive Plan for the same reason. These plans limit the amount of bonuses, stock awards and stock options that may be granted to any person in any year.

Further, in 1994, the Committee created stock ownership goals for executives at the vice president level and above. The goals are for these executives to own common stock worth a multiple of salary, ranging from one times salary to up to five times salary for the CEO, within five years. The CEO and most other key managers have achieved their stock ownership goals.

Annual Compensation

General

Annual compensation for Ford executives includes salary and bonus. This is similar to the compensation programs of most leading companies.

The Committee aims to pay salaries at the average of the survey companies, adjusted for company size and performance. The Committee also looks at the specific job duties, the person's achievements, and other criteria.

Bonuses

The Annual Incentive Compensation Plan provides for annual cash awards to participants based on achievement of specific performance goals relating to a specific year.

For 1998, the Committee set a bonus formula using performance goals based on corporate pre-tax income, automotive after-tax return on sales, Ford Motor Credit Company return on equity and quality (based on warranty performance and customer satisfaction). Awards may be less than or greater than 100% of the target award. The limit, approved by you, on the amount of a bonus award for any of the Named Executives for any year under the plan is $10,000,000. This limit is not a target. The Committee, in its discretion, may make awards to Named Executives that are less than the annual limit. [Name omitted]'s bonus for 1998 was $10,000,000. All other 1998 bonuses to Named Executives were below the limit.

The Committee also set target awards for the Company officers based on each person's level of responsibility. Using business data, the Committee reviewed Ford's performance during 1998 against the goals. The Committee decided that Ford exceeded the corporate pre-tax income goal, exceeded the automotive after-tax return on sales goal, partially achieved the Ford Motor Credit Company return on equity goal and achieved the quality goal. Based on this performance, the Committee decided to award 157% of the target awards to the officers and then make adjustments for individual performance for awards to officers who are not Named Executives.

The total amount set aside for bonuses in a given year depends on Ford's performance during the year against the performance goals. In 1998, the Committee set aside $483 million. Individual awards depend on each person's level of responsibility. For persons other than the Named Executives, the Committee increases or decreases awards from a formula amount, based on rank and salary, to reward a person's or group's performance.

Long-Term Compensation

General

Today's business decisions affect Ford over a number of years. This is why the long-term incentive awards are tied to Ford's performance and the value of Ford's common stock over several years.

In general, the amount of the long-term incentive awards does not change as much as the amount of the annual bonus awards.

The charts on pp. 24 and 25 [of the Proxy] show the long-term performance of Ford's common stock.

Stock Options

Stock options are an important part of Ford's long-term incentive program. The managers who get them gain only when you gain—when the common stock value goes up.

In 1996, 1997 and 1998, the Named Executives and other employees received ten-year options in amounts generally similar to prior years. In deciding the size of individual option grants for 1998, the Committee considered the number of options granted to the person in prior years, as well as the total number of options awarded to all employees. A formula approved by you limits the number of options that may be granted to any Named Executive. This limit, which is not a target, is 2.5% of the highest number of shares available in any year for grants under the 1998 Long-Term Incentive Plan, as adjusted under the Plan. All 1998 stock option grants to the Named Executives were below this limit.

Stock Awards

Common stock awards are based on performance against goals created by the Committee over a period of years.

In 1998, the Committee granted Performance Stock Rights to Company officers and certain other top executives. These Performance Stock Rights cover the performance period 1998-2000. Up to 150% of these rights may be awarded in the form of common stock after this period ends. The awards are made if goals relating to total shareholder returns relative to the stock of all other Standard & Poor's 500 companies are met.

The size of a person's Performance Stock Right award depends on competitive long-term compensation values determined by the outside consultant, the person's job, and the person's expected role in Ford's long-term performance. In general, the Committee grants less than the maximum number of shares covered by the Performance Stock Right award if the goals are only partly met.

The 1998 Long-Term Incentive Plan sets a limit, approved by you, on the number of shares available as stock awards under Performance Stock Rights to any Named Executive in any year. This limit is 500,000 shares, as adjusted under the Plan. The Performance Stock Rights granted in 1998 for the Named Executives are below the limit. For the 1998-2000 period, the Committee decided to pay Dividend Equivalents in cash on the Performance Stock Rights granted in 1998.

The Final Awards of common stock in 1998 under the 1990 Long-Term Incentive Plan covered the performance periods 1993-1997 and 1995-1997. Under that plan, up to 100% of the Contingent Stock Rights awarded may be granted in the form of common stock after the period ends. Using business data, the Committee reviewed Ford's performance during the 1993-1997 period against goals for product programs (25%), cost reduction (25%), product quality and customer acceptance worldwide (35%), and relationships with employees (15%). The Committee decided that Ford partly achieved the product program and product quality goals, met the cost reduction goals, mostly met the customer acceptance goals, and met the employee relationships goals. Based on this performance, the Committee decided to award 83% of the shares covered by the Contingent Stock Rights and then make adjustments for individual performance.

Using business data, the Committee also reviewed Ford's performance during the 1995-1997 period against goals for corporate return on equity (25%), product programs (25%), product quality and customer acceptance worldwide (35%), and relationships with employees (15%). The Committee decided that Ford partly achieved the return on equity, product program and product quality goals, mostly met the customer acceptance goals, and met the employee relationships goals. Based on this performance, the Committee decided to award 81% of the shares covered by the Contingent Stock Rights and then make adjustments for individual performance.

For the Named Executives, the adjusted awards for 1993-1997 and 1995-1997 were 100% of the initial grants. The Final Awards for the period ending in 1998 will be made in mid-1999 after Company performance data are available. These amounts will appear in next year's proxy statement.

Restricted Stock Units

The Committee granted Restricted Stock Units to ten executives in 1998. Three of the ten—Messrs. [names omitted]—are Named Executives.

A Restricted Stock Unit is worth one share of common stock. Again, this ties the executive's interests to your interests as stockholders. If the executive meets certain goals decided by the Committee, Ford pays the executive cash for each Restricted Stock Unit equal to the then-current value of a share of common stock.

The Committee grants the Restricted Stock Units and decides the goals, the restriction period, and the other terms of each Unit. The Committee also decides the extent to which the goals have been met and the final number of Units to award after the restriction period ends. During the restriction period, the Units cannot be sold or otherwise disposed of, and they are subject to conditions under the 1998 Long-Term Incentive Plan.

The grant of Restricted Stock Units depends on the achievement of several major Ford goals:

- worldwide product excellence,
- low-cost producer,
- industry leadership in customer satisfaction,
- empowered people,
- nimble through process leadership,
- industry leadership in corporate citizenship, and
- worldwide growth.

The Committee also reviews each person's contribution to meeting these goals.

Restricted Stock Units generally may not be paid out until 18 months after retirement and are subject to conditions under the 1998 Long-Term Incentive Plan. Dividend Equivalents are paid in cash until the payout of the Units. The Units have no voting rights.

Select Retirement Plan

To speed up the development of future leaders and reduce the number of top manager jobs, the Committee supported making offers under the Select Retirement Plan, a voluntary retirement program for certain U.S. management employees, in 1998. In general, the program added three years of age and contributory service for retirement benefits purposes. To be eligible, employees generally had to be at least age 52 with 10 or more years of service. The Committee reviewed and approved Select Retirement Plan offers for certain executives. Some of the executives retired during 1998 under this program. More information on the program is on p. 27 [of the proxy].

CEO Compensation

Annual Compensation

[Name omitted]'s salary, paid in 1998, as reported in the Summary Compensation Table, reflects a 25% increase over the amount paid in 1997. Prior to 1998, the Committee last increased his salary in 1996, the first increase since 1993. In deciding to increase [name omitted] salary, the Committee considered his job duties as well as the pay practices of the survey companies.

[Name omitted]'s bonus for 1998 was based on Ford's performance, using the method described above under "Bonuses." The Committee also considered other factors in applying its "negative discretion" permitted under the Internal Revenue Code (section 162(m)). It also considered his job as head of a restructured global company with a wide area of control and broad duties. The Committee and other nonemployee directors of Ford reviewed his 1998 accomplishments, and the Committee considered these combined views. [Name omitted]'s bonus for 1998 was below the formula limit in the bonus plan; however, it was capped at the $10,000,000 plan limit.

Long-Term Compensation

The Final Award of common stock in 1998 for [name omitted] was based on Ford's performance from 1993 to 1997 and 1995 to 1997, using the method described above under "Long-Term Compensation—Stock Awards." (The amount of the Final Award is shown in column (h) of the Summary Compensation Table on p. 18, under the heading "LTIP Payouts.") The Committee adjusted the amount based on the factors described above. The Final Award was in shares of common stock, a portion of which [name omitted] elected to defer.

The value of the stock options and Performance Stock Rights granted to [name omitted] in 1998 also depends on Ford's future success—and whether that success is reflected in the value of the common stock. For the Performance Stock Rights, the value of any Final Award also depends on the level of achievement of total shareholder return goals created by the Committee for 1998–2000.

In applying its "negative discretion" under the Internal Revenue Code in deciding the number of stock options to grant [name omitted] (shown in column (b) of the Options/SAR Grants Table on p. 20), the Committee considered the value of his other long-term incentive compensation compared with competitive long-term compensation values. It also considered the complexity and duties of his job.

Finally, the Committee considered the deductibility of [name omitted]'s compensation under the tax laws. As discussed above, you approved plan amendments and new plans allowing Ford to deduct, for federal income tax purposes, certain parts of [name omitted]'s compensation (as well as that of other Named Executives) for tax years starting with 1995.

Compensation of Executive Officers

The table below shows the before-tax compensation for the last three years for Alex Trotman, who served as CEO in 1998, and the four next highest paid executive officers at the end of 1998.

Summary Compensation Table

[Table contained in Proxy omitted]

Notes to Table

(1) Amounts shown as Restricted Stock Awards for 1997 and 1996 represent Dividend Equivalents paid in restricted stock under the Long-Term Incentive Plans. Restrictions on this stock generally lapsed in 1998. Holders of restricted stock received the same cash dividends as other stockholders owning common stock.

Listed below are the total number of shares represented by Ford Stock Fund Units credited to the Named Executives under a deferred compensation plan and the market values of these shares (determined by the closing price of common stock on the New York Stock Exchange on December 31, 1998). These shares will be distributed after termination of employment.

[Table contained in Proxy omitted]

The ultimate worth of the restricted stock depends on the value of common stock when the restrictions lapse. Under the long-term Incentive Plans generally, the Compensation Committee determines any restriction period for shares included in each Final Award. For each of the Named Executives, restrictions ended on January 1, 1998 on up to 18,000 shares awarded for the 1991-95 performance period. Restrictions ended on February 13, 1998 on all remaining shares of restricted stock held by the Named Executives.

(2) In general, under the 1985 Stock Option Plan, the 1990 Long-Term Incentive Plan and the 1998 Long-Term Incentive Plan, stock appreciation rights may be granted along with the grant of options to

executive officers. Exercise of a stock appreciation right cancels the related stock option, and vice versa.

(3) These amounts represent Final Awards under the Long-Term Incentive Plans. The Final Awards for the performance periods ending in 1996 were in restricted stock and the Final Awards for the performance periods ending in 1997 generally were in unrestricted stock. Final Awards are based on the attainment of performance goals and on individual performance. (See note 1 for more details on restricted stock.) The amounts shown represent Final Awards for performance periods ending in 1996 and 1997. No amount is shown for the performance period ending in 1998 because the awards will not be decided until the middle of 1999. Those amounts will appear in next year's proxy statement.

(4) These amounts are (1) matching contributions by Ford under the Savings and Stock Investment Plan ("SSIP") and (2) the values of certain credit provided to the Named Executives under the Benefit Equalization Plan ("BEP"). Under the BEP, Ford provides benefits substantially equal to benefits that could not be provided under the SSIP because of limitations under the Internal Revenue Code. For 1998, the amounts shown in column (i) as SSIP matching contributions and BEP credits, respectively, are as follows:

[Table contained in Proxy omitted]

(5) [Name omitted] retired from the Company effective January 1, 1999.

(6) 83% of [name omitted]'s 1996 compensation was for his service as Executive Vice President. The rest of his 1996 compensation and all of his 1997 and 1998 compensation was for his service as Vice Chairman.

(7) 83% of [name omitted]'s 1996 compensation was for his service as President of Ford Automotive Operations. The rest of his 1996 compensation and all of his 1997 and 1998 compensation was for his service as Vice Chairman. [Name omitted] retired from the Company effective January 1, 1999.

(8) 80% of [name omitted]'s 1996 compensation was for his service as Group Vice President, Product Development. The rest of his 1996 compensation and all of his 1997 and 1998 compensation

was for his service as Executive Vice President and President of Ford Automotive Operations.

(9) [Name omitted] retired from the Company effective January 1, 1999.

Stock Options

The Long-Term Incentive Plan allows grants of stock options and other rights relating to common stock. In general, whether exercising stock options is profitable depends on the relationship between the common stock's market price and the options' exercise price, as well as on the grantee's investment decisions. Options that are "in the money" on a given date can become "out of the money" if prices change on the stock market. For these reasons, we believe that placing a current value on outstanding options is highly speculative and that placing a current value on outstanding options is highly speculative and may not represent the true benefit, if any, that may be realized by the grantee.

The following two tables give more information on stock options.

Option/SAR Grants In Last Fiscal Year (1)

[Table contained in Proxy omitted]

Notes to Table

(1) The exercise price of the stock options is the average selling price on the New York Stock Exchange on the grant date. Stock appreciation rights were granted in tandem with these stock options.

In general 33% of a stock option grant can be exercised one year after the grant date, 66% after two years, and 100% after three years. Any unexercised options expire after ten years.

If a grantee retires, becomes disabled, or dies, his or her options continue to be exercisable up to the normal expiration date. In most other instances of employment termination, all rights end upon termination.

Options are subject to certain conditions, including not engaging in competitive activity. Options generally cannot be transferred except through inheritance.

In general, each grantee agrees to remain a Ford employee for at least one year from the grant of the option.

(2) 20% of this stock option grant can be exercised three years after the grant date, 40% after four years, 60% after five years, 80% after six years and 100% after seven years. The other terms of this option are generally similar to those referred to in Note 1 above.

(3) These values were determined using the Black-Scholes methodology and the assumptions described in Note 11 to Ford's Consolidated Financial Statements contained in Ford's 1998 Annual Report. The ultimate value of the options, if any, will depend on the future value of the common stock and the grantee's investment decisions, neither of which can be predicted.

Aggregated Option/SAR Exercises In Last Fiscal Year
And Fy-End Option/SAR Values

[Table contained in Proxy omitted]

Notes to Table

(1) The numbers shown include shares of common stock with respect to which stock appreciation rights were exercised for cash, as follows: 1,408,865 shares for [name omitted]; 127,982 shares for [name omitted]; 174,802 shares for [name omitted]; and 79,090 shares for [name omitted]. No shares of common stock were acquired in connection with the exercise of these stock appreciation rights.

(2) These year-end values represent the difference between the fair market value of common stock subject to options (based on the stock's closing price on the New York Stock Exchange on December 31, 1998) and the exercise prices of the options. "In-the-money" means that the fair market value of the stock is greater than the option's exercise price on the valuation date.

Performance Stock Rights And Restricted Stock Units

Under the Long-Term Incentive Plan, eligible employees may receive nontransferable Performance Stock Rights. A Performance Stock Right is the right to receive, after a specified performance period, a Final Award of up to a certain number of shares of common stock. The number of shares depends on whether the Performance Stock Right's performance goals are achieved and, for employees who are not Named Executives, on the employee's individual performance.

Under the Long-Term Incentive Plan, eligible employees also may receive nontransferable Restricted Stock Units. A Restricted Stock Unit is the right to receive, after the restriction period expires and subject to the achievement of certain goals, cash equal in value to one share of common stock. The final number of Restricted Stock Units that can be paid out in cash depends on whether the goals are achieved and on the employee's individual contribution.

The following table shows information on 1998 grants of Performance Stock Rights and Restricted Stock Units to the Named Executives.

Long-Term Incentive Plan-Awards In Last Fiscal Year (1)

[Table contained in Proxy omitted]

Notes to Table

(1) These entries represent the number of shares specified in Performance Stock Rights or Restricted Stock Units granted in 1998.

(2) No specific payout targets were created in connection with these grants.

Performance Stock Rights

The Compensation Committee decides the number of shares to be included in a Final Award by determining how completely certain performance goals were achieved. Usually, Performance Stock Rights are granted each year. The performance period is ordinarily three years. For 1998, performance goals for the Performance Stock Rights reported in column (b) of the table cover the 1998-2000 period and include essentially the same performance measures for each of the Named Executives. The performance goals and the mechanics of receiving a Final Award are more fully discussed on pp. 15 and 16 [of the proxy].

Dividend Equivalents paid in 1998 to the Named Executives in cash are reported in column (e) of the Summary Compensation Table on p. 18 [of the proxy]. Final Awards of common stock made to the Named Executives for the 1993-97 and 1995-97 performance periods are reported in column (h) of the Summary Compensation Table.

The amount ultimately realized for a Final Award will depend on the value of the common stock when the award is made, or if restricted, when the restrictions lapse and on the "earning out conditions." Under these conditions, if an employee quits, retires without Company approval, is released in Ford's best interest, is discharged, or engages in competition activity after termination, all of the employees' undistributed Final Awards, as well as outstanding Performance Stock Rights, will be forfeited and canceled unless a waiver is granted by the Committee. Further, all of the employee's rights under any award will be forfeited if the Committee determines that the employee acted in a manner inimical to Ford's best interest. After any restriction period ends, however, shares of common stock representing a Final Award are distributed to the employee free of restrictions and conditions.

Restricted Stock Units

The Committee creates the performance goals for the Restricted Stock Units and selects the persons who receive the Units. The 1998 grants, reported in column (b) of the table on p. 22 [of the proxy], depend on the achievement of seven major Company goals described on p. 16 [of the proxy]. Dividend Equivalents paid to the Named Executives are included in column (e) of the Summary Compensation Table. No Restricted Stock Units were paid out in 1998 to any of the Named Executives.

As with Performance Stock Rights, the amount ultimately realized under a Restricted Stock Unit depends on the achievement of performance goals, the compliance with certain conditions, and the value of common stock when the restrictions end.

Stock Performance Graphs

SEC rules require proxy statements to contain a performance graph comparing over a five-year period, the performance of our common stock against Standard & Poor's 500 Stock Index and against either a published industry or line-of-business index or a group of peer issuers. Ford chose the principal U.S. auto manufacturer—General Motors—as its peer issuer for the graph. We think this approach is more informative since relevant line-of-business indexes merely combine the U.S. automakers. In the past, we have also included Chrysler as a peer issuer. However, we have not included Chrysler this year due to its merger with Daimler-Benz. In addition to the five-year graph, we are providing a similar performance graph covering a ten-year period. Both graphs assume an initial investment of $100, quarterly reinvestment of dividends and, in the case of Ford common stock, an adjustment to reflect the impact of the April 7, 1998 spin-off of Ford's interest in Associates First Capital Corporation.

Comparison of Five-Year Cumulative Shareholder Return
Ford, General Motors And S&P 500 Stock Index

[Table contained in Proxy omitted]

Comparison of Ten-Year Cumulative Shareholder Return
Ford, General Motors And S&P 500 Stock Index

[Table contained in Proxy omitted]

Retirement Plans

Ford's General Retirement Plan ("GRP") provides a benefit for each year of noncontributory participation, and added benefits for those who make additional contributions. Ford also has two other retirement plans, the Supplemental Executive Retirement Plan ("SERP") and the Benefit Equalization Plan ("BEP"). Under the SERP, certain executives, including the Named Executives, may receive (1) an additional monthly benefit after retirement based on years of credited service and final average base salary, and (2) annuities based on Company earnings, the executive's performance, and other factors. In addition, for retirements effective October 1, 1998 or later, for certain U.S. Vice Presidents and above whose careers include subsidiary service, the SERP will provide an additional monthly benefit to equalize the total retirement benefits payable from the Company's retirement plans to an amount that would have been payable under the GRP/BEP if the executive's total service had been recognized as contributory service under those plans. Under the BEP, eligible employees, including the Named Executives, receive benefits substantially equal to those that would have been provided under the GRP but that could not be provided because of Internal Revenue Code limitations.

The following table shows the annual retirement benefits that would be payable at normal retirement (age 65 or later) on January 1, 1999. Benefits are shown for various rates of final average base salary and assume that employee contributions were made for the indicated periods. Employees contribute at the rate of $1\frac{1}{2}$% of base salary up to $160,000. The table shows total annual amounts payable under the GRP, SERP and BEP, including amounts relating to employee contributions.

Annual Contributory Pensions

Final Average Base Salary	Years of Service				
	20 Years	25 Years	30 Years	35 Years	40 Years
$ 200,000	$ 83,300	$ 104,400	$ 125,000	$ 146,700	$ 166,100
400,000	194,000	243,000	292,300	341,500	386,700
600,000	304,000	381,900	459,100	536,300	607,300
800,000	423,000	530,600	637,900	745,200	843,900
1,000,000	530,000	664,300	798,700	933,000	1,056,500
1,200,000	636,700	798,100	959,400	1,120,800	1,269,100
1,400,000	743,400	931,800	1,120,200	1,308,600	1,481,700
1,600,000	850,100	1,065,500	1,281,000	1,496,500	1,694,300
1,800,000	956,800	1,199,300	1,441,800	1,684,300	1,906,900
2,000,000	1,063,400	1,333,000	1,602,600	1,872,100	2,119,500

GRP and BEP benefits are computed by averaging the employee's highest five consecutive annual base salaries in the ten years immediately before retirement. SERP benefits generally are computed by averaging the employee's final five year-end annual base salaries immediately before retirement. No annuities were awarded in 1993 and 1994. [Name omitted] received annuities for 1995, 1996 and 1997. Assuming a retirement age of 65 and satisfaction of all conditions, the estimated percentage of total annual retirement benefits to be paid to [name omitted] from his annuities is 4%.

As of December 31, 1998, the credited years of service for each of the Named Executives were as follows: [name omitted], 43 years; [name omitted], 40 years; [name omitted], 34 years; [name omitted], 31 years; and [name omitted], 40 years.

The GRP and BEP benefits are computed as a joint-and-survivor annuity. The SERP benefit is computed as a straight-life annuity. Benefits payable under the plans are to be reduced for Social Security or other offsets.

In addition to the GRP and BEP, Ford maintains a voluntary retirement program for select U.S. management employees called the Select Retirement Plan ("SRP"). The SRP adds three years of age and contributory service to the employee for retirement benefits purposes, with a 15% floor on the increase of the employee's monthly benefits under any applicable retirement plans. The SRP generally calculates five-year final average salary by using final salary for three of the five years. To participate in the SRP, an employee must be selected by management and generally must be at least age 52 and have ten or more years of credited service under the retirement plans.

Sprint Corp.

1999 Proxy Statement

Board Committees

The Organization, Compensation and Nominating Committee. The principal responsibilities of the Organization, Compensation and Nominating Committee, as they relate to matters of executive compensation, are to: (1) assess and appraise the performance of the Chief Executive Officer and review the performance of executive management; (2) recommend to the Board of Directors base salaries, incentive compensation and other benefits for the Chief Executive Officer and other key officers; (3) counsel and advise management on plans for orderly development and succession of executive management; (4) take any and all action required or permitted to be taken by the Board of Directors under the stock option and restricted stock plans, stock purchase plans, incentive compensation plans and the deferred compensation plans of Sprint; and (5) review recommendations for major changes in compensation and benefit and retirement plans that apply to significant numbers of Sprint's total employees and which require review or approval of the Board of Directors.

The principal responsibilities of the Organization, Compensation and Nominating Committee, as they relate to the Director nomination process, are to: (1) periodically review the size and composition of the Board and make recommendations to the Board with respect to such matters; (2) recommend to the Board proposed nominees whose election at the next Annual Meeting of Stockholders will be recommended by the Board; and (3) recommend persons proposed to be elected to fill any vacancy on the Board of Directors between Stockholder meetings. The committee will consider qualified nominees recommended by Stockholders. Such recommendations should be sent to the Organization, Compensation and Nominating Committee, c/o Corporate Secretary at the corporate headquarters of Sprint, 2330 Shawnee Mission Parkway, Westwood, Kansas 66205.

The Chairman of the Organization, Compensation and Nominating Committee is [name omitted]. Other members are [names omitted]. The Organization, Compensation and Nominating Committee met six times in 1998.

Compensation of Directors

Annual Retainer and Meeting Fees. Directors who are not employees of Sprint (the Outside Directors) are each paid $35,000 annually plus $1,250 for each meeting attended and $1,000 for each committee meeting attended. Under the 1997 Long-Term Stock Incentive Program, Outside Directors can elect to use these fees to purchase FON Stock and PCS Stock. They can also elect to have the purchased shares deferred and placed in a trust. Sprint also maintains the Directors' Deferred Fee Plan under which Outside Directors may elect to defer all or some of their fees.

Stock Options. On April 21, 1998, each Outside Director was granted an option to purchase 2,000 shares of Sprint common stock at an option price equal to 100% of the fair market value on that date. The options expire ten years from the date of grant. Twenty-five percent of the shares subject to the option become exercisable on December 31, 1998, and an additional 25% become exercisable on December 31 of each of the three succeeding years. Following the Recapitalization, the options were converted into options to purchase 2,000 shares of FON Stock and 1,000 shares of PCS Stock. Under the 1997 Long-Term Stock Incentive Program, as amended and approved at the Special Stockholders Meeting on November 13, 1998, future option grants are made at the discretion of the Organization, Compensation and Nominating Committee.

Retirement Benefits. In 1982 Sprint adopted a retirement plan for its Outside Directors. Any Director of Sprint who served five years as a Director without simultaneously being employed by Sprint or any of its subsidiaries is eligible to receive benefits under the plan on retirement. The retirement plan was amended in December of 1996 to eliminate the retirement benefit for any Director who had not served five years as of the date of the amendment. An eligible Director retiring after March 30, 1989, will receive monthly benefit payments equal to the monthly fee (not including meeting fees) being paid to Directors at the time of the Director's retirement. The monthly retirement benefit would be $2,917 for any Director retiring while the current $35,000 annual fee remains in effect. The number of monthly benefit payments to a Director under the plan will equal the number of months served as a Director without simultaneously being employed by Sprint or any of its subsidiaries, up to a maximum of 120 payments.

Outside Directors not eligible for benefits under the retirement plan after the December 1996 amendment received units representing 2,500 shares of Sprint common stock credited to their accounts under the Director's Deferred Fee Plan upon becoming a Director of Sprint. Upon the Recapitalization, these units were converted into units representing FON stock and PCS Stock. Half of these units will vest on each succeeding anniversary.

Other Benefits. In addition, Outside Directors are provided with Sprint residential long distance service valued in the following amounts for 1998: [name omitted], $5,047; [name omitted], $1,213; [name omitted], $894; [name omitted], $373; [name omitted], $3,535; [name omitted], $6,000; and [name omitted], $3,427.

Organization, Compensation and Nominating Committee

Report on Executive Compensation

The Organization, Compensation and Nominating Committee of the Board, which is composed of independent, non-employee Directors and has the principal responsibilities described on page 7 of this Proxy Statement, has furnished the following report on executive compensation:

Sprint's compensation philosophy is to link, by using specific objectives, executives' compensation to the short-term and long-term performance of Sprint so as to maximize long-term Stockholder value. Sprint's executive compensation program consists of four elements: (1) base salary, (2) short-term incentive compensation, (3) long-term incentive compensation and (4) stock options. To develop a competitive compensation package, both base salary and total compensation (i.e., the sum of all four elements) are compared to market data from similarly sized companies in the telecommunications industry as well as other industries from surveys conducted by independent compensation consultants and from proxy data. The Committee believes that the comparison groups accurately reflect the market in which Sprint competes for executive talent. The companies in the S&P(R) Telephone Utility Index and the S&P(R) Telecommunications (Long Distance) Index, which are used in the Stock Performance Graph on page 19 of this Proxy Statement, are included in the comparison groups. The Committee's policy is to target base salaries at the 50th percentile for base pay of similar positions within the comparison group, and total compensation at the 75% percentile provided certain performance objectives are achieved.

Section 162(m) of the Internal Revenue Code denies a tax deduction to any publicly held corporation, such as Sprint, for compensation in excess of $1 million paid to any Named Officer unless such compensation is performance-based under Section 162(m). Sprint took all action required under Section 162(m) for Sprint's incentive compensation plans to be performance-based so as to preserve Sprint's tax deduction for compensation earned under such for 1998.

Base Salary. Each year the Committee makes a recommendation to the Board establishing base pay for all Named Officers. In making this recommendation for 1998, the Committee considered the salaries of other executives within the comparison group and the executives' performance during 1997. With respect to the latter, the Committee exercised its judgment in evaluating the executives' accomplishments during the year. As a result of his performance evaluations during his tenure as Chief Executive Officer, [name omitted]'s base salary exceeds the median of the comparison group.

Short-Term Incentive Compensation. Sprint's short-term incentive compensation (STIC) is a performance-driven annual incentive designed to promote the near term objectives of the organization. For the Named Officers, the material terms of the performance goals under STIC were approved by the Stockholders at the 1997 Annual Meeting.

Target incentive opportunity for STIC is based on job level and potential impact on organization results. The STIC payout is based on the achievement of ten financial objectives—three for the Local Telecommunications Division (LTD), three for the Long Distance Division (LDD), two for Sprint PCS/SprintCom, one for Global One, and one for National Integrated Services (NIS). For each objective, targets were established and compared to actual 1998 results.

- The objectives for the LTD related to operating income (45% weighting), net collectible revenue (30%), and economic value added (EVA) (25%). Actual results were 43.8% of target on a weighted average basis.

- The objectives for the LDD related to operating income (35% weighting), net collectible revenue relative to market growth (40%), and EVA (25%). Actual results were 179.3% of target on a weighted average basis.

- The objectives for Sprint PCS/SprintCom related to operating income (505 weighting) and net collectible service revenue (50%). Actual results were 72.8% of target on a weighted average basis.

- The objective for Global One related to operating income. The actual result was 0.0% of target.

- The CEO and COO objective for NIS was expense and capital spending. The actual result was 150.0% of target. The objectives for NIS for the remaining executive officers were the completion of key milestones the Sprint ION(SM) (Sprint's Integrated On-Demand Network) and competitive local exchange carrier electronic interface projects. The actual results were 150.0% of target on a weighted average basis.

The weights assigned for a particular executive among the LTD, LDD, Sprint PCS/SprintCom, Global One, and NIS depended on an executive's responsibilities with Sprint. The entire STIC payout for [names omitted] was based on the achievement of these financial objectives.

Based on the financial results described above, and the achievement of their personal objectives, the executive officers earned STIC payouts, on average, of 109.3% of target. [Name omitted]'s STIC payout was based on the financial results described above using relative weights for objectives by division as follows: 30% for the LTD, 40% for LDD, 15% for Sprint PCS/SprintCom, 5% for Global One, and 10% for NIS. Based on these factors, [name omitted] earned a payout of 110.8% of target.

Long-Term Incentive Compensation. Sprint's long-term incentive compensation (LTIP) is a three-year performance-driven incentive plan designed to promote the long-term objectives of the organization and to pay out in FON and PCS common stock. For the Named Officers, the material terms of the performance goals under LTIP were approved by the Stockholders at the 1997 Annual Meeting. Target incentive opportunity is established as a percentage of the three-year average salary range midpoint and is based on job level and potential impact on organization results.

LTIP payouts were based entirely on the achievement of EVA. This financial objective related to the LTD, the LDD, and Sprint consolidated.

- For the LTD, the actual result was 187.9% of target.
- For the LDD, the actual result was 200.0% of target.
- For Sprint consolidated, the actual result was 200.0% of target.

As with the STIC, the relative weights assigned to the LTIP objectives among the LTD, the LDD, and Sprint consolidated depend on an executive's responsibilities with Sprint.

The specific amounts of the LTIP payouts were determined by comparing actual financial results to the pre-established targets for each objective. The payout is also adjusted by a stock price factor under which the payout based on financial objectives as described above is multiplied by a fraction, the numerator of which is the market price of FON Stock and one-half the market price of PCS Stock on the last day of the performance period and the denominator of which is the market price of Sprint common stock on the first day of the performance period. The three-year increase in the price of FON Stock and PCS Stock resulted in a multiplier of 296.2%

[Name omitted]'s LTIP payout was based on the financial results described above using relative weights for each objective as follows: 25% for the LTD, 50% for the LDD, and 25% for Sprint consolidated. Based on the financial results and the methodology described above, [name omitted] received a payout of 583.4% of target. The LTIP payouts, if not deferred under the Executive Deferred Compensation Plan, were paid in restricted or unrestricted shares of FON Stock and PCS Stock.

Stock Options. Stock option grants combined with LTIP comprise long-term incentive compensation awarded to executive officers of Sprint. Total long-term incentive compensation is targeted at the 75th percentile of the comparison group. The Committee does not consider any measures of corporate or individual performance in determining option grants and does not consider the number of options already held by an executive. The telecommunications industry is going through tremendous changes and industry leaders are in high demand, both inside and outside the industry. In 1997, Sprint granted performance options to buy 1,000,000 and 500,000 shares to [name omitted] and [name omitted], respectively. These options become exercisable if the combined trading price of FON stock and one-half the trading price of PCS stock equals or exceeds $95.875 per share for a period of 30 trading days within a consecutive period of 45 days after June 9, 2001 and on or before June 9, 2003. Since the performance vesting criteria will most likely be met and in order to obtain more favorable accounting treatment the Board amended the vesting provision of these grants. The amendment provides that, if the performance vesting provisions have not already been achieved, these options will automatically vest on February 9, 2007. The Board of Directors believes that granting options and other stock awards to officers and other key employees enhances Sprint's ability to attract, retain and provide incentives to individuals of exceptional talent necessary for the continued success of Sprint.

During 1998 certain executive officers elected under Sprint's Management Incentive Stock Option Plan (MISOP) to receive options in lieu of receiving up to 50% of their target opportunity under Sprint's management incentive plans. For each $5.69 reduction in an executive's target opportunity resulting from such election, the executive received an option to purchase one share of FON Stock and one-half share of PCS Stock. The MISOP is in keeping with Sprint's philosophy of increasing the percentage of compensation tied to stock ownership. The Committee believes stock options more closely align Stockholder and employee interests by focusing executives on profitability of Sprint and its common stock.

Summary Compensation Table

The following table reflects the cash and non-cash compensation for services in all capacities to Sprint by those persons who were, as of December 31, 1998, the chief executive officer and the other four most highly compensated executive officers of Sprint, and [name omitted], who served as an executive officer until February 12, 1998 (the Named Officers):

[Table contained in Proxy omitted]

Option Grants

The following tables summarize options granted during 1998 under Sprint's stock option plans to the Named Officers. Options granted before the Recapitalization were converted into separate options to purchase FON Stock and PCS Stock. The exercise prices of the original options were allocated between the FON Stock and PCS Stock options based on the proportionate market values of FON Stock and PCS Stock over a ten-day trading period following the Recapitalization. This was intended to ensure that the aggregate intrinsic value of the original options was preserved. Following the conversion, the vesting and option periods of the FON Stock and PCS Stock options remained the same as for the original options that were converted.

The amounts shown as potential realizable values on these options are based on arbitrarily assumed annualized rates of appreciation in the price of FON Stock and PCS Stock of five percent and ten percent over the term of the options, as set forth in SEC rules. The Named Officers will realize no gain on these options without an increase in the price of FON Stock and PCS Stock that will benefit all holders of these stocks proportionately.

Unless otherwise indicated, each option listed below has a reload feature. Vesting is accelerated in the event of an employee's death or permanent disability. In addition, if an option has been outstanding for at least one year, vesting is accelerated upon a change in control or an employee's normal retirement at age 65 or older. A change in control is deemed to occur if (1) DT and FT acquire additional stock of Sprint that would result in their owning 35% or more of the voting power of Sprint stock, (2) someone acquires 20% or more of the outstanding stock of Sprint, or (3) there is a change of a majority of the Directors within a two-year period. No stock appreciation rights were granted during 1998.

Option Grants in Last Fiscal Year

FON Stock Options

[Table contained in Proxy omitted]

Notes to Table

(1) The dollar amounts in these columns are the result of calculations at the five percent and ten percent rates set by the SEC and are not intended to forecast future appreciation of FON Stock or PCS Stock.

(2) Twenty-five percent of this option became exercisable on February 9, 1999, and an additional 25% will become exercisable on February 9 of each of the three successive years.

(3) This option was granted in lieu of a potential award under the LTIP for the three-year period ending on December 31, 2000. The option becomes exercisable on December 31, 2000.

(4) This option was granted under the Management Incentive Stock Option Plan (MISOP). Under the MISOP, the optionee elected to receive options in lieu of receiving a portion of his bonus under the management incentive compensation plans. The MISOP benefits Sprint by reducing the cash bonus paid to the executive.

It further increases the percentage of compensation tied to stock ownership, in keeping with Sprint's philosophy to more closely align stockholder and employee interests. This option became exercisable on December 31, 1998.

(5) This option is a reload option. A reload option is an option granted when an optionee exercises a stock option and makes payment of the purchase price using shares of previously owned FON Stock or PCS Stock. A reload option grant is for the number of shares utilized in payment of the purchase price and tax withholding, if any. The option price for a reload option is equal to the market price of FON Stock or PCS Stock on the date the reload option is granted. A reload option becomes exercisable one year from the date the original option was exercised and does not have a reload feature.

(6) The amounts shown as potential realizable value for all Stockholders, which are presented for comparison purposes only, repre-

sent the aggregate net gain of all holders of record, as of February 22, 1999. The calculation for FON Stock assumes a hypothetical option granted at $52.86 per share on February 9, 1998 and expiring on February 9, 2008, if the price of FON Stock appreciates at the rates shown in the table. The calculation for PCS Stock assumes a hypothetical option granted at $11.52 per share on February 8, 1998 and expiring on February 8, 1008, if the price of PCS Stock appreciates at the rates shown in the table. There can be no assurance that the potential realizable values shown in the table will be achieved. Sprint will neither make nor endorse any predictions as to future stock performances.

Option Exercises and Fiscal Year-end Values

The following tables summarize the net value realized on the exercise of options in 1998, and the value of the outstanding options at December 31, 1998, for the Named Officers.

Aggregated Option Exercises in 1998
and Year-end Option Values

[Table contained in Proxy omitted]

Notes to Table

(1) The value realized upon exercise of an option is the difference between the fair market value of the shares of FON Stock or PCS Stock received upon the exercise, valued on the exercise date, and the exercise price paid.

(2) The value of unexercised, in-the-money options is the difference between the exercise price of the options and the fair market value, at December 31, 1998, of FON Stock ($83.625) or PCS Stock ($22.3125).

Pension Plans

The following table reflects the estimated annual pension benefit payable to an individual retiring in 1999 at age 65. The amounts include all prospective benefits under Sprint's plans, whether tax-qualified or not.

Pension Plan Table

Remuneration (1)	*Years of Service (2)*				
	15	20	25	30	35
$ 500,000	$114,518	$152,690	$ 190,863	$ 229,035	$ 267,208
700,000	161,018	214,690	268,363	322,035	375,708
900,000	207,518	276,690	345,863	415,035	484,208
1,100,000	254,018	338,690	423,363	508,035	592,708
1,300,000	300,518	400,690	500,863	601,035	701,208
1,500,000	347,018	462,690	578,363	694,035	809,708
1,700,000	393,518	524,690	655,863	787,035	918,208
1,900,000	440,018	586,690	733,363	880,035	1,026,708
2,100,000	486,518	648,690	810,863	973,035	1,135,208
2,300,000	533,018	710,690	888,363	1,066,035	1,243,708
2,500,000	579,518	772,690	965,863	1,159,035	1,352,208
2,700,000	626,018	834,690	1,043,363	1,252,035	1,460,708
2,900,000	672,518	896,690	1,120,863	1,345,035	1,569,208
3,100,000	719,018	985,690	1,198,363	1,438,035	1,677,708

Notes to Table

(1) Compensation, for purposes of estimating a pension benefit, includes salary and bonus (paid under Sprint's short-term incentive plans) as reflected under Annual Compensation in the Summary Compensation Table on page 12 [of the proxy]. The calculation of benefits under the pension plans generally is based upon average compensation for the highest five consecutive years of the ten years preceding retirement under a grandfathered benefit.

(2) These amounts are straight life annuity amounts and would not be subject to reduction because of Social Security benefits. For purposes of estimating a pension benefit, the years of service credited are 34 years for [name omitted], 15 years for [name omitted], 18 years for [name omitted], 35 years for [name omitted], 26 years for [name omitted], and 12 years for [name omitted].

In addition, Sprint has a Key Management Benefit Plan that permits a participant to elect a supplemental retirement benefit. More information on the plan is provided in the following section under "Employment Contracts".

Employment Contracts

Sprint has contingency employment agreements with [names omitted] that provide for separation pay and benefits if employment is involuntarily terminated following a change in control. A change in control is deemed to occur if someone acquires 20% or more of the outstanding voting stock of Sprint or if there is a change of a majority of the Directors within a two-year period. Benefits will include monthly salary payments for 35 months (or until the officer reaches age 65 if this occurs earlier) and three payments each equal to the highest short-term plus the highest long-term incentive compensation awards received during the three years preceding termination. In addition, life, disability, medical and dental insurance coverage will be provided for 35 months. For purposes of the Key Management Benefit Plan, an officer will be deemed to have remained a Key Executive (as defined in the plan) until age 60; interest will be credited under the Executive Deferred Compensation Plan at the maximum rate allowed under the plan. Retirement benefits will be determined assuming three years of additional service and no early retirement pension reduction will be imposed. If any excise tax is imposed by Section 4999 of the Internal Revenue Code, Sprint will make the executive whole with respect to any additional taxes due. The agreements are not intended as an anti-takeover provision but could discourage an attempt to acquire control of Sprint by increasing the cost.

The Named Officers have each signed non-competition agreements with Sprint which provide that he or she will not associate with a competitor for an 18-month period following termination of employment. In addition, the agreements provide that each executive will receive 18 months of compensation and benefits following an involuntary termination of employment.

Sprint has a Key Management Benefit Plan providing for a survivor benefit in the event of the death of a participant or, in the alternative, a supplemental retirement benefit. Under the plan, if a participant dies prior to retirement, the participant's beneficiary will receive ten annual payments each equal to 25% of the participant's highest annual salary during the five-year period immediately prior to the time of death. If a participant dies after retiring or becoming permanently disabled, the participant's beneficiary will receive a benefit equal to 300% (or a reduced percentage if the participant retires before age 60) of the participant's highest annual salary during the five-year period immediately prior to the time of retirement or disability, payable either in a lump sum or in installments at the election of the participant. At least 13 months before retirement, a participant may elect a supplemental retirement benefit in lieu of all or a portion of the survivor benefit. The supplemental retirement benefit will be the actuarial equivalent of the survivor benefit. Each Named Officer is a participant in the plan.

Appendix C

Sample Severance and Noncompetition Agreement

The following Securities and Exchange Commission-filed document, which has been provided by the Bombay Company, may be used for top officers.

Dear _____:

The Board of Directors (the "Board") of The Bombay Company, Inc. (the "Company") recognizes that you have made and are expected to make a substantial contribution to the profitability, growth, and financial strength of the Company. In addition, the Board has determined that it is appropriate to induce you to enter into an agreement (the "Agreement") with the Company containing certain post-employment restrictions and providing for the continuation of certain benefits and income to you in the event you leave the employ of the Company.

1. *Term of Agreement; Termination Date.* The term of this Agreement is three years, commencing on the date of execution by both parties. At the end of the first year, which shall be the anniversary of the effective date hereof (the "Anniversary Date") and thereafter upon each Anniversary Date, this Agreement will be automatically renewed for an additional year, unless the Company has delivered to you a notice that it does not wish to renew the Agreement at least 30 days prior to such Anniversary Date. Upon notice of nonrenewal, you are entitled to the protection of this Agreement for the remaining

term of the Agreement, subject to all other provisions of this Agreement.

2. *Compensation upon Termination of Employment.* As set forth herein, your employment with the Company may be terminated prior to the expiration of the term specified in Section 1 of this Agreement. However, the provisions of Sections 2 through 18 will continue in full force and effect regardless of whether you continue to be employed by the Company and regardless of the reason your employment is terminated.

(a) *Termination for Cause.* Your employment may be terminated by the Company for Cause, evidenced by a duly adopted resolution of the Board. Unless made subject to an arbitration proceeding as set forth below, such termination will be effective immediately upon delivery to you of a Notice of Termination. "Notice of Termination" means a notice, timely delivered, which indicates the specific provisions in this Agreement relied upon for termination. It will set forth in reasonable detail the facts and circumstances claimed provide a basis for termination of your employment under the provisions so indicated. If the Company terminates you for Cause, you are entitled to receive your Base Salary and Calculated Bonus to the termination date as specified in the Notice of Termination (the "Termination Date"). "Calculated Bonus" means your bonus calculated based upon Company performance (the elements, criteria and formula of which shall be determined by the executive bonus plan for the fiscal year as approved by the Board) on a year-to-date basis through the Termination Date, the computation of which shall be made by the Company consistent with generally accepted accounting practices and past practices.

"Cause" means (i) the willful and continued failure by you to perform your duties with the Company (other than failure resulting from incapacity due to physical or mental illness) after a written demand for substantial performance is delivered to you by the Board which specifically identifies the manner in which the Board believes that you have not substantially performed your duties; (ii) a final, nonappealable determination by a court that you committed an act of dishonesty, fraud, or willful misconduct involving the Company; (iii) your conviction of any felony; or (iv) the material breach by you of any provision of this Agreement. For purposes of this definition of

"Cause," no act, or failure to act, on your part will be considered "willful" unless done, or omitted to be done, by you not in good faith and without reasonable belief that this action or omission was in the best interest of the Company.

In the event there is a dispute over the basis for a termination for Cause pursuant to (i) or (iv) in the preceeding paragraph, and provided you request in writing to the Company within 7 days following the Date of Termination, the dispute will be made the subject of compulsory arbitration, which you agree will be final, binding and nonappealable absent gross fraud or misconduct by one or more of the arbitrators. You agree that such arbitration will be in accordance with the rules and procedures of the American Arbitration Association, by three arbitrators designated by such Association, will be held in Fort Worth, Texas unless mutually agreed to the contrary, and shall be held within 90 days following the Date of Termination. You shall continue to be paid your normal compensation and receive normal benefits during the pendency of the arbitration. If the arbitration decision concludes that Cause did not exist for the termination, then the termination shall automatically become a termination other than for Cause, and the compensation specified in this Agreement shall commence. If arbitration is selected, then for purposes of this Agreement, the Date of Termination shall become the date of the arbitration decision.

"Base Salary" means your annual base salary, payable bi-weekly in accordance with Company policy, plus any increases in salary as established in the executive compensation program approved by the Board for a given fiscal year.

(b) *Mutual Consent.* At any time during the term of this Agreement, the parties hereto may terminate your employment by mutual consent. Such termination by mutual consent must be in writing, signed by both parties, and must set forth the mutual agreement of the parties regarding the terms and conditions for the continuation of income or benefits payments, if any, from the Company to you.

(c) *Termination by You.* You may terminate your employment with the Company. In the event that you do so, termination will be effective (i) for voluntary resignation, thirty days after you deliver a Notice of Termination or comparable notice to the Company; (ii) for

"Good Reason" (defined below), on the tenth day after you deliver a Notice of Termination to the Company, specifying in detail the reasons therefor, provided the Company has not, during such ten day period, cured the event or events causing such "Good Reason"; or (iii) for the Company's material breach of this Agreement, on the thirtieth day after written notice to the Company of such alleged breach, provided the Company has not, during such thirty day period, cured such breach. In the event you voluntarily resign, you are entitled to receive your Base Salary and Calculated Bonus to the Termination Date.

"Good Reason" means any of the following:

> (i)   without your express written consent, the assignment to you of material duties inconsistent with or the removal of material duties normal to your position, responsibilities and status with the Company, a material adverse change in your reporting responsibilities, titles or offices, or your removal from or any failure to re-elect you to any of such positions, except in connection with the termination of your employment for Cause or termination by you other than for Good Reason;

> (ii)   any reduction by the Company in your level of Base Salary and Target Bonus as in effect on the date hereof, which is inconsistent with a broad-based compensation reduction involving all or substantially all corporate and divisional officers of the Company and their equivalents;

> "Target Bonus" means the amount of bonus dollars you would receive pursuant to the executive bonus plan if the Company achieved its planned objectives set forth in the annual business plan, as approved by the Board for a given fiscal year.

> (iii)   the Company's requiring you to be based anywhere other than the Company's corporate offices in Fort Worth, Texas, except for required travel on the Company's business to an extent substantially consistent with your present business travel obligations, or, if you consent to any relocation, the failure by the Company to pay (or reimburse you) for all reasonable moving expenses incurred by you relating to a change of your principal residence in connection with such relocation and to indemnify you against any loss (defined as

the difference between the actual sale price of such residence and the higher of (A) your aggregate investment in such residence or (B) the fair market value of such residence as determined by a real estate appraiser mutually acceptable to both parties) realized on the sale of your principal residence in connection with any such change of residence;

(iv)   any failure of the Company to obtain, in accordance with Section 12 of this Agreement, the assumption of the agreement to perform this Agreement by any successor to the Company; or

(v)   any purported termination of your employment which is not effected pursuant to a properly delivered Notice of Termination; for purposes of this Agreement, no such purported termination shall be effective.

(d)   *Termination Without Cause; Good Reason.* If the Company terminates your employment other than for Cause, or if you terminate your employment for Good Reason or because of the material breach by the Company of this Agreement which is not timely cured, then the Company agrees to make payments and provide the following benefits:

(i)   The Company agrees to pay you your Base Salary for a period of 24 months following the Termination Date, provided, however, if you obtain New Employment (as defined below) any compensation attributed to such employment shall reduce the required payments herein on a dollar for dollar basis after the completion of 12 months following the Termination Date, such payment period hereinafter called the "Continuation Period." For fiscal years beginning subsequent to the Termination, Date but during the Continuation Period, you shall be paid, on a pro rata basis, your Target Bonus as set by the Board of Directors for such subsequent year. The payments described in this Section 2(d)(i) shall be defined as "Continuance Amount(s)." The Continuance Amount will be paid in installments in accordance with the regular payroll of the Company, and each installment will be subject to regular payroll deductions and all applicable taxes.

"New Employment" means your acceptance of a compensated position of employment with another person, entity or organization, or the creation or establishment of a business causing you to be self-employed during the Continuation Period. If you accept employment during the Continuation Period with a level of compensation or attributed earnings less than the Continuance Amount, then the Company shall, on a monthly basis, pay any discrepancy between your compensation or earnings and the Continuance Amount until the earlier of (i) the final day of the Continuation Period, or (ii) the discrepancy no longer exists. For purposes of this Section 2(d)(i), compensation or earnings from New Employment shall include, but not be limited to, any sign-on bonuses, other bonuses, guarantees or value given to you in connection with the employment. You agree to provide the Company appropriate documentation describing the employment and establishing the discrepancy, the failure of which shall serve to excuse any future payment by the Company under this Section 2(d)(i). The Company shall have the right to determine, in its sole discretion, acting reasonably, the value of the compensation or earnings for purposes of satisfying any discrepancy.

(ii) Within 45 days following the Termination Date, you will also receive, in a lump sum, your bonus for the fiscal year during which the termination occurred, based on the greater of either (i) your prorated Target Bonus to the Date of Termination or (ii) your Calculated Bonus.

(iii) The Company also agrees that you will be entitled to continue to participate in the Company's group health plan (medical, dental, and basic life insurance) on the same terms as other Company employees until the earlier of: (i) the expiration of the Continuation Period or (ii) your eligibility for similar plans by a subsequent employer. In accordance with the plan's provisions, your coverage will cease on the Termination Date under the Key Executive Disability Plan and the Family Security Plan. Anything to the contrary notwithstanding, the Company will have no obligation to continue to maintain during the Continuation Period any plan solely as a result of the provisions of this Agreement.

(iv) Any front-loaded stock options previously granted to you under any stock option plan of the Company will vest as of the Termination Date, provided the date of grant is at least 12 months prior to the Termination Date, in the following proportionate amount: the numerator being the number of months elapsed since the date of the grant of the option and the denominator being 24. All other outstanding stock options granted to you at least 12 months prior to the Termination Date under any of the Company's stock option plans will automatically be accelerated and fully vested as of the Termination Date. For options granted under the 1986 Stock Option Plan, you will be entitled to continue to hold these options and to exercise them for a period of three months after the Termination Date, after which period such options will expire and be cancelled. Upon completion of three months following the Date of Termination, you shall be granted a cash-only stock appreciation right (SAR) for each stock option exercised during the three month period, exercisable by you at any time during the following 21 months for any stock appreciation from the date of exercise of the option to the date of exercise of the SAR. Your exercise of the SAR shall be by written notice to the Company, which notice shall be irrevocable when given and shall be based upon the closing price of the Company's Common Stock on the date of the notice. Upon receipt of the notice, which shall specify the number of rights being exercised and the cash value of such rights, the Company shall redeem the rights tendered and shall become obligated to pay to you the value of the SAR exercised. The Company may, at its option, pay such amount in equal quarterly payments over a period of 12 months following its receipt of your notice. Any SAR not exercised in accordance with this Agreement within the time period required shall expire and be cancelled, and shall only be transferable to the extent that the underlying stock option was transferable. Notwithstanding the three month exercise period set forth above, in the event the Company elects to amend any existing stock option plan or adopts a new stock option plan which would permit a post termination exercise period greater than three months, then you shall, for any options granted under such amended or new plan, be entitled to exercise the options for the full period allowed, provided, however, in such event, the SAR grant shall be reduced for such options such that for any option granted, the combined exercise period and SAR period shall not exceed 24 months. Upon written request, the Company may consent to provide you registration rights (which consent may not be unreasonably withheld) whereby you could register some or all of the shares of the Company's common stock owned by you.

(v) Additionally, your participation in and the Company's contributions for you in the Stock Purchase Program, Employee 401(k) Savings and Stock Ownership Plan, Supplemental Stock Program (or similar plans adopted for the Company's executives subsequent to this Agreement) will cease on the Termination Date. The Company agrees to provide you, however, a cash payment equal to (A) the amount of such contribution not previously paid or credited to you attributable to the portion of your Base Salary (in effect on the Termination Date) that accrues up to and including the Termination Date and any bonus accrued as of the Termination Date, which will be payable in one lump sum, and (B) the amount of the Company's contribution attributable to the Continuance Amount payable to you under subparagraph (i) above, to which you are entitled under this Agreement, and which the Company will pay monthly as long as such Continuance Amount is required to be made to you by the Company.

(e) *Withholdings From Payment/Offset.* Any payments made by the Company to you under this Section 2 will be subject to all applicable local, state, federal or foreign taxes, including income tax, withholding tax, and social security tax. Further, to the extent you have, on the Termination Date, any outstanding debts or financial obligations to the Company, the Company shall be entitled to set off against payments due you hereunder for such debts or obligations.

(f) *Parachute Payments.* Notwithstanding any other provision to the contrary herein, payments made pursuant to this Agreement shall be reduced to the extent necessary to prevent such payments from constituting "excess parachute payments" within the meaning of Section 280G(b) of the Internal Revenue Code of 1986, as amended, if, and only if, the Board of Directors determines that such reduction will have the likely effect of increasing your after-tax benefit. Such determination, and the determination of any reduction pursuant to this paragraph, shall be based upon the opinion of the Company's outside counsel or a nationally recognized accounting firm selected by the Company.

(g) *Payments After Death.* All payments of Continuance Amounts shall cease upon the latter of your death or the expiration of the twelfth month after the Termination Date. Any such payments after your death that may be due hereunder will be paid to your named beneficiary provided to the Company in connection with this Agreement, or if no such designation has been made by you, then to your executors, administrators, heirs, personal representatives, successors, or assigns, as the case may be.

3. *Additional Perquisites.* Upon termination of your employment with the Company for any reason other than for Cause or mutual agreement, the Company agrees to provide you with executive outplacement services up to a maximum expense of $20,000 or 10% of your Base Salary, whichever is greater. Additionally, the Company will continue to pay, for a period of one year after the Termination Date or until you obtain New Employment (whichever occurs first), all of your club membership dues to the same extent to which dues were previously paid by the Company. For a period of 45 days following the Termination Date, you will have the opportunity to purchase, for the lesser of fair market or book value, the automobile which the Company provided to you. Any car allowance you previously received, however, will cease immediately on the Termination Date.

4. *Conditions Applicable to Severance Benefits.* In consideration of the payments and benefits provided to you hereunder by the Company, you agree as follows:

(a) *No Competing Employment.* You agree that during the term of your employment and for a period commencing on the Termination Date (or the date a court of competent jurisdiction enters a final judgment enforcing this provision, whichever is later), and ending on the second anniversary thereof, you will not, directly or indirectly, either as an employee, employer, consultant, agent, principal, partner, stockholder, corporate officer, director, or in any other individual or representative capacity, work for, engage or participate in any business which is a Direct Competitor with the Company (as defined below) within the United States, Canada or other country where the Company conducts business as of the Termination Date, provided, however, that you may own, directly or indirectly, solely as an investment, securities of any entity that is registered under the Securities Exchange Act of 1934, as amended, if you (a) are not a controlling person of, or a member of a group which controls such entity or (b) do not, directly or indirectly, own 5% or more of any class of securities of such entity. You represent to the Company that the enforcement of this restriction would not be unduly burdensome to you. If a court of competent jurisdiction determines that this Section 4 meets the requirements of Section 15.50(1) of the Texas Business & Commerce Code ("TBCC") but not the requirements of Section 15.50(2) of the TBCC, then the Company and you each agree that the Company is deemed to have requested reformation by such court pursuant to Section 15.51(c) of the TBCC.

For the purposes of this Section 4, "Direct Competitor" shall mean any of the following: (i) any business that is principally engaged in, or any subsidiary, division, operating unit or department within another business in which such subsidiary, division, operating unit or department is principally engaged in the wholesale, mail order or retail sale of traditional-style or country-style home furniture, whether such operation is conducted in shopping malls, strip centers, free standing locations or through mail order catalogs; and (ii) any business that is the same or substantially similar to any new business unit developed or being developed by, or entity acquired by the Company after the effective date of this Agreement and prior to the Termination Date. "Being developed" as used herein shall mean either (i) the expenditure of $25,000 or more directly in connection with the business or concept being developed or (ii) a Board resolution approving the development of the business.

(b) *Confidentiality.* You will not disclose to any person at any time during or following your employment, any proprietary information, trade secrets, systems, manuals, confidential reports or lists of vendors, suppliers, manufacturers or clients, the nature and type of product design and development or services rendered by the Company, or equipment and methods used by the Company (the "Confidential Information"). Notwithstanding the foregoing, Confidential Information will *not* be deemed to include information which (i) is or becomes available to the public other than as a result of disclosure by you in violation of this Section 4(b) or (ii) you are required to disclose under any applicable laws, regulations or directives or any governmental agency, tribunal or authority having jurisdiction in the matter or under subpoena or other process of law.

You agree that all Confidential Information is and will remain the exclusive property of the Company. Upon termination of your employment for any reason, you agree to return to the Company all Confidential Information (including any copies or reproductions thereof), and any other property belonging to the Company, that is in your possession or control. You agree to provide the Company with written verification that all of the Confidential Information provided to you has been returned to the Company, that all memoranda, notes or other documents in any way relating to the Confidential Information and the business affairs of the Company have either been returned to the Company or destroyed and that you have not retained any copies of such Confidential Information, memoranda or notes.

(c)   *No Interference.* You will not, for a period commencing upon the Termination Date and ending upon the second anniversary thereof, either directly or indirectly, (i) make known to any person, firm or corporation the names and addresses of any of the vendors, suppliers or manufacturers of the Company or other proprietary contacts of the Company within the specialty retailing industry or any other information pertaining to such persons; (ii) call on, solicit, or take away, or attempt to call on, solicit, or take away any of the employees of the Company whether for you or for any other person, firm or corporation; or (iii) call on, solicit, or take away, or attempt to call on, solicit, or take away any customer, vendor, supplier, or manufacturer of the Company which has, within the current or previous fiscal year, produced goods tor, or provided services to the Company in an amount in excess of 2% of the Company's total purchases of resale merchandise (at cost), whether for you or for any other person, firm or corporation.

You will not make or publish, or cause to be made or published, any written or oral statements which may cause damage, financial or otherwise, to the Company, including, but not limited to, damage to the Company's goodwill.

(d)   *Use of Name.* After the Termination Date, you shall be indefinitely restricted and forbidden from using the names "Bombay", "Alex & Ivy" or any other names being used by the Company as of the Termination Date, or any other names deceptively similar thereto in any venture in which you are or may become directly or indirectly involved.

(e) *Equitable Remedies.* You acknowledge that a breach of any of the covenants contained in Sections 4(a) through 4(d) may result in material irreparable injury to the Company for which there is no adequate remedy at law and that it will not be possible to measure precisely damages for such injuries. You agree that, in the event of such a breach threat thereof, the Company shall be entitled, in addition to any other rights or remedies it may have, to obtain a temporary restraining order and/or a preliminary or permanent injunction enjoining or restraining you from engaging activities prohibited by Sections 4(a) through 4(d).

The parties to this Agreement agree that the limitations contained in this Section 4 with respect to geographic area, duration, and scope of activity are reasonable. However, if any court of competent jurisdiction shall determine that the geographic area, duration, or scope of activity of any restriction contained in this Section 4 is unenforceable, it is the intention of the parties that such restrictive covenant set forth herein shall not thereby be terminated but shall be deemed amended to the extent required to render it valid and enforceable.

You agree that the representations and covenants contained in this Section 4 pertaining to you shall be construed as ancillary to and independent of any other provision of this Agreement, and the existence of any claim or cause of action you may have against the Company or any officer, director, or stockholder of the Company, whether predicated on this Agreement or otherwise, shall not constitute a defense to the enforcement by the Company of the covenants contained in this Section 4.

5. *Consulting.* Except in the event of voluntary resignation, for a period of 90 days following the Termination Date, you shall be available, on a reasonable basis, to the Company for up to 5 days for the purpose of providing consultation to the Company's management and performing other transition assignments. The Company shall reimburse you for reasonable travel and other business expenses incurred by you at the Company's request during such period, but no additional compensation shall be payable to you for such services.

6. *Nonpayment Upon Breach.* Notwithstanding anything in this Agreement to the contrary, at any time after the Termination Date, if you, by any action or omission to act, breach any covenant, agreement, condition or obligation contained herein, the Company is entitled to cease making any payments and cease providing any of the benefits to you as contemplated in this Agreement.

7. *Legal Fees and Expenses.* The Company will pay the reasonable legal fees and expenses that you may incur as a result of the Company's contesting the validity, enforceability or your interpretation of this Agreement. If the Company is the successful party to such action, however, the Company has no obligation to pay such legal fees and expenses incurred by you. If the Company is required to pay your reasonable legal fees and expenses, the Company will promptly pay such expenses upon your submission to the Company of invoices or other written evidence of the legal fees or expenses incurred by you.

8. *Mediation; Arbitration.* Notwithstanding anything herein to the contrary, if a dispute or disagreement arises out of or in connection with this Agreement, prior to submission of the controversy to arbitration or for resolution by a court of competent jurisdiction, the parties hereto shall submit the controversy to mediation in a proceeding to be conducted in Fort Worth, Texas.

9. *Period of Limitations.* No legal action shall be brought and no cause of action shall be asserted by or on behalf of the Company or any affiliate of the Company against you, your spouse, heirs, executors, or personal or legal representatives after the expiration of two years from the date of accrual of such cause of action, and any claim or cause of action of the Company or its affiliate shall be extinguished and deemed released unless asserted by the timely filing of a legal action within such two-year period, provided, however, that if any shorter period of limitations is otherwise applicable to any such cause of action such shorter period shall govern.

10. *Nonexclusivity.* Your rights hereunder shall be in addition to any other rights you may have under the Company's Bylaws, the Delaware General Corporation Law, or otherwise.

11. *Amendments.* No supplement, modification or amendment of this Agreement shall be binding unless executed in writing by both

of the parties hereto. No waiver of any of the provisions of this Agreement shall be deemed or shall constitute a waiver of any other provisions hereof (whether or not similar), nor shall such waiver constitute a continuing waiver.

12. *Binding Effect; Assignment.* Except as provided otherwise herein, this Agreement shall be binding upon and inure to the benefit of and be enforceable by the parties hereto and their respective successors and assigns, including any direct or indirect successor by purchase, merger, consolidation or otherwise to all or substantially all of the business or assets of the Company, provided, however, you hereby acknowledge that this Agreement is a personal services contract and that you will not be entitled to assign any rights or obligations hereunder. The Company will require and cause any successor (whether direct or indirect by purchase, merger, consolidation or otherwise) to all, substantially all, or a substantial part, of the business or assets of the Company, by written agreement in form and substance satisfactory to you, expressly to assume and agree to perform this Agreement in the same manner and to the same extent that the Company would be required to perform if no such succession had taken place.

13. *Severability.* The provisions of this Agreement shall be severable if any of the provisions hereof are held by a *court* of competent jurisdiction to be invalid, void or otherwise unenforceable, and the remaining provisions shall remain enforceable to the fullest extent permitted by law.

14. *Governing Law.* This Agreement shall be governed by and construed and enforced in accordance with the laws of the State of Texas applicable to contracts made and to be performed in such state without giving effect to the principles of conflicts of laws. Subject to the provisions of this Agreement regarding mediation, the appropriate state or federal court located in Fort Worth, Texas shall have exclusive jurisdiction over all matters arising under this Agreement and will be the proper forum in which to adjudicate those matters.

15. *Notices.* All notices and communications which are required by this Agreement, or which may be given pursuant to this Agreement, shall be in writing and shall be transmitted to the following addresses:

The Bombay Company, Inc.
550 Bailey Avenue, Suite 700
Fort Worth, Texas 76107

Attn: Michael J. Veitenheimer

Either party may change the address to which such notices and communications shall be sent by written notice to the other party.

16. *Multiple Counterparts.* This Agreement may be executed in any number of counterparts, all of which taken together shall constitute one and the same document, and each of which shall be deemed an original, and any of the parties hereto may execute this Agreement by signing any of the counterparts.

17. *Legal Counsel.* The Company and its legal counsel have prepared this Agreement. You hereby acknowledge that you have had the opportunity to consult with and seek the advice of independent legal counsel of your choice regarding the terms of this Agreement and its subject matter.

18. *Entire Agreement.* This Agreement sets forth the entire agreement and understanding of the parties relating to the subject matter hereof, and supersedes all prior agreements, arrangements and understandings, written or oral, relating to the subject matter hereof.

Very truly yours,

THE BOMBAY COMPANY, INC.

By:_____

ACCEPTED AND AGREED as of
the ___ day of ___ , 199_.

Appendix D

Sample Employment Agreements

Four sample employment agreements are provided here for your information. Many clauses in these agreements provide sample language for related issues of executive compensation found within this book.

The first employment agreement that follows was drafted pursuant to a merger. The second agreement is between a company and a sole shareholder. The third agreement was drafted pursuant to an asset purchased. The fourth agreement is between a company and its president.

These forms have been provided by Julie M. Edmond, Esq., a partner in the law firm of Shea & Gardner, Washington, DC.

SAMPLE EMPLOYMENT AGREEMENT I: PURSUANT TO A MERGER

EMPLOYMENT AGREEMENT, dated September 19_, by and between _____ a ___ corporation (the "Company") and _____ (the "Executive").

The Executive was a shareholder of _____, a Corporation (_____), and was its President and the Chairman of its Board of Directors. Pursuant to an Agreement and Plan of Merger, dated September __, 19_ (the "Merger Agreement"), by and among _____ (the "Buyer"), the Company, the Executive, and the other stockholders of _____, was merged into the Company. The Buyer was and is the sole stockholder of the Company. This Agreement is being entered into pursuant to paragraph 7(b) of the Merger Agreement.

In consideration of the foregoing, and of the mutual covenants and agreements hereinafter set forth, the parties hereto agree as follows:

1. *Employment, Duties, and Acceptance.*

1.1 *Employment by the Company.* The Company hereby employs the Executive for the term provided in Section 2 (the "Term") to render exclusive and full-time services to the Company as President thereof and, in connection therewith, to perform the duties provided in Section 1.4 (the "Duties").

1.2 *Acceptance of Employment by the Executive.* The Executive hereby accepts such employment and agrees to perform the Duties for the Company. The Executive shall devote his entire working time and his best efforts to the business of the Company during the Term.

1.3 *Place of Employment.* The Executive's principal place of employment shall be in _____, subject to such reasonable travel, not in excess of that customary in the past, as the performance of the Duties may require.

1.4 *Duties.* The Executive shall hold the position and title, and exercise the responsibilities, of President of the Company. The Executive shall have the right and obligation, in his capacity as President, to perform the duties of the President as are described in the By-Laws of the Company and such other duties as may be assigned to him by the Board of Directors of the Company, in accordance with the policies and procedures promulgated for operating companies owned by the Buyer. The Executive shall report solely to the Chief Executive Officer of the Buyer, in his capacity as a member of the Board of Directors of the Buyer.

2. *Term of Employment and Other Employment.*

2.1 *Term of Employment.* The Term of the Executive's employment under this Agreement shall commence on the date of this Agreement and shall end on the third anniversary date thereof, unless extended as provided in this Section 2. The Company shall have the option, on the third anniversary date, to extend the Term of the Executive's employment until the fourth anniversary date; and, if the Company shall exercise such option, it shall on the fourth anniversary date have the option to extend the Term of such employment until the fifth anniversary date. The Company shall exercise such options by notifying the Executive in writing at least thirty (30) days prior to the corresponding anniversary date. On or after the third anniversary date or, if the Company shall exercise the first (or first and second) option(s) noted above, after the fourth (or fifth) anniversary date, as the case may be, the Executive's employment under this Agreement shall continue until terminated by either party. Such termination, if by the Executive, shall be only upon at least 90 days' prior written notice. Such termination, if by the Company, shall be by written notice; *provided, however,* notwithstanding the date of such termination, the Company shall continue to pay the Executive's salary for a period of one year following such date. The Term of such employment, as extended or continued, shall be treated for all purposes hereunder as the Term. Notwithstanding the foregoing, the termination of the Executive's employment under this Agreement, as provided elsewhere herein, shall end the Term.

2.2 *Other Employment.* In the event that the employment of the Executive is terminated by the Company pursuant to Section 2.1, the Executive shall have no obligation to accept employment offered to him by others, and the Company shall not interpose any defense against the payment of amounts due under Section 2.1 based on the refusal of the Executive to seek or accept any such employment, *provided, however,* if the Executive shall accept such employment, the Company may offset the amount of any compensation received from such employment from the amount otherwise due under Section 2.1.

3. *Compensation.*

3.1 *Salary.* As compensation for all services to be rendered pursuant to this Employment Agreement, the Company shall pay the Executive during the Term a salary of at least $___ per annum and such additional compensation as may be provided for in this Section 3. All of the Executive's compensation shall be payable in accordance with the payroll policies of the Company as from time to time in effect, less such appropriate deductions as shall be required to be withheld by applicable law and regulations, or by written election of the Executive.

3.2 *Bonus.* The Company shall pay to the Executive a bonus of $___ over the first three years of the Term. The Company shall place such bonus in a special expense fund earmarked for the Executive's exclusive discretionary use within ten (10) days after the date of this Agreement. The Executive shall have the right to apply all or part of this fund as he deems appropriate over the Term, except that he shall apply no more than $___ of such fund over the first year of the Term, and no more than one-half (1/2) of the remaining balance at the completion of the first year of the Term over the second year of the Term. In addition, the Executive and up to four (4) other executives of the Company shall be entitled to participate in a management incentive plan to be established for the calendar year 1986, and for each year thereafter during the Term, as the Board of Directors of the Company shall provide. Such plan shall be established on a basis similar to that provided in bonus programs adopted by other companies owned by the Buyer.

3.3 *Participation in Employee Benefit Plans.* The Executive shall be permitted during the Term, to the extent eligible, to participate in any group life, medical, or disability insurance plan, health program, dental program, pension plan or similar benefit plan, stock option plan thrift plan, or other fringe benefit plan of the Company, which participation shall be on a basis that is at least equivalent to that which is then made available to other executives of the Company.

3.4 *Expenses.* Subject to such policies as may from time to time be established by the Board of Directors of the Company, the Company shall pay or reimburse the Executive for all reasonable expenses actually incurred or paid by the Executive during the Term in the performance of his Duties upon presentation of expense statements or vouchers or such other supporting information as the Company may require.

3.5 *Salary Adjustments.* Effective October 1, 19_, and thereafter during the Term effective on every succeeding October 1, the annual salary of the Executive then in effect shall be reviewed by the Board of Directors of the Company in accordance with generally applied normal corporate policy and practice.

3.6 *Paid Vacation.* During each year of the Term of this Agreement, the Executive shall be entitled to four (4) weeks vacation, during which vacation period he shall continue to receive the salary and other compensation provided in this Section 3.

3.7 *Interest Free Loan.* The parties hereto acknowledge that the Executive has received an unsecured interest free loan from the Company in the amount of $___. The Executive shall repay to the Company within ten (10) days after the date of this Agreement the full amount of such loan, as well as the full amount of any and all other unpaid loans received by the Executive from the predecessor of the Company.

3.8 *Insurance.* The Company shall provide life insurance for the Executive on a basis similar to that on which it is provided to executives in other companies owned by the Buyer. The Company shall have the option to maintain a key-employee life insurance policy on the life of the Executive and may elect to continue as that insurance policy the insurance policy upon the life of the Executive in the amount of $___ of which the Company is currently the owner and partial beneficiary, *provided, however,* the Executive shall have the option for thirty (30) days after the date of this Agreement to purchase that policy from the Company for a sum equal to the current cash surrender value of that policy.

3.9 *Car.* The Company shall continue to make available to the Executive, until the second anniversary date of this Agreement, the _____ more fully identified by the copy of the Registration Statement previously delivered to the Buyer, currently being used by the Executive. On the second anniversary date of this Agreement, and on every third anniversary of that date during the Term, the car shall be replaced by an _____ 4-door sedan or other car of equivalent cost, as normally provided by the Buyer to equivalent executives of its U.S. subsidiaries, which car shall be made available to the Executive by the Company (by lease) for his full time use, *provided, however,* the Executive shall have the option on the second anniversary date of this Agreement and on every third anniversary of that date during the Term of applying the payments to be made by the Company for the lease of such car to the lease of a higher-priced car, the additional cost of the lease of such higher-priced car to be paid from the bonus provided in Section 3.2 or from the Executive's personal funds at his option, and such higher-priced car to be made available to the Executive for his full time use. The Executive shall have the option to purchase each car replaced under this Section for its estimated end-of-term wholesale value as reflected in the Agreement for the lease of such car. The Company shall be responsible for the maintenance of the car that it makes available to the Executive for his use, shall maintain full casualty and personal liability insurance with respect to such car, and shall provide the Executive, free of charge, with parking space at a parking garage near the corporate headquarters of the Company.

4.   *Termination.*

4.1   *Termination upon Death.* The Executive's employment under this Agreement shall terminate upon the Executive's death, subject to the Company's continuing obligation to make payment of salary or other compensation to the Executive's legal representatives to the extent then generally provided in the compensation programs of other companies owned by the Buyer. Such payments shall not affect any other amounts payable as insurance or other death benefits under any plan or arrangement then in force and effect with respect to the Executive.

4.2   *Termination upon Disability.*

(a)   If, during the Term of his employment, the Executive becomes physically or mentally disabled, so that the Executive is unable substantially to perform his duties hereunder, the Company may terminate his employment after a period of disability determined on the same basis as that generally applied by the Buyer with respect to the termination of the employment of executives of other companies owned by the Buyer on grounds of physical or mental disability.

(b)   During the first half of the period of disability that must pass before the Company may terminate the Executive's employment under subsection (a) above, the Company shall continue to pay the Executive the full amount of his annual salary (as then in effect) and any bonus that may have accrued. Thereafter, and until the termination of his employment, the Company shall pay the Executive fifty percent (50%) of his annual salary (as then in effect) and of any bonus that may have accrued. Any amounts payable as disability benefits under any plan or arrangement then in force and effect with respect to the Executive shall be deducted from the payments provided for in this subsection (b). Nothing in this Section 4.2 shall be deemed to extend the Term of this Agreement.

(c) In case of any disagreement between the Executive and the Board of Directors of the Company as to whether the Executive is disabled so as to permit the Company to terminate the Executive's employment hereunder in accordance with this Section 4.2, the question of such disability shall be submitted for determination to an impartial and reputable physician selected either by mutual agreement of the Executive and the Company or, failing such agreement, at the request of the Company by the then President of the Medical Society of _____ (or by such Society under the procedures it may have for such selection), and such determination of the question of such disability by such physician shall be final and binding on the Executive and the Company. The Company shall pay the fees and expenses of such physician.

4.3 *Termination for Cause.* The Board of Directors of the Company shall have the right to terminate the Executive's employment and discharge him for cause, which shall mean and be limited to the following events:

(a) An act or acts of dishonesty on the part of the Executive intended or reasonably likely to result directly or indirectly in substantial gain or personal enrichment at the expense of the Company or any of its subsidiaries, or the commission of a felony under the laws of the State of New York (other than a Class E felony);

(b) A determination by a licensed physician in New York State that the Executive is a chronic alcoholic or a narcotics addict (as that term is defined under the Mental Hygiene Law of the State of New York, as amended, or any successor statute). The Executive shall submit to an examination by such licensed physician upon the reasonable request of the Company;

(c) An act or omission which constitutes a substantial failure to perform his Duties hereunder, *provided, however,* no discharge shall be deemed for cause under this subsection (c) unless the Executive shall have first received written notice from the Board of Directors of the Company advising the Executive of the specific acts or omissions alleged to constitute a substantial failure to perform his Duties hereunder, and such failure continues after the Executive shall have had a reasonable opportunity to correct the acts so complained of;

(d) A determination by the Company that the Executive actually knew that the Merger Agreement contained a material misrepresentation or breach of warranty at the Effective Date.

Upon termination of his employment for cause, as provided herein, the Company shall pay the Executive his annual salary (as then in effect) accrued up to the last day of the month in which such termination occurs.

5. *Protection of Confidential Information; Non-competition.*

5.1 In view of the fact that the Executive's work as an employee of the Company hereunder will bring him into close contact with many confidential affairs of the Company, including information about costs, profits, sales, trade secrets, and other information not readily available to the public (hereinafter collectively referred to as "confidential matters"), the Executive agrees to keep secret all confidential matters of the Company and not to disclose them to anyone outside of the Company or otherwise use his knowledge of them for his own benefit, either during or after his employment with the Company.

5.2 The parties incorporate herein by reference the restrictive covenant contained in Section 13 of the Merger Agreement as it applies to the Executive, *provided, however,* the restrictive covenant contained therein shall not apply to the Executive if he shall voluntarily terminate his employment during the Term because of a breach of this Agreement by the Company.

5.3 If the Executive commits a breach, or threatens to commit a breach, of any of the provisions of this Section 5, the Company shall have the following rights and remedies:

(a) The right and remedy to have the provisions of this Section 5 specifically enforced by any court having equity jurisdiction, it being acknowledged and agreed that any such breach or threatened breach will cause irreparable injury to the Company and that money damages will not provide an adequate remedy to the Company; and

(b) The right and remedy to require the Executive to account for and pay over to the Company all compensation, profits, monies, accruals, increments, or other benefits (hereinafter collectively referred to as the "Benefits") derived or received by the Executive as the result of any transactions constituting a breach of any of the provisions of this Section 5, the Executive hereby agreeing to account for and pay over the Benefits to the Company.

5.4   If any covenant contained in this Section 5, or any part thereof, is held to be unenforceable because of the duration of such covenant or the area covered thereby, the parties agree that the court making such determination shall have the power to reduce the duration and/or area of such covenant and, in its reduced form, said covenant shall then be enforceable.

6.   *Indemnification.* The Company shall indemnify the Executive to the full extent authorized by law in the event he is made or threatened to be made a party to any action, suit or proceeding, whether criminal, civil, administrative or investigative, by reason of the fact that he is or was a director, officer or employee of the Company or any predecessor of the Company or serves or served any other enterprise as a director, officer or employee at the request of the Company or any predecessor of the Company.

7.   *Other Provisions.*

7.1   *Notices.* Any notice or other communication required or permitted hereunder shall be in writing and shall be delivered personally, telegraphed, telexed, sent by facsimile transmission, or sent by certified, registered, or express mail, postage prepaid. Any such notice shall be deemed given when so delivered personally, telegraphed, telexed, or sent by facsimile transmission or, if mailed, two days after the date of deposit in the United States mails addressed as follows:

(i) if to the Company, to:

Attention: The Board of Directors

with a copy to:

Attention:

(ii) if to the Executive, to:

with a copy to:

Attention:

7.2 *Entire Agreement.* This Agreement, and any other agreements incorporated therein by reference, sets forth the entire agreement and understanding of the parties relating to the subject matter hereof, and supersedes all prior agreements (including the Employment Agreement, dated March ___ 19_ between the Company and the Executive), arrangements, and understandings, written or oral, relating to the subject matter hereof.

7.3 *Waivers and Amendments.* This Agreement may be amended, superseded, cancelled, renewed, or extended, and the terms hereof may be waived, only by a written instrument signed by the parties or, in the case of a waiver, by the party waiving compliance. No delay on the part of any party in exercising any right, power, or privilege hereunder shall operate as a waiver thereof, nor shall any waiver on the part of any party of any such right, power, or privilege, nor any single or partial exercise of any such right, power, or privilege, preclude any other or further exercise thereof or the exercise of any other such right, powers, or privilege.

7.4 *Governing Law.* This Agreement shall be governed by and construed in accordance with the laws of the State of New York applicable to agreements made and to be performed entirely within such State.

7.5 *Assignment.* The provisions of this Agreement shall be binding upon and inure to the benefit of the parties hereto and their respective heirs, legal representatives, successors, and assigns. This Agreement, and the Executive's rights and obligations hereunder, may not be assigned by the Executive. The Company may assign this

Agreement and its rights, together with its obligations hereunder, in connection with any sale, transfer, or other disposition of all or substantially all of its respective assets or business, whether by merger, consolidation, or otherwise.

7.6 *Headings*. The headings in this Agreement are for reference only and shall not affect the interpretation of this Agreement.

IN WITNESS WHEREOF, the parties have executed this Agreement the date first above written.

ATTEST: By: _____

By: _____

                                     By: _____

SAMPLE EMPLOYMENT AGREEMENT II:
WITH SOLE SHAREHOLDER

EMPLOYMENT AGREEMENT, dated ____, 19_ by and between _____ a corporation (the "Company"), and _____ (the "Executive").

The Executive is the sole shareholder of the Company, its President and the Chairman of its Board of Directors. Pursuant to an Agreement of even date herewith (the "Acquisition Agreement"), by and between the Executive and _____, 100% of the issued and outstanding capital shares of the Company will be acquired by _____. This Agreement is being entered into pursuant to paragraph 5(b) of the Acquisition Agreement.

In consideration of the foregoing, and of the mutual covenants and agreements hereinafter set forth, the parties hereto agree as follows:

1. *Employment, Duties and Acceptance.*

1.1 *Employment by the Company.* The Company hereby employs the Executive for the term provided in Article 2 (the "Term") to render exclusive and full-time services to the Company as President and, in connection therewith, to perform the duties provided in Section 1.4 (the "Duties").

1.2 *Acceptance of Employment by the Executive.* The Executive hereby accepts such employment and agrees to perform the Duties diligently to the best of his abilities and in the best interests of the Company. The Executive shall devote his entire working time and his best efforts to the business of the Company during the Term.

1.3 *Place of Employment.* The Executive's principal place of employment shall be at _____ or such other location in the Washington, DC metropolitan area as the Company may designate upon reasonable notice to the Executive. The Company may direct the Executive to engage in such reasonable travel as the performance of the Duties may require.

1.4 *Duties.* The Executive shall hold the position and title, and exercise the responsibilities, of President. The Executive shall have the right and obligation, in his capacity as President, to perform the duties of that office to the extent they are described in the By-laws of the Company, as well as such other duties as from time to time may be assigned to him by the Company.

2. *Term of Employment.* The Term of the Executive's employment under this Agreement shall commence on the day of this Agreement and shall end on the third anniversary date thereof, unless extended as provided in this Article 2. The Company shall have the option, on the third anniversary date, to extend the Term of the Executive's employment until the fourth anniversary date; and, if the Company shall exercise such option, it shall on the fourth anniversary date have the option to extend the Term of such employment until the fifth anniversary date. The Company shall exercise such options by notifying the Executive in writing at least ninety (90) days prior to the corresponding anniversary date. On or after the third anniversary date or, if the Company shall exercise the first (or first and second) option(s) noted above, after the fourth (or fifth) anniversary date, as the case may be, the Executive's employment under this Agreement shall continue until terminated by either party. Such termination, if by the Executive, shall be only upon at least 30 days' prior written notice. Such termination, if by the Company, shall be only upon at least 30 days' prior written notice. The period of such employment, as extended or continued, shall be treated for all purposes hereunder as the Term. Notwithstanding the foregoing, the Executive's employment under this Agreement may be terminated as provided elsewhere herein, and such termination shall end the Term.

3. Compensation.

3.1 *Salary.* As compensation for all services to be rendered pursuant to this Agreement, the Company shall pay the Executive during the Term a salary of at least $___ per annum. All of the Executive's compensation shall be payable in accordance with the payroll policies of the Company as from time to time in effect, less such appropriate deductions as shall be required to be withheld by applicable law and regulations, or by written election of the Executive if agreed to by the Company.

3.2 *Participation in Employee Benefit Plans.* The Executive shall be permitted during the Term, to the extent eligible, to participate in any group life, medical, or disability insurance plan, health program, dental program, profit-sharing or pension or similar benefit plan, thrift plan, or other fringe benefit plan of the Company, participation shall be on a basis that is at least equivalent to that which is then made available to other executives of the Company. The Company shall continue to provide the Executive with the car that the Company now leases and provides for his use. The Company shall pay for the upkeep, maintenance, repair, normal operating expenses, and parking at the office for such automobile as well as all taxes associated with its registration and use. Upon expiration of the current lease of such automobile by the Company, the Company will provide the Executive with the use of an automobile pursuant to the Company's normal and usual policy then in effect.

3.3 *Incentive Plan.* The Executive shall be eligible to participate in Buyer's Senior Management Incentive Plan, starting with the 19_ Plan *pro rata,* in accordance with its terms and conditions.

3.4 *Expenses.* Subject to such policies as may from time to time be established by the Company, the Company shall pay or reimburse the Executive for all reasonable expenses actually incurred or paid by the Executive during the Term in the performance of his Duties upon presentation of expense statements or vouchers or such other supporting information as the Company may require.

3.5 *Salary Adjustment.* Effective June 1, 19_ and thereafter during the Term effective on every succeeding June 1, the annual salary of the Executive then in effect shall be reviewed by the President of Buyer in accordance with generally applied normal corporate policy and practice; except, however, the Executive's compensation shall not be less than $___ per annum as provided in Section 3.1 hereof.

3.6 *Paid Vacation.* During each year of the Term of this Agreement, the Executive shall be entitled to a vacation of the greater of twenty (20) working days or the time allowed under the Company's policies and practices then in effect, in addition to other holidays designated by the Company, during which vacation period he shall continue to receive the salary and other compensation provided in this Article 3. Such paid vacation must be taken at a time and in a manner consistent with his Duties.

4. *Termination of Employment.*

4.1 *Termination upon Death.* The Executive's employment under this Agreement shall terminate upon the Executive's death. The Company shall continue to make payment of salary or other compensation to the Executive's legal representatives in accordance with the Company's general policies and practices then in effect.

4.2 *Termination upon Disability.*

(a) If, during the Term of his employment, the Executive becomes physically or mentally disabled, so that he is unable substantially to perform his duties hereunder, the Company may terminate his employment after a period of disability determined on the same basis as that generally applied by the Company with respect to the termination of the employment of executives of the Company on grounds of physical or mental disability.

(b) In the case of any disagreement between the Executive and the Company as to whether the Executive is disabled so as to permit the Company to terminate the Executive's employment hereunder in accordance with this Section 4.2, the question of such disability shall be submitted for determination to an impartial and reputable physician selected by the mutual agreement of the Executive (or his legal representative) and the Company. Failing such agreement, the Company shall request a physician referral from the Medical Society of _____ and the Executive and the Company hereby agree in advance to accept the first name provided in that referral. The determination of the question of disability by such physician selected consistent with this subsection (b) shall be final and binding on the Executive and the Company. The Company shall pay the fees and expenses of such physician.

(c) If, with respect to the first ninety (90) days of the period during which the Executive suffers a disability of the kind described in subsection (a) above, the total amount of payment received by the Executive pursuant to sick leave and similar practices and policies generally followed by the Company is less than 100% of the amount of the salary that the Executive would have received with respect to the same period, the Company shall pay him the difference.

4.3 *Termination for Cause.* The Company may terminate the Executive's ernployment for cause. "Termination for cause" shall mean discharge from employment for committing an unlawful, deceitful or fraudulent act, for knowingly withholding from the Company's Board of Directors information material to the Company's interests, for knowingly making any misrepresentation to the Company's Board of Directors regarding a matter material to the Company's interests, for knowingly failing to carry out the instructions of the Company's Board of Directors, or for knowingly failing to abide by or to enforce any material policy or procedure of the Company. Upon termination of his employment for cause, as provided herein, the Company shall pay the Executive his salary (as then in effect) accrued up to the last date of the month in which such termination occurs.

5. *Confidentiality and Proprietary Materials.*

5.1 *Confidentiality.* The Executive shall not at any time during his employment with the Company or at any time after the termination of the same for any reason (including expiration of the Term) disclose, impart, divulge, or otherwise reveal in any manner whatsoever, directly or indirectly, in writing or orally, whether by counsel, discussion, recommendation, suggestion, or otherwise, any "Protected Information" except in the course of the proper discharge of his Duties or as expressly authorized by the Company's Board of Directors.

(a) As used in this Agreement "Protected Information" means any confidential or proprietary information (in whatever form recorded) about the Company, any Affiliate of the Company, or any customer or client of the Company or any such Affiliate, that the Executive has obtained, had access to, or gained knowledge of in the course of his employment with the Company. An Affiliate of the Company is any entity controlling, controlled by, or under common control with, the Company. Protected Information shall include, without limitation:

(i) Information concerning or relating to properties, organization, operations, procedures, plans, projects, programs, prod-

ucts, processes, systems, profitability, finances, and business relationships and opportunities;

(ii) Any trade secret or other similar information including, without limitation, the identity of customers or clients, customer
or client lists, mailing lists, software programs, databases, coding
information, standard forms, market analysis and strategies, and
pricing and cost information, except to the extent that such information is lawfully and readily available to the general public;

(iii) Information relating to any litigation including, without limitation, attorney work product and any data, documents, or
other information that may be subject to the attorney-client privilege.

(b) As used in this Agreement, the phrase "any Customer or
Prospective Customer of the Company" means any person or entity
(including, without limitation, any department, agency, or bureau of
the federal or any state or local government) with whom the Company currently is doing business, is engaged in negotiations, to whom
the Company has submitted a bid, or from whom the Corporation is
otherwise seeking to obtain or renew a contract, *provided* that in the
event of any termination of the Executive's employment with the
Company, the phrase shall apply to any person or entity who was a
Customer or Prospective Customer of the Company during the two
years prior to the date of such termination. Promptly upon the
Executive's written request made within thirty (30) days of termination of his employment with the Company, the Company shall give
him a list of its Customers and Prospective Customers as defined
herein.

(c) The Executive will not, without the prior express written
consent of the Company's Board of Directors, use any Protected
Information for his own benefit or the benefit of any person or entity
other than the Company.

(d) Upon termination of employment with the Company for
any reason, including the expiration of the Term, the Executive shall
return all books, records, lists, computer programs, documents,
notes, and other materials of any kind and in any form whatsoever,
including all copies thereof, which contain any Protected Information
(hereinafter "Protected Materials"). All Protected Materials shall be
returned whether initially (i) furnished by the Company or any

Affiliate of the Company, or any Customer or Prospective Customer of the Company or any such Affiliate, (ii) prepared by the Executive or any officer, director, employee, or agent of the Company, any Affiliate of the Company, or any Customer or Prospective Customer of the Company or any such Affiliate, or (iii) otherwise obtained in the course of the Executive's employment with the Company.

5.2 *Proprietary Materials.* All discoveries made, inventions created, and all ideas, concepts, designs, formulas, proposals, projects, programs, products, processes, systems, techniques, and improvements of whatever kind conceived or developed by the Executive directly or indirectly, alone or jointly with others, in the course of employment with the Company, whether during normal business hours or otherwise (hereinafter "Proprietary Materials"), shall be and remain the sole and exclusive property of the Company. The Executive shall fully and promptly disclose to the Company all such Proprietary Materials, together with all information and data necessary to impart a full understanding of the same. Upon request and without further compensation from the Company, but at the Company's expense, the Executive will (i) execute, acknowledge, and deliver all such papers and instruments as the Company may deem necessary in order for it to perfect, secure, and maintain all rights, title, and interest in and to any Proprietary Materials, including, without limitation, any and all patent, copyright, trademark, and trade secrets rights and protections in the same, and (ii) aid and assist the Company in any litigation involving the maintenance or establishment of such rights and protections, including, if necessary, testifying on behalf of the Company.

5.3 *Enforcement.* The Executive agrees that, having regard to the importance of the Duties hereunder and his position in relation to the Company's business, the obligations undertaken by him in this Article 5 are reasonable and necessary for the protection of the legitimate interests of the Company and do not work harshly upon him. If the Executive commits a breach, or threatens to commit a breach, or any of the provisions of this Article 5, the Company shall have the following rights and remedies:

(a) the right and remedy to have the provisions of this Article 5 specifically enforced by any court having equity jurisdiction, it being acknowledged and agreed that any such breach or threatened breach will cause irreparable injury to the Company and that money damages will not provide an adequate remedy to the Company; and

(b) the right and remedy to require the Executive to account for and pay over to the Company all compensation, profits, monies, accruals, increments, or other benefits (hereinafter collectively referred to as the "Benefits") derived or received by the Executive as the result of any transactions constituting a breach of any of the provisions of this Article 5, the Executive hereby agreeing to account for and pay over the Benefits to the Company.

6. *Indemnification.* The Company shall indemnify the Executive to the full extent authorized by law in the event he is made or threatened to be made a party to any action, suit, or proceeding, whether criminal, civil, administrative or investigative, by reason of the fact that he is or was a director, officer, or employee of the Company or serves or served any other enterprise as a director, officer, or employee at the request of the Company.

7. *Other Provisions.*

7.1 *Notices.* Any notice or other communication required or permitted hereunder shall be in writing and shall be delivered personally, telegraphed, telexed, sent by facsimile transmission, or sent by certified, registered, or express mail, postage prepaid. Any such notice shall be deemed given when so delivered personally, telegraphed, telexed, or sent by facsimile transmission or, if mailed, three days after the date of deposit in the United States mails addressed as follows:

(i) if to the Company, to:

with a copy to:

(ii) if to the Executive, to:

Copy to:

7.2 *Entire Agreement.* This Agreement and any other agreements incorporated herein by reference set forth the entire agreement and understanding of the parties relating to the subject matter hereof, and supersede all prior agreements, arrangements, and understandings, written or oral, relating to the subject matter hereof.

7.3 *Waivers and Amendments.* This Agreement may be amended, superseded, cancelled, renewed, or extended, and the terms hereof may be waived, only by a written instrument signed by the parties or, in the case of a waiver, by the party waiving compliance. No delay on the part of any party in exercising any right, power, or privilege hereunder shall operate as a waiver thereof, nor shall any waiver on the part of such party of any such right, power, or privilege, nor any single or partial exercise of any such right, power, or privilege, preclude any other or further exercise thereof or the exercise of any other such right, power, or privilege.

7.4 *Governing Law.* This Agreement shall be governed by and construed in accordance with the laws of the State of _____ without regard to its conflict of laws rules.

7.5 *Assignment.* The provisions of this Agreement shall be binding upon and inure to the benefit of the parties hereto and their respective heirs, legal representatives, successors, and assigns. This Agreement, and the Executive's rights and obligations hereunder, may not be assigned by the Executive. The Company may assign this Agreement and its rights, together with its obligations, hereunder, in connection with any sale, transfer, or other disposition of all or substantially all of its respective assets or business, whether by merger, consolidation, or otherwise.

7.6 *Headings.* The headings in this Agreement are for reference only and shall not affect its interpretation.

7.7 *Severability.* In the event that one or more of the provisions contained in this Agreement, or any part thereof, shall be determined to be invalid, illegal, or unenforceable in any respect under any applicable statute or rule of law, only such provision(s) shall be considered invalid, illegal, or unenforceable (and then only to the extent of such invalidity, illegality, or unenforceability), and the rest of the provisions shall remain in full force and effect. The Executive agrees that if any provision contained herein shall be adjudged to be invalid, illegal, or unenforceable for any reason, but would be adjudged to be valid, legal, and enforceable if part of the wording thereof were deleted and/or the time period thereof and/or the geographic area thereof were reduced, the said provision shall apply with such modification(s) as may be necessary to make it valid, legal, and enforceable.

IN WITNESS WHEREOF, the parties have executed this Agreement the date first above written.

ATTEST:

By:_____   By:_____
WITNESS:

By:_____   By:_____

GUARANTY

_____ hereby guaranties the payment by the Company of the compensation of the Executive pursuant to Article 3 of the foregoing Employment Agreement.
ATTEST:

By:_____   By:_____
[Corporate Seal]

SAMPLE EMPLOYMENT AGREEMENT III:
PURSUANT TO ASSET PURCHASED

This EMPLOYMENT AGREEMENT (this "Agreement") is made as of the ___ of November 1993, by and between _____ corporation with principal offices located at _____ (the "Company"), and _____ ("Executive").

WHEREAS, the Company and _____ corporation have entered into an Asset Purchase Agreement as of _____ (the "Purchase Agreement"), pursuant to which the Company is acquiring and _____ is selling substantially all of _____ assets; and

WHEREAS, Executive is the majority shareholder of _____ and is presently serving as President of _____ and it is a condition precedent to the closing of the Purchase Agreement that Executive and the Company enter into an employment agreement satisfactory to each and that Executive enter into a covenant not to compete with the Company; and

WHEREAS, the Company and Executive desire to enter into such an employment agreement and such a covenant not to compete subject to the terms and conditions set forth herein;

NOW, THEREFORE, in consideration of the foregoing premises and of the mutual covenants and agreements hereinafter set forth, the receipt and sufficiency of which are hereby acknowledged, the Company and Executive hereby agree as follows:

Section 1. *Employment.* The Company agrees to employ Executive, subject to the terms and conditions of this Agreement, to render full-time services to the Company as Vice President and Director of the Company's _____ Division/Operation. Executive agrees to such employment and agrees to perform the duties provided in Section 3 with reasonable diligence to the best of his abillties and in the best interests of the Company. Executive may continue, in his free time, to engage in private business transactions and provide minimal services on behalf of _____, *provided, however,* that Executive shall not engage in any business or perform any services in any capacity whatsoever in violation of Section 7 hereof.

Section 2. *Term.* The term of Executive's employment by the Company under this Agreement shall be for a period of three years commencing on the date hereof, and shall thereafter automatically be renewed on a year-to-year basis unless terminated by either party by 90 days' prior written notice to the other party. Notwithstanding the foregoing, Executive's employment under this Agreement may be terminated as hereinafter provided.

Section 3. *Duties.* Executive shall hold the positions and titles, and exercise the responsibilities, of Vice President and Director of the Company's _____ Division/Operation. Executive shall have such powers and duties as may from time to time be prescribed by the Company or its Board of Directors or mutually agreed upon by the Company and Executive. During his employment hereunder, Executive shall devote his full time, skill and efforts to the performance of his duties and the business and affairs of the Company as is customary for a person in his positions and/or with his duties and responsibilities at a comparable company and shall use his reasonable best efforts to advance the best interests of the Company at all times. Executive may engage in other private business transactions so long as they are not in violation of Section 7 hereof and so long as they do not affect Executive's full-time performance of his duties hereunder.

Section 4. *Place of Performance.* Executive shall perform his duties hereunder at _____ the headquarters of the Company's _____ Division/Operation, or at such other location mutually agreed upon by the parties, *provided, however,* that the Company may reasonably require Executive to travel and render services in different locations from time to time incident to the performance of such duties.

Section 5. *Compensation.* The Company agrees to pay Executive the following compensation for all services rendered by Executive to the Company:

(a) *Salary:* The Company shall pay Executive an annual salary of ___ Dollars ($___). Such salary shall be subject to withholding by the Company on account of payroll taxes and similar matters as are required by applicable law, rule or regulation of any appropriate govemmental authority, and shall be payable in accordance wlth the payroll policies of the Company from time to time in effect (such payments are, as of the date of this Agreement, made in bi-weekly installments).

(b) *Incentive Plan:* Executive shall receive incentive compensation up to a maximum annual award of ___ payable within 60 days after the end of each calendar year during the term of Executive's employment by the Company. Such incentive compensation will be based upon performance in relation to stated performance goals mutually agreed upon by the Company and Executive in Executive's annually reviewed incentive plan.

(c) *Bonus:* The Company shall establish a bonus pool constituting ten percent (10%) of the before tax profit (as determined by contract accounting in accordance with GAAP) earned on (i) any contract resulting from a ___ proposal or bid for any of the following seven contracts: (A) ___, (B) ___, (C) ___, (D) ___, (E) ___, (F) ___, or (G) ___, which are each identified in Schedule A attached hereto and (ii) each of the following four contracts for which the Company and _____ have jointly bid in 1993 or for which the Company, through its _____ Division/Operation, may bid or re-bid in the remainder of 1993 or in 1994: (A) ___, (B) ___, (C) ___, and (D) ___, which are each identified in Schedule A attached hereto. Executive shall allocate such bonus pool in any manner he deems advisable to one or more employee(s), including Executive, of the Company's _____ Division/Operation, *provided, however,* that, in the event of Executive's death, the entire applicable bonus pool shall be paid to his estate. Bonus payments shall be made by the Company directly to the employee(s) specified by Executive, subject to such withholding described above as required by law, and shall be income only to the employee(s) actually receiving such payments. Such bonus payments shall continue until the end of the pertinent initial contract and any exercised options on such contract, shall not be calculated or made based on any follow-on contracts, and shall be contingent upon Executive's continued compliance with the material terms of this Agreement. The share of before tax profit to be paid into the bonus pool shall be determined by the Company's accountant on or before the 60th day following the last day of each fiscal year of the Company during the term of this Agreement, and a written statement by the Company's chief financial officer, certifying such amount, shall be delivered to Executive on or before each such date. Payment of the amount due to the bonus pool shall be made by the Company on or before the 75th day following the last day of each such fiscal year of the Company, subject to such withholding described above as may be required by law.

(d) *Expenses:* The Company shall pay the reasonable expenses incurred by Executive (within limits that may be established by the Board of Directors of the Company, which limits shall not be unreasonable) in the performance of his duties hereunder (or shall reimburse Executive on account of such expenses paid directly by Executive) promptly upon the submission to the Company by Executive of appropriate vouchers prepared in accordance with Company rules and applicable regulation of the Internal Revenue Service.

(e) *Vacation:* Executive shall be entitled to a certain number of paid vacation days in each calendar year in accordance with the vacation policies and practices of the Company as determined by the Board of Directors of the Company, but not less than 15 business days in any calendar year, prorated appropriately on account of any calendar year during which Executive renders services hereunder for less than the entire such year. In addition, Executive shall be entitled to take, at any time reasonably acceptable to the Company during the term of his employment by the Company, up to thirty working days of paid vacation accrued while working for _____. Executive shall also be entitled to all paid holidays given by the Company to its senior executive employees. If, at the time of the termination (for any reason) of his employment with the Company, Executive has accrued but unused vacation time Executive shall be compensated for such time based upon his salary.

(f) *Other Benefits:* Executive shall be permitted, during the term of his employment with the Company, to participate in any group life, medical or disabillty insurance plan or program, profit-sharing or pension or similar benefit plan, or other fringe benefit plan of the Company as the Company may from time to time establish and in which Executive would be entitled to participate pursuant to the terms the thererof, *provided, however,* that the Company's medical plan shall cover any pre-existing condition of Executive or his dependents that was covered under Executive's medical plan in effect immediately prior to the date of this Agreement and providing that any known existing condition has been disclosed in a confidential letter to the Company's health plan administrator, _____ prior to the date of this Agreement. The foregoing, however, shall not be construed to require the Company to establish any such plans or to prevent the Company from modifying or terminating such plans once established, and no such action or lack thereof shall affect this Agreement.

Section 6. *Confidential Information and Proprietary Materials.*

(a) *Confidentiality:* (i) Executive shall not at any time during his employment with the Company or at any time after the termination of the same for any reason (including expiration of the term of Executive's employment hereunder) disclose, impart, divulge, or otherwise reveal in any manner whatsoever, directly or indirectly, in writing or orally, whether by counsel, discussion, recommendation, suggestion, or otherwise, any "Protected Information" except in the course of the proper discharge of his duties hereunder or as expressly authorized by the Company's Board of Directors.

(ii) As used in this Agreement, "Protected Information" means any confidential or proprietary information (in whatever form recorded) about the Company, any subsidiary of the Company, or any Customer or Prospective Customer of the Company or any subsidiary of the Company, that Executive has obtained, had aceess to, or gained knowledge of in the course of his employment with the Company or any subsidiary of the Company. Protected Information shall include, without limitation, except as provided in Subsection (vi) below:

(A) Information concerning or relating to properties, organization, personnel, operations, procedures, plans, projects, programs, products, processes, systems, profitability, finances, and business relationships and opportunities, except to the extent that such information is lawfully available to the public;

(B) Any trade secret or other similar information including, without limitation, the identity of customers or clients, customer or client lists, mailing lists, software programs, engineering or technical data, databases, coding information, market analysis and strategies, processes, systems, plans, projects, programs, and pricing and cost information, except to the extent that such information is lawfully available to the public; and

(C)   Information relating to any litigation including, without limitation, any attorney work-product and any data, documents, or other information that may be subject to the attorney-client privilege.

(iii)   As used in this Agreement, the phrase "any Customer or Prospective Customer of the Company or any subsidiary of the Company" means any person or entity (including, without limitation, any department, agency, or bureau of the federal or any state or local or foreign government) with whom the Company or any subsidiary of the Company currently is doing business or is engaged in negotiations, to whom the Company, or any subsidiary of the Company has submitted a bid or made a presentation, or from whom the Company or any subsidiary of the Company has sought to or is otherwise seeking to obtain or renew a contract, *provided, however,* that in the event of any termination of Executive's employment with the Company, the phrase shall also apply to any person or entity who was a Customer or Prospective Customer of the Company or any subsidiary of the Company during the one year prior to the date of such termination.

(iv)   Executive will not, without the prior express written consent of the Company's Board of Directors, use any Protected Information for his own benefit or the benefit of any person or entity other than the Company or any subsidiary of the Company.

(v)   Upon termination of Executive's employment with the Company for any reason, Executive shall return all books, records, lists, computer programs, documents, notes, and other materials of any kind and in any form whatsoever, including all copies thereof, which contain any Protected Information (hereinafter "Protected Materials"). All Protected Materials shall be returned whether initially (A) furnished by the Company or any subsidiary of the Company, or any Customer or Prospective Customer of the Company or any subsidiary of the Company; (B) prepared by Executive or any officer, director, employee, or agent of the Company, any subsidiary of the Company, or any Customer or Prospective Customer of the Company or any subsidiary of the Company; or (C) otherwise obtained in the course of Executive's employment with the Company.

(vi)   The term "Protected Information" shall not include information (A) available to the public, (B) disclosed with the prior approval of the Company or its customers, (C) made available to a third party by the Company without restriction, or (D) ordered to be disclosed by a court or administrative agency of competent jurisdiction.

(b) *Proprietary Materials:* Unless offered to the Company by Executive and refused by the Company, all discoveries made, inventions created, and all ideas, concepts, designs, formulas, proposals, projects, programs, products, processes, systems, techniques, and improvements of whatever kind conceived or developed by Executive directly or indirectly, alone or jointly with others, during the term of his employment with the Company, whether during normal business hours or otherwise (hereinafter "Proprietary Materials"), shall be and remain the sole and exclusive property of the Company. Executive shall fully and promptly disclose to the Company all such Proprietary Materials, together with all information and data necessary to impart a full understanding of the same. Upon request and without further compensation from the Company, but at the Company's expense, Executive will (i) execute, acknowledge, and deliver all such papers and instruments as the Company may reasonably deem necessary in order for it to perfect, secure, and maintain all rights, title, and interest in and to any Proprietary Materials, including, without limitation, any and all patent, copyright, trademark, and trade secrets rights and protections in the same; and (ii) aid and assist the Company in any litigation involving the maintenance or establishment of such rights and protections, including, if necessary, testifying on behalf of the Company during his term of employment by the Company.

Section 7. *Non-Competition.* (a)   In conjunction with and as an integral component of the sale to the Company under the Purchase Agreement of the Assets (as defined in the Purchase Agreement) and _____ business relating to such Assets, Executive agrees that during the period of Executive's employment by the Company (including any extensions of the original three year term) or for a period of three (3) years beginning on the date hereof, whichever is longer, Executive will not, directly or indirectly:

(i)   within any state, district, city, town, or marketing area in the United States or any foreign country in which the Company or any subsidiary of the Company is doing business or is qualified to do business, own, manage, operate, control, consult for, perform services for, be employed by or participate in the ownership, management, operation or control of, or be connected in any manner with or have any interest in, any person, firm, company or other entity engaged in any business of the type and character engaged in and competitive with that conducted by the Company or any subsidiary of the Company, *provided, however,* that Executive may become a member of professional organizations and societies and serve on the Board of Directors of one or more companies. If he first obtains the consent of the Company to such membership or services, and *provided, further,* that Executive may maintain ownership of any number of shares of the capital stock of _____ and provide minimal services on behalf of _____ so long as (A) ___ sole business activity consists of performing the existing work under and follow-on to ___ existing Contract and ___ does not actively pursue any other business, and (B) Executive has no active role in the day-to-day management of business of _____. The Executive may continue to direct the use and investment of the assets of _____. Executive shall exercise his best efforts to ensure that _____ and Executive act in conformity with this subsection 7(a)(i). For these purposes, ownership of securities of not in excess of 1% of any class of securities of a company whose stock is publicly traded shall not be considered to be competition with the Company or any subsidiary of the Company; or

     (ii)   persuade or attempt to persuade any Customer or Prospective Customer of the Company or any subsidiary of the Company not to hire the Company or any Subsidiary of the Company, or to hire another company, or

     (iii)   without the advance consent of the Company, persuade or attempt to persuade any employee of the Company or any subsidiary of the Company to leave the Company's or any such subsidiary's employ, or to become employed by any person, firm or company other than the Company or any subsidiary of the Company.

     (b)   In exchange for Executive's non-competition covenants contained in this Section 7, the Company shall pay Executive ___ Dollars ($\_\_\_ per year in calendar years 1994, 1995, and 1996, payable as follows: (A) the 1994 payment shall be made in full on December 29, 1993; and (B) the 1995 and 1996 payments shall be made in eight quarterly installments of \_\_\_ Dollars ($___ each on the last day of March, June, September, and December of 1995 and 1996, *provided, however,* that any such payments may be offset against any amounts payable to the Company by _____ and Executive under Section 6.2, Indemnification, of the Purchase Agreement as a result of any failure on the part of _____ or Executive to pay any applicable taxes payable prior to the closing of the Purchase Agreement.

(c) Executive acknowledges and recognizes that this covenant not to compete is ancillary to the sale to the Company by _____ of the Assets and _____ business related to the Assets, and that such covenant contain reasonable limitations as to time, geographical area and scope of activity to be restrained necessary to protect the Company's business interests.

Section 8. *Termination.*

(a) *Termination After Original Three-Year Term:* Beginning three years after the date of this Agreement, either Executive or the Company may terminate Executive's employment by the Company under this Agreement upon 90 days' prior written notice to the other.

(b) *Termination Upon Death:* Executive's employment under this Agreement shall terminate upon Executive's death.

(c) *Termination Upon Disability:*

(i) If, during the term of his employment hereunder, Executive becomes physically or mentally disabled, so that he is unable to substantially perform his duties hereunder even with reasonable accommodation, the Company may terminate his employment after a period of disability determined on the same basis as that generally applied by the Company with respect to the termination of the employment of executives of the Company on grounds of physical or mental disability.

(ii) In case of any disagreement between Executive and the Company as to whether Executive is disabled so as to permit the Company to terminate Executive's employment hereunder in accordance with this subsection 8(c), the question of such disability shall be submitted for determination to an impartial and reputable physician selected by the mutual agreement of Executive (or his legal representative) and the Company. Failing such agreement, the Company shall request a physician referral from the _____, and Executive and the Company hereby agree in advance to accept the first name provided in that referral. The determination of the question of disability by such physician selected consistent with this subsection (ii) shall be final and binding on Executive and the Company. The Company shall pay the fees and expenses of such physician.

(d) *Termination for Cause:* The Company may terminate Executive's employment for cause. Termination for "cause" shall include discharge from employment for (i) failing or refusing to perform his duties in material breach of this Agreement, including, but not limited to, violating any of the provisions of Section 6 or 7 hereof, (ii) committing a deceitful or fraudulent act in connection with his employment, (iii) conviction of any crime or offense (other than a minor misdemeanor or motor vehicle violation) in connection with his employment, (iv) conviction of any felony, (v) knowingly and intentionally withholding from any officer or agent of the Company information material to the Company's interests, (vi) knowingly and intentionally making any material misrepresentation to any officer or agent of the Company, or (vii) knowingly and intentionally failing to carry out the instructions of the Company's Board of Directors or senior executive officers, or (viii) knowingly and intentionally failing to abide by or to enforce any policy or procedure of the Company, which failure would normally be considered grounds for dismissal of any employee of the Company. Any disputes regarding the Company's termination of Executive under this subsection 8(d) shall be submitted to binding arbitration pursuant to Section 12 hereof. No amounts otherwise payable by the Company to the Executive under this Agreement shall be withheld by the Company during the first thirty (30) days after termination of Executive's employment for cause under this subsection 8(d); upon the expiration of such thirty-day period, the Company may withhold payments in accordance with subsection 8(e)(iii) hereof unless Executive has initiated an arbitration proceeding in which case the Company shall not withhold any amounts otherwise payable to Executive under this Agreement until completion of the arbitration, and the arbitration panel's issuance of a ruling in favor of the Company, *provided, however,* that any payments made subsequent to the termination may be recoverable by the Company if the arbitration panel finds in the Company's favor.

(e) *Payments Upon Termination:*

(i)   If Executive elects to terminate Executive's employment pursuant to subsection 8(a) hereof, (A) the Company shall pay Executive his salary and all other compensation set forth in Section 5 hereof accrued up to the date such termination occurs and (B) the Company shall pay the payments for his non-competition covenants set forth in subsection 7(b) hereof and (C) Executive shall have no right to receive any compensation from the Company for any period subsequent to the date of such termination. If the Company elects to terminate Executive's employment pursuant to subsection 8(a) hereof, (A) the Company shall pay Executive his salary and all other compensation set forth in Section 5 hereof accrued up to the date such termination occurs, (B) the Company shall continue to pay Executive and/or his designee(s) the bonus compensation to which they are entitled under subsection 5(c) hereof, (C) the Company shall pay the payments for his non-competition covenants set forth in subsection 7(b) hereof, and (D) Executive shall have no right to receive any other compensation from the Company for any period subsequent to the date of such termination.

(ii)   In the event of termination of Executive's employment under subsection 8(b) or 8(c) hereof, (A) the Company shall pay Executive or, if applicable, his estate, his salary and all other compensation set forth in Section 5 hereof accrued up to the date such termination occurs and (B) the Company shall continue to pay Executive or, if appiicable, his estate the payments for his non-competition covenants set forth in subsection 7(b) hereof on the schedule set forth in such sections so long as no provision of Section 6 or 7 of this Agreement is violated. In the event of the Executive's death, the Company shall continue to pay to his estate the bonus in subsection 5(c) contingent upon the ability to obtain a Term Life Insurance Policy on the Executive, payable to the Company for a mutually agreed upon face value amount. If the total bonus pursuant to subsection 5(c) is less than 50% of the face amount of this policy, the difference will be paid to the Executive's estate from the proceeds of the policy. The Company and the Executive will equally share the cost of this insurance. If the Executive becomes disabled as defined in subsection 8(c) of this agreement, the Company will continue to pay the Bonus Payments listed in subsection 5(c) of this agreement.

(iii)   If the Company terminates Executive's employment under subsection 8(d) hereof, (A) the Company shall pay Executive his salary and all other compensation set forth in Section 5 hereof accrued up to the date such termination occurs; (B) the Company shall continue to pay Executive the amounts due him for his non-competition covenants on the schedule set forth in subsection 7(b) hereof so long as Executive continues to abide by all the material terms of Sections 6 and 7 of this Agreement, *provided, however,* that Executive shall receive no such payments for his non-competition covenants if the Company terminates his employment under subsection 8(d)(ii) or 8(d)(iii) hereof; and (C) Executive shall have no right to receive any compensation, including, but not limited to, any bonus under subsection 5(c) hereof (other than non-competition payments under subsection 8(d)(iii)(B) hereof) from the Company for any period subsequent to the date of such termination.

(f) *Non-exclusive Rights:* The Company's right of termination shall be in addition to and shall not affect its rights and remedies under Sections 6, 7, and 12 of this Agreement, and such rights and remedies under such Sections shall survive termination of this Agreement and Executive's employment.

Section 9. *Notice.* Any notice or other communication required or permitted hereunder shall be in writing and shall be sufficiently given if delivered in person or sent by telex, telecopy, registered or certified mail with postage prepaid, Federal Express or Express Mail, addressed as follows:

(a) If to Executive, to:

(b) If to the Company, to:

Such addresses and numbers may be changed by written notice. Such notice or communication shall be deemed to have been given as of the date so delivered in person or sent by telex or telecopier wlth receipt confirmed, or as of two days after the date mailed, registered or certified, postage prepaid or sent by Federal Express or Express Mail.

Section 10. *Entire Agreement.* This Agreement and the Purchase Agreement set forth the entire agreement and understanding of the parties relating to the subject matter hereof, and supersede all prior agreements, arrangements, and understandings, written or oral, relating to the subject matter hereof.

Section 11. *Waivers and Amendments.* This Agreement may be amended, superseded, canceled, renewed, or extended, and the terms hereof may be waived, only by a written instrument signed by Executive and, on behalf of the Company, by an officer other than Executive specifically designated by the Board of Directors of the Company or, in the case of a waiver, by such party waiving compliance. No delay on the part of any party in exercising any right, power, or privilege hereunder shall operate as a waiver thereof, nor shall any waiver on the part of such party of any such right, power, or privilege, preclude any other or further exercise thereof or the exercise of any other such right, power, or privilege.

Section 12. *Enforcement, Arbitration, and Governing Law.*

(a)   It is the desire and intent of the Company and Executive that the provisions of this Agreement shall be enforced to the fullest extent permissible under the laws and public policies applied in each jurisdiction in which enforcement is sought. If any particular provision or portion of this Agreement shall be adjudicated to be invalid or unenforceable, this Agreement shall be deemed amended to delete therefrom such provision or portion adjudicated to be invalid or unenforceable. Executive agrees that, having regard to the importance of his duties hereunder and his position in relation to the Company's business, the obligations undertaken by him in this Agreement including, but not limited to, the obligations in Sections 6 and 7 hereof, are reasonable and necessary for the protection of the legitimate interests of the Company and do not work harshly upon him.

(b)   All disputes relating or in any way connected to this Agreement shall be submitted to binding arbitration in lieu of all other remedies available at law or in equity. Any matter submtttted to arbitration shall be arbitrated in _____ or in such other location as shall be mutually agreed upon by the Company and Executive, in accordance with the commercial Arbitration Rules of the American Arbitration Association ("AAA") then in effect. The arbitration shall be conducted by a tripartite tribunal with the Company and Executive each selecting one arbitrator with technical expertise in the area of dispute and such two arbitrators selecting a third, mutually agreeable, neutral arbitrator who shall act as chair of the tribunal. If either the Company or Executive fails to select an arbitrator, the AAA shall appoint an arbitrator on such party's behalf. The arbitration panel may order specific performance of any provision of this Agreement and a court may order injunctive relief to make such agreements effective. Notwithstanding the foregoing, the parties agree that, upon application thereto, a court of competent jurisdiction may issue preliminary injunctive relief to preserve the status quo or otherwise enforce or provide for the effectiveness of the terms and conditions of this Agreement pending the outcome of the arbitration hereunder. The decision rendered by the arbitrators shall be final and binding upon all parties to this Agreement, and judgment upon that award may be entered in any court having jurisdiction thereof and may be enforced by either party to the arbitration. The tribunal shall determine which party to the arbitration shall bear the cost of the arbitration or the proportion of such cost that each party shall bear, and the prevailing party shall have his or its attorneys' fees paid by the non-prevailing party.

(c) The interpretation and construction of this Agreement and all matters relating thereto shall be governed by the laws of the State (excluding its conflict of laws rules) applicable to agreements executed and to be performed solely within such State.

(d) Subject to the arbitration requirements of subsection 12(b), any appropriate judicial proceeding brought against any of the parties to this Agreement may be brought in the courts of the State _ or in the United States District Court for the _____ and, by execution and delivery of this Agreement, each of the parties hereto expressly consents to the jurisdiction of such courts, waives any defense of inconvenient forum, and irrevocably agrees to be bound by any judgment rendered thereby in connection with this Agreement. The parties consent to service of process by registered mail, return receipt requested. The foregoing consents to jurisdiction shall not constitute general consents to service of process in the State of Texas for any purpose except as provided above and shall not be deemed to confer rights on any person other than the respective parties to this Agreement. The prevailing party in any such judicial proceeding shall have his or its attomeys' fees paid by the non-prevailing party.

Section 13. *Parties and Assignment.* The provisions of this Agreement shall be binding upon and inure to the benefit of the parties hereto and their respective heirs, legal representatives, successors, and assigns. This Agreement, and Executive's rights and obligations hereunder, may not be assigned by Executive. The Company may assign this Agreement and its rights, together with its obligations, hereunder, in connection with any sale, transfer, or other disposition of all or substantially all of the assets or business of the Company whether by merger, consolidation, or otherwise.

Section 14. *Headings.* The headings in this Agreement are for reference only and shall not affect its integration.

Section 15. *Severability.* In the event that one or more of the provisions contained in this Agreement, or any part thereof, shall be determined to be invalid, illegal, or unenforceable in any respect under any applicable statute or rule of law, only such provision(s) shall be considered invalid, illegal, or unenforceable (and then only to the extent of such invalidity, illegality, or unenforceability), and the rest of the provisions shall remain in full force and effect. Executive agrees that if any provision contained herein shall be adjudged to be invalid, illegal, or unenforceable for any reason, but would be adjudged to be valid, legal, and enforceable if part of the wording thereof were deleted and/or the time period there and/or the geographic area thereof were reduced, the said provision shall apply with such modification(s) as may be necessary to make it valid, legal, and enforceable.

Section 16. *Counterparts.* This Agreement may be signed in separate counterparts, each of which shall be deemed an original and both of which together shall constitute one and the same instrument.

Section 17. *Effective Date.* This Agreement shall be effective as of the Closing (as defined in the Purchase Agreement) of the Purchase Agreement, and shall be null, void, and of no effect if such Closing does not take place.

IN WITNESS WHEREOF, this Agreement has been duly executed and delivered by Executive and by the duly authorized officer of the Company as of the date first above written.

[Corporate Seal]

Attest:

By:_____   By:_____
          Secretary   Executive Vice President
                                              Chief Financial Officer

SCHEDULE A

CONTRACTS

_____

_____

_____

_____

_____

_____

_____

_____

_____

_____

_____

SAMPLE EMPLOYMENT AGREEMENT IV:
WITH A COMPANY PRESIDENT

EMPLOYMENT AGREEMENT, dated March 19_, by and between _____ a ___ corporation (the "Company") and _____ (the "Executive").

In consideration of the mutual covenants and agreements hereinafter set forth, the parties hereto agree as follows:

1.   *Employment, Duties and Acceptance.*

1.1   *Employment by the Company.* The Company hereby employs the Executive for the term provided in Article 2 (the "Term") to render exclusive and full-time services to the Company as President and, in connection therewith, to perform the duties provided in Section 1.4 (the "Duties").

1.2   *Acceptance of Employment by the Executive.* The Executive hereby accepts such employment and agrees to perform the Duties diligently to the best of his abilities and in the best interests of the Company. The Executive shall devote his entire working time and his best efforts to the business of the Company during the Term.

1.3   *Place of Employment.* The Executive's principal place of employment shall be at _____ or such other location in the Washington metropolitan area as the Company may designate upon reasonable notice to the Executive. The Company may direct the Executive to engage in such reasonable travel performance as the Duties may require.

1.4   *Duties.* The Executive shall hold the position and title, and exercise the responsibilities, of President. The Executive shall have the right and obligation, in his capacity as President, to perform the duties of that office to the extent they are described in the By-Laws of the Company, as well as such other duties as from time to time may be assigned to him by the Company.

2.   *Term of Employment.* The Executive's employment under this Agreement shall commence on January 1, 19_, and shall continue

until terminated by either party. The period of such employment shall be treated for all purposes hereunder as the Term. The Executive's employment may be terminated by the Company as provided elsewhere in this Agreement or by the Executive upon at least 90 days' prior written notice. Termination of the Executive's employment hereunder shall end the Term.

3. *Compensation.*

3.1 *Salary.* As compensation for all services to be rendered pursuant to this Agreement, the Company shall pay the Executive during the Term a salary of at least $___ per annum. All of the Executive's compensation shall be payable in accordance with the payroll policies of the Company as from time to time in effect, less such appropriate deductions as shall be required to be withheld by applicable law and regulations, or by written election of the Executive if agreed to by the Company.

3.2 *Participation in Employee Benefit Plans.* The Executive shall be permitted during the Term, to the extent eligible, to participate in any group life, medical, or disability insurance plan, health program, dental program, profit-sharing or pension or similar benefit plan, thrift plan, or other fringe benefit plan of the Company, which participation shall be on a basis that is at least equivalent to that which is then made available to other executives of the Company.

3.3 *Car.* The company shall make available to the Executive for his full-time use a car leased by the Company that is at least as expensive as the cars then normally provided to Presidents of other operating companies owned by _____. The Company shall be responsible for the maintenance of such car, shall maintain full casualty and personal liability insurance with respect to such car, and shall provide the Executive, free of charge, with a parking space within reasonable walking distance of the Company's principal offices at _____.

3.4 *Incentive Plan.* The Executive shall be eligible to participate in the Company's Management Incentive Plan in accordance with its terms and conditions.

3.5 *Expenses.* Subject to such policies as may from time to time be established by the Company, the Company shall pay or reimburse the Executive for all reasonable expenses actually incurred or paid by the Executive during the Term in the performance of his Duties upon presentation of expense statements or vouchers or such other supporting information as the Company may require.

3.6   *Salary Adjustment.* Effective January 1, 19_, and thereafter during the Term effective on every succeeding January 1, the annual salary of the Executive then in effect shall be reviewed by the Board of Directors of the Company in accordance with generally applied normal corporate policy and practice.

3.7   *Paid Vacation.* The Executive shall be entitled to a vacation of twenty (20) working days during 19_ and, during each subsequent year of the Term of this Agreement, the time allowed under the Company's policies and practices then in effect, in each case in addition to other holidays designated by the Company. During each such vacation period the Executive shall continue to receive the salary and other compensation provided in this Article 3. Such paid vacation must be taken at a time and in a manner consistent with his Duties.

4.   *Termination of Employment.*

4.1   *Termination upon Death.* The Executive's employment under this Agreement shall terminate upon the Executive's death. The Company shall continue to make payment of salary or other compensation to the Executive's legal representatives in accordance with the Company's general policies and practices then in effect.

4.2   *Termination upon Disability.*

(a)   If, during the Term of his employment, the Executive becomes physically or mentally disabled, so that he is unable substantially to perform his duties hereunder, the Company may terminate his employment after a period of disability determined on the same basis as that generally applied by the Company with respect to the termination of the employment of executives of the Company on the grounds of physical or mental disability.

(b)   In case of any disagreement between the Executive and the Company as to whether the Executive is disabled so as to permit the Company to terminate the Executive's employment hereunder in accordance with this Section 4.2, the question of such disability shall be submitted for determination to an impartial and reputable physician selected by the mutual agreement of the Executive (or his legal representative) and the Company. Failing such agreement, the Company shall request a physician referral from the Medical Society of the City _____ and the Executive and the Company hereby agree in advance to accept the first name provided in that referral. The determination of the question of disability by such physician selected consistent with this subsection (b) shall be final and binding on the Executive and the Company. The Company shall pay the fees and expenses of such physician.

(c) If, with respect to the first ninety (90) days of the period during which the Executive suffers a disability of the kind described in subsection (a) above, the total amount of payments received by the Executive pursuant to sick leave and similar practices and policies generally followed by the Company is less than 100% of the amount of the salary that the Executive would have received with respect to the same period, the Company shall pay him the difference.

4.3   *Termination for Cause.* The Company may terminate the Executive's employment for cause. "Termination for cause" shall mean discharge from employment for committing an unlawful, deceitful or fraudulent act, for knowingly withholding from the Company's Board of Directors information material to the Company's interest, for knowingly making any misrepresentation to the Company's Board of Directors regarding a matter material to the Company's interests, for knowingly failing to carry out the instructions of the Company's Board of Directors, or for knowingly failing to abide by or to enforce any material policy or procedure of the Company. Upon termination of his employment for cause, as provided herein, the Company shall pay the Executive his salary (as then in effect) accrued up to the last date of the month in which such termination occurs.

4.4   *Termination by the Board of Directors.* The Company may terminate the Executive's employment other than for cause or disability upon resolution by the Board of Directors in its sole discretion. The Company shall give at least ninety (90) days' prior written notice of such termination. Upon termination of his employment, as provided in this Section 4.4, other than for cause or disability:

(a)   The Company shall pay the Executive as severance an amount equal to his annualized salary at the time his employment with the Company ends. The Company shall pay this severance amount within thirty (30) days after the date the Executive's employment ends.

(b)   The Company shall provide to the Executive, at the Company's expense, for the period of one year from the date the Executive's employment with the Company ends, such health (including dental), life and long-term disability insurance coverage then generally provided to employees of the Company. The insurance coverage that the Executive would otherwise receive pursuant to this subparagraph shall be reduced by an amount equal to any insurance coverage received by the Executive in connection with other employment performed by the Executive during the one year period following the end of his employment with the Company.

(c)   The Company shall obtain professional outplacement services for the Executive, at the Company's expense, to be performed by a nationally recognized outplacement firm.

(d)   The Company shall provide to the Executive clear title to his supplemental retirement insurance contract releasing him from the requirement to repay any portion of the gain or company paid premium. Additionally, the Company will make one annual premium payment for the year following the Executive's termination and cover all tax consequences resulting from these actions.

(e)   The Company shall continue to provide the Executive, at the Company's expense, for the period of one year from the date the Executive's employment with the Company's ends, with the use of his leased car and be responsible for the maintenance of such car, and shall provide the Executive, free of charge, with a parking space within reasonable walking distance of the Company's principal offices.

5.   *Confidential Information Restrictive Covenant.*

5.1   *Confidential Information.* In view of the fact that the Executive's work as an employee of the Company hereunder will bring him into close contact with many confidential affairs of the Company, including information about costs, profits, sales, trade secrets, and other information not readily available to the public (hereinafter collectively referred to as "confidential matters"), the Executive agrees to keep secret all confidential matters of the Company and not to disclose them to anyone outside of the Company or otherwise use his knowledge of them for his own benefit, either during or after his employment with the Company.

5.2 *Restrictive Covenant.* During the Term and for one (1) year after the termination of the Executive's employment with the Company for any reason, the Executive shall not, unless acting with the Company's prior written consent or as an officer, employee or agent of the Company, or of any corporation controlled by, controlling, or under common control with the Company, (i) induce or attempt to induce any client or prospective client of the Company to cease doing business with, or not to do business with the Company; or (ii) induce or attempt to induce any officer or employee of the Company to terminate his or her employment with the Company.

5.3 *Proprietary Materials.* All discoveries made, inventions created, and all ideas, concepts, designs, formulas, proposals, projects, progress, products, processes, systems, techniques, and improvements of whatever kind conceived or developed by the Executive directly or indirectly, alone or jointly with others, in the course of employment with the Company, whether during normal business hours or otherwise (hereinafter "Proprietary Materials"), shall be and remain the sole and exclusive property of the Company. The Executive shall fully and promptly disclose to the Company all such Proprietary Materials, together with all information and data necessary to impart a full understanding of the same. Upon request and without further compensation from the Company, but at the Company's expense, the Executive will (i) execute, acknowledge, and deliver all such papers and instruments as the Company may deem neeessary in order for it to perfect, secure, and maintain all rights, title, and interest in and to any Proprietary Materials, including, without limitation, any and all patent, copyright, trademark, and trade secrets rights and protections in the same, and (ii) aid and assist the Company in any litigation involving the maintenance or establishment of such rights and protections, including, if necessary, testifying on behalf of the Company.

5.4 *Remedies.* If the Executive commits a breach, or threatens to commit a breach, of any of the provisions of this Article 5, the Company shall have the following rights and remedies:

(a) The right and remedy to have the provisions of this Article 5 specifically enforced by any court having equity jurisdiction, it being acknowledged and agreed that any such breach or threatened breach will cause irreparable injury to the Company and that money damages will not provide an adequate remedy to the Company; and

(b) The right and remedy to require the Executive to account for and pay over to the Company all compensation, profits, monies, accruals, increments, or other benefits (hereinafter collectively referred to as the "Benefits") derived or received by the Executive as the result of any transactions constituting a breach of any of the provisions of this Article 5, the Executive hereby agreeing to account for and pay over the Benefits to the Company.

5.5 *Judicial Modification.* If any covenant contained in this Article 5, or any part thereof, is held to be unenforceable because of the duration of such covenant or the area covered thereby, the parties agree that the court making such determination shall have the power to reduce the duration and/or area of such covenant and, in its reduced form, said covenant shall then be enforceable.

6. *Indemnification.* The Company shall indemnify the Executive to the full extent authorized by law in the event he is made or threatened to be made a party to any action, suit, or proceeding, whether criminal, civil, administrative or investigative, by reason of the fact that he is or was a director, officer, or employee of the Company or serves or served any other enterprise as a director, officer, or employee at the request of the Company.

7. *Other Provisions.*

7.1 *Notices.* Any notice or other communication required or permitted hereunder shall be in writing and shall be delivered personally, telegraphed, telexed, sent by facsimile transmission, or sent by certified, registered, or express mail, postage prepaid. Any such notice shall be deemed given when so delivered personally, telegraphed, telexed, or sent by facsimile transmission or, if mailed, three days after the date of deposit in the United States mails addressed as follows:

(a) if to the Company, to:

with a copy to:

(b) if to the Executive, to:

7.2 *Entire Agreement.* This Agreement and any other agreements incorporated herein by reference set forth the entire agreement and understanding of the parties relating to the subject matter hereof, and supersede all prior agreements, arrangements, and understandings, written or oral, relating to the subject matter hereof.

7.3 *Waivers and Amendments.* This Agreement may be amended, superseded, cancelled, renewed, or extended, and the terms hereof may be waived, only by a written instrument signed by the parties or, in the party waiving compliance. No delay on the part of any party in exercising any right, power, or privilege hereunder shall operate as a waiver thereof, nor shall any waiver on the part of such party of any such right, power, or privilege, nor any single or partial exercise of any such right, power, or privilege, preclude any other or further exercise thereof or the exercise of any other such right, power, or privilege.

7.4 *Governing Law.* This Agreement shall be governed by and construed in accordance with the laws of the State of _____ without regard to its conflict of laws rules.

7.5 *Assignment.* The provisions of this Agreement shall be binding upon and inure to the benefit of the parties hereto and their respective heirs, legal representatives, successors, and assigns. This Agreement, and the Executive's rights and obligations hereunder, may not be assigned by the Executive. The Company may assign this Agreement and its rights, together with its obligations, hereunder, in connection with any sale, transfer, or other disposition of all or substantially all of its respective assets or business, whether by merger, consolidation, or otherwise.

7.6   *Headings.* The headings in this Agreement are for reference only and shall not affect its interpretation.

7.7   *Severability.* In the event that one or more of the provisions contained in this Agreement, or any part thereof, shall be determined to be invalid, illegal, or unenforceable in any respect under any applicable statute or law, only such provision(s) shall be considered invalid, illegal, or unenforceable (and then only to the extent of such invalidity, illegality, or unenforceability), and the rest of the provisions shall remain in full force and effect. The Executive agrees that if any provision contained herein shall be adjudged to be invalid, illegal, or unenforceable for any reason, but would be adjudged to be valid, legal, and enforceable if part of the wording thereof were deleted and/or the time period thereof and/or the geographic area thereof were reduced, the said provision shall apply with such modification(s) as say be necessary to make it valid, legal, and enforceable.

IN WITNESS WHEREOF, the parties have executed this Agreement the date first above written.

ATTEST:

By:_____   By:_____
                                              Director

Witness:

_____   _____

Appendix E

Sample Shareholder-Approved Annual Incentive Compensation Plan

This appendix shows the shareholder-approved annual incentive plan for the company Fortune Brands, Inc. Because this plan provides for payment in cash, it would not require shareholder approval; however, most companies like Fortune Brands, Inc. would still obtain shareholder approval as a means of authorizing plan administration by the board compensation committee.

The stock exchanges require executive compensation plans that pay in stock to be approved by shareholders. In addition, other regulations also require shareholder approval of compensation plans. For example, the Internal Revenue Code Section 162(m) requires that companies with "performance-based" compensation have plans that award this compensation approved by shareholders if they wish to qualify for an exception to the $1 million cap on company tax deductions for any performance-based compensation.

Fortune Brands, Inc. Annual Executive Incentive Compensation Plan

ARTICLE I

GENERAL

SECTION 1.1 Purpose. The purpose of this Annual Executive Incentive Compensation Plan (the "Plan") is to advance the interests of the stockholders of Fortune Brands, Inc. (the "Company") by providing performance-based incentives to senior executives of the company.

SECTION 1.2 Definitions. As used in the Plan, the following terms shall have the following meanings:

(a) "Award" means, for each Participant, a specific dollar amount payable as determined by the Committee pursuant to Section 2.2 of the Plan after application of the Committee's discretion pursuant to Section 2.4(b) of the Plan;

(b) "Board of Directors" means the Board of Directors of the Company;

(c) "Code" means the Internal Revenue Code of 1986, as amended;

(d) "Committee" means the Compensation and Stock Option Committee of the Board of Directors;

(e) "Incentive Pool" means, with respect to each Performance Period, the total amount of dollars available to be paid to all Participants. This amount shall be based on an objective formula established by the Committee in accordance with Section 2.2 of the Plan using one or more of the Performance Measures. It shall be allocated among the Participants in the manner determined by the Committee in accordance with the Plan;

(f) "Participants" means, with respect to each Performance Period, the group of all persons elected to the office of Vice President of the Company or any office senior thereto except any officer covered by an annual incentive compensation plan of any subsidiary of the Company. A person who during part of such Performance Period has held such office shall participate on a proportional basis reflecting the portion of the

Performance Period during which he or she has held such office;

(g) "Performance Period" means performance goals and objectives, which shall be based on any of the following performance criteria, either alone or in any combination, as the Committee may determine: cash flow; cash flow from operations; earnings per Common share; earnings per Common share from continuing operations; income before income taxes; income before income taxes, depreciation, and amortization; income from continuing operations; net asset turnover; net income; operating income; operating margin; return on equity; return on net assets; return on total assets; return on total capital; sales; economic value added; and total return to stockholders. For any Performance Period, Performance Measures may be determined on an absolute basis or relative to internal goals or relative to levels attained in years prior to such Performance Period or related to other companies. For any Performance Period, the Committee shall provide whether and how the Performance Measures shall be adjusted in the event of any or all of the following items: extraordinary, unusual, or non-recurring items; effects of changes in applicable laws, regulations, or accounting principles; effects of currency fluctuations; effects of financing activities (e.g., effect on earnings per share of issuance of convertible debt securities); realized or unrealized gains and losses on securities; expenses, charges, or credits for restructuring initiatives, producing initiatives, or for impaired assets; non-cash items (e.g., amortization, depreciation, or reserves); other non-operating items; writedowns of intangible assets, property, plant, or equipment, investments in business units and securities resulting from the sale of business units; spending for acquisitions; and effects of any recapitalization, reorganization, merger, acquisition, divestiture, consolidation, spin-off, split-off, combination, liquidation, dissolution, sale of assets, or other similar corporate transaction or event; and

(h) "Performance Period" means each consecutive twelve-month period commencing January 1 of each year.

SECTION 1.3 Administration of the Plan. The Plan shall be administered by the Committee; provided, however, that

(i) The number of directors on the Committee shall not be less than two and

(ii) Each member of the Committee shall be an "outside director" within the meaning of Section 162(m)(4) of the Code. The Committee may adopt its own rules of procedure, and the action of a majority of the Committee, taken at a meeting, or taken without a meeting by unanimous written consent of the members of the Committee, shall constitute action by the Committee. The Committee shall have the power and authority to administer, construe, and interpret the Plan, to make rules for carrying it out and to make changes in such rules.

ARTICLE II

AWARDS

SECTION 2.1   Awards. The Committee may make Awards to Participants with respect to each Performance Period, subject to the terms and conditions set forth in the Plan.

SECTION 2.2   Terms of Awards. Within 90 days after the commencement of each Performance Period (or prior to such later date as permitted by, or such earlier date as required by, Section 162(m) of the Code and the regulations promulgated thereunder), the Committee shall establish in writing for such Performance Period (i) the objective formula for determining the Incentive Pool for the Performance Period (using one or more of the Performance Measures) and (ii) the allocable percentage of the total Incentive Pool to which each Participant shall be entitled, provided that the total of all such percentages for all Participants for any Performance Period shall not exceed 100 percent. The Committee shall cause each Participant to be notified in writing of (i) his or her selection as a Participant and (ii) the formula for determining the Incentive Pool for the Performance Period.

SECTION 2.3   Limitations on Awards. The maximum amount of an Award to any Participant for any Performance Period shall not exceed $2.5 million. No part of the amount of any Incentive Pool for any Performance Period which is not awarded in such performance Period may be carried forward for award in subsequent Performance Periods.

SECTION 2.4   Determination of Awards

(a) The Committee shall, promptly after the date on which all necessary financial or other information for a particular Performance Period becomes available, in the manner required by Section 162(m) of the Code, certify (i) the degree to which each of the Performance Measures has been attained and (ii) with respect to each Participant, the amount of the Participant's Award, if any.

(b) Notwithstanding anything in the Plan to the contrary, the Committee may, in its sole discretion, reduce or eliminate, but not increase, any Award. In exercising its discretion, the Committee may use such objective or subjective factors as it determines to be appropriate in its sole discretion. The determination by the Committee as to the terms of any of the foregoing adjustments shall be conclusive and binding. No part of any potential Award for any Performance Period that is not actually awarded to a Participant because of any reduction permitted by this Section 2.4(b) or required by Section 2.3 shall be available for award to any other Participant whose actual compensation for such period is subject to Section 162(m) of the Code.

(c) After the end of each Performance Period when the amount of each Participant's Award has been determined, the Committee shall cause each Participant to be provided with written notice of the amount of his or her award, if any. Awards shall become payable in cash as promptly as practicable after the certifications described in this Section 2.4 have been made by the Committee.

SECTION 2.5   Deferral of Payment of Awards. Notwithstanding Section 2.4(c), the Committee may, in its sole discretion, upon the request of a Participant, determine that the payment of an Award (or any portion thereof) to the Participant shall be deferred and when such deferred Award shall be paid and over what period of time. The Committee shall have discretion to provide for the payment of an amount equivalent to interest, at such rate or rates fixed by the Committee or based on one or more predetermined investments selected by the Committee, on any such deferred Award.

ARTICLE III

MISCELLANEOUS

SECTION 3.1   Restriction on Transfer. The rights of a Participant with respect to amounts under the Plan shall not be transferable by such participant, otherwise than by will or the laws of descent and distribution.

SECTION 3.2   Tax Withholding. The Company shall have the right to deduct from all payments made under the Plan to a Participant or to a Participant's beneficiary or beneficiaries any federal, state, or local taxes required by law to be withheld with respect to such payments.

SECTION 3.3   Source of Payments. The Company shall not have any obligation to establish any separate fund or trust or other segregation of assets to provide for payments under the Plan. To the extent any person acquires any rights to receive payments hereunder from the Company, such rights shall be no greater than those of an unsecured creditor.

SECTION 3.4   Employment Rights and Other Benefit Programs. The provisions of the Plan shall not give any Participant any right to be retained in the employment of the Company. In the absence of any specific agreement to the contrary, the Plan shall not affect any right of the Company, or of any affiliate of the Company, to terminate, with or without cause, any participant's employment at any time. The Plan shall not replace any contract of employment between the Company and any Participant, but shall be considered a supplement thereto. The Plan is in addition to, and not in lieu of, any other employee benefit plan or program in which any Participant may be or become eligible to participate by reason of employment with the Company.

SECTION 3.5   Amendment and Termination. The Board of Directors may at any time and from time to time alter, amend, suspend, or terminate the Plan in whole or in part. No termination or amendment of the Plan may, without the consent of the Participant to whom an Award has been determined for a completed Performance Period but not yet paid, adversely affect the rights of such participant in such Award, nor shall any amendment increase the amount payable to a Participant for a Performance Period if such amendment is made after the final day of the period for establishing the objective formula for determining the Incentive Pool for the Performance Period set forth in Section 2.2 of the Plan.

SECTION 3.6 Governing Law. The Plan and all rights and Awards hereunder shall be construed in accordance with and governed by the laws of the State of Delaware.

SECTION 3.7 Severability. If any provision of the Plan is or becomes or is deemed to be invalid, illegal, or enforceable in any jurisdiction such provision shall be construed or deemed amended to conform to applicable laws, or if it cannot be so construed or deemed without, in the determination of the Committee, materially altering the purpose or intent of the Plan, such provision shall be stricken as to such jurisdiction, and the remainder of the Plan shall remain in full force and effect.

SECTION 3.8 Effective Date. The Plan shall be effective as of January 1, 1997, subject to the approval thereof by the stockholders of the Company at the 1997 annual meeting of stockholders. Such approval shall meet the requirements of Section 162(m) of the Code and regulations thereunder. If such approval is not obtained, then the Plan shall not be effective and any formula for determining the Incentive Pool for any Performance Period, any percentage thereof to which any person otherwise may be entitled and any notice given pursuant to Section 2.2 of the Plan shall be void *ab initio*.

Appendix F

Sample Compensation Plan for Outside Directors

This plan of the Dupont Company includes the authorization of stock grants plus a deferred compensation program for outside directors.

Dupont Stock Accumulation and Deferred Compensation Plan for Directors

1. PURPOSE OF THE PLAN

The Purpose of the Dupont Stock Accumulation and Deferred Compensation Plan for Directors (the "Plan") is (1) to further identity of interests of members of the Board of Directors of E.I. Dupont de Nemours and Company (the "Company") with those of the Company's stockholders generally through the grant of common stock of the Company (the "Stock"); and, (2) to permit Directors to defer the payment of all or a specified part of their compensation, including any grant of Stock by the Company, for services performed as Directors.

2. ELIGIBILITY

Members of the Board of Directors of the Company who are not employees of the Company or any of its subsidiaries or affiliates and who do not receive a form of compensation for Board services in lieu of customary Director's fees shall be eligible to receive grants of Stock under the Plan. Members of the Board of Directors of the Company who are not employees of the Company or any of its subsidiaries or affiliates shall be eligible under this Plan to defer compensation for services performed as Directors.

3. ADMINISTRATION AND AMENDMENT

The Plan shall be administered by the Compensation and Benefits Committee of the Board of Directors (the "Committee"). The decision of the Committee with respect to any question arising as to the interpretation of this Plan, including the severability of any and all of the provisions thereof, shall be final, conclusive, and binding. The Board of Directors of the Company reserves the right to modify the Plan from time to time, or to repeal the Plan entirely, provided, however, that (1) no modification of the Plan shall operate to annul an election already in effect for the current calendar year or any preceding calendar year; and, (2) to the extent required under Section 16 of the Securities Exchange Act of 1934 ("Exchange Act"), Plan provisions relating to the amount, price, and timing of stock grants and options shall not be amended more than once every six months, except that the foregoing shall not preclude any amendment necessary to conform to changes in the Internal Revenue Code or the Employee Retirement Income Security Act.

The Committee is authorized, subject to the provisions of the Plan, from time to time to establish such rules and regulations as it deems appropriate for the proper administration of the Plan, and to make such determinations and take such steps in connection therewith as it deems necessary or advisable.

4. COMPLIANCE WITH SECTION 16 OF THE EXCHANGE ACT/CHANGE IN LAW

It is the Company's intent that the Plan comply in all aspects with Rule 16b-3 of the Exchange Act, or its successor, and any regulations promulgated thereunder. If any provision of this Plan is found not to be in compliance with such rule and regulations, the provision shall be deemed null and void, and the remaining provisions of the Plan shall continue in full force and effect. All transactions under this Plan shall be executed in accordance with the requirements of Section 16 of the Exchange Act and regulations promulgated thereunder.

The Board of Directors may, in its sole discretion, modify the terms and conditions of this Plan in response to and consistent with any changes in applicable law, rule, or regulation.

5. ANNUAL STOCK GRANT

Effective with the 1996 Annual Meeting and annually thereafter, each Director eligible under Article 2 hereof shall be awarded an annual grant of two hundred (200) shares of Stock following his/her election to the Board of Directors at the Annual Meeting of Stockholders. A Director elected to the Board at a time other than at the Annual Meeting shall receive a grant of two hundred (200) shares of Stock following his/her first attendance at a Board meeting, provided, however, that no Director shall receive more than two hundred (200) shares of Stock in any given calendar year. A Director may use shares of Stock granted hereunder to satisfy withholding taxes related to grants under this Plan in accordance with terms and conditions established by the Committee.

6. ELECTION TO DEFER

On or before December 31 of any year, a Director may elect to defer, until a specified year or retirement as a Director of the Company, the receipt of the Stock granted under Article 5 or the payment of all or a specified part of all fees payable to the Director for services as a Director during the calendar year following the election and succeeding calendar years in the form of cash or stock units, provided, however, that Stock may only be deferred as stock units. Any person who shall become a Director during a calendar year, and who was not a Director of the Company on the preceding December 31, may elect, within thirty days after election to the Board, to defer in the same manner the receipt of the Stock granted under Article 5 or the payment of all or a specified part of fees not yet earned for the remainder of that calendar year and for succeeding calendar years in the form of cash or stock units. Elections shall be made by written notice delivered to the Secretary of the Committee.

7. DIRECTORS' ACCOUNTS

Fees deferred in the form of cash shall be held in the general funds of the Company and shall be credited to an account in the name of the Director. On the first day of each quarter, interest shall be credited to each account calculated on the basis of the cash balance in each account on the first day of each month of the preceding quarter at the Prime Rate of Morgan Guaranty Trust Company of New York (or at such other rate as may be specified by the Committee from time to time) in effect on the first day of each month. Stock granted under Article 5 to be deferred in the form of stock units, or fees to be deferred in the form of stock units, shall be allocated to each Director's account based on the closing price of the Company's common stock as reported on the Composite Tape of the New York Stock Exchange ("Stock Price") on the effective date of the Stock grant or the date the fees would otherwise have been paid. The Company shall not be required to reserve or otherwise set aside shares of common stock for the payment of its obligations hereunder, but shall make available as and when required a sufficient number of shares of common stock to meet the needs of the Plan. An amount equal to any cash dividends (or the fair market value of dividends paid in property other than dividends payable in common stock of the Company) payable on the number of shares represented by the number of stock units in each Director's account will be allocated to each Director's account in the form of stock units based upon the Stock Price on the dividend payment date. Any stock dividends payable on such number of shares will be allocated in the form of stock units. If adjustments are made to outstanding shares of common stock as a result of split-ups, recapitalizations, mergers, consolidations, and the like, an appropriate adjustment will also be made in the number of stock units in a Director's account. Stock units shall not entitle any person to rights of a stockholder unless and until shares of Company common stock have been issued to that person with respect to stock units as provided in Article 8.

8. PAYMENT FROM DIRECTORS' ACCOUNTS

The aggregate amount of Stock granted under Article 5 which has been deferred and deferred fees, together with interest and dividend equivalents accrued thereon, shall be paid in the year specified or after a Director ceases to be a Director of the Company. Amounts deferred to a specified year shall only be paid in a lump sum and shall be paid promptly at the beginning of that specified year. Amounts deferred to retirement shall be paid in a lump sum or, if the Director elects, in substantially equal annual installments over a period of years specified by the Director. The delivery election must be made by written notice delivered to the Secretary of the Committee prior to the date of retirement, and the first installment (or lump sum payment) shall be paid promptly at the beginning of the following calendar year. Subsequent installment shall be paid promptly at the beginning of each succeeding calendar year until the entire amount credited to the Director's account shall have been paid. Amounts credited to a Director's account in cash shall be paid in cash and amounts credited in stock units shall be paid in one share of common stock of the Company for each stock unit, except that a cash payment will be made with any final installment for any fraction of a stock unit remaining in the Director's account. Such fractional share will be valued at the closing Stock Price on the date of settlement.

9. PAYMENT IN EVENT OF DEATH

A Director may file with the Secretary of the Committee a written designation of a beneficiary for his/her account under the Plan on such form as may be prescribed by the Committee, and may, from time to time, amend or revoke such designation. If a Director should die before all deferred amounts credited to the Director's account have been distributed, the balance of any deferred Stock and fees and interest and dividend equivalents then in the Director's account shall be paid promptly to the Director's designated beneficiary. If the Director did not designate a beneficiary, or in the event that the beneficiary designated by the Director shall have predeceased the Director, the balance in the Director's account shall be paid promptly to the Director's estate.

10. TERMINATION OF ELECTION

A Director may terminate his/her election to defer payment of fees in cash or stock units by written notice delivered to the Secretary of the Committee. Termination shall become effective as of the end of the calendar year in which notice of termination is given with respect to fees payable for services as a Director during subsequent calendar years. Amounts credited to the account of a Director prior to the effective date of termination shall not be affected thereby and shall be paid only in accordance with Articles 7 and 8.

11. NONASSIGNABILITY

During the Director's lifetime, the right to any deferred stock or fees including interest and dividend equivalents thereon shall not be transferable or assignable.

12. GOVERNING LAW

The validity and construction of the Plan shall be governed by the laws of the State of Delaware.

13. EFFECTIVE DATE

This Plan shall become effective as of January 1, 1996, provided it is approved by stockholders at the Company's 1996 Annual Meeting, and shall continue in full force and effect until terminated by the Board of Directors.

Appendix G

Sample Proposal to Increase the Number of Shares Used in an Executive Compensation Plan

This is a generic example of a proposal to shareholders that requests approval to increase the number of shares used in a company's executive compensation plans. It was developed from similar proposals that were sent to the Digital Equipment Corporation shareholders and The Boeing Company shareholders in 1997.

Proposal to Amend the 1992 Executive Long-Term Incentive Plan by Increasing the Number of Shares Available for Issuance

The Board of Directors recommends that the number of shares available for use in the Company's Executive Long-Term Incentive Plan (the "Plan") be increased thereto by 5,000,000 shares. This recommendation is contained on Page 1 of the Company's 1997 Annual Meeting Proxy and will become effective, if approved by stockholders, on the date of the Annual Meeting of Stockholders this year. The increase in shares is needed to enable the Company to meet the Plan's objectives of (1) attracting and retaining high quality executive talent; and (2) providing executives with ownership of company stock so that their interests efforts, and results are linked to the long-term interests of stockholders.

The Board of Directors recommends a vote FOR approving this amendment to the Executive Long-Term Incentive Plan.

A description of the 1992 Executive Long-Term Incentive Plan follows:

> In 1992 the Plan was approved by stockholders, and at that time 5,000,000 shares were authorized for issuance to executives. Since adoption of the Plan, 4,280,000 shares have been issued and/or have been made available for purchase.

> The Plan is administered by the Compensation Committee of the Board of Directors (the "Committee"), which is composed of non-employee Directors. They determine eligible participants and the type and level of all awards. The Committee may authorize Incentive Stock Options that comply with the provisions of Section 422 of the Internal Revenue Code and therefore provide Company executives with opportunity for capital gains tax rates; Non-Qualified Stock Options, which do not comply with Section 422 of the Internal Revenue Code and therefore do not provide the Company executives with the opportunity for capital gains tax; Stock Appreciation Rights, Phantom Shares, and Cashless Exercise Rights, which can provide executives with cash and/or cash and stock equal to the appreciation in specified amounts of company stock; Restricted Stock Awards that may contain a tenure and/or performance restriction that the executive must meet in order to take possession of the shares without any restriction on their sale; Performance Shares and Performance-Based Stock Options, which provide the executive either with shares or the opportunity to purchase shares if specified company long-term performance goals are achieved; and Performance Units that provide executives with specified cash and/or stock payments if specified company long-term goals are achieved.

> The Board of Directors may terminate or amend the Plan provided that no amendment shall, without stockholder approval, increase the number of shares of Common stock to be offered under the Plan or change the class of employees eligible to participate in the Plan.

Appendix H

Sample Proposal of Shareholder-Approved Performance-Based Compensation Plan as Defined under Code Section 162(m)

This example describes how The Boeing Company presented shareholders with an amendment to their executive compensation plans that describes the performance-based feature of their incentive compensation. Payments from the executive compensation plan are intended to qualify as "performance-based" under Internal Revenue Code Section 162(m) and therefore be tax-deductible to the company even if they exceed $1 million total compensation for any one of the top five executives. (Code Section 162(m) does not permit a company to take tax deductions on compensation over $1 million for the top five executives [as reported in public company proxies] unless they are performance-based.) By obtaining shareholder approval of the performance measures to be used in the plan, a public company can retain tax deductibility of all compensation paid.

Amendment to the Incentive Compensation Plan for Officers of the Boeing Company

The Board of Directors, subject to approval of the Company's shareholders, has adopted resolutions to amend and restate the Incentive Compensation Plan for Officers and Employees of The Boeing Company and Subsidiaries (the "Incentive Plan"). The Incentive Plan was originally approved by the Company's shareholders in 1947 and was last submitted to shareholders for approval of an amendment and restatement in 1957. The Incentive Plan has subsequently been amended and restated by the Board of Directors. The purpose of the Incentive Plan is to attract, retain, and motivate key employees by recognizing, motivating, and rewarding contributions to the Company and the accomplishment of Company objectives.

The proposed Incentive Plan amendments (the "Incentive Plan Amendments") were prepared primarily to qualify certain payments to employees under the Incentive Plan as performance-based compensation under Section 162(m) of the Code. Section 162(m) provides that compensation in excess of $1 million paid in any year to the chief executive officer and the four other highest paid executive officers of a public company (for purposes of the Incentive Plan, "Covered Employees") will not be deductible by the Corporation for federal income tax purposes unless certain conditions are met. One condition is that the compensation qualify as "performance-based compensation." In addition to other requirements for qualification as performance-based compensation, shareholders must be advised of and approve the material terms of the performance goals under which such compensation is to be paid.

Set forth below is a summary of certain important features of the Incentive Plan and the Incentive Plan Amendments, which summary is qualified in its entirety by reference to the full text of the Incentive Plan, as amended and restated, which is published in the 1997 proxy statement as Attachment #1. The proposed substantive amendments are shown in italics in the Attachment.

The Incentive Plan will continue to be administered by the Compensation Committee. Officers and employees of the Company and its 50-percent-owned subsidiaries who hold executive, administrative, supervisory, technical, or other key positions are eligible to participate in the Incentive Plan. In certain cases, employees in other positions within the Company and certain former employees may receive awards under the Incentive Plan. As of February 24, 1997, approximately 2,000 employees were eligible to participate in the Incentive Plan.

The Incentive Plan provides the Committee with complete discretion to make awards of cash, Boeing common stock, "Boeing Stock Units" (the right to receive Boeing common stock and the dividends thereon at the end of a three-year vesting period), or a combination thereof to employees who are eligible for awards under the Incentive Plan. The Committee may also establish programs under the Incentive Plan to provide for long-term incentive awards to selected senior executives. The long-term incentive program previously in effect under the Plan is currently being phased out. The Committee has authority to establish a long-term incentive program in the future, at which time performance criteria and employee maximums may be specified. The Committee may authorize the chief executive officer of the Company (who may in turn authorize other executive officers of the Company) to make awards under the Incentive Plan to certain eligible employees. Awards under the Incentive Plan may be deferral arrangements, and the Company may deduct from the payment of an award withholdings required by law or amounts owed by the award recipient to the company or to a subsidiary of the Company.

The Incentive Plan Amendments provide that payments to participants in the Incentive Plan are limited each year to an aggregate of 6 percent of "Plan Earnings" for the previous year. Plan Earnings are defined as the net earnings of the Company for the year, as reported by the Company in its consolidated financial statements, adjusted to exclude income tax, certain non-recurring and extraordinary items, the Company Share Value Trust, and the Incentive Plan. The amount paid to Covered Employees under the Incentive Plan Amendments is limited to 1 percent of Plan Earnings, with a maximum of 0.3 percent of Plan Earnings for the chief executive officer, 0.2 percent of Plan Earnings for the second most highly compensated Covered Employee and 0.167 percent of Plan Earnings for each of the other three Covered Employees. The Committee has the discretion to reduce amounts awarded to Covered Employees below these maximum levels, but does not have the discretion to increase the amount awarded to a Covered Employee beyond the maximum levels of compensation established by the Incentive Plan. Prior to the Incentive Plan Amendments, the Incentive Plan provided that the Company's Board of Directors could set aside each year for awards under the Incentive Plan a fund in an amount not in excess of 6 percent of "profit subject to the plan" for such year, as such term was defined in the Incentive Plan, and that no person could receive from the fund for any one-year awards in excess of 5 percent of the fund.

The Incentive Plan Amendments provide that the Incentive Plan may be amended by a majority vote of the Company shareholders or Board of Directors, except that the Company's shareholders must approve any amendment that would increase the number of shares available for issuance under the Incentive Plan, change the performance criterion or goal governing the amount that may be paid to Covered Employees, or change the requirements for amending the Incentive Plan. Prior to the Incentive Plan Amendments, a two-thirds vote by the Company's shareholders or Board of Directors was required to amend the Incentive Plan, with shareholder approval required for any amendment that would increase the amount that could be set aside for any year, increase the percentage of the Incentive Plan fund set aside for any year that could be awarded to one participant, or change the requirements for amending the Incentive Plan.

The Incentive Plan Amendments identify the total of 5 million shares of Boeing common stock that continue to be available under the Incentive Plan and may be used for making awards under the Incentive Plan. Prior to the Incentive Plan Amendments, an aggregate share limit was not required to be stated under the Incentive Plan.

The Board of Directors Unanimously Recommends a Vote FOR this Amendment.

Attachment 1

Incentive Compensation Plan for Officers and Employees of The Boeing Company and Subsidiaries (As Amended and Restated)

1. Definitions. As used in this plan (the "Plan"), the following terms have the meanings set forth below:

"Board of Directors" means the Board of Directors of The Boeing Company;

"BSU" means Boeing Stock Unit, as described in Section 5.2;

"Common Stock" means the common stock of The Boeing Company;

"Company" means The Boeing Company;

"Committee" means the Compensation Committee of the Board of Directors;

"Covered Employee" means each of (i) an employee of the Company who on the last day of the year with respect to which an award is made is (or serves in the capacity of) the Company's Chief Executive Officer and (ii) the four most highly compensated executive officers of the Company, other than the Company's Chief Executive Officer, whose total compensation for that year is reported to Company's shareholders in accordance with the provisions of the Securities Exchange Act of 1934, as amended;

"Earnings Credit BSUs" has the meaning given in Section 5.2;

"Exchange" means The New York Stock Exchange;

"Fair Market Value" means, as to a particular day, the mean of the high and low per-share trading prices for the Common Stock as reported for such day in *The Wall Street Journal* or in such other source as the Committee deems reliable;

"Plan Earnings" for a particular year means the net earnings of the Company for such year, as reported on the Company's consolidated financial statement included in its Annual Report on Form 10-K for such year, adjusted to eliminate the following:

(i)   Federal and state taxes on income,

(ii) Awards under the Plan,

(iii) Restructuring or similar charges to the extent they are separately disclosed in such annual Report,

(iv) The effect of changes in accounting principles,

(v)   The effect on net earnings for the accrued distributable appreciation of the Company's Share Value Program, and

(vi) "extraordinary items" determined under generally accepted accounting principles.

"Subsidiary" means any corporation or association more than 50 percent of the voting securities of which are owned directly or indirectly by the Company or by one or more of its other Subsidiaries and the accounts of which are customarily consolidated with those of the Company for the purpose of reporting to stockholders.

2. Committee. The Committee shall have full power and authority to administer the Plan, and to construe and interpret its terms and provisions. Decisions of the Committee shall be final and binding upon all parties.

3. Eligibility.

3.1 Key Employees. Officers and employees of the Company and its Subsidiaries who hold executive, administrative, supervisory, technical, or other key positions shall be eligible for participation under the Plan, and participants shall for the most part be selected from among Company or of a Subsidiary who is not also an officer or employee of the Company or of a Subsidiary shall be eligible for participation under the Plan.

3.2 Special Contributors; Former Employees. Awards may also be made under the Plan to employees not holding executive, administrative, supervisory, technical, or other key positions who have, nevertheless, made a substantial contribution to the success of the

Company and its Subsidiaries. In addition, a former employee who has either:

(a) Retired under the employee retirement plan of the Company or of a Subsidiary; or

(b) Left the service of the company or of a Subsidiary to enter the armed services and, who would have been eligible for an award but for such retirement or termination of service, may be eligible for an award for the year in which such employee retires or so leaves the service of the Company or of a Subsidiary. In the case of a former employee who would have been eligible for an award but for death, an award may be granted to the surviving spouse or children or to the estate of such former employee, as the Committee may determine in its sole discretion.

4. Making Awards.

4.1 Committee Authority. The Committee shall make awards, subject to the limitations herein, to such individuals within the eligible group and in such amounts and at such times as, in the Committee's judgment, shall best serve the interest of the Company and its Subsidiaries at that time, taking into account each individual's job performance and contributions to the success of the Company and its Subsidiaries.

Except as provided in Section 4.2, the Committee shall have complete discretion in determining to whom awards under the Plan shall be made and when awards shall be paid, including whether all or any portion of any award shall be paid in installments over two or more years, provided, however, in making awards the Committee shall request and consider the recommendations of the Chief Executive Officer of the Company and others whom it may designate.

4.2 Delegation of Award-Making Authority and Award Recommendations. The Committee may, at such times or times as it elects, authorize the Chief Executive Officer of the Company who in turn may authorize other executives of the Company to make additional awards subject to the limitations herein provided, in amounts not exceeding an aggregate amount and under conditions determined by the Committee. In making recommendations to the Committee and in making awards authorized by the Committee, the Chief Executive

Officer of the Company shall request and consider the recommendations of other officers and supervisory employees of the Company and its Subsidiaries.

4.3 Forms of Awards. Awards may be made entirely in cash, in Common Stock, in stock units, or on any combination thereof as determined by the Committee, provided, however, awards made by the Chief Executive Officer or authorized executives of the Company shall be made only in cash or Common Stock or a combination thereof.

4.4 Limits on awards.

4.4.1 Limit on the Number of Shares Awarded. Not more than five million (5,000,000) shares of Common Stock may be used for the purpose of making awards under the Plan. The number of shares awarded under the Plan in any one year shall be consistent with the total number of shares identified in this Section 4.4 being available over the projected twenty-year minimum life of the Plan.

4.4.2 Annual Limit on Value of Awards. The aggregate value of all awards granted under the Plan (including awards granted under Section 4.5 to Covered Employees) in any one calendar year shall not exceed 6 percent of Plan Earnings for the previous year.

4.5 Awards to Covered Employees. Notwithstanding any other provisions of this Section 4, any award under the Plan to a Covered Employee must satisfy the requirements of this Section 4.5. The purpose of this Section 4.5 is to ensure compliance by this Plan with the requirements of Section 162(m) of the Internal Revenue Code of 1986, as amended, related to performance-based compensation. Covered Employees status is determined for the year with respect to which the award is made, rather than the year of payment.

Awards to Covered Employees are subject to:

(a) Approval of this Plan and of the criterion stated in Section 4.4.1 by the shareholders of the Company;

(b) The maximum amount that may be awarded to any Covered Employee under the Plan for any year as stated in Section 4.5.1; and

(c) Approval by the Committee.

4.5.1 Criterion; Maximum Awards. The maximum potential awards under the Plan to Covered Employees for any year shall be the respective percentages of Plan Earnings for such year as follows:

Covered Employee	*Maximum Potential Award as* Percentage of Plan Earnings
Chief Executive Officer	Three-tenths of one percent (0.3%)
The most highly compensated Covered Employee other than the Chief Executive Officer	Two-tenths of one percent (0.2%)
Each other Covered Employee	One-sixth of one percent (0.167%)
Total	One Percent

4.5.2 Shareholder Approval of Performance Goal. The criterion established in Section 4.5.1 on which awards under the Plan are based shall first apply in the year 1997, but such criterion and any awards based thereon shall be conditional upon a vote of the shareholders of the Company approving the Plan and the criterion and performance goal stated herein.

4.5.3 Approval; Committee Discretion. The Committee shall make a determination in writing as to whether the Covered Employees have met the performance goal for the year. The Committee may, in its sole discretion, reduce amounts of awards to all or any of the Covered Employees from the maximum potential awards allocated by application of Section 4.5.1. No such reduction shall increase the amount of the award payable to any other Covered Employee. The Committee shall determine the amount of any reduction in a Covered Employee's award on the basis of such factors as it deems relevant, and it shall not be required to establish any allocation or weighting component with respect to the factors it considers. The Committee shall have no discretion to increase an award above the amount determined by application of Section 4.5.1.

5. Certain Types of Awards

5.1 Long-Term Incentive Program. Subject to the other terms and conditions of this Plan, the Committee may make awards, in capital stock of the Company or otherwise, to selected senior executives within the eligible group pursuant to a program adopted by the Committee providing for long-term incentive awards; and the Committee may in connection therewith reduce other awards under the Plan to such executives.

5.2 BSUs. Subject to other terms and conditions of the Plan, the Committee may direct that all or part of an award shall be made in the form of BSUs. BSU awards shall be subject to the following terms and conditions:

5.2.1 Calculation of Award Amount. A participant shall be credited with BSUs equal in number to either:

(i) The number of shares specified in the grant of the award; or

(ii) The number of shares of Common Stock that could be purchased with the BSU portion of an award otherwise denominated in cash, based on the Fair Market Value of such stock on the day of the award (or on the next business day on which the Exchange is open, if the Exchange is closed on the day of the award) excluding commissions, taxes, and other charges. Such number shall be carried to two decimal places.

For purposes of the Plan, a "participant" includes an employee or former employee having a BSU account under the Plan; and the number of BSUs in a participant's account shall be appropriately adjusted to reflect stock splits, stock dividends and other like adjustments in the Common Stock.

5.2.2 Participant Accounts. The Company shall maintain accounts for each participant to whom BSUs have been credited, and shall annually report to each participant his or her BSU account balance.

5.2.3 Vesting of BSU Awards. BSUs shall vest three years after the date the award is made or (if earlier) on the date the participant dies, retires, is laid off, or becomes disabled and entitled to Disability Retirement Income under the Company's employee retirement plan or under comparable provisions of a Subsidiary's retirement plan.

5.2.4 Earnings Credit on BSU Awards. Each participant's BSU account shall be credited with Earnings Credit BSUs equal in number to the number of shares of Common Stock that could be purchased with cash dividends that would be payable on the number of shares of Common Stock that equals the number of BSUs in each participant's account. Determination of the number of shares so credited shall be made in the manner described in Section 5.2.1 as to cash-denominated awards, as of each dividend payment date for the Common Stock. Participants shall be notified annually of the number of Earnings Credit BSUs in their accounts. Earnings Credit BSUs shall vest at the same time as the BSUs with which they are associated.

5.2.5 Forfeiture of Non-Vested BSU Awards. If a participant's employment with the Company or a Subsidiary terminates prior to the expiration of three years from the date an award is made, for any reason other than death, retirement, layoff, or disability, the participant's BSUs from such award shall be forfeited and canceled. Earnings Credit BSUs shall be forfeited and canceled along with the BSUs with which they are associated.

5.2.6 BSU Awards Payable in Cash or Stock. Distributions from a participant's BSU account shall be made as soon as reasonably possible after the vesting date of the BSUs. In the absence of an election to the contrary by the participant, distributions shall be in cash. A cash distribution shall equal the cash value, on the date as of which the distribution is calculated (which shall be the vesting date, unless some other date is prescribed by the Committee), of that number of whole shares of Common Stock equal to the whole number of vested BSUs in the participant's account on such date, based on the Fair Market Value of such stock on that date (or on the next day on which the Exchange is open, if the Exchange is closed on the date as of which the distribution is calculated). Any distribution in stock shall be in whole shares of Common Stock equal in number to the whole number of vested BSUs in the participant's account, adjusted in accordance with Section 5.2.7. No fractional shares shall be distributed, and any account balance remaining after a stock distribution shall be added to the required withholdings provided for in Section 5.2.7.

5.2.7 Deferral of BSU Awards. Participants may elect to defer distribution of vested BSUs through the Company's Deferred Compensation Plan. Such deferral elections must be made in the manner and at the times prescribed in that plan.

6. Distribution of Awards

6.1 Terms; Deferred Payment. Distribution of awards shall be governed by the terms and conditions applicable to such awards, as determined by the Committee or its delegate. An award, the payment of which is to be deferred pursuant to the terms of an employment agreement, shall be paid as provided by the terms of such agreement. Awards or portions thereof deferred pursuant to the Company's Deferred Compensation Plan or other deferral arrangement shall be paid as provided in such plan or arrangement. Any other awards the payment of which has been deferred, in whole or in part, shall be paid as determined by the Committee.

6.2 Deductions. The Company shall deduct from the payment of each award any withholdings required by law or required by Section 5.2.6; and the Company may deduct any amounts due from the recipient to the Company or a Subsidiary.

6.3 Notice; Distribution Date. The Committee or its delegates shall advise participants of their awards under the Plan, and shall fix the distribution date or dates for such awards. Awards shall be paid on the distribution date or as soon thereafter as reasonably possible. The number of shares of stock to be issued in payment of awards otherwise denominated in cash shall be determined based on the closing trading price per share of the Common Stock as reported for the business day immediately preceding the applicable distribution date in *The Wall Street Journal* or in such other source as the Committee deems reliable.

7. Repeal; Amendments. The Plan and any and all provisions hereof may be repealed or amended either:

(a) By the affirmative vote of the holders of record of a majority of the shares of stock present in person or by proxy and entitled to vote at any meeting of the shareholders of the Company at which a quorum is present if the notice of such meeting sets forth the form of the proposal for such repeal or amendment or a summary thereof; or

(b) The affirmative vote of a majority of the Board of Directors at any meeting if the notice of such meeting sets forth the form of the proposal for such repeal or amendment or a summary thereof, provided, however, that the Company's shareholders must approve, by a vote meeting the requirements of clause (a) above, any amendment that would:

   (i) Amend Section 4.4.1 so as to increase the number of shares available for issuance under the Plan,

(ii) Amend Section 4.5.1 so as to change the criterion or goal governing the amount which may be awarded to any Covered Employee or the formula used to determine such amount,

(iii) Change the definition of Covered Employee, or

(iv) Amend this Section 7.

No repeal or amendment of the Plan shall operate to annul or modify any award previously made under the Plan.

8. Nonassignability. No awards authorized or made pursuant to the Plan shall be subject in any manner to anticipation, alienation, sale, transfer, assignment, pledge, encumbrance, charge, execution, attachment, garnishment, or any other legal process, and any attempt to subject an award to any of the foregoing shall be void.

Appendix I

Economic Value-Added Bonus Plan

This appendix includes the Eli Lilly Economic Value-Added (EVA) bonus plan, which is a rare attachment to any company proxy. Value-added plans are a significant trend today, and many companies may want to use this example as a reference in developing their own share-holder-approved plan.

Article I: Bonus Plan Statement of Purpose and Summary

1.1 The purpose of the Plan is to provide a system of bonus compensation for selected employees of Eli Lilly and Company and subsidiaries which will promote the maximization of shareholder value over the long term, by linking performance incentives to increases in shareholder value. The Plan ties bonus compensation to Economic Value Added ("EVA"), and thereby rewards employees for long-term, sustained improvement in shareholder value. The Plan is intended to satisfy the requirements for providing "performance-based" compensation under Section 162(m) of the Internal Revenue Code.

1.2 EVA will be used as the performance measure of value creation. EVA reflects the benefits and costs of capital employment. Employees create economic value when operating profits from a business exceed the cost of capital employed.

Article II: Definitions of Certain Terms

Unless the context requires a different meaning, the following terms shall have the following meanings:

2.1 "Company" means Eli Lilly and Company and its subsidiaries.

2.2 "Committee" means the Compensation and Management Development Committee, the members of which shall be elected by the Board of Directors from among its members. Each Committee member shall, at all times while serving, satisfy the requirements of an "outside director" within the meaning of Section 162(m) of the Internal Revenue Code.

2.3 "Participant" means any employee of the Company designated by the Committee as a participant in the Plan with respect to any Plan year. In its discretion, the Committee may designate Participants either on an individual basis or by determining that all employees in specified job categories, classification or levels shall be Participants.

2.4 "Plan" means this Eli Lilly and Company EVA Bonus Plan.

2.5 "Plan Year" means the applicable calendar year.

2.6 "Retirement" means the cessation of employment upon the attainment of at least eighty age and service points, as determined by the provisions of The Lilly Retirement Plan as amended from time to time, assuming eligibility to participate in that plan.

2.7 "Disability" means the time at which a Participant becomes eligible for a payment under The Lilly Extended Disability Plan, assuming eligibility to participate in that plan.

2.8 "Section 162(m)" means Section 162(m) of the Internal Revenue Code of 1986, as amended.

2.9 "Section 162(m) Participant" means a Participant who, in the determination of the Committee, is or may in the future become a "covered employee" under Section 162(m).

Article III: Definitions and Components of EVA

The following terms set forth the calculation of EVA and the components of calculating EVA. The calculation of EVA for a Plan

Year is used in determining the bonuses earned by Participants under the Plan, as set forth in Article IV.

3.1 "Economic Value Added" or "EVA" means the excess NOPAT that remains after subtracting the Capital Charge.

3.2 "Net Operating Profit After Tax" or "NOPAT" means the after tax operating earnings of the Company for the Plan Year. NOPAT is determined by adding net sales plus other net income (excluding interest income from operating cash) and subtracting the following: cost of goods sold, selling, general and administrative expenses (excluding goodwill amortization and interest expense), amortization of research and development, taxes (excluding the tax benefit of interest expense) and amounts associated with discontinued operations.

3.3 "Capital Charge" means the deemed opportunity cost of employing Capital for the Company. The Capital Charge is calculated by multiplying Capital times the Cost of Capital (C*).

3.4 "Capital" means the net investment employed in the operations of the Company produced by operations and financing activities. Capital is calculated by adding together current assets (excluding operating cash), net property, plant and equipment, gross goodwill, net intangibles, other assets, and capitalized research and development, and the present value of operating leases, and subtracting the following: non-interest bearing liabilities and capital associated with discontinued operations.

3.5 "Cost of Capital" or "C*" is the percentage calculated from the weighted average of Cost of Debt and Cost of Equity. Cost of Capital for each Plan Year is determined by referencing to the percentage calculated at the end of October of the prior Plan Year.

3.6 "Cost of Debt" capital is the marginal long-term borrowing rate of the Company times (one minus the tax rate).

3.7 "Cost of Equity" capital is the risk-free rate plus (beta times the market risk premium). For this purpose, (I) "risk free rate" is the 30-year U.S. Treasury Bond rate, (ii) "beta" represents the 5 year historical average variation of the Company's earnings versus the S&P 500, and (iii) "market risk premium" represents the average risk of an equity return versus a bond return.

Article IV: Definition and Computation of the EVA Bonus

Bonuses earned under the Plan for a Plan Year are determined based on a comparison of actual EVA to the "Target EVA" for the year, which is established as described below to ensure improvement in EVA from year to year. The result of this comparison is adjusted by a "Leverage Factor" measuring the volatility of industry returns. The factor produced is referred to as the "Bonus Multiple," which is multiplied by the Participant's "Target Bonus" amount established for the year to produce the actual bonus earned. This amount, referred to as the "Declared Bonus," is credited to the Participant's Bonus Bank balance and paid out in the manner provided below.

4.1 "Target Bonus." The Target Bonus Awards will be determined by the Committee on a basis that takes into consideration a Participant's salary grade level, job responsibilities as well as past and expected future job performance. Target Bonus Awards are expressed as a percentage of annual base salary as in effect on the first day of the Plan Year. If a Participant moves from any salary grade level to a G-6 or above salary grade level during a Plan Year, he/she will receive an award that is pro-rated according to time based on the Target Bonus percentage and base salary applicable to each such salary grade. The Target Bonus will be based on the currency in which the highest portion of base salary is regularly paid. The Committee shall determine the appropriate foreign exchange conversion methodology in its discretion.

4.2 "Declared Bonus." A Declared Bonus is the Target Bonus times the Bonus Multiple.

4.3 "Bonus Multiple." The Bonus Multiple is the difference (positive or negative) between Actual EVA and Target EVA, divided by the Leverage Factor, plus one.

4.4 "Bonus Bank." All bonus payments are made from the Bonus Bank. Each Participant's beginning Bonus Bank balance in his/her first year of participation is zero. The Bonus Bank is increased or decreased for any Plan Year by the amount of Declared Bonus. If the available Bonus Bank balance is positive, the Participant will be paid from such balance up to the Target Bonus amount, plus one third of any such balance that remains after subtracting the Target Bonus from available Bonus Bank balance. If the available Bonus Bank balance is negative, no payment will occur.

4.5 "Target EVA." The Target EVA for each year will be calculated as follows:

$$\text{Target EVA} = [\text{Prior Year's Actual EVA} + \text{Prior Year's Target EVA}],$$
$$\div\, 2, + \text{Expected Improvement}$$

4.6 "Expected Improvement." The Expected Improvement is the additional EVA amount determined by the Committee that is used to assure that a minimum level of improvement is achieved in order to earn target awards.

4.7 "Leverage Factor." The Leverage Factor determines the rate of change in bonuses as EVA surpasses or falls short of Target EVA, determined by the Committee from an evaluation of the long-term volatility of industry returns.

4.8 "Section 162(m) Requirements, Bonus Maximum." In the case of Section 162(m) Participants, all determinations necessary for computing Declared Bonuses for a Plan Year, including establishment of all components of the EVA calculation and of the Target Bonus percentages, shall be made by the Committee not later than 90 days after the commencement of the Plan Year. As and to the extent required by Section 162(m), the terms of a Declared Bonus for a Section 162(m) Participant must state, in terms of an objective formula or standard, the method of computing the amount of compensation payable to the Section 162(m) Participant, and must preclude discretion to increase the amount of compensation payable that would otherwise be due under the terms of the award. Notwithstanding anything elsewhere in the Plan to the contrary, the maximum amount of the Declared Bonus that may be paid from the Bonus Bank to a Section 162(m) Participant during any one calendar year shall be $5 million.

4.9 "Working Plan Example." Examples of the mechanics of the Plan are shown on Schedule A.

Article V: Plan Administration

5.1 Time of Payment. Payment from the Bonus Bank will be made before March 1 of the year following the Plan Year.

5.2 Certification of Results. Before any amount is paid under the Plan, the Committee shall certify in writing the calculation of EVA for the Plan Year and satisfaction of all other material terms of the calculation of the Declared Bonus.

5.3 New Hires, Promotions. New hires or individuals promoted who are first selected for participation by the Committee effective on a date other than January 1 will participate on a pro-rata basis in their first year of participation, based on the Declared Bonus determined for the Plan Year, pro-rated for that period of the year during which the Participant was selected for participation in the Plan. Any such Participant's Target Bonus Award will be determined based on his or her annual base salary as in effect on the date of hire or promotion, as applicable. Notwithstanding the foregoing, in the case of any Section 162(m) Participant who first becomes eligible to participate in the Plan after January 1 of a Plan Year, such participant's Declared Bonus may be determined, at the discretion of the Committee exercised at the time such participation begins, in a manner that complies with the requirements for "performance-based compensation" under Section 162(m).

5.4 Termination of Employment, Demotions. If a Participant ceases employment with the Company before the end of a Plan Year for reasons other than Retirement, Disability or death, or is demoted to a non-global job level with the Company during a Plan Year, the Participant shall receive no Declared Bonus for that Plan Year, and his/her Bank Balance shall be forfeited. The Committee may make complete or partial exceptions to this rule, in its sole discretion. Notwithstanding the foregoing, with respect to the Declared Bonus for a Section 162(m) Participant, any such termination of employment or demotion shall result in payment of a bonus based on the Declared Bonus determined for the Plan Year but pro-rated for the period of the year prior to such event, subject to the Committee's discretion to forfeit all or any portion of such bonus.

5.5 Leave of Absence. If a Participant takes an approved leave of absence from employment during a Plan Year, the Participant will not be eligible for the Declared Bonus for the Plan Year. The Committee may make complete or partial exceptions to this rule, in whatever manner it deems appropriate. The Participant will retain his/her Bonus Bank balance if he/she returns to employment following the period of leave of absence. Notwithstanding the foregoing, with respect to the Declared Bonus for a Section 162(m) Participant, any such leave of absence shall result in payment of a bonus based on the Declared Bonus determined for the Plan Year but pro-rated for the period of the year that the Participant was actively employed by the Company, subject to the Committee's discretion to forfeit all or any portion of such bonus.

5.6 Retirement, Disability or Death. If a Participant ceases employment with the Company because of Retirement, Disability, or death, the Participant or personal representative, as the case may be, shall receive full payment of his/her Bank Balance and a bonus based on the Declared Bonus determined for the Plan Year but pro-rated for that period of the year during which the Participant was an active employee of the Company.

5.7 Plan Participation. A Participant may not participate in this Plan for any portion of a year for which he/she is entitled to receive payment under the Eli Lilly and Company Contingent Compensation Plan, and shall be treated in accordance with 5.3.

5.8 Forfeiture Events. Notwithstanding any other provisions of this Plan to the contrary, the Committee may, in its sole discretion, upon the occurrence of a Forfeiture Event (as defined below), forfeit all or any portion of a Participant's Declared Bonus and Bonus Bank balance and terminate such Participant's future participation in the Plan. For purposes hereof, a "Forfeiture Event" shall mean the occurrence of one or more of the following events with respect to a Participant: (I) the termination or forced resignation from employment of the Participant for "misconduct" (as defined in the Company's Employee Information Handbook), (ii) any violation by the Participant of the Guidelines of Company Policy (the "Redbook") that is detrimental to the Company, (iii) any breach of a noncompetition, nonsolicitation, nondisclosure or other restrictive covenant that may apply by written agreement between the Company and the Participant or (iv) Participant's having engaged in any other activity that, in the judgement of the Committee, is detrimental to the business, affairs or reputation of the Company (including, without limitation, engaging in any criminal activity).

Article VI: General Provisions

6.1 Withholding of Taxes. The Company shall have the right to withhold the amount of taxes which in the sole determination of the Company are required to be withheld under law with respect to any amount due or payable under the Plan.

6.2 Expenses. All expenses and costs in connection with the adoption and administration of the Plan shall be borne by the Company.

6.3 No Prior Right or Offer, No Right to Future Participation. Participation in the Plan for Plan Years is determined from year-to-year by the Committee in its sole discretion. Except and until expressly granted pursuant to the Plan, nothing in the Plan shall be deemed to give any employee any contractual or other right to participate in the benefits of the Plan. No award to any such Participant in any Plan Year shall be deemed to create a right to receive any award or to participate in the benefits of the Plan in any subsequent Plan Year.

6.4 Rights Personal to Employee. Any rights provided to an employee under the Plan shall be personal to such employee, shall not be transferable, except by will or pursuant to the laws of descent or distribution, and shall be exercisable during his/her lifetime, only by such employee, or a court-appointed guardian for the employee.

6.5 Non-Allocation of Award. In the event of a suspension of the Plan in any Plan Year, as described in Section 11.1, no awards under the Plan for the Plan Year during which such suspension occurs shall affect the calculation of awards for any subsequent period in which the Plan is continued.

Article VII: Limitations

7.1 No Continued Employment. Neither the establishment of the Plan nor the grant of an award thereunder shall be deemed to constitute an express or implied contract of employment of any Participant for any period of time or in any way abridge the rights of the Company to determine the terms and conditions of employment or terminate the employment of any employee with or without notice or cause at any time.

7.2 No Vested Rights. Except as expressly provided herein, no employee or other person shall have any claim of right (legal, equitable, or otherwise) to any award, allocation, or distribution or any right, title, or vested interest in any amounts in his/her Bonus Bank and no officer or employee of the Company or any person shall have any authority to make representations or agreements to the contrary. No interest conferred herein to a Participant shall be assignable or subject to claim by a Participant's creditors.

7.3 Non-alienation. Except as provided in Subsection 5.1, no Participant or other person shall have any right or power, by draft, assignment, or otherwise, to mortgage, pledge or otherwise encumber in advance any payment under the Plan, and every attempted draft, assignment, or other disposition thereof shall be absolutely void.

Article VIII: Committee Authority

8.1 Authority to Interpret and Administer. Except as otherwise expressly provided herein, full power and authority to interpret and administer this Plan shall be vested in the Committee. The Committee may from time to time make such decisions and adopt such rules and regulations for implementing the Plan as it deems appropriate for any Participant under the Plan. Except as to Participants who are treated by the Committee as executive officers of the Company for federal securities law reporting purposes (including any Section 162(m) Participant), the Committee may delegate in writing to officers or employees of the Company the power and authority granted by this Section 8.1 to interpret and administer this Plan. Any decision taken by the Committee or officer or employee to whom authority has been delegated, arising out of or in connection with the construction, administration, interpretation and effect of the Plan shall be final, conclusive and binding upon all Participants and any person claiming under or through Participants.

8.2 Adjustments for Significant Events. Prior to the beginning of a Plan Year, the Committee may specify with respect to Declared Bonuses for the Plan Year that EVA will be determined before the effects of acquisitions, divestitures, restructurings or changes in corporate capitalization, accounting changes, and/or events that are treated as extraordinary items for accounting purposes; provided that such adjustments shall be made only to the extent permitted by Section 162(m) in the case of Section 162(m) Participants.

8.3 Financial and Accounting Terms. Except as otherwise provided, financial and accounting terms, including terms defined herein, shall be determined by the Committee in accordance with generally accepted accounting principles and as derived from the audited consolidated statements of the Company, prepared in the ordinary course of business.

8.4 Section 162(m) Deferrals. To the extent that, notwithstanding the terms of the Plan, the Company's tax deduction for remuneration in respect of the payment of bonuses under the Plan to a Section 162(m) Participant would be disallowed under Section 162(m), either exceeds or, if such bonus were paid, would exceed the $1,000,000 limitation in Section 162(m), any such excess (as determined by the Committee in its sole discretion) shall be automatically deferred under the terms of The Lilly Deferred Compensation Plan. Payment of any deferred amounts shall be made to the Participant in the first year thereafter that the Company's tax deduction in respect of the payment would not be disallowed under Section 162(m).

Article IX: Notice

9.1 Any notice to be given to the Company or Committee pursuant to the provisions of the Plan shall be in writing and directed to Secretary, Eli Lilly and Company, Lilly Corporate Center, Indianapolis, IN 46285.

Article X: Effective Date

10.1 This Plan, as amended and restated herein, shall be effective for the Plan Year commencing January 1, 1999, subject to the approval of the Plan at the Company's 1998 annual meeting of stockholders. The terms of this restated Plan shall apply to Declared Bonuses earned in 1999 and future years. All Declared Bonuses earned in years prior to 1999 shall be payable in accordance with the terms of the Plan as in effect for the year to which the Declared Bonus relates. The final Plan Year of this Plan, unless amended by the Board (or the Committee) and approved by the stockholders as provided in Article XI, shall be the 2003 Plan Year.

Article XI: Amendments and Termination

11.1 This Plan may be amended, suspended or terminated at any time at the discretion of the Board of Directors of Eli Lilly and Company, and may, except for this Section 11.1, be amended at any time by the Committee. Solely to the extent deemed necessary or advisable by the Board (or the Committee) for purposes of complying with Section 162(m), the Board (or the Committee) may seek the approval of any such amendment by the Company's stockholders. Any such approval shall be by the affirmative votes of the stockholders of the Company present, or represented, and entitled to vote at a meeting duly held in accordance with applicable state law and the Articles of Incorporation and By-laws of the Company. The material terms of EVA must be disclosed to and reapproved by the stockholders of the Company no later than the Company's annual meeting of stockholders that occurs in the year 2003.

Article XII: Applicable Law

12.1 This Plan shall be governed by and construed in accordance with the provisions of the laws of the State of Indiana.

Eli Lilly and Company EVA Bonus Plan

Schedule A

Year 1:   Target EVA = $150 million
            Actual EVA = $200 million
            Leverage Factor = $100 million

Economic Value Added Grid:

Bonus Multiple	EVA
1.0	$150 million (Target EVA)
1.5	$200 million (Actual EVA)
2.0	$250 million

Declared Bonus:

Actual EVA – Target EVA = $50 million
Bonus Multiple = 1 + (Actual EVA – Target EVA) ÷
              Leverage Factor
              1 + $50 ÷ $100 = 1.5
Target Bonus = $20,000
Declared Bonus = $30,000 ($20,000 × 1.5)

Bonus Bank:

Declared Bonus	$30,000
Beginning Bank Balance	$ 0
Available Bank Balance	$30,000
Target Bonus Paid	$20,000
Remaining Balance	$10,000
Pay ⅓ Remaining Balance	$ 3,333
Ending Bank Balance	$ 6,667

Total Bonus Paid = $20,000 + $3,333 = $23,333

EVA Target Reset for Year 2 = $175 million
                           ($200 million + $150 million
                           ÷ 2 + 0 = $175)

Year 2: Target EVA = $175 million
        Actual EVA = $140 million
        Leverage Factor = $100 million

Economic Value Added Grid:

Bonus Multiple	*EVA*
.65	$140 million (Actual EVA)
1.0	$175 million (Target EVA)
2.0	$275 million

Declared Bonus:

Actual EVA – Target EVA = $35 million

Bonus Multiple = 1 + (Actual EVA – Target EVA) ÷
                    Leverage Factor
                    1 + $35 ÷ $100 = .65

Target Bonus = $20,000

Declared Bonus = $13,000 ($20,000 × .65)

Bonus Bank:

Declared Bonus	$13,000
Beginning Bank Balance	$ 6,667
Available Bank Balance	$19,667
Target Bonus Paid	$19,667
Remaining Balance	$ 0
Pay ⅓ Remaining Balance	$ 0
Ending Bank Balance	$ 0

Total Bonus Paid = $19,667 + $0 = $19,667

EVA Target Reset for Year 3 = $157.5 million
                    ($140 million + $175 million ÷
                    2 + 0 = $157.5)

Appendix J

W. R. Grace Stock Incentive Plan

1. *Purposes.* The purposes of this Plan are (a) to enable Key Persons to have incentives related to Common Stock, (b) to encourage Key Persons to increase their interest in the growth and prosperity of the Company and to stimulate and sustain constructive and imaginative thinking by Key Persons, (c) to further the identity of interests of Key Persons with the interests of the Company's stockholders, and (d) to induce the service or continued service of Key Persons and to enable the Company to compete with other organizations offering similar or other incentives in obtaining and retaining the services of the most highly qualified individuals.

2. *Definitions.* When used in this Plan, the following terms have the meaning set forth in this section 2.

Board of Directors: The Board of Directors of the Company.

Cessation of Service (or words of similar import): When a person ceases to be an employee of the Company or a Subsidiary. For purposes of this definition, if an entity that was a Subsidiary ceases to be a Subsidiary, persons who immediately thereafter remain employees of that entity (and are not employees of the Company or an entity that is a Subsidiary) shall be deemed to have ceased service.

Change of Control: Shall be deemed to have occurred if:

(a) the Company determines that any "person" (as such term is used in Sections 13(d) and 14(d) of the Exchange Act), other than a trustee or other fiduciary holding securities under an employee benefit plan of the Company or a corporation owned, directly or indirectly, by the stockholders of the Company in substantially the same proportions as their ownership of stock in the Company, has become the "beneficial owner" (as defined in Rule 13d-3 under the Exchange Act), directly or indirectly, of 20% or more of the outstanding Common Stock of the Company;

(b) individuals who are "Continuing Directors" (as defined below) cease to constitute a majority of any class of the Board of Directors;

(c) there occurs a reorganization, merger, consolidation or other corporate transaction involving the Company (a "Corporate Transaction"), in each case, with respect to which the stockholders of the Company immediately prior to such Corporate Transaction do not, immediately after the Corporate Transaction, own more than 60% of the combined voting power of the corporation resulting from such Corporate Transaction; or

(d) the stockholders of the Company approve a complete liquidation or dissolution of the Company.

Change in Control Price: The higher of (a) the highest reported sales price, regular way, as reported in *The Wall Street Journal* or another newspaper of general circulation, of a share of Common Stock in any transaction reported on the New York Stock Exchange Composite Tape or other national exchange on which such shares are listed or on NASDAQ during the 60-day period prior to and including the date of a Change of Control or (b) if the Change of Control is the result of a tender or exchange offer or a Corporate Transaction, the highest price per share of Common Stock paid in such tender or exchange offer or Corporate Transaction; provided, however, that in the case of Incentive Stock Options, the Change of Control shall be the date such Incentive Stock Option is exercised. To the extent that the consideration paid in any Corporate Transaction or other transaction described above consists in whole or in part of securities or other noncash consideration, the value of such securities or other noncash consideration shall be determined in the sole discretion of the Board of Directors.

Code: The Internal Revenue Code of 1986, as amended.

Committee: The Compensation, Employee Benefits and Stock Incentive Committee of the Board of Directors of the Company or any other committee designated by the Board of Directors to administer stock incentive and stock option plans of the Company and the Subsidiaries generally or this Plan specifically.

Common Stock: The Common Stock of the Company, par value $.01 per share, or such other class or shares or other securities or property as may be applicable pursuant to the provisions of section 8.

Company: W. R. Grace & Company, a Delaware corporation.

Corporate Transaction: The meaning set forth in the definition of "Change of Control" above.

Exchange Act: The Securities Exchange Act of 1934, as amended.

Exercise Period: The meaning set forth in section 14(b) of this Plan.

Fair Market Value: (a) The mean between the high and low sales price of a share of Common Stock in New York Stock Exchange composite transactions on the applicable date, as reported in the *Wall Street Journal* or another newspaper of general circulation, or, if no sales of shares of Common Stock were reported for such date, for the preceding date for which such sales were so reported, or (b) the fair market value of a share of Common Stock determined in accordance with any reasonable method approved by the Committee.

Incentive Stock Option: A stock option that states it is an incentive stock option and that is intended to meet the requirements of Section 422 of the Code and the regulations thereunder applicable to incentive stock options, as in effect from time to time.

Issuance (or words of similar import): The issuance of authorized but unissued Common Stock or the transfer of issued Common Stock held by the Company or a Subsidiary.

Key Person: An employee of the Company or a Subsidiary who, in the opinion of the Committee, contributed or can contribute significantly to the growth and successful operations of the Company or one or more Subsidiaries. The grant of a Stock Incentive to an employee shall be deemed a determination by the Committee that such person is a Key Person.

Nonstatutory Stock Option: An Option that is not an Incentive Stock Option.

Option: An option granted under this Plan to purchase shares of Common Stock.

Option Agreement: An agreement setting forth the terms of an Option.

Plan: The 1998 Stock Incentive Plan of the Company herein set forth, as the same may from time to time be amended.

Service: Service to the Company or a Subsidiary as an employee. "To serve" has a correlative meaning.

Spread: The meaning set forth in section 14(b) of this Plan.

Stock Award: An issuance of shares of Common Stock or an undertaking (other than an Option) to issue such shares in the future.

Subsidiary: A corporation (or other form of business association) of which shares (or other ownership interests) having 50% or more of the voting power regularly entitled to vote for directors (or equivalent management rights) are owned, directly or indirectly, by the Company, or any other entity designated as such by the Board of Directors; provided, however, that in the case of an Incentive Stock Option, the term "Subsidiary" shall mean a Subsidiary (as defined by the preceding clause) that is also a "subsidiary corporation" as defined in Section 424(f) of the Code and the regulations thereunder, as in effect from time to time.

3. Grants of Stock Incentives.

(a) Subject to the provisions of this Plan, the Committee may at any time and from time to time grant Stock Incentives under this Plan to, and only to, Key Persons.

(b) The Committee may grant a Stock Incentive to be effective at a specified future date or upon the future occurrence of a specified event. For the purposes of this Plan, any such Stock Incentive shall be deemed granted on the date it becomes effective. An agreement or other commitment to grant a Stock Incentive that is to be effective in the future shall not be deemed the grant of a Stock Incentive until the date on which such Stock Incentive becomes effective.

(c) A Stock Incentive may be granted in the form of:

    (i)   an Option, or

(ii) a combination of a Stock Award and an Option

4. *Stock Subject to this Plan.*

(a) Subject to the provisions of paragraph (c) of this section 4 and the provisions of section 8, the maximum number of shares of Common Stock that may be issued pursuant to Stock Incentives granted under this Plan shall not exceed seven million (7,000,000).

(b) Authorized but unissued shares of Common Stock and issued shares of Common Stock held by the Company or a Subsidiary, whether acquired specifically for use under this Plan or otherwise, may not be used for purposes of this Plan.

(c) If any shares of Common Stock subject to a Stock Incentive shall not be issued and shall cease to be issuable because of the termination, in whole or in part, of such Stock Incentive or for any other reason, or if any such shares shall, after issuance, be reacquired by the Company or a Subsidiary from the recipient of such Stock Incentive, or from the estate of such recipient, for any reason, such shares shall no longer be charged to the limitation provided for in paragraph (a) of this section 4 and may again be made subject to Stock Incentives.

(d) Of the total number of shares specified in paragraph (a) of this section 4 (subject to adjustment as specified herein), during the term of this Plan as defined in section 9, (i) no more than 10% may be subject to Options granted to any Key Person and (ii) no more than 15% may be subject to Stock Incentives granted to any Key Person.

5. *Stock Awards.* Except as otherwise provided in section 12, Stock Incentives in the form of Stock Awards shall be subject to the following provisions:

(a) For purposes of this Plan, all shares of Common Stock subject to a Stock Award shall be valued at not less than 100% of the Fair Market Value of such shares on the date such Stock Award is granted, regardless of whether or when such shares are issued pursuant to such Stock Award and whether or not such shares are subject to restrictions affecting their value.

(b) Shares of Common Stock subject to a Stock Award may be issued to a Key Person at the time the Stock Award is granted, or at any time subsequent thereto, or in installments from time to time. In the event that such issuance shall not be made at the time the Stock Award is granted, the Stock Award may provide for the payment to such Key Person, either in cash or shares of Common Stock, of amounts not exceeding the dividends that would have been payable to such Key Person in respect of the number of shares of Common Stock subject to such Stock Award (as adjusted under section 8) if such shares had been issued to such Key Person at the time such Stock Award was granted. Any Stock Award may state that the value of any shares of Common Stock subject to such Stock Award may be paid in cash, on each date on which shares would otherwise have been issued, in an amount equal to the Fair Market Value on such date of the shares that would otherwise have been issued.

(c) The material terms of such Stock Award shall be determined by the Committee. Each Stock Award shall be evidenced by a written instrument consistent with this Plan. It is intended that a Stock Award would be:

   (i) made contingent upon the attainment of one or more specified performance objectives, and/or

   (ii) subject to restrictions on the sale or other disposition of the Stock Award or the shares subject thereto for a period of three or more years, provided, however, that (x) a Stock Award may include restrictions and limitations in addition to those provided herein and (y) of the total number of shares specified in paragraph (a) of section 4 (subject to adjustment as specified therein), up to 3% may be subject to Stock Awards not subject to clause (i) or (ii) of this sentence.

(d) A Stock Award shall be granted for such lawful consideration as may be provided for therein.

6. *Options*. Except as otherwise provided in section 12, Stock Incentives in the form of Options shall be subject to the following provisions:

(a) The purchase price per share of Common Stock shall not be less than 100% of Fair Market Value of a share of Common Stock on the date the Option is granted. The purchase price and any withholding tax that may be due on the exercise of an Option may be paid in cash, or, if so provided in the Option Agreement:

    (i) in shares of Common Stock (including shares issued pursuant to the Option being exercised and shares issued pursuant to a Stock Award granted subject to restrictions as provided for in paragraph (c) of section 5), or

    (ii) in a combination of cash and such shares, provided, however, that no shares of Common Stock delivered in payment of the purchase price may be "immature shares" as determined in accordance with generally accepted accounting principles in effect at that time. Any shares of Common Stock delivered to the Company in payment of the purchase price or withholding tax shall be valued at their Fair Market Value on the date exercised. No certificate for shares of Common Stock shall be issued upon exercise of an Option until the purchase price for such shares has been paid in full.

(b) If so provided in the Option Agreement, the Company shall, upon request of the holder of the Option and at any time and from time to time, cancel all or a portion of the Option then subject to exercise and either:

    (i) pay the holder an amount of money equal to the excess, if any, of the Fair Market Value, at such time or times, of the shares subject to the portion of the option so canceled over the purchase price of such shares, or

    (ii) issue shares of Common Stock to the holder with a Fair Market Value, at such time or times, equal to such excess, or

    (iii) pay such excess by a combination of money and shares.

(c) Each Option may be exercised in full at the time of grant, or may become exercisable in one or more installments at such time or times or upon the occurrence of such events, as may be specified in the Option Agreement, as determined by the Committee. Unless otherwise provided in the Option Agreement, an Option, to the extent it is or becomes exercisable, may be exercised at any time in whole or in part until the expiration of such Option.

(d) Each Option shall be exercisable during the life of the holder only by him and, after his death, only by his estate or by a person who acquires the right to exercise the Option by will or the laws of descent and distribution. An Option, to the extent that it shall not have been exercised or canceled, shall terminate as follows after the holder ceases to serve:

(i) if the holder shall voluntarily cease to serve without the consent of the Committee or shall have his service terminated for cause, the Option shall terminate immediately upon cessation of service;

(ii) if the holder shall cease to serve by reason of death, incapacity or retirement under a retirement plan of the Company or a Subsidiary, the Option shall terminate three years after the date on which he ceased to serve;

(iii) except as provided in the next sentence, in all cases the Option shall terminate three months after the date on which the holder ceased to serve unless the Committee shall approve a longer period (which approval may be given before or after cessation of service) not to exceed three years. If the holder shall die or become incapacitated during the three-month period (or such longer period as the Committee may approve) referred to in the preceding clause (iii), the Option shall terminate three years after the date on which he ceased to serve. A leave of absence for military or governmental service or other purpose shall not, if approved by the Committee (which approval may be given before or after the leave of absence commences), be deemed a cessation of service within the meaning of this paragraph (d). Notwithstanding the foregoing provisions of this paragraph (d) or any other provision of the Plan, no Option shall be exercisable after expiration of a period of ten years and one month from the date the Option is granted. Where a Nonstatutory Option is granted for a term of less than ten years and one month, the Committee may, at any time prior to the expiration of the Option, extend its term for a period ending not later than ten years and one month from the date the Option was granted. Such extension shall not be deemed the grant of a new Option under this Plan.

(e) No Option nor any right thereunder may be assigned or transferred except by will or the laws of descent and distribution and except, in the case of a Nonstatutory Option, pursuant to a qualified domestic relations order (as defined in the Code), unless otherwise provided in the Option Agreement.

(f) An Option may, but need not, be an Incentive Stock Option. All shares of Common Stock that may be made subject to Stock Incentives under this Plan may be made subject to Incentive Stock Options, provided, however, that:

(i) no Incentive Stock Option may be granted more that ten years after the effective date of this Plan, as provided in section 9, and

(ii) the aggregate Fair Market Value (determined as of the time an Incentive Stock Option is granted) of the shares subject to each installment becoming exercisable for the first time in any calendar year under Incentive Stock Options granted on or after January 1, 1987 (under all plans, including this Plan, of his employer corporation and its parent and subsidiary corporations) to the Key Person to whom such Incentive Stock Option is granted shall not exceed $100,000.

(g) The material terms of each Option shall be determined by the Committee. Each Option shall be evidenced by a written instrument consistent with this Plan, and shall specify whether the Option is an Incentive Stock Option or a Nonstatutory Option. An Option may include restrictions and limitations in addition to those provided for in this Plan.

(h) Options shall be granted for such lawful consideration as may be provided for in the Option.

7. Combination Stock Awards and Options. Stock Incentives authorized by paragraph (c)(iii) of section 3 in the form of combinations of Stock Awards and Options shall be subject to the following provisions:

(a) A Stock Incentive may be a combination of any form of Stock Award and any form of Option, provided, however, that the terms and conditions of such Stock Incentive pertaining to a Stock Award are consistent with section 5 and the terms and conditions of such Stock Incentive pertaining to an option are consistent with section 6.

(b) Such combination Stock Incentive shall be subject to such other terms and conditions as may be specified therein, including without limitation a provision terminating in whole or in part a portion thereof upon the exercise in whole or in part of another portion thereof.

(c) The material terms of each combination Stock Incentive shall be determined by the Committee. Each combination Stock Incentive shall be evidenced by a written instrument consistent with this Plan.

8. *Adjustment Provision.*

(a) In the event that any reclassification, split-up or consolidation of the Common Stock shall be effected, or the outstanding shares of Common Stock are, in connection with a merger or consolidation of the Company or a sale by the Company of all or a part of its assets, exchanged for a different number or class of shares of stock or other securities or property of the Company or for shares of the stock or other securities or property of any other corporation or person, or a record date for determination of holders of Common Stock entitled to receive a dividend payable in Common Stock shall occur,

(i) the number, kind and class of shares or other securities or property that may be issued pursuant to Stock Incentives thereafter granted,

(ii) the number, kind or class of shares or other securities or property that have not been issued under outstanding Stock Incentives,

(iii) the purchase price to be paid per share or other unit under outstanding Stock Incentives, and

(iv) the price to be paid per share or other unit by the Company or a Subsidiary for shares or other securities or property issued pursuant to Stock Incentives that are subject to a right of the Company or to a Subsidiary to re-acquire such shares or other securities or property, shall in each case be equitably adjusted as determined by the Committee.

(b) In the event that there shall occur any spin-off or other distribution of assets of the Company to its shareholders (including without limitation an extraordinary dividend),

    (i) the number, kind and class of share or other securities or property that may be issued pursuant to Stock Incentives thereafter granted,

    (ii) the number, kind and class of share or other securities or property that have not been issued under outstanding Stock Incentives,

    (iii) the purchase price to be paid per share or other unit under outstanding Stock Incentives, and

    (iv) the price to be paid per share or other unit by the Company or a Subsidiary for shares or other securities or property issued pursuant to Stock Incentives that are subject to a right of the Company or a Subsidiary to re-acquire such shares or other securities or property, shall in each case be equitably adjusted as determined by the Committee.

9. *Term*. This Plan shall be deemed adopted and shall become effective on the dates on which it is approved by the W. R. Grace & Company, a New York corporation, as sole shareholder of the Company. No Stock Incentives shall be granted under this Plan after the tenth anniversary of such date.

10. *Administration*.

(a) This Plan shall be administered by the Committee. No director shall be designated as or continue to be a member of the Committee unless he shall at the time of designation and at all times during service as a member of the Committee be an "outside director" within the meaning of Section 162(m) of the Code. The Committee shall have full authority to act in the matter of selection of Key Persons and in granting Stock Incentives to them and such authority as is granted to the Committee by this Plan. Notwithstanding any other provision of this Plan, the Board of Directors may exercise any and all powers of the Committee with respect to this Plan, except to the extent that the possession or exercise of any power by the Board of Directors would cause any Stock Incentive to become subject to, or lose an exemption from Section 162(m) of the Code or Section 16(b) of the Exchange Act.

(b) The Committee may establish such rules and regulations, not inconsistent with the provisions of this Plan, as it deems necessary to determine eligibility to be granted Stock Incentives under this Plan and for the proper administration of this Plan, and may amend or revoke any rule or regulation so established. The Committee may make such determinations and interpretations under or in connection with this Plan as it deems necessary or advisable. All such rules, regulations, determinations and interpretations shall be binding and conclusive upon the Company, its Subsidiaries, its shareholders and its directors, officers and employees, and upon their respective legal representatives, beneficiaries, successors and assigns, and upon all other persons claiming under or through any of them.

(c) Members of the Board of Directors and members of the Committee acting under this Plan shall be fully protected in relying in good faith upon the advice of counsel and shall incur no liability in the performance of their duties, except as otherwise provided by applicable law.

11. *General Provisions.*

(a) Nothing in this Plan or in any instrument executed pursuant hereto shall confer upon any person any right to continue in the service of the Company or a Subsidiary, or shall affect the right of the Company or of a Subsidiary to terminate the service of any person with or without cause.

(b) No shares of Common Stock shall be issued pursuant to a Stock Incentive unless and until all legal requirements applicable to the issuance of such shares have, in the opinion of counsel to the Company, been complied with. In connection with any such issuance, the person acquiring the shares shall, if requested by the Company, give assurances, satisfactory to counsel to the Company, in respect of such matters as the Company or a Subsidiary may deem desirable to assure compliance with all applicable legal requirements.

(c) No person (individually or as a member of a group), and no beneficiary or other person claiming under or through him, shall have any right, title or interest in or to any shares of Common Stock allocated or reserved for the purposes of this Plan or subject to any Stock Incentive except as to such shares of Common Stock, if any, as shall have been issued to him.

(d) In the case of a grant of a Stock Incentive to a Key Person who is employed by a Subsidiary, such grant may provide for the issuance of the shares covered by the Stock Incentive to the Subsidiary, for such consideration as may be provided, upon condition or understanding that the Subsidiary will transfer the shares to the Key Person in accordance with the terms of the Stock Incentive.

(e) In the event the laws of a country in which the Company or a Subsidiary has employees prescribe certain requirements for Stock Incentives to qualify for advantageous tax treatment under the laws of that country (including, without limitation, laws establishing options analogous to Incentive Stock Options), the Committee, may, for the benefit of such employees, amend, in whole or in part, this Plan and may include in such amendment additional provisions for the purpose of qualifying the amended plan and of a Stock Incentive granted thereunder under such laws, provided, however, that:

(i) the terms and conditions of a Stock Incentive granted under such amended plan may not be more favorable to the recipient than would be permitted if such Stock Incentive had been granted under this Plan as herein set forth,

(ii) all shares allocated to or utilized for the purposes of such amended plan shall be subject to the limitations of section 4, and

(iii) the provisions of the amended plan may restrict but may not extend or amplify the provisions of sections 9 and 13.

(f) The Company or a Subsidiary may make such provisions as either may deem appropriate for the withholding of any taxes that the Company or a Subsidiary determines as required to be withheld in connection with any Stock Incentive.

(g) Nothing in this Plan is intended to be a substitute for, or shall preclude or limit the establishment or continuation of, any other plan, practice or arrangement for the payment of compensation or benefits to directors, officers or employees generally, or to any class or group of such persons, that the Company or any Subsidiary now has or may hereafter put into effect, including without limitation, any incentive compensation, retirement, pension, group insurance, stock purchase, stock bonus or stock option plan.

12. *Acquisitions*. If the Company or any Subsidiary should merge or consolidate with, or purchase stock or assets or otherwise acquire the whole or part of the business of, another entity, the Company, upon the approval of the Committee,

(a) may assume, in whole or in part and with or without modifications or conditions, any stock incentives granted by the acquired entity to its directors, officers, employees or consultants in their capacities as such, or

(b) may grant new Stock Incentives in substitution thereof. Any such assumed or substitute Stock Incentives may contain terms and conditions inconsistent with the provisions of this Plan (including the limitations set forth in paragraph (d) of section 4), including additional benefits for the recipient, provided, however, that if such assumed or substitute Stock Incentives are Incentive Stock Options, such terms and conditions are permitted under the plan of the acquired entity. For the purposes of any applicable plan provision involving time or a date, a substitute Stock Incentive shall be deemed granted as of the date of grant of the original Stock Incentive.

13. *Amendments and Terminations*.

(a) This Plan may be amended or terminated by the Board of Directors upon recommendation of the Committee, provided, however, that, without the approval of the stockholders of the Company, no amendment shall be made which:

(i) causes this Plan to cease to comply with applicable law,

(ii) permits any person who is not a Key Person to be granted a Stock Incentive (except as otherwise provided in section 12),

(iii) amends the provisions of paragraph (d) of section 4, paragraph (a) of section 5, or paragraph (a) or paragraph (f) of section 6 to permit shares to be valued at, or to have a purchase price of, respectively, less than the percentage of Fair Market Value specified therein,

(iv) amends section 9 to extend the date set forth therein, or

(v) amends this section 13.

(b) No amendment or termination of this Plan shall adversely affect any Stock Incentive theretofore granted, and no amendment of any Stock Incentive granted pursuant to this Plan shall adversely affect such Stock Incentive, without the consent of the holder thereof.

14. *Change in Control Provisions.*

(a) Notwithstanding any other provision of this Plan to the contrary, in the event of a Change of Control:

(i) Any Options outstanding as of the date on which such Change in Control occurs, and which are not then exercisable and vested, shall become fully exercisable and vested to the full extent of the original grant; and

(ii) All restrictions and deferral limitations applicable to Stock Incentives shall lapse, and Stock Incentives shall become free of all restrictions and become fully vested and transferable to the full extent of the original grant.

(b) Notwithstanding any other provision of this Plan, during the 60-day period from and after a Change of Control (the "Exercise Period"), unless the Committee shall determine otherwise at the time of grant, the holder of an Option shall have the right, in lieu of the payment of the purchase price for the share of Common Stock being purchased under the Option, by giving notice to the Company, to elect (within the Exercise Period) to surrender all or part of the Option to the Company and to receive cash, within 30 days after such notice, in an amount equal to the amount by which the Change in Control Price per share of Common Stock on the date of such election shall exceed the purchase price per share of Common Stock under the Option (the "Spread") multiplied by the number of shares of Common Stock subject to the Option as to which the right subject to this section 14(b) shall have been exercised.

(c) Notwithstanding any other provision of this Plan, if any right granted pursuant to this Plan to receive cash in respect of a

Stock Incentive would make a Change of Control transaction ineligible for pooling-of-interests accounting that, but for the nature of such grant, would otherwise be eligible for such accounting treatment, the Committee shall have the ability to substitute for such cash Common Stock with a Fair Market Value equal to the amount of such cash.

Appendix K

Apple Computer, Inc. Senior Officers Restricted Performance Share Plan

1. Purpose

This annual performance-based incentive plan (the "Performance Share Plan" or the "Plan") is designed to reward executive officers of Apple Computer, Inc. and its subsidiaries (the "Company") for achieving performance objectives. The Performance Share Plan is intended to provide an incentive for superior performance and to motivate participating officers toward even higher achievement and business results, to tie their goals and interests to those of the Corporation and its shareholders, to promote the maintenance of substantial stock ownership levels by officers of the Corporation, and to enable the Corporation to attract and retain highly qualified executive officers. The Performance Share Plan is also intended to secure the full deductibility of incentive compensation payable to the Corporation's Chief Executive Officer and the four highest compensated executive officers (collectively the "Covered Employees") whose compensation is required to be reported in the Corporation's proxy statement and all compensation payable hereunder to such persons is intended to qualify as "performance-based compensation" as described in Section 162(m)(4)(C) of the Internal Revenue Code of 1986, as amended (the "Code").

2. Eligibility and Participation

Only (i) those executive officers of the Corporation at the level of senior vice president or above and (ii) such other key employees of the Company as are recommended by management to and designated by the Compensation Committee shall be eligible to participate in the Performance Share Plan. Prior to or at the time performance objectives are established for a "Performance Period", as defined below, the Compensation Committee (the "Committee") of the Company's Board of Directors (the "Board") will designate in writing which executive officers and other key employees among those who may be eligible to participate in the Plan shall in fact be participants for such Performance Period (the "Participants"). The initial Participants in the Performance Share Plan shall be the individuals holding the positions identified in Appendix A.

3. Plan Year and Performance Objectives

(a) Plan Year: The fiscal year of the Performance Share Plan (the "Plan Year") shall be the fiscal year beginning on the first day of the Company's fiscal year and ending on the last day of the Company's fiscal year. The performance period (the "Performance Period") with respect to which awards may be payable under their Plan shall be the Plan Year. The initial Plan Year shall commence on September 30, 1996 and end on September 26, 1997.

(b) Performance Goal Setting Period: Within the first ninety (90) days of each Performance Period the Committee shall establish in writing, with respect to such Performance Period, one or more performance goals, a specific target objective or objectives with respect to such performance goals and an objective formula or method for computing the amount of performance shares payable to each Participant under the Plan if the performance goals are attained. Notwithstanding the foregoing sentence, for any Performance Period, such goals, objectives and compensation formulae or methods must be established within that number of days, beginning on the first day of such Performance Period, which is no more than twenty-five percent (25%) of the total number of days in such Performance Period.

(c) Performance Measurement: Performance goals shall be based upon one or more of the following business criteria for the Company:

- earnings per share
- share price
- revenue growth
- return on equity
- return on net assets
- timing objectives for delivery of new products
- retention of key employees

The Committee may adopt other performance goals in its sole and absolute discretion, provided, however, that in the event the Committee determines to adopt performance goals based on criteria other than those stated above, the Committee shall obtain shareholder approval of such criteria. All performance goals adopted by the Committee shall be preestablished, objective performance goals as described in Reg. Sec. 1.162-27(e)(2), promulgated under Section 162(m) of the Code. Measurements of the Company's or a Participant's performance against the performance goals established by the Committee shall be objectively determinable and, to the extent any performance goal is expressed in standard accounting terms, such performance goal shall be determined according to generally accepted accounting principles as in existence on the date on which the performance goals are established and without regard to any changes in such principles after such date.

4. Determination of Performance Share Awards

(a) Shares Covered by the Plan: Shares awarded under the Performance Share Plan shall be shares of the Company's common stock ("Shares"). The maximum number of Shares that may be awarded under the Plan shall be 2,000,000 in the aggregate and, in any single Plan Year, 300,000 to any one individual, subject to adjustment as provided in Section 6(k). Shares that are converted to cash in accordance with Section 5 shall be treated as shares awarded under the Plan for purposes of the aggregate and individual limits in the previous sentence. Any increase in the number of Shares allocated to the Plan must be approved by the Company's shareholders. Any Shares deliverable under the Plan may be made available from authorized but unissued Shares or Shares reacquired by the Company, including Shares purchased in the open market or in private transactions.

(b) Grants of Performance Shares: At the beginning of each Plan Year, each Participant will be granted the target number of Shares (see Appendix A) that can be earned based on performance with respect to that Plan Year (the "Conditional Grant"). At the time the Conditional Grant is made on behalf of a Participant, certificates representing the target number of Shares will be registered in the name of the Participant. During the Plan Year, the certificates representing those Shares will be held by the Company. The Committee may specify that the Conditional Grant for a Plan Year will be earned if the applicable target is achieved for one goal or for any one of a number of goals. The Committee may also provide that the Conditional Grant for a Plan Year will be earned only if targets are achieved for more than one performance goal. The Committee may also provide that the Conditional Grant to be earned for a given Plan Year will vary based upon different levels of achievement of the applicable performance targets.

As soon as practicable after the end of each Performance Period, the Committee shall certify in writing to what extent the Company and the Participants have achieved the performance goal or goals for such Performance Period, including the specific target objective or objectives and the satisfaction of any other material terms of the Performance Share Award and the Committee shall calculate the amount of each Participant's actual award for such Performance Period based upon the performance goals, objectives and computation formulae or methods for such Performance Period (the "Actual Grant"). The Committee shall have no discretion to increase the maximum amount of any Participant's Actual Grant as so determined, but may reduce the amount of or totally eliminate such award, as it determines, in its absolute and sole discretion, in an amount appropriate to reflect the Participant's performance.

No Participant's Actual Grant for any Plan Year shall exceed the number of Shares stated in Appendix A.

Only after the Actual Grant has been awarded to a Participant will he or she have the rights of a shareholder in the Company with respect to any of the Shares covered by the Conditional Grant, including the right to vote the Shares and the right to receive any distributions with respect to such Shares.

5. Payment of Awards

Approved Performance Share Awards shall be payable by the Company to each Participant in Shares, or, at the election of the Participant, fifty percent (50%) in Shares and fifty percent (50%) in cash ("Cash Election"), as soon as reasonably practicable after the last day of the relevant Performance Period (the "vesting date"), provided that the Committee has first certified in writing that the relevant performance goals were achieved. In the event that a Participant makes a Cash Election, the amount of cash to be awarded shall be determined by the Committee as of each vesting date, such that (subject to the performance goals for that Performance Period being fully satisfied), the Participant receives fifty percent of the total value of the Shares earned as of the vesting date in cash and the remainder in Shares, based on the closing price of the Company's common stock on the vesting date. Cash Elections for any Performance Period shall be made on a form provided for the purpose by the Committee within sixty (60) days of the date an employee is notified by the Committee that he or she has been designated as a Participant in the Plan for that Performance Period. Except in the case of an Actual Grant made to a Participant's Beneficiary (as hereinafter defined), a participant is precluded from selling or otherwise disposing of any interest in Actual Grant Shares until such time as the Shares are distributed to the participant.

If a Participant ceases to be employed by the Company prior to the end of any Plan Year, award payment rights will be determined as follows:

A. Involuntary termination by the Company for cause or voluntary termination by a Participant would lead to a Participant's forfeiture of all Performance Share Plan awards for that Plan Year. Termination for cause is defined as follows: conviction of (i) a felony, (ii) embezzlement from the Company or (iii) other business fraud.

B. Termination on account of death, disability, or involuntary termination not for cause by the Company entitles a Participant, or the Participant's Beneficiary, to a prorated share of the Performance Share Award. Prorated awards are determined based on the number of completed months that the Participant was employed in the Plan Year divided by 12 months and are subject to reduction as provided in Section 4(b). Prorated awards shall be paid at the same time as if the Participant had remained employed until the end of the Plan Year.

6. Other Terms and Conditions

(a) Term of Plan: The Performance Share Plan shall become effective upon its adoption by the Board, subject to the subsequent approval thereof by the shareholders of the Company in accordance with Section 6(b). It shall continue in effect for a term of five (5) years unless sooner terminated under Section 7 of the Plan.

(b) Shareholder Approval: No Actual Grants shall be awarded under the Performance Share Plan unless and until the material terms (within the meaning of Section 162(m)(4)(C) of the Code) of the Plan, including the business criteria described in the Plan, are disclosed to the Company's shareholders and are approved by the shareholders by a majority of votes cast in person or by proxy (including abstentions to the extent abstentions are counted as voting under applicable state law).

(c) No Participation Rights: No person shall have any legal claim to be granted an award under the Performance Share Plan and the Committee shall have no obligation to treat Participants uniformly. Participation in the Performance Share Plan in any Plan Year does not entitle any Participant to participate in the Plan in any other Plan Year. The right to receive a targeted number of performance shares in any given year does not entitle a Participant to participate with respect to the same number of Shares in any subsequent year.

(d) No Rights to Specific Property: Except as may be otherwise required by law, Conditional Grants and Actual Grants under the Performance Share Plan shall not be subject in any manner to anticipation, alienation, sale,. transfer, assignment, pledge, encumbrance, charge, garnishment, execution, or levy of any kind, either voluntary or involuntary. No Participant shall have any claim with respect to any specific assets of the Company or to stock certificates registered in the Participant's name prior to the vesting of the shares represented by such certificates.

(e) No Employment Rights: Neither the Performance Share Plan nor any action taken under the Plan shall confer upon any Participant any right with respect to continuation of employment by the Company (or any subsidiary or affiliated company) or to maintain any Participant's compensation at any level, nor shall it interfere in any way with any Participant's right or the right of the Company (or any subsidiary or affiliated company) to terminate a Participant's employment at any time or for any reason.

(f) Other Benefits: Performance Share Awards shall not be considered as part of a Participant's salary or used for the calculation of any other pay, allowance, pension or other benefit unless otherwise permitted by other benefit plans provided by the Company or its subsidiaries, or required by law or by contractual obligations of the Company or its subsidiaries.

(g) Beneficiary: The term "Beneficiary" shall mean the person or persons designated by a Participant to whom Performance Share Awards are to be paid pursuant to the terms of the Performance Share Plan in the event of the Participant's death. The designation shall be on a form provided by the Committee, executed by the Participant, and delivered to the Committee. A Participant may change his or her Beneficiary designation at any time. If no Beneficiary is designated, the designation is ineffective, or in the event the Beneficiary dies before the balance of the Performance Share Award is paid, the balance shall be paid to the Participant's spouse, or if there is no spouse, in equal shares to the Participant's lineal descendants, or if there is no surviving spouse or lineal descendant, to the Participant's estate.

(h) Permanent Disability: For purposes of the Performance Share Plan, a permanent disability shall mean a disability which would qualify a Participant to receive benefits under the Apple Computer, Inc. Long-Term Disability Plan (after satisfying the elimination period thereunder) as now or hereafter in effect.

(i) Incapacity of Participant or Beneficiary: If the Committee finds that any Participant or Beneficiary to whom a Performance Share Award is payable under the Performance Share Plan is unable to care for his or her affairs because of illness or accident or is under a legal disability, any Performance Share Award due (unless a prior claim therefore shall have been made by a duly appointed legal representative) at the discretion of the Committee, may be paid to the spouse, child, parent or brother or sister of such Participant or Beneficiary or to any person whom the Committee has determined has incurred expense for such Participant or Beneficiary. Any such payment shall be a complete discharge of the obligations of the Company under provisions of the Performance Share Plan to the extent of such payment.

(j) **Tax Withholding:** The Company will withhold from each Actual Grant at the time of payment thereof all applicable state, local and federal withholding taxes, as required by law, as determined by Apple in its sole discretion. Such withholding will be made first from the amount of the Participant's Cash Election, if any, and second from the Participant's Shares, to the extent required. Alternatively, in lieu of withholding from Shares, the Participant may elect to fund the payment of withholding taxes determined by Apple to be due by making payment of the full amount of the withholding taxes to Apple on or before the due date of the withholding taxes.

(k) **Adjustments Due to Changes in Capitalization:** If the outstanding Shares are increased, decreased, or exchanged for a different number of kind of shares or other securities, or if additional Shares or other securities are distributed with respect to such Shares or other securities, through merger, consolidation, sale of all or substantially all of the property of the Company, reorganization, recapitalization, reclassification, stock dividend, stock split, reverse stock split or other distribution with respect to such Shares or other securities, an appropriate and proportionate adjustment may be made in (i) the maximum number and kind of Shares provided for in Section 4(a) of the Plan, (ii) the annual individual maximum grant limit provided for in Section 4(a), (iii) the number and kind of Shares subject to each then outstanding Performance Share Award, and (iv) each Participant's target number of Shares as provided in Appendix A.

Adjustments under this Section 6(k) will be made by the Committee, whose determination as to what adjustments will be made and the extent thereof will be final, binding and conclusive on all interested persons. No fractional Share or other interest will be issued under the Plan on account of any of such adjustments

(l) **Change in Control:** In the event of a change in control (as defined below) of the Company, the Committee shall make equitable adjustments to the Participant's Performance Shares in a manner intended to preserve their economic value as of the date of the change in control, including modifications to performance measures and performance goals if necessary; provided, however, that if a Participant's employment with the Company is terminated without cause in connection with a change in control, then any other provision of the Plan to the contrary notwithstanding, the Participant shall be entitled to receive the maximum annual number of Performance Shares for the year in which the change-in-control occurs following such termination regardless of whether the Performance Goals are achieved. For purposes of this Plan, change in control is defined as follows:

A. When any "person", as such term is used in Section 13(d) and 14(d) of the Exchange Act (other than the Company, a Subsidiary or a Company employee benefit plan, including any trustee of such plan acting as a trustee) is or becomes the "beneficial owner" (as defined in Rule 13d-3 under the Exchange Act), directly or indirectly, of securities of the Company representing fifty percent (50%) or more of the combined voting power of the Company's then outstanding securities; or

B. The occurrence of a transaction requiring shareholder approval and involving either the sale of all or substantially all of the assets of the Company or the merger of the Company with or into another entity.

(m) Conditions Upon Issuance of Shares: Shares shall not be issued with respect to an Award unless the issuance and delivery of such Shares pursuant thereto shall comply with all relevant provisions of law, including, without limitation, the Securities Act of 1933, as amended, the Exchange Act, the rules and regulations promulgated thereunder, and the requirements of any stock exchange or quotation system upon which the Shares may then be listed or quoted, and shall be further subject to the approval of counsel for the Company with respect to such compliance.

Inability of the Company to obtain authority from any regulatory body having jurisdiction, which authority is deemed by the Company's counsel to be necessary to the lawful issuance of any Shares hereunder, shall relieve the Company of any liability in respect of the non-issuance of such Shares as to which such requisite authority shall not have been obtained.

(n) Governing Law: The place of administration of the Performance Share Plan shall be in the State of California and the validity, construction, interpretation, administration and effect of the Performance Share Plan and the rules, regulations and rights relating to the Performance Share Plan, shall be determined solely in accordance with the laws of the State of California.

7. Administration

(a) Administrator: The Plan shall be administered by a Committee designated by the Board to administer the Plan, which Committee shall be constituted in such a manner as to permit the Plan and grants and awards thereunder to comply with Rule 16b-3 as it applies to grants to officers and in such a manner as to satisfy the Applicable Laws. All members of the Committee shall be persons who qualify as "outside directors" as defined under Section 162(m) of the Code. Until changed by the Board, the Compensation Committee of the Board shall constitute the Committee hereunder.

(b) Powers of the Administrator: The Committee shall have full power, authority and discretion to administer and interpret the provisions of the Performance Share Plan and to adopt such rules, regulations, agreements, guidelines and instruments for the administration of the Plan and for the conduct of its business as the Committee deems necessary or advisable. Without limitation of the foregoing, subject to the provisions of the Plan and such limitations as are necessary or desirable in order for incentive awards paid to Covered Employees to constitute qualified performance-based compensation under Section 162(m) of the Code, the Committee shall have the authority, in its discretion: (i) to determine the amount of cash to be awarded pursuant to any Cash Election under Section 5 above; (ii) to determine the employees who shall be Participants in the Plan; (iii) to interpret the Plan; (iv) to determine the terms and conditions, not inconsistent with the terms of the Plan, of any Conditional Grant or Actual Grant awarded hereunder (including, but not limited to, any restriction or limitation, or any waiver of forfeiture restrictions regarding any Grant and/or the Shares relating thereto, based in each case on such factors as the Administrator shall determine, in its sole discretion); (v) to approve forms of agreement for use under the Plan; (vi) to prescribe, amend and rescind rules and regulations relating to the Plan; (vii) to modify or amend each Grant (with the consent of the Participant); (viii) to authorize any person to execute on behalf of the Company any instrument required to effectuate any Grant previously granted by the Administrator; and (ix) to make all other determinations deemed necessary or advisable for the administration of the Plan.

(c) Effect of Decisions by the Administrator: All decisions, determinations and interpretations of the Administrator shall be final and binding on all Participants.

8. Amendment and Termination

The Board may at any time amend, alter, suspend or terminate the Plan, as it may deem advisable; provided that except as otherwise required by law, any amendment required to conform the Performance Share Plan to the requirements of Section 162(m) of the Code or to conform the Performance Share Plan or any grant made thereunder to the requirements for exemption under Rule 16b-3 promulgated under the Securities Exchange Act of 1934, as amended, or any successor thereto ("Rule 16b-3"), shall be made by the Committee, and provided that, to the extent necessary and desirable to comply with Section 162(m) of the Code (or any other applicable law, regulations or rules), the Company shall obtain shareholder approval of any Plan amendment in such a manner and to such a degree as is required, including, without limitation, any amendment to the class of individuals who are eligible to participate in the Performance Share Plan, to the performance criteria specified in Section 2 hereof or to the maximum incentive award payable to any Participant, unless shareholder approval is not required in order for incentive awards paid to Covered Employees to constitute qualified performance-based compensation under Section 162(m) of the Code. Any such amendment, alteration, suspension or termination of the Plan shall not impair the rights of any Plan Participant under any grant theretofore made without his or her consent. Such grants shall remain in full force and effect as if this Plan had not been amended or terminated, except as may otherwise be required by applicable law.

Appendix A

Position	Maximum Total Award of Performance Shares	Annual Maximum Performance Share Awards
Chief Executive Officer	1,000,000	200,000
Chief Operating Officer	100,000	20,000
Chief Financial Officer	100,000	16,000
Chief Technology Officer	80,000	16,000
Chief Administrative Officer	80,000	16,000

Appendix L

Code Section 162(m): Recent IRS Rulings

For tax years commencing on or after January 1, 1994, a publicly held corporation will be denied a deduction for any compensation over $1 million paid to a CEO or any other officer whose compensation must be reported under SEC proxy disclosure rules. Following are brief summaries of selected recent IRS letter rulings under Code Section 162(m).

Letter Ruling 9924007

A Company's plan permits directors and officers to defer a defined minimum percentage of total annual compensation, including performance-based compensation, earned each year. At the end of a deferral period, a participant is entitled to receive shares of Company common stock equal to the number of units then credited to his or her deferred compensation account. The Company wished to amend the plan to allow the Company to enter into participant agreements that would allow for the purchase of future shares of stock directly from the participant and would entitle the participant to cash payment in exchange for the stock equal to the average trading price of the stock during the term of the agreement. The IRS ruled that any performance-based income payable under the deferred compensation accounts will not fail to satisfy Code Section 162(m) as a result of the proposed amendment.

Letter Ruling 9921032

A Company has co-CEOs and questions the method for determining which employees are "covered employees" under Code Section 162(m). The IRS ruled (1) whichever co-CEO is more highly compensated will be a "covered employee" and (2) the other co-CEO will be a "covered employee" if that co-CEO's compensation makes him or her among the four highest compensated officers other than the CEO designated in (1).

Letter Ruling 9910011

Company is a publicly held corporation with a calendar year as the taxable year. Several of the Company's officers who are "covered employees" for purposes of Code Section 162(m) will resign their officer positions midyear. Such individuals will continue to be employed by Company for the remainder of the year (and possibly future years). The regulations under Code Section 162(m) provide that a person must be employed as an officer on the last day of the taxable year in order to be a "covered employee." The IRS ruled that officers of the Company who resign their position as officers prior to the last day of the tax year without the intent to resume their duties as officers in the future will not be considered "covered employees" for that year for purposes of Code Section 162(m).

Letter Ruling 9811029

Company maintains a stock option plan. The compensation committee of the Board of Directors consists of at least two "outside" directors and other directors who are not "outside" directors. The IRS ruled that for purposes of meeting the "performance-based compensation" exception to the Code Section 162(m) $1 million cap on compensation deductions, such a committee satisfies the compensation committee requirements as long as the directors who do not qualify as outside directors abstain or recuse themselves with respect to administration of the plan.

Letter Ruling 9801043

Company A merged with and into Company B. Company B is the surviving corporation. Prior to the merger, Company A maintained a performance (primarily stock-based) award plan. The plan was approved by Company A's shareholders prior to the merger. The merger agreement was approved by shareholders of Company A and shareholders of Company B. Company B's Board of Directors approved amendments to the Plan to reflect certain adjustments as a result of the merger: (1) a company name change, (2) plan references to company stock of Company B, and (3) the number of shares reserved for issuance under the plan and the number of shares subject to options or stock appreciation rights (SARs) were adjusted by the merger consideration multiplication factor. The regulations do not require a plan such as this to be resubmitted to the shareholders of the surviving corporation after the merger. Treasury Regulations Section 1.162-27(e)(4)(vi) provides that once the material terms of a performance goal are disclosed to and approved by shareholders, no additional approval is required unless material terms of the performance goal are changed. If a compensation committee can change target goals under the plan after shareholder approval for the plan is received, material terms of the performance goal are subject to disclosure to and reapproval by shareholders no later than the first shareholder meeting that occurs in the fifth year following the year of the previous shareholder approval. The IRS ruled that this plan will continue to meet the "performance-based compensation" exception under Code Section 162(m) based on the approval of the plan by the shareholders of Company A prior to the merger. Additional approval by the shareholders of Company B, the surviving corporation, is not required.

Appendix M

Code Section 280G: Cases and IRS Rulings

Selected IRS rulings and court cases under the golden parachute rules of Code Section 280G are summarized briefly here.

Letter Rulings 9920009, 9915021

If, following a merger, the acquiring shareholders do not act in concert to control target company's management, the merger does not constitute a change of control for purposes of Code Section 280G.

Letter Ruling 9905012

A merger of two companies results in the acquisition by the target's shareholders of more than 50 percent of the stock of the acquiring corporation, which is the surviving corporation. A change of control occurs with respect to the acquiring corporation; however, a change in control under Code Section 280G does not occur with respect to the target corporation as long as the acquiring corporation's shareholders do not act in concert to control the target.

Letter Ruling 9822029

The value of restricted stock awards granted during the "base period" and included in the employee's income pursuant to a Code

Section 83(b) election is included when determining the employee's "base amount" for purposes of parachute calculations under Code Section 280G.

Letter Ruling 9610022

A transfer of assets is a change of ownership for Code Section 280G purposes if shareholders of one of the merging companies own, following the merger, a 50 percent or less interest in the surviving corporation.

Sullivan v. Easco Corporation (662 F Supp 1396 (D Md 1987))

An executive's employment agreement was entered into in contemplation of a takeover attempt; however, the court ruled that the compensation payable thereunder was not "contingent on a change in ownership" because such payments were irrevocable regardless of the occurrence of a change of control.

Worth v. Huntington Bancshares, Incorporated (43 Ohio St 3d 192, 540 NE2d 249 (1989))

Employment contract provided that benefits were payable upon a change of control if, in the employee's determination, his or her status or responsibilities have diminished. The court ruled that golden parachute agreements are not void as against public policy and the court should consider the employee's subjective reasoning and the surrounding facts and circumstances.

Cline v. Commissioner (34 F3d 480 (7th Cir 1994))

A post-acquisition bonus payment was found to be a parachute payment where the executive's severance agreement was amended to reduce payments thereunder to avoid the application of the Code Section 280G excise tax, but after the takeover, the acquiring company paid the executive a termination bonus equal to the difference between his or her amended severance agreement payments and higher severance amounts payable under the original severance agreement.

Appendix N

Sample Deferred Compensation Plan for Non-Profit Organization

A sample Code Section 457(f) ineligible deferred compensation plan is provided here for your information. This sample plan is drafted to include the concept of a "substantial risk of forfeiture" and a "rolling" vesting concept.

[Name of Organization]

Deferred Compensation Program

This Deferred Compensation Program (the "Program") is hereby established this _____ day of _____, 19__, by [Name of Organization] (the "Employer") to reward the continued service of the Employer's key employees.

1. Effective Date.

The Program shall become effective as of January 1, 19__.

2. Eligible Employees.

The Executive Committee of the Board of Directors of the Employer (the "Committee") shall be entitled to designate the employees of the Employer that shall be eligible to participate in the Program from time to time. It is intended that the Program shall constitute an unfunded arrangement maintained for the purposes of providing deferred compensation for a select group of management or highly compensated employees of the Employer. The names of the eligible employees shall be set forth in Exhibit A to the Program, which may be revised from time to time to reflect the additions or deletions of individuals from the class of eligible employees and to reflect any action taken pursuant to Section 6 below. Exhibit A, as revised from time to time, shall be attached hereto and constitute a part of the Program.

3. Deferral of Bonus.

Each Eligible Employee shall be entitled to elect to forego all or any portion, as either a dollar amount or a percentage, of the bonus that may become payable to the Eligible Employee from the Employer for a calendar year. Any such election shall be made prior to the commencement of the calendar year for which the bonus may become payable and shall be evidenced by a written agreement between the Eligible Employee and the Employer in a form acceptable to the Employer. Any such election shall be irrevocable and shall apply to the actual bonus that becomes payable to the Eligible Employee for the calendar year. To the extent an Eligible Employee elects to defer a dollar amount of the bonus that may become payable for a calendar year and this amount exceeds the amount of the actual bonus that becomes payable to the Eligible Employee for such calendar year, the election shall be deemed to cover 100% of the actual bonus amount that becomes payable to the Eligible Employee for such calendar year.

4. Accounts.

(a) A bookkeeping account (the "Account") shall be established and maintained on behalf of each Eligible Employee that has made an election pursuant to Section 3 above. Such Account shall be credited with an amount equal to the bonus amount deferred by the Eligible Employee pursuant to Section 3 above for any given calendar year.

(b) As of the last day of each Plan Year, the amount credited to each Eligible Employee's Account as of the last day of the prior Plan Year shall be increased to reflect deemed interest calculated using the 3-Year Treasury Bill rate that is published for the month of December for the current Plan Year, credited from the last day of the preceding Plan Year.

5. Vesting.

The right of an Eligible Employee to receive payment of an amount equal to the balance of an Account maintained on behalf of the Eligible Employee pursuant to Section 4 above shall be conditioned upon the Eligible Employee being employed by the Employer on the earlier to occur of the following dates:

(a) The date specified on Exhibit A hereto with respect to such Eligible Employee's Account; or

(b) The date on which the Eligible Employee dies or incurs an illness or injury that completely prevents the Eligible Employee from performing his or her occupation, as determined by the Committee in its sole discretion.

The Eligible Employee shall have no right to receive payment of an amount equal to the balance of, or have any other rights with respect to, his or her Account until such date. If, for any reason, the Eligible Employee is not employed by the Employer on such date, the Eligible Employee shall forfeit all rights under the Program to receive payment of an amount equal to the balance of his or her Account and the balance of such Account shall be reduced to zero.

6. Rolling Vesting.

No later than the December 31 which is three (3) years prior to the date specified in Exhibit A pursuant to Section 5(a) hereto with respect to an Account, the Eligible Employee and the Employer may agree to postpone the date specified in Exhibit A pursuant to Section 5(a) with respect to such Account. Exhibit A shall be amended to reflect this new date, which shall be treated as the date specified in Section 5(a) with respect to such Account for all purposes hereunder unless and until such date is further postponed in accordance with this Section 6.

7. Distributions.

(a) An Eligible Employee shall receive payment of an amount equal to the balance of his or her Account maintained on the Eligible Employee's behalf pursuant to Section 4, reduced as necessary pursuant to Section 11 below, in a lump sum as soon as administratively practicable following the date specified in Exhibit A pursuant to Section 5(a) with respect to such Account.

(b) Notwithstanding the foregoing, an amount equal to the balance of the Eligible Employee's Account that has not previously been paid to such Eligible Employee, reduced as necessary pursuant to Section 11 below, shall be paid to the Eligible Employee's designated beneficiary in a lump sum as soon as administratively practicable following the date specified in Section 5(b). The Eligible Employee shall be entitled to designate a beneficiary for this purpose on a form provided by the Committee for this purpose. If no beneficiary has been designated by an Eligible Employee prior to the date on which the balance of his or her Account becomes distributable pursuant to this Section 7, the balance of the Eligible Employee's Account shall be paid to the Eligible Employee's estate.

8. Administration.

The Committee shall determine the rights of any individual hereunder and shall otherwise administer the Program in its sole discretion. Any decision or action of the Committee hereunder shall be final and binding on all parties.

9. Successors.

The Program shall be binding upon any successor (whether direct or indirect, by purchase, merger, consolidation or otherwise) to all or substantially all of the business and/or assets of the Employer, and the Employer shall require any such successor to expressly assume and agree to perform this Program. As used in this Program, "Employer" shall mean the Employer as defined herein and any successor to its business and/or assets.

10. No Rights to Continued Employment.

The Program shall not be construed to give an Eligible Employee a right of continued employment with, or the right to be retained in the employ of, the Employer.

11. Taxes.

To the extent required by law, the Employer shall withhold any federal, state or local taxes from payments made under the Program, including FICA and FUTA taxes.

12. Amendment and Termination.

The Employer shall be entitled to amend or discontinue this Program at any time; provided, however, that any such amendment or discontinuance does not adversely effect an Eligible Employee's rights with respect to any Accounts with outstanding balances hereunder. In the event that the Program is discontinued, the Program shall continue to apply to any Accounts with outstanding balances hereunder.

13. Miscellaneous.

(a) All payments shall be paid in cash from the general assets of the Employer such that the Program shall constitute an unfunded arrangement for purposes of the Employee Retirement Security Act of 1974, as amended. An Eligible Employee who has made an election pursuant to Section 3 hereof shall have no right, title or interest whatsoever in or to any investments which the Employer may make to aid it in meeting its obligations hereunder. To the extent that any person acquires a right to receive payments from the Employer, such right shall be no greater than the right of an unsecured creditor.

(b) The benefits provided for Eligible Employees hereunder are in addition to benefits provided by any other plan or program of the Employer and shall supplement and not supersede any other plan, program or arrangement between the Employer and any Eligible Employee.

(c) No Eligible Employee or his or her beneficiary or heir shall have any right to commute, sell, transfer, assign or otherwise convey the right to receive any payment under the terms of this Program. Any such attempted assignment shall be considered null and void. The interest of any such person in receiving a payment hereunder shall not be subject to anticipation, nor to voluntary or involuntary alienation, until such payment is actually made.

(d) If any provision of this Program shall be determined to be void by any court of competent jurisdiction, then such determination shall not affect any other provision of the Program, all of which shall remain in full force and effect.

(e) The Program shall be construed and enforced in accordance with the laws of the State of _____.

(f) All headings herein have been inserted solely for reference and shall not constitute a part of this Program nor affect its meaning, construction or effect.

(g) Where appropriate, words in the masculine gender herein shall include the feminine gender.

IN WITNESS WHEREOF, the Employer has executed the Program this _____ day of _____, 19__.

[Name of Organization]

By: _____

Title: _____

Index

[References are to question numbers.]

A

Accounting considerations

accounting statements containing compensation expenses, 1:44

annual incentives, 4:8

APB 25, 1:45–1:48, 1:54

book value appreciation rights, 7:14

book value purchase plans, 6:43

combination performance share/stock option plans, 8:7

compensation forms, 1:43

convertible debentures, 6:50

EPS calculations, 1:52, 1:53

executive perquisites, 10:22

fair value calculation models, 1:50

FAS 123, 1:45–1:49, 1:51, 20:17

fundamental issues, 1:43–1:52

ISOs, 6:9

long-term incentive plans, 5:25

nonstatutory stock options, 6:16

option reloads, 6:38

performance-based stock options, 6:64

performance share plans, 7:48

performance unit plans, 7:41

phantom stock plans, 7:23

premium stock options, 6:33

restricted stock grants, 7:32

restricted stock/stock option plan combination, 8:14

SARs, 7:7

SAR/stock option plans, 8:22

stock awards, 1:45

stock options, FAS 123, 20:17

Accumulation. *See* Capital

Acquisition. *See* Restructuring

Administration of plan. *See* Plan administration

Alternative minimum tax

defined, 1:42

ISO, 6:8, 20:20

Amendment

long-term incentive plan, 5:58

Annual incentives

accounting treatment, 4:8

appropriateness, 1:20

approving annual payments, 23:18

award levels, corporate restructuring, 23:14

as base salary percentage, 22:5

bonus levels, 20:4, 20:5

changing practices, 20:6, 20:7

characteristics of appropriate organizations, 1:21

defined, 4:1

[References are to question numbers.]

Annual incentives (*cont'd*)
  division executives, 21:3–21:5, 21:13
  economic profit plan use with, 19:9
  eligibility, 4:4
  establishing, small company, 12:2
  for expatriates, 16:23
  funding incentive plans, 4:57–4:65
  general considerations, 4:1–4:9
  vs. long-term incentives, 1:23, 1:29
  market competition, 3:9
  meeting needs of executives and company, 1:3
  nonprofit organization, 14:9–14:13
  payment forms, 4:5
  pensionable, 4:6
  performance maximums, 4:54
  performance measures, 4:35–4:48
  performance standards, 4:49–4:56
  plan design, 4:10–4:34, 12:10, 22:6
  prevalence, 4:2
  public sector, 17:8
  rationale, 4:3
  restructured companies
    achieving equity despite different business unit goals, 23:16
    approving payments, 23:18
    award levels, 23:14
    performance target plan for one unit and discretionary plan for another, 23:17
  shareholder approval, 4:9
  short-term vs. long-term performance, 1:22
  size of company, 22:3
  tax impact, 4:7
Annual salary increase. *See* Salary increases
APB 25. *See* Accounting considerations
Appreciation plans
  book value appreciation rights, 7:13–7:17

  defined, 7:1
  examples, 7:2
  generally, 7:1, 7:2
  stock appreciation rights, 7:3–7:12
Appreciation right. *See* Stock
Approval
  total compensation strategy, 11:24
Assets. *See also* Return on assets
  sample employment agreement, Appendix D
Award
  annual incentive, 23:14
  economic profit, 19:12
  long-term incentive, 20:8, 23:21, 23:23
  plan design, 5:29
    salary multiple approach, 5:30
    targeted income approach, 5:31
  performance plan
    tax effect, 5:45
  performance unit plans, 7:43
  size
    annual incentive plans, 4:57
    nonprofit organization annual incentive, 14:10
  stock
    accounting, 1:45
    outside directors, 20:26
    public sector, 17:9
    temporary executives, 18:12

B

Banding. *See* Salary banding; other increases
Base salary
  above average, 3:10
  annual incentives as percentage of, 22:5
  change in mix with annual incentives, 20:7
  classifications, following a restructuring, 23:9
  establishing, 3:1, 3:2

[References are to question numbers.]

determining total compensation
mix, 1:18
division executives, 21:2
fundamental issues, 1:16–1:18
geographic location, 1:16
job evaluation, 3:3–3:10
large company considerations, 22:2
market competition, 3:9
merit increase, nonprofit
organization, 14:8
needs of executives vs. those of
company, 1:2
new venture businesses, 12:13
vs. other total compensation
elements, 1:17
public companies, 17:2
range
alternatives to, 3:13
nonprofit organization, 14:7
salary banding; other increases,
3:13–3:16
salary increases, 3:11, 3:12
small company considerations,
12:5, 22:2
temporary executives, 18:10
trends
large companies, 20:1
$1 million deduction cap and,
20:3
small companies, 20:2
Benefits. *See also* Excess benefit
plans; Executive benefit plans
corporate restructuring and
change in benefits and
perquisites during, 23:24
change in eligibility during, 23:25
costs, total compensation strategy
statement, 11:12
insured, temporary executives, 18:14
new venture businesses, 12:13
programs, total compensation
strategy statement, 11:11
retirement
temporary executives, 18:15

total compensation strategy
statement, 11:13
satisfying executive needs, 1:4
small versus large companies, 22:14
Black-Scholes option pricing model,
1:45, 1:47, 1:49, 1:50, 5:26
Board of directors compensation
choosing board members, 13:1
compensation methods, 13:7–13:13
deferred compensation, 13:8
general considerations, 13:1, 13:2
Keogh plans, 13:16, 13:17
other benefits, 13:14–13:19
outside vs. inside directors,
13:3–13:6
performance-based plans, 13:9
perquisites, 13:19
retirement benefits, 13:15
role, 13:2
stock options, 13:10–13:13
taxation of income, 13:7
Bonus
annual levels, trends in
large companies, 20:4
small companies, 20:5
completion, 16:19
plans, long-term, for expatriates,
16:22
small company considerations, 12:5
trends in bonus levels
large companies, 20:4
small companies, 20:5
Book value appreciation rights
accounting impact, 7:14
advantages, 7:16
defined, 7:13
disadvantages, 7:17
tax treatment, 7:15
Book value purchase plans
accounting impact, 6:43
advantages, 6:45
appropriate companies, 6:47
defined, 6:42
disadvantages, 6:46
tax treatment, 6:44

[References are to question numbers.]

Building a total compensation strategy. *See* Total compensation

Business plan
total compensation strategy, 11:7

Business unit. *See also* Division
executives
affecting total compensation
strategies, 11:16
restructured company
compensation levels, 23:6, 23:7
long-term incentive plans, 23:20
short-term incentive plans, 23:13, 23:16
use of economic profit in, 19:8

Buy-back agreement
conditions typically included, 2:9

C

Capital. *See also* Return on capital
accumulation
plans, total compensation
strategy statement, 11:15
stock-based, 2:6
costs
determining, 21:12
executive's influence on, 19:7
and executive's influence on
economic profit, 19:6, 19:11
gains
avoiding, expatriates, 16:17
defined, 1:37
rationale for favorable treatment, 1:38
tax decrease, 20:19, 20:20

Car programs. *See* Perquisites and other benefits

Cash compensation. *See* Total compensation

Cashless exercise
cashless option exercise defined, 5:51
vs. SAR, 7:6

Cellular phone. *See* Perquisites and other benefits

Checklist
executive expatriate compensation
program, 16:32

Classification system, 3:5

Closely held company
defined, 2:3
privately held company as, 2:4

Club membership. *See* Perquisites and other benefits

Code Section 83
election, 5:48, 7:34
substantial vesting of stock, 5:41
tax property transfer, 9:25

Code Section 162(m)
limitations issued by IRS in 1996, 1:34
company response to pay caps, 1:34
recent IRS rulings, Appendix L

Code Section 280G
recent cases and IRS rulings, Appendix M

Code Section 457
nonqualified deferred compensation
plan, 9:16
tax consequences, 9:26

COLI
vs. retail life insurance contracts, 9:35

Combination long-term plans. *See* Long-term incentive plans

Communications
economic profit plans, 19:13
total compensation strategy, 11:25

Company car programs. *See* Perquisites and other benefits

Company merger. *See* Merger

Company performance
effect on total compensation, 1:14
graph requirement, 2:31

Company philosophy. *See* Corporate philosophy

Company plane. *See* Perquisites and other benefits

[References are to question numbers.]

Company size. *See* Size of company
Comparison of plans. *See* Plan
comparisons
Compensation
  agreements, sample, Appendix B
  compensation committee, defined,
    2:25
  for division executives. *See* Division
    executives
  economic profit performance vs,
    19:11
  golden parachutes, 10:35
  mix of elements, 22:9
  philosophy. *See* Corporate
    philosophy
  reviewing during restructuring, 23:3
Competitive market. *See* Market
competition
Completion bonus
  defined, 16:19
Computers. *See* Perquisites and other
benefits
Constructive receipt
  and long-term incentives, 5:39, 5:46
  nonqualified deferred compensation
    plan contributions, 9:23
Contracts. *See* Executive contracts
Contributions
  funded vs. unfunded top-hat plan,
    9:65
  nonqualified deferred compensation
    plan
    constructive receipt, 9:23
    economic benefit doctrine, 9:24
  qualified plan limits, 9:6
Control of company
  change of control
    defined, 10:32
    golden parachute rules, Appendix
      M
    outside director benefits, 20:28
Convertible debentures
  accounting impact, 6:50
  advantages, 6:53
  appropriate companies, 6:55

defined, 6:48
disadvantages, 6:54
EPS impact, 6:52
shareholder approval, 6:49
tax treatment, 6:51
Corporate level. *See also* Division
executives
  classification, 3:5, 3:6
  effect on total compensation, 1:10
  performance measures, 4:45
  ranking, 3:4
Corporate philosophy
  compensation method chosen, 1:27
  plan design, 5:27
  primary disadvantage of long-term
    performance plans, 5:28
  total compensation strategy, 11:5
Cost of living allowance, 16:5
Costs
  benefits, total compensation
    strategy statement, 11:12
  of capital, effect of executives on,
    21:12
  retirement plans
    small company considerations,
      12:6
    special early retirement
      programs, 15:5
Currency fluctuation
  expatriate protection, 16:18

D

Debentures. *See* Convertible
debentures
Deferred compensation
  board of directors, 13:8
  constructive receipt, 5:46
  integration during company merger,
    5:61, 5:62
  nonqualified deferred compensation
    plan, 9:6–9:26
  primary approaches, 9:8

[References are to question numbers.]

Design. *See* Plan design
Dilution
  incentive stock options, 6:10
  nonqualified stock option, 6:17
Directors. *See* Board of directors
  compensation
Disability. *See also* Executive
  disability income insurance plans
  executive disability income
    insurance plans
     funding, 9:53
     operation, 9:48
     premium rates, 9:52
     tax considerations, 9:49–9:51
     total compensation strategy
      statement, 11:14
  for expatriates, 16:26
  insurance, small versus large
    companies, 22:14
Disclosure
  excess benefit plans, 9:68
  FAS 123, 1:51
  proxy statement
    Code Section 162(m), recent
     rulings, Appendix L
    information charts, 2:27
    long-term incentive, 5:59
    other information, 2:28
Discounted stock options
  accounting impact, 6:26
  advantages, 6:27
  defined, 6:23
  depth of discount, 6:29
  disadvantages, 6:28
  prevalence, 6:24
  tax treatment, 6:25
Discretionary plan
  advantages, 4:28
  defined, 4:27
  disadvantages, 4:29
  restructured company, 23:17
Divestiture. *See* Restructuring
Dividends
  phantom stock plans, 7:21

  sample wage dividend plan,
    Appendix B
Division executives
  annual incentives, 21:3–21:5
  base salary, 21:1, 21:2
  benefits and perquisites, 21:17–21:20
  defined, 21:1
  disadvantages of division-based
    incentive compensation plans,
    21:16
  use of economic profit in, 19:8
  long-term incentives, 21:6–21:16
  regulatory constraints, 21:18
Downsizing. *See* Restructuring

E

Early retirement. *See* Special early
  retirement programs
Earnings per share
  calculations
    and definition, 4:38
    FASB guidelines, 1:52
  and convertible debentures, 6:52
  incentive stock option, 6:10
Economic benefit doctrine
  defined, 5:47
  nonqualified deferred compensation
    plan contributions, 9:24
Economic pay increases, 3:13
Economic profit
  award payments, long-term
    incentive plan, 19:12
  and cost of capital, 19:7
  defined, 19:1
  in divisions or strategic business
    units, 19:8
  executive impact on, 19:6
  performance vs compensation, 19:11
  plan
    advantages, 19:4
    for business turnaround, 19:17
    communicating to executives, 19:13

[References are to question numbers.]

example of unsuccessful plan,
19:19
examples of companies that have
used, 19:16
disadvantages, 19:5
fixed term, 19:15
implementing, 19:10
to overcome competition, 19:18
participation of non-executives,
19:14
use in executive compensation
plans, 19:3
use with other annual or long-term
incentive plans, 19:9, 19:12
Economic value-added
defined, 5:9, 19:2
examples of companies that have
used, 19:16
plan implementation, 5:10
plans that have not worked, 19:5
trends, 20:11
**Economic value-added/shareholder
value plans**
vs. performance plans, 5:23
vs. stock plans, 5:22
Education allowance, 16:9
Election
Code Section 83(b), 5:48, 7:34
S corporation status, 2:12, 2:13
Emerging company. *See* Start-up
company
Employee-owned life insurance, 9:36
Employment agreements. *See also*
Executive contracts
company president, Appendix D
pursuant to merger, Appendix D
sample, Appendix D
with sole shareholder, Appendix D
Entrepreneurial company. *See also*
Size of company
total compensation strategy
statement, 11:28
versus large company practices,
22:1–22:14

Equity. *See* Return on equity
ERISA considerations
early retirement incentive program
outside qualified plan, 15:11
excess benefit plans, 9:66–9:68
funded vs. unfunded plan, 9:58–9:60
nonqualified deferred compensation
plan, 9:54–9:68
special early retirement program,
15:8
split-dollar life insurance, 9:38
top-hat plan, 9:54, 9:61–9:65
Estate planning
split-dollar life insurance, 9:44
EVA. *See* Economic value-added
Excess benefit plans
ERISA requirements, 9:66–9:68
tax considerations, 9:21, 9:22
Excess parachute payment. *See*
Golden parachute
Executive benefit plans
ERISA considerations, 9:54–9:68
excess benefit plans, 9:66–9:68
executive disability income
insurance, 9:48–9:53
failure of traditional benefit
programs, 9:2
funding arrangements, 9:28–9:32
general considerations, 9:1–9:3
importance, 9:1
insurance-related nonqualified
deferred compensation plans,
9:33–9:36
nonqualified deferred compensation
plans, 9:54–9:60
nonqualified retirement plans,
9:7–9:20, 9:69
overall compensation, 9:3
qualified plans, 9:4–9:6
split-dollar life insurance, 9:37–9:47
tax considerations, 9:21–9:27
top-hat plans or SERPs, 9:61–9:65
Executive contracts
employment agreement
advantages, 10:25

[References are to question numbers.]

Executive contracts (*cont'd*)
employment agreement (*cont'd*)
disadvantages, 10:26
enforcement, 10:28
golden parachutes, 10:29–10:46
noncompete clauses, 10:27
retirement contract
advantages and disadvantages, 10:49
example, 10:50
provisions, 10:47
reason for using, 10:48
selection, 10:24
types, 10:23
Executive disability income insurance plans. *See* Disability
Executive performance
effect on total compensation, 1:15
Executive perquisite. *See* Perquisites and other benefits
Executives
small and large company definition, 22:1
Expatriates
annual incentives, 4:30
cost of living allowance, 16:5
defined, 16:1
education allowance, 16:9
foreign service premium, 16:3
general considerations, 16:1–16:11
hardship allowance, 16:4
home leave, 16:11
home rental program, 16:8
housing allowance, 16:6
language training, 16:10
reimbursement, home sale or other relocation costs, 16:7
special compensation
annual incentive plans, 16:23
checklist, 16:32
completion bonus, 16:19
currency fluctuation, 16:18
free-standing stock appreciation rights, 16:21

home country balance sheet compensation program, 16:31
life insurance and disability, 16:26
long-term bonus plans, 16:22
medical benefits, 16:24
net to net compensation program, 16:30
pension plan, 16:25
perquisites, 16:27
repatriation, 16:28
second assignment, 16:29
stock options, 16:20
tax considerations
avoiding taxes, 16:16, 16:17
foreign earned income exclusions, 16:15
spendable income, 16:14
tax equalization, 16:12
tax-free income, 16:13
temporary executives, 18:9
typical compensation elements, 16:2
Expenses
accounting statements, 1:44
expense accounts. *See* Perquisites and other benefits; Reimbursement

F

Factor comparison, 3:7
Fair value calculation. *See* Valuation
Family-owned company
stock provision to non-family members, 12:7
FAS 123. *See* Accounting considerations
FASB
EPS calculations, 1:52
FAS 123, 1:45–1:49, 1:51, 20:17
Fees
board of directors, 13:6
FICA and FUTA taxes
deferred compensation arrangements, 9:27

[References are to question numbers.]

Fiduciary issues
nonqualified deferred compensation plan, 9:56
Financial institutions
performance measures, 4:47
Financial performance measures
in annual incentive plans, 4:37
Financial planning programs
perquisites, 10:6
First class travel. *See* Perquisites and other benefits
Foreign earned income exclusions. *See* Tax considerations
Foreign service premium, 16:3
Forfeiture. *See* Substantial risk of forfeiture
Free-standing stock appreciation rights, 16:21
Full-value plans
choice, 7:19
defined, 7:18
generally, 7:18, 7:19
performance share plans, 7:46–7:48
performance unit plans, 7:39–7:45
phantom stock plans, 7:20–7:29
restricted stock grants, 7:30–7:38
Fundamental concepts
accounting considerations, 1:43–1:52
base salary, 1:16–1:18
incentive plans, 1:19–1:30
tax considerations, 1:31–1:42
total compensation issues, 1:1–1:15
Funding arrangements
annual incentive plans
factors driving amounts, 4:58
maximums or caps, 4:65
participant method, 4:62–4:64
pool method, 4:59–4:62
size of award, 4:57
excess benefit plans, 9:67
executive disability income insurance plans, 9:53
funded plan
contributions, 9:20

excess benefit plans, taxation, 9:21
top-hat plan, 9:64, 9:65
vs. unfunded plan, 9:59, 9:60, 9:65
life insurance, 9:32
nonqualified deferred compensation plan, 9:55, 9:58
rabbi escrow agreement, defined, 9:28
rabbi trust
defined, 9:29
vs. secular trust, 9:31
secular trust
defined, 9:30
vs. rabbi trust, 9:31
special early retirement programs, 15:5
top-hat plans or SERPs, 9:64

G

Geographic location
effect on base salary, 1:16
Golden parachute
advantages and disadvantages, 10:33
change of control
contingent payments, 10:40, 10:46
defined, 10:32, 10:42
court cases, Appendix M
defined, 10:29
disqualified individual, 10:36
example of golden parachute payment, 10:46
excess parachute payment
avoiding excise tax, 10:45
calculation, 10:41
defined, 10:38
tax rules, 10:37
exempt payments, 10:39
government regulations affecting, 10:34
IRS rulings, Appendix M

[References are to question numbers.]

Golden parachute (*cont'd*)
  payments contingent on change of
    control, 10:40
  payments "in the nature of
    compensation," 10:35
  recent court cases and IRS rulings,
    Appendix M
  silver parachute, 10:30
  stock options, 10:43
  tax rules, 10:37, 10:41, 10:44, 10:45
  tin parachute, 10:31
Group term life. *See* Life insurance
Growth company
  total compensation strategy
    statement, 11:28
Growth or improvement plan
  advantages, 4:16
  disadvantages, 4:17
  operation, 4:15
Guidelines
  EPS calculations, 1:52
  incentive plan design, 1:24

H

Hardship allowance, 16:4
High-growth company
  competitive values despite growth,
    12:9
  total compensation strategy
    statement, 11:28
Hiring bonus. *See* Bonus
Home leave, 16:11
Home office. *See* Perquisites and
  other benefits
Home rental program, 16:8
Housing allowance, 16:6

I

Incentives
  annual
    accounting treatment, 4:8

appropriateness, 1:20
  approving annual incentive
    payments, 23:18
  award levels, 23:14
  business unit issues, 23:16, 23:17
  characteristics of appropriate
    organizations, 1:21
  and corporate restructuring,
    23:12–23:18
  defined, 4:1
  economic profit plan and, 19:9
  eligibility, 4:4
  establishing, small company, 12:2
  for expatriates, 16:23
  funding incentive plans, 4:57–4:65
  general considerations, 4:1–4:9
  vs. long-term incentives, 1:23,
    1:29
  market competition, 3:9
  meeting needs of executives and
    company, 1:3
  nonprofit organization, 14:9–14:13
  payment forms, 4:5
  pensionable, 4:6
  performance maximums, 4:54
  performance measures, 4:35–4:48
  performance standards, 4:49–4:56
  plan design, 4:10–4:34, 12:10
  prevalence, 4:2
  public sector, 17:8
  rationale, 4:3
  restructured companies, 23:14,
    23:16–23:18
  shareholder approval, 4:9
  short-term vs. long-term
    performance, 1:22
  tax impact, 4:7
eligibility, 1:25
fundamental issues, 1:19–1:30
guidelines for plan design, 1:24
long-term incentives
  vs. annual, 1:23, 1:29
  common forms in private
    companies, 2:7
  determining, 11:22, 23:21

[References are to question numbers.]

economic profit plans and, 19:9,
  19:11, 19:12
meeting needs of executives and
  company, 1:3
negative effect of not providing in
  privately held company, 2:10
nonprofit organizations, 14:14
performance plan vs. other
  long-term incentives, 5:19
restructured company,
  23:19–23:23
small company, 12:4
stock-based plan vs. other
  long-term incentives, 5:20
new venture businesses, 12:13
rationale, 1:19
short-term
  and corporate restructuring
    considerations, 23:12–23:18
  determining, 11:21
stock plans, 1:30, Appendix J
temporary executives, 18:11
Incentive stock options
accounting impact, 6:9
advantages, 6:12
AMT effect on tax treatment, 6:8,
  20:20
defined, 6:6
disadvantages, 6:13
fully diluted EPS, 6:10
vs. nonstatutory stock options, 6:22
prevalence, 6:11
tax treatment, 6:7
Income
ordinary, 1:36
Independent contractor
temporary executives, 18:2–18:4,
  18:19
Indexed stock options
defined, 6:65
Industry type
effect on total compensation, 1:11
salary range determination by, 23:10

Insurance. *See also* Executive
  disability income insurance plans;
  Life insurance
  insurance-related nonqualified
    deferred compensation plans
    COLI vs. retail life insurance, 9:35
    employee-owned life insurance,
      9:36
    funding with life insurance other
      than COLI, 9:34
    life insurance to fund promise,
      9:33
    plan termination insurance, 9:57
  public sector, 17:10
  temporary executives, 18:14
International business
division-based incentive plans, 21:15
total compensation strategies, 11:17
IRS
golden parachute rules, recent
  rulings, Appendix M
limitations under Code Section
  162(m), 1:34, Appendix L

J

Job evaluation
base salary above average
classification system, 3:5
defined, 3:3
factor comparison, 3:7
labor market values, 3:8
market competition, base salary
  and annual incentive, 3:9
point factor approach, 3:6
public vs. private companies, 17:3
ranking system, 3:4
Junior stock plans
advantages, 6:57
defined, 6:56
disadvantages, 6:58
prevalence, 6:59

[References are to question numbers.]

K

Keogh plans
board of directors, 13:16, 13:17

L

Language training
expatriates, 16:10
Large company. *See* Size of company
Level within the corporation. *See* Corporate level
Life cycle
total compensation strategy, 11:8
Life insurance
for expatriates, 16:26
funding promise, 9:32–9:36
insurance-related nonqualified deferred compensation plans, 9:32–9:36
perquisites
supplemental life insurance, 10:9
split-dollar
common applications, 9:43
defined, 9:37
enhancing nonqualified retirement plan, 9:47
ERISA, 9:38
estate planning, 9:46
executive payment of part of premium, 9:40
policy splitting, 9:39–9:41
problems of group term life insurance plans, 9:44
replacing group coverage, 9:45
retirement, 9:42
total compensation strategy statement, 11:14
Loans. *See* Perquisites and other benefits
Local nationals
annual incentives, 4:31

Long-term bonus plans. *See* Bonus
Long-term compensation plan
division executives, 22:7–22:11
sample, Appendix B
trends in
economic value-added plans, 20:11
executive loans, 20:14
noncompete clauses, 20:10
other trends, 20:16
performance-based stock options, 20:9
reload stock features, 20:12
stock award levels, 20:8
stock cancel and reissue plans, 20:15
stock ownership guidelines, 20:13
Long-term incentive plans
appreciation plans, 7:1–7:17
characteristics, 5:2
combination long-term plans
common compensation combinations, 8:5
general considerations, 8:1–8:5
parallel plans, 8:2, 8:3, 8:4
performance share/stock option plans, 8:6–8:11
restricted stock/stock option plans, 8:12–8:18
SAR/stock option plans, 8:19–8:23
tandem plans, 8:1, 8:3, 8:4
compensation philosophy, 5:27, 5:28
considerations, 5:6
currently emerging, 5:8
defined, 5:1
division executives, 22:7–22:11
economic profit plan and, 19:9, 19:11, 19:12
economic value-added
defined, 5:9
implementation, 5:10
eligibility, 5:3
full-value plans, 7:18–7:48
general considerations, 5:1–5:14

[References are to question numbers.]

long-term performance plan,
  defined, 5:13
objectives, 1:28
omnibus plan, 5:38
plan administration, 5:57–5:62
plan comparisons
  basic accounting issues, 5:25
  Black-Scholes option pricing
    model, 5:26
  getting executives to own stock,
    5:21
  performance plan vs. other
    long-term incentives, 5:19
  shareholder value/economic
    value-added plans vs.
    performance plans, 5:23
  shareholder value/economic
    value-added plans vs. stock
    plans,
    5:22
  stock-based plans vs. other
    long-term incentives, 5:20
  stock option plan vs. long-term
    performance plan, 5:15, 5:17
  stock option plan vs. restricted
    share plan, 5:16, 5:18
  tax rules, 5:24
plan design, 5:29–5:31
prevalence, 5:4
principal types, 5:7
rationale, 5:5
restructured company and, 23:19
  business units vs. departments,
    23:20
  changes in award frequency and
    terms, 23:23
  determining size of awards, 23:21
  number of shares as percentage
    of total shares outstanding, 23:22
shareholder value
  defined, 5:11
  plan operation, 5:12
stock options, 5:14, 5:32–5:37, 5:49–
  5:56
tax considerations, 5:39–5:48

Long-term incentives
  vs. annual, 1:23, 1:29
  common forms in private
    companies, 2:7
  determining, 11:22
  division executives, 21:6–
    21:16
    change from stock options to
      incentives, 21:8
    payout schedule, 21:9
    value-added performance
      measures, 21:10
  meeting needs of executives and
    company, 1:3
  negative effect of not providing in
    privately held company, 2:10
  nonprofit organizations, 14:14
  performance plan vs. other
    long-term incentives, 5:19
  small company, 12:4
  stock-based plan vs. other
    long-term incentives, 5:20
Long-term performance plan
  defined, 5:13
  primary disadvantage, 5:28
  public sector executive
    compensation, 17:9
  small and large companies,
    22:11
  stock option plan vs, 5:15, 5:17
Look back approach, 4:52
Look forward approach, 4:50

M

**Management variable compensation
plan**
  sample, Appendix B
Managers. *See* Mid-level managers
Manufacturing organization
  performance measures, 4:46
Market competition
  determining, 11:19

[References are to question numbers.]

Market competition (*cont'd*)
economic profit plans overcoming, 19:18
effect on total compensation, 1:12
executive perquisites, 10:11
50th percentile strategy, 11:20
high-growth company, 12:9
valuing executives, 3:8

Matrix plan
advantages, 4:25
disadvantages, 4:26
key features, 4:24

Measures. *See* Performance

Medical benefits
for expatriates, 16:24
small versus large companies, 22:14
special early retirement programs, 15:10

Merger
golden parachute rules, Appendix M
long-term incentive plan
administration, 5:60
deferred compensation
integration, 5:61, 5:62
sample employment agreement, Appendix D
short-term incentive plan
integration, 4:34

Merit increase
nonprofit organization, 14:8
public companies, 17:4

Merit pay
alternatives, 3:13

Mid-level managers
annual incentives, 4:33

Mission statement
total compensation strategy, 11:6

Model agreement
rabbi trust, Appendix A

Models
fair value determination, 1:50

Modified home country balance sheet compensation program, 16:31

N

Net to net compensation program
elements, 16:30

New ventures. *See* Start-up company

Noncompete agreement
in executive contract, 10:27
sample, Appendix C
special early retirement conditions, 15:9
use in stock award plans, 20:10

Non-litigation agreements
special early retirement conditions, 15:9

Nonprofit organizations
annual incentives
award size, 14:10
eligibility, 14:12
performance measures, 14:11
prevalence, 14:9
regulations, 14:13
base salary, 14:7, 14:8
business objectives, 14:3
company size, 14:4
compensation mix, 14:2
defined, 14:1
division-based incentive plans, 21:14
general considerations, 14:1–14:6
geographical location, 14:6
long-term incentives, 14:14
perquisites, 14:15, 14:16
type of organization, 14:5

Nonqualified deferred compensation plan
appropriateness, 9:17
beneficiary, 9:15
constructive receipt, 9:23
contributions to funded vs. unfunded plan, 9:20
defined, 9:9
economic benefit doctrine, 9:24
ERISA considerations, 9:54–9:68
fiduciary issues, 9:56
insurance-related, 9:33–9:36

[References are to question numbers.]

participation, vesting, and funding
  requirements, 9:55
plan termination insurance, 9:57
vs. qualified plan, 9:10
rationale, 9:12
SEC registration, 9:69
tax considerations, 9:18–9:27
types, 9:16
typical benefits, 9:11
typical company objectives, 9:14
typical objectives of deferring
  income, 9:13
Nonqualified retirement plans
deferred compensation, 9:7–9:20,
  9:69
split dollar enhancement, 9:47
Nonstatutory stock options
accounting treatment, 6:16
advantages, 6:19
calculating dilution, 6:17
defined, 6:14
disadvantages, 6:20
vs. ISOs, 6:22
offsetting withholding burden, 6:21
prevalence, 6:15
tax treatment, 6:18

O

Omnibus plan
defined, 5:38
Option reloads
accounting impact, 6:38
advantages, 6:40
defined, 6:37
disadvantages, 6:41
tax treatment, 6:39
trends, 20:12
Options. *See* Stock
Ordinary income
defined, 1:36
Outside directors
benefits, 20:27
change-of-control benefits, 20:28
changing remuneration levels, 20:24

retirement plans, 20:25
stock awards, 20:26
Outsourcing
alternatives, 18:7
defined, 18:6
Overseas executives. *See* Expatriates

P

Parallel grant
restricted share and stock option
  shares, 8:13
Parallel plans
advantages, 8:3
defined, 8:2
disadvantages, 8:4
parallel SAR/stock option plan
  defined, 8:20
Participant method, incentive pools
advantages, 4:63
disadvantages, 4:64
use of method, 4:62
Pay limits
company response, 1:35
Peer company performance plan
advantages, 4:22
disadvantages, 4:23
operation, 4:21
Peer group approach
performance comparison, 4:51
Pension plan
expatriate, 16:25
Percentage of profits approach
performance standards, 4:53
Performance. *See also* Matrix plan;
Performance plans
company performance
  effect on total compensation, 1:14
  graph requirement, 2:31
  SEC reporting regulations, 20:18
economic profit plans, 19:4, 19:5,
  19:11
executive performance
  effect on total compensation, 1:15

[References are to question numbers.]

Performance (*cont'd*)
measures
    annual incentive plans, 4:35–4:48
    nonprofit organization annual
      incentive, 14:11
    performance unit plans, 7:40
    small company, 12:2
performance-based stock awards,
    20:16
performance-based stock options
    accounting treatment, 6:64
    advantages, 6:61
    defined, 6:60
    disadvantages, 6:62
    indexed stock option defined, 6:65
    tax consequences, 6:63
    trends, 20:9
restructured companies, 23:15
standards, annual incentives
    appropriateness, 4:56
    basic, 4:49
    look back approach, 4:52
    look forward approach, 4:50
    peer group approach, 4:51
    percentage of profits, 4:53
    performance maximums for
      annual incentive plans, 4:54
    threshold performance level, 4:55

Performance plans. *See also*
Long-term performance plan
award, tax effect, 5:45
    long-term, public sector, 17:9
    vs. other long-term incentives,
      5:19
board of directors, 13:9
economic profit plan advantages,
    19:4
peer company performance plan,
    4:21–4:23
performance share plan
    accounting treatment, 7:48
    defined, 7:46
    stock option plan combination,
      8:6–8:11
    tax treatment, 7:47

performance unit plans
    accounting impact, 7:41
    advantages, 7:44
    defined, 7:39
    disadvantages, 7:45
    establishing performance
      measures, 7:40
    tax treatment, 7:42
    typical award period, 7:43
shareholder value/economic
    value-added plans vs, 5:23
target performance plan
    advantages, 4:19
    disadvantages, 4:20
    operation, 4:18
    restructured company, 23:17

Perquisites and other benefits. *See
also* Executive benefit plans
accounting treatment, 10:22
board of directors, 13:19
cellular phones, 10:3, 10:18
company car programs, 10:4, 10:17
company planes and first class
    travel, 10:20
company selection, 10:13
competitive analysis, 10:11
computers, laptop, 10:18
corporate restructuring and
    change in eligibility during
      restructuring, 23:25
    change in perquisites during
      restructuring, 23:24
    perquisites most commonly
      added or improved, 23:26
country club/luncheon club
    perquisites, 10:5, 10:16
division executives, 21:17
entertainment expense
    reimbursement, 10:15
examples, 10:2
executive contracts, 10:23–10:50
expatriate, 16:27
expense accounts for
    entertainment, 10:7

[References are to question numbers.]

financial planning programs, 10:6, 10:21
general considerations, 10:1–10:13
large company, 22:12–22:14
nonprofit organizations, 14:15
perquisite defined, 10:1
public sector executive compensation, 17:14
restructuring company, 23:8
satisfying executive needs, 1:4
SERP
  nonprofit organizations, 14:16
  typical plan benefits, 10:10
severance, 10:8, 23:26
small company, 12:11, 22:12–22:14
supplemental life insurance, 10:9, 10:19
tax regulations, 10:14–10:21
temporary executives, 18:13
travel expense reimbursement, 10:14
valuation, 10:12
Phantom stock plans
accounting impact, 7:23
advantages, 7:25
appropriate companies, 7:28
defined, 7:20
disadvantages, 7:26
dividends, 7:21
prevalence, 7:22
shadow stock plan defined, 7:29
tax treatment, 7:24
vesting, 7:27
Philosophy. *See* Corporate philosophy
Phone benefits. *See* Perquisites and other benefits
Plan administration, long-term incentive plans
amending, 5:58
instituting, 5:57
merger, 5:60, 5:61
proxy statements, 5:59, Appendix L
Plan comparisons
basic accounting issues, 5:25
Black-Scholes option pricing model, 5:26
getting executives to own stock, 5:21
performance plan vs. other long-term incentives, 5:19
shareholder value/economic value-added plans
  vs. performance plans, 5:23
  vs. stock plans, 5:22
stock-based plans vs. other long-term incentives, 5:20
stock option plan
  vs. long-term performance plan, 5:15, 5:17
  vs. restricted share plan, 5:16, 5:18
tax rules, 5:24
Plan design
annual incentives
  basic plan designs, 4:11
  company merger, 4:34
  discretionary plan, 4:27–4:29
  executives vs. mid-level managers, 4:33
  expatriates, 4:30
  growth or improvement plan, 4:15–4:17
  key issues, 4:10
  local nationals, 4:31
  matrix plan, 4:24–4:26
  new ventures/start-ups, 4:32
  peer company performance plan, 4:21–4:23
  profit sharing plan, 4:12–4:14
  small company, 12:10
  target performance plan, 4:18–4:20
compensation philosophy, 5:27
determining amount of long-term incentive payout or grant, 5:29
incentive plans, guidelines, 1:24
salary multiple approach in determining size of long-term incentives, 5:30
targeted income approach, 5:31

[References are to question numbers.]

Plan termination. *See* Termination of plan

Planning
tax rate considerations, 1:39

Point factor approach, 3:6

Policy splitting. *See* Life insurance

Pool method, incentive funds
advantages, 4:60
disadvantages, 4:61
operation, 4:59
participant method, 4:62–4:64

Premium. *See* Executive disability income insurance plans; Life insurance; Premium stock options

Premium stock options
accounting impact, 6:33
advantages, 6:35
defined, 6:30
disadvantages, 6:36
establishing premium, 6:31
prevalence, 6:32
tax treatment, 6:34

President of company
sample employment agreement, Appendix D

Private vs. public company considerations
closely held company, 2:3, 2:4
executive compensation program differences, 2:5
general considerations, 2:1–2:5
private or privately held company, defined, 2:2
proxy rules, 2:23–2:32, 21:19, Appendix L
public or publicly traded company defined, 2:1
future value of stock options, 2:29
S corporations, 2:11–2:14
SEC regulations, 2:15–2:22
stock-based plans, 2:6–2:10

Profit sharing plan
advantages, 4:13
disadvantages, 4:14
operation, 4:12

Proxy rules
board compensation committee, 2:25
change in treatment of executive compensation, 2:32
Code Section 162(m), Appendix L
company performance graph, 2:31
disclosure information charts, 2:27, 21:19
effect of reporting requirements, 2:24
future value of stock options, 2:29
media/shareholder reaction to stock option exercise, 2:30
other proxy statement disclosures, 2:28, Appendix L
regulatory base and effective dates, 2:26
shareholder proxy and proxy statement defined, 2:23

Proxy statement
defined, 2:23
long-term incentive information, 5:59
other proxy statement disclosures, 2:28, 21:19, Appendix L

Public company. *See* Private vs. public company considerations

Public sector executive compensation
annual incentives, 17:8
base salary, 17:2
insured benefits, 17:10
job evaluation systems, 17:3
long-term performance plans, 17:9
merit increases, 17:4
perquisites, 17:14
vs. private sector programs, 17:1
recruitment, 17:15
regulations, 17:13
retirement plans, 17:11
salary ranges, 17:7
stock award plans, 17:9
supplemental retirement plans, 17:12

[References are to question numbers.]

tenure-based pay increase systems,
17:5, 17:6
Purchase plans
book value purchase plans,
6:42–6:47
convertible debentures, 6:48–6:55
defined, 6:1
differences between types, 6:3
discounted stock options, 6:23–6:29
general considerations, 6:1–6:5
incentive stock options, 6:6–6:13
junior stock plans, 6:56–6:59
nonstatutory stock options,
6:14–6:22
option reloads, 6:37–6:41
performance-based stock options,
6:60–6:65
premium stock options, 6:30–6:36
stock option exercise
setting prices, 6:4
typical exercise period, 6:5
types, 6:2
Pyramiding stock swap. *See* Stock

Q

Qualified plan
ERISA and Code considerations,
special early retirement program,
15:8
vs. nonqualified deferred
compensation plan, 9:10
qualification considerations, 9:4–9:6

R

Rabbi escrow agreement
defined, 9:28
Rabbi trust
defined, 9:29
model agreement, Appendix A
vs. secular trust, 9:31

Range banding, 3:13
Ranking system, 3:4
Recapitalization. *See* Restructuring
Recruitment
and public sector, 17:15
Registration. *See* SEC registration
Regulation T
defined, 5:52
Reloads. *See* Option reloads
Relocation costs
reimbursement, 16:7
Remuneration. *See* Total remuneration
Rental
home rental program, expatriate
benefit, 16:8
Reorganization. *See* Restructuring
Reporting
excess benefit plans, 9:68
proxy rules, 2:23–2:32, Appendix L
Responsibility
effect on total compensation, 1:9,
21:20
Restricted share plan
restricted performance share plan,
Appendix K
stock option plan vs, 5:16, 5:18
Restricted stock grants
accounting impact, 7:32
advantages, 7:36
appropriate companies, 7:38
Code Section 83(b) election, 5:48,
7:34
defined, 7:30
disadvantages, 7:37
prevalence, 7:31
tax considerations, 5:44, 7:33
vesting, 7:35
Restricted stock plans
stock option plan combination,
8:12–8:18
Restructuring
acquisition issues, 23:4
base salary classifications, 23:9
benefits and
change during restructuring, 23:24

[References are to question numbers.]

Restructuring (*cont'd*)
benefits and (*cont'd*)
change in eligibility during
restructuring, 23:25
compensation levels in separate
business units or departments,
23:6, 23:7
defined, 23:1
economic profit plans and, 19:17
examples of companies that have
undergone, 23:2
long-term incentive plans
between business units or
departments, 23:20
changes in award frequency and
terms, 23:23
determining size of award,
23:21
effect of restructuring on, 23:19
number of shares used as
percentage of total shares
outstanding, 23:22
merger issues, 23:5
perquisites and
additions or improvements
during restructuring, 23:26
changes during restructuring,
23:24
changes in eligibility during
restructuring, 23:25
reviewing executive pay, 23:3
salary administration practices,
23:11
salary ranges, 23:10
short-term incentives
approving annual incentive
payments, 23:18
business unit issues, 23:13,
23:16, 23:17
eligibility, 23:12
performance measures used,
23:15
potential award levels, 23:14
supplemental benefits and
perquisites, 23:8

Retirement benefits
board of directors, 13:15, 20:25
retirement contracts. *See* Executive
contracts
temporary executives, 18:15
total compensation strategy
statement, 11:13
Retirement plans. *See also* Special
early retirement programs
outside directors, 20:25
public sector executive
compensation, 17:11
supplemental, small and large
companies, 22:13
Return on assets
definition and calculation, 4:39
Return on capital
calculation, 4:41
Return on equity
calculation, 4:40

S

Salary administration
and corporate restructuring, 23:11
Salary banding; other increases
alternatives to base salary ranges
and merit pay, 3:13
economic pay increases, 3:13, 3:16
negative experiences, 3:15
positive experiences, 3:14
Salary increases
inflation, 3:12
motivating effect, 3:11
Salary multiple approach, 5:30
Salary ranges
public sector, 17:7
restructuring, 23:10
Sale of home
reimbursement, 16:7
Sample compensation agreements,
Appendix B
S corporation
defined, 2:11

[References are to question numbers.]

election, 2:12, 2:13
unreasonable compensation, 2:14
SEC registration
nonqualified deferred compensation
plan, 9:69
SEC regulations
reporting of company performance
comparisons, 20:18
Securities Act of 1933, 2:15, 2:17
Securities Exchange Act of 1934,
2:16, 2:18–2:22
SEC Section 16 of the 1934 Act
actions needed to benefit, 2:21
basic rules, 2:18
board of directors options, 13:11
clarifications, 2:22
major changes, 2:19
paying for stock, 5:50
SARs, 7:4
significant effects, 2:20
Secular trust
defined, 9:30
vs. rabbi trust, 9:31
Securities Act of 1933
avoiding application, 2:17
generally, 2:15
Securities Exchange Act of 1934
generally, 2:16
Section 16 rules, 2:18–2:22
**SERP (supplemental executive
retirement plans).** *See* Top-hat plans
or SERPs
Service company
performance measures, 4:48
Severance agreement
changes during corporate
restructuring, 23:26
golden parachutes, 10:29–10:46
sample, Appendix C
special early retirement programs,
15:3, 15:4
typical severance amount, 10:8
Shadow stock plan. *See* Phantom
stock plans

Shareholder. *See also* Proxy rules
approval
annual incentives, 4:9
convertible debentures, 6:49
sample employment agreement,
Appendix D
shareholder value
defined, 5:11
economic value-added plans, vs.
performance plans, 5:23
economic value-added plans, vs.
stock plans, 5:22
operation, 5:12
Short-term incentive. *See* Incentives
Silver parachute. *See* Golden
parachute
Size of award
nonprofit organization annual
incentive, 14:10
Size of company
effect on total compensation, 1:13
large company
annual bonus levels, 20:4
base salary levels, 20:1
total compensation strategy
statement, 11:27
nonprofit organization, 14:4
small company
annual bonus levels, 20:5
annual incentive plan design,
12:10
base salary levels, 20:2
competition and
cost-containment, 12:6
establishing annual incentives,
12:2
executive benefits and
perquisites, 12:11
family-owned companies, 12:7
general considerations, 12:1–12:11
less sophisticated business
performance measures, 12:2
long-term incentives, 12:4
mix of compensation elements,
12:1

[References are to question numbers.]

Size of company (*cont'd*)
  small company (*cont'd*)
    new venture businesses, 12:12,
      12:13
    parachute provisions, 10:37
    recruitment without competitive
      salary and bonus, 12:5
    small, high-growth companies
      and competitive values, 12:9
    small human resources staff, 12:3
    total compensation strategies,
      12:8
    total compensation strategy
      statement, 11:26
  small company versus large
    company practices, 22:1–22:14
    benefits and perquisites,
      22:12–22:14
    long-term plans, 22:7–22:11
    total cash compensation,
      22:1–22:6
Small company. *See* Size of company
Special early retirement programs
  as a result of corporate
  restructuring, 23:26
  ERISA and Code implications, 15:8,
    15:11
  funding, 15:5
  medical benefits, 15:10
  negative consequences
    to companies, 15:6
    to employees, 15:7
  noncompete or non-litigation
    agreements, 10:27, 15:9
  rationale, 15:2
  severance, 15:3, 15:4, 15:11
  under existing retirement plan, 15:1
Spendable income, 16:14
Split-dollar life insurance. *See* Life
 insurance
Standards. *See* Performance
Start-up company
  base salary and benefits, 12:13
  compensation programs, 1:26
  incentive compensation, 12:12

  incentive plans, 4:32
Stock
  awards
    accounting, 1:45
    levels, changes, 20:8
    noncompete clauses, 20:10
    outside directors, 20:26
    public sector, 17:9
    temporary executives, 18:12
  Black-Scholes option pricing model,
    5:26
  cancel and reissue plans, 20:15
  from family-owned company to
    non-family members, 12:7
  getting executives to own stock, 5:21
  incentive plan, W. R. Grace,
    Appendix J
  option exercise
    cashless option exercise, 5:51
    exercise period, 6:5
    negative reaction, 2:30
    paying the exercise price, 5:49
    pyramiding stock swap exercise,
      5:54
    Regulation T, 5:52
    Section 16 rules, 5:50
    setting exercise price, 6:4
    stock swap, 5:53
  options. *See also* Incentive stock
    options; Nonstatutory stock
    options
    board of directors compensation,
      13:10
    conditions, 5:35, 5:36
    discounted, 6:23–6:29
    exercise period, 5:33
    to expatriates, 16:20
    FASB regulations, 20:17
    future value, 2:29
    golden parachute treatment, 10:43
    incentive, 6:6–6:13
    long-term incentives, 21:8
    new regulations pending, 20:21
    nonstatutory, 6:14–6:22
    option reloads, 6:37–6:41, 20:12

[References are to question numbers.]

performance-based, 6:60–6:65,
  20:9
premium, 6:30–6:36
rationale of using stock-based
  plans, 5:34
reserved shares, 5:37
tax considerations, 5:42
transfer, 20:22
types, 5:32
value, 22:10
plans
  board of directors, 13:10–13:13
  buy-back agreement, 2:9
  dilution, 20:23
  FAS 123, 1:48, 20:17
  incentive plans, 1:30
  long-term incentive, 2:7, 2:10
  vs. other long-term incentives,
    5:20
  performance share/stock option
    plan combination, 8:6–8:11
  phantom stock, 7:20–7:29
  privately held companies, 2:6
  problems with use in private
    companies, 2:8
  rationale, 5:34
  restricted stock grants, 7:30–7:38
  restricted stock plan/stock option
    plan combination, 8:12–8:18
  SAR/stock option plan
    combinations, 8:19–8:23
  shareholder value/economic
    value-added plans vs., 5:22
stock appreciation rights
  accounting impact, 7:7
  advantages, 7:10
  appropriate company, 7:12
  vs. cashless exercise, 7:6
  combined with stock options,
    board of directors
    compensation, 13:13
  defined, 7:3
  disadvantages, 7:11
  free-standing, 16:21
  prevalence, 7:5

SEC Section 16 rules, 7:4
tandem SAR/stock option plans,
  8:19–8:23
tax considerations, 5:43, 7:8
vesting, 7:9
stock option plan
  defined, 5:15
  vs. long-term performance plan,
    5:15, 5:17
  performance share plan
    combination, 8:6–8:11
  vs. restricted share plan, 5:16,
    5:18
  restricted stock plan
    combination, 8:12–8:18
  SAR plan combination, 8:19–8:23
stock ownership guidelines, 20:13
stock swap
  defined, 5:53
  drawbacks, 5:56
  pyramiding stock swap exercise,
    5:54–5:56
  tax considerations, 5:55
Strategic business units
  economic profit used in, 19:8
Substantial risk of forfeiture
  long-term incentives, 5:40, 5:41
**Supplemental executive retirement
  plan (SERP).** *See* Top-hat plans or
  SERPs
Supplemental life insurance. *See*
  Perquisites and other benefits
Supply and demand. *See* Market
  competition
Swap. *See* Stock

T

Tandem plans. *See also* Long-term
  incentive plans
  advantages, 8:3
  defined, 8:1
  disadvantages, 8:4

[References are to question numbers.]

Tandem plans (*cont'd*)
restricted stock/stock option plan,
defined, 8:12
SAR/stock option plan
defined, 8:19
to directors, 13:13
Targeted income approach
plan design, 5:31, 21:3, 22:5
Target performance plan
advantages, 4:19
disadvantages, 4:20
operation, 4:18
Tax considerations
alternative minimum tax, 1:42
annual incentives, 4:7
board of directors compensation,
13:7
book value appreciation rights, 7:15
book value purchase plans, 6:44
capital gains, 1:37, 1:38, 20:19,
20:20
Code Section 83 tax property
transfers, 9:25
Code Section 162(m), 1:34, 1:35
Code Section 457 plan, 9:26
combination performance
share/stock option plans, 8:8
compensation forms, 1:31
compensation planning, 1:39
congressional pay limits, 1:35
convertible debentures, 6:51
effective tax rate, 1:40
excess benefit plans, 9:21, 9:22
excise tax on excess parachute
payments, 10:45
executive disability income
insurance plans, 9:49–9:51
expatriates
avoiding taxes, 16:16, 16:17
equalization, 16:12
foreign earned income
exclusions, 16:15
spendable income, 16:14
tax-free income, 16;13

FICA and FUTA tax, deferred
compensation arrangements, 9:27
fundamental issues, 1:31–1:42
golden parachutes
application of tax rules, 10:37
avoiding excise tax, 10:45
calculation of excess payment,
10:41
withholding rules, 10:44
ISOs, 6:7, 6:8, 20:20
long-term incentive plans, 5:24
Code Section 83(b), 5:48, 7:34
constructive receipt, 5:39, 5:46
deferred compensation, 5:46
economic benefit theory, 5:47
performance plan award, 5:45
restricted stock grant, 5:44
stock appreciation right, 5:43
stock option, 5:42
substantial risk of forfeiture,
5:40, 5:41
marginal tax rate, 1:41
nonqualified plans, 9:18, 9:19
nonqualified deferred compensation
plan contributions, 9:23, 9:24
nonstatutory stock options, 6:18
option reloads, 6:39
ordinary income, 1:36
performance-based stock options,
6:63
performance share plans, 7:47
performance unit plans, 7:42
perquisites and other benefits
car and cellular phone and laptop
payments, 10:18
club membership reimbursement,
10:16
company car reimbursement,
10:17
company planes and first class
travel, 10:20
entertainment expense
reimbursement, 10:15
financial planning assistance,
10:21

[References are to question numbers.]

supplemental life insurance, 10:19
travel expense reimbursement, 10:14
phantom stock plans, 7:24
premium stock options, 6:34
pyramiding exercise, 5:55
restricted stock grants, 7:33
restricted stock/stock option plan combination, 8:15
SARs, 7:8
SAR/stock option plans, 8:23
stock options, 8:23
  combination performance share/stock option plans, 8:8
  ISOs, 6:7, 6:8
  long-term incentive plans, 5:42
  nonstatutory, 6:18
  option reloads, 6:39
  performance-based, 6:63
  premium, 6:34
  restricted stock/stock option plan combination, 8:15
  SAR/stock option plans, 8:23
stock swap, 5:55
unreasonable compensation, 1:32, 1:33
Temporary executives
alternatives to outsourcing, 18:7
as independent contractors, 18:2, 18:19
  advantages and disadvantages, 18:3, 18:4
base salary, 18:10
conversion to full-time status, 18:18
current litigation, 18:19
defined, 18:1
incentive compensation, 18:11
insured benefits, 18:14
Microsoft case, 18:19
obtaining an assignment, 18:8
outsourcing, 18:6, 18:7
overseas assignment, 18:9
perquisites, 18:13
regulations, 18:16
retirement benefits, 18:15

short-term vs. long-term assignment, 18:5
stock awards, 18:12
Tenure-based pay increases, 17:5, 17:6
Termination of plan
nonqualified plan, termination insurance, 9:57
Tin parachutes. *See* Golden parachutes
Top-hat plans or SERPs
SERPS
  executive perquisites, 10:10
  nonprofit organizations, 14:17
  public sector, 17:12
  small versus large companies, 22:13, 22:14
top hat plan
  benefit payment, 9:62
  ERISA requirements, 9:54, 9:61–9:64
  funding, 9:64, 9:65
  future benefit payment, 9:63
  inadvertent creation, 9:61
Total compensation
annual and long-term incentives, 1:3
base salary, 1:2
  determining mix of elements, 1:18
  vs. other elements, 1:17
benefits and perquisites, 1:4
cash, 1:6, 20:1–20:7, 21:4, 22:1–22:6
company performance, 1:15
company size, 1:13
corporate level, 1:10
defined, 1:7
division executives, 21:20
executive performance, 1:14
executive responsibility, 1:9
factors, 1:8
industry type, 1:11
small company strategies, 12:8
strategy building
  approval and implementation, 11:24, 11:25
  benefit factors, 11:11–11:15

[References are to question numbers.]

Total compensations (*cont'd*)
  strategy building (*cont'd*)
    business purposes, 11:3
    compensation factors, 11:4–11:10
    determining the mix, 11:18–11:22
    developing a total strategy, 11:23
    elements of executive
      compensation, 11:2
    examples of strategy statements,
      11:26–11:28
    external factors, 11:10
    general considerations, 11:1–11:3
    internal factors, 11:9
    other factors, 11:16, 11:17
    total compensation strategy
      defined, 11:1
  supply and demand, 1:12
  total cash compensation, 1:6
  total compensation defined, 1:7
  total compensation factors, 1:8
  total remuneration defined, 1:1
  valuation of all compensation
    elements, 1:5
Total remuneration
  defined, 1:1
Transfers
  property tax, Code Section 83, 9:25
  stock options, 20:22
Travel. *See* Perquisites and other
  benefits
Trends in executive compensation
  long-term compensation, 20:8–20:16
    economic value-added plans,
      20:11
    executive loans, 20:14
    noncompete clauses, 20:10
    other trends, 20:16
    performance-based stock options,
      20:9
    reload stock features, 20:12
    stock award levels, 20:8
    stock cancel and reissue plans,
      20:15
    stock ownership guidelines, 20:13
  outside directors

    benefits, 20:27
    change-of-control benefits, 20:28
    remuneration levels, 20:24
    retirement plans, 20:25
    stock awards, 20:26
  regulatory issues
    capital gains tax rate decrease,
      20:19, 20:20
    dilution, 20:23
    pending new regulations, 20:21
    public company performance
      comparisons, 20:18
    reaction to FAS 123, 20:17
    stock option transfers, 20:22
  total cash compensation
    annual incentive practices, 20:6
    base salary levels, 20:1–20:3, 20:7
    bonus levels, 20:4, 20:5, 20:7

U

Unfunded plan
  contributions, 9:20
  vs. funded plan, 9:59, 9:60, 9:65
  top-hat plan, 9:64, 9:65
U.S. executives working overseas.
  See Expatriates
Unreasonable compensation
  consequences of determination, 1:33
  defined, 1:32
  public vs. private company and S
    corporation, 2:14

V

Valuation
  all executive compensation
    elements, 1:5
  executive perquisites, 10:12
  executive positions, 3:8
  fair value
    FAS 123, 1:49
    models, 1:50

[References are to question numbers.]

stock option future value, 2:29,
22:10
Value added performance measures
example, 21:11
use in long-term compensation
plans, 21:10
Variable compensation plan. *See*
Management variable compensation
plan
Venture. *See* Start-up company
Vesting
economic profit awards from
long-term incentive plan, 19:12
excess benefit plans, 9:67
nonqualified deferred compensation
plan, 9:55
phantom stock plans, 7:27

restricted stock grants, 7:35
SARs, 7:9
substantial, Code Section 83, 5:41

W

Wage dividend plan
sample, Appendix B
Withholding
offsetting, nonstatutory stock
options, 6:21
parachute payments, 10:44
W. R. Grace stock incentive plan,
Appendix J